Muslim Peoples

Muslim Peoples

A World Ethnographic Survey

Second Edition,
Revised and Expanded

Edited by **Richard V. Weekes**

Maps by John E. Coffman
Paul Ramier Stewart, consultant

Maba–Yoruk

Greenwood Press
Westport, Connecticut

Library of Congress Cataloging in Publication Data

Main entry under title:

Muslim peoples.

Bibliography: p.
Includes index.
Contents: [1] Acehnese—Lur — [2] Maba—Yoruk.
1. Muslims.   2. Ethnology—Islamic countries.
3. Islamic countries—Social life and customs.
I. Weekes, Richard V., 1924-
DS35.625.A1M87   1984   305.6′971   84-   83-18494
ISBN 0-313-23392-6 (lib. bdg.)
ISBN 0-313-24639-4 (lib. bdg. : v. 1)
ISBN 0-313-24640-8 (lib. bdg. : v. 2)

Library of Congress Catalog Card Number: 83-18494
ISBN 0-313-23392-6   (set)

First published in 1984

Greenwood Press
A division of Congressional Information Service, Inc.
88 Post Road West
Westport, Connecticut 06881

Printed in the United States of America

10 9 8 7 6 5 4 3 2 1

CONTRIBUTORS

Partap C. Aggarwal
SHRI RAM CENTER FOR INDUSTRIAL
   RELATIONS
New Delhi, India

Irshad Ali
DEPARTMENT OF ANTHROPOLOGY
Gauhati University

Tahir Ali
DEPARTMENT OF ANTHROPOLOGY
Wesleyan University

J. C. Anceaux
University of Leiden

Jane Monnig Atkinson
DEPARTMENT OF ANTHROPOLOGY
Stanford University

Jerome H. Barkow
DEPARTMENT OF SOCIOLOGY AND
   ANTHROPOLOGY
Dalhousie University

R. H. Barnes
INSTITUTE OF SOCIAL ANTHROPOLOGY
Oxford University

Daniel G. Bates
DEPARTMENT OF ANTHROPOLOGY
Hunter College of City University of New York

Ulku U. Bates
DEPARTMENT OF ART
Hunter College of City University of New York

Lois Beck
DEPARTMENT OF ANTHROPOLOGY
Washington University

Burton Benedict
DEPARTMENT OF ANTHROPOLOGY
University of California, Berkeley

Henri Berre (*deceased*)
CENTRE NATIONAL DE LA RECHERCHE
   SCIENTIFIQUE
Valbonne, France

Peter J. Bertocci
DEPARTMENT OF ANTHROPOLOGY
Oakland University

U. B. Bhoite
DEPARTMENT OF POLITICAL SCIENCE
Maharathwada University

R. M. Blench
DEPARTMENT OF SOCIAL
   ANTHROPOLOGY
University of Cambridge

Christian Bouquet
DEPARTMENT OF GEOGRAPHY
University of Bordeaux III

John Bowen
HARVARD INSTITUTE FOR INTERNA-
   TIONAL DEVELOPMENT
Harvard University

James L. Brain
DEPARTMENT OF ANTHROPOLOGY
State University of New York at New Paltz

Harald Beyer Broch
ETHNOGRAPHICAL MUSEUM
University of Oslo

Philip Burnham
DEPARTMENT OF ANTHROPOLOGY
University of London

70528

Robert L. Canfield
DEPARTMENT OF ANTHROPOLOGY
Washington University

B. M. Das
DEPARTMENT OF ANTHROPOLOGY
Gauhati University

Thomas R. DeGregori
DEPARTMENT OF ECONOMICS
University of Houston

Leland Donald
DEPARTMENT OF ANTHROPOLOGY
University of Victoria

Paul Doornbos
AFRICAN STUDIES CENTRE
University of Leiden

Vernon R. Dorjahn
DEPARTMENT OF ANTHROPOLOGY
University of Oregon

Louis Dupree
DEPARTMENT OF ANTHROPOLOGY
Princeton University

Svetlana Rimsky-Korsakoff Dyer
FACULTY OF ASIAN STUDIES
The Australian National University

Pat Emerson
DEPARTMENT OF SOCIOLOGY
University of Washington

Richard M. Emerson (*deceased*)
DEPARTMENT OF ANTHROPOLOGY
University of Washington

Janet Ewald
DEPARTMENT OF HISTORY
Duke University

James C. Faris
DEPARTMENT OF ANTHROPOLOGY
University of Connecticut

Golamreza Fazel
DEPARTMENT OF ANTHROPOLOGY
University of Massachusetts, Boston

Robert A. Fernea
DEPARTMENT OF ANTHROPOLOGY
University of Texas, Austin

Gregory A. Finnegan
UNIVERSITY LIBRARY
Roosevelt University

James J. Fox
DEPARTMENT OF ANTHROPOLOGY
The Australian National University

C. Magbaily Fyle
INSTITUTE OF AFRICAN STUDIES
University of Sierra Leone

David P. Gamble
DEPARTMENT OF ANTHROPOLOGY
San Francisco State University

Frederick C. Gamst
DEPARTMENT OF ANTHROPOLOGY
University of Massachusetts, Boston

Gene R. Garthwaite
DEPARTMENT OF HISTORY
Dartmouth College

William H. Geoghegan
DEPARTMENT OF ANTHROPOLOGY
University of California, Berkeley

Alfred G. Gerteiny
DEPARTMENT OF HISTORY
University of Bridgeport

Byron J. Good
SCHOOL OF MEDICINE
University of California, Davis

Mary-Jo DelVecchio Good
SCHOOL OF MEDICINE
University of California, Davis

Peter G. Gowing (*deceased*)
DANSALAN RESEARCH CENTER
Iligan City, Philippines

Kathryn Green
DEPARTMENT OF HISTORY
Indiana University

Gunnar Haaland
DEPARTMENT OF SOCIAL STUDIES AND
    DEVELOPMENT
The CHR-Michelsen Institute (Norway)

John Hamer
DEPARTMENT OF ANTHROPOLOGY
University of Alabama

Robert L. Hardgrave, Jr.
DEPARTMENT OF GOVERNMENT
University of Texas, Austin

Donn V. Hart (*deceased*)
DEPARTMENT OF ANTHROPOLOGY
Northern Illinois University

Robert V. Haynes
DEPARTMENT OF HISTORY
University of Houston

LeVell Holmes
DEPARTMENT OF MULTI-CULTURAL
    STUDIES
California State College at Sonoma

Svend E. Holsoe
DEPARTMENT OF ANTHROPOLOGY
University of Delaware

Ladislav Holy
DEPARTMENT OF SOCIAL
    ANTHROPOLOGY
University of St. Andrews

C. Edward Hopen
DEPARTMENT OF ANTHROPOLOGY
University of Toronto

William G. Irons
DEPARTMENT OF ANTHROPOLOGY
Northwestern University

Alfred Janata
MUSEUM FUR VOLKERKUNDE
Neue Burg, Austria

Allen K. Jones
TRANSCENTURY CORPORATION
Washington, D.C.

Lidwien Kapteijns
AFRICAN STUDIES CENTRE
University of Leiden

R. Lincoln Keiser
DEPARTMENT OF ANTHROPOLOGY
Wesleyan University

Martin A. Klein
DEPARTMENT OF HISTORY
University of Toronto

R. M. Koentjaraningrat
DEPARTMENT OF ANTHROPOLOGY
University of Indonesia

Kim Kramer
DEPARTMENT OF ANTHROPOLOGY
Stanford University

Ruth Krulfeld
DEPARTMENT OF ANTHROPOLOGY
George Washington University

Herbert S. Lewis
DEPARTMENT OF ANTHROPOLOGY
University of Wisconsin, Madison

William G. Lockwood
DEPARTMENT OF ANTHROPOLOGY
University of Michigan

Deborah L. Mack
PROGRAM OF AFRICAN STUDIES
Northwestern University

Paul Magnarella
DEPARTMENT OF ANTHROPOLOGY
University of Florida

L. K. Mahapatra
DEPARTMENT OF ANTHROPOLOGY
Utkal University

Clarence Maloney
Rajshahi University

Peter Mark
DEPARTMENT OF HISTORY
Yale University

Gail Minault
DEPARTMENT OF HISTORY
University of Texas, Austin

Mattison Mines
DEPARTMENT OF ANTHROPOLOGY
University of California, Santa Barbara

David C. Montgomery
DEPARTMENT OF HISTORY
Brigham Young University

H. S. Morris
University of Cambridge

Larry W. Moses
CENTER FOR URALIC AND ALTAIC
    STUDIES
Indiana University

Victor L. Mote
DEPARTMENT OF GEOGRAPHY
University of Houston

Satoshi Nakagawa
DEPARTMENT OF ANTHROPOLOGY
The Australian National University

Merun H. Nasser-Bush
Boulder, Colorado

H. Arlo Nimmo
DEPARTMENT OF ANTHROPOLOGY
California State University at Hayward

J. Noorduyn
ROYAL INSTITUTE OF LINGUISTICS AND
ANTHROPOLOGY
Leiden, The Netherlands

Jennifer W. Nourse
DEPARTMENT OF ANTHROPOLOGY
University of Virginia

S. R. Nur
FACULTY OF LAW
Hasanuddin University

Arye Oded
FACULTY OF HUMANITIES
Tel Aviv University

Robert Olson
DEPARTMENT OF HISTORY
University of Kentucky

Maxwell Owusu
DEPARTMENT OF ANTHROPOLOGY
University of Michigan

Stephen L. Pastner
DEPARTMENT OF ANTHROPOLOGY
University of Vermont

Barbara L. K. Pillsbury
DEPARTMENT OF ANTHROPOLOGY
University of California, Los Angeles

Ronald Provencher
DEPARTMENT OF ANTHROPOLOGY
Northern Illinois University

Lanfranco Blanchetti Revelli
INSTITUTE OF PHILIPPINE CULTURE
Manila University

S. P. Reyna
DEPARTMENT OF SOCIOLOGY AND
ANTHROPOLOGY
University of New Hampshire

Rosemary E. Ridd
DEPARTMENT OF ANTHROPOLOGY
Oxford University

Carlton L. Riemer
Iligan City, Philippines

Richard Roberts
DEPARTMENT OF HISTORY
Stanford University

Frank A. Salamone
DEPARTMENT OF ANTHROPOLOGY
Mount Saint Mary College

Jeffrey T. Sammons
DEPARTMENT OF HISTORY
University of Houston

Ruth Laila Schmidt
CENTER FOR SOUTH AND SOUTHEAST
ASIAN STUDIES
University of California, Berkeley

Henry G. Schwarz
CENTER FOR EAST ASIAN STUDIES
Western Washington University

Kerrin Gräfin Schwerin
DEPARTMENT OF HISTORY
University of Heidelberg

Ray Scupin
DEPARTMENT OF ANTHROPOLOGY
The Lendenwood Colleges

William A. Shack
DEPARTMENT OF ANTHROPOLOGY
University of California, Berkeley

M. Nazif Shahrani
DEPARTMENT OF ANTHROPOLOGY
Pitzer College

Moin Shakir
DEPARTMENT OF POLITICAL SCIENCE
Maharathwada University

J. C. Sharma
DEPARTMENT OF ANTHROPOLOGY
Panjab University

Abdi A. Sheik-Abdi
DEPARTMENT OF ANTHROPOLOGY
University of Massachusetts, Boston

Sergei A. Shuiskii
Princeton University

Carol Silverman
DEPARTMENT OF ANTHROPOLOGY
University of Oregon

Michael Sims
AFRICAN STUDIES ASSOCIATION
Brandeis University

Susan Rodgers Siregar
DEPARTMENT OF SOCIOLOGY AND
    ANTHROPOLOGY
Ohio University

David H. Spain
DEPARTMENT OF ANTHROPOLOGY
University of Washington

Jay Spaulding
Kean College of New Jersey

William Spencer
DEPARTMENT OF POLITICAL SCIENCE
Rollins College

James C. Stewart
California State College at Sonoma

Richard F. Strand
Chicago, Illinois

Nina Swidler
DIVISION OF SOCIAL SCIENCES
Fordham University

Richard Tapper
SCHOOL OF ORIENTAL AND AFRICAN
    STUDIES
University of London

Robin Thelwall
DEPARTMENT OF LINGUISTICS
New University of Ulster

Akbarali H. Thobani
Metropolitan State College, Denver

Elly Touwen-Bouwsma
DEPARTMENT OF ANTHROPOLOGY
Free University, Amsterdam

Joseph Tubiana
CENTRE NATIONAL DE LA RECHERCHE
    SCIENTIFIQUE
Valbonne, France

Marie-José Tubiana
CENTRE NATIONAL DE LA RECHERCHE
    SCIENTIFIQUE
Valbonne, France

Dennis Tully
DEPARTMENT OF ANTHROPOLOGY
University of Washington

Ch. F. van Fraassen
ROYAL INSTITUTE OF LINGUISTICS AND
    ANTHROPOLOGY
Leiden, The Netherlands

Leo F. Van Hoey
DEPARTMENT OF SOCIOLOGY AND
    ANTHROPOLOGY
Lake Forest College

Jacob Vredenbregt
Hasanuddin University

Sidney R. Waldron
DEPARTMENT OF SOCIOLOGY AND
    ANTHROPOLOGY
State University of New York at Cortland

Harry H. Walsh
DEPARTMENT OF RUSSIAN
University of Houston

Peter R. Watson
Summit, New Jersey

Ava S. Weekes (deceased)
Houston, Texas

Richard V. Weekes
DEPARTMENT OF ANTHROPOLOGY
University of Houston

Robert Wessing
DEPARTMENT OF ANTHROPOLOGY
Northern Illinois University

Sigrid Westphal-Hellbush (deceased)
Bochorn, Germany

Ronald Wixman
DEPARTMENT OF GEOGRAPHY
University of Oregon

John A. Works, Jr.
DEPARTMENT OF HISTORY
University of Missouri, St. Louis

Robert M. Wren
DEPARTMENT OF ENGLISH
University of Houston

Donald R. Wright
DEPARTMENT OF HISTORY
State University of New York at Cortland

Theodore P. Wright, Jr.
DEPARTMENT OF POLITICAL SCIENCE
State University of New York at Albany

Inger Wulff
DANISH NATIONAL MUSEUM
Copenhagen, Denmark

Moshe Yegar
Jerusalem, Israel

CONTENTS

Volume 1

MAPS SHOWING
LOCATION OF
MUSLIM GROUPS

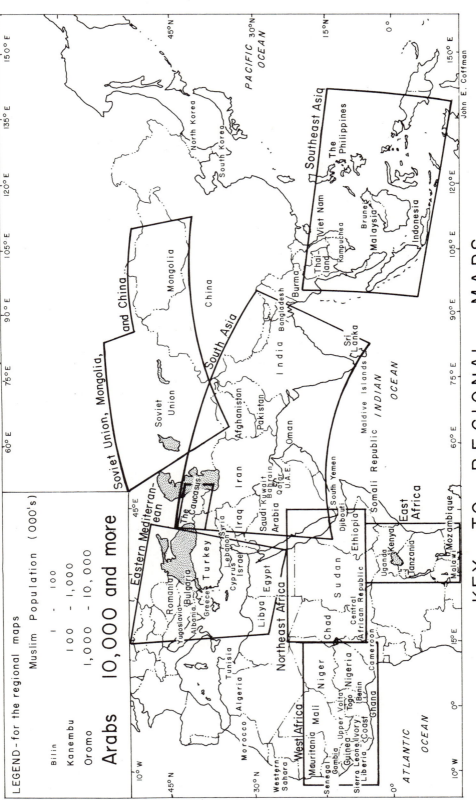

KEY TO REGIONAL MAPS

LEGEND – for the regional maps

Muslim Population (000's)

Bilin   1 – 100

Kanembu   100 – 1,000

Oromo   1,000 – 10,000

Arabs   10,000 and more

Soviet Union, Mongolia, and China

Eastern Mediterranean

The Caucasus

South Asia

Southeast Asia

Northeast Africa

West Africa

East Africa

Mongolia

China

Soviet Union

Afghanistan

Pakistan

Iran

Iraq

Syria

Lebanon

Israel

Cyprus

Turkey

Greece

Bulgaria

Albania

Yugoslavia

Romania

Tunisia

Algeria

Morocco

Western Sahara

Libya

Egypt

Chad

Niger

Mali

Mauritania

Senegal

Gambia

Guinea

Upper Volta

Sierra Leone

Liberia

Ivory Coast

Togo

Benin

Ghana

Nigeria

Cameroon

Central African Republic

Sudan

Ethiopia

Djibouti

South Yemen

Kuwait

Bahrain

Qatar

U.A.E.

Oman

Saudi Arabia

Somali Republic

Uganda

Kenya

Tanzania

Malawi

Mozambique

India

Bangladesh

Burma

Sri Lanka

Maldive Islands

Thailand

Kampuchea

Viet Nam

Malaysia

Brunei

Indonesia

The Philippines

North Korea

South Korea

PACIFIC OCEAN

INDIAN OCEAN

ATLANTIC OCEAN

John E. Coffman

150° E   135° E   120° E   105° E   90° E   75° E   60° E   45° E   15° E   0°   10° W

45° N   30° N   30° N   15° N   0°   45° N

30°N   15°N   0°

EASTERN MEDITERRANEAN

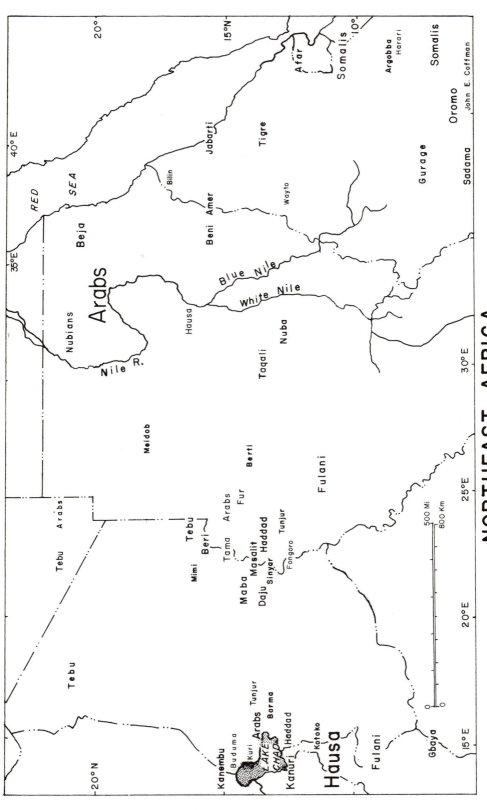

NORTHEAST AFRICA

RED SEA

Arabs

Beja

Nubians

Nile R.

Meidob

Tebu Arabs

Tebu

Tebu

Mimi

Beri

Maba

Daju

Masalit

Sinyar

Haddad

Tama

Fur

Berti

Arabs

Tunjur

Fongoro

Fulani

Hausa

Blue Nile

White Nile

Taqali

Nuba

Bilin

Beni Amer

Jabarti

Tigre

Wayto

Gurage

Sadama

Afar

Somalis

Argobba

Harari

Somalis

Oromo

John E. Coffman

Fulani

Gbaya

Kanembu

Buduma

Kuri

Arabs

Tunjur

Barma

Haddad

Kotoko

Kanuri

Hausa

LAKE CHAD

500 Mi

800 Km

20°N

40°E

35°E

30°E

25°E

20°E

15°E

20°

15°N

10°

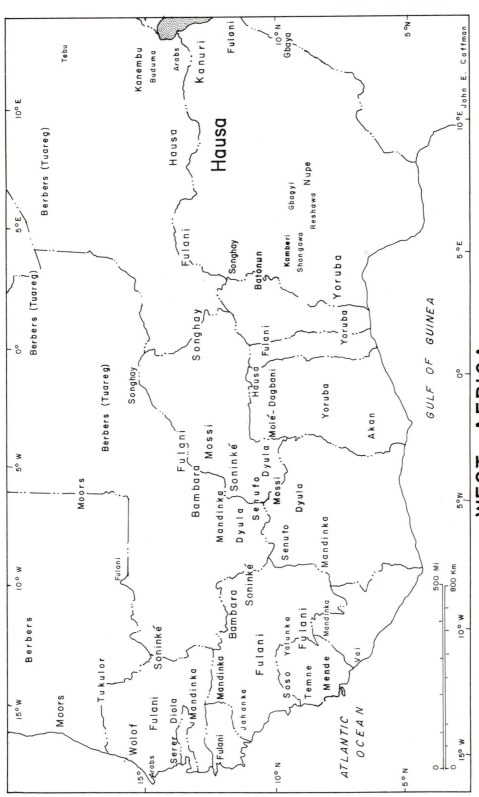

WEST AFRICA

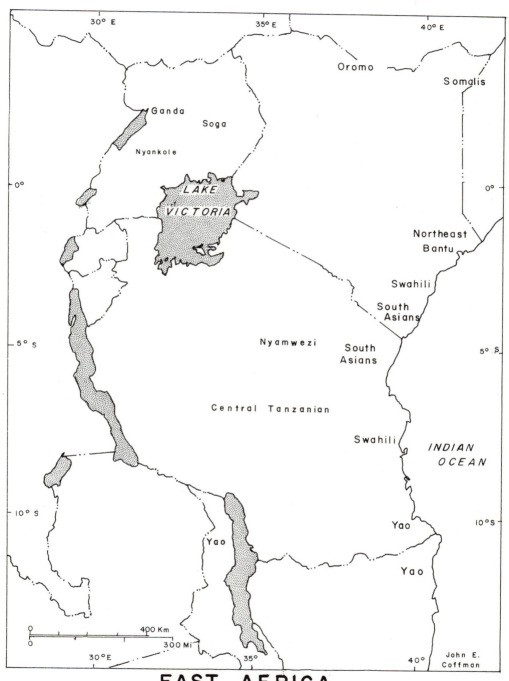

EAST AFRICA

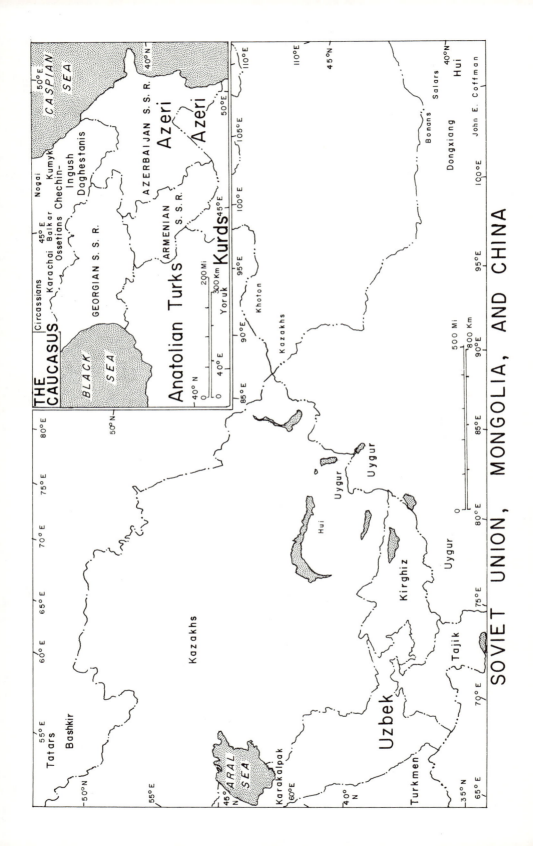

SOVIET UNION, MONGOLIA, AND CHINA

THE CAUCASUS

Circassians
Nogai
Kumyki
Karachai Balkar Chechin-
Ossetians Ingush
Daghestanis

CASPIAN SEA

BLACK SEA

GEORGIAN S. S. R.

AZERBAIJAN S. S. R.

ARMENIAN S. S. R.

Azeri

Azeri

Anatolian Turks

Kurds

Yoruk

John E. Coffman

Hui

Bonans

Salars

Dongxiang

Khoton

Kazakhs

Uygur

Uygur

Uygur

Hui

Kirghiz

Kazakhs

Tatars

Bashkir

Karakalpak

ARAL SEA

Uzbek

Turkmen

Tajik

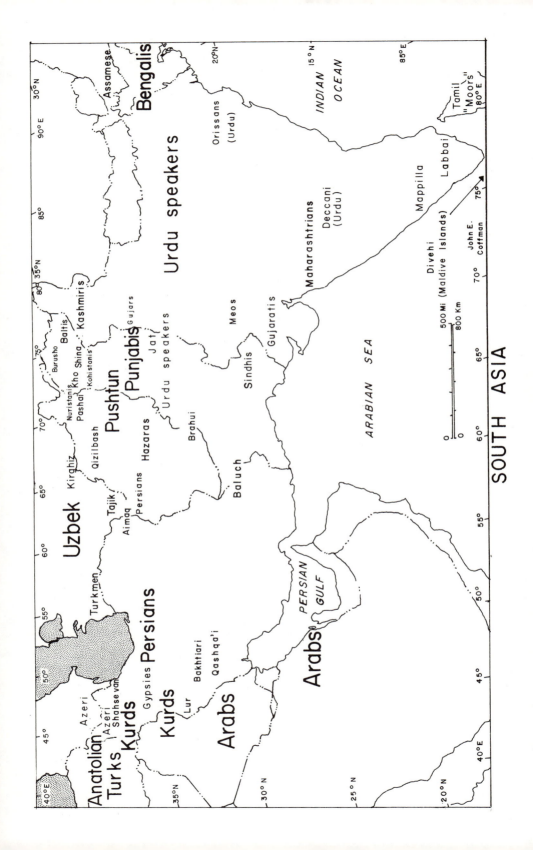

SOUTH ASIA

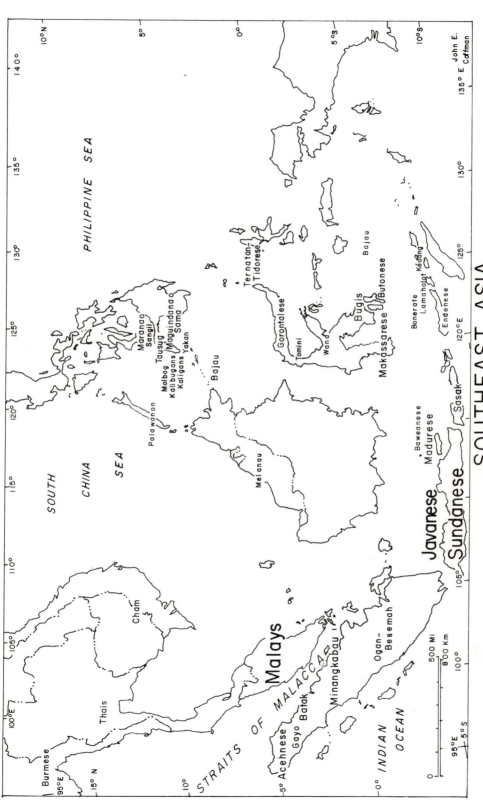

SOUTHEAST ASIA

Muslim Peoples

M

MABA The Maba of eastern Chad constitute that nation's largest non-Arab Muslim group. Like other Chadian Muslims, they are universally Sunni following the Maliki rite. Primarily a farming population, they number some 200,000 people in Chad, with several thousands living as immigrants or refugees in neighboring Sudan. Since their conversion to Islam in the seventeenth century, they have formed the nucleus of Wadai, today a province, but earlier a Muslim sultanate which came to dominate the eastern Chad Basin in the nineteenth century. After years of resistance, the Maba of Wadai were conquered by the French in 1911. A half-century of colonial rule did little to change their culture or to integrate them into the larger nation. For the past 15 years, the Maba and other Chadian Muslims have been involved in a complex civil war which remains unresolved.

The Maba homeland is located on the plateau which slopes upward from the Chad Basin and continues into Sudan. The mean altitude is 1,500 feet, but the landscape is punctuated with isolated granite peaks and highlands which hamper communication. The climate and vegetation are Sahelian, with an average rainfall of 18 inches between May and September. This rainy season is crucial to the Maba farmers, for there are no permanent streams or rivers. Their very name is said to derive from an Arabic phrase meaning ''water is our father,'' although a more likely derivation is ''people of the hills.'' During the rains, the savanna is covered with wild grasses, providing an important supplement to the diet as well as forage for cattle, sheep and goats. Acacia and doum palms are the most common trees, with groves of larger shade trees limited to dry stream beds.

Maba is a collective name for several groups who share a common culture and speak Bora Mabang, a Nilo-Saharan language closely related to Masalit and Runga, spoken to the northeast and south, respectively. The most important Maba subgroups are the Kodoi, Awlad Jema, Malanga, Mandala and Madanga. All of these groups claim to be indigenous, and they intermarry. Traditionally, the sultan's wives came from among them, and they played important roles as notables and soldiers. A second stratum of Maba including the Marfa, Karanga, Kashméré, Koniéré, and Kadianga seem to be clients or immigrants who over the centuries have adopted Bora Mabang. All of these groups formerly held slaves who have been largely assimilated, but there remains one group known as Daramdé or Kultu who serve as a distinct caste of hunters, potters and sometimes smiths while living on the edge of Maba villages (see Haddad). Wadaian often appears as a synonym for Maba, underlining the close connection between the sultanate and people, but the term lacks precision. Unrelated peoples such as Zaghawa, Masalit and even Chadian Arabs often fall under this classification (see Arabs, Chadian; Beri; Masalit).

The heritage of Arab immigration, political centralization and Islam are linked in the area. Local traditions begin with a shadowy Daju dynasty replaced by the Tunjur Arabs at the end of the fifteenth century. Both of these groups play a part in the political traditions of the Fur and, hence, may indicate the appropriation of a neighboring dynastic history. Clearly, small groups of Arab nomads had begun to move onto the Maba plateau in the fourteenth century. An alternating pattern of conflict and cooperation between nomad and farmer began (and continues to the present). Beyond dominating the Maba core area, the Tunjur apparently had little impact upon their subjects (see Tunjur).

Liberation and conversion to Islam is said to have come at one stroke in the seventeenth century. A small group of Arabs led by Abd al-Karim, reputedly an Abbasid prince, allied themselves with Maba chiefs and overthrew the Tunjur. This victory and the foundation of Wadai represents an increase in Arab migration and Islamic influence in the region. The resulting kingdom, however, was not exclusively Arab, the bulk of whom remained nomadic and somewhat marginal to political life. From the capital of Wara and later Abéché, the rulers of Wadai and their Maba supporters enlarged their territory and hence their position as middlemen in the trans-Saharan and trans-continental trade. Military campaigns, particularly in the south, provided ivory and the hundreds of slaves exported northward each year. Pilgrims and merchants came from the west on their way to Red Sea ports. By the mid-nineteenth century, Wadai was the strongest state in central Sudan, and Abéché was a cosmopolitan Muslim capital. The presence there today of regional Sufi orders such as the Mirghaniyya (Sudan), Sanusiyya (Libya), Qadiriyya and the dominant Tijaniyya (West Africa) reflects Wadai's central position.

The colonial conquest was traumatic. The French dismantled the traditional administrative system; drought, famine and epidemics reduced the population by an estimated 50 percent by 1918; in the previous year the French massacred about 100 Muslim scholars and their followers in Abéché. Despite its former prominence, Wadai became a remote corner of French Equatorial Africa. Its population remained largely semi-subsistence farmers and herdsmen. Children were far more likely to attend Quranic classes than the handful of colonial schools serving 1,000 students in a population of 455,000. Literacy (in French) was estimated at less than 5 percent. Colonial neglect was not rectified in the early independence government, dominated as it was by Christian southerners. The attitudes and policies of both groups have fueled the current rebellion.

In Chad, the bulk of the Maba remain rural; Abéché is the only town, with a permanent population estimated at 32,000, of which the Maba constitute less than 50 percent. Nevertheless, the town remains an important regional focus. The sultan's court, reestablished by the French in 1935, vies with the central government for the people's allegiance. The daily market attracts Maba from more remote areas. Others settle in Abéché during the dry season as laborers or artisans. Here they encounter Muslims from a wider world. Chadian Arabic is the lingua franca, and Islamic practice is more rigorous. Until direct air travel to Saudi Arabia replaced land pilgrimage in the 1970s, as many as 80,000 West African pilgrims passed through the town each year. Muslim scholars, many of whom come from Sudan and Nigeria, provide advanced instruction not available in the countryside. Sufism in various forms is firmly entrenched. All of these influences have spread to the surrounding villages. By contrast, the modest network of modern institutions, government offices, shops, schools and a hospital have had a limited impact on the surrounding Maba villages.

The typical Maba village contains 200 to 1,800 people. Households consist of a handful of round straw huts with high, peaked roofs enclosed by mat fences. Huts are reserved for sleeping and storing grain in large clay pots. All other activities take place in the courtyard. The household unit is usually small, headed by a mature male, one wife and their children. The husband's younger, unmarried siblings and his older female relatives may also share the compound. Polygyny is common, but more than three wives is rare; co-wives never share the same compound. Individual households are compactly arranged in honeycomb fashion along narrow lanes, which all lead to a large, central square. Here, there is a straw-roofed pavilion for the elders as well as a mosque demarcated by stones and a thorn hedge. The square serves a variety of communal purposes: dances, assemblies and occasional markets. Villages traditionally are located at the foot of a hill, testifying to their original habitat. Today, as in the past, many Maba have returned to the hills for security against attack.

During the short rainy season farmers cultivate the sandy soil around each village. Millet and sorghum are the staple grains; maize, peanuts and vegetables are grown on smaller plots frequently tended by women who have separate fields. The universal tools are the short-handled hoe and an ax to clear brush. Where suitable soil is in short supply, some villagers establish temporary hamlets in the surrounding area, returning to the main village after harvest. This also appears to be the way in which new settlements are founded. The dry season witnesses a dispersion of villagers, leaving only the elderly and the very young. Young men may move southward with the village herds or set off for Abéché or Sudan as migrant laborers or students. Entire households occasionally move to areas where they can grow tobacco or vegetables on irrigated plots. The Maba, therefore, can be classified as semi-sedentary. The recent political instability has added to this population movement.

Although the Maba have been Muslims for over three centuries, village social organization and customs reflect their pre-Islamic past. There is a rudimentary division of the village population into four age grades beginning with circumcision between the ages of 10 and 12. Young girls submit to clitoridectomy at the same age and become marriageable. After circumcision, the boys usually attend a village Quranic school until the age of 18, helping their teacher with farm labor. Thereafter, the young men serve as shepherds or become migrant laborers. Formerly, this second grade supplied the recruits for the sultan's armies. Full maturity comes with marriage, and from this group the village chief is chosen. At 50, one becomes an elder and spends most of the day under the shelter in the village square. The elders settle local disputes according to traditional law. Centralized authority in the sultanate and later colonial reforms have altered local administration, but age grades continue to function. Despite Quranic injunction, the local millet beer remains popular, and its consumption marks all festivals. Those at harvest undoubtedly had earlier religious significance, but Islamic prayer, fasting and holidays have largely superseded them.

A good deal of the credit for the increased Islamization of the Maba must go to the local teachers, or *fuqura* (singular, *faqi*). Itinerant or settled, Maba or Arab, the *faqi* is the local religious specialist. He teaches, advises, makes charms, collects alms and frequently farms. Nineteenth-century travellers were generally impressed with their network of Quranic education. Admittedly, few of the *fuqura* are scholars or even well versed in the Maliki rite, but they have enhanced religious observance throughout Wadai. Their influence explains the reticence felt by many Maba in sending their children to modern schools as well as the growing number of Chadian students seeking a higher Islamic education in the Sudan or Egypt. The *fuqura* have also served as prime agents of Arabization among the Maba.

The Arab population of Wadai today numbers well over 100,000, while throughout Chad they form the largest ethnic group. Their dark complexion reflects the high degree of intermarriage over the past centuries, and cultural borrowings have been equally common. On the one hand, the Arab ruling class introduced by Abd al-Karim assimilated Maba culture, while on the other Maba gradually adopted Islam and Arab clothing. Until the colonial period, however, the two populations remained distinct although frequently interdependent. Maba farmers exchanged grain for Arab livestock and dairy products, and their settlements were frequently interspersed in much of Wadai.

Under French rule, Arab nomads were encouraged to settle and Maba began to accumulate herds, joining Arabs in seasonal migration. Increased allegiance to Islam and the diffusion of the Arabic language became a form of cultural resistance. The *fuqura* have been involved in both activities. In Maba villages near Abéché, Arabic has become the sole language, and villagers have established an Arab identity complete with fictive genealogies. In remoter areas, Arabic has become universally known. Arabization has continued since independence. The tradition of labor migrations to Sudan has reinforced ties with the larger Arab community, as has the revolt against the national government.

Armed opposition to the government of François Tombalaye began in central

Chad in 1965, and then rapidly spread to the north and east including Wadai. Motives are complex. To the general resentment of northern Muslims towards a southern-dominated government must be added opposition to the corruption of traditional chiefs and government bureaucrats, sectionalism and Islamic resurgence. The conflict has been obscured by political rivalry, banditry and the changing foreign patrons of various factions. Maba participation was initially limited to emigrés in the Sudan who formed the Chadian Liberation Front (FLT), but the call for Muslim solidarity has appealed to more and more Maba. In the first months of 1982, Abéché became the center for Hissene Habré's forces, who have subsequently established tenuous control over the northern two-thirds of the country. Today, the Maba's destiny in the war-torn country remains unclear.

BIBLIOGRAPHY

Books

Decalo, Samuel. *Historical Dictionary of Chad*. London: Scarecrow Press, 1977.
Fisher, Humphrey J., and Fisher, Allan G. B. *Slavery and Muslim Society in Africa*. London: C. Hurst, 1970.
Lapie, Pierre Oliver. *My Travels Through Chad*, translated by Leslie Bull. London: John Murray, 1943.
Nachtigal, Gustav. *Sahara and Sudan*, vol. 4, *Wadai and Darfur*, translated with an introduction by Allen G. B. Fisher and Humphrey J. Fisher. Berkeley: University of California, 1971.
Nelson, Harold D., ed. *Area Handbook for Chad*. Washington, D.C.: Government Printing Office, 1972.
Thomason, Virginia M., and Adlook, Richard. *The Emerging States of French Equatorial Africa*. Stanford: Stanford University Press, 1960.
Works, John A. *Pilgrims in a Strange Land, Hausa Communities of Chad*. New York: Columbia University Press, 1976.

Article

Decalo, Samuel. "Chad, the Roots of Centre-Periphery Strife." *African Affairs* 79:317 (1980): 490–509.

Unpublished Manuscripts

Lemarchand, Rene. "Chad: Background to Conflict." Paper presented to the Colloquium on Chad, Department of State, Washington, D.C., October 1979.

Works, John A. "Wither Chad? Scenarios and Prospects." Paper presented to the Colloquium on Chad, Department of State, Washington, D.C., October 1979.

John A. Works, Jr.

MADURESE   Less than one-third of the Madurese live on their island of Madura off the north coast of East Java. While the inhabitants of the small islands along the south coast of Madura and those living on the Sapudi and Kangean archipelagos east of Madura are also known as Madurese or Orang Madura, most Madurese are dispersed to other parts of Indonesia. Those in and around Madura number perhaps 3 million; nearly 8 million live elsewhere, making the Madurese (10.9 million) Indonesia's third largest ethnic group. Nearly all are Muslim.

Since the second half of the eighteenth century, many Madurese have settled as farmers in East Java, which was underpopulated due to frequent wars between Balinese and Javanese. In the nineteenth century a great number migrated to areas in East Java in search of temporary work on the large sugar and tobacco plantations. In the course of time, thousands settled permanently. Today, the eastern regencies of East Java are mostly inhabited by Madurese, with many more now migrating to the cities of Surabaya and Jakarta as well as to the islands of Bali and Kalimantan.

The Madurese language is related to the Javanese language, the largest subgroup in the Malayo-Polynesian language family. It is also spoken by the inhabitants of the island of Bawean northwest of Madura (see Baweanese). The main dialects are Western Madurese and Eastern Madurese. Within Western Madurese the dialects of Gangkalan and Pamekasan are distinguishable. The Madurese spoken on the islands of Sapudi and Kangean is considered to be a distinct dialect within Eastern Madurese. An indigenous Madurese literature has barely developed. Most Madurese manuscripts are translations of Javanese literary works.

Only 10 percent of the population on Madura lives in the capital cities of the four regencies into which the island of Madura is divided. By far the largest part of the Madurese live in rural villages. These villages were formed by administrative fiat and do not form a social unit. A Madurese village rather consists of a collection of small social units based on kinship and territorial alliances. Compounds are scattered over the farm land. A cluster of 5 to 15 compounds constitutes a hamlet, or *pedukoan*. The inhabitants of such a hamlet are often connected by kinship and marriage.

The majority of the Madurese subsist on agriculture, although fishing, salt production and maritime trade are also important economic activities. Fruit and tobacco cultivation is an important source of income, and the breeding of cattle and animal husbandry are widespread. There are no large industries on Madura; small-scale industry, like the production of tiles, bricks and lime, is only found where the raw materials are.

Due to the shortage of water, rice can be cultivated only once a year on rain-dependent *sawah*. Besides rice, maize, cassava and peanuts are important for direct subsistence. The average landholding is small, and the yield is not sufficient to supply the daily needs of the farmers. Many must seek work in trade or handicrafts. The women gain subsidiary earnings in petty trading and agrarian labor for rich farmers.

Madurese working in other parts of Indonesia keep in touch with their families on the island. They send them money, and for important events like childbirth and marriage they return to their villages temporarily. On major Islamic holidays such as Maulud and Id al Fitr most migrants return to Madura to celebrate with their relatives.

Madurese kinship system is bilateral, and this finds expression in kinship terms. Cousins from both the father and mother's side are called *sapopo*. The smallest social unit is the extended family, usually made up of two or three generations: parents, children and grandchildren. The family lives together on the *pekarangan*, a compound enclosed by fences. The houses are built on the northern part of the compound, the front side facing south. Kitchens and stables are alternately built on the eastern and southern part. The *langgar*, built on the western side, is the center for religious and social activities. Here the men perform their daily prayers, pass the night and see their male guests. Most daily life takes place on the *tanean*, the open space in front of the buildings. The *selamatan*, a communal meal held on Islamic holidays and in celebration of major changes in life stages of family members, takes place in the *langgar*. The house is the domain of the women, in which they say their daily prayers and sleep together with the small children. Their female guests are welcomed on the front verandah of the house.

The Madurese prefer a marriage between relatives, especially between first and second cousins. Usually a marriage is arranged by the respective parents with the parents of a boy proposing for a girl. This proposal is accompanied by the mutual exchange of presents and sweets. The date of the wedding is fixed by the parents of the bridegroom-to-be. Most of the rites connected with a wedding are according to Madurese custom. The *kiyai*, a religious teacher and leader, plays an important part in the ceremony. He says the prayers and solemnizes the marriage; he conducts the wedding procession from the compound of the bridegroom to that of the bride and back again. A marriage is rarely solemnized by officials such as the *modin* or the *pengulu*, an official of the government's Office of Religious Affairs.

Although men are allowed to have four wives at a time according to Islamic law, polygyny is rare. Only among village officials does it occur. Ordinary Madurese cannot afford more than one wife.

The settlement pattern after marriage is predominantly matrilocal. The newlyweds often live on the compound of the wife's parents until they are able to provide for themselves and set up a compound of their own. One of the married children, usually a daughter, stays permanently on the parental compound. She is responsible for taking care of her parents in their old age and after their death, she conducts the *selamatan* cycle, held on the third, seventh, fortieth, and hundredth days and the first and second year after their deaths, and finally on the thousandth day. She then inherits the parents' house and takes over the compound.

During the lifetime of the parents, parts of the inheritance, such as land and cattle, are divided among the children. Not until the death of both parents is the entire inheritance divided. The *ahli waris*, usually the eldest son, plays a major part in the division. All children receive an equal share, despite Islamic inheritance rules to the contrary.

The members of the village council are the formal leaders in the village. Their influence and authority depend on personal qualities and the degree to which they have been successful in gaining the support of the informal leaders. One of these is the local *kiyai*, who takes care of the religious education of the children. He is also invited to say the prayers at the *selamatan*, held on Islamic holidays, marriages and funerals. In all family matters people look to the *kiyai* for advice.

On the whole the informal leaders gain more respect and influence among the rural population than the local officials. Their strong social and political position is reflected in the support given to the orthodox Islamic political party, Nahdatul Ulama, in the 1971 elections. Of the total number of votes in Madura, 67 percent went to this party.

Madurese are Sunni Muslims and adhere to the tenets of the Shafi school. In the course of the sixteenth century, Islam was spread over Madura from the Islamic centers of Giri, Gresik and Ampel in Surabaya on the north coast of Java. In contrast to the Javanese, the distinction between the *abangan* (nominal Muslims) and *santri* (those who endeavor to keep the Five Pillars of Islam) cannot be drawn among the Madurese (see Javanese). Madurese perform the five daily prayers, pay their yearly *zakat* and fast during Ramadan. To be a *hajji* means not only the performance of the pilgrimage but also an increase of status in the community and even the improvement of their economic position. The Islamic holidays of Maulud and Id al Fitr are celebrated within the family circle. It is the custom on Id al Fitr to visit the graves of dead relatives and pray at the tomb of local saints. Lailat al Miraj (Isra Miraj), the ascension of Muhammad, is celebrated in the mosque or in the open square. A good speaker is invited to recite the experiences of the Prophet during his journey through the heavens.

Despite the fact that the Madurese are strict Muslims, their religious conceptions are intertwined with non-Islamic elements. Any change in the life of an individual has to be attended by *selamat* to make things go well. To avert bad influences, a *selamatan* is organized for all sorts of occasions. The prayers said during these *selamatan* are addressed not only to Allah but also to the ancestors.

The Madurese are noted not only for their bullracing (their ancestors are considered to have invented bullfighting) but for their practice of *carok*, which involves eliminating an adversary with a sickle-shaped knife. To commit *carok*, the attacker strikes his victim from behind with his knife so as to cut his carotid arteries or his belly. The threat of *carok* is always present among Madurese when prestige and honor are at stake. The motives for *carok* include adultery, quarrels about goods and cattle and losing face in public. Rarely does a victim of *carok* survive, and a feud between the families or parties involved can be the consequence. (Javanese believe the Madurese are a violent people and express fear about visiting the island of Madura.) To protect oneself from the threat of *carok*, or to find help in a village election or a bullrace, one consults a *dykun* or a *kiyai*.

The modernist Islamic movement, Muhammadiya, has followers only among intellectuals, officials and teachers in the regional capitals. The reformist ideas of this movement, namely, adherence to the Quran only and rejection of ancestor and saint worship, find little appeal among rural Madurese, who are more oriented to the local *kiyai* and their religious conceptions.

Change in the sense of adaptation of modern values is slow in the rural areas of Madura. Secular education has not yet been fully accepted. In 1974 more than 50 percent of the population was illiterate. The Madurese prefer religious education to secular education. Some of the religious schools, especially in the interior of Madura, are centers of the Naqshbandiyya *tariqa* (Sufi brotherhood).

Traditional values are strong among the Madurese. The rules given by the ancestors represent the *adat*, custom, and must be respected to gain health and prosperity. On the other hand people are expected to be good Muslims and gain *selamat* in this life and afterwards. In short, both religion and *adat* hold essential values for life. As the Madurese say: "Whereas religion is my soul, *adat* is my breath."

BIBLIOGRAPHY

Books

Atmosoedirdjo. *Vergelijkende Adatrechtelijke Studie van Oost-javase Madoerezen en Oesingers*. Amsterdam: Poortpers, 1952.

Farjon, I. *Madura and Surrounding Islands: An Annotated Bibliography, 1860–1942*. Koninklijk Instituut voor Taal-, Land-en Volkenkunde, Bibliographic Series, No. 7. The Hague: Martinus Nijhoff, 1980.

Graaf, H. J. de, and Pigeaud, Th. G. Th. *De eerste Moslimse Vorstendommen op Java. Studiën over de staatkunige Geschiedenis van de 15de en 16de eeuw*. Verhandelingen van het Koninklijk Instituut voor Taal-, Land-en Volkenkunde, No. 69. The Hague: Martinus Nijhoff, 1974.

Leunissen, J. *Monografi Daerah Jawah Timur*. Vols. 1–3. Jakarta: Department Pendidikan dan Kebudayaan Republik Indonesia, 1977.

Niehof, A. "The Family Planning Fieldworker and Village Politics on Madura, Indonesia." In *Local Leadership and Program Implementation in Indonesia*, edited by Quarles van Ufford et al. Amsterdam: Vrije Universiteit, 1981.

Touwen-Bouwsma, E. *De Barisanorganisatie van Madura: Nieuwe eisen aan een oud kader*. Medeldelingen van de Subfakulteit der Sociaal-Kulturele Wetenschappen van de Vrije Universiteit, No. 6. Amsterdam: Vrije Universiteit, 1977.

———. "Historical and Contemporary Fallacies Affecting the Position of the Village Head in Sampang, Madura." In *Local Leadership and Program Implementation in Indonesia*, edited by Quarles van Ufford, et al. Amsterdam: Vrije Universiteit, 1981.

Uhlenbeck, E.M.A. *A Critical Survey of Studies on the Languages of Java and Madura*. Koninklijk Instituut voor de Taal-, Land-en Volkenkunde, Bibliographical Series, No. 7. The Hague: Martinus Nijhoff, 1964.

Articles

Bijlmer, J. "Pencarian Nafkah di Surabaya." *Madura II, Proyek Penilitian Madura* (1978): 194–210.

Halim Kahn, M. "The Economic Geography of Madura." *Madjalah Geografi Indonesia* 5 (1965): 22–32.

Jonge, H. de. "Juragans and Bandols: Intermediaries in Tobacco-trading on Madura." *Madura II, Proyek Penilitian Madura* (1978): 194–210.

———. "Staatsvorming per contract Het Madurese Regentschap Sumenep, de V.O.C. en Nederlands-Indie 1680–1883." *Symposion* 2 (1979): 170–187.

Jordaan, R. E. "Tombuwan in the 'Dermatology' of Madurese Folk-Medicine." *Bijdragen tot de Taal-, Land-en Volkenkunde* 138 (1982): 9–29.

Unpublished Manuscripts

Koesnoe, M. "Kedudukan Wanita menurut Adat beberapa Masyarakat Pedesaan di Madura." Laporan Penilitian, Universitas Airlangga Surabaya, 1972.

Kuntowijoyo. "Social Change in an Agrarian Society: Madura 1850–1940." Ph.D. dissertation, Columbia University, 1980.

Soesang Obeng, H. "Perkawinan menurut Hukum Adat Madura, di Kabupaten Sumenep." Laporan Penelitian, Universitas Airlangga Surabaya, 1972.

Touwen-Bouwsma, E. "Cara mewariskan Tanah di salah satu Desa Pertanian di Madura." Paper presented at the Seminar Penilitian Madura, Batu, Indonesia, July 1979.

———. "Carok, een vorm van dreiging en geweld in boerengemeen-schappen op Madura." Paper presented at the KOTA III Conference, "Geweld in Aziatische Maatschappijen," Amsterdam, May 1982.

Elly Touwen-Bouwsma

MAGUINDANAO   The Maguindanao are the largest Muslim ethnic group in the Philippines. They number approximately 885,000, or about 1.7 percent of the population. Nearly all live in the province of Cotabato on the large southern island of Mindanao.

Just north of the Maguindanao are two other major Muslim groups—the Maranao of the region around Lake Lanao and the Iranon, who live along the coast of Illana Bay (see Maranao). The three groups are closely related culturally and linguistically, suggesting a possible common origin, probably in pre-Islamic times. In fact, the Iranon are sometimes treated merely as a subgroup of the Maranao, although they regard themselves as culturally distinct.

The Maguindanao have been called the "people of the flood plain." They inhabit the vast river basin of Pulangi, or Rio Grande de Mindanao, an expanse of marshlands interlaced with serpentine waterways. In former times, most of their settlements were located on the banks of the many rivers and streams and on higher ground in and around the marshes. The two largest settlements were near present-day Cotabato City and what is now Dulawan, or Datu Piang.

For the past several centuries the Maguindanao have been united by a common language, Maguindanao of the Malayo-Polynesian family, and have shared social and political institutions, visible outward symbols of dress and ornamentation and a faith in Islam. Over the years, many neighboring peoples have been absorbed into Maguindanao society, and it appears that the two specific requisites for such absorption have been acceptance of the group's sociopolitical organization and conversion to Sunni Islam. To be a Maguindanao is to be a Muslim.

The symbols of ethnic identity are many, although not all are as widely used as they were in the past. Many Maguindanao men have shaved heads or close-cropped hair, and the head is normally bound in public with a kerchief or a turban, which may be topped with a woven hat. *Hajjis* wear a particular type of white decorated turban. Some men wear the tubular, wraparound skirt. In the past, members of ruling families and other persons of high status could be identified by several symbols—among the men by a certain type of rounded hat and most notably by an ivory-handled, gold- and silver-ornamented *kris*, or curved sword.

Older Maguindanao communities often include several large wooden houses containing multiple dwelling units. These houses may be occupied by a single extended family or, as is more often the case, by several nuclear families related by varying degrees of kinship. Many Maguindanao are quite mobile and take up residence with kinsmen for indefinite periods. There is a marked sense of commonality in the use of land and resources in areas where some common ancestry has been established.

In traditional times the Maguindanao practiced a crude form of slash cultivation, sometimes accompanied by burning. Their staple foods were rice, tubers, sago and, later, corn. Coconuts and an abundant variety of fruits were grown. Chickens and goats were kept, and fish were obtained in great quantities from the rivers and marshes. Some spices were cultivated, as were coffee, betel nut and, later, cacao and tobacco. The principal change in recent times is that many Maguindanao have shifted to plow and harrow methods of wet rice cultivation.

The conversion of these and other nearby peoples from animism to Islam is shrouded in legend. Traditional accounts attribute their conversion to the teachings of Sarip Kabungsuwan, a Muslim prince of Johore (Malay peninsula) who claimed direct decent from the Prophet Muhammad. Kabungsuwan is said to have arrived at Mindanao around 1500 accompanied by a small group of Sama warriors (see Sama). Legends persist that through a combination of his wisdom, the force of his personality and the great appeal of his message Kabungsuwan was able to win converts peacefully. The accuracy of these legends remains unknown, but it is interesting that both the Maranao and Maguindanao families of higher rank trace their genealogical descent from Sarip Kabungsuwan.

Tradition holds that the Malay prince assumed the local title *datu*, which may be loosely translated as lord or chieftain. His direct successors, however, were known as *sulutan* (sultan). At times, there were several sultanates in Cotabato. A *sulutan* was advised and supported by a council of *datus* known as the *ruma bechara*, which played a significant role in the selection of an heir to the sultanate. Numerous military and civilian posts associated with the sultanate were often held by relatives of the *sulutan*.

The joint processes of Islamic conversion and political consolidation early in the sixteenth century appear to have initiated an expansionist phase in Maguindanao history. The Maguindanao controlled most of the trade between the seacoast and the interior of Mindanao, and at various times they dominated most of the southern part of the island from the Zamboanga peninsula on the west to the coast of Davao on the east. The powerful Muslim lowlanders were able to exact tribute and taxes from the pagan hill tribes and often took slaves from among these peoples.

When the Spanish began to colonize the northern and central Philippine islands from 1565 onward, they came into direct conflict with the Maguindanao and other Muslim people of the south. The Spaniards identified the Islamized natives with their traditional enemies, the Moors of North Africa, and thus called them Moros, a term which is now regarded as derogatory and is resented by contemporary Muslim Filipinos. Spanish attempts to conquer and subjugate these Muslims led to the prolonged, although intermittent, hostilities known as the Moro Wars, which spanned more than 300 years of Philippine history. In the notorious tradition of divide and conquer, the Spanish manned their armies for these wars with Christian converts from the northern islands. This was to have profound and lasting consequences, for it led to a bitter enmity between Christian and Muslim Filipinos, even though these peoples probably shared a similar cultural heritage in pre-Islamic, pre-Christian times.

The Spanish never fully subdued the Maguindanao, although they were able to contain them from about 1850 until the end of their colonial rule in 1898. The Americans finally ended major armed resistance in Cotabato with the defeat of the Muslim hero Datu Ali in 1905. From that time on the major effort of the American colonial government, and later the Philippine government, was to integrate the Maguindanao into the rest of the nation politically and to encourage resettlement in Cotabato by non-Muslim Filipinos.

A distinctive characteristic of Maguindanao social organization is a system of social rank known as *maratabat*. Those persons most directly descended from Kabungsuwan have the greatest *maratabat* and are accorded the highest rank, *datu*. The *sulutan* was traditionally chosen from among the *datus*. The next highest rank is that of the *dumatu*, or lesser nobles. Below them are the *sakop*, who are followers, or freemen. Lowest in rank are the *ulipan*, who are freemen indentured for debts or crimes. Not included in the system of social rank, but providing an important base for Maguindanao society in traditional times, were the *banyaga*, or chattel slaves.

The social categories based upon *maratabat* are conceived and described by the Maguindanao as discrete, endogamous social classes. In actual practice, however, marriages between persons of varying rank are common, and children are assigned to a rank intermediate between those of their parents. This leads to an integrated spectrum of rank rather than to sharply defined social classes.

Maratabat is central to Maguindanao social and political organization because it gives the *datus* special claim to power and privilege. It directly affects the organization of labor as well as much of everyday social interaction. It provides the basis for determining the proper amount of *sunggod*, or bridewealth, to be exchanged at marriage. Finally, in cases of homicide or accidental killing, it is used to reckon the amount of blood money, or *wergild*, needed to avert a feud.

Like most Philippine ethnic groups, the Maguindanao have a bilateral kinship system, and males and females usually inherit equally. One exception is that descent from Kabungsuwan is considered more direct through male ancestors. The personal kindred has many important social functions in connection with rights to land, residence rights, marriage negotiations and feuding. The Maguindanao favor and frequently practice second cousin marriage, producing a sort of kindred endogamy which promotes solidarity within this otherwise somewhat amorphous group. *Datus* and others of high rank may take plural wives, but polygyny is rare among common people. Divorce occurs among those of all ranks, especially in cases of infertility, incompatibility, adultery or non-payment of promised amounts of *sunggod*. Nevertheless, the marriage bond appears strong following the birth of children.

The Islam of the Maguindanao is distinctly a folk Islam. Especially in rural areas the religion is imperfectly understood, and frequently there is only limited observation of rituals and obligations. The formal religious convictions of rural villagers tend to coexist with strong ancient beliefs in environmental spirits. There is common conviction about the efficacy of certain magical rituals and healing ceremonies. Sarip Kabungsuwan himself is said to have had miraculous powers of magic and healing.

These beliefs are sometimes accepted even by the local religious leaders, known as *panditas*, who conduct religious ceremonies and who otherwise attempt to teach a basic understanding of the Quran. In recent years, however, there has been increased awareness of, and interest in, orthodox Islamic beliefs and practices. This has been accompanied by a growing sense of community with Muslim peoples outside the Philippines. Indicative of this trend is the fact that many new mosques and *madrasas* have been constructed in Cotabato, and the number of young people receiving a formal religious education has increased sharply.

The Maguindanao are now a minority even in their home region of Cotabato, which in recent years has been divided by the national government into several provinces for political reasons. Like other Muslims in the country, the Maguindanao have been subject to special laws allowing them to maintain certain of their cultural traditions, most notably the practices of polygyny and divorce. These laws have been renewed or extended repeatedly, but they have always specified a termination date at some time in the near future. The assumption of the central government in granting such short-term exceptions to national laws appears to be that they, along with other Filipino Muslims, must sooner or later accept the norms of the larger society.

Economic development has been rather limited in predominantly Muslim areas of the Cotabato provinces. Maguindanao attribute this to government neglect, while non-Maguindanao blame it on the traditionalism of the Muslims, including what outsiders view as an archaic social and political system which continues to favor the few of higher rank. The political power of the *datus* has declined in recent years, due in part to acculturative pressures upon their society and in part to the changing population of these provinces. For a time, some were able to attain elective political office at the national and provincial levels, but this has become increasingly rare with the influx of settlers and changed electorate.

The political future of the Maguindanao and other Muslim peoples of Mindanao and Sulu has remained uncertain for several years. A secessionist movement which came to be known as the Moro National Liberation Front (MNLF) emerged in the early 1970s and became militarily active after the declaration of martial law in 1972. The armed conflict between MNLF forces and government troops caused considerable social disruption in Cotabato and elsewhere during the 1970s and into the 1980s. Like the Spanish and American colonial governments, the present Philippine government has experienced difficulty in bringing lasting peace to this region and ensuring harmonious relations among its numerous ethnic groups, including the Maguindanao.

BIBLIOGRAPHY

Books

Chaffee, Frederic H., et al. *Area Handbook for the Philippines*. The American University FAS, DA Pam 550–72. Washington, D.C.: Government Printing Office, 1969.
Forrest, Captain Thomas. *A Voyage to New Guinea and the Moluccas, from Balambangan: Including an Account of the Maguindanao, Sooloo and Other Islands*. London: 1780. Selected portions reprinted in *Travel Accounts of the Islands*. Manila: Filipiniana Book Guild, 1971.
Gowing, Peter G., and McAmis, Robert D. *The Muslim Filipinos: Their History, Society and Contemporary Problems*. Manila: Solidaridad Publishing House, 1974.
Ileto, Reynaldo C. *Magindanao, 1860–1888: The Career of Dato Uto of Buayan*. Southeast Asia Program Data Paper, No. 82. Ithaca: Cornell University Press, 1971.

Majul, Cesar A. *Muslims in the Philippines*. Quezon City: University of the Philippines Press, 1973.

Saleeby, Najeeb M. *Studies in Moro History, Law and Religion*. Manila: Bureau of Public Printing, 1905.

Articles

Costa, Hoacio de la. "A Spanish Jesuit Among the Magindanaus." *Comment* 12 (1961): 19–41.

Enoc, Pasandalan. "Marriage Among the Magindanaws." *Philippines Today* 9:3 (1963): 13–15.

Hunt, Chester L. "Ethnic Stratification and Integration in Cotabato." *Philippine Sociological Review* 5:1 (1957): 13–38.

Mednick, Melvin. "Some Problems of Moro History and Political Organization." *Philippine Sociological Review* 5:1 (1957): 39–52.

Stewart, James C. "The Cotobato Conflict: Impressions of an Outsider." *Solidarity* 7:4 (1972): 31–42.

Unpublished Manuscript

Stewart, James C. "People of the Flood Plain." Ph.D. dissertation, University of Hawaii, 1977.

James C. Stewart

MAHARASHTRIANS   Muslims constitute one of the small, yet significant cultural and social segments of the population of the west Indian state of Maharashtra and its capital, Bombay. It is the largest minority in the state. Although the various parts of the state were once under Muslim rule, the extent of Muslim cultural impact on Maharashtra is much less than on northern India. Some of the factors limiting this impact are the state's geographical location far south of the Muslim-dominated areas, the Hindu influence on former Muslim rulers, continuity of revenue administration, compostion of the armies and the relative absence of intolerance.

The number of Muslims in Maharashtra (5.7 million) is only 8.4 percent of the total state population. Rural Muslims constitute 5 percent of the population while urban Muslims make up 15.8 percent. In no district of Maharashtra do Muslims form more than 15 percent of the population. In Bombay and Aurangabad, they constitute 14.7 and 14.2 percent respectively; in Poona, 5 percent.

The overwhelming majority of Maharashtrian Muslims are converted from Hinduism, but a small number are descended from the original Muslim migrants who settled in the coastal region of Kakan around A.D. 700. These are known as Kufas and originally lived in Egypt, but fled from persecution there. Even today, surnames such as Khalib and Fakhi show the Arab origins.

Conversion began in the twelfth century in the wake of the Muslim invasion from north India. This period also witnessed the continuous flow of Arabs, Turks and Persians into western India. In addition to the Moghuls, some Muslims also migrated from south India. After the establishment of British rule, some left western India, but many who had come as camp followers settled in the area. Muslim communities of Kakars, Bedras, Mukris and Gaokasais are instances of those who came from different parts of India and stayed in Maharashtra. Except in Marathwada, a large number of converts belonged to the lower stratum of Hindu society. In Marathwada, which was a part of the old Hyderabad state, high-caste Brahmins and Marathas embraced Islam in order to safeguard their traditional rights and privileges. During the British period, Shia Muslim communities, such as Bohra, Khoja and Memon, migrated from Kutch Gujarat and became Maharashtrians.

As there is variety in the heritage of Maharashtrians, so too is there no common language among them. The Muslims in rural areas communicate in the language of the areas. Thus the language of the Muslims in Vidharba is Hindi; in western Maharashtra, Marathi; in the Konkan region, Konkani; in Marathwada, Marathi and Urdu; and in Bombay, Gujarati and Hindustani.

The Muslim social structure in Maharashtra is hierarchical, but unlike the Hindu caste system, it is not very elaborate or rigid. Many similarities do exist, however. In fact, the community is not a single, homogeneous, well-knit group, but rather a conglomeration of various sub-communities. They are different from each other in matters of faith, beliefs, social customs and rituals. They marry within the group and are ranked hierarchically. The whole stratification appears to be a part of the wider Hindu organization. For example, the Muslim Bagban (fruit and vegetable trader) serves both Muslim and Hindu customers. The Hindus also consider them as a separate caste. In the same way, certain castes, such as Dhobis, Halal or Hajjam, which are looked down upon by Hindus because of their low rank, are also considered to be low by Muslims. The *ashraf* (descendants of the Prophet Muhammad or his followers) feel that these groups are inferior.

A large number of Muslims belong to the Sunni sect and are followers of the Hanafi school. The Khojas and the Bohras belong to the Shia (Ismaili) sect. Various Sunni groups in Konkan follow the Shafi school. Among the various well-known castes or sub-communities found within Muslim society are the Sayyids (in all districts of Maharashtra except in Konkan); Shaikhs, who claim descent from Aku Bakr, Siddiqi, Omar Farooq and Abbas (one of Muhammad's uncles); Pathans; and Moghuls. The Khojas, Bohras and Memons (who originally belonged to the Lohana community of the Hindus) are heavily concentrated in Bombay and speak Gujaratis (see Gujaratis). They have their own caste associations. Their dress and social customs are different from the rest of the Muslim population. The Bohras and Khojas have separate mosques. Members of these communities marry among themselves and constitute a large trading community in Bombay.

Among other occupational Muslim groups are the Monins (who once belonged to Salis and Koshti caste of the Hindus and are in Malegaon, Yeola, Manmad

and Bhivandi); Attars (perfumers); Kaligars (tinsmiths); Rafugars (clothes dar-
ners); Barudgars (manufacturers of fireworks); Takaras (stone carvers originally
belonging to the Dhondphoda community of Hindus); Misgaras (copper and
brass smiths); Saltankars (tanners and the descendants of the untouchable Cham-
bhar caste); Mukris (moneylenders and traders in grain, who were part of the
Hindu Laman tribe); Mahavats (elephant drivers); Kafshgars (makers of embroidered slippers worn by Muslims during marriage ceremonies); Hajjams (barbers); Phanibands (makers of combs from wood or bone); Multanis (sellers of
dried fish); Garudi or Madari (village magicians); Dharads (ironsmiths); Dar-
veshis (mendicants); Sikkalgars (traditionally, makers of metal arms, such as
swords, daggers and spears, but now grinders of knives and scissors); Naqarchees
(drum beaters); Gaokasai (beef butchers); Bakar Kasai (goat and sheep butchers);
Halalkhors (sweepers originally belonging to the Bhangi caste); Tambolis (sellers
of betel leaves, tobacco and betel nuts); Dhobis (washermen); Bhatyaras (cooks);
and Kanjars (sellers of chickens and eggs).

Also Bedras (hunters and husbandmen); Kagazis (paper makers); Nalbands
(who shoe horses and bullocks); Naikwaris (messengers); Sarbans (camel drivers); Pinjaris (cotton cleaners); Lakarharas (suppliers of wood); Teli (sellers of
sweet oil); Labbayars (dealers in leather goods, found in Kolhapur); Dalal (brokers in horse trading); Darzis (tailors); Goniwalas (grain sellers); Pakhalis (water
carriers); Patregars (silk tassel twisters); Bojgaras (who distill and sell millet
beer, found in Sholapur); Rachiharas (needle fitters); Bhadbhunjas (grain parch-
ers); Bhois (fishermen); Bhishtis (peddlers); Rangrez (dyers); Maniyars (bracelet
makers); Gaundi (bricklayers); Dhuldhoyas (collectors of ashes from goldsmiths'
shops or ashes of Hindu bodies to sift for particles of gold and silver); Jamati
Muslims (Kokani-speaking upper-class Muslims); Daldis (fishermen in Kokan);
Habshis (descendants of Abyssinian slaves); and Chorvad (illegitimate children
of Kokani and Siddiqi landlords).

Barring those in trading communities, such as Bohras or Khojas in Bombay
who are quite well off, and certain landlord families in Vidharba, Marathwada
and western Maharashtra, most Muslims are poor artisans or landless laborers.
They have been migrating to industrial towns, particularly Bombay, in search
of jobs in factories and industries. This is one of the factors accounting for their
small rural population; but however small their actual rural percentage, they are
treated as part of the village community. Their customs are not very different
from those of the Hindus. There are even many similarities in religious observances; Muslims follow quite a few Hindu customs and offer vows to Hindu
deities. In the same way, Muslim saints or *pirs* (dead or alive) are treated with
deep respect by Hindus. Both groups participate in some of each other's festivals,
such as Holi and Muharrum. Muslims do not always eat beef or mutton, or if
the Hindus, particularly the dominant caste in Maharashtra, want to eat mutton,
the animal is killed by Muslim butchers.

In those urban areas where their population is large, say, over 15,000, Muslims
form separate identifiable groups. Notwithstanding the similarities in the cele-

bration of marriage and other rituals, they celebrate Muslim holy days in their own traditions. They have separate educational institutions. Even in urban areas, social divisions persist, strengthened by the caste-oriented and faction-ridden politics of the state, despite the political and religious leadership's insistence upon a united community.

Although the Muslim contribution to the cultural life of Maharashtra is limited, Marathwada has always been a preserve of Urdu language and literature. Urdu prose and poetry are widely read, and a few Muslims have made notable contributions to the enrichment of Marathi language and literature. Prominent among them are Amar Shaikh, Hamid Dalwai and Mrs. Mumtaz Rahmatpure.

However much Hindu and Muslim have lived in harmony in the past, increased incidents of communal violence in certain parts of Maharashtra and deepening feelings of economic discrimination are causing disillusion among urban Muslims with leading national parties. Increasing numbers are joining such parties as the Muslim League. The league has already become a strong force in Bombay and in certain parts of Marathwada and Vidharba. This separatist political consciousness cannot help but have an adverse effect on the socio-cultural life in Maharashtra.

BIBLIOGRAPHY

Books

Ahmed, Imtiaz, ed. *Caste and Social Stratification Among the Muslims*. Delhi: Manohar Book Service, 1973.
Davis, Kingsley. *The Population of India and Pakistan*. Princeton: Princeton University Press, 1951.
Gibb, H.A.R., and Kramers, J. H., eds. *Shorter Encyclopedia of Islam*. Ithaca: Cornell University Press, 1965.
Karve, Irawati. *Maharashtra: Land and Its People*. Bombay: Directorate of Government Printing, 1968.
Orenstein, Henry. "Leadership and Caste in a Bombay Village." In *Leadership and Political Institutions in India*, edited by Richard L. Park and Irene Tinker. Princeton: Princeton University Press, 1959.
Siddiqui, N. A. *Population Geography of Muslims in India*. New Delhi: Directorate of Government Printing, 1976.

Article

Morrison, William A. "Family Types in Badlapur: An Analysis of a Changing Institution in a Maharashtrian Village." *Sociological Bulletin* 8 (1959): 45–67.

Moin Shakir
U. B. Bhoite
Population figures updated by Richard V. Weekes

MAKASSARESE   The Makassarese (or Mangkasara', as they call themselves) number an estimated 2.5 million and form one of the major groups in the

Indonesian province of South Sulawesi (formerly South Celebes). They inhabit the coastal plains and mountainous interior of the southern regions as well as the island of Salayar lying off the south coast. Ujung Pandang, called Makassar until 1971, which is the capital and largest city of this province, is located in the Makassarese area. About half of its population is Makassarese.

The culture of the Makassarese is basically similar to that of the Bugis, who live to their north, and the whole of the Bugis-Makassar peninsula may appropriately be considered a single cultural area (see Bugis). The principal difference between the two groups is the languages they speak, which, though closely cognate, differ considerably in vocabulary. Traditional Makassar and Bugi literature, on the other hand, are largely similar, while the pre-Muslim script, which is still in use, is the same for both.

The Makassarese have a longstanding tradition of seafaring, fishing and overseas trade. In the seventeenth century, Gowa, the main Makassar kingdom, expanded into a maritime empire dominating the South Sulawesi peninsula, the coasts of the whole of Sulawesi and some neighboring islands. Its power was based on the wealth accumulated through an overseas trade extending over the entire Indonesian archipelago and beyond.

After this Makassar empire was destroyed by the Dutch in 1669, large Makassar fleets for years roamed the intra-island seas in search of spoils and action.

A Makassar venture combining fishery and commerce was first started in the eighteenth century, when there was a growing demand for trepang or *bêche-de-mer*, a small edible marine animal, for the Chinese cuisine. Makassarese fishermen took part in collecting trepang from where it grew on the seabed in shallow water and brought large quantities to Makassar, mainly for export to China. Their search for trepang led them to the southern seas and eventually to the coastal waters of northern Australia, which became their principal trepang grounds. For about a century and a half, until 1906 when Australia closed its coasts to them, a fleet of their vessels used to set out annually from Makassar with the northwest monsoon and return six months later with the southeast wind. Artifacts found on the northern Australia coasts and traces of Makassarese influence on the culture and languages of the local aborigines testify to their former presence and activities there.

A traditional shipbuilding center still exists in the southeastern salient of South Sulawesi, near villages such as Ara and Bira, where the Bugis-Makassar sailing vessels are still built. The age-old technology, details of which are orally transmitted, is kept alive by a population speaking a Makassarese dialect.

Ships of the *pinisi'* type, locally developed with some Western influences, may weigh some 100 tons and reach a length of about 70 feet. They are constructed of hardwood timber in boatyards on the beach with the aid of nothing but an adze but supported by magic spells and symbolic ceremonies at crucial stages.

Ever since the king of Gowa adopted Islam in 1605, the life and society of the Makassarese have been marked by this religion, including its more and its less rigidly orthodox elements. The most revered saint is the seventeenth-century mystic Shaikh Yusuf (1626–1699), whose tomb in the center of the old kingdom of Gowa is an object of pilgrimage. He not only was a learned Sufi who had studied in Mecca but also is commemorated as a national hero. He was one of the leaders of the resistance against the Dutch in Java until his capture and banishment first to Ceylon and later to South Africa. He is venerated as a great Muslim leader both in South Africa, where he died and was buried, and in South Sulawesi, where his remains were transferred in 1705. One of the local Sufi orders, the Khalwatiyya Yusuf, traces its origins to Shaikh Yusuf. The people of certain villages even believe that a visit to his grave is the equivalent to a pilgrimage to Mecca.

Among the mountain people there are groups, called Patungtung, who still retain partially pre-Islamic religious beliefs and have special ceremonies and religious leaders of their own. In the eastern district of Kajang there lives a similar group under their chief, titled *ammatoa* ("old father"), as guardians of the sacred wood of Tombolo.

BIBLIOGRAPHY

Books

Andaya, A. Y. *The Heritage of Arung Palakka: A History of South Sulawesi (Celebes) in the Seventeenth Century.* The Hague: Martinus Nijhoff, 1981.
Horridge, G. A. *The Konjo Boatbuilders and the Bugis Prahu of South Sulawesi.* Marine Monograph and Reports, No. 40. London: National Maritime Museum, 1979.
MacKnight, C. C. *The Voyage to Marege': Macassan Trepangers in Northern Australia.* Melbourne: University Press, 1976.

J. Noorduyn

MALAYO-POLYNESIAN-SPEAKING PEOPLES   Several different geographical groups are represented by populations that speak Malayo-Polynesian languages. Although these various populations speak languages of a single family of languages and share certain cultural traits associated with an ancient horticultural technology, they are culturally diverse.

Malayo-Polynesian languages are spoken by native populations of Madagascar, the Malay peninsula, Indonesia, the Philippine islands, Taiwan, the islands of the Pacific Ocean and isolated areas of southern Vietnam and Kampuchea (Cambodia). Before the rapid spread of Indo-European languages beginning about four centuries ago, no other language family was spread so widely as Malayo-Polynesian. It was probably even more widespread in ancient times, having been represented among languages of the East African mainland before the great migration of Bantu speakers and perhaps among languages of the southern coastal areas of mainland China before the last great southward spread of Sinitic languages.

The place of origin of Malayo-Polynesian is not known. Some prehistorians have placed its beginnings in southern China and associate its spread with that of an ancient system of food production (the Southeast Asian Horticultural Neolithic—beginning perhaps 12,000 years ago). Other scholars have pointed out that Malayo-Polynesian is not now represented by any language of the Chinese mainland and only by Cham and its dialects and Malay and its dialects in mainland Southeast Asia. According to these latter scholars the greatest diversity of Malayo-Polynesian languages is in the Melanesian area near Fiji, which may be the place from where Malayo-Polynesian languages dispersed. Both theories are based on incomplete data.

A number of Muslim ethnic groups not treated separately here have been grouped together into a single cultural complex by some authors. The Abung (864,000) and their cultural allies, Besemah (395,000), Kerinci (311,000), Rejang (778,000), Lampungers (662,000) and Batinese (105,000) belong to a so-called Rejang-Lampung complex of ethnic groups which occupy most of the southern third of Sumatra. Groups of this complex seem to have a Batak-like substratum of culture based originally on a religion of megalithic initiation rites, human sacrifice and headhunting (see Batak). The substratum has been deeply modified through intensive contact with Malay, Minangkabau and Javanese culture.

The Abung and the closely allied Paminggir and Pubian, for example, speak dialects that are virtually identical to standard (Riau-Johore) Malay, but they have a strongly developed patrilineal clan organization that closely resembles that of the Batak. Moreover, they and the Malays agree that several centuries ago the Abung were driven from the highlands of southern Sumatra by coastal Malays who were impatient and fearful of their beliefs in human sacrifice and headhunting. Remnants of these beliefs are still evident in some of their rituals, but they are all nominally Muslims of the Shafi rite.

The Besemah and Rejang were closely allied in the recent past, and they have been more influenced by Javanese culture than other ethnic groups of the Rejang-Lampung complex. They differ from each other in language. Besemah speak a dialect of Malay. Rejang speak a language that is closely related to Malay. Until the 1930s and the world depression both the Rejang and the Besemah were strongly patrilineal, but since that time, matrilineal institutions apparently have developed among the Rejang.

The Batinese occupy the area around Djambi, which is near the ancient capital of the Malay world, Melayu. They are so thoroughly assimilated into Malay culture that they refer to themselves as Djambi Malays.

The influence of Minangkabau culture is most apparent among the Kerinci (see Minangkabau). Some scholars have classified their language as a southern dialect of Minangkabau. Moreover, the Kerinci have matrilineal social organization, but it differs in detail from typical Minangkabau matrilineal organization.

All of these groups are Muslims of the Shafi school of the Sunni sect. They are somewhat less orthodox and thorough in their practice of Islam than the Acehnese, Malays and Minangkabau. Their patterns of subsistence and their general life-styles are similar to those of Malays and Acehnese, who were largely responsible for the spread of Islam into southern Sumatra in particular and throughout Southeast Asia in general. Although the people of the Rejang-Lampung complex are less orthodox than the Malays, Acehnese and Minangkabau, they, in turn, are generally more orthodox than Muslims of the eastern islands of Indonesia, such as the Butinese, Gorontalese, Laki, West Toraja and Bolaang-Mongondo of Sulawesi (Celebes) or the Tidorese and Ternatans of Halmahera. These more eastern groups were near the most distant edges of the trading empire of the Melaka Malays. Islam arrived later there than in the center of the empire, and it was not so intensively proselytized.

Islam spread into Southeast Asia within a century or two of the Prophet's lifetime, but it was not immediately successful. Marco Polo noted that it was the religion of Pasai, in northern Sumatra, at the end of the thirteenth century, but Hindu-Buddhism was elsewhere the major religion. Probably, native chiefs came to view Islam as an ideology that might focus support for overthrowing traditional empires, such as Javanese Majapahit, that were overbearing and that interfered with chiefly interests in local and long-distance sea trade. Moreover, Islam provided a means for claiming special trading privileges with Gujarati, Arab, Persian and Turkish traders who controlled so much of Western commerce in the fourteenth and fifteenth centuries. Melaka was not the first city-state in the area to become Islamic, but it was the most successful and was most responsible for the further spread of Islam throughout Southeast Asia. The Acehnese were probably converted earlier to Islam, and they developed an important trading empire that existed along with that of Johore and Portugal after the fall of Melaka to the Portuguese in 1511. The Acehnese did not succeed in assimilating many other ethnic groups to their culture, not even those whom they conquered, such as the Gayo (who still maintain much of their Batak culture) or the northern Minangkabau, but their capital city, Kota Raja, did become a center of Islamic learning that was important not only to Southeast Asia but to the Islamic world generally.

Ronald Provencher

MALAYO-POLYNESIAN-SPEAKING PEOPLES (EASTERN INDO-NESIA)

The Indonesian province of Nusa Tenggara Timur (NTT) is one of two in this "Muslim" country in which Muslims are a minority (the other is Bali). According to the 1980 census, NTT had a population of 2.7 million people, only 8.5 percent of whom were Muslim, or 230,000. Despite their numbers, the diverse Muslim peoples of NTT are of interest because of their long historical association with Islam dating from the sixteenth and seventeenth centuries.

More than 80 percent of the Muslim population of NTT is concentrated in five regencies, or *kabupaten*: 1) East Flores, which includes the islands of Solor, Adonara and Lembara, 2) Alor, which includes the island of Pantar, 3) Ende on the south central coast of the island of Flores, 4) Manggarai on the western end of Flores and 5) Kupang, the regency at the western end of Timor which incorporates the present provincial capital. These regencies are precisely the areas with the oldest links to Islam.

Islam reached these islands from various directions in the sixteenth and seventeenth centuries at a time when the Muslim community consisted of peoples of many ethnic groups whose specific origins were less important than their adherence to Islam. Historical evidence suggests that one of the earliest sources of contact with Islam was with Muslim traders from the north coast of Java, particularly Gresik. A second source of contact was with Muslims from the sultanate of Ternate in the northern Moluccas (see Ternatan-Tidorese). A third source was with Muslims from the sultanate of Bima on the island of Sumbawa. Since both Ternate and Bima looked to the north coast of Java for their religious traditions, these three sources of contact represent a similar tradition. The Sultan of Ternate claimed sovereignty over Timor and the islands to the east of Flores, whereas the Sultan of Bima claimed Flores and the island of Sumba. Later, in the seventeenth century, Islamic influence emanating from Makassar came to predominate as Makassarese, Bugis and Butonese sailors, accompanied by groups of Bajau, began to penetrate the area and occasionally settle in or near established Muslim communities (see Bajau; Bugis; Butonese; Makassarese).

The Portuguese reached these islands by the middle of the sixteenth century, just as Islam was beginning to become established in various coastal settlements. The Portuguese established Christian settlements in opposition to Islam, and this resulted in clashes involving the local population, particularly on the islands of Solor and Adonara and on the south coast of Flores and Ende (see Endenese). The Dutch arrived early in the seventeenth century and immediately aligned themselves with the Muslims in opposition to their trading rivals, the Portuguese. They signed contracts of trade and alliance with the Sultans of Ternate and Bima as well as with the Muslim rulers of Solor and Adonara, but eventually they were able to compel the sultans of Ternate and Bima to relinquish their claims to these islands, and thereafter the Dutch dealt exclusively with local Muslim rulers. When, in the middle of the seventeenth century, they founded their principal settlement at Kupang on Timor, they ceded a portion of beach near their fort to their Muslim allies. This beach, known as Pantai Solor with its associated settlement, Kampung Solor, has remained an Islamic residence to this day.

The complicated history of Dutch, Portuguese and Islamic relations accounts for the location and distribution of the Muslim peoples of NTT as well as the occurrence of Christian and Muslim members of the same ethnic group. Furthermore, the scattering of Muslim communities throughout the islands has facilitated the historical migration of Bugis and Makassarese, which has increased considerably in recent years. The traditional and still predominant occupations of the Muslim peoples of NTT as fishermen, sailors and traders also have their bases in the history of these islands.

In the regency of East Flores, Muslims, who according to the 1980 census number 53,255, are most numerous in the districts of East Solor, East Adonara and East Lembata. These Muslims belong mainly to the somewhat diverse ethnic group known as Solorese (see Lamaholot). A portion of the Kédangese population of Lembata is, however, also Muslim, and there are a number of Sama-speaking Bajau Laut settlements of Adonara and Lembata (see Kédang).

In the Alor Regency, Muslims, who number 27,397, are concentrated on the coast of Pantar and on the northwestern corner of Alor, which includes the port and regency capital of Kalabahi. Here the Muslim population (sometimes confusingly referred to as Alorese) consists primarily of Solorese settlers with one or possibly more Bajau settlements. Recently, however, there has been a substantial migration of Bugis and Makassarese to the area around the town of Kalabahi. Official statistics list one-third of the population of Kalabahi as Muslim.

The approximately 52,106 Muslims in the Ende Regency make up half the population of the town of Ende and of the district of Nanagapanda and approximately one-third the population of the district of Wolowaru. The Endenese are part of a single ethnic group, a majority of whom are now Catholic. In the nineteenth century, Muslim Endenese migrated to the north coast of Sumba and have maintained their settlements there.

In the regency of Manggarai, where Muslims number some 33,898, the ethnic composition of the population is mixed. Manggarai is located directly across the Sape Straits from the old sultanate of Bima, on Sumbawa. For several centuries the coast of Manggarai was dominated by Bima and was settled not only by Bimanese but also by Makassarese and Bugi, and a considerable number of Bajau. In contemporary Manggarai, Muslims can be found along the coast but are most numerous in the districts of Komodo, which faces Sumbawa, and Reo and Elar on the north coast. In Komodo, whose capital is Lauan Bajo ("Bajau Harbor"), Muslims make up over 40 percent of the population.

The majority of the 19,816 Muslims in the Kupang Regency are to be found in the town of Kupang. This urban population includes members of all the Muslim ethnic groups of the province, including an increasing number of Bugis traders as well as Muslim government officials from all over Indonesia. The President of Indonesia recently provided funds to build a large mosque in the center of the town which now dwarfs other smaller but historically important mosques in the area.

The other regencies of the province have a smaller proportion of Muslims. In the regency of Sikka on Flores, which has an Islamic population of 14,930, Muslims are to be found mainly in the district of Maumere and in the town of Maumere itself. The Bay of Maumere, which faces in the direction of South Sulawesi, has long been open to trade and influence from this important Islamic center. Bugis established a settlement there in the nineteenth century, as did Bajau at Geliting near Maumere in a somewhat earlier period. A similar pattern is evident in the regency of Ngada, which has a Muslim population of 11,466, more than half of which is concentrated in the north coast districts of Riung and Aesesa.

Throughout NTT most Muslims are settled along the coast; few live in the interior, and virtually none of the population of the interior has converted to Islam. One exception occurred recently, just after 1965, when a sizable group of Timorese or Atoni Pah Meto in the highland district of East Amanuban in the regency of South Central Timor converted to Islam. This community of Muslim Timorese numbers less than 3,000 people within an ethnic group of 600,000, but it represents the first change in a pattern that has persisted for over 300 years.

James J. Fox

MALAYS   Malays call themselves Orang Melayu (Malay persons). Others refer to them as Melayu (or a cognate term, such as Malay in English). The basic meaning of *melayu*, except as it applies to Malays and to their ancient center of empire near present-day Djambi in Sumatra, is lost. Various folk explanations of the term depend on the possible meanings of the apparent root word *layu* in related dialects and languages, such as "flee," "fade," "parch" or "sail."

Malays comprise almost half of the 15 million inhabitants of the Federation of Malaysia, whom they dominate politically. They are the majority population of the four southernmost provinces of Thailand, but their exact numbers there can only be estimated because of their similarity to southern Thai Muslims and because Malay-Thai bilingualism is fairly common. Estimates are as high as 1.8 million Malays living in Thailand. They are important minorities in Singapore (375,000) and Indonesia (7.6 million), and there are smaller communities of several thousands in Sri Lanka, Saudi Arabia, India and Malagasy. In all, their population exceeds 16 million.

Many of the Malays of the Malay peninsula are descendants of immigrants from the Indonesian islands, principally Sumatra, who assimilated to Malay ethnic identity during the first three decades of this century. All speak the Malay language (of which modern Indonesian is a variety), but many also speak the dialects and languages of their non-Malay ancestors—Minangkabau, Javanese, Korinci, Boyanese, Buginese, Mandailing or Acehnese. The wide variety of dialects of Malay language in the peninsular states of coastal enclaves throughout Southeast Asia provides further evidence of the tremendous number of subvarieties of Malay culture.

Geographical dispersal has been as effective as assimilation of other populations in creating diversity within Malay culture. The dispersal of Malays was well underway by the fifth century A.D., when they began to dominate local trade in Southeast Asia and long-distance sea trade between northwestern India and southern China. Their domination of sea trade continued until the sixteenth century, and even into the early European colonial period before the onset of the Industrial Revolution.

Malays founded several trading empires, among which Sri Vijaya, Melayu and Melaka were most important, and their language became the major language of commerce in Southeast Asian ports. Melaka, successor of fourteenth-century Melayu, which lost its empire to the Javanese kingdom of Majapahit, was instrumental in converting many Southeast Asian kingdoms to Islam in the fifteenth century.

In the idiom of the Malay language, to be converted to the Islamic faith is to enter Malay ethnicity (*masok melayu*). And many non-Malays have become Malays through conversion to Islam and residence in a Malay community. According to folk definition and according to the constitution of the Federation of Malaysia, anyone who habitually speaks Malay language, follows Malay custom, and adheres to the religion of Islam is a Malay. The folk ideal is that all Malays are Muslims.

Malays belong to the Shafi school of the Sunni tradition. They are orthodox in their conception and practice of Islam, but in addition they have some beliefs and rituals that are clearly Hindu-Buddhist or animistic in origin and are a continuation of pre-Islamic (pre-fourteenth-century) traditions in Malay culture. In this syncretism Islamic elements are not distorted or diminished by animistic or Hindu-Buddhist elements; rather, each religious tradition has appropriate places within the whole of Malay religious belief and practice.

Animistic beliefs include conceptions of spiritual energy or soul substance (*semangat*), disembodied spiritual essence (*badi*), place spirits (*hantu*) and demonic presences, such as vampire crickets (*pelesit*), thumb-sized manikins (*polong*) and monstrous childbirth hags (*pontianak*). The rituals of birth, illness and death, as well as agricultural rituals, are especially rich in animistic symbolism. Hindu-Buddhist symbols are important in the rituals of Malay royalty and in ceremonies which utilize metaphors of royalty, such as weddings and certain types of curing séances.

Islamic rites begin and end virtually all ceremonies, even those which are predominantly animistic or Hindu-Buddhist in content. Moreover, Islamic ritual is more commonplace than animistic or Hindu-Buddhist ritual. The ritual includes five daily prayers, the Friday sermons, the several Islamic holy days, the occasional Islamic religious feasts (*khenduri*) to celebrate good fortune or security or remembrance of the dead, the annual month of fasting and the return of family and friends from pilgrimage to Mecca. They outweigh the animistic and Hindu-Buddhist portions of curing rituals and elaborate weddings.

Approximately 80 percent of all Malays live in rural villages. Most of them farm wet rice and work small plantations of rubber trees. Others work as laborers on large agricultural estates, as laborers on tin mining dredges or as inshore salt water fishermen. Many urban Malays are government clerks. Others are laborers, technicians, factory workers, sales persons, small businessmen or members of police or military units or government officials. Very few have professional occupations. Rural or urban, rubber tapper or government official, almost all are orthodox in the everyday practice of Islam. And there is little variance in their animistic and Hindu-Buddhist beliefs and practices except as these relate to the special ritual of the rice farmer, the ritual language of the tin miner, the taboos of the fisherman or the weekend feasts of high-ranking government bureaucrats.

Acts of courtesy comprise a very important aspect of Malay social organization. Most groups, including many households, are loosely structured, that is, the commitments of members to a group are usually tentative and may be easily altered. Within a household, sibling relationships and daughter–parent relationships are relatively strong, but group loyalty (except recently to Malay ethnic identity) is not as important as a source of social conformity as adherence to the rule of Malay courtesy. Formal ceremonies provide important contexts for affirmation of the rules of courtesy and of the status relationships that structure Malay social organization. Moreover, much of the symbolism of curing rituals relates the oral pleasures of feasting to the social pressures of status courtesy.

Various Islamic reform movements have been represented in the Malay world during the twentieth century, but the most revolutionary in its effect appears to be the *dakwah* ''missionary'' movement of the 1970s, which has convinced some devout Malays that parts of their own traditional world as well as the modern Westernized world are not in conformity with the orthodox practice of Islam. Malays interested in retaining their Malay culture as well as their devotion to Islam comprise a social category separate from that of the *dakwahs*, and both of these are distinct from ''secular'' Malays, who are concerned with modernization. The *dakwah* movement is heavily involved in a persuasive missionary campaign. One manifestation of this is the magazine *Dakwah*, which has been published (in Latin script Malay) since 1977.

Except in rare instances, such as in Sungei Penchala (within the limits of the metropolitan area of Kuala Lumpur), the *dakwah* movement has not resulted in physically separating Malay communities. Traditional, *dakwah* and secular Malays live side by side in the same communities. Throughout this ideological fissioning they have remained together residentially and segregated from other ethnic communities of Malaysia. Malay ethnic identity has become more important during this period in part because of the government's efforts to provide opportunities to recover from the low economic status they held as colonial wards of the British before independence. Many members of the other ethnic communities, principally the Chinese and Indians, object to the present advantages afforded Malays.

BIBLIOGRAPHY

Books

Ali, Syed Husin. *Malay Peasant Stories and Leadership*. Kuala Lumpur: Oxford University Press, 1975.

————. *The Malays: Their Problems and Future*. Kuala Lumpur: Heinemann Asia, 1981.

Bader, A. Kahar. "Social Rank, Status-Honor, and Social Class Consciousness Amongst the Maylays." In *Modernization in South-East Asia*, edited by Hans Dieter-Evers. Singapore: Institute of South-East Asian Studies, 1973.

Evers, Hans-Dieter, ed. *Modernization in South-East Asia*. Singapore: Institute of South-East Asian Studies, 1973.

Firth, Raymond. *Malay Fishermen: Their Peasant Economy*. London: Routledge and Kegan Paul, 1946.

Firth, Rosemary. *Housekeeping Among Malay Peasants*. 1943. Reprint ed. London: Athalone Press, 1966.

Fraser, Thomas W. *Rusembilan: A Malay Fishing Village in Southern Thailand*. Ithaca: Cornell University Press, 1960.

Ginsburg, Norton Sydney, and Roberts, Chester F., Jr. *Malaya*. Seattle: University of Washington Press, 1958.

Gullick, John M. *Indigenous Political Systems of Western Malaya*. 1958. Reprint ed. New York: Humanities Press, 1965.

————. *Malaysia*. New York: Praeger, 1969.

————. *Malaysia and Its Neighbors*. New York: Barnes and Noble, 1967.

Harrison, Thomas H. *The Malays of South-West Sarawak Before Malaysia*. London: Macmillan, 1970.

————. "Tribes, Minorities, and the Central Government of Sarawak, Malaysia." In *Southeast Asian Tribes, Minorities, and Nations*, edited by P. Kunstadter. Princeton: Princeton University Press, 1966.

Henderson, John W., et al. *Area Handbook for Malaysia*. The American University FAS, DA Pam 550–45. Washington, D.C.: Government Printing Office, 1970.

LeBar, Frank M., ed. *Ethnic Groups of Insular Southeast Asia*. New Haven: Human Relations Area Files Press, 1972.

————. *Ethnic Groups of Mainland South-East Asia*. New Haven: Human Relations Area Files Press, 1964.

Malm, William P., and Sweeny, Anil. *Studies in Malaysian Oral and Music Traditions*. Ann Arbor: University of Michigan Press, 1975.

Nash, Manning. *Peasant Citizens: Politics, Religion, and Modernization in Kelantan, Malaysia*. Athens: Ohio University Center for International Studies, 1974.

Peacock, James L. *Muslim Puritans*. Berkeley: University of California Press, 1978.

Provencher, Ronald. "Islam in Malaysia and Thailand." In *Crescent in the East*, edited by R. Israeli. London: Curzon Press, 1982.

————. "Orality as a Pattern of Symbolism in Malay Culture." In *The Imagination of Reality: Essays on Southeast Asian Coherence Systems*, edited by A. L. Beck and A. A. Yengoyan. Norwood, N.J.: ABLEX, 1979.

————. *Two Malay Worlds: Interaction in Urban and Rural Settings*. Berkeley: University of California Center for South and Southeast Asia Studies, 1971.

Skeat, Walter William. *Malay Magic: An Introduction to the Folklore and Popular Religion of the Malay Peninsula*. New York: Barnes and Noble, 1966.

Strange, Heather. *Rural Malay Women in Tradition and Transition*. New York: Praeger, 1981.

Swift, Michael G. *Malay Peasant Society in Jelebu*. New York: Humanities Press, 1965.

————. "Men and Women in Malay Society." In *Women in the New Asia*, edited by Barbara Ward. Paris: UNESCO, 1963.

Thomas, M. Ladd. "Political Socialization of the Thai-Islam." In *Studies on Asia*, edited by Robert K. Sakai. Lincoln: University of Nebraska Press, 1966.

————. "The Thai Muslims." In *Crescent in the East*, edited by R. Israeli. London: Curzon Press, 1982.

Articles

Husin, S. Ali. "Patterns of Rural Leadership in Malaya." *Journal of the Malaysian Branch of the Royal Historical Society* 41 (1968): 45–145.

Ibrahim, Ahmad B. Mohamad. "Islam Customary Law/Malaysia." *Intisari* 2:2 (1964): 34–45.

Majul, Cesar A. "Theories on the Introduction and Expansion of Islam in Malaysia." *Silliman Journal* 11:4 (1964): 335–398.

McGree, T. G. "The Cultural Role of Cities: A Case Study of Kuala Lumpur." *Journal of Tropical Geography* 26 (1968): 178–196.

McTaggart, W. D. "The Distribution of Ethnic Groups in Malaysia, 1947–57." *Comparative Politics* 1:2 (1969): 264–268.

Standish, W. A. "South Thailand: Malay-Moslem Mixtures." *Far East Economic Review* (1967): 19–22.

Suhrke, Asti. "The Thai Muslims: Some Aspects of Minority Integration." *Pacific Affairs* 43:4 (1970–71): 531–547.

Unpublished Manuscripts

Maeda, Narifumi. "The Changing Peasant World in a Melaka Village: Islam and Democracy in the Malay Tradition." Ph.D. dissertation, University of Chicago, 1974.

McKinley, Robert H. "A Knife Cutting Water: Child Transfers and Siblingship Among Urban Malays." Ph.D. dissertation, University of Michigan, 1975.

Yusof, Abdul Maulud. "Cultural Adaptations in an Urbanizing Malay Community." Ph.D. dissertation, Rice University, 1976.

Ronald Provencher

MANDING-SPEAKING PEOPLES Manding speakers make up one of the largest groups of West African peoples speaking closely related forms of the same language. Mostly rural, agricultural peoples, those who speak the Manding languages inhabit the western savannas in a broad area around a geographical and cultural center on the upper Niger River in eastern Guinea and southwestern Mali. Although Manding speakers share a strong cultural identity in addition to their often mutually intelligible languages, they have no common name for themselves or their languages. The word "Manding," which scholars in increasing numbers have been using in the past decade to refer to the group of languages, comes from the name "Mandingue," which French colonial officials used when referring to all speakers of the languages. The French took Mandingue from Manden or Mande, the name for the traditional heartland on the upper Niger to which most Manding speakers look for their common heritage.

Linguists call the group of Manding languages Mande-kan and divide them into two major subgroups: Mande-tan and Mande-fu. Speakers of Mande-tan languages form the more northerly and larger portion of the group; in fact, anthropologists and others have sometimes considered speakers of the Mande-tan languages to be *the* "Manding people," excluding the Mande-fu group.

Mande-tan speakers are almost always divided into three major regional groupings: Mandinka, Bambara and Dyula. These names have come to be thought of as the names of separate ethnic groups. The Mandinka (Maninka, Mandinko, Mandingo, Malinké) are the central and westernmost of the Manding speakers. They occupy an area in the shape of an arc about 800 miles long from lower Gambia to northwestern Ivory Coast, and they remain the residents of the area of Manden near the Guinea–Mali border. The Bambara (Bamana) live northeast of the central Mandinka, occupying much of the savanna region of modern Mali. The Dyula are primarily residents of northern Ivory Coast and western Upper Volta, though some have spread across the borders into Ghana and Mali (see Bambara; Dyula; Mandinka).

Speakers of the Mande-fu languages are the more southerly Manding speakers. They inhabit regions bordering on the heavier forests in Guinea, Sierra Leone, Liberia and Ivory Coast. Included in this group are the Soso and Yalunka of Guinea (see Soso; Yalunka); the Mende and Loko of Sierra Leone (see Mende); the Kpelle, Loma and Mano of Liberia; and the Dan and Kweni (Guro) of Ivory Coast. The Mande-fu languages differ from the Mande-tan in such characteristics as formation of plurals, consonant changes and sentence intonation.

A number of small, related ethnic groups exist around the fringe of the major Manding-speaking regions. They speak dialects of one of the Manding languages. Many of the so-called Fringe Mandinka are indentified by their regional location in combination with the Mandinka suffix -*nka* or -*ka*, meaning "originating from." Thus a Khasonka is a Manding speaker from Khaso on the upper Senegal River around Kayes; a Wasulunka is from Wasulu, south of the Niger River along the Mali–Guinea border; and so on for the Manyanka (sometimes called Comendi) in eastern Sierra Leone, Konyaka and Mauka in northwestern Ivory Coast.

Although all of these groups speak variants of the Manding language, the Khasonka and Wasulunka maintain traditions of having descended from the Fulani (Fulbe, Fula, Peul) in the distant past (see Fulani). Groups that differ still but share close linguistic affinity and traditions of Manding origins include the Kuranko of northeastern Sierra Leone, the Kono of Sierra Leone's eastern highlands and the Vai of southeastern Sierra Leone and northeastern Liberia (see Vai). Other Fringe Mandinka include the Boza, Dafi, Samo, Nono, Tienga, Bisa and Sia. A "Fringe Bambara" exist, too, the most notable being the Kagoro of the Karta region of Mali, north of Bamako. And the Somono fishing people, who live along the Niger in Mali, speak Bambara as a first language.

Approximately 11 million people in nine modern African nations speak a Manding language, with about two-thirds of these speaking it as a first language. The Manding languages are part of the large Niger-Congo language family and as such are related to many other West African languages (Akan of Ghana, Yoruba of Nigeria) and even distantly to the Bantu languages spoken in much of central, eastern and southern Africa (see Bantu-speaking Peoples).

Mande-kan has simple and direct grammatical structures. As with many African languages, tone is important for meaning. Identical words often are distinguished by nothing more than the differences in relative pitch of the voice when saying them. Aside from some recent publications in Latin script (many of which have been products of national literacy programs), local records using modified Arabic script and fairly extensive use of traditional graphic symbols and ideograms for mystical purposes, the Manding languages remain important only in the oral mode. Indeed, Manding speakers preserve their vital historical traditions and practice their oral art through the medium of the spoken word. The oral literature of Manding speakers is widely noted as some of the best in the world.

In addition to language, what gives Manding speakers a sense of unity is their knowledge of having common origins and a common cultural heritage. At the root of this heritage is the once-great Mali Empire. A small state of Mali—al-Bakri, the Arab geographer of the mid-eleventh century, called it "Malil"— founded by several Mandinka clans and centered on the upper Niger, existed from early in the second millenium, but its period of expansion and greatness came later. In the thirteenth century the "lion king," Sundiata, unified the Mandinka, conquered others and took advantage of the lucrative trade passing between the Sahara Desert and the goldfields of the more southerly forests to make Mali strong and its leading families wealthy.

Foreign merchants from across the Sahara came to Mali's leading cities, and with them came Islam. The religion blended with local religious practices and maintained an importance, particularly among the Mandinka and Dyula, down through the centuries. Mali's famous ruler, Mansa Musa, provided evidence of Islam's influence when in 1324 he made a pilgrimage to Mecca. In Cairo he spent or gave away so much gold that he disrupted the monetary standard of the eastern Mediterranean. Evidence of Islam's penetration among Manding speakers today is reflected in the fact that over 90 percent of Senegambia Mandinka and Ivory Coast–Guinea Dyula are Muslims. Such percentages decline considerably among the Bambara and some fringe groups.

It was out of Manden, the core area of the Mali Empire, that Manding speakers and Manding influences spread. Mandinka moved west and southwestward from the upper Niger. Manding influences moved southward primarily with traders, a word for which in all Manding languages is *dyula*. Many of these itinerant merchants were "Mandingized" Soninké (Sarakolé) who were moving between

Mali proper and the southern goldfields and sources of kola nuts (see Soninké). Consolidation of these Manding elements with those over whom they had a strong influence led to the emergence of the Dyula ethnic group in Ivory Coast and Upper Volta.

Identification of the Bambara as a distinct ethnic and linguistic group was associated in part with the seventeenth- and eighteenth-century political kingdoms centered on Segou and Kaarta downriver from old Mali. In many areas of the more central parts of Manding territory considerable intermingling of Mandinka, Bambara and Dyula has occurred and continues. For this reason it is impossible to draw distinct ethno-linguistic boundaries for the various groups of Manding speakers.

Although differences exist in the social structures of specific Manding groups, they hold many traits in common. Manding speakers are patrilineal, patriarchal and polygynous, whether Muslim or not. Patronymic groups, usually called clans, which consist of individuals who share a common surname, are recognized across ethnic boundaries throughout the Manding world. Such groups are normally associated with distinct totems, animals or plants, and with food prohibitions. Individuals travelling away from home can make claims of hospitality on strangers who share nothing more with the traveller than his last name.

Most Manding speakers recognize three basic divisions of society. At the top of the social hierarchy are the so-called free-born, a group that traditionally included rulers and warriors as well as farmers and hunters. Below these are members of such endogamous occupational groups as blacksmiths, leatherworkers and praise singers. At the bottom are those who sometimes are referred to as slaves. This group consists mainly of individuals and families who in one way or another are dependent on other, higher-class members of society for their economic viability and social integration into the larger group.

Most Manding speakers are sedentary farmers. Across the landscape of seemingly endless stretches of grasses and trees they grow millet, rice and garden vegetables for consumption, peanuts or cotton to sell for cash. They keep chickens, goats and sheep and enjoy such fruits as mangoes, bananas, oranges and papayas. In the edges of the more southerly forests, where rainfall is considerably heavier, root crops are more important. Like most West Africans, Mandinka regularly chew kola nuts. These forest products, imported into the Manding areas from the south, act as a stimulant and thirst-quencher.

Villages of Manding speakers tend to be small and compact. Typical houses are round with mud walls and thatched roofs. In recent years more corrugated metal and less thatch has been used in roofing.

Village organization rests on the lineage structure. The eldest male of the founding lineage is normally made village head; elders of prominent village families sit as a council and settle disputes. Family elders also oversee such rites of passage as naming ceremonies for infants, initiation (which often includes circumcision and a period of education in customs and traditions) and marriages.

Throughout the Manding-speaking world, commerce is an occupation held in high regard. Markets thrive in many villages, and travelling merchants pass regularly across the expanse of the Manding area and beyond, conducting an interregional trade of significant proportions.

Language, heritage and basic social and economic forms are not all that Manding speakers share. When Manding speakers travel or migrate, as they have done over the centuries, they spread many of their noteworthy art forms. Through the land where Manding-kan is spoken one hears Manding music and oral literature, recited to the music of the *kora* (a harp-lute), *blafon* (a xylophone) or distinctive drums. There are also common forms of weaving, carving, dyeing, metalworking and dancing. Thus, the large area between northern Ghana and the Gambian Atlantic, and between northeastern Liberia and the central Niger, is a region where Manding culture predominates. Speakers of the Manding languages recognize their common culture, bearing evidence of this recognition in their saying: "Manding is without end until the day of resurrection."

BIBLIOGRAPHY

Books

Atkins, Guy, ed. *Manding: Focus on an African Civilisation*. London: School of Oriental and African Studies, University of London, 1972.
Bird, Charles. *The Dialect of Mandekan*. Bloomington: Indiana University Press, 1982.
———, and Kendall, Martha B. "The Mande Hero." In *Explorations in African Systems of Thought*, edited by Ivan Karp and Charles S. Bird. Bloomington: Indiana University Press, 1980.
Bovill, E. W. *The Golden Trade of the Moors*. 2nd ed. London: Oxford University Press, 1968.
Bravmann, Rene. *Islam and Tribal Art in West Africa*. New York: Cambridge University Press, 1974.
Dalby, David. "Distribution and Nomenclature of the Manding People and Their Language." In *Papers on the Manding*, edited by Carlton T. Hodge. New York: Humanities Press, 1971.
Goody, Jack. "The Mande and the Akan Hinterland." In *The Historian in Tropical Africa*, edited by Jan Vansina, R. Mauny, and L. V. Thomas. London: International African Institute, 1964.
Levtzion, Nehemia. *Ancient Ghana and Mali*. London: Methuen, 1973.
———. *Muslims and Chiefs in West Africa*. London: Oxford University Press, 1971.
McCall, Daniel F. "The Cultural Map and Time-Profile of the Mande-speaking Peoples." In *Papers on the Manding*, edited by Carleton T. Hodge. New York: Humanities Press, 1971.
Niane, D. T. *Sundiata: An Epic of Old Mali*. London: Longman, 1965.
Westernmann, D., and Bryan, M. A. *The Languages of West Africa*. 2nd ed. London: Dawsons, 1970.

Article

Dieterlen, G. "The Mande Creation Myth." *Africa* 27 (1957): 124–138.
Donald R. Wright

MANDINKA   Although they collectively look to "Manden," the small region
near where the Niger River crosses the Guinea–Mali border, as their cultural
homeland, the Mandinka are widely dispersed throughout a considerable portion
of West Africa's westernmost savannas. They inhabit eastern Guinea, extreme
southern Mali, northwestern Ivory Coast, eastern Guinea-Bissau, southeastern
Senegal and most of Gambia. There are small groups of Mandinka in eastern
Sierra Leone and Liberia as well. Sometimes called Malinké (as they are known
to the Fulani and many French-speaking Africans), Maninka, Mandinko or Mandingo, and often identified locally by place of origin (a Mandinka from Kaabu
in Guinea-Bissau is called a Kaabunka, for instance), they number approximately
4 million. As with most groups where ethnic mixture has been extreme, it is not
easy to determine just who is and who is not a Mandinka. Population figures
are little more than rough estimates.

Mandinka is one of the Manding languages, part of the Niger-Congo language
family of West and Central Africa (see Manding-speaking Peoples). Until recently, nearly all those literate in Mandinka wrote the language with a local
form of Arabic script. Numbers of the literate were small, consisting mainly of
Muslim clerics and scholars. But in recent years, literacy programs in some
countries have led to the writing of Mandinka in phonetic or Latin scripts, and
the number of literate Mandinka has grown slightly. Still, most Mandinka who
achieve literacy today read French or English, the language of their particular
schools. Mandinka remains largely an oral language.

The location and distribution of Mandinka today is a result of movements of
people and cultural diffusion over the last millennium and especially during the
period of greatness of the Mali Empire from the thirteenth to the fifteenth centuries. For social, political and economic reasons, and also because long periods
of drought seem to have made support of a large population difficult in the more
central portions of Mali, Manding speakers gradually spread from the upper
Niger River homelands into their present locations. The Mandinka movement
was primarily west and southwest. Where they moved, they mixed with local
peoples, while keeping the essence of Mandinka culture, so that Mandinka
today—especially those on the periphery of the major Mandinka culture area—
have a heritage of mixed ethnicity.

Although changes commonly associated with colonialism, modernization, urbanization and formal schooling have altered Mandinka ways of life for some
over recent decades, basic aspects of Mandinka society remain traditional. There
have always been three clear divisions of Mandinka society: free-born, artisans
and slaves. The free-born class is the most variegated. Traditionally it included

a surclass of noble lineages who provided the rulers of Mandinka states. Everyone in Mandinka society today knows which lineages made up this elite group. Indeed, many members of the one-time ruling lineages are prominent persons in regional and national society and politics. But there is much more to the free-born class than the former rulers. Larger numbers of farmers, merchants, Muslim clerics and others are among this group of "free" people.

The occupational groupings of artisans, sometimes ambiguously termed "castes," are endogamous lineages of blacksmiths, leatherworkers and praise singers (*griots*). Artisans are set apart in society and are held in fear and awe. Blacksmiths and workers of leather are revered for their craft secrets and expertise, which involve spiritual rituals others are incapable of performing. *Griots* are social separates, living on the edges of villages and traditionally not allowed to defile the ground by burial therein. In past days *griots* were buried in the enormous trunks of baobab trees. The separation of the *griot* from the rest of society is a result of being an entertainer, an occupation of low status in many societies, and of having intimate ties with persons in positions of power. Over the years *griots* have been particularly important members of Mandinka society, for they have borne the primary responsibility of perpetuating the oral traditions and cultural heritage of the Mandinka.

Many Mandinka today prefer not to discuss the social category of "slaves." Nevertheless, there remain persons and lineages identified as slaves, or at least as descendants of individuals who were slaves in the not too distant past. But as in most African societies, slavery among the Mandinka is different from the chattel slavery once practiced in the Americas. During the years of the Atlantic slave trade, there were indeed "trade slaves," who in most instances were slaves captured in warfare or otherwise obtained from other societies. However, "domestic" slavery seems to have been more a state of social and economic dependence. Some think of it as the status of the kinless in a society where kinship is vital for social position and economic viability. In fact, there is evidence of virtually kinless Mandinka nuclear families having "enslaved" themselves to prominent lineages in times of social upheaval or economic want. Today, although slavery is outlawed in all countries where Mandinka live, the knowledge of who is of a slave lineage continues to affect Mandinka social relations. It is rare for a free-born Mandinka to marry a "slave" boss, regardless of relative skills and qualifications. Among contemporary rural Mandinka, whether called slavery or not, dependence, and with it a degree of social inferiority, remains commonplace.

What makes the various social groupings fit into a larger Mandinka whole is the seemingly simple ingredient of kinship. The largest common descent group among the Mandinka is the patrilineally identified clan, which includes all persons with the same surname who trace their ancestry to the same man. Geographically dispersed clans are too broad to be effective social units, however; the effective units are made up of extended patrilineages living together in the same village. Each such patrilineage has a leader, usually the eldest male member, who presides over social and religious rites, mediates differences and oversees collection and redistribution of income.

Beyond the patrilineage is the age-set, which brings together all men or women of the same approximate age and gives them a common identity. Each age-set includes all those who pass initiation rites together, usually every five years or so. This normally means circumcision and a period of training prior to the entry to adulthood. Age-sets provide several functions. Each active age-set also performs the dual functions of providing intensive labor for individual farms and providing for the general welfare of their villages. Modernization has altered age-sets and initiation in recent years. Many males are circumcised earlier, traditional training periods have been shortened to meet vacations in school calendars and age-sets tend to be less active and important in urban areas.

Modern Mandinka are sedentary farmers. Their compact rural villages dot the landscape. Around the villages are the farmlands upon which the Mandinka grow the staples of their diet: millet and rice. Since the mid-nineteenth century peanuts have been grown in Senegambia as a cash crop, and small amounts of cotton are grown in Senegal and Guinea. Cash crops and millet are the produce of Mandinka men. Women grow rice. Such small animals as sheep, goats and chickens abound in the vicinity of Mandinka villages, and their meat adds protein to the Mandinka diet. Millet in sweetened sour milk is a popular breakfast. A typical main meal consists of steamed rice covered with a spicy stew of vegetables and, if available, meat or fish. Mangoes, bananas, oranges, papayas and cashew fruits add balance.

Mandinka villages are organized along lineage lines. A major lineage will make up a village ward or hamlet, an exogamous group that lives together in a specific area. Villages can have as few as two or three or as many as several dozen wards. Within each ward are subgroupings made up of brothers and their families, and within such groups are the minimal lineages of a man, his wife or wives (the Mandinka are polygynous) and their children. Normally children live in their mother's house. Male children can be intensely competitive with their fathers; closer, more supportive relationships often develop with maternal uncles. Once through initiation, young Mandinka are more free to marry and form households of their own. In recent generations, marriage has sometimes been put off for a number of years so that young men and women can finish their educations and accumulate wealth.

Mandinka marriage involves payment of a brideprice, usually in more than one installment. A traditional practice of betrothing girls at birth to a matrilineal cross-cousin is less prevalent than it once was. Still, marriages are frequently arranged between families. In addition to the drawn-out marriage ceremonies, one of the biggest festive occasions is the naming ceremony for an infant, which takes place about a week after the child is born. Women play major roles in both marriage and naming ceremonies. Divorce is permitted; both divorced parties can remarry.

A fundamental concept of Mandinka social organization is that age is synonymous with respect and authority. Each village has a village head, an elder of a prominent (usually said to be the founding) lineage, who presides over meetings. Such meetings are conventions of village elders, who meet to adjudicate matters involving crime and local disputes. Each village also had an *imam*, who leads prayers at the village mosque and serves as the religious leader of the community. Other men in a village can achieve positions of authority by having large families, bountiful supplies of food, considerable wealth and a large following of dependents and supporters. Such persons are known as *kandas*. "When a *kanda* talks," the Mandinka put it simply, "people listen."

Mandinka women work hard—some say harder than men. Women do all the domestic chores in addition to seasonal rice farming, and through childbearing age they perform these tasks frequently with infants tied to their backs. Mandinka men tend to regard their female counterparts as less intelligent, less educated and less serious in their practice of Islam. Strong-willed women, however, exert an important influence in the lives of their families, and men are sometimes not the dominant figures at home that they consider themselves. Like men, women who achieve old age are treated with great respect. There are several women's organizations on the village level, and women tend to enjoy the company of other women as they work around the home or in the rice fields.

Opposing forces in the minds of Mandinka, especially males, affect their behavior and often have strong effects on the ways they lead their lives. One of these forces is called *fadenya* ("father-childness"), a strong urge to build one's reputation beyond that of one's father. Mandinka children are born with reputations. Society automatically has certain expectations of children based upon the general regard of the children's fathers and their fathers' lineages. To be considered noteworthy persons, children have to exceed, and usually far exceed, people's expectations of them. Children of successful fathers or respected patrilineages thus find it difficult to achieve renown. Sometimes they try to do so in antisocial ways, and here the other, opposing force comes into play. *Badenya* ("mother-childness") is pressure to behave in ways that are acceptable to one's society. Violation of group norms in behavior brings shame, which often stifles the activities of individuals concerned with what people in the group think of them. Thus, Mandinka men are pressed strongly to achieve success beyond that of their fathers and their patrilineages, but when they seek success in ways that violate group norms, they are socially scorned.

Islam has been penetrating Mandinka society since the days of Mali or perhaps before. Muslim scribes and clerics played important roles in the affairs of the Malian court for many years. However, conversion of an individual ruler and influence in the centers of Mandinka political power did not mean conversion of most Mandinka. Into the eighteenth century, there were pockets of Muslim clericalism within small Mandinka states, but the majorities of people in these states practiced pre-Islamic religions that involved worship of spirits of the land upon which they live. Muslim clerics were valued at court for their literacy and for their abilities to make protective amulets. Otherwise, Islam was a minority religion.

It was largely a series of Islamic *jihads* among the Mandinka that led to their general conversion. Catalysts for these movements of religious revival were members of a Fulani clan, the Torodbe, many of whom lived among the larger Mandinka population. Mandinka in Guinea felt the effects of a Fulani-led *jihad* in the first half of the eighteenth century, and most Mandinka were influenced much more directly by Al-Hajj Umar Tall's great movement of Islamic revival in Guinea and eastern Senegal in the 1850s. Mandinka in Guinea-Bissau were converted forcefully by the Fulani of Futa Jalon in Guinea in the 1860s. A series of wars, led by Muslim clerics of varying religious fervor, brought Islam to many Mandinka in Gambia in the last half of the nineteenth century. Most of those who did not convert as a result of the *jihad* movements came to accept Islam because clerics—especially Jahanka—spread the religion in the early decades of the colonial period. Today the degree of Islamization among the Mandinka varies from about 90 percent in Senegambia to less than 50 percent in certain parts of Guinea and Sierra Leone (see Jahanka).

Although most Mandinka consider themselves Muslims (Sunni, Maliki rite), their religion is heavily syncretized with their earlier beliefs. A Mandinka can pray in the village mosque and then just a few hours later sacrifice a chicken at the base of a large silk-cotton tree to seek assistance from the spirits of the village. Healing, magic and divination are important parts of Mandinka Islam. Most persons consult *marabouts* for cures, to obtain protective amulets, to learn what is in store for them in the future or to gain favorable treatment in business or legal matters. *Marabouts* also deal in "offensive magic"—praying against or making charms that will do harm to others. Many educated Mandinka conceal their belief in such magic, but it is a rare individual, formally educated or not, who does not have a charm or two in his car or under his bed.

Mandinka belong to both the Tijaniyya and Qadiriyya Sufi brotherhoods. The Ahmadiya have also been effective in a few cities. Most Muslim Mandinka pray regularly and attempt to fast; making the Haj is important to those with means. Celebration of three Islamic holy days is widespread. There are festivals at the end of Ramadan (Id al Fitr); on Tabaski (Id al Kabir), which normally involves the slaughtering of a ram; and on the Prophet's birthday, Maulud, which involves night-long prayers and songs. Parents who want their children to become Muslim clerics send them to Quranic schools, where teachers care for the children's needs, often perfunctorily, and where the children beg if younger or work for their teachers if older.

For Mandinka, success in life is usually measured in economic and social terms, in that order. A man who becomes an economic success by accumulating wealth from successful farming or trading gains considerably in status and gains a following of dependents, some through marriage ties and some through functional economic arrangements. A wealthy person is respected only as long as he remains generous, however. A person with means who hoards his wealth, gives small gifts on festive occasions and does not see to it that his relatives and dependents live well merits scorn. In fact, generosity is so highly prized and stinginess so contemptible that many Mandinka feel it necessary to leave home and live among foreign societies, farming or trading away from relatives and friends, to begin accumulating brideprice and wealth for its own sake.

Personal characteristics that are especially valued are honesty, logical thinking and the ability to express oneself in front of a group. Mandinka disapprove of dishonesty, but manipulation of others through guile is a trait found in many and the ability to so manipulate others often leads to success. Perhaps it is for this reason that Mandinka are particularly suspicious people. Close personal relationships between men are rare. Many expect cunning and deceit from even their closer friends.

In cities and even in a number of smaller towns, the effects of modernization on the Mandinka life-style is increasing. Many Mandinka children now are able to get some formal education in a secular school, where a French or English curriculum is still followed. Some few are able to graduate from secondary school and to obtain jobs in business or their country's civil service. Fewer still get scholarships for advanced training or education. Opportunities for secondary school are strictly limited, however, and many young Mandinka are forced to leave school around early adolescence. This group of young school-leavers forms a potential problem, for after six or seven years of school, their aspirations go beyond the lineage compound, the millet field and the village. Many head for urban areas and try, often unsuccessfully, to find jobs. The drain of some of the most able youth from Mandinka villages hinders efforts at rural development.

BIBLIOGRAPHY

Books

Curtin, Philip D. *Economic Change in Precolonial Africa: Senegambia in the Era of the Slave Trade*. Madison: University of Wisconsin Press, 1975.
Gamble, David P. *Elementary Mandinka Sentence Book*. Rev. ed. London: Colonial Office Research Department, 1955.
Haswell, Margaret R. *The Changing Pattern of Economic Activity in a Gambia Village*. London: Her Majesty's Stationary Office, 1963.
Hopkins, Nicolas S. "Mandinka Social Organization." In *Papers on Manding*, edited by Carleton T. Hodge. New York: Humanities Press, 1971.
Innes, Gordon. *Kelefa Saane: His Career Recounted by Two Mandinka Bards*. London: School of Oriental and African Studies, 1978.
Leary, Frances Anne. "The Role of the Mandinka in the Islamization of the Casamance." In *Papers on the Manding*, edited by Carleton T. Hodge. New York: Humanities Press, 1971.
Quinn, Charlotte A. *Mandingo Kingdoms of the Senegambia: Traditionalism, Islam and European Expansion*. Evanston: Northwestern University Press, 1972.
Sanneh, Lamin O. "The Muslim Education of an African Child: Stresses and Tensions."

In *Conflict and Harmony in Education in Tropical Africa*, edited by Godfrey N. Brown and Marvyn Hiskett. London: Allen and Unwin, 1975.

Schaffer, Matt, and Cooper, Christine. *Mandinko: The Ethnography of a West African Holy Land*. New York: Holt, Rinehart and Winston, 1980.

Weil, Peter M. "Political Structure and Process Among the Gambian Mandinka: The Village Parapolitical System." In *Papers on the Manding*, edited by Carleton T. Hodge. New York: Humanities Press, 1971.

Wright, Donald R. *The Early History of Niumi: Settlement and Foundation of a Mandinka State on the Gambia River*. Athens: Ohio University Press, 1977.

————. *Oral Traditions from the Gambia*, vol. 1, *Mandinka Griots*; vol. 2, *Family Elders*. Athens: Ohio University Press, 1979.

Articles

Jebate, Muhammed. "Traditional Mandinka Male Circumcision," translated by Abdoulie Bayo. *The Gambia Museum Bulletin* 1 (1981): 1–7.

Klein, Martin A. "Social and Economic Factors in the Muslim Revolution in Senegambia." *Journal of African History* 13 (1972): 419–441.

Nyandu, Alhaji Nfamara Omar. "Marabouts and Jujus," translated by Sheriffo Bojang. *The Gambia Museum Bulletin* 1 (1981): 49–58.

Weil, Peter M. "The Masked Figure and Social Control: The Mandinka Case." *Africa* 41 (1971): 279–293.

Wright, Donald R. "The Western Manding: A Bibliographical Essay." *Africana Journal* 6 (1975): 291–302.

Unpublished Manuscripts

Howard, Allen M. "Big Men, Traders and Chiefs: Power, Commerce and Spacial Change in the Sierra Leone-Guinea Plain." Ph.D. dissertation, University of Wisconsin, 1972.

Weil, Peter M. "Mandinka Mansaya: The Role of the Mandinka in the Political System of the Gambia." Ph.D. dissertation, University of Oregon, 1968.

Wright, Donald R. "Niumi: The History of a Western Mandinka State Through the Eighteenth Century." Ph.D. dissertation, Indiana University, 1976.

Donald R. Wright

MAPPILLA   The Muslims of Kerala along the Malabar coast in south India are known as Mappilla, often transliterated into English as Moplah. The term is variously interpreted, but is taken by Kerala Muslims as deriving from *maha pillai*, great person, referring to the respected status of the early Muslim settlers. The nearly 5.8 million Mappilla traditionally trace their origin in Kerala to the ninth century A.D., when Arab traders brought Islam to the west coast of India. The community has been characterized as consisting of those of pure Arab ancestry, of the descendants of Arabs and Hindu women of the country and of converts to Islam, mainly from among the lower castes.

At the beginning of the sixteenth century, when Portuguese and Arab chronicles provide the first descriptions of the Malabar coast, the Mappilla were largely a mercantile community concentrated along the coast of what is now northern Kerala in urban centers, dominating intercoastal and overseas trade. Segregated from the Hindu population in separate settlements, the Mappilla had considerable autonomy, and under the patronage of the Zamorin of Calicut, they enjoyed prestige as well as economic power. With the rise of Portuguese power in challenge to Mappilla commercial interests, many Mappilla moved inland in search of new economic opportunities, and in time, through intermarriage and conversion (especially from the most depressed Hindu castes), they increasingly came to be agricultural tenants, low in status and desperately poor. Reduced to insecure tenancy and vulnerable to rack renting and eviction at the hands of Hindu landlords, the Mappilla responded in a series of violent outbreaks during the nineteenth and early twentieth centuries, culminating in 1921 in the Mappilla Rebellion. Extending over some 2,000 square miles of Malabar District, the rebellion, nurtured by the ideology of the Khilafat movement, was carried on for six months by peasant bands in what was described by British authorities as open war against the king.

The Mappilla today remain concentrated in those areas of northern Kerala which were the scene of the rebellion. In 1969, in response to the demands of the Muslim League in Kerala and as a reward for its political support, the government of the state redrew district boundaries so as to carve out the new, predominantly Muslim district of Malappuram. The Muslim population of Kerala—overwhelmingly Mappilla—is 5.7 million, approximately 20 percent of the population of the state. In the district of Malappuram, however, the Muslims constitute over 50 percent of the population. In addition to the Mappilla of Kerala, almost all of the 37,000 people of the Lakshadweep (Laccadive) Islands lying off the Malabar coast are Mappilla.

The Mappilla speak Malayalam, the Dravidian language of Kerala, but they use Arabic script in a form of writing known as Arabi Malayalam. They have no knowledge of Urdu and no social ties to the Muslims of north India. Of all the religious communities of Kerala, the Mappilla have the least education, with a rate of literacy only one-third that of the state's 60 percent average.

Socially, reflecting the pattern of earlier conversions among different Hindu castes, the Mappilla retain caste distinctions and are divided between those who follow the matrilineal (*marumakkathayam*) joint family system and those who follow the patrilineal (*makkathayam*) system, which in conformity with Islamic law involves the division of property among all heirs. The Muslims of Kerala are predominantly Sunni and followers of the Shafi school, although there is a small Shia sect centered in the town of Kondotti, where a shrine is tended by a family of *thangals* (Sayyids) who migrated from Iran. The *thangals*, who claim direct descent from the Prophet, are held in great reverence and many serve as *qadi* (*kazi*), or heads of congregations. The Kazi of Calicut is regarded by Mappilla as their religious head. Itinerant preachers are known as *musaliars*.

The mosques of Kerala are distinctive, rectangular in shape with sloping tiled roofs and ornamental gables in the manner of Hindu temples of the region.

The northern coastal towns of Kerala, particularly Calicut, are centers of Mappilla trading activity. Mappilla merchants, especially petty traders and shop-keepers, have established themselves in towns and cities throughout south India and are represented in substantial numbers in Bombay. In earlier years, Mappilla migrated to Burma, Malaya and Singapore, as well as to the gulf sheikhdoms and Saudi Arabia. In the countryside of Malabar, where their numbers were expanded by conversion, the Mappilla are less prosperous. The coastal fishermen of Malabar are Mappilla, as are many of the poorest peasants and landless laborers.

Politically, the Mappilla of Kerala command a pivotal position. Although both in Congress and Communist (Marxist) parties have a degree of Muslim support, the Mappilla majority constituencies have regularly elected Muslim League candidates to the state assembly. In the delicate balance between opposing parties, the league has been able to exert an influence disproportionate to its numerical strength, and the inclusion of the Muslim League has been a vital ingredient in the formation of stable ministerial coalitions.

BIBLIOGRAPHY

Books

Choudhary, Sukhbir. *Moplah Uprising (1921–23)*. Delhi: Agam Prakashan, 1977.
Dale, Stephen F. *Islamic Society on the South Asian Frontier: The Mappilas of Malabar, 1498–1922*. New York: Oxford University Press, 1980.
D'Souza, Victor S. "Status Groups Among the Moplahs of the Southwest Coast of India." In *Caste and Social Stratification Among the Muslims*, edited by Imtiaz Ahmed. Delhi: Manohar Book Service, 1973.
Dube, Leela. *Matriliny and Islam: Religion and Society in the Laccadives*. Delhi: National Publishing House, 1969.
Gough, Kathleen. "Mappilla: North Kerala." In *Matrilineal Kinship*, edited by David M. Schneider and Kathleen Gough. Berkeley: University of California Press, 1961.
Kutty, A. R. *Marriage and Kinship in an Island Society (Laccadive Islands)*. Delhi: Publishing House, 1972.
Mayer, Adrian. *Land and Society in Malabar*. Bombay: Oxford University Press, 1972.
Miller, Roland E. *Mappila Muslims of Kerala: A Study in Islamic Trends*. Bombay: Orient Longman, 1976.
Woodcock, George. *Kerala: A Portrait of the Malabar Coast*. London: Faber & Faber, 1967.

Articles

Abdulla, V. "The Moplahs." *Illustrated Weekly of India* 95 (1970): 6–13.
Dale, Stephen F. "The Islamic Frontier in Southwest India: The Shahid as a Cultural

Ideal Among the Mappillas of Malabar.'' *Modern Asian Studies* 11 (1977): 57–99.

———. ''The Mappilla Outbreaks: Ideology and Social Conflict in Nineteenth-Century Kerala.'' *Journal of Asian Studies* 35 (1975): 85–97.

D'Souza, Victor S. ''Social Organization and Marriage Customs of the Moplahs on the Southwest Coast of India.'' *Anthropos* 54 (1959): 487–516.

Hardgrave, Robert L., Jr. ''Caste in Kerala: A Preface to the Elections.'' *Economic and Political Weekly* 16 (1964): 1841–1847.

———. ''The Mappilla Rebellion, 1921: Peasant Revolt in Malabar.'' *Modern Asian Studies* 11 (1977): 57–99.

Manickam, S. ''The Moplahs of Malabar.'' *Journal of Kerala Studies* 1 (1974): 267–286.

Pillai, Suranad Kunjan. ''Marriage Customs in Kerala.'' *Mythic Society Quarterly Journal* 58 (1967–1968): 17–24.

Wood, Conrad. ''Historical Backgrounds of the Moplah Rebellion: Outbreaks, 1836–1919.'' *Social Scientist* (India) 3 (1974): 5–33.

Wright, Theodore P., Jr. ''The Muslim League of South India Since Independence: A Study of Minority Group Political Strategies.'' *American Political Science Review* 60 (1966): 579–599.

Robert L. Hardgrave, Jr.

MARANAO   The Maranao are a Philippine Muslim group living predominantly around Lake Lanao in the northwest portion of the island of Mindanao. The word "Maranao" means "people of the lake," and it is used to designate not only the people, but also the language spoken by the people.

Closely associated with the Maranao is a group or subgroup of people variously called Iranon, Iranun, Illanun and Ilanon. Iranon sometimes refers specifically to people living in and around Balabagan, which is southwest of Lake Lanao on the coast of Illana Bay. Scholars disagree on whether or not the Iranon are of the same ethno-linguistic stock as the Maranao. Most consider the Iranon to be rather recent antecedents of the Maranao. No adequate study has been done to determine the exact numbers of the Iranon or their precise relationship to the Maranao.

Racially the Maranao, like most other Filipinos, are of Malayan and Indonesian stock, so that they are physically indistinguishable from other Filipinos.

Linguistically, Maranao is closely related to the major Filipino languages, since it too belongs to the central Philippine subgroup. It is generally not understood by other Mindanao groups, with the exception of the Maguindanao.

Lake Lanao, the largest lake in Mindanao and the second largest fresh water lake in the Philippines, is approximately 2,300 feet above sea level. It empties into the Agus River, which feeds the Maria Christina Falls about 18 miles north of it. The southern tip of the lake is approximately 21 miles from the municipality of Malabang on the southwestern coast of Mindanao. Thus the Maranao are predominantly a non-coastal inland group relatively isolated from coastal Filipinos and foreign colonial powers until recently. The mountainous terrain between the coast and Laka Lanao has made it difficult for outsiders to influence the Maranao. A cement road between Marawi City and Iligan City and improved roads elsewhere in the area are changing this situation.

Of the major Muslim ethnolinguistic groups in the Philippines the Maranao were the last to be Islamized. They were also a major center of fierce resistance against the Spanish, the Americans, the Japanese and the Republic of the Philippines, especially after martial law was declared in September 1972.

The population of the Maranao in 1983 is estimated to be around 840,000, making them numerically the second largest Muslim group after the Maguindanao in the Philippines. About 90 percent of the Maranao live in the province of Lanao del Sur, while the remaining 10 percent live in Lanao del Norte and parts of Cotabato, Zamboanga del Sur and Bukidnon.

The Maranao are primarily agriculturalists and fishermen. The land on the eastern side of Lake Lanao is a fertile rice-growing area. With modern techniques, using irrigation and new seed varieties, it is estimated that the rice yield from this area could be tripled annually. In other areas of Lanao the combination of fertile soil, abundant rainfall and a pleasant climate makes it possible for farmers to produce a surplus of corn, peanuts, sweet potatoes, coffee, citrus fruits and exotic tropical fruits. Besides the staple, which is rice, the most common food of the Maranao is fish.

Other economic activities of the Maranao include such cottage industries as cloth and mat weaving, wood carving, and metalwork in brass, silver and gold. One of the ways that other ethnic groups of the Philippines become aware of the Maranao is through the Maranao merchants who travel throughout the Philippines selling straw mats, yard goods, blankets and metalwork.

The commercial, cultural and educational center of the Maranao is Marawi (formerly called Dansalan), on the northern tip of Lake Lanao. With a population of around 50,000 people in 1970, it is the largest city in Lanao del Sur. It is also the provincial capital. Maranao from all around the lake travel by water or by land to sell their products at Marawi's market, so that they can buy clothes, household utensils, farm tools and other items not available in the villages.

The cultural value system of the Maranao revolves around such principles as hospitality, *maratabat* (a sociopsychological force involving notions of pride, honor, self-esteem, face and rank) and the centrality of kinship relationships. Islamic values are strong.

The Maranao village is made up of several nucleated households. Several nuclear families may live together under one roof or join together with other families in a food-sharing relationship. A typical traditional Maranao house has no partitions inside. Along both walls of the house are sleeping areas with an aisle down the center. Each nuclear family occupies one sleeping area made up of a kapok mattress, straw mats, embroidered pillows and a cloth canopy from which is suspended a mosquito net. In the rear of the house is a common kitchen, shared by all occupants of the house. Usually all the occupants are related directly or indirectly to one another, and this relationship is carefully recorded in an individual's genealogy. Thus the Maranao live closely not only with the members of their immediate family, but also with their more distant relatives. As a result, they develop strong ties of loyalty to their kinsmen.

Special occasions, such as marriage, death or a unique individual achievement (finishing an Islamic course at Al Azhar University in Cairo, for example), call for a feast, at which there may be all or some of the following activities: chanting the individual's genealogy, playing musical instruments, singing folk tunes, telling folk tales, playing games, dancing. All these are highly developed folk arts among the Maranao. The gathering together of all the relatives at such a feast serves to renew and strengthen kinship ties.

By virtue of the prominence of a bilateral descent system, a Maranao possesses membership in several villages at the same time. Membership is based on kinship, not on residency, and an individual inherits kinship both from his father's and from his mother's side. This is complicated by the tendency toward exogamy, i.e., people tend to marry outside their own traditional descent group. Obviously an individual can live in only one village at a time, even though he can claim membership, with its concomitant rights, privileges, duties and responsibilities, in several villages. There may also be people whose residence is in the territory of a village community, but they are not members of that traditional village community because they do not have the lineage required for membership in that particular village. Thus Maranao perceive of villages as communities of persons who share a descent group or a set of descent groups rather than places or spatial territories. Furthermore, there is fluidity and change in the active membership of a particular village, since an individual Maranao usually claims only a portion of his descent group duties some of the time. His personality and the amount of his energy and ambition determine the number of village communities he can participate in and the extent of his participation.

While an individual's rights and duties are determined by his descent line, his personal prestige and his ultimate ranking in the total society as seen by himself and by others will largely be determined by acquired skills (as an orator, a Quran reader, an authority on law) and his performance as a leader in his village community (settling disputes, bravery in battle, avenging an insult or killing of a close relative). A person with a low-ranking lineage may achieve high status in the society by virtue of his personal skills and attributes. This arrangement allows for social mobility and accounts for the competitiveness and the tendency toward conflict in Maranao society.

Maranao Islam (Shafi school) shows vestiges of Sufi influence, notably in some loan words and in some group chants at religious ceremonies. Pre-Islamic beliefs and practices, especially those related to agriculture, the cycles of nature and the spirit world, are more prevalent in the rural areas than in the urban centers. The Maranao practice of the Islamic religion has been influenced by Arab teachers who lived among and taught the Maranao, by young men and women who have studied Islamic subjects in Middle East Arab schools and have returned to teach in local *madrasa* and by non-Muslim agencies, both in the government and from the private sector, who are interested in the development of the area. As a result, the folkways of the Maranao are gradually and steadily being changed, because the Maranao are sensitive to the criticism made by Muslim and non-Muslim groups and individuals that these practices are not in line with orthodox Islamic principles. This is causing considerable tension between the old and the young, the conservative and the liberal, the tolerant and the fanatic, the traditional and the modern in the everyday life of the Maranao.

Many Maranao are vehemently opposed to the Republic of the Philippines, especially the feature of martial law, and a number of Maranao are in armed revolt against it. They prefer a federated system of government, which would allow for more local autonomy; or they prefer to secede from the republic completely in order either to align themselves with a Muslim country or to be independent altogether. Loyalty to descent groups causes many Maranao to tolerate, shelter or support the rebels, whom they affectionately refer to as "the children."

BIBLIOGRAPHY

Books

Chaffee, Frederic H., et al. *Area Handbook for the Philippines*. The American University FAS, DA Pam 550–72. Washington, D.C.: Government Printing Office, 1969.

Filipinas Foundation. *An Anatomy of Philippine Muslim Affairs*. Makati, Rizal, Philippines: Filipinas Foundation, 1971.

Gowing, Peter G. *Mosque and Moro: A Study of Muslims in the Philippines*. Manila: Philippine Federation of Christian Churches, 1964.

————, and McAmis, Robert D., eds. *The Muslim Filipinos: Their History, Society, and Contemporary Problems*. Manila: Solidaridad Publishing House, 1974.

Isidro, Antonio, and Saber, Mamitua, eds. *Muslim Philippines*. Marawi City, Philippines: Mindanao State University Research Center, 1968.

Majul, Cesar Adib. *Muslims in the Philippines*. Quezon City: University of the Philippines Press, 1973.

McAmis, Robert Day. *An Introduction to the Folk Tales of the Maranao Muslims of Mindanao in the Southern Philippines*. Philippine Studies Program, Department of Anthropology Transcript Series, No. 9. Chicago: University of Chicago, 1966.

————. "Muslim Filipinos: 1970–1972." In *The Muslim Filipinos: Their History, Society, and Contemporary Problems*, edited by Peter G. Gowing and Robert D. McAmis. Manila: Solidaridad Publishing House, 1974.

Mednick, Melvin. *Encampment of the Lake: The Social Organization of the Moslem-Philippine (Moro) People*. Chicago: University of Chicago Press, 1965.

————. "Sultans and Mayors: The Relation of a National to an Indigenous Political System." In *The Muslim Filipinos: Their History, Society, and Contemporary Problems*, edited by Peter G. Gowing and Robert D. McAmis. Manila: Solidaridad Publishing House, 1974.

Riemer, Carlton L. *Maranao "Maratabat" and the Concepts of Pride, Honor, and Self-Esteem.* Occasional Paper No. 4. Marawi City, Philippines: Dansalan Research Center, 1976.

Saber, Mamitua. "Muslim Filipinos in Unity Within Diversity." In *Muslim Philippines*, edited by Antonio Isidro and Mamitua Saber. Marawi City, Philippines: Mindanao State University Research Center, 1968.

————, and Madale, Abdullah T., eds. *The Maranao.* Manila: Solidaridad Publishing House, 1975.

Articles

Baradas, David B. "Conflict in the 'Land of Promise.' " *Philippine Sociological Review* 20:4 (1972): 363–366.

Isidro, Antonio. "Education of the Muslim." *Solidarity* 4:3 (1969): 8–12.

Madale, Nagasura T. "Kashawing: Rice Ritual of the Maranaos." *Mindanao Journal* 1:1 (1974): 74–80.

Rivera, Generoso F. "The Maranaw Muslims of Lumbayao, Lanao." *Philippine Sociological Review* 14:3 (1966): 127–134.

Saber, Mamitua. "Some Observations on Maranaws and Social and Cultural Transition." *Philippine Sociological Review* 11:1–2 (1963): 51–56.

————; Tamano, Mauyag; and Warriner, Charles K. "The Maratabat of the Maranao." *Philippine Sociological Review* 8:1–2 (1960): 10:–15.

Warriner, Charles K. "Myth and Reality in the Social Structure of the Philippines." *Philippine Sociological Review* 8:3–4 (1960): 26–32.

————. "Myths, Moros, and the Maranao." *Exchange News Quarterly* 10 (1959): 2–3, 20.

————. "Traditional Authority and the Modern State: The Case of the Maranao of the Philippines." *Social Problems* 12:1 (1964): 51–56.

Unpublished Manuscript

Baradas, David B. "Maranao Law: A Study of Conflict and Its Resolution in a Multicentric Power System." Ph.D. dissertation, University of Chicago, 1971.

Carlton L. Riemer
Population figures updated by Richard V. Weekes

MASALIT The Masalit live in the most remote and unknown areas of Sudan and Chad. While great trading empires were conquered on their east and west, Dar ("home of") Masalit won its independence and maintained it into the twentieth century. The people developed a reputation for fiercely protecting their autonomy; they produced everything they needed, had their own language and customs and were capable of defending their borders. Yet in these more peaceful days, the Masalit are becoming increasingly integrated into global systems of exchange, power and thought. These forces of transformation cannot be defeated by military means. Economic, political, environmental and cultural processes are at work, and the Masalit are becoming a peripheralized people.

The Masalit, and a group of the same people called "Masalat," number more than 300,000. The largest group straddles the Chad–Sudan border, with some 200,000 Masalit speakers in Dar Masalit District of Northern Darfur Province, Sudan, and 50,000 in the Adre District of Chad. To the west in the Oum Hadjer-Am Dam area of Chad live approximately 23,000 Masalat. To the southeast of Dar Masalit, in the vicinity of Gereida, Southern Darfur, live Masalit and Masalat numbering in the tens of thousands. In recent decades, Masalit populations have grown up in Khartoum, the Gedaref-Kassala area and other eastern Sudan locations as a result of migration and resettlement.

It is unclear whether the Masalit/Masalat distinction represents a significant ethnic or linguistic difference or a mere linguistic artifact due to Arabization of names. The Masalat of Gereida and the people of Dar Masalit are in contact; they have some common clans and recently joined in paying compensation for an act of homicide against a non-Masalit in Southern Darfur.

Although French sources consider the Masalat of Chad an offshoot of the Dar Masalit people, the oral traditions of Sudanese Masalit trace Masalat origins to the west. The Masalit and Masalat of Sudan consider that the original Masalit population migrated from Tunis and came to Sudan via present-day Chad. Linguistically, Masalit is part of the Maba branch of Nilo-Saharan, and languages of this branch are spoken in the Am Dam area. This fact, in combination with oral traditions, suggests that Masalit and Maba languages became distinct in the Am Dam area of Chad; thereafter, some Masalit migrated to the current Dar Masalit and Gereide locations and populated them. Linguistic research is needed to unravel the sequence and timing of events (see Maba).

Masalit are in contact with Arab and non-Arab populations in all regions, and Arabic is widely used as a lingua franca. This is especially true of townspeople in all areas and of the Gereida and Am Dam populations generally. Within Dar Masalit many women and children speak only the Masalit language, but men tend to learn more Arabic in the course of labor migration to eastern Sudan. The use of Arabic appears to be spreading, especially in towns where children attend school and market activities bring different language groups together.

In Dar Masalit the Masalit are the majority ethnic group, outnumbering the Gimr, Jebel (Mileri), Sinyar and Arab populations (see Sinyar; Tama-speaking Peoples). They inhabit most of the southern part of the Dar, a Sahelian region with mean annual rainfall of approximately 20 inches in recent years. This represents a decline of over 4 inches average rainfall since 1969 and appears to be a permanent condition in spite of the widely accepted view that the Sahel drought ended in 1974. The area appears to be in a process of desertification, as are other areas of Sudan.

Masalit engage in mixed agriculture, primarily cultivation of millet and peanuts in the northern sandy areas and sorghum in the southern wadis. They keep moderate numbers of cattle, sheep and goats and are able to manure some of their fields. In recent years camels purchased from Arab nomads have become an important form of transport, supplementing the large number of donkeys.

Hunting and gathering activities, while significant in the past, have become limited due to the increased population and reduction of forest resources.

While most grain is grown for domestic use, some is bartered or sold to nomadic Arabs and townspeople throughout the Dar. In areas south of Geneina, the district capital, peanuts, sesame, okra, mangos, coriander and other crops are grown for sale to meet the increasing cash needs of the Masalit. Other cash resources are sale of animals, tanning hides, sewing, transport, brewing and wood gathering.

The greatest involvement in cash economy is through labor migration to the eastern Sudan. For many, migration to new Masalit villages is permanent. For others, especially in the 15–40 age group, migration is temporary. While their wives and children farm and support themselves, men take employment for one to five years on mechanized agricultural schemes in the east. Ideally, they will meet the cash needs of their families and return with clothing and perhaps some investment capital. In practice, many migrants are unsuccessful and are lucky to meet their own needs for the period of absence.

Within Dar Masalit both men and women cultivate, own lands and animals and make consumption decisions. As among many Nilo-Saharan-speaking peoples, the individual is the most important economic unit. Most men and women farm and store their harvests separately. Older children may also have their own fields. The family is not united in a joint estate under one person's control, but rather a system of rights and duties between husband and wife, parent and child. Men must provide housing and most cash goods for their wives and children, while women are primarily responsible for the domestic needs and food for the family. Children should help their parents, especially their mothers, with labor, and in young adulthood with gifts of cash or clothing if they do well in labor migration; parents should provide children with subsistence needs, ceremonial and marital expenses and, eventually, land.

Masalit houses are made from forest products, which are increasingly hard to obtain. The frame of the round, conical-roofed house requires strong, sizable wooden posts and poles; the roof is thatched with wild grasses, the best of which are now scarce. Walls are made from mats from another wild grass. Millet stalks may also be used for walls and are the usual material to make a fenced compound around the houses, kraals and granaries of the family.

Men and women are usually married by their early twenties. The groom, with the assistance of his family, pays a bridewealth of approximately three cows, ten goats and a variable amount of cash; this is primarily distributed to the bride, her mother and more distant relatives. The groom must build a house in the bride's mother's compound and live there with his wife for at least a year, working in the fields of her mother. In the second year he will cultivate his own field, but the couple stays on until at least one child is born, and they may stay permanently. If and when the couple moves out, they may settle near the husband's or wife's family, depending usually on the availability of fields.

Men frequently have two wives simultaneously, sometimes more. The second wife's mother still expects a house and bridewealth, but in the case of a second marriage she can command less labor from the groom. Approximately half of polygynously married men have their wives' households in separate villages. Polygynous joint compounds are rare.

Divorce is common. A divorced woman usually retains the house and compound of the couple, and she is entitled to assistance in feeding the small children who stay with her until they are about ten years old. Bridewealth may be returned in part for a short marriage. Many divorced and widowed women never remarry, but few men remain single for long.

Households are aggregated into villages, which are constantly reshaped by marriages, divorces and shifts of residence. Within the village, most interactions are structured by ties of kinship and neighborliness. Frequently one or several large extended families of cognatically related men and women and their spouses make up the majority of a village population. However, non-kin or distant relatives who move in can develop close reciprocal relationships on the basis of neighborliness alone. Ideal relationships among co-villagers include mutual assistance, cooperative labor exchange and sharing of ideas and values. Men eat, pray and socialize in a central *masik*, usually a shaded clearing, while women visit each other in their homes and at the well. Villages may, however, be divided into several neighborhoods with their own *masiks*. Alcohol use and religious piety also divide some villages into informal factions.

Political organization beyond the village is currently in a state of transition. The Native Administration structure from the colonial era continues to function for purposes of tax collection and informal adjudication. This is composed of a hierarchy of offices, from that of the village *shaikh*, through those of *dimlij* and *fursha* (titles from Fur administration) to the sultanate, which originated after the fall of Dar Fur. This "native" system of offices is superimposed upon a system of segmentary patrilineages with territorial rights, which may not have had offices or chiefs before Dar Fur imposed them. The Native Administration structure is being replaced by a system of rural councils, courts, cooperatives and Sudan Socialist Union chapters along the same lines as the rest of Sudan. *Dimlij* territories are ignored in the new system, but *fursha* territories are being kept intact, and the *furshas* or members of their families are frequently office holders in the organization.

The Masalit are Muslims, and the idiom of Islam dominates political and social life and values. By the seventeenth century, Islam had been introduced to Dar Fur by itinerant holy men, and they probably also came to Dar Masalit. One observer in 1874 noted "an unusual number of *faqis*" (clerics). However, Islam had made considerable accommodation to pre-Islamic practices such as divination and ceremonies to avoid locusts or to cause rains.

Sultan Ismail brought more orthodox teachings, including Mahdist reforms, to Dar Masalit such as observation of the Ramadan fast, prohibition of alcoholic beverages and certain pre-Islamic ceremonies and the reduction of bridewealth. While Islamic practice in Dar Masalit was not reformed in his lifetime, Sultan

Ismail began a process of increasing orthodoxy that continues to this day. While the village *faqi* remains important, there is a growing role for the town-based, better-educated *imams*. The Ramadan fast is rigorously observed, and many abstain from alcohol, pray the five daily prayers and seek religious instruction. Many accommodations to local practices continue, such as group recitation of the names of god or using portions of the Quran to affect the weather. Amulets and potions with powers to cause conception, make one loved, protect or harm are prepared from Muslim holy texts. The trend appears to be towards closer ties with the pious community of Dar Masalit and that of the rest of the Islamic world.

The tendency towards increasing external direction and linkages is apparent not only in religious but also in political, cultural and economic life. Dar Masalit is no longer an isolated region, self-sufficient and independent. It is dependent on national and global markets for its continued existence; it is part of the same political system as the rest of Sudan, and it is increasingly aware of its place in the Islamic world. Dar Masalit will retain a local character in the future, but it is irreversibly involved in these larger systems. This involvement will be accelerated by the environmental and ecological problems which beset the area and further reduce self-sufficiency. In these ways the Masalit, for all their uniqueness, are proceeding in the same directions as most people living in the peripheral areas of the world.

BIBLIOGRAPHY

Books

Haaland, G. "Ethnic Groups and Languages in Darfur." In *Aspects of Language in the Sudan*, edited by R. Thelwall. Coleraine: New University of Ulster, 1980.
Lebeuf, A.M.D. *Les Populations du Tchad*. Paris: Presses Universitaires de France, 1959.
Le Rouvreur, A. *Sahariens et saheliens du Tchad*. Paris: Berger-Levrault, 1962.
Nachtigal, G. *Sahara and Sudan*, vol. 4, *Wadai and Darfur*, translated by A.G.B. and H. J. Fisher. Berkeley: University of California Press, 1971.
O'Fahey, R. S. *State and Society in Dar Fur*. London: C. Hurst, 1980.
Tully, D. "Dar Masalit Today: Dynamics of Ecology, Society and Politics." In *Peoples and Cultures of the Ethio-Sudan Borderlands*, edited by M. L. Bender. East Lansing: African Studies Institute, Michigan State University, 1981.

Articles

Davies, R. "The Masalit Sultanate." *Sudan Notes and Records* 9 (1926): 49–62.
Greenberg, J. H. "Nilo-Saharan and Meroitic." *Current Trends in Linguistics* 7 (1971): 421–442.

Kapteijns, L. "The Emergence of a Sudanic State: Dar Masalit, 1874–1905." *International Journal of African Historical Studies* 16 (1983): 601–613.
———, and Spaulding, J. "Precolonial Trade Between States in the Eastern Sudan, ca. 1700–ca. 1900." *African Economic History* 11 (1982): 29–62.

Unpublished Manuscripts

Kapteijns, L. "Mahdist Faith and Sudanic Tradition: History of Dar Masalit, 1870–1930." Ph.D. dissertation, Universiteit van Amsterdam, 1982.
Tully, D. "Culture and Context: The Process of Market Incorporation in Dar Masalit, Sudan." Ph.D. dissertation, University of Washington, 1984.
———. "Dual Economy or Dual Population: A Western Sudanese Case." Paper presented at the Eightieth Annual Meeting of the American Anthropological Association, Baltimore, March 1982.
———. "Labor Migration in the Economy and Society of Dar Masalit." Paper presented at the First Annual Meeting of the Sudan Studies Association, Baltimore, 1982.

Dennis Tully

MEIDOB   Five hundred miles west of the confluence of the Blue and White Niles, across a monotonous landscape, broken only by random granite outcrops, rise the Meidob hills of western Sudan in Darfur Province. Comprising an area of 240,000 square miles, including the surrounding plains to the south and east, these volcanic peaks and the pleasant upland plateaus between them is Dar Meidob, the home of the Meidob people. They number about 45,000, spread evenly with a concentration in the administrative center of Malha. They call themselves Tiddi in their own language.

To the north lies the Libyan desert, uninhabited save when the jizzu—a rich pasture of mixed vegetation—appears after the rains and pastoralists bring their animals to graze. A traditional caravan route leads through this area, splitting to Libya and the camel markets of Egypt. Camels and salt have been the traditional commodities which have been exploited by the Meidob and led them to trade outside their own Dar. To the east, the Meidob compete for pasture with the Kababish Arab camel nomads and to the south and west with Zaghawa, Rizeygat and other nomads (see Beri). A small section of the Meidob occupies the northern fringes of the Tagabo hills, 80 miles to the southwest, where they neighbor on the sedentary Berti (see Berti). With all these groups, they maintain a posture of more or less open mutual hostility, and the Meidob reputation among their neighbors is one of untrustworthy animal thieves.

Meidob pastoralism does not entail extensive movement in terms of distance. Camels and sheep are herded separately by the adolescents and young adult men and are kept continuously moving from pasture to pasture, while the cattle and goats are kept, by the women, in the settlements within easy reach of water supplies. The Meidob have traditionally practiced agriculture as well, normally growing enough sorghum and basic vegetables to satisfy all local needs. With the addition of milk and goat meat, these products form the basic diet.

The Meidob language, which is still spoken by all Meidob, is a member of the Nubian language group, which is included in the Eastern Sudanic sub-phylum of the Nilo-Saharan family of African languages. The historically and politically most important members of this group are the Nile Nubian tribes—the Mahas and the Dongolawi (see Nubians). Links with these groups are preserved in Meidob traditions, and certain kinship patterns are also parallel.

The Meidob recognize three internal divisions: the Urrti, Shalkota (or Kargeddi) and Torti. Linguistically, there are two distinguishable dialects, Urrti and Shalkota/Torti. Differences have been noted in sound distribution and vocabulary, but these do not impede mutual intelligibility and show that communication and cohesion within the whole group has prevented extreme linguistic differentiation. In the past, each division had its own *malik*, or leader. The Urrti and Shalkota both claim to have come to Dar Meidob from Nubia and to be related to the Mahas. The Torti claim to have come with the Shalkota. Whatever the truths behind these claims, the divisions remain active and are fueled by hostility and feuding between them. The Torti, though now subordinates to the Shalkota, should be noted for having held custody of various ritual objects and offices of pre-Islamic nature which only disappeared in the last 100 years. Of some historical significance, also, is the matrilineal succession, which was probably exclusive in pre-Islamic times and now coexists with other culture patterns. No other tribes in this area of Darfur Province illustrate any traces of this, though the Nile Nubians practiced it, at least until medieval times.

Islam first effectively entered Darfur with the conversion of the Fur Sultan Suleiman Solong (1660–1680). Traditions state that the Meidob *malik* was one of 20 chiefs subordinate to the Fur (see Fur). While several prominent Meidobi individuals held important posts at court, it seems that Meidob isolation allowed them to retain a great measure of independence. They do not appear to have become effectively Islamized until well into the nineteenth century. The Mahdiyya was not welcomed among the Meidob, though various temporary alliances were made with Mahdist forces, largely to further local rivalries. Active conversion to Islam spread when the last Fur sultan, Ali Dinar (1898–1916), incorporated the Meidob effectively under his political control. The incorporation of Darfur into the Anglo-Egyptian Condominium in 1916 was followed by the British administrators recognizing the Shalkota *malik* as overall leader. The Urrti malikdom was abolished in 1923, that of the Torti in 1944, and that of the Shalkota technically in 1971, when the Sudan government abolished the vestiges of the "native administration" with the Peoples Local Government Act. In reality, the power of the *maliks* had been considerably reduced since the time of Ali Dinar, and the territorial sections which became tax-collecting areas had an *omda* appointed as their head. These *omdas* formed a group of political leaders who exercised effective power, and a similar situation persists at the present time, when political and moral leadership rests more on individual prestige and wealth than on hereditary status.

In Dar Meidob today, the five tenets of Islam are strictly followed, and the men observe all the main Muslim festivals. Mosques, often consisting of simple marked plots of ground, are found throughout the Dar. Quranic schools are uncommon, and women, who are less in contact with Arabic and outside influences, are the focus of the maintenance of certain traditional practices such as fertility rites, other marriage rituals and divination and oracular consultation in connection with illness. Since public non-Islamic rituals have ceased, there appears to be no pressure to avoid these remaining traditional practices, parallel to the situation in most parts of Sudan.

Prior to the Mahdiyya, the Meidob seem to have practiced matrilineal succession and inheritance exclusively. This is borne out by the genealogies of the various *maliks* and other oral traditions. There are 13 matriclans with totemic names of animals or insects, and these are found among all the three sections of the group. In addition, patriclans and groups of descending kin (*dirria*) based on male and female links are now recognized. The *dirria* comprise a group of from three to five generations back to a male ancestor. Close kin marriage is preferred among the Meidob, excluding members of the same matriclan, with father's brother's daughter/son as the ideal. Polygyny is practiced, with a strict exclusion on taking two wives from the same section of the matriclan. This exclusion is linked with residence patterns. Polygyny is linked with wealth and status, and its incidence increases with age. Residence after marriage does not depend on matriclan or patriclan affiliation but seems to depend primarily on the needs (other things being equal) at the basic settlement level (*kar*). In this context, the *dirria* operates as a residence group, and as such an individual, whose matriclan and patriclan affiliations are determined by birth, may choose to identify with one of a number of *dirria*, since they have overlapping membership. The choice then is usually based on residence, and if a member moves away from that locality, his membership ceases to be effective.

Residence is conditioned by two factors: the physical settlement pattern and the marital/kin status. The basic settlement unit, the *kar*, consists of a small number (typically four to five) of separate huts. These huts are permanent, and a nomad group would have three different *kar* associated with the grazing and watering patterns of the year: *sagan-kar* (rainy season hamlet), where the longest continuous residence is kept; *iccin-kar* (winter hamlet) for the coolest, post rains residence and *pargan-kar* (dry season hamlet) for the least abundant grazing period. Each adult woman has her own hut and lives with her children and possibly her husband. While virilocal residence is the norm, a number of other patterns are common, and the demands of herding and herd size condition the residence patterns and following from these needs also affect the choice of marriage partner. For example, in a family which needs manpower for herding, a daughter may be married as a second wife, in which case she and her future children would commonly remain in her parental settlement and provide continuing labor for them. Thus, the cross-cutting kinship and residence patterns enable maximum flexibility to be maintained with the needs of animal husbandry playing at least as important an underlying role as kinship and marriage in the choice of residence.

Another important sphere of activity in which kinship plays an important role is inheritance and payment of compensation for death or injury. While this was previously through matrilineal relationships, today the patriclan links play an equally important role, and both the devolution of property and the payment of compensation is shared equally between matri- and patriclans. Gifts of animals to children of both sexes are given at various stages of their life and are outside these inheritance rules. Much of the transfer of livestock takes place during the life of the owner, and thus inheritance on death has less importance than it might otherwise.

The patriclan, which has clearly grown up in the context of Islam and Islamic legal practice, also provides the main context for men to gain political power, through which they can acquire status and wealth.

The Meidob are Sunni, and the traditional juridical rite has been Maliki, although due to Ottoman and Egyptian traditions at the national level Hanafi operates. In fact, for the Meidob as for all but the most dedicated urban Muslims, *adat* or customary law is followed and has been institutionally recognized by the government. *Adat* is accepted for all local cases (other than those covered by the Penal Code) instead of Shariah law if both parties to a suit agree.

The physical isolation of Dar Meidob is more apparent than real. The Meidob are extremely cosmopolitan in outlook and well informed both locally and nationally. Regular contact with Omdurmani, Egyptian and recently Libyan markets connected with camel sales has kept the Meidob abreast of current economic and political affairs, and a number of supernational entrepreneurs have achieved significant success. This is based on the steady increase in herds, which is founded on the political stability and the exclusion of non-Meidob from grazing in the area between 1930 and 1950. The drought of the last ten years or so led to a temporary exodus from the Dar. The expansion of labor migration to Libya by young men is having a significant effect, but it is too early to say if this will lead to a permanent shift of a significant part of the population from pastoralism. At present, much of the wealth thus acquired is reinvested in herd expansion.

BIBLIOGRAPHY

Book

Thelwall, R. "Meidob Nubian: Phonology, Grammatical Notes and Basic Vocabulary." In *Sahelian Language Studies*, edited by M. L. Bender. East Lansing: Michigan State University Press, 1983.

Articles

Lampen, G. D. "A Short Account of Meidob." *Sudan Notes and Records* 11 (1928): 55–67.
MacMichael, H. "Nubian Elements in Darfur." *Sudan Notes and Records* 1 (1918): 30–118.

Unpublished Manuscripts

Ali, Yusuf Adam. "Some Aspects of Meidob History." B.A. thesis, Khartoum University, 1980.
Hales, E. A. "Meidob Kinship, Marriage and Residence." Ph.D. dissertation, Cambridge University, 1979.
Hales, J. M. "The Pastoral System of the Meidob." Ph.D. dissertation, Cambridge University, 1978.

Robin Thelwall

MELANAU The coastal area of northwestern Sarawak in Borneo is a low-lying swampy plain extending from 3 to 20 miles inland, often below sea level. Its poor peat soil, covered with dense rain forest, does not easily allow the inhabitants to grow rice by shifting cultivation, the characteristic mode of farming in the interior districts. The area is transversed by meandering rivers, all flowing roughly northwest into the South China Sea. These rivers are tidal for long distances upstream; and during the monsoon, from November to March, they are likely to overflow their banks and flood the surrounding land. Swamp rice, a strain of hill rice that tolerates wet soil but not flooding, can be grown on the raised river banks. Rice grown in such conditions is an uncertain crop and is frequently ruined before it can be harvested.

The inhabitants of these inhospitable coastal swamps, in an area stretching from the delta of the Rejang River along the coast northeastward for roughly 100 miles, are known as the Melanau. The name, they say, was given to them by the people of Brunei. They call themselves *a-likou*, meaning "people of the river." They number perhaps 89,000 (based on a 1960 census), three-quarters of whom are Muslim (67,000), the rest animist (15,000) and Roman Catholics. Their language is Austronesian, akin to but distinct from Malay.

Melanau Muslims are a traditional people, poor and without significant education. Their conception of Islam is strongly animistic, as are many of their rituals. With education and the new wealth of Malaysia, combined with a resurgence of Islam, these traditional views and practices are now in the process of rapid change.

The only plant that grows in the swamp environment of Sarawak is the sago palm, and for centuries the Melanau have cultivated it as their principal food and cash crop. The flour produced from it is used for subsistence and export. Certain essential commodities such as salt, iron, copper and stone are not found in the area so the Melanau trade sago and forest products—rattan, gums and resins, beeswax, camphor, birds' feathers and timber—for the things they need in such cities as Brunei and Pantianak on the coast of Borneo, in Johore in Malaya and in markets in Indonesia, Indo-China and China. Trade is indispensable to their lives.

The traditional Melanau village once consisted of two or three longhouses, massive wooden fortresses built on piles, often 30 feet high, usually situated at the confluence of a strategically important stream with the main river. In front of each was a long veranda, much like a street. Each village was politically independent within its own territory and often on terms of active hostility with its neighbors. When peaceful conditions were established in the latter part of the nineteenth century, the houses were gradually abandoned and the villagers built separate family dwellings along the banks of the rivers.

Although physically a single structure, a longhouse was made up of separate apartments, each ideally owned and inhabited by one married couple and perhaps one married child, often the youngest. A large part of village life took place on the veranda, and when small separate houses came to replace the longhouses much of the culture, especially the performance of communal ceremonies, fell into disuse.

Political control of the villages was in the hands of aristocratic elders whose families usually owned the central longhouse apartments and who were the descendants of the villages' founders. On each side of this core were apartments owned by freemen, and at each end were the apartments of freed slaves or field slaves, in contrast to household slaves, who lived in the apartments of their owners. An elaborate set of customary rules (*adat*) regulated the behavior of the ranks to one another and most other aspects of social life. The *adat*, one of the community's most valued possessions, was in the custody of the self-appointed aristocratic elders. No single elder was superior to the others, although one might have special knowledge that fitted him for particular tasks. For example, a man with unusual abilities in war might be put in charge of defense and raids, and another with knowledge of rituals might assume leadership on ceremonial occasions. A man with charismatic qualities might rise to preeminence during his lifetime and maintain a loose alliance of villages. Such local leaders, however, were never able to establish kingdoms, and their rule invariably broke up at their deaths, if not before.

Melanau society made use of three distinct criteria in organizing social life. The first was that of local grouping; the second was that of kinship; and the third was that of hereditary rank. An individual thought of himself in each of these social dimensions. He was closely identified with a particular locality, especially a village whose inhabitants were thought to be, and often were, unique in matters of dialect and custom. As an individual, a person was the focal point of kin with whom he or she shared a wide range of social and economic interests, regulated by principles of bilateral descent. Lastly he had, by virtue of birth, a rank status. At birth a Melanau was placed in the theoretically unalterable and named rank category of his father. Although each rank was ideally endogamous, marriage between individuals of different rank were not uncommon, and among Muslim immigrants this fact led to a very slow increase in their numbers.

In any context the behavior of an individual toward another was largely determined by whether the two were neighbors or strangers, kinsmen or not, of equal or unequal rank. In addition, behavior was also regulated by age and sex and was further constrained by the concept of *adat*.

Traditional social organization and ideas, in spite of the abandonment of the longhouse and extensive conversion to Islam, are still central to the organization of Melanau life. Muslims, pagans and Christians alike still maintain traditional forms of household, kinship behavior and observance of rank distinctions. Visiting Muslim teachers sometimes try to correct what they hold to be mistaken practices and beliefs, especially in the conduct of weddings, when the proper ordering of society in its correct ranks is prominently on display, and also in the treatment of illness by shamans. Such visitors are listened to with respect, but on their departure what they said is usually forgotten.

For at least four centuries the Melanau have been under the influence and, at one time, nominal jurisdiction of the Muslim sultans of Brunei. Representatives of the sultans lived at the mouths of the more important sago-producing rivers to control trade revenues. These representatives and their families were assimilated by the local population and came to speak Melanau instead of Malay as their first language. They lived as hereditary elders in longhouse fortresses; and though the one selected as the sultan's representative at any one time carried prestige and could sometimes successfully claim to be ruler of the river, he was, as much as were the elders in the wholly pagan villages upriver, merely *primus inter pares*.

The Muslim settlers from Brunei almost completely adopted Melanau values, especially those concerning rank. They imposed themselves on local society as a superior rank and regarded the pagan upper ranks as second-class aristocrats. Even more than religion, it was rank in all sections of society that counted most. At birth a Melanau acquired not only a place in a village and a circle of kinsmen; he was also placed in his rank category. Muslims from Brunei brought with them the titles *pengiren*, *awang* and *dayang*. In many respects these titles marked them off more significantly than their religion, since the preferred Melanau marriage, among pagans as much as Muslims, was with a second cousin of any kind, provided marriage was not across any of the three main rank barriers— aristocrats, middle ranks and slaves.

The establishment of Singapore as an international market in 1819 introduced fundamental changes in the trade of the whole region of the Indonesian archipelago and in particular in the trade of the Melanau sago. Until then, most sago had been exported as a high starch food in the form of a baked biscuit prepared in the villages. When European textile industries demanded industrial starch, the market for sago flour biscuits decreased in favor of sago flour. Malay traders from Kuching in Sarawak began competing with the established merchants from Brunei in supplying the new flour in Singapore. Piracy was part of the game.

In 1839 James Brooke, an Englishman, arrived in Kuching on the river Sarawak, where a section of the local Malay aristocracy was in revolt against the representative of the Sultan of Brunei. Brooke helped suppress the revolt and in 1841 had himself appointed Raja of Sarawak on the understanding that the state would remain Muslim in perpetuity and that the Muslim Malay-speaking inhabitants were to provide most of the civil service. For the next 20 years, Brooke and his successor, his nephew, were engaged in war. By the late 1850s, the Raja found himself short of money and still at war. To save himself and the solvency of Sarawak, Brooke annexed the sago-producing districts and in 1861 forced the sultan to grant him title to the whole area. Brooke's family ruled Sarawak until World War II; in 1946, Sarawak was ceded to Great Britain, and in 1963, Sarawak joined the Republic of Malaysia.

As the coastal district settled down after Brooke's conquest, production increased, as did trade with Singapore. The reasons for living in longhouses disappeared with the advent of peace and security, and Melanau began moving to villages with separate houses. Under Brooke, the Malay community was privileged and the Muslim religion protected, if not actively pushed. For the Melanau, many of whom could speak Malay, to become Muslim was *masok melayu*—to become Malay, with all its privileges.

After the turn of the century, the situation changed. It had been the policy of the Raja never to allow Christian missionaries to threaten the interests of his Muslim subjects. But around 1900 he permitted the Roman Catholics to set up schools and churches. One particular aristocrat in Brooke's administration, on returning home from the pilgrimage to Mecca, was disturbed to find a Roman Catholic mission on his river. His father, one of the Raja's most influential administrators, joined with his son, and for the next 40 years they and other Muslims recruited by them conducted a steady and covert campaign of proselytization, supported by the governmental benefits accruing to Muslims. The results were dramatic. In 1900 it is estimated that only one-third of the Melanau were Muslim; in 1964, three-fourths of them were. The percentage is probably higher today.

Like most Muslims in the Indonesian area, the Melanau are Sunni and follow Shafi law, although rather loosely. When Sarawak acceded to the Malaysian federation in 1963, Islam did not, as in other parts of Malaysia, become the official religion, although it was allotted a highly privileged position with a state department and official funds to manage its interests. Money was supplied for building mosques and salaries of religious officials. Less money was contributed to other religions, and many inducements were made to persuade pagans and others to become Muslim.

Under the Brooke regime, Muslims in all parts of the country were governed in all matters, except those directly concerning the state, by the *undang undang melayu*, a code of Malay customary law compiled by Muslim administrative officers and religious officials in the capital. The requirements laid down in this code were not always strictly orthodox, and among the Melanau observance was usually lax. It remains so today. Public prayers are held on Fridays, but virtually no one, except a few mosque officials, performs other public prayers. The month of fasting is nominally observed, and the last day is a general holiday. A few people go on pilgrimage every year, and boys are circumcised at the age of 15, when they become adults. Girls are sometimes symbolically clitoridectomized by having an incision made on the sarong they wear at the ceremony. Marriage is in front of the *imam* but is, so to speak, an appendage to the full pagan rituals that unambiguously state the ranks of the parties. Muslim laws of inheritance are disregarded, and the pagan custom of dividing property equally among all children is universally followed. In their proselytization of pagans, Muslim administrative officers unofficially introduce the rule that only Muslims may inherit Muslim property and so convert sons and daughters by converting an elderly parent.

In other aspects of ritual life Muslims and pagans differ very little in essentials. Pagans believe that in death a man paddles a canoe to the afterworld and that after passing through a gate he is directed to his proper part of that afterworld by the guardian. A Muslim, too, paddles to the afterworld, but on arrival must walk on a sword across a cauldron of burning coals to a road that leads to the place for Muslims, for Christians or for pagans.

Muslims and pagans alike believe that this present world is duplicated by others above and below it, inhabited, like this one, by humans, animals, vegetation and spirits. The universe as a whole is orderly, governed by *adat*, and though spirits have powers that humans lack, humans have powers that plants and animals do not. These facts do not mean that any order of being is superior to any other. All depends on the others, and if one offends another, trouble ensues until matters are put right. In general, this can be done only by experts or shamans, who for various reasons have become friends with other orders of being. If it is pointed out to a Melanau that orthodox Islam does not permit dealings with spirits, he will agree, but will add, as did one old man, "Allah is busy and far away. We are unimportant people and have to deal with things as they are."

BIBLIOGRAPHY

Books

Baring-Gould, S., and Bamfylde, C. A. *A History of Sarawak Under Its Two White Rajahs, 1839–1908*. London: Southeran, 1909.

Morris, H. S. "The Coastal Melanau." In *Essays on Borneo Societies*, edited by V. T. King. Oxford: Oxford University Press, 1978.

———. *Report on a Melanau Sago Producing Community in Sarawak*. London: Her Majesty's Stationary Office, 1953.

———. "Shamanism Among the Oya Melanau." In *Social Organization: Essays Presented to Raymond Firth*, edited by M. Freedman. London: Cass, 1967.

———. "Slaves, Aristocrats and Export of Sago in Sarawak." In *Asian and African Systems of Slavery*, edited by J. L. Watson. Oxford: Blackwell, 1980.

Pringle, Robert. *Rajahs and Rebels*. Ithaca: Cornell University Press, 1970.

Runcilman, Steven. *The White Rajahs*. Cambridge: Cambridge University Press, 1960.

H. S. Morris

MENDE One of the two largest ethnic groups in Sierra Leone is the Mende, who comprise some 31 percent of the population. The other is the Temne, who are perhaps 35 percent (see Temne). Less than one-third—346,000—of the 1.2 million Mende are Muslim. Mende inhabit roughly 12,000 square miles of coastal bush and central forest country in southern Sierra Leone, where they are grouped into more than 60 chiefdoms. A few thousand live in Liberia, most in Guma Mendi chiefdom.

Specialists recognize three major subgroups on the basis of dialectical and cultural differences: Kpa-Mende in the west, Sewa Mende in the center and east and Ko-Mende in the north and the center. Linguistically, they belong to the Manding-speaking subgroup of Greenberg's Congo-Kordofanian family; culturally, they are included by Murdock in his Kru and Peripheral Mande culture province (see Manding-speaking Peoples).

The Mende, like most Sierra Leone peoples, welcomed itinerant Muslims, often traders, who settled among them. Known as *mori* men, they provided a valued service such as in making charms and divining for the Mende, especially chiefs and warriors. These traders were Sunni Muslims of the Maliki rite, but prior to the twentieth century there seem to have been few converts. In this century, the spread of Islam among the Mende and other Sierra Leone peoples is probably related to anti-colonial feelings.

The Ahmadiya sect of Islam was introduced to Sierra Leone in 1937 and into the Mende area in 1939 at Baomahun, then a gold-mining center. By 1945, the Ahmadis moved to Bo, which remains their base. A 1960 estimate indicated about 3,000 Ahmadis in Sierra Leone, the majority being Mende.

More than 80 percent of the Mende are primarily farmers who produce a range of food and cash crops. Rice, both wet and dry varieties, is the staple; cassava is virtually a co-staple in some areas. Dried fish, various leaves and vegetables are added to a stew base of palm oil to flavor the rice. The diet of most non-elite Mende is starchy and often protein deficient. The labor demands of cash crops, such as palm kernels, coffee, cocoa and ginger together with an expanding, urban-based, wage-labor market have created an agricultural labor shortage in some areas that has not been overcome through technological innovation. It becomes progressively more difficult for a growing population to feed itself. Nearly all food and cash crop production is in the "domestic mode," although traditionally the work force of the farming household was augmented at times of peak labor input by cooperative work groups, "by-turn labor" arrangements (where, for example, five men farm each other's land in turn over a period of five days) and, more recently, by agricultural wage laborers.

The western Mende were early drawn into contact with coastal trading interests and the Freetown settlement. The building of the Sierra Leone Government Railway early in the twentieth century opened up the Mende area to further influences. Settlements expanded around the stations, some of which developed into provincial towns that grew largely through rural–urban migration. The development of a diamond industry in and adjacent to Mende chiefdoms has had important influences since the early 1950s.

Traditionally, each Mende farming settlement was comprised of a number of households or domestic units, each known as a *mawe*. The larger households had a patrilineally extended or joint family as a core and often included more distant agnates as well as affines and dependents of the head who were unrelated, including domestic slaves. Members of a household made a "family farm," the produce of which the head controlled. Each married man, at least, made a *bulei*, a small farm from which he fed his family. Households whose heads were related agnatically combined to form a *kuwui*, a compound, which might constitute an entire village, a section of a town or, together with other such units, a section of the city. The head, a *kulokwui*, settled disputes, served as representative of the compound on the town council and mobilized support for council actions. On occasion, a capable woman succeeded her deceased husband as *kulokwui*. Connected with each *kuwui* in a town were villages outside in which were housed some members of the compound.

The colonial British labeled the largest enduring sociopolitical units they encountered among the Mende as "chiefdoms"; each ruled by an *ndomahei*, a figure referred to as "paramount chief," assisted by a council of section chiefs, town chiefs and other notables. There appeared to be in pre-colonial times no rule of hereditary succession producing dynasties, although instances of father–son succession have occurred. The prime consideration seems to have been ability to administer and lead in war, a common occurance in the nineteenth century. In Sierra Leone, only the Mende had some female paramount chiefs, apparently as a result of the practice of putting forward women as chiefs to the British colonial administration so as to escape punishment for male participation in the "Hut Tax Wars" of 1898. This was possible since chiefship was more secular among Mende than other ethnic groups in Sierra Leone, where sacred/ritual considerations precluded women.

Individual behavior among the Mende is sanctioned by a number of societies or associations. Those societies, or certain officers of them, control supernatural power, define acceptable and unacceptable conduct and deal with code violations. Most important, in that they embrace the largest portions of the population, are the *poro* for men and the *sande* for women. Both have structured initiation procedures which involve considerable instruction and training in traditional values and "education for life." Sir Milton Margai, a medical doctor and Sierra

Leone's first head of state (and a Christian Mende), once designed and implemented a program utilizing *sande* training sessions to introduce such modern practices as health education and trained midwifery. The *humoi* society specifically regulates men–women relations; "incest" is conceived as breaches of *humoi* laws. Christian missions and Muslims oppose these associations, and adherents who have been initiated often become inactive; some refuse to let their sons be initiated into *poro*. For Muslims and Christians, sanctions of behavior stem from their faith, not the traditional societies, and conflict is inevitable. There are other societies of more limited membership devoted to such efforts as healing/counseling and mutual aid (some were labeled subversive by the colonial government). Muslim influence is shown in that insurance and mutual-aid societies are called *malodi* (from the Arabic *mawlid*).

Mende have traditionally believed in a supreme creator deity, Ngewo, who is contacted indirectly through a *ngafa*, a spirit. Ancestral spirits, non-ancestral spirits and the spirits of the societies or associations suffice. Ngewo invest many objects with supernatural power, *hale*, usually glossed as "medicine", which can be utilized. Specialist practitioners are qualified to use *hale*; specifically, the officers of the societies who cure individuals and ensure the prosperity of the chiefdom, and the *halemoi*, a term covering diviners, private practitioners and sometimes including *mori* men, Muslims who work with Islamic paraphernalia. The word *honei* refers to a "witch-spirit" in the body of a witch, a *honamoi*, those who have the ability and means to attack a victim with the supernatural power (*honei*) in their own bodies, and sorcerers, who use magical devices of extracorporeal origin. Some argue, however, that Mende take a "practical attitude" towards life, concern themselves with today's problems and are little interested in metaphysics.

Like other West Africans, Mende have taken over an Arabic/Islamic vocabulary, the use of which does not necessarily imply extensive knowledge of Islam. For example, the ancestral spirits come to be viewed as intermediaries between Allah and the living and so continue to be propitiated. Similarly, traditional rites are often continued while being supplemented by Islamic practices; thus commemorative ceremonies on the seventh and fortieth days following a funeral are added to the traditional fourth-day rite. In funeral ceremonies and elsewhere Mende Muslims replace the old red rice sacrifice (made with red palm oil) with the white rice offering (made with honey, sugar and/or coconut oil). The wide range of traditional charms utilizing *hale* have been supplemented by Islamic forms such as *sura* written on paper or *nesi*, "holy water," obtained by washing a Quranic text off the board or slate on which it has been written, bottling the water and subsequently using it as medicine. Charms are used for a wide variety of purposes. Is is possible that conversion to Islam reduces the frequency of autopsies to determine whether or not the deceased was a witch. The more obvious manifestations of Mende Islam are the praying places outlined on clear ground, the mosques, plus the Quranic schools; Mende call the students in the latter "children around the fire," an apt description of a common village scene.

BIBLIOGRAPHY

Books

Abraham, A. *Mende Government and Politics Under Colonial Rule*. London: Oxford University Press, 1978.

Harris, W. T., and Sawyer, H. *The Springs of Mende Belief and Conduct*. Freetown: Sierra Leone University Press, 1968.

Issac, B. L. "The Economic, Ethnic and Sexual Parameters of Petty Trading in Pendembu, Sierra Leone." In *Essays on the Economic Anthropology of Liberia and Sierra Leone*, edited by V. Dorjahn and B. L. Isaac. Newark, Del.: Liberian Studies Association, 1979.

Kaplan, Irving, et al. *Area Handbook for Sierra Leone*. Washington, D.C.: Government Printing Office, 1976.

Little, K. L. "The Mende in Sierra Leon." In *African Worlds: Studies in the Cosmological Ideas and Social Values of African Peoples*, edited by Daryll Forde. London: Oxford University Press, 1954.

Murdock, George P. *Africa: Its Peoples and Their Culture History*. New York: McGraw-Hill, 1959.

McCulloch, M. *Peoples of Sierra Leone*. Ethnographic Survey of Africa, Western Africa, Part 2. London: International African Institute, 1950.

Nyoku, A. A. "The Economics of Mende Upland Rice Farming." In *Essays on the Economic Anthropology of Liberia and Sierra Leone*, edited by V. Dorjahn and B. L. Isaacs. Newark, Del.: Liberian Studies Association, 1979.

Reeck, Darrell. *Deep Mende: Religious Interactions in a Changing African Rural Society*. Leiden: E. J. Brill, 1976.

Trimingham, J. Spencer. *Islam in West Africa*. London: Oxford University Press, 1959.

Articles

Fisher, Humphrey. "Ahmadiyya in Sierra Leone." *Sierra Leone Bulletin of Religion* 11:1 (1960): 1–10.

Harris, W. T. "Mende Marriage and the Law of Inheritance." *Sierra Leone Bulletin of Religion* 1:1, 10–19, and 1:2 (1959): 33–36.

Hoffer, Carol P. "Mende and Sherbro Women in High Office." *Canadian Journal of African Studies* 6:2 (1972): 151–164.

Isaac, B. L. "Female Fertility and Marital Form Among the Mende of Rural Upper Bambara Chiefdom, Sierra Leone." *Ethnology* 19:3 (1980): 297–313.

Ijagbemi, E. A. "The Mende of Sierra Leone." *Tarikh* 5:1 (1974): 46–56.

Kilson, Marion D. de B. "Social Relationships in Mende Domeisia." *Sierra Leone Studies* 15 (1961): 168–172.

Richards, J.V.O. "Some Aspects of the Multivariate Sociocultural Roles of the Sande of the Mende." *Canadian Journal of African Studies* 9:1 (1975): 103–113.

Unpublished Manuscripts

Getaweh, S. M. "The Conceptualization of Family-Size Goals Among the Mende in Sierra Leone and the Vai in Liberia." Ph.D. dissertation, Boston University, 1978.

Isaac, B. L. "Traders in Pendembu, Sierra Leone." Ph.D. dissertation, University of
    Oregon, 1969.
Skinner, D. E. "Islam in Sierra Leone During the Nineteenth Century." Ph.D. disser-
    tation, University of California, Berkeley, 1971.

Vernon R. Dorjahn

MEOS   Muslims of the north Indian state of Rajasthan, who number about 2.7
million, are concentrated with one exception in urban centers. They can be
divided into four major categories: traders, the service class, the Rajputs and
the rural community of the Meos. Each is distinct in regard to its origin, occupation, social position and relationship with the wider Muslim culture. Nearly
one-half are immigrants who came to Rajasthan at different times and for different
reasons.

All over Rajasthan, in such cities and towns as Jaipur and Jodhpur, there are
communities of Muslim traders, among them the Bohras and the Khojas. Most
of them migrated from Gujarat into Rajasthan during the past 200 years (see
Gujaratis). The local Hindu trading communities, such as the Marwaris, had left
Rajasthan for better opportunities elsewhere, and Muslim merchants came in to
fill the gap in small retail trading of consumer goods, such as cloth, soap, oils
and hardware. They grew to be quite successful. Many are well educated, and
their sons have entered white collar professions.

Comprising some 15 percent of the Muslims of Rajasthan, the Muslim traders
are believed to be mostly converts from the Hindu Bania (trading caste). They
have remained relatively isolated from the mainstream of Muslim culture in
northern India because of their association with Shiism. As Shia, they have
managed to retain separate identities by forming distinct communities with hereditary religious leadership. They marry among themselves and tend to be
extremely conservative in their social customs. After the partition of India in
1947, many migrated to Pakistan, where they became influential in business,
especially in Karachi. The founder of Pakistan, Mohammed Ali Jinnah, was a
Khoja.

A second group of Muslims in Rajasthan is composed of the service castes.
It includes Manihars (bangle sellers), Rangrez (dyers), Kasai (butchers), Sakka
(water carriers), musicians and others. They are all immigrants from the Ganges
River valley, but unlike the traders, they came during Muslim rule preceding
the British colonial period. Northern India was at that time the center of culture,
art, crafts, industry and trade. Activities such as music and painting were considered prestigious, and crafts, including embroidery, weaving and dyeing, were
in great demand among the Rajput elite in Rajasthan. Hence, groups of Muslim
artists and craftsmen were attracted into the area from their native homes in the
United Provinces or Bihar. Some of the famous *gharanas* (families) of musicians
who have recently come into the limelight were settled in Rajasthani princely
states. Under the patronage of the Rajputs they preserved and enhanced the

ancient *raga* traditions of India. The work of Muslim artists and craftsmen was appreciated, and they were given due respect and protection. They enjoyed full freedom to practice their religion and customs. Many Sufi saints had both Hindu and Muslim followings, and on special occasions Hindus made offerings at Muslim shrines. The Muslims on their part accommodated their Hindu patrons in a variety of ways. For instance, they spoke local dialects, adopted many Hindu customs, remained loyal against Muslim invaders and participated in Hindu festivals. A recent case involved a Muslim family in Suratgarh, who had continued to maintain a Hindu temple for several generations as a hereditary right. Also, many of the Rajasthani butcher communities eschewed beef butchering in deference to their Hindu patrons. In fact, they went so far as to treat beef butchers as untouchables. Clearly, there was a strong attitude of religious tolerance on both sides.

A third category is that of the Rajput converts. Despite a strong sense of rivalry, the Rajputs (Hindu military caste) and the Muslims established a variety of friendly contacts with each other. Often Rajput rulers formed alliances with the Muslim kings. Rajputs were eagerly sought by Muslim kings as mercenaries because of their reputation as loyal and brave soldiers. Emperor Akbar married a Rajput princess to strengthen the alliance between the two communities. As a result of these contacts, some Rajput families were converted to Islam. Such conversions, however, were not easily condoned locally, and the tendency was for the convert Rajputs to move out of Rajasthan and settle elsewhere. There are many Rajput Muslim families in north India as well as Pakistan. They are still distinguishable because of their pride in Rajput ancestry, retention of many Hindu customs and strict endogamy. Some even retain their *gotra* (clan) name or use Rajput as a surname. This incongruence of the Rajputs is tolerated even in predominantly Muslim environments because of their high socioeconomic status. The number of Rajput Muslims living in Rajasthan is small, but groups survived even until recently. The Khanzadas of Alwar were one such group, but they all migrated to Pakistan after 1947.

Meos

The largest section of the Muslim population in Rajasthan is the community known as the Meos. Numbering nearly 600,000, they are the only native community of Muslims in Rajasthan. They are concentrated in the Alwar and Bharatpur districts in the northeastern part of the state and also in the Gurgaon District of the neighboring state of Haryana. The parts of the three districts where they live is popularly referred to as Mewat, derived from the Meos because of their predominance in the area. Until 1947 the Meos were even more dominant in Mewat than they are today. About that time they suffered the trauma of dislocation, forced conversion and violence. A number of Meos migrated to Pakistan, but by the early 1950s the ones who remained were resettled, and their land and property were restored to them.

The Meos were originally Hindus; when and how they were converted is still unclear. It seems probable on the basis of popular belief that they were converted in stages: first by Salar Masud in the eleventh century, by Balban in the thirteenth century and again during Aurangzeb's reign in the seventeenth century. Being close to Delhi, the Meos apparently took an active interest in politics, sometimes by giving refuge to dissidents, occasionally by raiding the capital for material gain and at other times by getting involved in intrigues for succession. More often than not they backed the wrong group and as a consequence suffered severe reprisals. At times conversion to Islam was part of the settlement after defeat. One clearly recorded incident of conversion occurred about the turn of the fifteenth century when Bahadur Nahar, a Hindu Rajput ruler of Mewat, embraced Islam. Other Rajput families followed his lead, and the clan of the Khanzadas was established. This probably stimulated conversion of other Hindu castes in Mewat.

The Meos claim Rajput descent for the entire community, feeling very proud and even defensive of this background. In a recent book on Meo history, its Meo author refers to Rajput ancestry in the title and devotes half the volume to prove it. Two major kinds of evidence are marshaled in support. One is the genealogical records supposedly maintained by the local *jagas* (Brahman genealogists). The link is invariably established all the way back to the mythical Hindu gods, Rama and Krishna. Another kind of evidence is derived from the folklore. Both of these stories conform more to the desire of the group rather than historical fact. The Meo community is divided into many (at least 800) *gotras* (exogamous clans). Some of these *gotras* resemble those of the Rajputs, but there are others which seem to link with such Hindu castes as Brahman, Mina, Jat and Bhatiara. Most probably, therefore, the Meos originally belonged to many different Hindu castes and not just to the Rajputs.

The Meos combine elements of both Hindu and Muslim traditions in their culture. In fact, until recently Hindu customs so predominated Meo life-style that the admixture was considered quaint by both Hindus and Muslims outside Mewat. For instance, the popular names of both males and females were like those of the Hindus. Muslim names were given occasionally and sometimes the Muslim title Khan was added to a Hindu name. The rituals performed in connection with the life cycle were mostly of the Hindu tradition, with only a few Muslim elements added. Marriage ceremonies used all of the Hindu rituals, including the worship of Hindu gods, performed together with the Muslim *nikah* ceremony. Two major Islamic rites adopted by the Meos were male circumcision and burial of the dead, but even these were recast into the local Hindu mold. Almost all of the local festivals and ceremonies associated with agriculture, health and change of seasons were retained. A few Muslim festivals, such as the two Ids, Shab-e-barat, and Muharram, were adopted. Reading of the Quran was less popular than reading the Hindu epics *Ramayana* and *Mahabharata*. Hindu shrines far outnumbered the mosques in Mewat. Few Meos prayed in the

Muslim manner, but most of them performed the Puja (worship) at the shrines of the Hindu gods and goddesses.

The Meos even now follow the traditional Hindu customs with regard to marriage and kinship. *Gotra* exogamy is strictly observed. Cousin marriage continues to be taboo among the Meos. Recent attempts to break this tradition have evoked strong opposition. Also, Meo women do not observe *purdah*.

Since 1947 a strong move towards Islamization has begun in Mewat. A religious revival movement initiated in Delhi a few years prior to independence suddenly became popular, and under its influence many of the Hindu rituals, ceremonies and festivals were abandoned by the Meos and substitutes from Muslim tradition adopted in their place.

There appear to be three reasons for Islamic revival in Mewat. First, when India was partitioned in 1947 to give the Muslims a separate state, antipathy between the Hindus and the Muslims was heightened to the point of violence. In Mewat, this led to attempts on the part of the Hindus to reconvert the Meos. For the Meos, this produced an identity crisis, and they felt that the very existence of the community was threatened. As soon as normal conditions returned, the Meos began to reassert their identity as Muslims.

Second, under the old system the Meos were the dominant caste and enjoyed high social prestige as well as economic and political power. In other words, the prevailing system of stratification favored the Meos so much that they did not like to disturb it even after conversion to Islam. The local Hindu castes, in their own interest, overlooked the change in religion of the Meos as long as their own economic and social life remained undisturbed. They continued to serve the Meos as a high caste in exchange for their fixed due in agricultural produce and gifts of various kinds. Even the Brahman continued to serve the Meos as priest. But following Independence, a variety of social, political and economic changes began to take place in India. The traditional caste system began to weaken as a result. Due to certain circumstances, such as emigration of some Meos to Pakistan, the impact of social change was more intense in Mewat. The untouchable castes were given representation in the village council as well as land abandoned by the Meos, which of course raised their status and changed their attitude towards the high castes. Furthermore, as agriculture became more market-oriented, the traditional relationship among various castes and their interdependence broke down. These and many other changes eroded the caste system to such an extent that the privileges of the Meos as the dominant caste were severely curtailed.

Third, with the improvement of communication and other developments, the Meos began to feel that they could no longer remain isolated from the outside world. They were drawn into the emerging nation through the electoral process, participation in the newly formed village *panchayats*, increased links with the wider market, higher education of their children, etc. The Meos discovered that the first natural step for them in this process of widening integration was to forge links with the Muslim community outside of Mewat. To do this, it was essential for them to adopt the culture of the Muslims on the one hand and abandon Hindu customs on the other. Hence, the Meos began to Islamize rapidly.

BIBLIOGRAPHY

Books

Aggarwal, Partap C. "Caste Hierarchy in a Meo Village in Rajasthan." In *Caste and Social Stratification Among the Muslims*, edited by Imtiaz Ahmad. Delhi: Manohar Book Service: 1973.
———. *Caste, Religion and Power: An Indian Case History*. New Delhi: Shri Ram Centre for Industrial Relations, 1971.
———. "The Meos of Rajasthan and Haryana." In *Caste and Social Stratification Among the Muslims*, edited by Imtiaz Ahmad. Delhi: Manohar Book Service, 1973.
Ali, Hashim Amir. *The Meos of Mewat, Old Neighbors of New Delhi*. New Delhi: Oxford, 1970.
Mujeeb, M. *The Indian Muslims*. London: Allen & Unwin, 1967.

Articles

Aggarwal, Partap C. "A Muslim Sub-Caste of North India: Problems of Cultural Integration." *Economic and Political Weekly* 1 (1966): 159–167.
Narain, Iqbal. "Technocrats as Head of the Block Team: Some Hypotheses about the Rajasthan Experiment." *Economic and Political Weekly* 5 (1970): 2041–2047.
Sharma, K. L. "Changing Class Stratification in Rural Rajasthan." *Man in India* 50 (1970): 257-267.

Partap C. Aggarwal
Population figures updated by Richard V. Weekes

MIMA-MIMI   The Mima of Sudan and the Mimi of Chad once constituted a unified ethnic group inhabiting the present territory of the Mima southeast of Darfur's provincial capital of El Fasher. Today, the approximately 50,000 Mima and Mimi live scattered in Sudan's Darfur and Kordofan provinces and in Chad's Wadai Province, in urban and market centers, as pastoral nomads or in rural sedentary colonies on a territory of their own. The main Mima centers in Darfur are Woda'a and Fafa; in Kordofan, Magrur in the center and the Abu Daza District in the west of the province. In Wadai their main territory encompasses about 60 villages to the north and northeast of the northern district capital of Biltine; Agan is one of the main centers for the sedentary Mimi.

The geographical origins of the Mima and Mimi are unclear. Both western and eastern origins are claimed, but there is no reason to deny the assumption that the groups as a whole is autochthonous to Darfur. Their own claim to be "Bani Umayya," that is, descendants of the Umayyads, based on alliteration, probably is unfounded.

Historians have not investigated the reasons for their present dispersal. Linguistic research has yielded interesting material which might throw light on the early history of the group. The Mima of Sudan and the pastoralist part of the Chadian Mimi have been Arabophone for a long time. The sedentary, cultivating Mimi of Chad (self-name: Amdang, or "people," and called Mututu by the Maba) speak a language related to the extensive Fur language spoken hundreds of miles to the east by more than one-half million people. Various other pieces of circumstantial evidence strongly point to a migration westwards of part of the original group in the fifteenth and sixteenth centuries at the latest. The Mima who stayed behind lived between the Nile Valley, the source of Islamization and Arabization from the seventeenth century onwards, and the Fur. They along with the Birgid and Berti, similarly located, adopted Arabic, and their languages became extinct. The majority of the migrated Mimi engaged in animal husbandry and frequent migrations, and contacts with Arab pastoral nomads led to their adopting Arabic as their mother tongue. Thus, of all Mima and Mimi, only the Amdang, who have stayed put in the Biltine region, still speak the original language of the group. They number 8,000 at the most.

The main written sources on the Mima and Mimi in the nineteenth and twentieth centuries stress a number of similarities. Both have been subject polities of the pre-colonial states of the region, the sultanates of Wadai and Darfur. Both groups were divided into 20 or 30 subsections headed by native chiefs. At the apex of this tribal organization stood Mima and Mimi "free" kings, who were in turn overseen by agents from the central government. Both Mima and Mimi are commended for their bravery in battle but are compared unfavorably with neighboring ethnic groups as regards religious dedication, civility in dealing with strangers and even physical appearance. Another similarity which emerges from the travel literature of the nineteenth century is the impact on both groups of external influences and the concomitant loss of ethnic identity. Finally, in the case of the Mimi of Wadai, there are indications that they were not highly regarded. As immigrants who converted to Islam around 1665 upon the overthrow of the then ruling pagan Tunjur dynasty, the Mimi have since been associated with the Zaghawa, a neighboring group with whom they exchanged women and who were held in contempt by the new Maba dynasty for their religious ignorance (see Beri; Maba; Tunjur).

The majority of the Chadian Mimi spend the larger part of the year in the southern part of Wadai, and many have chosen this region as their permanent habitat. These pastoralist Mimi have lost their cultural identity and are virtually indistinguishable from Arab pastoral nomads with whom they compete for grazing and water. The sedentary Mimi of the Biltine area inhabit the hilly eastern part of Dar ("home of") Mimi, where they cultivate cereals, beans, sesame and a number of other crops; they also keep livestock, but much less than their pastoralist brothers.

The entire Mimi area—the eastern hills and western plains—is sandy and almost treeless. Seasonal shortages of water limit the number of animals of the settled Mimi and force the pastoralists to migrate south and west.

The Chadian Mimi are bounded to the north by Mahamid Arabs, to the northeast by the Durayn and Zaghawa, to the east by the Mararit, to the southeast by the Tama, and to the south by various Maba-speaking groups (see Tama-speaking Peoples). To the west lies a waterless area which is exploited in the winter by various livestock-owning groups. The sedentary Mimi marry mostly among themselves and occasionally with Maba and Arabs. The pastoralist Mimi marry the Zaghawa and Abu Sharib. Neither Mimi group marries the Tama. Judging from the differences in means of subsistence, residence pattern and marriage alliances, it is doubtful whether the Mimi can be considered a corporate entity. Whereas the pastoralists live like pastoral Arabs, the Amdang farm. Their culture and social organization show many traces of borrowing from neighboring sedentary groups, for example, in cultivating techniques, cultural artifacts and vocabulary.

The Sudanese Mima are engaged in a far wider variety of economic activities than their Chadian counterparts with whom intermittent contacts exist. Whereas in Chad, education, administration and trade have been disrupted by the civil war, the Sudanese Mima have benefitted from the proliferation of trade and government services as much as any group in the country. The Mima work as teachers, officials, craftsmen and traders.

BIBLIOGRAPHY

Books

Gaudefroy-Denombynes, M. *Documents sur les langues de l'Oubangui-Chari*. Actes du XIVe Congrès des Orientalistes, Algiers, 1905, Paris, 1907.
MacMichael, H. A. *A History of the Arabs of the Sudan*. Vol. 1. 1922. Reprint ed. London: Frank Cass, 1967.
Le Rouvreur, Albert. *Sahéliens et sahariens du Tchad*. Paris: Berger-Levrault, 1962.

Articles

Greenberg, Joseph H. "On the Identity of Jungraithmayr's Mimi." *African Marburgensia* 2 (1972): 45–49.
Jungraithmayr, H. "How Many Mimi Languages Are There?" *African Marburgensia* 4:2 (1971): 62–69.
Lukas, J., and Volckers, O. "G. Nachtigal's Aufzeichnungen über die Sprache der Mimi in Wadai." *Zeitschrift für Eingebohrenen-sprachen* 29 (1938–39): 145–154.

Paul Doornbos

MINANGKABAU The Minangkabau (also "Menangkabau") are closely related in culture and language to the Malays, from whom they differ in certain important characteristics of social organization (see Malays). Unlike Malays and unlike most other Islamic peoples, the Minangkabau are matrilineal, organized into kinship groups according to the principle of descent through women. Folk explanations of their name refer symbolically to this fact. For example, one such folk etymology of the term *minangkabau* is based upon its resemblance to the words *menang* (winning) and *kerbau* (water buffalo). This similarity has been elaborated into a story about an ancient time in which an unweaned and starving female calf owned by the Minangkabau unwittingly castrated and thereby defeated a champion Javanese bull. The incident is supposed to have given the Minangkabau their name (''buffalo victory''). Another folk etymology notes that *minang* refers to the harness that prevents a calf from nursing, and yet another notes that *minang* refers to the ceremony before marriage in which engagement gifts are offered, both noting the importance of water buffalo for milk, capital and labor in the settled agriculture of the Minangkabau.

Among themselves, the Minangkabau usually subdivide their ethnic identity according to particular areas within the Minangkabau realm. The Orang Padang, for example, are the people of Padang Panjang, which is the capital of West Sumatra; the Orang Batang Kapas are the people of the Batang Kapas River valley, which lies south of the Padang Panjang area. There are as many such sub-ethnic identities as there are named areas within the traditional homeland in the highlands of west central Sumatra.

Approximately one-half of the 6 million Minangkabau live in the Indonesia province of West Sumatra, where they comprise more than 80 percent of the population. Hundreds of thousands have migrated to other provinces of Sumatra (especially Riau, Djambi and North Sumatra), and they are usually a conspicuous minority in cities throughout Indonesia because of their success in commerce and their high positions in government. Altogether, they account for more than 4 percent of the population of Indonesia.

More than 125,000 Minangkabau live in the peninsular Malaysian state of Negri Sembilan, an island area near Melaka. The first immigrants from Minangkabau lands in Sumatra settled there in the fourteenth or fifteenth century. In the last quarter of the eighteenth century they established a royal court in Sri Menanti by inviting a prince of the royal blood from Pagar Ruyong, one of the three traditional capitals of the Minangkabau in Sumatra. In the eighteenth, nineteenth and early twentieth centuries, more Minangkabau immigrants settled in the Malaysian states of Perak, Selangor, Johore and Pahang.

Perhaps 500,000 of the descendants of these later immigrants recognize their Minangkabau ancestry and heritage, but most are more or less assimilated to Malay culture. Even in Negri Sembilan, where about one-third of the population is Minangkabau, many descendants of the Sumatran immigrants have become Malays. Their assimilation into Malay ethnicity has been easy because of similar customs and the mutual intelligibility of Malay and Minangkabau dialects. Matrilineal institutions survive in Negri Sembilan but are becoming less relevant as commercial agricultural production and wage labor, both dominated by males, increase in importance.

Wherever possible, the Minangkabau are wet rice agriculturalists who farm permanent, irrigated fields. Women perform most of the tasks of cultivating wet rice, preparing the soil with hoes, transplanting the rice seedlings and weeding the fields, which they own. Men usually help with harvesting the rice, and they plow in the areas where water buffalo are used for that purpose. Both in the traditional and in the modern economy, the work of men has included extensive involvement in commerce. This was clearly a major factor in the eighteenth-century conquest of Johore, on the Malay peninsula, by the Minangkabau state of Siak, based in eastern Sumatra, and in the Padri movement of Minangkabau proper during the late nineteenth and early twentieth centuries. However, the traditional agricultural economy, which is dominated by women, is of equal or greater importance.

Buffalo are kept for their milk, which is consumed as a thin yogurt, and only infrequently are buffalo slaughtered to provide meat for important feasts. Fish are a large part of the diet even in inland areas, where they are raised in artificial ponds and in the rice fields. Market gardening is important in the well-watered and fertile volcanic soils of the northwestern part of West Sumatra, near Bukit Tinggi, but much less so in the relatively poor soils farther south, near Batang Kapas. Land is crowded in the fertile areas of the north, and there is very little slash-and-burn agriculture. Harvested rice fields are quickly planted in peanuts and vegetables. In the more thinly populated south, timbered land is still available for slash-and-burn agriculture, which entails cutting trees and brush and burning the dried debris (to provide ash fertilizer) before planting. Dry rice, tapioca and maize are usually planted in the first year, and following the harvest the new fields are planted in commercial crops, such as rubber, clove or coffee. Rubber plantations are more important in Negri Sembilan than in any other area of West Sumatra.

Just as subsistence patterns vary somewhat from region to region in the Minangkabau realm, so demography and social organization vary. Communities encourage their young adolescent males to leave home and gain experience. In all communities, men are thought to be interested in travel because they cannot own the best established agricultural fields and can only use the fields of their sisters or must establish their own unirrigated agricultural lands in the least desirable locations. However, the percentage of men who remain away from home during long periods of the year varies from area to area.

In villages where the soil is rich, the population dense and the fields and irrigation system well established, men are scarce except at the time of the rice harvest, when they return from their *rantau* (places to which they migrated more or less temporarily) to help their sisters and mothers and to visit their wives. At other times of the year, there is an overwhelming presence of women in such villages. There are children, of course, and a few old men. The women do virtually all of the work and make the day-to-day practical decisions. When men return, they are treated with great respect. Many of them are traders who have sought personal fortunes far afield, and some of them have other wives and families in distant towns where they conduct their businesses.

In the poorer villages of the Batang Kapas area, however, many men (having previously made their adolescent *merantau*) remain at home throughout the year. They contribute more labor to the tasks of subsistence, more often own a small piece of land in their own right and make most of the day-to-day decisions. A similar situation is common in the villages of Negri Sembilan. The importance of male labor and of newly opened (nontraditional) lands in many commercial agricultural enterprises lessens the relevance of traditions that give only women property rights to irrigated rice fields.

Many Western scholars, noting that Quranic law seemingly places women at social and economic disadvantage, have wondered at the zeal and orthodoxy with which the Minangkabau embrace Islam, but the Minangkabau see no conflict between their matrilineal customs and the strong patrilineal bias of Islam. The right to use ancestral property, such as wet rice land or a longhouse, is inherited through females, but individually earned property, such as a bus or a newly opened bit of jungle land, may be inherited through males in accordance with Quranic rules of inheritance (which provide larger portions for male heirs).

Thus, customary law (*adat perpateh*) and Shariah (*adat temenggong*) are not necessarily contradictory. However, disputes do occur regarding inheritance of property, particularly with regard to disposition of property acquired through the efforts of a male, which might be claimed by his sisters' children as property of his matrilineage, by his own children as their father's personal property or by his widow as common property of their marriage (*hak suarang*).

The widow's right, *hak suarang*, to inheritance of common property of her marriage is not uncommon in urban contexts, where the nuclear family is a more important and immediate economic unit than the matrilineage. This difference from usual expectations regarding inheritance in rural areas may also reflect the higher levels of education and later marriages of urban women, which enhance their capacity to claim their own personal property.

The similarity of Malay and Minangkabau cultures and the folk wisdom and folklore of both cultures hint at a not very distant common past. Some of the "clues" may deal with differences in rules of inheritance. *Melayu*, the Malay and Minangkabau term for English "Malay," is the name of one of the major *suku* (matriclans) of the Minangkabau. Moreover, one of the origin myths of the Minangkabau refers to the first Minangkabau persons as twins with names corresponding to the names of the systems of law and inheritance (*adat*) of the Minangkabau (*perpateh*) and the Malays (*temenggong*). Finally, in the Malay peninsula there is a commonly told story that the first settled communities were the result of marriages between native women and immigrant princes. This same story openly asserts the rights of natives to the land and might thereby also imply the special right of women to land. The story also asserts the right of the immigrant men to rule and might thereby refer to the male-oriented rule of Islam.

Despite the matrilineal orientation of the Minangkabau, royal ties are inherited through males. A single royal patrilineage that is symbolically superior to (four or eight) matriclans helps to neutralize competition among the matriclans for resources and political power.

All Minangkabau are Sunni, adhering to the Shafi school of Muslim law. They accept the propriety of formally submitting to Allah, praying five times daily, giving alms and tithe, fasting in the month of Ramadan and making the pilgrimage to Mecca. An ancient residue of Hindu-Buddhism is apparent in such major rites of passage as birth rituals, naming ceremonies and marriage. Funerals are simple and Islamic. Some agricultural and curing rituals have strong animist elements. Most rituals are virtually the same as those of the Malays. However, the special sister's child–mother's brother relationship (between a person and a parental generation male of one's own matrilineage) is celebrated ritually. For example, in the ritual giving of the male dowry before marriage, the Minangkabau add a verbal duel between the mother's brothers of the bride and groom.

BIBLIOGRAPHY

Books

Abdullah, Taufik. "Modernization in the Minangkabau World: West Sumatra in the Early Decades of the Twentieth Century." In *Cultures and Politics in Indonesia*, edited by Claire Holt. Ithaca: Cornell University Press, 1972.

Bachtiar, Harsja "Negeri Taram: A Minangkabau Village Community." In *Villages in Indonesia*, edited by R. M. Koentjaraningrat. Ithaca: Cornell University Press, 1967.

Johns, Anthony H. *Rantjak Dilabueh: A Minangkabau Kaba*. Southeast Asia Program Data Paper, No. 32. Ithaca: Cornell University Press, 1958.

Josselin de Jong, P. E. de. *Minangkabau and Negri Sembilan: Socio-Political Structure in Indonesia*. Leiden: Eduard Ijdo, 1951.

LeBar, Frank M., ed. *Ethnic Groups of Insular Southeast Asia*. New Haven: Human Relations Area Files Press, 1972.

Marsden, William. *The History of Sumatra*. 3rd ed. 1811. Reprint ed. London: Oxford University Press, 1966.

McVey, Ruth T., ed. *Indonesia*. New Haven: Human Relations Area Files Press, 1963.

Peacock, James L. *Indonesia: An Anthropological Perspective*. Pacific Palisades, Calif.: Goodyear, 1973.

Schrieke, B. *Indonesian Sociological Studies*. The Hague: W. Van Hoeve, 1955.

Swift, Michael G. *Malay Peasant Society in Jelebu*. New York: Humanities Press, 1965.

Vreeland, Nena, et al. *Area Handbook for Indonesia*. The American University FAS, DA Pam 550-39. 3rd ed. Washington, D.C.: Government Printing Office, 1975

Articles

Abdullah, Taufik. "Adat and Islam: An Examination of Conflict in Minangkabau." *Indonesia* 2 (1966): 1–24.

————. "Some Notes on the Taba Tjindua Mato: An Example of the Minangkabau Traditional Literature." *Indonesia* 9 (1970): 1–22.

Dobbin, Christine. "Economic Change in Minangkabau as a Factor in the Rise of the Padri Movement, 1784–1830." *Indonesia* (1977): 1–39.

Gullick, J. M. "The Negri Sembilan Economy of the 1890's." *Journal of the Malayan Branch of the Royal Asiatic Society* 22:38 (1951): 38–55.

Hanna, Willard. "The Role of the Minangkabau in Contemporary Indonesia." *Southeast Asia Series. American Universities Field Staff* 2:7 (1959): 35–49.

Josselin de Jong. P. E. de. "Islam Versus Adat in Negri Sembilan (Malaya)." *Bijdragen tot de Taal-, Land- en Volkenkunde* (Netherlands) 116:1 (1960): 158–203.

Junus, Umar. "The Payment of Zakat Al-Fitrah in a Minangkabau Community." *Bijd* (Netherlands) 122 (1966): 447–454.

————. "Some Remarks on Minangkabau Social Structure." *Bijd* 120 (1964): 293, 326–332.

Kato, Tsuyoshi. "Change and Continuity in the Minangkabau Matrilineal System." *Indonesia* 25 (1978): 1–16.

Mitchell, Istutiah Gunawan. "The Socio-Cultural Environment and Mental Disturbance: Three Minangkabau Case Histories." *Indonesia* 7 (1969): 123–163.

Tanner, Nancy. "Disputing and Dispute Settlement Among the Minangkabau of Indonesia." *Indonesia* 8 (1969): 21–67.

————. "The Nuclear Family in Minangkabau Matriliny: The Mirror of Disputes." *Bijdragen tot de Taal-, Land- en Volkenkunde* 138:1 (1982): 129–151.

Unpublished Manuscript

Kennedy, Raymond. "The Ethnology of the Greater Sunda Islands." Ph.D. dissertation, Yale University, 1935. (University Microfilms 67-4797.)

Ronald Provencher

MOGHOLS   Two elements distinguish the Moghols of Afghanistan. They no longer speak their original Mongol language, and within a generation or two they will have lost their ethnic identity. Demographically unimportant—they number no more than 10,000, dispersed in fewer than 50 villages—they once played a major role in the history of Afghanistan. Their language fascinates linguists, who now study the development and change of a language separated by thousands of miles for over half a millenium from the main body of Mongol speakers.

The forefathers of the Afghan Moghols were once the military and political leaders of a thirteenth-century multi-ethnic coalition known as Nikudari or Qarawunas. Nikudar Oghlan was a Chagatai general of Hulagu, founder of the Mongol Il Kahn dynasty, who came to Persia in 1256. Marco Polo mentioned him as "king of the Qarawunas." Nikudar planned to defect, was imprisoned and died in Mesopotamia. Many of his troops aligned themselves with the Kurt dynasty of Herat in their successful struggles for independence from Il Khan rule. This union lasted for a century until Timur (Tamerlane) captured Herat in 1380.

The Nikudari soon disappeared from historical records, to be mentioned only once again, in 1562, by Babur, founder of the Moghul dynasty in India, who referred to them as "inhabitants of Ghor." It was in this mountainous tract of west central Afghanistan that the Afghan Moghols lived until around 1900.

It was while they were allied with the Kurt rulers in Herat that the Nikudari or Moghols established themselves in Afghanistan. An unruly group of princes, the Kurts were often attacked by Il Khanid troops and on these occasions retreated to their castle, the "stronghold of Qaisar," in southern Ghor. The ruins of this castle and a number of nearby Moghol villages remain to this day. In 1886, British intelligence reported 18 Moghol villages with a population of some 5,000 still living in the area. The publication of a vocabulary of their Moghol language in 1838 caused a sensation among linguists of the time. They were forgotten again until 1955, when a team of U.S. and Japanese linguists discovered what has been called the "Zirni Manuscript," which prompted renewed interest. Further linguistic research has been carried out by a German team.

The Kurts disappeared from history after Timur captured Herat in 1380. Under Timurid and Arghunid rule, the Moghols of Ghor exerted political power in the mountain regions of west central Afghanistan. Then, in 1650, a Pushtun immigrant from Baluchistan named Taiman shaped a coalition of peoples in southern Ghor that has become known as the Taimani tribe of the Char Aimaq (see Aimaq). Taiman and his successors seem to have gotten along well with the Moghols until around 1900, when a quarrel about marriage contracts arose that started a blood feud. The ensuing fight caused the diaspora of the majority of the Moghols from Ghor. That case was not settled until 1930 through an exchange of wives in marriage between the Taimani chiefs of Nili and the leading family of the Moghols in neighboring Zirni. By then only eight villages with Moghol populations had survived in Ghor near Qaisar; the rest of the population had emigrated to Obeh and Herat oases on the Heri-rud River and at least five villages in northern and northeastern Afghanistan.

Strict observation of the rule of endogamy by the Moghols preserved their Mongolian language and physical features. Mongolian appearance is still strong today, whereas linguistic missions between 1955 and 1971 found it difficult to trace even elderly individuals who still remembered fragments of the original language. The Moghols of Ghor and Herat have become Farsi-Dari speakers, while others have adopted Pashto. Their numbers may have risen since the British estimates of 1886 by 100 percent, amounting to a maximum of 10,000 individuals.

Although the Moghols were able to preserve their own language in a Farsi-Dari speaking environment for more than 700 years, their culture was assimilated in all other respects, probably early during their history in the west. Recent research affirms their Sunni creed, in contrast to nineteenth-century, second-hand statements as to their "paganism" or Shiism. They have adapted themselves to a semi-nomadic way of life and the mixed pastoral and agricultural economies of their neighbors to the north and east, the Taimani, in contrast to the fully sedentary "Mountain Tajiks" of Ghor to their west and south.

The Moghols of Ghor live in open villages, their one-story houses being built usually of sun-dried mud-bricks, frequently on a stone foundation. A peculiar feature Moghol houses have in common with Taimani houses is the frequent occurrence of gabled roofs, an unusual feature in Afghanistan and unlike the flat roofs of the usual two-storied houses in the compact villages of the neighboring Tajik. Moghol tents show the same specific characteristics as the tents of the southern Taimani in Farsi District, quite different from the structure of the latter people's traditional tent with straight walls and gables.

During the annual migration of the Moghols, the whole village moves in early April from their houses at the bottom of the valleys some 30 to 90 miles up into the hills. This movement coincides with the lambing season, and milk processing is the main occupation for the months to come. Patches of the hillsides are plowed, and wheat is sown on this non-irrigated land. Part of the male population has to return to the village in late July for a week or two to harvest the winter wheat on the irrigated patches in the valley. Immediately after their return to the campsite, the spring wheat is ripe for harvest. In early September the community returns to the outskirts of the permanent settlement and pitches the tents on the harvested fields, where their sheep and other animals also graze. This step in the annual cycle provides a minimal amount of manure before the fields are plowed in October and winter wheat is sown. Just before the plowing the winter quarters are occupied and the tents stored until next spring.

The compound in the village is usually occupied by an extended family (paternal or fraternal), whereas there usually is a separate tent for each nuclear family during the summer. The economic entity for agriculture and animal husbandry ideally is the greater unit of the extended family as well.

The Moghols of Ghor are structured in two subtribes, Burquti and Arghuni. The former is further divided into Kalanzai and Khurdagzai ("Clan of the Elder," and "Clan of the Younger"), the ancient tradition of the steppes, reminiscent of the nobility of the "White Bones" and the commoners of the "Black Bones." This is one of the arguments supporting the belief that the Burquti (literally and according to oral tradition, "descendants of the Buraq Khan," great-grandson of Chagatai) are the original core of the Moghols of Afghanistan.

The two main divisions of the Arghuni are the Marda and Khudaydad ("Given by God"). These groups are of lower status. The Marda supposedly are followers of the Khan. Khudaydad is a name given either to a son born much later than his elder brothers or to a son of an elderly couple, born as a single child.

The settlement pattern of the Moghols of Ghor strengthen these suppositions. Those living closest to the former castle of Qaisar are the Kalanzai, for example, the Khans and their personal following. Next to them are Khurdagzai villages and in the outer circle the two "commoner" groups of the Arghuni. Marda in large numbers also exist as Taimani and Aimaq-Hazara clans.

The Moghols of Afghanistan are now in a process of total assimilation with the Tajik and Pushtun. It can be foreseen that they will have lost their ethnic identity within a generation or two.

BIBLIOGRAPHY

Books

Iwamura, Shinobu, ed. *The Zirni Manuscript: A Persian-Mongolian Glossary and Grammar*. Transcribed and translated in collaboration with Natsuki Osada and Tadashi Yamasaki. Preliminary remarks on the Zirni manuscript by N. Poppe. Results of the Kyoto University Expeditions to the Karakoram and the Hindukush, 1955. Kyoto: University of Kyoto, 1961.
Iwamura, Shinobu, and Schurmann, H. F. "Notes on Mongolian Groups in Afghanistan." In *Silver Jubilee Volume of the Zinbun-Kagaku-Kenkyusya*. Kyoto: University of Kyoto, 1954.
Schurmann, Herbert Franz. *The Mongols of Afghanistan: An Ethnography of the Moghols and Related Peoples of Afghanistan*. The Hague: Mouton, 1962.

Articles

Bacon, Elizabeth. "Review of H. F. Schurmann: The Mongols of Afghanistan." *Central Asiatic Journal* 8:1 (1963): 62–67.
Ferdinand, Klaus. "Ethnographic Notes on Chahar Aimaq, Hazara and Moghol." *Acta Orientalia* 28:1–2 (1964): 175–203.
Leech, Robert. "A Vocabulary of the Moghal Aimaks." *Journal of the Asiatic Society of Bengal* 7 (1838): 785–787.

Alfred Janata

MOLBOG   The Molbog, one of the minor Muslim groups of the Philippines, are the aboriginal population of Balabac Island, located between Palawan and Borneo. The Molbog constitute the majority of the overall local population. In the outer islands of the Balabac archipelago, the Molbog are intermixed with other Muslim groups, mainly the Sama. Molbog can also be found in the southernmost tip of Palawan proper, where they have blended with Islamized Palawanon, and in Banggi, a big island south of Balabac that is in Malaysian territory.

The Molbog in Balabac Municipality number a little over 6,000. There are perhaps 830 in Batarasa Municipality and no more than 250 on Banggi Island, altogether not exceeding 7,100.

The Molbog language is classified in the South Palawan linguistic stock, which includes the languages of Palawanons, Tagbanuas and Bataks. Similarities are particularly accentuated between Molbog and Palawanon, which have a certain level of mutual comprehensibility. A majority also speak Tagalog (see Palawanon).

The name "Molbog" derives from *malubog*, which means "unclear/turbid water.'' Tradition says that the name was given by early sailors and merchants and referred to the island as well as its inhabitants.

The Molbog share Balabac with other ethnic groups: Muslims (Jama Mapun, Sama and a few Tausug) and Christians (Cuyonens, Ilongos, Ilocanos, Bicolanos and Tagalogs). Interethnic relationships vary according to the demographic distribution and particular social position of the individual involved but generally can be defined as an asymmetric one with the Molbog always playing the inferior role.

The main discriminants of this relationship are economic and religious. It is economic in the sense of market production versus subsistence production. The immigrant groups are merchants, coconut planters, government employees and, at least partially, market-oriented agriculturalists, while the Molbog are direct producers of their means of livelihood. In the case of religion, two factors are significant: Christian versus Muslim and more orthodox forms of the latter versus the less doctrinally strict. This second distinction, resting on the grade of Islamization, is not perceived in the same way by Molbog and other immigrant Muslims. The Molbog, a group more superficially Islamized, tend to identify themselves in the same category as other Muslims who have a deeper knowledge of Islamic doctrine. However, the latter always attempt to portray the Molbog as more primitive and ignorant, if not, as they say, as ''imitators'' of the ''real'' Islam.

The Molbog are one of the groups last Islamized. According to tradition, the first Islamic missionaries arrived in Balabac from Borneo seven *pangkat* (generations) ago, more or less during the last half of the eighteenth century.

The story of the conversion is painted with the shades of legend. Many figures common to Sulu Muslims such as *alims* walking on the water from Mecca, *hajjis* gifted with powerful amulets and mighty sultans are credited for almost instantaneous conversion, while proselytization was undoubtedly long and uneven. Spanish sources report the existence of ''pagans'' at the end of the nineteenth century.

Contact between Molbog and Muslim developed in three stages. At first it was occasional. Balabac was visited by Muslim merchants, provided a refuge for Sama pirates and was sometimes subjected to slave raids. No stable and continuous relationship was established.

As a result of the expansion of Sulu at the expense of Brunei, the second stage began. Around the beginning of the nineteenth century, some Tausug and Jama Mapun settled in Balabac. These individuals, possibly former slave traders or merchants, were able to obtain the subjection of some groups of Molbog in exchange for protection from other foreign intruders. Using the title *Datu*, they imposed taxation and ruled the local population. In this period, new Islamic elements penetrated deeper into Molbog culture. The newcomers generally merged with the local population; they married Molbog women and introduced part of their former cultural heritage.

A third stage is characterized by the successful spread of Islam throughout the island as well as by a more direct control of Balabac by the Sulu sultanate. The local *kalibugan* (mestizo) rulers in Balabac were the offspring of marriages between the first Tausug settlers and the Molbog. They used the title *panglima* (official representative of the sultan) and collected taxes to send once a year to Batarasa, in the mainland Palawan, where part of the Sulu royal family transferred during the nineteenth century.

The control by the sultan was strict; he had ultimate word in questions of succession, and his emissaries directly and frequently interfered with local problems. After American rule was established at the beginning of this century, the process of Islamization was still in progress. In different periods, *imams* and Islamic teachers came to Balabac for short visits, and it was only after the first years of the century that all the Molbog came to profess the Islamic faith.

The Molbog's productive activities are shifting cultivation and fishing. Hunting and gathering are of secondary importance, but especially in the case of gathering, they can acquire considerable relevance as a substitute source of livelihood when rice is lacking.

The staple food is rice. Additional crops are cassava, sweet potato and corn. Other vegetables such as taro, yams and beans are cultivated but in lesser quantities, and not regularly. Fruit trees are planted but seldom reach the productive age for lack of care.

Fish is the main source of protein. The most common fishing techniques are hook and line, which are used from the dugout, underwater speargun fishing and fishing by light during the last and the first quarters of the moon cycle. While the latter is performed usually in small groups, the other two are essentially individual activities.

In traditional times, the idea of private ownership of land was completely alien to the Molbog. Land was considered the property of God, and no one could claim permanent right to it. Right to usufruct was exercised by the farmer until the land was cultivated. At the end of the agricultural cycle, when the land was abandoned, he no longer had any claim to it. While the government has instituted processes for individual titles which can be bought and sold, the basic concept that land is a public good still holds. No Molbog will refuse permission for another Molbog to cut trees on the land for which he pays taxes, and rent payment is never required.

The Molbog kinship system is bilateral. The descent lines of both the father and the mother are biologically and socially recognized. Descent groups are totally absent, and a strong genealogical amnesia worsened by a taboo called *busung busung* that forbids naming parents, elders and the dead makes it impossible for the Molbog to recall names of ancestors who died even two generations earlier.

Marriage is prohibited between first degree patrilineal or matrilineal cousins. Polygynous marriages are rare. Post-marital residence is uxirilocal for the first year of marriage, at which time the husband will help the father-in-law with the cultivation of the field. After the fulfillment of this obligation, the new family builds its own house, usually beside the field. For a certain number of years until the children are adults, the family will keep on moving the place of residence every year and will build the new house alternatively near the husband's or the wife's parents.

The underlying principle of the Molbog social organization is the *usbawaris*, or ego-centered kindred. The *usbawaris* is composed of all the bilateral "blood relatives" of ego and sets a series of diadic ties based on mutual obligations between ego and each of the relatives. Except for two siblings, every person is theoretically at the center of such a set of ties different from those of others. Since every individual is simultaneously the center of his own kindred as well as a part of the kindred of someone else, kinship relations will overlap and compete.

The basic social groups are the *sonkosawan*, or elementary family, the *koporonakan*, or restricted kindred, and the *kampung*, or extended kindred.

The *sonkosawan* ("set of spouses") is constituted by a couple and their unmarried children. Instituted by marriage, it can be dissolved by divorce or death or enlarged through the marriage of a child to a temporary extended family. It is the only enduring corporate unit of production and consumption. Following a pattern of generalized reciprocity, its members share labor, the products of work and social responsibility. They live together under one roof.

The *koporonakan*, or limited kindred, defines a category of persons who can trace their ascendants to a common living ancestor. The term is always used referentially (*koporonakan* of...). As a group, it is not discrete because its members are always members of other identical entities.

Besides these social categories based on kinship, the Molbog recognize another category, the *rurungan*, or neighborhood. The *rurungan* is a group of persons who live in proximity, exchange work and participate together in religious ceremonies. It is the only group with functional characteristics beyond the elementary family.

The Molbog consider themselves Muslims in every respect. For them Islam is the most powerful element of group identification, so much so that in daily language the term "Molbog" is often confused with the term "Muslim." In common conversation, it is not rare to hear Molbog say that they are speaking "Muslim," or that the people living in Mecca are "Molbog." When questioned, they explain their logic as follows: "If the Arabs are Muslims they must be like Molbog because the Molbog are also Muslims." Cultural and linguistic differences seem to be secondary to the common religion.

Yet Islam has not penetrated the Molbog as deeply as it has other Philippine Muslim groups. Their knowledge of Muslim doctrine is shallow and limited to what the *pakir* (Arabic, *faqi*, "religious official") tells them. There are no *madrasas*, and no person speaks Arabic. Religious education is formal and consists mainly in learning how to read Arabic and how to perform the rituals.

For the Molbog, to be a Muslim means essentially believing in Allah and avoiding pork. All the other prescriptions of Islamic orthodoxy are secondary and only vaguely observed. The five daily prayers are never performed, and the rule of fasting during Ramadan is never respected. Only the *imams* pray once a week on Fridays and fast at the beginning and the end of Ramadan. No Molbog has the money to visit Mecca so no one uses the title *hajji*. Islamic taxes, *zakat* and *sadakat*, are paid irregularly.

The content of the Molbog's Islam is syncretic, and many pre-Islamic beliefs and practices are present, blending with Islam in a unique religious body. Under Allah and Tuhan, (God) the omnipotent and ultimate cause of everything, a large number of spirits and beings (*jinn*, Saitan, Gargasi, Hantu) populate the supernatural world of the Molbog. Besides orthodox Islamic festivals, traditional rituals and ceremonies are performed to propitiate the good spirits and keep away the evil ones. Together with the *pakir*, traditional shamans and practitioners (*balian*) worship the divinities.

Islam has not changed traditional religion, it just reshaped it to make it compatible with a monotheistic nature. Some of the names of the supernatural beings were changed and to the traditional magical spellings and prayers was adjoined the profession of faith: *"La ilaha illa' Llah wa Muhammad Rasullullah"* ("There is no God but Allah and Muhammad is His Prophet"). The entire complex of beliefs and prayers existing before the conversion has been maintained, but simultaneously submitted to the ultimate authority of Allah.

BIBLIOGRAPHY

Books

Casino, Eric S. *The Jama Mapun: A Changing Samal Society in the Southern Philippines*. Quezon City: Ateneo de Manila University Press, 1975.

Gowing, Peter G. *Muslim Filipinos: Heritage and Horizon*. Manila: New Day Publishers of the Christian Literature Society of the Philippines, 1979.

———, and McAmis, Robert D. *The Muslim Filipinos: Their History, Society and Contemporary Problems*. Manila: Solidaridad Publishing House, 1974.

Kiefer, Thomas M. *The Tausug: Violence and Law in a Philippine Moslem Society*. New York: Holt, Rinehart and Winston, 1972.

Lebar, Frank M., ed. *Ethnic Groups of Insular Southeast Asia*. Vol. 2. New Haven: Human Relations Area Files Press, 1975.

Majul, Cesar A. *Muslims in the Philippines*. 3rd ed. Manila: St. Mary's Publishing House, 1979.

Saleeby, Najeeb M. *The History of Sulu*. 1908. Reprint ed. Manila: Filipiniana Book Guild, 1963.

Article

Kuder, Edward M. "The Moros of the Philippines." *Far Eastern Quarterly* 4:2 (1945):
    119–126.

                                                          Lanfranco Blanchetti Revelli

MOLÉ-DAGBANE-SPEAKING PEOPLES   The many societies of the Molé-
Dagbane-speaking peoples of northern Ghana and the adjacent parts of neighboring countries are built upon a common linguistic and historical base. Numbering approximately 7.7 million people, the societies range from small isolates
of a couple of thousand to the 5 million Mossi, most of whom live in Upper
Volta. Most of the other 30 or so societies number in the tens of thousands, the
largest being the Grusi (473,000) and Dogamba (350,000), population estimates
being based on inaccurate census figures of 1960 and 1967. Muslims account
for no more than 35 percent of the entire Molé-Dagbane-speaking peoples, with
the largest concentration among the Mossi (see Mossi).

The Molé-Dagbane-speaking peoples are not so much "Muslim" as they are
"influenced by Muslims." They affect the economy and society of the entire
region without being politically or numerically dominant. Indeed, so ethnically
pluralist is the region that the leading historian of Islam in the region has distinguished the "dispersion of Muslims" from "the spread of Islam."

Molé-Dagbane is a linguistic term for a group of related languages. Alternate
terms for the language family are Voltaic and Gur; Molé-Dagbane is sometimes
applied to a subgrouping of the Gur family. Molé-Dagbane languages are found
in the basin drained by the middle and upper parts of the Volta River, which
rises in three branches in Upper Volta and crosses Ghana to the sea. The head-
waters of the river are in Mossi country. It is the so-called Middle Volta Basin
that is home to the Molé-Dagbane peoples. A few outlying groups include the
Dogon, famous for their art, in the Bandiagara Escarpment in Mali, northwest
of the Mossi, who forced them there. Others are the Bassari, Batonun and related
peoples who live east of the Volta Basin in northern Togo Benin and Nigeria.

In structure, Molé-Dagbane societies range from "acephalous" groups with
no greater authority than the patriarch of an extended family to a string of
genealogically related kingdoms, each with complicated internal organizations.
Kingdoms include a variety of ethnic groups, not all of them Molé-Dagbane-
speaking, the result being a lack of any fixed individual identity. A given ethnic
group may occur in more than one kingdom, or both in and out of such organized
states. A particular clan may spread lineal kinship connections across several
ethnic groups. However, in contemporary southern Ghanian usage, the term
"Northerner" is virtually synonymous with Molé-Dagbane.

The Volta Basin location is important to the Molé-Dagbane peoples, both in
terms of their general history and specifically with respect to Islam. Since ancient
times long-distance trade routes have crisscrossed the West African savanna,

linking its peoples with each other and with the culturally distinct populations of the coastal rain forests to the south and with the Mediterranean world across the Sahara. Three major routes converge in Molé-Dagbane territory. One starts in the land of the Akan peoples, the most well-known and powerful of whom are the Asante (see Akan). A second begins in the northwest part of the Middle Volta, where a succession of Manding empires and their cities of Jenne, Mopti and Timbuktu have been centers of Islamic learning as well as trade. A third connects with the great Hausa cities and states of northern Nigeria: Sokoto, Kano, Zaria and Katsina, all major Islamic and economic centers.

In the past, the Akan peoples traded gold and kola nuts (a caffeine-rich stimulant much sought throughout the savanna, especially by Muslims denied alcohol by their faith). In return, the savanna states traded for salt (from the Saharan mines) and slaves. The latter were in great demand once the trans-Atlantic slave trade developed. Except for some gold and slaves (often Molé-Dagbane), the Middle Volta peoples controlled trade routes rather than resources. But those routes and their trade were very important. The Akan "Gold Coast" was the main source of gold for Europe and the Arab world through the Middle Ages until the Spanish conquest of Peru and Mexico. It was the trade through the Middle Volta which brought the cavalry and traders from elsewhere who introduced state government and Islam to the Molé-Dagbane farming peoples.

The original Middle and Upper Volta Basin peoples were farmers living in scattered homesteads of adobe-like houses. (Later, under slave-raider pressure, some of these compounds were walled to the point of low-grade fortification.) The farmers were organized in localized kinship groups, to which individuals were affiliated through male lines of descent. Subsistence agriculture, using hoe cultivation, was based upon millet in the Upper Volta, to which yams were added in those parts of the Middle Volta where sufficient rain fell to grow them. Land was vested in the family group down through time; living family members held it in trust for their descendants, having in their turn received it from ancestors who owned it by virtue of having cleared uninhabited ground.

This was reinforced by a religion which possessed earth shrines that influenced rain and soil fertility but whose main focus was the solicitation of benevolent ancestral intervention in one's affairs by means of prayers and sacrifices on graves. The natural and supernatural worlds were directly linked on a kinship continuum. Most but not all of these "autochthonous" peoples were speakers of Molé-Dagbane languages. The Bisa, for example, who formed the population base for the first Mossi state of Tenkodogo, were non-Muslim Manding.

Sometime around the thirteenth century, cavalry, possibly from Nigeria, entered the Middle Volta Basin. Militarily superior, they were able to conquer local people and establish states. Defining dates and sequences is still difficult, not least because the traditionally "senior" state of Mamprusi was in recent centuries weak in power and in oral tradition. Also, "Mossi" cavalry were in the region some two centuries before the earliest known state. ("Mossi" in a historical context is frequently applied to all these immigrant state-founding cavalry.) By the fourteenth and fifteenth centuries, datable references to wars with Mossi appear in records of Mali and Songhay. Nevertheless, none of the currently existing states can be reliably dated earlier than about 1480, the approximate date for foundation of Mamprusi and Dagomba. The northern (modern) Mossi states were founded a generation or so later. In each case, "founding" means establishing a state over pre-existing farming groups, whose Molé-Dagbane languages became the languages of the "Mossi" cavalry elite as well.

The various Manding-speaking peoples moved outwards from their Upper Niger River homeland at different times. The rise of the Mali Empire and its successors added greater importance to Manding movements. They were the source for the diffusion of Islam into the western Sudan savanna, including the Hausa, and their traders, the Dyula, known also as Wangara, who figure heavily in early accounts of the West African interior (see Manding-speaking Peoples; Dyula).

Dates for these developments are not firmly established, but it has been argued that the Dyula from Mali brought Islam into the Volta Basin beginning in the late fourteenth century, with the pace accelerating in the next century. The late fifteenth century saw the founding of the Molé-Dagbane "Mossi" states out of the somewhat earlier cavalry influx. Gonja, a state with a Mande elite south of Dagomba, rose in the late 1500s. The first Akan state, to the south, arose roughly contemporaneously with the Molé-Dagbane states. Hausa histories from Kano first mention kola nuts, which come only from the Akan forests, in the early fifteenth century. The period 1350–1600, then, saw the rise of trade between the Akan forest peoples and the Mali Mandinka to their northwest and the Hausa to the northeast. The traders were Muslim.

State formation was founded upon a particular technology, the military uses of the horse. Long-distance trade, for its part, was made possible by the superior "technology," as it were, of Islam. Islam provided two unrivaled advantages. One was writing, which allowed superior record keeping, communication by letter and extended spheres of influence by safe-conduct letters and certificates of Islamic learning. Even more important, the universalist framework of Islam and its legal codes made easier the ongoing commerce between distant and diverse peoples.

The three components of the Molé-Dagbane societies have been long established: peasant farmers, Muslim traders and political-military elites who both exploited trade and made it all possible by maintaining civil and economic order. This techno-economic view of Islam is important in understanding the essential role of Islam in societies that were, overall, not Muslim.

Muslims were another specialized group, similar to blacksmiths, drummers, potters and soldiers. The skills of trade and Islam were concentrated in ethnically and clan-related descent groups. The main difference was that the Muslim's tool kit was intellectual. Muslims lived in socially separate and distinct communities associated with trade routes. Throughout the region lived pagan farmers, some of whom lived within states, some not. Among them were political centers with kings or chiefs and economic centers, "Dyula trading towns," of Muslims. The underlying peasant society, based on kinship, was relatively unaffected by the states and trade networks, which existed "above" them.

During the development of this regional system, the great Muslim reformer Uthman don Fodio wrote off the Volta Basin states and peoples as "countries where infidelity is overwhelming and Islam is rare." The fact that the societies were not Muslim obscures the importance of Islam to them. Several writers note the importance of charms containing Quranic writing, which were in demand in the Akan forest states and the savanna cavalry-based ones. Indeed, an early European observer of Asante noted that this trade was such that a Muslim could be supported for a month by a piece of paper. The economic and spiritual power of Islam caused Muslims to receive formal recognition and participation in official pagan administrations. *Imams* became court functionaries by the early eighteenth century. Their influence was out of proportion to the percentage of Muslim citizens. Pagan fathers sent sons to Muslim schools for the advantages they would gain, and entire pagan villages would sometimes invite a Muslim scholar to found a school. In the northwest corner of the basin in the eighteenth century the small state of Wa was founded upon a Dyula trading town.

The persistence of "stateless" Molé-Dagbane peoples alongside and between organized states may be accounted for by two factors. One is that states taxed trade, not farmers. Expanding boundaries to incorporate peasants did not necessarily pay. Second, from the sixteenth through the nineteenth centuries, slaves were important in the regional economy. Since a Muslim cannot be enslaved by another Muslim, and since the trading aspects of the states were the most Islamized, there was a positive benefit in having handy populations who were outside the formal protections of the state.

Throughout African states, Islamized and not, there is a tendency towards undefined boundaries that shade off into zones of weaker and weaker control. This is the case of the Molé-Dagbane "stateless" peoples like the Talensi (Tale; Fra-Fra), Sisala (Isala), Lobi, Lowiili, Birifor and Dagari (Dagabaa), who cannot be understood as societies without taking into account their proximity to states. One common "tribe" in the literature, the Grusi (in widely varying spellings), are nothing more than the congeries of stateless peoples south of the Mossi and north and east of the Mamprusi and Dagomba; the word is the Mossi collective noun labelling all the assorted stateless peoples to their south. It is an identity with meaning only to those who bestowed it on peoples whose societies sharply contrasted to their own.

Complete population figures for the Molé-Dagbane peoples are lacking. Among the stateless groups, in fact, merely defining ethnic identity, much less counting members, is difficult and controversial. The 1960 Ghana census was the last one to publish ethnic enumerations, and those for Molé-Dagbane people are often "supertribalized" aggregations. In that census, there were 217,640 Dagomba, 186,970 of whom were living in their homeland. There were 58,710 Mamprusi, 46,500 of whom were in their territory. The stateless societies included 59,000

Sisala, lumped with their neighbors, the Dagari (201,680), the Talensi (138,370) and the Kusai (121,610), in the northeast corner of Ghana. There were 110,150 Konkomba and 37,550 Lobi in Ghana, with large populations of the former in Togo and the latter in Upper Volta and Ivory Coast.

In 1960 what had been ruled by the British from the turn of the century to 1957 as the "Northern Territories" comprised the Upper and Northern Regions. The former included most of the stateless peoples, the latter the state of Mamprusi, Dagomba and Gonja. The 1960 Upper Region population was 862,000 and the Northern Region was 427,000, for a combined total of 1,289,000 out of a national population of 6,727,000. Of those 1,289,000 Northerners, some 186,000 (14.4 percent) were Muslims, not all of whom were Molé-Dagbane people.

Post-1960 ethnic and religious figures are not available, save for a 1967 estimate of 267,907 in the six constituencies corresponding to the Dagomba state. The 1970 census counted 727,618 in the Northern Region and 862,723 in the Upper Region, for a total of 1,590,341.

The meaning of the 14 percent Muslim figures varies as regional data are disaggregated. Muslims tend to concentrate in towns and cities. A study of the Sisala, for example, found that of Sisala living in towns larger than 5,000 population, 49.4 percent were Muslims in 1960, as opposed to only 8.4 percent for Sisala in rural locations. In this case, most of the town-dwelling Sisala were migrants in southern Ghanian cities. These migrants, like others leaving the savanna with its broadly similar cultures and religion based upon ancestral graves, found that a universalist religion served them better in the culturally and ecologically different southern Ghana. (Parallel shifts in proportions existed for the far smaller Christian Sisala community.) Not all urban Sisala were considered deeply or even permanently converted.

The Sisala figures, however, do indicate that when Molé-Dagbane peoples participate in the Ghanian nation they are both likely to be considered Muslim by southerners and to be in a situation where it would indeed be advantageous to identify oneself as Muslim. The north of Ghana is far less developed than the rest of the country and suffered further for having been in the political opposition during the Nkrumah years.

A quirk of politics in 1979 gave the north its first substantial access to political power. The circumstances of the return to civilian rule meant that the leader of the People's National Party was ineligible to stand for the presidential election. His replacement, Dr. Hilla Limann, a diplomat, won the election despite being a virtual unknown within Ghana. He is a Sisala, from the border with Upper Volta. When his government in its turn was overthrown by another military *coup d'état* in December 1981, a contributing factor, if not the major one, was southern Ghanian opposition to a shift in regional importance. Significantly, that shift was seen as benefitting a "Muslim" population. A commentator on the regional split in the Limann regime noted that "by 1981 some people were grumbling that 'each new appointment is Alhaji This or Issaka That.' " The historical association of the Muslim minority with the economic and political elite in the Volta Basin carried over to the modern, national arena.

Among the Molé-Dagbane-speaking peoples, then, are a series of ethnically complicated societies incorporating Muslims and depending on them despite their numerical minority. The same circumstances that favor the spread of Islam in contemporary savanna West Africa are adding increasing numbers of converts to the original Mandinka/Dyula and Hausa traders. A literate and skilled elite is managing to exert an influence not only in the Volta Basin but throughout the savanna, out of proportion to their numbers.

BIBLIOGRAPHY

General Works

Books

Fage, J. D. "Reflections on the Early History of the Mossi-Dagomba Group of States." In *The Historian in Tropical Africa*, edited by Jan Vansina, et al. London: International African Institute, 1964.
Goody, Jack. *The Ethnography of the Northern Territories of the Gold Coast West of the White Volta*. London: Her Majesty's Stationary Office, 1954.
———. "The Mande and the Akan Hinterland." In *The Historian in Tropical Africa*, edited by Jan Vansina, et al. London: International African Institute, 1964.
Ladouceur, Paul Andre. *Chiefs and Politicians: The Politics of Regionalism in Northern Ghana*. London: Longmans, 1979.
Levtzion, Nehemia. *Muslims and Chiefs in West Africa: A Study of Islam in the Middle Volta Basin in the Pre-Colonial Period*. Oxford: Clarendon Press, 1968.
Manoukian, Madeline. *Tribes of the Northern Territories of the Gold Coast*. Ethnographic Survey of Africa: Western Africa, Part 5. London: International African Institute, 1951.
Skalnik, Peter. "Early States in the Voltaic Basin." In *The Early State*, edited by H.J.M. Claessen and P. Skalnik. The Hague: Mouton, 1978.
Wilks, Ivor. "The Mossi and the Akan States 1500–1800." In *History of West Africa*, edited by J. F. Ade Ajayi and Michael Crowder. Vol. 1. New York: Columbia University Press, 1972.
———. "The Transmission of Islamic Learning in the Western Sudan." In *Literacy in Traditional Societies*, edited by Jack Goody. Cambridge: Cambridge University Press, 1968.

Articles

Goody, Jack. "Rice-burning and the Green Revolution in Northern Ghana." *Journal of Development Studies* 16:2 (1980): 136–155.
Holden, Jeffrey J. "The Zabarim Conquest of North-West Ghana, Part I." (Part II did not appear.) *Transactions of the Historical Society of Ghana* 8 (1965): 60–86, 9 (1965): 119–120 (maps).

States: Dagomba

Books

Ferguson, Phyllis. "Patterns of Succession to High Office in Dagomba." In *West African Chiefs: Their Changing Status Under Colonial Rule and Independence*, edited by Michael Crowder and Obaro Ikime. New York: Africana, 1970.

Staniland, Martin. *The Lions of Dagbon: Political Change in Northern Ghana*. Cambridge: The University Press, 1975.

Articles

Ladouceur, Paul Andre. "The Yendi Chieftaincy Dispute and Ghanaian Politics." *Canadian Journal of African Studies* 6:1 (1972): 97–115.

Wilks, Ivor. "A Note on the Early Spread of Islam in Dagomba." *Transactions of the Historical Society of Ghana* 8 (1965): 87–98.

Unpublished Manuscripts

Ferguson, Phyllis. "The Dynamics of Muslim and non-Muslim Interaction: The Case of the Molé Walis of Dagbon." Communicating paper, Conference on the Maintenance and Transmission of Islamic Culture in Tropical Africa, Boston, April 27–28, 1973.

———. "Islamization in Dagbon: A Study of the Alfanema of Yendi." Ph.D. dissertation, Cambridge University, 1972.

States: Mamprusi

Books

Brown, S. D. *Ritual Aspects of the Mamprusi Kingship*. Leiden: Afrika-Studiecentrum, 1975.

———. "Structure of the Mamprusi Kingdom and the Cult of *Naam*." In *The Study of the State*, edited by H.J.M. Claessen and Peter Skalnik. The Hague: Mouton, 1981.

States: Wa

Book

Wilks, Ivor. "Patterns of Succession to High Office in Wa." In *West African Chiefs: Their Changing Status Under Colonial Rule and Independence*, edited by Michael Crowder and Obaro Ikime. New York: Africana, 1970.

Stateless Peoples

Books

Fortes, Meyer. *The Dynamics of Clanship Among the Tallensi*. Oxford: Oxford University Press, 1945.

———. *Time and Social Structure and Other Essays*. London: Athlone Press, 1970. (Talensi.)

———. *The Web of Kinship Among the Tallensi*. Oxford: Oxford University Press, 1949.

Goody, Jack. *Death, Property and the Ancestors: A Study of the Mortuary Customs of the LoDagaba of West Africa*. Stanford: Stanford University Press, 1962.

———. *The Myth of the Bagre*. Oxford: Clarendon Press, 1972. (Dagari.)

———. *The Social Organization of the LoWiili*. 2nd ed. London: International African Institute, 1967. (Dagari.)

Griaule, Marcel. *Conversations with Ogotemmeli: An Introduction to Dogon Religious Ideas*. London: International African Institute, 1965.

Grindal, Bruce. *Growing up in Two Worlds: Education and Transition Among the Sisala of Northern Ghana*. New York: Holt, Rinehart and Winston, 1972.

Hart, Keith. "The Economic Basis of Tallensi Social History in the Early Twentieth Century." In *Research in Economic Anthropology*, edited by George Dalton. Vol. 1. Greenwich, Conn.: JAI Press, 1979.

———. "Migration and the Opportunity Structure: A Ghanaian Case Study." In *Modern Migrations in Western Africa*, edited by Samir Amin. London: International African Institute, 1974. (Fra-Fra.)

———. "Swindler or Public Benefactor? The Entrepreneur in His Community." In *Changing Social Structure in Ghana: Essays in the Comparative Sociology of a New State and an Old Tradition*, edited by Jack Goody. London: International African Institute, 1975. (Fra-Fra.)

Mendonsa, Eugene. *The Politics of Divination: A Processural View of Reactions to Illness and Deviance Among the Sisala of Northern Ghana*. Berkeley: University of California Press, 1982.

Spini, Tito, and Spini, Sandro. *Togu Na: The African Dogon: "House of Men, House of Words."* New York: Rizzoli, 1977.

Tait, David. *The Kinkomba of Northern Ghana*. London: International African Institute, 1961.

Verdier, Raymond. "Ontology of the Judicial Thought of the Kabre of Northern Togo." In *Law in Culture and Society*, edited by Laura Nader. Chicago: Aldine, 1969.

Articles

Bourdier, Jean-Paul, and Trinh T. Minh-Ha. "The Architecture of a Lela Compound." *African Arts* 16:1 (1982): 68–72, 96. (Gurunsi.)

Fortes, Meyer. "Some Aspects of Migration and Mobility in Ghana." *Journal of Asian and African Studies* 6:1 (1971): 1–20. (Fra-Fra.)

Hart, Keith. "Informal Income Opportunities and Urban Employment in Ghana." *Journal of Modern African Studies* 11:1 (1973): 61–89. (Fra-Fra.)

————. "Migration and Tribal Identity Among the Frafras of Ghana." *Journal of Asian and African Studies* 6:1 (1971): 20–36.

Hilton, T. E. "Frafra Resettlement and the Population Problem in Zuarungu." *Bulletin de l'Institut Française d'Afrique Noire* (series B) 22:3–4 (1960): 426–442. (Fra-Fra.)

————. "Notes on the History of Kusasi." *Transactions of the Historical Society of Ghana* 6 (1962): 79–86.

Hunter, John M. "The Clans of Nangodi: A Geographical Study of the Territorial Basis of Authority in a Traditional State [sic] of the West African Savanna." *Africa* 28:4 (1968): 1–36. (Fra-Fra.)

————. "Population Pressure in a Part of the West African Savanna: A Study of Nangodi, NE Ghana." *Annals of the American Association of Geographers* 57 (1967): 101–114. (Fra-Fra.)

Tait, David. "An Analytical Commentary on the Social Structure of the Dogon." *Africa* 20:3 (1950): 175–199.

Unpublished Manuscripts

Blier, Suzanne Preston. "Architecture of the Tamberma (Togo)." Ph.D. dissertation, Columbia University, 1981.

Hagaman, Barbara L. "Beer and Matriliny: The Power of Women in a West African Society." Ph.D. dissertation, Northeastern University, 1977. (Lobi.)

Nunley, John Wallace. "Sisala Sculpture of Northern Ghana." Ph.D. dissertation, University of Washington, 1976.

Smith, Fred Thomas. "Gurensi Architectural Decoration in Northeastern Ghana." Ph.D. dissertation, Indiana University, 1979. (Fra-Fra.)

Gregory A. Finnegan

MOORS   The Moors, who are almost totally Sunni Muslim, live in western North Africa. Numbering nearly 4 million, they constitute about 58 percent of Mauritania's population, or 1 million; 10 percent of Morroco's, or 2.2 million; 3 percent of Mali's, or 200,000 and about 60,000 in Senegal and The Gambia. A Moor is regarded as any person, irrespective of skin color, who speaks any of the numerous dialects of Hassaniya, a language which, in its purest form, draws heavily on the original Yemeni Arabic spoken by the Bani Hassan tribe which invaded northwest Africa during the sixteenth and seventeenth centuries.

Largely nomadic, Moorish society is hierarchical, composed of tribal confederations, tribal and clan segments, subsegments and tent units. The social system resembles that of other Saharan and Arab desert societies with variation due to West African ecology and history. The complex structure of society, developed in nomadic life, emerged from the constant state of insecurity in a harsh desert environment characterized by fratricidal wars, banditry and organized raids.

The Moors recognize four major divisions, based upon elements of heritage, race and occupation. At the top are those called the white Moors, composed of an aristocracy and its tributaries, then two types of slaves and finally occupational castes.

A *bidan* (white Moor) is ethnologically defined as a nomad of Berber-Arab origin. Living primarily in Saharan Mauritania and Mali, the *bidan* becomes progressively darker in skin color toward the south as a result of black African admixtures. (Other elements entering the Moorish ethnic group include the non-Negroid Fulani and the Negroid Wolof and Soninké.)

The *bidan* upper elements of Moorish society are divided into two strata. The nobility, or the suzerains, are generally referred to as *'adma*, or bones; the second, commoners or tributaries, are called *lahma*, or flesh. The *'adma* is composed of the *hassan* (warriors) and the *zawya* (religious leaders). Before the French "pacification," the *hassan* generally had political preeminence over the *zawya*.

Traditionally, the function of the *hassan* is to protect the *zawya*; each *zawya* tribe has its particular *hassan* protector. An important *zawya* tribe may have several *hassani* tribes as protectors or vice versa. Such arrangements and verbal treaties do not, however, imply any kind of *zawya* vassalage to the *hassan*. The *zawya* provide moral, spiritual, legal and political services to their protectors, instruct their children, minister to their sick and wounded, act as intercessors between God and man, chase away evil spirits, prevent curses and the evil eye and settle disputes. The *hassan* and *zawya* complement each other.

Below the two *'adma* aristocratic classes come the *lahma*, or tributaries, who are in a position similar to that of the clients in ancient Rome. They are grouped into tribes which may be vassals of either the *hassan* or *zawya* tribes. They must marry at their social level. They, too, may be men of war or of religion, although those with martial traditions serve as auxiliary forces. Modern government injunctions to disarm have led most of them to a life of monasticism. Many still in remote areas pay tribute to their *'adma* overlords.

The *sudan* (black) Moors form the lower classes of Moorish society. They live in a world of their own, usually in slavery. Although slavery has been outlawed, it remains basic in the social and economic structure of the Moors. The juridical abandonment of the term *'abd* (slave) and its replacement by that of *hartani* (freedman) for a *sudan* Moor cannot hide the continued survival of slavery in northwest Africa.

Two kinds of slaves exist: the *'abd-le-tilad*, who belongs to the tent and constitutes membership in the family, and the *'abd-le-tarbiya*, an acquired slave. Many Moors, whether in Mauritania or Mali, remain oblivious to governmental provisions outlawing slavery. Those who are aware of them consider the laws impractical. In their view, owners would be ruined without slaves and many slaves would not know what to do with their freedom. Many freed slaves refuse to leave their masters, while others form a destitute proletariat in the urban centers.

The fourth element in Moorish society is represented by the occupational castes, usually regarded as aliens by both *'adma* and *lahma*, although they have similar characteristics. Among them are the *m'allmin* (craftsmen), the *aghazazir* (salt miners), the *ighyuwn* (bards) and two fast disappearing tribes of *namadi* (hunters) and *imraguen* (fishermen). These are not castes in the traditional sense of the term, but remnants (about 300 persons each) of aborigines who have kept their ethnic purity through insularity.

Moors follow the Maliki school of Islamic law. Two main *tariqa* flourish among them. The Qadiri is the most widespread, characterized by a multitude of secret societies replete with mysticism. The Tijani is a second major brotherhood. Less important is the Shadhiliyya *tariqa*.

BIBLIOGRAPHY

Books

Curran, Brian Dean, and Schrock, Joann. *Area Handbook for Mauritania*. The American University FAS, DA-Pam 550-161. Washington, D.C.: Government Printing Office, 1972.

Gerteiny, Alfred G. "Islamic Influences on Politics in Mauritania." In *Aspects of West African Islam*, edited by Daniel F. McCull and Normal Bennett. Boston University Papers on Africa, Vol. 5. Boston: Boston University African Studies Center, 1971.

————. *Mauritania*. New York: Praeger, 1967.

————. "Mauritania." In *Islam in Africa*, edited by James Kritzeck and William H. Lewis. Princeton: Van Nostrand, 1969.

Moorehouse, Geoffrey. *The Fearful Void*. Philadelphia: Lippincott, 1974.

Stewart, C. C., and Stewart, E. R. *Islam and Social Order in Mauritania*. Oxford: Clarendon Press, 1973.

Articles

Gerteiny, Alfred G. "The Racial Factor and Politics in the Islamic Republic of Mauritania." *RACE: Journal of the Institute of Race Relations* 8 (1967): 263–275.

Moore, Clement Henry. "One Partyism in Mauritania." *Journal of Modern African Studies* 3:3 (1965): 409–520.

Wolff, Ursula. "Mauritania's Nomadic Society Preserves Its Lifestyle." *Africa Report* 17:8 (1972): 11–16.

Alfred G. Gerteiny
Population figures updated by Richard V. Weekes

MOSSI   The Mossi are one of the major peoples living in the basin of the Volta River, south of the great bend of the Niger River. They number nearly 4.9 million, nearly all of whom live—or have their family homes—in Upper Volta, where they constitute about half the population. Some one-half million Upper Volta Mossi work in Ivory Coast, Ghana and other neighboring countries.

A conservative estimate is that slightly more than one-third, or 1.8 million, are Muslim. (Mossi is often spelled "Moshi" in British and Ghanaian writing.)

Mossi speak Moore, sometimes written Moré or Molé, which is a member of the Gur or Voltaic subfamily of Niger-Congo. The Voltaic culture area includes much of Upper Volta, northern Ghana, northern Togo and adjacent small areas of Ivory Coast, Mali and Benin. Besides the Mossi, the Voltaic peoples include such culture groups as the Talensi, the Konkomba, the Dogon and the Lobi, as well as the Dagomba and Mamprusi kingdoms in northern Ghana (see Molé-Dagbane-speaking Peoples).

It was in this area that the Mossi kingdom of Tenkodogo was founded in the fifteenth century by cavalry from the Dagomba and Mamprusi states. From Tenkodogo, in turn, the Mossi states of Ouagadougou and Yatenga, and the related Gourmantche state of Fada N'Gurma, were established. These three Mossi states, along with various interstitial buffer states and dependencies, formed the Mossi homeland.

Basic Mossi culture is shared with all Voltaic societies, both those with centralized governments and those with lineage elders or village chiefs as the highest authorities. Mossi live in dispersed settlements in which segments of extended families dwell within walled compounds about 300 feet apart. Villages are formed of partrilineally related males and their wives. A proportion of households may consist of men who have settled instead in their wife's or, more usually, their mother's village. Over time, the descendants of such men (and even of outright immigrants without kin ties) will be absorbed as full members of the village kinship core.

Traditionally, a senior male presided over a large compound containing himself, his wives and children, his younger brother and their families and married sons. The family was held together by an ideology of kinship based on a religion in which ancestral spirits influenced the fortunes of their descendants, enforced by the fact that land was held collectively by families. Even in states (like Mossi) where chiefs controlled access to land, rights were vested in families, not individuals. Except for the families who were clients of a chief or king (and who were usually descended from war captives or immigrants), an individual's place in society was determined by kinship. Even the often overlooked ability of individuals to exploit alternative opportunities through their kinship links to their mother's family did not undercut the dominant patrilineal organization as much as it reinforced the overall sense that individuals existed as part of larger families.

Economic development in the region, especially the internationally funded Volta valley project, which is opening new and fertile lands for cultivation, is inducing change in the traditional family structures. There is a trend towards nuclear families in which a man, his wives and children form a social and economic unit better able to conserve their own gains.

Most Mossi, indeed over 90 percent of the Upper Volta population, live by subsistence hoe farming in rural villages. The countryside is flat and arid, covered by brush, scattered trees and a few mesas or smaller outcroppings. The thin soil is red with laterite. Daily activities depend on the season. During the April–September rainy season, men and women work in the fields, either in their own gardens and fields or as members of cooperative work groups which assist each other in heavy tasks like cultivating, weeding, harvesting and threshing. The dry season is devoted to threshing millet, the staple crop, repairing their adobe-like houses and rethatching roofs. Some have craft skills such as weaving and pottery making. Men weave and sew; women spin thread from indigenous cotton.

Despite having populations consisting mostly of farmers, the power of Mossi states in the past was based on control of trade routes. Between the Akan forest states, such as Asante (Ashanti), and the Niger River cities of Gao, Mopti and Timbuktu, there was a heavy trade in livestock, cotton cloth, salt and kola nuts. The Mossi not only taxed the trade, they participated in it as well.

The Mossi came into contact with Islam through the Songhay empire (see Songhay). From 1328 through 1333 the Yatenga Mossi sacked the Songhay capital of Timbuktu. The Songhay defeated them in 1477, and in 1498 the great Songhay emperor, Askia, proclaimed a *jihad* against the Mossi when their leaders refused to adopt Islam. Despite these Songhay attacks, the Mossi were never conquered until the coming of the French in 1896. The Mossi remained too strong to be conquered on their home ground but were not strong enough to conquer other areas.

Mossi resisted conversion to Islam in part because of the close association of their political and religious systems. A Mossi ruler required the aid of his ancestors, approached through the ancestor cult; a Muslim chief would have to forfeit this basis for his rule. Since the Mossi states were strong enough to resist conquest, Islam could only reach them through diffusion or persuasion. In the late 1700s several Ouagadougou kings were converted to Islam, but without lasting effect and without insisting that their heirs be Muslims.

Because of this history, the Mossi are often noted as the most important people of the West African savanna to have resisted Islam, although somewhere between one-fourth and one-third are now Muslim. Their conversion has come through their contact, beginning around 1684, with Mande traders who settled among them (see Manding-speaking Peoples). In 1780 a Mogho Naba (Ouagadougou king) who had a Mande mother granted these immigrants, known as Dyula or (especially) Yarsé, the right to settle throughout his realm. Today the Yarsé have completely assimilated Mossi culture; they speak Moore and live as do other Mossi. However, they have remained Muslim, since Islam is an essential attribute in long-distance trade.

Not all Yarsé are traders; many live as farmers. While some writers describe the Yarsé in the Mossi kingdom of Yatenga as marrying only other Yarsé, other data show them freely marrying ordinary Mossi. Indeed, Tenkodogo Mossi draw a distinction between Yarsé and Mossi converts to Islam; the latter are seen as more purely Muslim. Yarsé Islamic practices are more syncretic. Census figures for 1961 show 9.8 percent of Yarsé as traditionalist in religion.

Diffusion of Islam into Mossi culture is not surprising given their location on the fringes of major Muslim states in the past and their position astride Muslim-dominated trade routes, but it is greater than one would expect from the conventional description of the Mossi as anti-Islamic. For example, days of the week have names which are cognates of the Arabic names. When a Mossi market occurs on a Friday, as it does every 21 days, that market is an especially large and active one. A Mossi eats with the right hand, reserving the left for toilet functions. The Arab *zagarid* (shrill, trilling cries of joy) is made by women at marriages, upon completion of group tasks like threshing and, significantly, to salute important chiefs.

The spread of Islam was aided by the French conquest in 1896–1897, which cast doubt on the efficacy of the traditional religion because it did not prevent the defeat. The close connection between the Mossi political system and religion had reinforced the latter when the former was strong; the linkage continued in defeat with opposite results. As a consequence, Mossi became more receptive to Muslim missionaries. These were largely from other African savanna peoples and were evidence that one could convert without seriously disrupting a familiar way of life. Christian missions suffered from association with the colonial rulers, from having mostly alien clergy and from their more striking demands (especially monogamy) upon prospective converts.

Islam continues to gain ground over Christianity as an alternative to Mossi traditional religion, even though Roman Catholic missions controlled the colonial schools which trained those who took power from the French. Many civil servants are Christian. The first president (1961–1966) of independent Upper Volta, Maurice Yaméogo, was a Catholic Mossi, as is the first African cardinal, Archbishop Zoungrana of Ouagadougou. The military presidents who followed were Muslim but not Mossi; General Sangoule Lamizana (1966–1980) and Colonel Saye Zerbo (1980–1982) are Samo, a Mande people. The November 1982 *coup d'état* leadership retained a non-Muslim as chief of the armed forces but installed a Catholic Mossi, Major Jean Baptiste Ouedraogo, as chair of the People's Provisional Salvation Council. In foreign policy, Upper Volta has become more conscious of its Muslim neighbors and citizens. Despite the overall minority status of Muslims, under President Lamizana Upper Volta applied at the 1973 Pan Islamic Conference in Pakistan to join the Islamic grouping.

Mossi Muslims are Sunni of the Maliki school of law. Like other West African Muslims, they tend to be followers of one or another *tariqa*. Two of these brotherhoods, the Qadiri and the stricter Tijani, are important. Despite their voluntary membership, though, membership in a *tariqa* is much more a consequence of family tradition or the affiliation of one's religious initiator than the result of conscious choice between schools of religious interpretation.

Large Mossi populations outside Upper Volta are the result of labor migration, especially during the savanna dry season, to work on cocoa farms in Ghana and, more recently, Ivory Coast. Mossi have long been accustomed to a variety of population movements and migration.

Mossi migration is important to Islamization in two ways. First, migration exposes individuals to the advantages Islam offers in terms of protection and aid from co-religionists of whatever ethnicity, while traditionalists lack a universal link to non-Voltaics. Second, not all Mossi immigrants have gone to laboring jobs. There are well-established Mossi trading communities in Ghanaian cities. One study found that second- and third-generation Mossi in Kumasi, Ghana, were increasingly assimilated into the Muslim Hausa-dominated *zongo* (stranger's quarter) and knew very little of Mossi culture or even the language, although they retained ethnic identity as Mossi in their own as well as others' eyes (see Hausa).

The impact of Islam on Mossi society and culture is considerable. Mossi Muslims are, however, enough of a minority and a historical and cultural novelty that they are conscious of being part of a non-Muslim whole. West African Islam in the savanna belt is known for embracing a continuum of believers ranging from urban Quranic scholars of great orthodoxy to rural farmers repeating prayers by rote alongside traditional shrines. But whereas a Hausa farmer, say, in Nigeria is part of a self-consciously Muslim society with institutional supports, a Mossi Muslim must rely on his own values and commitments to "Islamize" his daily life. The continuing incorporation of Mossi and Upper Volta into regional and world economic and political systems favors universalistic religions, and Islam offers Mossi many advantages. Both Christianity and Islam are expanding at the expense of traditional religion, but Islam has the greater momentum.

BIBLIOGRAPHY

Books

Bricker, Gary, and Traoré, Soumana. "Transitional Urbanization in Upper Volta: The Case of Ouagadougou, a Savannah Capital." In *Urban Systems in Africa*, edited by Robert A. Obudho and Salah El-Shaikh. New York: Praeger, 1979.

Fage, J. D. "Reflections on the Early History of the Mossi-Dagomba Group of States." In *The Historian in Tropical Africa*, edited by J. Vansina, R. Mauny, and L. V. Thomas. London: International African Institute, 1964.

Finnegan, Gregory A. "Employment Opportunity and Migration Among Mossi of Upper Volta." In *Research in Economic Anthropology*, edited by George Dalton. Vol. 3. Greenwich, Conn.: JAI Press, 1980.

————, and Delgado, Christopher L. "Cachez la Vache: Mossi Cattle, Fulbe Keepers and the Maintenance of Ethnicity." In *Image and Reality in African Interethnic Relations: The Fulbe and Their Neighbors*, edited by Emily A. Schultz. Williamsburg, Va.: College of William and Mary, 1980.

Goody, Jack R. *Technology, Tradition and the State in Africa*. London: International African Institute, 1971.

Hammond, Peter B. "Economic Change and Mossi Acculturation." In *Continuity and Change in African Cultures*, edited by W. R. Bascom and M. J. Herskovits. Chicago: University of Chicago Press, 1959.

————. "Technoeconomic Innovation and Mossi Religious Change." In *African Reli-*

gious Groups and Beliefs: Papers in Honor of William R. Bascom, edited by Simon Ottenberg. Cupertino, Calif.: Folklore Institute, 1982.

———. *Yatenga: Technology in the Culture of a West African Kingdom*. New York: Free Press, 1966.

Izard, Michael. "The Yarsé and Pre-Colonial Trade in Yatenga." In *The Development of Indigenous Trade and Markets in West Africa*, edited by C. Meillassoux. London: International African Institute, 1971.

Levtzion, Nehemia. *Muslims and Chiefs in West Africa: A Study of Islam in the Middle Volta Basin in the Pre-Colonial Period*. Oxford: Clarendon Press, 1968.

Schildkraut, Enid. *People of the Zongo: The Transformation of Ethnic Identities in Ghana*. Cambridge: Cambridge University Press, 1978.

Skalnik, Peter. "The Dynamics of Early State Development in the Voltaic Area." In *Political Anthropology*, edited by S. L. Seaton and H.J.M. Claessen. Chicago: Aldine Press, 1979.

———. "Early States in the Voltaic Basin." In *The Early State*, edited by H.J.M. Claessen and P. Skalnik. The Hague: Mouton, 1978.

Skinner, Elliot P. *African Urban Life: The Transformation of Ougadougou*. Princeton: Princeton University Press, 1974.

———. "Intergenerational Conflict Among the Mossi: Father and Son." In *Peoples and Cultures of Africa*, edited by Elliot P. Skinner. Garden City, N.Y.: Doubleday, 1972.

———. "Islam in Mossi Society." In *Islam in Tropical Africa*, edited by I. M. Lewis. 2nd ed. Bloomington: Indiana University Press, 1966.

Zoanga, J. B. "The Traditional Power of Mossi *Nanamse* of Upper Volta." In *The Nomadic Alternative*, edited by W. Weissleder. The Hague: Mouton, 1978.

Articles

Butler, Herbert. "The Absorption of Strangers and Cultural Change Among the Mossi." *Proceedings of the Central States Anthropological Society, Selected Papers* 3 (1977): 17–22.

Saul, Mahir. "Beer, Sorghum and Women: Production for the Market in Rural Upper Volta." *Africa* 51 (1981): 746–764.

Skinner, Elliott P. "Christianity and Islam Among the Mossi." *American Anthropologist* 60 (1958): 1102–1119.

Unpublished Manuscripts

Butler, Herbert W. "The Structuring Process in a Mossi Village." Ph.D. dissertation, Michigan State University, 1974.

Finnegan, Gregory A. "Population Movement, Labor Migration and Social Structure in a Mossi Village." Ph.D. dissertation, Brandeis University, 1976.

Ford, Robert Elden. "Subsistence Farming Systems in Semi-Arid Northern Yatenga (Upper Volta)." Ph.D. dissertation, University of California, Riverside, 1982.

Tarr, Delbert Howard. ''Indirection and Ambiguity as a Mode of Communication in West Africa: A Descriptive Study.'' Ph.D. dissertation, University of Minnesota, 1979.

Gregory A. Finnegan

N

NOGAI Increasing assimilation by Russian culture appears to be threatening the survival of Islam among the Nogai. They are a scattered people in the Soviet Union, numbering 65,000, although they may still be classified as Muslims of the Volga. The Nogai are also referred to as the Nogailar, Nogaitsy and Mangkyt. There are also small groups in Bulgaria, Romania and Turkey, for whom no valid population estimates exist but who number probably no more than 50,000. In the Soviet Union, there are Nogai in the Volga steppe region between the Terek and Kuma rivers; others live in the Crimea near the town of Perekop. In Romania, Nogai are found in the Dobruja.

The Nogai are found in two loose federations: the Kara-Nogai (Black Nogai) and Ak-Nogai (White Nogai). They speak two dialects that differ widely from each other but are both usually classified as Kipchak-Turkic. For a time both dialects were classified as literary languages by the Soviet authorities, but eventually a single literary Nogai was established, based on the Crimean Nogai dialect. The use of Nogai is declining in the Soviet Union today.

The name "Nogai" is often linked with the historical name "Nogai," an identification that is of dubious validity. Nogai ("dog" in Mongol) seems to be derived from the Emir Nogai, a general of the Golden Horde at the end of the thirteenth century. His territory, centered on the Ponto-Caspian steppes between the Caspian and the Dobruja, acquired his name in the traditional fashion of steppe nomads, who used a heroic name to identify an entire federation of loosely united tribes. In further traditional fashion, whatever unity existed seems not to have long survived the death of the Emir in 1300. Two large, loosely organized groups emerged, the northern, "lesser" Nogai and the southern, "greater" Nogai. It is out of this division of peoples that today's Nogai emerge. The difficulty lies in identifying what role the later groups calling themselves Nogai played in the earlier confederation. The "lesser" Nogai seem to have formed the nucleus out of which the present-day Nogai of the Dobruja emerged, while the "greater" Nogai seem to have been the antecedents of the more nomadic Nogai of the Volga steppes. There is thus great diversity among the modern Nogai, especially in terms of their dialects.

Islam came to the Nogai Horde early in its history, with references to the faith occurring as early as the sixteenth century. The close association of the Nogai with the Turkic khanates of the Crimea and with the Ottoman sultans led to a firm Sunni faith among them. Today, as the Nogai become increasingly assimilated by the Russian culture which surrounds them, it seems doubtful that Islam will long survive as a major element in Nogai society.

BIBLIOGRAPHY

Books

Allen, William Edward David, and Muratoff, Paul. *Caucasian Battlefields*. Cambridge: The University Press, 1953.
Baddeley, John F. *The Rugged Flanks of Caucasus*. 2 vols. London: Oxford University Press, 1942.
Benningsen, Alexandre. *The Evolution of the Muslim Nationalities of the USSR and Their Linguistic Problems*. London: Central Asian Research Centre, 1961.
Geiger, Bernhard, et al. *Peoples and Languages of the Caucasus*. The Hague: Mouton, 1959.
Menges, Karl H. *The Turkic Languages and Peoples*. Wiesbaden, Germany: Harrassowitz, 1968.
Nekrich, Aleksandr J. *The Punished Peoples*. New York: Norton, 1978.
Smirnov, N. A. *Islam and Russia*. London: Central Asian Research Centre, 1956.
Wurm, Stefan. *Turkic Peoples of the USSR*. London: Central Asian Research Centre, 1954.
Zenkovsky, Serge A. *Pan-Turkism and Islam in Russia*. Cambridge: Harvard University Press, 1960.

Larry W. Moses

NUBA The term ''Nuba'' refers to the approximately 800,000 to 1 million non-Arab inhabitants of the more than 80 small hill communities in the Nuba Mountains of Kordofan Province, Sudan. This term, known to everyone familiar with the region and commonly used in government publications and censuses, is not a term used by any specific local group, each of whom has its own term for itself and acknowledges no necessary common kinship or political unity with any other. There is no ''Nuba'' ethnic group.

''Nuba'' actually has a varied history and should be distinguished from ''Nubia,'' although some of the northernmost of the many languages of the Nuba are indeed related to the languages of the Nubia of the Upper Nile Valley (see Nubians). Culture histories, however, are much more difficult to specify, and it is safest at the stage of current knowledge to discourage speculation on the origins of the Nuba or their relationships elsewhere. Certainly there are relationships to others in such elements as language and culture traits. But the inhabitants of the hill communities themselves (as well as historians) have claims, demonstrations, myths and speculations on the origins of specific Nuba groups from north to south (Ghulfan, Dair, Dilling), from west to east (Nyimang, Tira), from east to west (Kao, Taqali, Kaduru) and even from the south to north (Fungor)!

There are perhaps up to 100 mutually unintelligible vernaculars in the Nuba hills and some ten distinct groups of languages representing at least two (Niger-Congo and Nilo-Saharan) of Africa's five distinct unrelated linguistic stocks (Malayo-Polynesian, Khoisan, Afro-Asiatic). The great majority of the people also speak Arabic. People speaking one of the language groups of the Nuba Mountains, especially the languages of Dair, Dilling, Kaduru, Ghulfan (the so-called Hill Nubian) once were found farther north in the plains of Kordofan. The western Nuba Mountains have a few communities of Daju speakers, probably migrants from the once powerful Daju rulers of Darfur (see Daju). Other major language groups of the Nuba Mountains are related to west, central and southern African languages.

The evidence of the great linguistic diversity and complexity of the Nuba Mountain peoples and the demonstrated similarity to languages elsewhere suggest the Nuba Mountains, if nothing else, were a refugee area over the past millenium or more for peoples from all directions finding security in and around and on the granite inselbergs that rise out of Kordofan. Here they could engage in rainfall agriculture and attempt to escape both slave raiders and oppressive state forms found farther north, west and east, partially secure in their isolation and in the defensive advantage of the rocky mountians themselves.

This security was only partial, for the Nuba Mountains became for many years a source of slaves by raiders from the north. As a consequence local people developed a marked distrust of outsiders as practically every contact was exploitive in some manner. Although some slaves were undoubtedly from the Nuba Mountains of Kordofan, the common literary and historical reference to all African slaves in the Middle East and Orient as "Nuba" or "Nubian" is hardly an accurate specification of origin. By literary license, Nuba or Nubian came to be synonymous with black or even African, especially from the northeast of Africa.

As there has been no overall political unity of the non-Arab inhabitants of the Nuba Mountains, no term, save Nuba, has emerged to refer to the entire population. In historical literature occasionally a term may be used to refer, mistakenly, to inhabitants of large portions of the area which stems from but one specific group of people, one hill community or small group of hill communities. One such term is *anag* (*anaq*), variously translated as "aborigine," "non-Muslim inhabitant" or "pagan." It is found particularly in reference to northern hill groups, argued by some to be Nubian migrants from farther north into the Nuba Mountains. Another term is *turuj*, referring to a small group of cultivators in southwest Kordofan, but formerly used to refer to pagans of the entire region, particularly western Nuba frequently slaved by rulers in Darfur and Sennar.

While some hill communities have specific histories and traditions, some have had distinct political developments and differential experiences with Islam and other Muslims. This is particulary true for the northeastern Nuba people of Taqali (Teqale, Taqwi) and, to a lesser extent, their neighbors of Dair, who developed a state form with distinct kingly genealogies during medieval time (see Taqali). This was allied with, if not derived from, the Funj state of Sennar. Both were Muslim kingdoms, and as a consequence the northern and eastern Nuba became progressively Islamic. The Taqali kingdom at its maximum in the eighteenth and nineteenth centuries extended well into the Tira hills to the south. And even today there is a tradition among some local people that they are not Nuba but really Funj (see Funj).

It is uncertain just how many indigenous Nuba Mountain peoples are today Muslims. The inhabitants of the western, northern and eastern hills are certainly converted to Islam, but the southerly hill communities plus the more isolated central mountain peoples maintain their own pre-Islamic belief systems. A few are Christians from colonial missionary efforts.

Conversion to Islam has a contradictory history, encouraged by force on the one hand and inhibited by force on the other. It was encouraged during the Mahdiyya (1885–1889) with the formation of the *jihadiya* with many Nuba troops and inhibited by later British colonial policy to stem Islamic influence in the Nuba Mountains. Local nomadic Baggara Arabs (the closest non-Nuba neighbors) have rarely been influential in conversion, and, of course, earlier slaving by Muslims discouraged conversion.

Islam in the Nuba Mountains has normally meant some form of Arabization (and vice versa). Mercantilists and traders as well as nomads throughout the area brought Arab culture. And relations generally have been cordial between the Nuba and these Arabs. Often friendships, treaties and close ties of mutual dependence developed, usually to be compromised by exploitive state forms and outside economic pressures. British colonial policy, with the Closed Districts Ordinances of the 1920s, sought to inhibit the spread of Islam with prohibitions on the movements of Muslim clerics and traders without special permission. This sometimes extended to the prohibition of Arabic names, Arab dress and Arabic as a medium of instruction. This last resulted in a series of misguided policies in which English and the local vernacular were used, neither of which was found commonly in Sudan outside the village.

The adoption of Islam, much like the adoption of Arabic and Arab culture traits, was mixed and syncretic. Subsequent to independence in 1956, Christian influence in the Nuba Mountains declined and Islam expanded ever more rapidly through the various channels of commerce, education and expanded contact with the Arab north. Specific conversion, however, most frequently took place at the hands of the *fuqura* (singular *faqi*, "cleric"), who were often of West African origin and not by specific proselytizing by government or neighboring Arabs. This is today undergoing some change.

Though exact figures are impossible, particularly because Islam sits so lightly on the shoulders of many converts (rather a mantle of Arab culture and syncretic religion), the Muslim population of the Nuba is probably over 30 percent, or as many as 300,000 people. Islam is rarely fervent and involves principally a series of what are Arab cultural adoptions: circumcising boys, abstaining from eating pigs or other animals not ritually slaughtered and observing exogamous clan marriage practices. Converts normally pray commonly. They do not usually undertake the Haj, and only a few stop drinking the abundant local beer. Though often converted by West African *fuqura*, their adherence is usually to one or more of the Sufi brotherhoods common to Sudan. They are rarely involved in ecstatic experiential practices.

Individual Nuba hill communities vary in size from small villages of only a thousand or fewer people to large groups with contiguous or closely adjacent or allied villages, such as Otoro, of more than 50,000 people. There is no political unity between the various hill groups, and though they may trade with one another, particularly if they share a language, the unity necessary for mobilization in offense, defense, economic or political commonality is absent. This has meant that the Nuba have not been easily converted to single political parties which stress their Nuba unity or local nationalism. Repeated attempts have usually resulted in failure. Divisions of language, history, religion and traditional social organization persist.

The traditional economic foundations of Nuba life are agricultural, as rainfall agriculture in the Nuba Mountains is normally adequate for a good subsistence crop with the most rudimentary techniques. Nuba cultivators are excellent, and surpluses of the staple, sorghum, are sold as well as made into beer. People also cultivate a series of other garden crops and tobacco for personal consumption. They also keep a variety of domestic animals, including pigs by those not Muslim. A small amount of cotton, sorghum, peanuts, plus gum arabic and gathered forestry products (dried *dom* palm for weaving) constitute the principal exports of the region.

Village communities are organized chiefly by kin group sodalities such as clans and clan sections. These may be the property-holding units which disperse land for cultivation by members of the clan group. Descent is matrilineal in the southern hills and patrilineal in the northern and eastern hills (and even duolineal in the extreme southeast).

Authority is in the hands of clan elders in most hills, as well as, especially in non-Islamic areas, ritual specialists or priests who are responsible for various phenomena such as rain control, ritual to insure successful crops and keeping the peace. These specialists have come to be known to outsiders as *kujur*, although the term comes from but a single Nuba language group. Many of these priests or kin group elders are guardians of residential shrines at which various paraphernalia is kept necessary to the ritual, such as rain stones for the rain magic. In some of the northern hills these specialists often also undergo spiritual possession.

There are no "chiefs" in most hill communities, although the colonial government created local leaders responsible to the state. Sometimes these were also the *kujur*, who were often labelled *mek* or *sultan* in distinction from the *omda* leaders created for Arab groups in Sudan. These *mek* have come to be "chiefs" and given small judicial powers and state sanction. But except for the Taqali kingdom, no other Nuba Mountain political structures extended beyond the elders of each community.

Men may be polygynous in most areas, but more commonly they have but a single wife. In most communities, especially in those not yet converted to Islam, women have considerable freedom and often farm on their own land. Indeed, they are probably among the freest women in Sudan.

There are various types of age organizations of young men in most hills which group boys into units for production activities and sports participation, such as wrestling and stick fighting, all important for constituting and marking boys as men. Chief celebrations are post-harvest festivals. At these there is much revelry, racing, dancing and sporting contests. This has generated a degree of tourist exploitation as Europeans focus on such celebrations out of context to emphasize the primitiveness and essential "Africanness" of the Nuba Mountains. Such exploitation has been viewed as promoting separatist ideologies. It has caused considerable embarrassment to the government and some local friction between local Muslims and non-Muslims. The competence of the Nuba and their potential for national benefit is underemphasized. Although earlier government practices (sanctioning slavery and later colonial inhibitions on Islam), then privatization of property and most recently tourists have exacerbated the difference between Kordofan Arabs and Nuba, Islam itself has been the potentially most unifying factor among the Nuba, a people whose unity heretofore can only be said to have been characterized by their common exploitation from the outside.

BIBLIOGRAPHY

Books

Faris, J. "Pax Britannica and the Sudan: S. F. Nadel." In *Anthropology and the Colonial Encounter*, edited by T. Asad. London: Ithaca Press, 1973.
———. "Southeastern Nuba Age Organization." In *Essays in Sudan Ethnography*, edited by W. James and I. Cunison. London: C. C. Hurst, 1972.
James, W. "Social Assimilation and Changing Identity in the Southern Funj." In *Sudan in Africa*, edited by Y. F. Hasan. Khartoum: Khartoum University Press, 1971.
Nadel, S. F. *The Nuba*. London: Oxford University Press, 1947.
Stevenson, R. C. "Some Aspects of the Spread of Islam in the Nuba Mountains (Kordofan Province, Republic of Sudan)." In *Islam in Africa*, edited by I. M. Lewis. London: Oxford University Press, 1966.

Articles

Nasr, Ahmed Abdel Rahim. "British Policy Towards Islam in the Nuba Mountains." *Sudan Notes and Records* 52 (1971): 23–32.
Stevenson, R. C. "Linguistic Research in the Nuba Mountains—I." *Suan Notes and Records* 43 (1962): 118–130.

Unpublished Manuscripts

O'Brien, J. "Agricultural Labor and Development in Sudan." Ph.D. dissertation, University of Connecticut, 1980.
Saeed, Abdel Baset. "The State and Socioeconomic Transformation in the Sudan: The Case of Social Conflict in Southwest Kurdufan." Ph.D. dissertation, University of Connecticut, 1982.
Stevenson, R. C. "The Nuba Peoples of Kordofan Province: An Ethnographic Survey." M.Sc. thesis, University of Khartoum, 1965.

James C. Faris

NUBIANS Nubian is the name commonly given to the people whose native villages were located between Aswan, Egypt, and the Dongola region of northern Sudan until the building of the High Dam at Aswan in the years 1962–1965. The building of the High Dam necessitated massive resettlement of the inhabitants of these villages. The Egyptian Nubian population was relocated in New Nubia, a government project located near Kom Omo, 20 miles north of Aswan; the Sudanese Nubians living near Wadi Halfa moved to Khasim al Ghurba, east of Khartoum.

Altogether, some 100,000 villagers were resettled before Lake Nasser covered their villages. Today more than three times this number of people are estimated to live in the new settlements. Many more people of Nubian origin live in the cities of Egypt, full participants in the national life of their country. As there is no formal obstacle to intermarriage between Nubians and other Sudanese and Egyptian Muslims, hundreds of thousands of persons in both countries share Nubian descent without being part of this ethno-linguistic group, of which there are perhaps three-quarters of a million.

The loss of their native lands is but the final development in a historical process which had profoundly affected the physical isolation of the traditional villages long before they were threatened by the building of the present dam. Over the last 100 years a tradition of labor migration to the cities of Egypt and Sudan had already introduced an important series of social changes into Nubia. These changes had effectively created a society which was part urban and part rural, part modern and part a reflection of an ancient traditional past. Throughout Nubia, elements of the Christian kingdoms once existing in the Nubian land had gradually blended with the Muslim traditions which came to prevail after the area's conversion to Islam, beginning in the sixteenth century.

Historically, the Nubians' physical situation on the Nile placed them in a strategic position between Egypt to the north and the African kingdoms on the southern stretches of the river. In the sixth century A.D., missionaries from Byzantium sent by Queen Theodora introduced a theocratic regime to the region. After a brief period of Arab conquests, this government was officially recognized by the Arab ruler of Egypt, Abdullah ibn Sa'd, in the seventh century, and a treaty was concluded which lasted for 600 years. Under the terms of the treaty, a tributary relationship was established between Christian Nubia and the much more powerful Muslim community of greater Egypt, a condition marked by an annual ritual exchange of goods between the two states. The kingdoms of Nubia were not to be the site of Muslim settlement, although merchants were allowed to visit the region. Thus Nubia became involved in the overland trade between Africa and the Egyptian world and was particularly important as a source of slaves. In *Tales of a Thousand and One Nights*, harem guards and slaves were often identified as Nubian, but it is possible that this name was broadly applied to Africans who had entered the Muslim world as part of the Nubian slave trade. Of course, Nubian villages themselves were subject to slave raids by Arab tribesmen, since they lacked the religious protection which prevents one Muslim from enslaving another. However, there were free Nubians who belonged to the guilds of medieval Egypt, specializing in porterage and transportation as well as other occupations and crafts. Nubians are also mentioned as agricultural overseers in the Nile delta, and many villagers may have come to Egypt as traders as well as slaves.

During the late nineteenth and early twentieth centuries, Nubian lands were flooded by waters from the dam constructed at Aswan in 1897 and subsequently heightened in 1912 and 1927. For these losses the Nubians received compensation, and many constructed elaborate homes for themselves, placed higher on the sand and rocks above the river. The styles of these homes involved large spacious courtyards and numerous rooms for guests as well as those for family use. Often such homes were built in anticipation of eventual retirement from city work and provided a luxurious contrast to the frequently crowded servant quarters where many Nubians lived in the cities. By this time the Nubians had responded to the demand for service occupations which developed during the colonial period in Egypt and Sudan. In many hotels and restaurants as well as private homes, Nubians from the same villages, often kinsmen, monopolized the job opportunities and established themselves as a mark of aristocratic elegance in both public and private settings.

Although Nubians were conspicuous in Egypt as doormen, waiters and servants in private homes, appearances were deceiving; by the mid-1960s there were proportionally as many Nubians working in the various occupational sectors of the economy as other Egyptians. Many Nubians had become educated in the cities of Egypt by accompanying their migrant fathers and attending school with the sons of their employers. Bilingualism became almost universal among Nubian men in this century.

Nubian women, many of whom remained in the traditional village, were slower to learn Arabic and thus preserved the Nubian languages (part of the eastern Sudanic group of the Nilo-Saharan family). Today in the new settlements, surrounded by Arabic speakers, with Arabic TV and radio and Arab social services, the use of Nubian is rapidly declining. At the same time, ethnic consciousness is greatly increasing among adult Nubians, and the preservation of Nubian traditions and languages has been an important factor in Nubian attempts to establish new communities along the shores of Lake Nasser, away from non-Nubian speakers. Nevertheless, the future of the unwritten languages is now in question.

In Old Nubia, the thin line of settlement which stretched nearly 500 miles along the Nile Valley above Egypt was divided into linguistically distinct and often unfriendly segments. Closest to Aswan lay the villages of the Kenuz, a population which took its name from Kanz al-Dawla, the chief of an Arab tribe, the Beni Kanz, in this region, and which intermarried with the Nubians in the thirteenth century. The language of the Kenuz is close to that of the Dongolawi villages several hundred miles to the south, and it seems reasonable to suppose that this group is descended from Dongolawi migrants who established a trade link between Dongola and Egypt, bypassing the intervening population through overland caravan routes on the desert.

The traditions of the Kenuz and their southern neighbors, the Egyptian Fedija and the Mahasi of the Sudan, suggest that hostile relations may once have prevailed between these groups. In addition to language, other cultural characteristics differentiate the groups. Before resettlement, the Kenuz villages were distinguished by barrel-vaulted mud-brick roofs which they built over their guest and bridal rooms, a feature not found in the southern part of Nubia, although historically these roofs were once part of Dongola architecture. The Kenuz also maintained active saint cults centered around the tombs of cenotaphs of holy men and Muslims of the past which drew the migrant villagers back to their communities for the annual feasts. These celebrations, or *mulids*, were sponsored by tribally organized people with extended kinship based on patrilineally reckoned lineages such as is characteristic of Arab groups. The tribal organizations were of great importance in helping organize the urban migration, providing jobs for kinsmen and help for newcomers to the cities—a far from antiquated service in modern times, and one which lessened the strains of this radical adaptation to local scarcity of resources. The organizations were also of great consequence during the difficult period of resettlement.

The Fedija-Mahasi people were less affected by the early dams constructed at Aswan, and they continued to cultivate substantial amounts of land near and beyond the Sudanese border until the actual resettlement began in the 1960s. The absence of saint cults in this area, in direct contrast to the Kenuz, and the noticeable difference in house styles and decor suggest a long period of relatively independent development for the two groups. Indeed, the Fedija reported that Kenuzi traders had become familiar in the area only in the 1940s and 1950s. The system of patrilineal descent and tribal organization was also much less pronounced in this area. Named kin groups—families, or *nogs*—were in fact bilateral descent groups in which both male and female ancestry were of consequence, particularly when the property and date palm ownership were part of the inheritance. One belonged to a descent group as long as one appeared, it was said, for divisions of the dates and for each other's weddings and funerals.

In addition, the remnants of the stratified social patterns which seemed to have prevailed here during the Christian period were to be found in the existence of the Kashafs. These people were descendants of Turkish rulers who were established during the Ottoman period, when southern Nubia was a frontier area and soldiers from throughout the Ottoman Empire were stationed in the garrisons of the region. Many of the soldiers married and remained in Nubia; resentment over the way in which this aristocracy expropriated lands and forced marriage to gain access to property still prevailed in the 1960s. However, little in the way of difference in standards of living could be seen which might distinguish these families from other Nubian groups.

The total conversion of Nubia to Islam, in the sixteenth and seventeenth centuries, was of overwhelming importance to the Nubians, ending forever the dangers of slavery from which the region had both profited and suffered in the past. Movements of Islamic conservatism were still evident throughout Nubia in the 1960s and continue to the present. These movements have ended many customs from the pre-Islamic period in villages. Even the songs and dances which were distinctive in style and form have come under attack from members of the Marghaniyya brotherhood, which is popular among many Nubian men.

By the 1960s the Nubian past could best be found in the stories and tales which Nubian women told their children of the spirits which were believed to inhabit the Nile and which formed a part of the supernatural world of Kenuzi men and women and in the frightening beings believed to inhabit the forbidding deserts and rocks behind the villages. Among some Nubians, these ancient beliefs coexisted with the experience of sophisticated city life as lived among the wealthiest Egyptians and foreigners. The two "styles" seemed to be well accommodated by the Nubians of this century in a pattern of life which granted full value to the advantages of both city and country while recognizing the dangers of too great dependence on either mode of existence.

Today, not only are New Nubia in Egypt and Khashm al-Ghurba in Sudan much closer to the urban centers where many Nubians live and work at least part of the time, but also foreign labor migration to the oil-rich countries of the Middle East has recently become of great economic importance. In New Nubia, there is much evidence of prosperity. New brick homes are found among the older government-built houses, most of which have been radically remodeled and decorated. TV antennas are a common sight. Many homes have electric refrigerators and other appliances. As experienced migrants, Nubians have modified old patterns of adjustment to new circumstances and have formed their own recruitment networks across national boundaries. Only inexperienced young men have trouble finding work and are of concern to the adults.

Intermarriage with other Muslims and permanent urban residence, which in the past resulted in the loss of Nubian connections for many thousands of persons, will undoubtedly continue at ever greater rates; the conditions of resettlement promote all forms of acculturation. However, in the 1980s Nubians are aware of a common identity surpassing tribal and village differences in a way which was not true 20 years ago. Pride in that identity and efforts to sustain it through establishing independent settlements, in the development of cultural and social centers exhibiting Nubian arts and crafts and by joining together in organizations to publicize Nubian causes and promote Nubian interests on both a local and national level are increasingly apparent. Ironic as it may seem, the loss of their homeland has done more to unify and increase self-consciousness among the Nubians than any other factors. Nubian ethnicity is becoming a social and political fact of increasing significance in Egypt and Sudan.

BIBLIOGRAPHY

Books

Adams, William Y. *Nubia, Corridor to Africa*. Princeton: Princeton University Press, 1977.

Burkhardt, John L. *Travels in Nubia*. London: John Murray, 1819.

Callender, Charles, and el Guindi, Fadwa. *Life Crisis Rituals Among the Kenuz*. Studies in Anthropology, No. 3. Cleveland: The Press of Case Western Reserve University, 1971.

Dafalla, Hassan. *The Nubian Exodus*. London: C. Hurst, 1975.

Fahim, Hussein M. *Dams, People and Development: The Aswan High Dam Case*. Elmsford, N.Y.: Pergamon, 1981.

————. *Nubian Resettlement in the Sudan*. Miami: Field Research Projects, 1972.

Fernea, Robert A. *Nubians in Egypt: Peaceful People*. Austin: University of Texas Press, 1973.

————, ed. *Contemporary Egyptian Nubia*. 2 vols. New Haven: Human Relations Area Files Press, 1966.

Hintz, Fritz, ed. *Africa in Antiquity: The Arts of Ancient Nubia and the Sudan, Meroitica 5*. Berlin: Akademie-Verlag, 1979.

Keating, Rex. *Nubian Rescue*. New York: Hawthorne Books, 1975.

Kennedy, John G. *Leadership and Change in a Nubian Village*. Palo Alto, Calif.: Mayfield, 1976.

————. *Nubian Ceremonial Life: Studies in Islamic Syncretism and Cultural Change*. Berkeley: University of California Press, 1979.

————. *Struggle for Change in a Nubian Community: An Individual in Society and History*. Palo Alto, Calif.: Mayfield, 1977.

McLaughlin, P.F.M. *Language-Switching as an Index of Socialization in the Republic of Sudan*. Berkeley: University of California Press, 1964.

Monneret de Villard, Ugo. *La Nubia Medioevale*. Vols. 1–2. Cairo: Institut Français d'Archéologie Orientale, 1935.

————. *La Nubia Medioevale*. Vols. 3–4. Cairo: Institut Française d'Archéologie Orientale, 1957.

Nadel, Harold D., et al. *Area Handbook for the Democratic Republic of Sudan*. The American University FAS, DA Pam 55-27. 2nd ed. Washington, D.C.: Government Printing Office, 1973.

Shinnie, P. L. "The Culture of Medieval Nubia and Its Impact on Africa." In *Sudan in Africa*, edited by Y. F. Hasan. Khartoum: Khartoum Sudan Research Unit, 1971.

————. *Meroe*. New York: Praeger, 1967.

Stevenson, R. C. "Some Aspects of the Spread of Islam in the Nubia Mountains." In *Islam in Tropical Africa*, edited by I. M. Lewis. London: Oxford University Press, 1966.

Trigger, Bruce. *History and Settlement in Lower Nubia*. Publications in Anthropology, No. 69. New Haven: Yale University Press, 1965.

Trimingham, J. Spencer. *The Influence of Islam Upon Africa*. New York: Praeger, 1968.

————. *Islam in the Sudan*. London: Frank Cass, 1965.

Wenzel, Marian. *House Decoration in Nubia*. London: Gerald Duckworth, 1972.

Articles

Adams, William Y. "J. L. Burckhardt, Ethnographer." *Ethnohistory* 20:3 (1973): 213–227.

Fahim, Hussein J. "Change in Religion in a Resettled Nubian Community, Upper Egypt." *International Journal of Middle East Studies* 4:2 (1973): 163–177.

Fernea, Robert A. "Nubian Migration: A Cultural Phenomenon." *VII Congrès international des sciences, anthropologiques et ethnologiques, Moscou* 9 (1970): 236–243.

————, and Kennedy, John G. "Initial Adaptations to Resettlement: A New Life for Egyptian Nubians." *Current Anthropology* 7 (1966): 349–354.

Geiser, Peter. "Some Differential Factors Affecting Population Movement: The Nubian Case." *Human Organization* 26:4 (1967): 164–177.

Kennedy, John G. "Aman Doger: Nubian Monster of the Nile." *Journal of American Folklore* 83:330 (1970): 438–445.

————. "Circumcision and Excision in Egyptian Nubia." *Man* 5:2 (1970): 175–191.

————. "Mushahra: A Nubian Concept of Supernatural Denger and Theory of Taboo." *American Anthropologist* 69:6 (1967): 685–702.

————. "Nubian *zar* Ceremonies as Psychotherapy." *Human Organization* 26:4 (1967): 185–194.

Kronenberg, A., and Kronenberg, W. "Parallel Cousin Marriage in Medieval and Modern Nubia." *Kush* 13 (1965): 241–260.

————. "Preliminary Report on Anthropological Fieldwork in Sudanese Nubia, 1961–1962." *Kush* 11 (1963): 302–311.

————. "Preliminary Report on Anthropological Fieldwork in Sudanese Nubia, 1962–1963." *Kush* 12 (1965): 282–290.

————. "Preliminary Report on the Anthropological Fieldwork in Sudanese Nubia, 1964." *Kush* 13 (1965) 205–212.

Lee, David R. "The Nubian House: Persistence of a Cultural Tradition." *Landscape* 18:1 (1969): 36–39.

Musad, Mustafa M. "The Downfall of the Christian Nubian Kingdoms." *Sudan Notes and Records* 40 (1959): 124–128.

———. "Islam in Medieval Nubia." *Nubie, Cahiers d'histoire egyptienne* (Cairo) 10 (1967): 165–176.

Rouchdy, Aleya. "Language in Contact—Arabic-Nubian." *Anthropological Linguistics* 22:8 (1980): 334–344.

Spaulding, J. "Kora—A Theme in Nubian Cultural History." *Africa Today* 28:2 (1981): 61–68.

                                                                    Robert A. Fernea

NUPE   The Nupe people live along the banks of the rivers Niger and Kaduna in west-central Nigeria between Lokoja at the rivers' confluence and New Busa near the new Kainji Dam. The reorganization of states dating from 1975 left the Nupe the majority in Niger State, although the capital was located in Minna, traditionally a Gbari area. The Nupe living on the south bank of the Niger River are presently in Kwara State.

The population of the Nupe is very tentatively estimated at half a million, a figure complicated by the confusion in previous ethnographies between those who speak Nupe as a first language and those who speak related but different languages yet find it convenient to speak Nupe as a lingua franca. Nupe is a Benue-Kwa language, related ultimately to Yoruba and Ibo but more closely to Ebira and Idoma, southwest of the main Nupe area.

When they enter the record of oral history, the Nupe seem to have been divided into a number of riverine kingdoms, drawing their wealth from trade in fish and transit goods passing up and down the Niger. Seventeenth-century Yoruba traditions mention them as already a political force. They must have been well organized when the *jihad* of Uthman dan Fodio began to impinge on their frontiers in the second decade of the nineteenth century. Some traditions make the conversion of the rulers of Nupe occur in the late eighteenth century, and certainly, previous to the military conquest by the Fulani, their involvement with the long-distance trade would have meant contact with Muslims (see Fulani).

The principal figure remembered in Nupe tradition as the purveyor of Islam is Mallam Dendo, an itinerant Fulani preacher and seller of charms who reached Nupeland around 1810. Mallam Dendo rapidly became a political figure of considerable importance and was intimately involved in the complex struggles that eventually wrested power from the Nupe rulers and placed it in the hands of the Fulani. A unified political capital was established for Nupe at Raba, and it was here that the first European travellers made contact with the Fulani rulers. Later in the century, the capital was moved to Bida, more central in Nupeland and, significantly, not on the river, reflecting a shift in economic base to grain growing and long-distance trade.

Islam was an essentially urban phenomenon among the Nupe, where it was the religion of the traders and ruling classes. As Hausa, not Nupe, was the language of these classes, Islam was strongly associated with "foreignness." Later in the century, as the Nupe element became stronger and the rulers began to identify themselves as Nupe, Islamic prayers and observances were translated into Nupe, and, indeed, Bida became a well-known locus of Islamic scholarship in the late nineteenth century. The Muslim legal system was Maliki.

Islam made little impression on the rural areas in this period for the simple reason that the urban Nupe/Fulani were raiding the countryside for slaves. Virtually all hinterland settlements were atop the inselbergs and mesa hill formations that abound in this area. Relations with the towns were hostile. Only with the suppression of slaving did Islam begin to penetrate the countryside, mostly through the agency of traders, but also through the conversion of villagers who had gone to cities to work. As a result, it was diffused principally along the roads, and today there is a strong correlation between the distribution of Muslims and the accessibility of the villages.

Another factor inhibiting the spread of Islam was Christianity. Mission stations were first established at Lokoja in the 1860s, and with the establishment of the authority of the Royal Niger Company at the end of the century they began to have a broader impact. The initial response to Christianity in Bida was entirely negative, but in the nearby villages it was widely adopted at a ceremonial level. Its expansion continues today. Part of the reason, undoubtedly, is the need for rural populations, who have defined themselves in opposition to the town for a century, also to define themselves ideologically. Christianity provides a coherent means of doing this.

A small Nupe village consists of a number of interlinked compounds, and these are structured so as to accommodate the extended family. All married men have their own rooms, and normally each of their wives also has a separate room. These rooms are single circular or rectangular chambers, built into or surrounded by an exterior wall. Traditionally, there was a single entrance to each compound through a large circular building, the *katamba*. The head of the household would meet and talk with his guests in this building, and only women were allowed to pass through to greet their relatives. When a son of the compound married, he might either reside patrilocally, if both farmland and housing were available, or else begin a new nuclear compound elsewhere. This neolocal tendency has become more common in recent years, both in the towns, where space is at a premium, and in rural areas, where access to fertile land is presently more important than defensive needs.

Children normally sleep in their mother's room until they are adolescents. Male children then sleep in the room of one of their male relatives, most commonly an older brother. Unmarried girls may sleep in the room of any female relative. Although there is ideally a premium on virginity among girls, it is not very strictly obeyed, and the custom of exhibiting the blood-stained underclothes of a newly married girl among urban Muslims was forbidden earlier in the century. Circumcision is practiced throughout Nupeland and is normally done at any age between seven days and three years without significant ceremony. This is probably a pre-Islamic practice.

Something less than 30 percent of the Nupe would even claim to be Muslims, and of these, perhaps only one-half could in any sense be said to practice their religion. Certainly the percentage is higher among Nupe of towns and cities and less than that among villagers. Where it does exist, it has features that reflect the compromise that had to be made between the purer, ascetic religion of the Fulani *mallamai* and the very different population on whom it was imposed. Perhaps its most significant aspect is the identification of the traditional deity, Soko, with the Allah of Islam, permitting ambiguity about the destination of prayers, libations and other utterances. Harvest offerings, charms to protect crops against theft and marriage songs all depend on the semantic fluidity of their terms to unite Islam, Christianity and traditional religion in their observance.

To this extent, Islam has responded to the demands of traditional society by providing alternative service to fill its needs. As divination, *eba*, is a crucial aspect of decision making in non-Islamic areas, so sand divining, *hati*, notionally Islamic but essentially magical, now competes with it in the towns. The charms sold by *mallamai* compete with the remedies proposed by the Nupe doctors. The traditional spirits of the bush have become the *alijenu* (*jinns*) that plague people.

Islam encompasses a nexus of cultural features, and in some ways these have made a broader impression on the whole of Nupe than the actual religion. The most important of these is probably the crystallization of political hierarchy. The Nupe traditionally had titles reflecting seniority, but with the Fulani these were massively expanded along the lines of other northern Nigerian emirates. The financial resources required for access to such titles permitted the formation of a more rigid class hierarchy than previously. Even so, rulers came to power by rotating succession, and there was thus considerably more flexibility than in Hausa areas. The position, therefore, became more a political post than in the earlier, smaller and more ritually constrained polities.

With this hierarchy went much of the material culture associated with Islam in the West African savanna. Traditional crafts were expanded, and new crafts were introduced to meet the need for social distinctions required by the new differences in wealth. The ranks of praise singers became more professionalized to meet the needs of clients who could afford to become permanent patrons. Hammered brass work, producing trays and vessels with Islamic motifs, became larger business while the keeping of the large Arab horses was the center of a supply industry, both for trappings and fodder. House building became more elaborate (the city wall of Bida is a typical product of this period). The coming of *mallamai* meant the institutions of Quranic schools, and this in turn implied a disruption of the work-training patterns of adolescent boys.

Similarly, many types of food and methods of food processing came to Nupe after the *jihad*. Among them were cakes known as *kara* (beancakes) and *bambara* (peanut cakes), citrus fruits, bananas and the custom of eating the green leaves of the baobab. The widespread Nupe prejudice against eating pork must date from this era as well. Certain crafts, such as the working of stained leather and making of wallets, bookbags and sandals, were introduced as well as the making of coil baskets from the leaves of the Borassus palm and furniture, beds and stools from dried raffia fibers.

These religious, political and material innovations have been absorbed by the Nupe and are, in fact, pictured by the Nupe as "traditional," and thus to be preserved. When the Nupe ruler (*etsu*) moves from place to place by Mercedes-Benz instead of on horseback, the Nupe see this as the destruction of an ancient tradition, when in fact the custom of the ruler riding on horseback is probably not more than 150 years old.

Islam is so strongly associated with urbanism among the Nupe that it is now difficult to disentangle the social aspects that were introduced at the time of the *jihad*. The Nupe have always been polygynous, and traditionally there was a strong correlation between status and the number of wives. This continues today, and the device of concubinage is used to circumvent the Islamic prohibition of more than four wives. A study in Bida showed 40 percent of compound heads were polygynous, while 59 percent of women lived in a polygynous family unit. Of compound heads of both sexes, 17 percent were unmarried, revealing an unusual feature of Nupe society, a tolerance of mature, unmarried female entrepreneurs. Some women traders have become wealthy enough to go on the Haj. This has been a source of controversy among more orthodox Muslims.

The life-crisis rituals typical of Nupe society have been adapted by Nupe Muslims to meet the requirements of Islam. When a child is born, it will undergo a *suna*, or naming ceremony, where prayers will be offered for its future health and success. Apart from the prayers, these are typically Nupe social occasions, turning on the redistribution of food and drink. The same is true of weddings and funerals, where Islamic prayers are made in addition to all the ceremonial characteristics of these occasions. A single innovation of Islam is the "charity" marriage, where a father gives away his daughter without demanding the customary bridewealth (1,000 *naira* at present). Traditionally, this is the act of a holy man towards a poor man. However, today it is frequently a device used by the wealthy polygynous household head to ally himself with a family of his choice. It is considered shameful to refuse a charity bride, although it is occasionally done, especially if an old aristocratic family suspects a newly wealthy family is using it as a device to upgrade its social status.

Bida and the other urban Nupe centers are still essentially ruled by the powerful Islamic elites that have controlled this area since the *jihad*. However, they have adopted an open door policy to immigrants from other parts of Nigeria, in contrast to the attitudes in cities farther north. According to one survey of Bida, more than 33 percent of the population came from elsewhere, mostly Yoruba from Oyo State. Nearly all of the immigrants are Christian, and this causes some rumbles of protest among the *mallamai*. But the Nupe allow them for they bring needed technical skills. The motorbike and car mechanics, the sellers and repairers of radios, the taxi drivers and sellers of Western clothing are all foreigners from other states.

Nupe compromise and adaptability may well explain why Bida and other Nupe towns have been free to date from the violent disturbances in other areas of northern Nigeria. The relatively weak observance of Islam among the Nupe has meant the Islamic sects have so far found little adherence. Similarly, because there is no active proselytism, the substantial Christian communities in some of the hinterland villages around Bida have not caused the friction that might be imagined from the experience of other areas. Both Islam and Christianity will continue to make progress over traditional religion in Nupe in the foreseeable future, but the increasing secularism of the Nigerian state as a whole makes it unlikely that there will be a regrowth of monolithic Islamic state institutions.

BIBLIOGRAPHY

Books

Hansford, K., et al. *An Index of Nigerian Languages.* Accra, Ghana: Summer Institute of Linguistics, 1976.
Nadel, S. F. *A Black Byzantium.* London: Oxford University Press, 1942.
———. *Nupe Religion.* London: Routledge and Kegan Paul, 1954.

Unpublished Manuscript

Blench, R. M. "The Ethnohistory of the Niger-Kaduna Peoples and Its Relation to Their Linguistic Subgroupings." Paper presented to the Colloquium on African Languages, Afrikaanse Taalkunde, Rijksunuversiteit te Leiden, September 7, 1982.

R. M. Blench

NURISTANIS   In the final decade of the nineteenth century a little-known people called the Kafirs became the last pawns in the "Great Game" between British and Russian imperialism in Afghanistan. The warlike Kafirs formed a hitherto impenetrable island of Aryan polytheism in the surrounding ocean of Islam. In the West their mysteriousness and steadfast resistance to Islam inspired Kiplingesque stories, and their geopolitical fate was chronicled in the headlines. Although the Kafirs lay in the westward path of the expanding British Raj, Britain conceded the Kafirs to the sphere of influence of the Amir of Afghanistan, whose kingdom formed a buffer between the converging British and Russian empires. In the winter of 1895–1896 the Amir's army subjugated the Kafirs, and his *mullahs* set about converting them to Islam. By 1898 all the Kafirs within the Amir's domain had embraced Sunni Islam. To commemorate their acceptance of the light of Islam, the Amir changed the name of their country from Kafiristan,

"Land of Infidels," to Nuristan, "Land of Light." Today the 60,000 to 100,000 descendants of the former Kafirs are known throughout the region as Nuristanis.

Nuristan lies on the southern watershed of the Hindu Kush range in northeastern Afghanistan. It comprises the area drained by three roughly parallel valley systems which arise at the crest of the Hindu Kush ridge and debouche southward into the Kunar and Kabul rivers. The easternmost valley system is drained by the Landay Sin, which joins the Kunar River near Barikot on the edge of Nuristan. The central drainage system flows into the Parun-Pech River, which turns east upon leaving Nuristan territory and skirts the southern flank of Nuristan before joining the Kunar at Chagha Saray. The Alishang River drains western Nuristan before passing through a defile into Laghman and thence to the Kabul River. Nuristan is bounded on the north by the crest of the Hindu Kush, on the east by the Afghan–Pakistan border, on the west by the watershed between the Alingar and Panjshir valleys and on the south by Laghman and the uplands of the Kunar and Pech valleys.

A temperate climate with abundant precipitation in the winter and spring provides Nuristan with sufficient water to support an irrigated agriculture and extensive arboriculture. The rugged terrain of the Hindu Kush limits the amount of arable land, but this deficiency is offset by an abundance of alpine pastureland that makes the region well suited for transhumant stockherding. Throughout Nuristan, subsistence rests on a mixed economy based on the production of cereal grains and dairy products.

Cultivated crops include maize, wheat, millet, barley, sorghum, beans, peas and squash. Tree crops are walnuts, mulberries, grapes, apricots, pomegranates, jujubes, figs, pears, persimmons and peaches. Dairy products include butter, ghee, buttermilk, buttermilk solids and various types of cheeses.

Nuristan is a linguistically and ethnically diverse region. Within Nuristan six mutually unintelligible and unwritten languages are spoken. Five of these languages constitute the Nuristani group of languages, which is a branch of the Indo-Iranian subfamily of Indo-European languages. The sixth language, Pashai, is spoken in westernmost Nuristan by groups of Pashai peoples who were converted to Islam with the rest of the Nuristanis and are a culturally distinct group living mostly outside Nuristan (see Pashai).

To outsiders Nuristani identify themselves simply as Nuristanis, but to each other they identify themselves by the name of their village or by a more encompassing ethnic name. Ethnic names usually indicate a village or a region from which a people traces its origin. On the basis of linguistic and cultural affinities the different Nuristani peoples fall into three groups. The first group consists of the diverse peoples inhabiting Nuristan's southern tier, all of whom call themselves Kalasha. They encompass three of the five Nuristani linguistic communities. Among them, the following ethnic divisions exist:

In southwestern Nuristan live the Ashkunu, Gramsana and Kalasha of the village of Sanu (Wama), who all speak dialects of a single language. The latter two peoples occupy small territories off the west bank of the Pech River in south-central Nuristan. The Ashkunu occupy the three valleys of Kolata, Titin and Badzaygal, which drain westward into the Alishang River.

To the east of these peoples live the Kalash of the Vaygal Valley, a major basin that drains southward into the Pech some 20 miles upriver from Chagha Saray. They speak an independent language that they call Kalasha-ala. A major dialect division of Kalasha-ala separates the Varjan ("Upper People"), who occupy the upper Vaygal basin and the Velagil and Tsuki valleys to the east, from the Chima-Nishey, who occupy the lower Vaygal basin. These two groups have separate historical origins, the Varjan coming from the east and the Chima-Nishey coming from Gramsana territory to the west.

East of the Vaygal Valley live the Tregami, who occupy three villages in the upper reaches of a small valley system that drains into the Pech about six miles upriver from Chagha Saray. They speak an independent language that is closely related to Kalasha-ala.

The second group includes the Kati, Mumo, Kshto and Kom peoples, each speaking dialects of a single language. The Kati are the most numerous Nuristani people. From their center in the Ktivi Valley in central Nuristan, they extend westward into numerous villages throughout the entire upper Landay Sin basin, overflowing into a few high valleys in Pakistan. The eastern Kati are separated from their western kinsmen by the intervening territory of the Vasi and Kalasha of Vaygal. The Mumo occupy two villages in a small territory to the south of the eastern Kati, in the central Landay Sin basin. The Kshto occupy two villages separated by Kom territory: one in the Nichingal Valley near its confluence with the Landay Sin and the other in the Dungal Valley on the Kunar side of the watershed. The remainder of the lower Landay Sin basin, along with some upland territory on both sides of the Kunar, belongs to the Kom.

The final group consists only of the Vasi, who occupy five villages in the Parun Valley. Their language is divided into dialects according to village. Culturally and linguistically the Vasi are the most distinctive of the Nuristani peoples.

Although the Nuristani peoples regard themselves to be as distinct from each other as they are from neighboring non-Nuristani peoples, comparative studies of their languages and cultures reveal a unity that transcends the cultural variation.

The Nuristani languages share a common phylogeny. Oral traditions of the Nuristani peoples indicate a long mutual interaction and a common belief that the Nuristanis formerly inhabited the lower Kunar basin, whence they were driven to their present location by the expansion of the Pushtun. Although historical details are lacking, the Nuristanis apparently have coexisted for millenia.

Before Islam, the Nuristanis shared a common Aryan religion. Their belief divided the world into pure and impure, corresponding to the division between divinities and mortals. The divinities determined one's destiny in accordance with the generosity with which one sacrificed to them and the purity with which one maintained himself and his dependents. The wills and wishes of the divinities were mediated to mortals by shamans. Sacrifices and purification rites were performed by hereditary specialists. The ideal of generosity in sacrifice was

symbolized in institutionalized feast-giving, through which the giver gained both
purity and formal social rank.

In contemporary Nuristan the basic sociopolitical unit is the village. Each
village is surrounded by agricultural land owned by the male heads of households,
and associated with each village are seasonally used alpine and lowland grazing
areas to which male residents have hereditary rights.

There are no formally constituted offices of political leadership in Nuristani
society. Within the village, leadership is dominated by men who have informally
distinguished themselves in fostering the cohesiveness of the community. Leaders
promote their views at open community conferences, which are convened whenever decisions affecting the entire community must be made. At such conferences
an adept leader may be delegated whatever authority he needs to resolve a
community crisis, as long as he has the consensus of the other political leaders.
When the crisis is resolved or his consensus wanes, he resumes his normal role
in the community.

Political leaders emerge primarily through their demonstrated ability to mediate
interpersonal conflicts that arise within the community. Nuristani society lacks
formal structures, such as courts, to resolve such conflicts, and the role of
mediator is crucial to the maintenance of social cohesion. In Nuristan conflicts
are always resolvable by appropriate compensation as determined through mediation. Blood money is required in disputes involving bloodshed. Such disputes
are considered particularly dangerous for the community, because until blood
payment is met, the aggrieved or his agnatic kinsmen may extract blood venge-
ance. The potential for unresolved disputes to escalate into bloodshed is the
major motivation for civic-minded men to step forward as mediators.

To enforce village laws enacted by the village leaders in community conferences, the men of the village annually choose a group of village policemen.
Such policemen are representatives of agnatic lineages or village divisions and
are primarily involved with regulating irrigation, harvesting and the transhumant
schedule. They are empowered to fine transgressors according to traditional rates.
Fines are usually split between the policemen and the village treasury, which is
maintained to subsidize expenses incurred in conducting external political affairs.

Kinship, especially agnatic kinship, is the basis for cooperation among Nuristanis. Agnates are obliged to support each other in time of crisis or need. One
also draws economic support from his mother's agnates. Nuristanis model ag-
nation by a tree metaphor in which agnatic lineages are the ''branches.'' Before
Islam, marriage to the daughter of an agnate was considered incestuous and a
cause for the ''branch to be split.'' Nowadays marriage between agnates is losing
its stigma because there is no such prohibition under Islamic law.

Because kinship is the fundamental interpersonal tie, Nuristanis who have
frequent dealings in other Nuristani villages will adopt men from such villages
as brothers. Along with intermarriages, such adoptive ties form the primary links
between the different Nuristani peoples.

Property and rights to grazing areas are inherited patrifilially, usually while the father is still alive. Traditionally only men could own property in Nuristan; under Islamic law women are entitled to a share of the patrimony, but in practice their share usually reverts to their brothers or close male agnates.

Nuristanis are divided into a land-owning upper caste and a lower caste of craftsmen, both endogamous. The lower caste were slaves until the advent of Islam, and they are still largely disenfranchised. Within the lower caste there is a further subdivision, the nature of which varies among the different Nuristani peoples. Lower-caste craftsmen produce the woodworking, blacksmithing, pottery, weaving and basketry used in daily Nuristani life.

Beyond occupation specialization by caste, the basic division of labor is by sex. Males and females are supposed to contribute equally to the production of the traditional Nuristani meal. The women provide bread, which entails responsibility for all agricultural production and the gathering of firewood. The men provide a dairy product, which entails the husbandry of goats and cattle.

Environment and the availability of territory determine some of the major differences between the Nuristani peoples. Irrigation and field-terracing techniques are somewhat more elaborate among the Kalasha peoples, who inhabit the lower and narrower valleys of the Hindu Kush, than among the remaining peoples, who inhabit the broader valleys of the higher elevations. The Vasi and most Kati live above the zone where two cereal crops will grow annually; these peoples rely on peas as a major supplement to their grain crops. Because of the elevation, these peoples also lack the abundant holly-oak stands that provide winter grazing for the goats of the lower inhabitants; the Vasi especially raise fodder grasses which they stall feed their livestock throughout the winter.

Among the most important cultural differences in Nuristan are variation in kinship organization. Kalasha and Kati recognize formalized groupings of close agnates that are lacking in the descent model of the Kom and Kshto. Corporate agnatic estates do not exist except among the Vasi, whose lineages each have a clan house in which resides the hereditary lineage leader; other Nuristani peoples do not recognize such hereditary roles. Although there is a common core of kinship terminology throughout Nuristan, wide variation is found in the designation of in-laws and aunts.

Other cultural differences that tend to coincide with the three major Nuristani ethnic divisions include variations in dress, house construction and music.

Since their incorporation into Afghanistan in 1896, the Nuristanis have regarded themselves as dominated by a corrupt and oppressive regime of their traditional enemies, the Pushtun. However, the Pushtun kings treated the Nuristanis nobly and provided the Nuristanis with opportunities for advancement in the military, exploiting their skill as mountain warriors. Several Nuristanis rose to the highest military ranks, and it was through these prominent Nuristanis that the otherwise isolated peoples of Nuristan felt any personal integration into the national community.

After the Communist coup of April 1978, many nationally prominent Nuristanis were liquidated in the ensuing purge. The Nuristanis saw no personal ties to a Communist Afghanistan, and fearing that the new regime would forcibly try to supplant Islam with Communist atheism, political leaders from throughout Nuristan convened and resolved to expel the Communist government from their region. In October 1978, the Nuristanis launched the attack that sparked the nationwide uprising against the Soviet-backed regime in Afghanistan.

BIBLIOGRAPHY

Books

Edelberg, Lennart, and Jones, Schuyler. *Nuristan*. Graz, Austria: Akademische Druck-u., 1979.
Robertson, George Scott. *The Kafirs of the Hindu-Kush*. London: Lawrence & Bullen, 1896.
Strand, Richard F. "The Evolution of Anti-Communist Resistance in Eastern Nuristan." In *Revolutions and Rebellions in Afghanistan, 1978–1982*, edited by Robert L. Canfield and M. Nazif Shahrani. In press.
———. "Principles of Kinship Organization Among the Kom Nuristani." In *Cultures of the Hindukush: Selected Papers from the Hindu-Kush Cultural Conference held at Moesgård, 1970*, edited by Karl Jettmar in collaboration with Lennart Edelberg. Wiesbaden, Germany: Franz Steiner, 1974.

Articles

Strand, Richard F. "The Changing Herding Economy of the Kom Nuristani." *Afghanistan Journal* 2:4 (1975): 123–134.
———. "Notes on the Nuristani and Dardic Languages." *Journal of the American Oriental Society* 93:3 (1973): 297–305.

Unpublished Manuscript

Katz, David J. "Kafir to Afghan: Religious Conversion, Political Incorporation and Ethnicity in the Waygal Valley, Nuristan." Ph.D. dissertation, University of California, Los Angeles, 1982.

Richard F. Strand

NYAMWEZI   The Nyamwezi are one of the major Bantu peoples of Tanzania who live south of Lake Victoria in the western and lake regions. Their population is about 3.7 million, of whom 478,000 (13 percent) are Muslim. Traditionally, but not entirely accurately, they have been divided into three cultural subgroups: the Nyamwezi "proper" (717,000, of whom 50 percent may be Muslim), Sukuma (2.7 million, with 4 percent Muslim) and Sumbwa (200,000, with 4 percent Muslim). In reality, these names reflect only the geographical locations of the Nyamwezi people.

The vast majority of the Nyamwezi (Banyamwezi, when using the Bantu prefix applied to ''people'') live by hoe agriculture (see Bantu-speaking Peoples). The Sukuma occupy an area of steppe country bordering Lake Victoria characterized by vast rolling plains with huge granite outcrops. Most of this area is cleared and occupied, and the population seems to have increased since World War I.

The major cash crop and one which is an important part of Tanzania's economy is cotton. The growing of cotton is subject to strict controls to prevent the spread of disease and pests. Its sale takes place through a system of producer cooperatives to which all cultivators must belong. In the southern and west areas (Nyamwezi and Sumbwa) much of the land is still quite heavily wooded by *miyombo* bush. The entire area has been subject to a series of ecological disasters since 1890, when a rinderpest pandemic killed 90 percent of the cattle. This was followed by a plague of jigger fleas and an epidemic of smallpox. The resultant drop in human and cattle populations allowed the bush to grow over previously cleared areas, which in turn allowed tsetse flies to breed. Tsetse flies carry trypanosomiasis, which has been a serious problem to both humans and bovines. There were severe outbreaks of sleeping sickness in the late 1920s, following heavy mortality from influenza epidemics in the years 1917–1920, which contributed to the low population growth in this area.

Tobacco has become another important cash crop in the southwestern wooded area, as has beeswax, yet another valuable product showing a high profit for a relatively small amount of labor, important in making high-grade polishes and lipsticks. The main food crops are maize, sorghum, millet and, to a lesser extent, rice, sweet potatoes, cassava and peanuts. There are many cattle in all areas and in Sukumaland in particular; overgrazing has become a problem. Cattle are important as a sign of wealth and in the payment of brideprice. In many cases, profits made from cotton have been invested in cattle.

In the nineteenth century, travellers reported that the Nyamwezi lived in large fortified villages, but with the coming of colonial rule these were abandoned. By the 1960s, most people lived in isolated homesteads based on some form of extended family. Since 1974 most of the rural peoples of Tanzania have been compelled to move into larger village groupings under an official policy of villagization. These groupings were originally called *ujamaa* villages. The word *ujamaa* means ''familyness'' and is used to translate the English term ''African socialism.'' However, there has been little popular enthusiasm for the idea so that although all rural Tanzanians are now required to live in ''registered villages,'' only about a dozen in the entire country are acknowledged to be of the *ujamaa* type. The rationale for the policy was to make adult education easier, to increase access to clean drinking water and other sanitation facilities and to improve communication and political control. Since most Tanzanians formerly lived in isolated homestead groupings, the new policy will probably have profound effects, especially when coupled with a policy of universal primary education which requires that all boys and girls, regardless of religious affiliation, receive at least six years of education in secular school.

House types of the Nyamwezi vary considerably. Some people continue to use the traditional circular house with a thatched roof; others build rectangular houses with mud and wattle or adobe bricks. The use of corrugated metal for roofs is increasing. At one time, kin and neighbors worked together in large groups to perform difficult tasks, and perhaps the village structure will encourage a return to this cooperation.

The Nyamwezi have probably occupied their present area for some 300 years, and there are traditions of origin from several geographical directions. There were many small chiefdoms, each with a ruling dynasty; many of these appear to have had a different ethnic origin from that of the people over whom they ruled, and in some cases, the chiefs observed matrilineal descent.

During the nineteenth century, when the caravan trade with the coast was at its height, estimates of as many as 1 to 2 million Nyamwezi men went to the coast annually as porters. It is significant that the Nyamwezi have a special joking relationship known as *utani* with peoples all the way across Tanzania. All Nyamwezi men and most women speak and understand the national language, Kiswahili, although their mother tongue is Kinyamwezi, a Central Bantu branch of the Niger-Congo language family.

Although the Nyamwezi practice patrilineal descent, clans and lineages are not at all important, except in chiefly lines. (The office of chief was legally abolished in Tanzania after independence.) Most unusual for this part of Africa is the custom that sons may move away from their father's homestead during the latter's lifetime, and it is quite common for close kin to live widely separated from each other. In consequence, there is considerable cooperation between affines and neighbors.

Marriage is of two kinds: with and without payment of bridewealth. In the former case, the husband obtains full rights over his wife and any children. Where no bridewealth is paid, the situation is similar to that in a matrilineal society in that the husband has no rights over the children. However, he can obtain such rights later by payments to his wife's people. Divorce is relatively common. Various forms of the levirate are possible but are not often practiced today. The Arab practice of preferred marriage to a parallel cousin (FaBrDa) would be regarded as incestuous.

Islam came into the area via the slave trade in the 1840s and was introduced by the Arab and Swahili caravan leaders, who set up an important center at what is today called Tabora (the Kazeh of Dr. David Livingstone). There was little attempt to proselytize, and it seems that most people became Muslim converts in imitation of particular chiefs, particularly in the Tabora area, or through contacts with this town and on expeditions to the coast.

The slow process continues to the present, and it has been noted that men who move to the major cities readily adopt Islam as a religion rather than

Christianity, probably because Christianity forbids polygyny. And since in Islam there are no clergy comparable to those of the Christian churches, there is no curb on the beer drinking that is so much a part of the traditional and modern culture of the Nyamwezi.

Most non-immigrant Muslims of the area (as elsewhere in East Africa) are Sunni of the Shafi school. In the major cities of Tabora and Mwanza, there are many Asians who are Shia Ismaili or Shia Ithna Ashari. Their numbers have decreased considerably in the past few years; many have migrated to Britain and Canada (see Asians of East Africa). There has been some activity in Tabora by the Ahmadiya sect. This may have been influenced in the early days of independence by the example of the regional commissioner, the late Shaikh Amri Abedi, who was a prominent Ahmadi. He was famous as a Swahili poet and for his concern with the translation of the Quran into Swahili.

Observance of the requirements of Islam is minimal. Only a small minority in the cities carry out daily prayer. Most people observe Ramadan, although not too strictly, and no more than a handful have made the Haj. There are no Islamic saints comparable to those in West Africa. Most Muslims continue to engage in rites directed towards ancestral spirits and in a large number of secret societies for both sexes, with functions ranging from snake charming to spirit possession.

The Nyamwezi people, particularly the Sukuma group, have undergone a series of vicissitudes in this century. Their agricultural and herding practices, which long dismayed Western agricultural and animal husbandry experts, have now been shown to be an entirely rational response to tsetse and tick-born diseases, even though the result has been serious soil erosion. The compulsory concentration into village communities may have as yet unforeseen results, one of which could well be a large-scale conversion to Islam and the development of fundamentalism as a response to economic deprivation, deteriorating natural resources and political discontent.

BIBLIOGRAPHY

Books

Abrahams, R. G. "Kahama Township, Western Province, Tanganyika." In *Social Change in Modern Africa*, edited by A. W. Southall. London: Oxford University Press, 1961.

————. *The Political Organization of Unyamwezi*. Cambridge: Cambridge University Press, 1968.

————. *The Nyamwezi Today*. New York: Cambridge University Press, 1981.

Cory, Hans. *Political System of the Sukuma*. Nairobi: Eagle Press, 1954.

————. *Sukuma Law and Custom*. 1953. Reprint ed. Westport, Conn.: Negro University Press, 1970.

Finucane, J. R. *Rural Development and Bureaucracy in Tanzania: The Case of Mwanza Region*. Uppsala: Scandanavian Institute of African Studies, 1974.

Ingham, K. A. *History of East Africa*. London: Longmans, 1962.

Kimambo, I. N., and Temu, A. J. *A History of Tanzania*. Nairobi: East African Publishing House, 1969.

Liebenow, J. G. "The Sukuma: A Tanganyika Federation." In *East African Chiefs*, edited by A. Richards. London: Oxford University Press, 1960.

Omari, C. K. *The Strategy for Rural Development*. Kampala: East African Literature Bureau, 1976.

Trimingham, J. Spencer. *Islam in East Africa*. Oxford: Clarendon Press, 1964.

Articles

Abrahams, R. G. "Neighborhood Organization: A Major Sub-system Among the Northern Nyamwezi." *Africa* 35:2 (1965): 168–186.

———. "Time and Village Structure in Northern Unyamwezi." *Africa* 47:4 (1977): 372–385.

Birley, M. H. "Resource Management in Sukumaland Tanzania." *Africa* 52:2 (1982): 1–30.

Moreau, H. E. "Joking Relationships in Tanganyika." *Africa* 14:7 (1944): 386–400.

Waziri, Juma. "The Sukuma Societies for Young Men and Women." *Tanganyika Notes and Records* 54 (1960): 27–29.

Unpublished Manuscript

Welch, E. A. "Life and Literature of the Sukuma in Tanzania, East Africa." Ph.D. dissertation, Howard University, 1974.

James L. Brain

NYANKOLE The Nyankole belong to the western Interlacustrine Bantu of Uganda that include also the Nyoro and Toro tribes. They all developed similar political cultures of kingship and centralized government and also share a common tradition about a group of alien gods who brought statecraft and cattle to the area. Historians question the tradition but agree that the states in this region were established about five centuries ago by pastoral people who founded their dynasties and dominated the agricultural inhabitants.

Ankole, the homeland of the Nyankole, was one of several ancient kingdoms that were abolished in 1967 and today forms a district in southwest Uganda. It borders the Kangera River on the south, Lake Edward and Lake George on the west, the former kingdom of Toro on the north and the western plateau of Buganda on the east. The area has considerable topographical variety, the eastern part consisting of green hills about 4,000 feet in elevation and several small lakes, among them Mburu and Nakivaly. To the west the elevation rises to 7,000 feet and then abruptly goes down to the western rift and the shores of lakes

Edward and George. The annual rainfall in the western part reaches 55 inches but in the east does not exceed 35 inches.

The population of Ankole District today is about 1 million, 8 percent of the total population of Uganda (13.7 million). Of this 1 million, perhaps 20,000 are Muslim. The Nyankole are divided into two distinct groups, the majority, about 90 percent, consisting of the sedentary Iru population in the west. Their subsistence crops include plantain and millet. The other group is the pastoral Hima, who subsist on milk. Both Irun and Hima are divided into numerous clans which are totemic and exogamous. Among the main cash crops are cotton, coffee and tea. The pastoral Hima export cattle, the major resource of the district, and also hides and skins.

The Hima are considered to have arrived here in one of the Hamitic invasions from the north. They established the kingdom of Ankole and ruled as an aristocratic class of herdsmen. The subservient Iru, Bantu peasantry, were free to cultivate their land provided they carried out the menial tasks expected of them by their Hima overlords. Hima domination was based on their military prowess. They were mobile and experienced in raiding and had better knowledge of the countryside. The Hima also had better collective organization in the cattle kraal than the family homestead of the Iru. The class distinction between Hima and Iru was social and legal and was maintained by strict prohibition of intermarriage.

During the colonial period the authority of the Mugabe was supreme, and people believed that he had magical and religious powers, although he was also bound by traditional customs. He nominated his chiefs mainly from the Hima clans, essentially from royal Hinda. The royal clan was not endogamous, and Hima ''commoners'' could marry into it to achieve high positions. The Iru also had some important positions in the kingdom as artisans and manufacturers of weapons. They were also magicians and diviners.

In the Nyankole religion, the cult of Bagyendnawa, the royal drum, is still active. The drum became a common focus of belief and ritual for all people, Hima and Iru alike, and thus it was a unifying factor which strengthened the political dominance of the Hima. The drum's shrine is in the Royal Enclosure near the town of Mbarara, and it is considered to be the guardian of the Ankole prosperity. It has the power of performing good or evil, and therefore the people offer it cattle, milk or beer to satisfy it and also to make it strong.

In 1901, the British and Ankole signed an agreement which consolidated the kingdom as autonomous within the Ugandan protectorate. British rule brought about great changes in traditional relations between the Hima and the Iru, which were previously based on serfdom and dominance. Legal and formal inequality was abolished, and intermarriage between the two groups became acceptable. The British also maintained greater number of Iru chiefs than before, which sometimes caused tension. The Mugabe was actually deprived of much of his political and magical powers. Nevertheless, the Hima, who generally adopted the Protestant religion, kept a larger proportion of the higher grades in the government service than the mostly Catholic Iru. This situation changed only after Uganda achieved its independence.

Islam was first brought to Ankole in the late 1880s by Arab and Swahili traders coming from the coast of East Africa. They entered the region via the caravan routes across Tanganyika and along the western shores of Lake Victoria. The Muslim traders' main interest was Buganda, but some of them went north and reached Ankole. Here they sold their merchandise, consisting of cloth, beads, guns, gunpowder and magical fetishes and bought mainly ivory. Although some of those traders stayed in Ankole for long periods, they did not leave any significant Islamic impression. Usually they lived alone and did not mix with the local population. Unlike Mutesa I of Buganda, the Mugabe of Ankole did not show any interest in the traders' religion (see Ganda).

As happened with other Interlacustrine Bantu, the main Islamic influence came from Buganda and by Ganda *shaikhs* and *walimu* (teachers). The first Ganda Muslims arrived as refugees during the religious wars of the 1880s and 1890s in Buganda, after being defeated by the Christians. Among those Ganda Muslims was Shaikh Kauzi, who reached Bukanga in Ankole during this period and established the first Muslim community there. Other Ganda refugees who befriended the Mugabe were given posts of chiefs and subchiefs, and in their position they could convert some of their servants and other dependents. After the British incorporated Ankole into the protectorate of Uganda, they used to send Ganda administrators to act as chiefs and help in the organization of the new district. Among these were some Ganda Muslims like Abdul Affendi, who arrived in 1900 and later became the chief of the Bukanga area. Another was Abdul Aziz Bulwada, who arrived in Ankole in 1905 as interpreter to the British officials and then was made chief of Mitoma. He became known for his efforts to eliminate witchcraft and other traditional beliefs among the local Muslims.

The expansion of Islam in Ankole was rather slow in comparison to Buganda or Busoga (see Soga). Today only about 2 percent of the population of the district are Muslims, and this percentage has not changed since the beginning of the present century. The actual number of the Muslims increased only in proportion to the general increase of the population. On the other hand, the percentage of Christians has grown gradually, and today they constitute 55 percent of the population. The rest observe the traditional religion. The number of Asians who profess Islam and other Asian faiths is insignificant.

The difficulties which Islam encounters in Ankole stem from various causes. The Nyankole have traditionally abhorred circumcision, a rite obligatory among most Muslims. While in Buganda and Busogo some of the converts became leaders of the Muslim community, no prominent member of the Nyankole royal clan has been converted. Muslims are opposed to the use of alcohol, while for the Nyankole, drinking beer is important in their social life. For a long time nearly all Muslim leaders in Ankole were foreigners from Buganda. They spoke Luganda and continued to keep their Kiganda customs and ways of life in their dress, homes, food and behavior. The Nyakole converts tried to imitate them, and Islam became associated with foreigners. To become a Muslim, so it seemed, was to adopt Ganda manners and language and follow their social and cultural life. This was not popular with the king and chiefs and Nyankole, who generally were at odds with rival Buganda. On the other hand, the Christian missionaries who arrived in Ankole at the turn of the century succeeded in converting the king, his household and most of the chiefs; many Nyankole adopted the new religion of their leaders. Besides, Christian missionaries, with their financial resources, built schools and hospitals all over the district and attracted people to their religion. The Muslims in Ankole lacked these facilities during most of the colonial rule.

Since the 1950s, some improvements have been carried out in Muslim education. Assistance has come from the East Africa Muslim Welfare Society, established by the Ismailis in 1945. The society started to give the Muslims of Ankole financial help, which enabled them to pay salaries to their teachers and *shaikhs*, who up to that time were dependent on the good will of Muslims and other voluntary contributions. The first Muslim secondary school was built in Kabwoke in 1950. More and more *walimu* and *shaikhs* were local Nyankole people who could teach in the indigenous tribal language.

During the regime of President Idi Amin (1971–1979) the Muslims of Ankole, as in other areas, enjoyed a privileged position, but Christianity remained the dominant religion in the district. It was Nyankole Christians who could organize the biggest and the most efficient Uganda military force, which joined the Tanzanians in the war which put an end to the Amin regime.

The Nyankole Muslims are mostly Sunnis of the Shafi school. The head of the community is the chief *shaikh*, whose main tasks are the ordaining of new *shaikhs* and supervising all Muslim affairs in the district. He keeps contact with the main Muslim center in Kampala. To be nominated a *shaikh* one must have some years of experience as a *walima* (teacher) and pass an examination in the theory and practice of Islam. In recent years, a few *shaikhs* have graduated from Al Azhar University of Cairo.

Because of the scarcity of *shaikhs* in Ankole, Islamic daily functions are organized mainly by the *walima*. He is expected to know Arabic, to recite the Quran, to lead the prayers on Fridays and to organize such ceremonies as births, marriages and funerals. He also supervises the meat sold in markets to ensure that it is *halal* (ritually slaughtered).

Conversion to Islam is usually conducted by the *shaikhs*, who instruct the new converts and ensure that they are circumcised. As in other areas in Uganda, conversion to Islam takes place, in many instances, during the Maulud festival (the birthday of Prophet Muhammad) which is among the most popular Islamic festivals.

The Sunni Muslims in Ankole, like their co-religionists in Buganda, are divided into Juma and Juma-Zukuli factions pertaining to Friday prayers (see

Ganda). These factions differ on such questions of how to decide the beginning of the Ramadan fast, whether by Western calendar or by moon phases.

Nyankole are divided into clans, and each clan has its own totem. Children belong to their father's clan. Clans are exogamous, and men are not allowed to marry women of their own clan. Family life is patriarchal.

The main communities of the Nyankole Muslims are in the counties of Isingiro, Igara, Sheema and Kazara and the town of Mbarara. Pastoral Nyankole live in cattle kraal, and their houses usually consist of grass huts built within the circle of the kraal. The chief occupation of the men is animal husbandry; the women cook their milk dishes and prepare the butter. Many live in trading centers, where they work as shopkeepers, butchers, bus conductors and taxi drivers. Muslims are also found in villages along the main roads selling their fruits and vegetables to travellers. Some are engaged in cattle trade with Buganda and other regions. Despite their small numbers, the Nyankole Muslims have achieved a marked success in their varied commercial ventures, both in the rural and urban areas.

BIBLIOGRAPHY

Books

Karugire, S. *History of the Kingdom of Nkore in Western Uganda to 1896*. Oxford: Clarendon Press, 1971.
King, N.; Kasozi, A.; and Oded, A. *Islam and the Confluence of Religions in Uganda, 1840–1966*. Tallahassee, Fla.: American Academy of Religion, 1973.
Morris, H. F. *A History of Ankole*. Kampala: East African Literature Bureau, 1962.
The Republic of Uganda. *Report on the 1969 Population Census*. Vol. 1. Entebbe: The Government Printer, 1971.
Roscoe, J. *The Banyankole*. Cambridge: Cambridge University Press, 1923.
———. *The Northern Bantu*. New York: Barnes & Noble, 1966.
Stenning, D. J. "The Nyankole." In *East African Chiefs*, edited by A. Richards. London: Faber and Faber, 1959.
Trimingham, J. Spencer. *Islam in East Africa*. Oxford: Clarendon Press, 1964.

Article

Bamunoba, Jr. "Islam in Ankole." *Dini na Mila* (Kampala) (1965): 5–17.
Mushanga, M. T. "The Clan System Among the Banyankole." *Uganda Journal* 34:1 (1970): 29–33.

Arye Oded

O

OGAN-BESEMAH   The term "Ogan-Besemah" designates an ethnic and linguistic family of peoples living in the province of South Sumatra, Indonesia. The Ogan-Besemah area covers most of the province, from the outskirts of Palembang in the east to the mountainous border with Bengkulu in the west. Members of the several societies comprising this family consider themselves more akin to each other than to other peoples inhabiting the province—the Komering to the south, Malay speakers to the east and Rejang to the north.

The Ogan-Besemah family is sometimes spoken of by residents of the area as simply the "Ogan" or "Dempo" people, but more often it is broken down into two subfamilies. The Besemah subfamily or grouping (often written "Pasemah") is centered in the western highlands regencies of Lahat and Muara Enim and includes the further ethnic and dialectical subdivisions of Lematang, Kikim, Besemah proper and Lingtang. The four of these together are often mentioned by Sumatrans with the acronym LEKIPALI. The Semende (or Semendo) people speak a distinct language within this grouping. It is estimated that within this grouping approximately 395,000 people speak Besemah languages.

The Ogan grouping lies immediately to the east of the Besemah area and includes the sub-divisions of Enim, Musi, Rawas and Ogan proper, situated in the regencies of Muara Enim, Oku, Oki, Muba and Mura. There are approximately 680,000 speakers of Ogan languages. Ogan-Besemah languages are mutually intelligible, but each is recognized by speakers as a separate language. The languages were once written in a local, Sanskrit-derived script (generally called the Ka-Ga-Nga script), but its use is dying out, and only Latin and Arabic scripts are taught in schools.

Although Palembang is represented in Malay myths as the site of the early kingdom of Srivijaya and the origin place of the Malay sultans, the interior Ogan-Besemah area was relatively independent of Palembang rulers. Dutch rule shakily commenced in 1816, but was long limited to the capital. In different areas of Ogan-Besemah, local leaders organized active resistance from the 1840s on, and formal annexation of Besemah into the Palembang residence was not until 1866.

Present provincial divisions place the area in South Sumatra, and western Besemah people play a particularly dominant role in provincial politics.

Social structure within Ogan-Besemah is best characterized by the variation from one society to the next in the emphasis or weighting given to each of several key social relations. Two types of marriage exist everywhere in the area. In one type (generally called *belaki*), payment of bridewealth before marriage establishes the couple's residence in the boy's household, and all children from the marriage remain affiliated to that household. In the second type (generally called *ambiq anaq*) the boy moves into the girl's household with no major payments; children are classified as part of the girl's descent line.

Because of differences in descent ideology, these two marriage alternatives are given varying valuations across the area. In the west (Lahat) the norm is the virilocal *belaki* marriage; the eldest son is required to take a wife into the patriline through an uxorilocal *ambiq anaq* marriage. In Enim society to the east both marriage types are correct, without clear normative preference. In all cases inheritance is within the lineage.

Throughout most of the area the *marga*, or subdistrict, has traditionally been the primary sociopolitical unit, ruled by an elected *pasirah*. Land rights were the prerogative of the *marga*, and the *pasirah* had judicial as well as customary (*adat*) authority. During the past decade the village (*dusun*) has gradually delegated some of these *marga* prerogatives in accordance with the nationwide reorganization of administration. *Dusun* each consist of 300 to 400 households, a small number by Indonesian standards. Houses are generally single-family dwellings of three or four rooms raised on stilts, with the lower part of the house used for storage or, in some cases, trade.

In some districts the village is structured by a descent category or lineage (often called *jurai*), which may rest on either patrilineal or matrilineal principles. In these cases village heads are often chosen from a line of traditional (*adat*) leaders and village affairs run by the descendants of elder lines. In other districts the focus of village unity is the grave and myths connected with a founding figure (not necessarily an ancestory), whose characteristics and occupations often lend a specific tone to present-day village life. In Oku, for example, woodworking is associated with a particular *dusun*, goldworking with another, and each village possesses stories of its founding and conversion to Islam that set it apart from every other village in the district.

Children are cared for by both parents and are viewed in terms of the reproduction of the household unit. Sons or daughters remaining in the household immediately after marriage thereby take on responsibility for caring for younger dependents, preserving family land or other wealth and contributing to ritual feasts. Conversely, children who marry out of the lineage break these ties of household responsibility.

Agriculture is the principal economic activity in the area and is based on three key crops: rice, rubber and coffee. Rice is grown only for producer consumption and nowhere produces yields consistently over 1.5 tons per acre. Much of the rice area is either in swamp (*lebak*) or in highland areas, where it competes with coffee for farmers' time and capital. Intensification of rice production has thus been relatively unattractive to local farmers.

Wet rice plots are worked by hoeing or plowing with oxen or water buffalo. Planting is carried out by groups of five to ten people working either for wages or as part of a rotating work group. Harvesting is done by mixed-sex work groups or by the farming family.

Rubber became an important cash crop early in this century, but in recent years declining international demand and the relatively poor quality of local rubber have led to rapidly falling prices (a 40 percent fall over 1981). Rubber is becoming a stop-gap occupation; when nothing else works, one can always tap the family trees. Rubber tapping is, however, a low-status occupation.

Coffee seedlings have long been planted as part of a swidden cycle, but the 1,000 percent increase in local Robusta prices in the late 1970s sent farmers to the hills to burn, clear and plant new coffee gardens. Both yields and quality of the coffee (Arabice and Robusta) are somewhat below those of other areas in Indonesia, however, and the recent (1981) drop in coffee prices has hurt these farmers more than most.

Ogan-Besemah peoples, particularly the Besemah group, have played a dominant role in South Sumatran politics, alternating with the Komering for control of the governor's office and consequent patronage posts. They occupy a full range of jobs both in South Sumatra and in Jakarta.

Nearly all Ogan-Besemah people are Muslims. Islam spread earliest into the eastern Ogan regions, beginning perhaps in the sixteenth century, but the western Besemah districts were converted mainly in the second third of the nineteenth century. Megalithic shrines on the Besemah plateau are still objects of vows and ritual feasts.

Much of the later conversion to Islam was the work of the Naqshbandiyya *tarekat* (in Arabic, *tariqa*), a Sufi order that has spread throughout Sumatra from centers in Medan and southern Aceh. In the 1950s leaders of the order formed a *tarekat*-based political party with South Sumatra as a major center; this group has since continued as a nonpolitical association.

Village *tarekat* practices have three major components. First, a chain of transmission of knowledge is cited as the guarantee for the order's authenticity. This chain, which runs from the angel Gabriel down to the current local head of the order, is recited out loud at all prayer sessions. Second, the name of God (Allah) is recited over and over by a *tarekat* devotee as a way to gnosis. Third, the past sins of the practitioners are redeemed by a variety of rituals, most commonly the repeating of the first part of the confession of faith ("*la ilaha illa' Llah*") 70,000 times. Such sessions are regularly held in many villages in the area.

Mosques serve as the formal religious center in each village, and most men attend Friday prayer at least some of the time. While the sermon itself is often read in a formal Indonesian incomprehensible to many worshippers, the prayer is an occasion for the transaction of official village affairs as well as an act of obedience to God.

The key intersection of social life and religious ritual is at the *sedekah*, the meal and prayer session held to celebrate a birth, commemorate a death, ward off danger or give thanks for a crop. At every *sedekah* there is a two-way transmission of spiritual goods between men and God. The assembled community recites prayers that are offered to the spirits of the dead ancestors, who in turn pass on the merit (*pahala*) of the prayers to God. The return is a blessing by God for the subject of the ritual: a newborn child, a crop or the spirit of the recently deceased.

In its village forms, both the doctrine and the organization of religious life are oriented towards the otherworldly rather than towards social or political action. No concrete blueprint for social reform emerges from the combination of *tarekat*, worship and *sedakah* that shapes traditional village religious life. Although reformist teachers have challenged this view and Muhammadiya schools have been established in some areas, neither the Muhammadiya organization nor the Nahdlatul Ulama have won substantial followings. Rather, villagers see their social identity and uniqueness as mediated by intervillage ties to the major Sumatran religious schools (*pesantren*), by links through kinship and marriage to other districts and by a common sense of shame (*maluan*) and the preservation of custom (*adat*).

BIBLIOGRAPHY

Books

Jaspan, M. A. "Rejang Complex." In *Insular Southeast Asia: Ethnographic Studies, Section 1, Sumatra*, compiled by Frank M. LeBar. New Haven: Human Relations Area Files, 1975.
Marsden, William. *The History of Sumatra*. 1783. Reprint ed. Kuala Lumpur: Oxford University Press, 1966.

Unpublished Manuscript

Collins, William. "Besemah Concepts: A Study of the Culture of a People of South Sumatra." Ph.D. dissertation, University of California, Berkeley, 1979.

John Bowen

ORISSANS   The Muslims of the Indian state of Orissa call themselves Mahomedan or Muslim. Non-Muslims call them Musalman or Pathan. They number perhaps 400,000, only 1.5 percent of the state's population of 26.8 million, based upon 1971 figures.

Orissan Muslims were converted from among the local population during the days of Moghul rule in India, beginning in the sixteenth century. As Moghul power was primarily along the coast (an area called Moghul Bandi) most Muslims are concentrated in the districts of Balasore, Cuttack and Puri. Nearly all speak Urdu as their mother tongue, although many speak Oriyan as a second language, especially if they attend regional secular schools instead of Muslim *madrasas*.

As throughout India, Orissan Muslims are divided into numerous social categories based upon descent, religious affiliation and occupation, these categories being so relatively rigid that they have the characteristics of ethnic groups. They are largely endogamous and exclusive. In the hierarchy, the Sayyids, self-claimed descendants of the Prophet Muhammad, rank highest, although there is controversy as to who is and is not a true descendant. Shaikhs rank second. They are leaders of the communities, presiding over meetings and trying certain personal law cases. Many hold religious positions.

Third in ranking are the Mirzas, descendants of revenue collectors during the Moghul regime. Most landlords and wealthy aristocrats come from this group. Other groups include Moghuls and Pathans, descendants of the old court and its functionaries. There is also a group called Khan, who are supposed to be the warriors and the best among the local soldiery. Low-status groups based upon occupation are the Kunjraa, traders in such foods as dried fish and vegetables, and the Kansei, the butchers. Throughout these groups there is increasing intermarriage because of the economic advancement of the relatively lower groups.

The overwhelming majority of Orissan Muslims are Sunni, divided between those of the Hanafi or Barelvi school of law, and the Wahhabi, or Deoband school. Some Shia are found in Cuttack, and they are divided among the Khoja, Dawoodi and Bohra groups. There are a number of Ahmadiyas.

Most Muslims in Orissa are farmers, yet Muslims have a higher percentage of urban dwellers than Hindus, roughly 30 percent to 10 percent. In towns and cities, they work in petty trades, construction and small industry, such as *bidi* making, a *bidi* being an Indian variant of a leaf-wrapped cigarette. Some Muslims have become teachers, lawyers, doctors and engineers.

Within the Muslim social structure, the *zamindar*, or landlord, sits at the top. He is followed in prestige by the *hajji*, who has made the pilgrimage to Mecca, then the *haafiz*, a person who can read and recite the Quran fluently, followed by the *maulvi*, the most learned of Muslim clerics. Below him rank the local secular leader, the *sardar*, who runs the *panchayat* or local council, and his *bhalabhaai*, who arranges meetings and collects fees. Then comes the local *mullah*, who is the working cleric, the *muezzin*, who calls the faithful to prayer at the mosque, and finally the *chhatiaa*, the local messenger.

The lineage of a Muslim family is known as *khandan*. The father's paternal grandfather is usually the first ancestor of the patrilineage, and boys are especially desired and pampered. Birth of children is an occasion for merriment. Both child and mother are given the first bath on the third day; the second bath is on the twenty-first day. On the fortieth day the third bath removes the birth pollution from the mother, the child and the woman who assisted in the birth. If breastfeeding is not possible for the mother, a neighbor or relative will act as wet nurse. A child may not marry anyone who has been wet-nursed by the same woman. A child usually breast-feeds up to two and a half years, or until the next child is born.

The first shaving of the child's head is done before its first birthday. The *mullah* or other qualified religious specialist reads the Quran while the barber paints the head with sandalwood paste. A castrated he-goat is slaughtered with the first stroke delivered by the *mullah*. The barber weighs the hair that is removed and receives money from the child's father equal to the weight of the hair. The barber also receives betel, betelnut and rice.

Male children are circumcised (*sunat*) between the ages of four and ten. The circumcisor, known as *khalifaa*, operates with an aseptic bamboo sliver. This is a festive occasion: the child is attired in new clothes and taken in a procession in which all relatives take part, including the women. Usually circumcision is combined with the marriage of a close relative.

Cousin marriage is common. A boy may marry his father's brother's daughter or mother's brother's daughter, provided the bride is younger in age than the bridegroom. A boy may not marry his father's sister or a girl her father's sister's husband (polygyny is allowed, but not common) or mother's brother. A boy may not marry a sister of his maternal aunt until the aunt is dead or divorced.

Betrothal, which usually takes place only a week before marriage, involves a ceremony called *zabaab* and takes place between the families of the bride and bridegroom in the presence of local notables. As among the Hindus, the bridegroom's party approaches the bride's party bringing such presents as *bhakur* (fresh-water fish), curds or yogurt, *bundi laddu* sweets and garlands of flowers as well as the bridal dress and marriage ring. The bride is annointed with turmeric paste and her hands bound by the *lagna-ganthi* or nuptial knot, consisting of *durvaa* grass, sun-dried rice and betelnut cracker. Each of the items used is ritually essential and has many symbolic meanings. At this meeting the amount of *mahr*, or the money to be compensated to the bride in case of divorce, is negotiated. The bride announces the amount of *mehr* at the wedding ceremony.

Following the *zabaab* ceremony at the home of the future bride, the two families, friends and officials proceed to the bridegroom's residence, where the ceremony is repeated with the bridegroom wearing the gown, nuptial knot and other ritual elements.

The groom is called *dullah* or *nausa*, and the bride is called *dulhan* or *bitia*. One day prior to the wedding, another ritual takes place, the *mehendi*. The bridegroom dresses in the new pajama-like shirt or *kurta* or, if he is well-to-do, a *sherwani* and *pugri* with red shoes provided by the bride's maternal uncle. The bride dresses in a red sari and avoids all black pigmentation (black being inauspicious in the regional ritual idiom). She wears flowers in her hairbraid, a transparent cover for her head and face and nuptial ornaments of silver or gold.

On the day of the wedding, the bridegroom arrives at his bride's house in a ceremonial procession called *baraat*. The procession includes family, relatives, friends and, above all, the headman of the ward in which the groom lives, the *sardar*. The bride's party, composed of similar individuals, welcomes the bridegroom with entertainment, sweets, betelnut and garlands of flowers.

In Orissa, the *nikah*, or wedding ceremony, takes place preferably before 11 A.M. (it is inauspicious to begin later as ceremonies around 12 noon are connected with burials.) The most crucial element is the mutual consent to the marriage by the bride and groom, such consent being given in the presence of the government-licensed *mullah* and community leaders. The bride must have at least two witnesses to her marriage. After the *mullah* asks her consent and she gives it, he recites the prescribed Quranic text and writes and records her consent, which she signs by signature or thumbprint if she is illiterate. The ceremony is then repeated with the groom. Thereafter, all members of the wedding party are treated to sweets, betel and floral garlands. The ceremony is over, the couple is now married before Allah and the Muslim public, and a sumptuous feast begins. Throughout, members of the families have ritual roles to play. In the Bhadrak region of Balasore District, even certain Hindu castes such as gardeners, oilmen and barbers have ritually important roles in Muslim marriages.

In Orissan Muslim practice, wives do not have a right to divorce their husbands. But as the marriage is considered a sacrament and a legal contract, the divorced wife may go to court to obtain her *mahr* and obtain maintenance for any children.

Upon death, the deceased's body is ritually washed in rose water or with soap and anointed with sandalwood paste in case of the well-to-do. It is dressed in a white gown-like cloth (not sewn) and carried in a wooden coffin to the mosque or an open field, where the *janaajaa* (last prayer) is recited by the *mullah*. The procession then goes to the burial ground in great ceremony; for example, it is auspicious to carry the coffin. At the cemetery, the deceased's eldest son (or brother's son or father if there is no son) digs the grave. While the *mullah* chants texts from the Quran, the body is put into the grave on its back with its head to the south. The *mullah*, then the others, throw clods of earth into the grave, and the ceremony is over. After three or four days, the grave is plastered over with mud. At home and at the mosque, *kulfaatiaa*, or prayer to go in the name of the deceased, is held for three days. The Quran is recited for 40 days, and on the fortieth day the soul is given a formal farewell in the *ruhbidaayee* ceremony, with relatives and friends invited to a feast, a practice notable among the Barelvi group. The destitute are also fed at this feast as an act of piety. Among the Deoband group of Muslims, the farewell to the soul ceremony is not observed.

As in many societies, a wide range of kin relationships is observed by members of the Muslim community. Joking relationships exist between the husband and his wife's younger siblings, grandparents and grandchildren. A respectful relationship exists between husband and wife's elder brother, the person most responsible for his sister's well-being. Orissan Muslims do not practice avoidance, as do Hindus.

As among Hindus, Orissan Muslims maintain ritual friendships. Flower friendship among girls is common: they call each other by flower names and treat each other like close relatives. If both are Muslim, they try to create marital ties between their families. Among boys, the relationships, called *dost* or *sangaat*, may be equally close and binding. Ritual friendships exist between Muslims and Hindus, who call each other god-brothers or god-sisters, god-fathers or god-mothers and invariably invite each other to important festivals and family rituals.

Many Orissan Muslims participate in Hindu festivals such as Raja Parab. In the Badrakh region of Balasore District, more Muslims than Hindus visit the Makar Jaatraa ritual affair. Conversely, Hindus frequently are invited to the major Muslim festivals of Bakr Id, Id al Adha and Sirate un Nabi (birthday of the Prophet.)

Muslim fundamentalism is nurtured by leaders of the Barelvi and Deoband schools and through such youth organizations as Tabliq Jamaat or Jamaat Islami. Sufism is strong, the great Sufi, Maulvi Habibur Rahman, having been an acknowledged national leader of the Barelvi group. Some holy shrines such as that of Kadam Rasul, which includes a holy footprint of the Prophet Muhammad, are venerated by Muslims and Hindus alike in Orissa.

It appears that Muslims of Orissa are more fervent in the practice of their religion than are Hindus. Yet they reflect the local culture in their belief, shared with Hindus, in magic and the occult. There is a strong belief in ghosts, who possess the power to do evil and whose presence must be exorcized. The devil, or Saitaan, interferes with the good and auspicious and misguides people.

For all Muslims, however, the highest ideals are those of Islam. The good Muslim is one who does not drink alcohol, eat pork or commit adultery or incest. He does not charge interest, gamble or accept dowry. Nor does he swear. He has his male children circumcised and married properly. He prays five times a day. Like people everywhere, Orissan Muslims violate the Shariah and seek forgiveness in prayer. The values of honor, piety and refraining from offensive behavior are common to all Muslims in Orissa.

(The author gratefully acknowledges information provided by Mohammed Farooq, M.A., Senior Secretary, OXFAM, Bhubaneswar, on the cultural practices of the Barelvi group.)

L. K. Mahapatra

OROMO   The Oromo occupy a substantial part of the land from northeastern Ethiopia to east central Kenya, and between the borders of Sudan and Somalia. They share a common language and a growing common identity.

The Oromo, commonly called the Galla, enter historical records in the middle of the sixteenth century, when they expanded to the north and northeast from an original homeland in what is today southern Ethiopia. For some reason, perhaps related to the wars and weakness of the Abyssinian/Ethiopian states at that time, Oromo began a series of raids which carried them, within a few decades, well into northern Ethiopia. During succeeding centuries they came to occupy much of the best land of highland Ethiopia, while other Oromo groups spread across the more barren lowland areas of southern Ethiopia and northern Kenya. When they began their great movements in the sixteenth century, they were apparently primarily pastoral and egalitarian and practiced their own religion. Over the past four centuries they have become remarkably diversified in social and political structure, economy and religion, although certain common underlying patterns are discernible among many of the Oromo groups.

It is often said that the Oromo represent 40 percent or more of Ethiopia's population, but because there has never been a census in Ethiopia there is no reasonable way to estimate their number. Guesses range from a cautious low of 7 million to the claim of 19 million by the Oromo Liberation Front. In any case, they comprise either the overwhelming majority or a very substantial portion of the population in 9 of 14 provinces: Wellega, Ilubabor, Kafa, Shoa, Arusi, Harar, Bale, Sidamo, Wollo. In addition, about 80,000 Oromo represent a major part of the inhabitants of the vast but thinly populated north central and northeastern districts of Kenya.

It would be misleading to suggest that there are fixed and definite Oromo "tribal" groupings. Subgroup names abound and may refer to various social realities. There are, however, some major Oromo group or territorial names that are often encountered and reflect some sense of identity and perhaps mark a distinctive way of life. In the southernmost Oromo areas there are the Boran (Borana), the Gabra or Garre (east of Lake Turkana/Rudolph) and the Orma (near the Tana River in southeastern Kenya), all of whom are egalitarian pastoralists. To the north of Borana are the Guji, who live to the east of Lake Abaya (Margherita) in southern Ethiopia, while to their north are the Arssi (Arusi) and various Oromo groups in Bale Province. Many of the Arssi and Bale Oromo are Muslim. There are Oromo groups around Harar such as Ittu, Anniya, and the so-called Afran Qallo, four groups known as the Obora, Nole, Babile and Alla. The Oromo around Harar are mostly Muslim and practice sedentary mixed agriculture. The Guji and Arssi combine cattle raising with varying degrees of cultivation.

The northernmost Oromo groups are the Wollo, the Yejju and the Raya (Azebo), who live in Wollo and southern Tigre provinces. They, too, are mostly Muslim. The other major groups are the Tulama of Shoa Province, the Mech'a of western Shoa and northern Kafa, and the Wellega Oromo of Wellega and Ilubabor. All of these are mixed agriculturalists, and the Mech'a of Kafa Province are Muslim. Perhaps 55 percent of the Oromo are Sunni Muslim with Shafi and, to a lesser degree, Hanafi the leading juridical rites. Sufi brotherhoods are active, the most common apparently being the Tijaniyya and Qadiriyya.

The preferred designation for this people today is Oromo, although most members of some groups are not accustomed to this usage and refer to themselves by the names of major constituent groups, such as Arssi, Guji and Boran. The name "Galla," which was so widely used in Ethiopia and in the literature, is an outsider's term, not a self-designation, and is considered to be derogatory by educated Oromo. It is ironic that Muslims formerly rejected the term "Oromo" because to them it connotes "pagan."

The Oromo language (*afan Oromo*, called Gallinya by the Amhara) belongs to the Eastern Cushitic branch of the Afro-Asiatic language family. Although there are dialect differences from region to region, the language is basically mutually intelligible from one end of Oromoland to the other. Linguistic evidence suggests that the Oromo had long resided in southern Ethiopia before their sixteenth-century expansion, and no other place of origin is indicated for them.

As the Oromo conquered new territories, their lives were modified. They moved into new environments and encountered new neighbors, political forces and religions. In the far north, the Wollo, Raya and Yejju became a prominent force in the politics of the Abyssinian state and played vital roles in the competition for power in the eighteenth and nineteenth centuries. It is said that today members of these groups are more likely to speak Amharic and Tigrinya than the Oromo language. Their leaders converted to Islam in the nineteenth century, and the people followed.

In Wellega and in the Gibe River region of southwest Ethiopia, the Oromo developed six kingdoms of their own. The rulers of the new state in Wellega, formed about 1850, became Ethiopian Christians, while the kings of the five Gibe states, Jimma, Limmu, Gera, Guma and Gomma, all converted to Islam in the first half of the eighteenth century. Islam was brought to this region primarily by merchants from northern Ethiopia. (All of these states were incorporated into the expanding Ethiopian empire by the 1890s.)

Most of the other Oromo groups, whether pastoral or sedentary agriculturalists, retain important elements of the original Oromo sociopolitical system and religion, subject, however, to many modifications and to control by the Ethiopian state. In the Harar area, however, the Oromo were heavily affected by the Muslim city-state of Harar and by the Egyptian occupation of that area in the period 1875–1885 (see Harari). The Oromo became Muslim at that time, either as a result of forced conversion or by choice. To the west and south of Harar, many Arsi and Bale Oromo also converted to Islam.

A central institution for the Oromo historically, and for many still today, is the *gada* system. There are many variations and manifestations of *gada*, but in essence its two major elements are generation sets of 40 years' duration and assemblies, with elected leaders, that organize and lead certain aspects of Oromo life. In *gada* theory each male enters the system exactly 40 years after his father. For each set there are five named periods, each eight years in duration, and the individual passes through these once he has entered the system. In theory each of these five periods also represents an age grade, with associated functions in war, law, leadership and ritual, but in practice the connection with instrumental organization and practical politics is complex and varies greatly from one place and time to another. What does seem to be the case is that, wherever the system has not been superseded by other political forces, the Oromo make use of the principles of assembly and elected leadership of assembly chairmen and organizers, councillors and judges, war leaders, ritual leaders and other functionaries. On the other hand, the ritual, ceremonials and symbolism of *gada* continue to be important to certain groups even where the political and instrumental significance has become accentuated or is lost entirely, as long as the religion has not been entirely replaced by Islam. For the Boran and the Guji, in particular, *gada* symbolism and ceremonials remain central to the society, marking the unity and the identity of groups. Currently, *gada* is enthusiastically supported, if not revived, by the newly developing political movement of the Oromo.

The original religion of the Oromo stressed a Creator God associated with the sky and recognized the existence of numerous spirits associated with various locations such as mountain tops, great trees and groves, river fords and wells. Apparently it has not been difficult to reconcile these beliefs with Islam. Today, however, Islam is also competing with the spread of new forms of spirit possession and spirit mediumship throughout Ethiopia and northeast Africa.

Islam spread fastest in the nineteenth century as a result of the conversion of rulers and their courts, whose people subsequently followed them. Then, and now, it also spread as individuals responded to the influence or missionary efforts of other Muslims, especially traders. Conversion is particularly marked among those Oromo who desire to join the community of merchants, since Muslims tend to dominate trade in many areas of Ethiopia.

Adherence to Islam and knowledge of the religion vary considerably from place to place. Unfortunately there is little ethnographic information available for the Muslim Oromo. In Jimma, where a state with a Muslim administration retained its internal autonomy until the 1930s, there were *qadis* and other learned men, and Muslim law and principles were applied in certain spheres of life. The kings had mosques built, at least one to each of the 60 administrative districts, and offered *waqf* land near the mosques to families whose men would agree to attend Friday prayers. Even in Jimma, however, observance of prayers is mostly for a relatively few older men, and knowledge of the religion is quite limited. While Ramadan fasting is observed by many, celebration of the other Muslim festivals is limited to self-selected men who gather to read and drum and chant verses from the Quran. There are Quranic schools in the countryside and Muslim practitioners of varying degrees of orthodoxy, including some who write inscriptions for amulets. In Jimma, Islamic usages influence the observances of the life cycle, from circumcision through marriage, death and burial and inheritance rules. There is also a general sense of identification with the world of Islam and community of believers.

Muslim Oromo from all over Ethiopia make pilgrimages to the tomb of Shaikh Husain in Harar Province, near the Webi Shebelli River. The saint's tomb consists of a complex of buildings and shrines, and it has long been a major Muslim shrine and pilgrimage center, especially for Oromo. Pilgrimage was also a feature of the Oromo religion itself, and there are still many who travel to sites south of Shaikh Husain to visit the center of the Abba Muda, or K'allu of the Boran and Guji.

Although there are so many different Oromo groups today, there are a few Oromo values and styles of social behavior which are common to all. Oromo values emphasize the importance of sociability and social solidarity, whether of communities, districts, voluntary associations, *gada* units or kin groups. This solidarity is manifest in an emphasis on the maintenance of peace and of reconciliation among members of the group. Peace among the members may be essential for ritual and religious as well as secular reasons.

Within such groups there is also a tendency to hold to a theory of the equality of all male members. Even though they live near, and often under the control of, the Amhara, who emphasize hierarchy and inequality, the Oromo value of equality continues to be important. This is not an ethic of political and economic levelling; various Oromo groups recognize and respect differences in wealth and power, the presence of war leaders, land and cattle owners, powerful religious leaders and even kings. Rather, it is an ideology which holds that any man's (i.e. male) voice may be heard in council and no man need bow and scrape before another. This principle is frequently upheld through the rotation of office, election for limited terms and drawing of lots in many social contexts. Neighborliness and friendship may be at least as important as kinship; cooperative groups, voluntary associations for mutual aid and sociability are common features in Oromo areas.

Oromo reckon descent patrilineally and speak in terms of named patrilineal descent groups whose actual social importance varies considerably from place to place. They also are noted for a distinct bias towards the male side and masculinity in attitude, ritual and symbolism. Virility and male attributes are evaluated positively, to the disadvantage of the female side and femininity. They stress bravery and warrior ethos. The martial arts of riding, spear throwing and fighting are emphasized, and men who have killed dangerous animals or human enemies are honored and have the right to sing and boast of their exploits. Whereas peace within the in-group is demanded, warfare against enemies is, or was, highly honored. War between opposing Oromo groups was common.

Since their expansion, dispersion and differentiation in the sixteenth century, the Oromo have never been united as a single people. The many local groups have had different ecologies, economies, religions, social organizations, political systems, involvements and interests. The degree of interaction with the Ethiopian state has varied, too. The northerners of Shoa, Wallo and Tigre provinces were deeply involved in Ethiopian state politics, as were the rulers and notables of Wellega. Many of the other groups, including the Muslims of Harar, Arussi, Bale and the Gibe states, were either antagonistic to the Christian rulers or, in the case of the Borana, were far enough from the center to escape very much involvement at all. Despite the weight of their numbers and strategic location, their disunity and lack of common interest and identity resulted in their being, for the most part, under the control of a culturally alien political elite and state.

In the late 1970s, after the fall of the Ethiopian monarchy and the entry of revolutionary programs and ideas to Ethiopian, the potential for concerted Oromo "nationalist" action greatly increased. As disenchantment with the new regime grew, some educated Oromo defected from the government, some left the country and an Oromo Liberation Front developed abroad. There had been an insurgent movement in Bale Province since the 1960s which included many Oromo. How far these "liberation movements" will progress cannot be predicted, but it is clear that the Oromo have the potential to become a major factor in the politics of Ethiopia and northeast Africa.

BIBLIOGRAPHY

Books

Baxter, P.T.W. "Acceptance and Rejection of Islam Among Boran of the Northern Frontier District of Kenya." In *Islam in Tropical Africa*, edited by I. M. Lewis. London: Oxford University Press, 1966.
———. "Boran Age-Sets and Generation-Sets: *Gada*, a Puzzle or a Maze?" In *Age, Generation and Time*, edited by P.T.W. Baxter and U. Almagor. London: Hurst, 1978.
———. "Repetition in Certain Boran Ceremonies." In *African Systems of Thought*, edited by M. Fortes and G. Dieterlen. London: Oxford University Press, 1965.
———. "Some Consequences of Sedentarization for Social Relationships." In *Pastoralism in Tropical Africa*, edited by T. Monod. London: Oxford University Press, 1975.
Blackhurst, H. "Continuity and Change in the Shoa Galla *Gada* System." In *Age, Generation and Time*, edited by P.T.W. Baxter and U. Almagor. London: Hurst, 1978.
Hinnant, John. "The Guju: *Gada* as a Ritual System." In *Age, Generation and Time*, edited by P.T.W. Baxter and U. Almagor. London: Hurst, 1978.
Huntingford, G.W.B. *The Galla of Ethiopia*. London: International African Institute, 1955.
Knutsson, K. E. *Authority and Change*. Göteborg, Sweden: Etnografiska Museet, 1967.
———. "Dichotomization and Integration." In *Ethnic Groups and Boundaries*, edited by F. Barth. Boston: Little, Brown, 1969.
Legesse, Asmarom. *Gada: Three Approaches to the Study of an Africa Society*. New York: Free Press, 1973.
Lewis, H. S. *A Galla Monarch: Jimma Abba Jifar, Ethiopia, 1830–1932*. Madison: University of Wisconsin Press, 1965.
———. "Wealth, Influence and Prestige Among the Shoa Galla." In *Social Stratification in Africa*, edited by A. Tuden and L. Plotnicov. New York: Free Press, 1970.
Torry, W. "Gabra Age Organization and Ecology." In *Age, Generation and Time*, edited by P.T.W. Baxter and U. Almagor. London: Hurst, 1978.
Trimingham, J. S. *Islam in Ethiopia*. London: Oxford University Press, 1952.

Articles

Abir, M. "The Emergence and Consolidation of the Monarchies of Enarea and Jimma in the First Half of the Nineteenth Century." *Journal of Africa History* 6:2 (1965): 205–219.

Hultin, J. "Social Structure, Ideology and Expansion: The Case of the Oromo in Ethiopia."
    Ethos 40 (1975): 273–284.
Knutsson, K. E. "Social Structure of the Mecca Galla." *Ethnology* 2:4 (1963): 506–
    511.
Lewis, H. S. "Neighbors, Friends and Kinsmen: Principles of Social Organization Among
    the Cushitic-speaking Peoples of Ethiopia." *Ethnology* 13:2 (1974): 145–157.
———. "The Origins of the Galla and Somali." *Journal of African History* 9:1 (1966):
    27–46.
———. "A Reconsideration of the Socio-Political System of the Western Galla." *Journal
    of Semitic Studies* 9:1 (1964): 139–143.

Unpublished Manuscripts

Baxter, P.T.W. "The Social Organization of the Galla of Northern Kenya." D.Phil.
    thesis, Oxford University, 1954.
Brooke, C. H. "A Study of Galla Settlements: Hararge Province, Ethiopia." Ph.D.
    dissertation, University of Nebraska, 1957.
Hassan, Muhammad. "The Relation Between Harar and the Surrounding Oromo Between
    1800–1887." B.A. thesis, Haile Sellasie I University, 1973.

Herbert S. Lewis

OSSETIANS   While Muslims are a minority among the Ossetians, a rural
people living in the Caucasus Mountains, they are the second largest group of
Indo-Iranian-speaking Muslims in the Soviet Union (after the Tajik). Ossetians
call themselves Iron and their land Iristan. One tribal division lives in the Digor
River valley, and its members call themselves Digiron. It is the Digiron who
comprise the Muslims among the Ossetians (Ossessians, Ossetes, Ossets).

The Iranic language, Ossetian, has two dialects, Iron (eastern) and Digor
(western), which is more archaic. Iron is the basis for Ossetian literature. There
are many influences and derivations from other Caucasian, Turkic and Russian
languages. Ossetian is written in the Cyrillic alphabet.

Most Ossetians live in the mountainous North Ossetian Autonomous Soviet
Socialist Republic, an area of peaks and valleys suitable primarily for stock-
breeding—cattle, sheep and goats. At least seven mountains in the area exceed
the two-mile mark. Aerial photographs reveal a maze of valleys and precipices
which provide the rich background for the events in Ossetian legends.

Another smaller group of Ossetians lives on the forested plains of the South
Ossetian Autonomous Oblast' in the Georgian Soviet Socialist Republic. These
Ossetians are traditional farmers, living on collective farms raising crops and
livestock.

In both northern and southern areas, Ossetians are known for their stone and
wood carving and metal craftsmanship as well as gold and silver embroidering.
A considerable number of Ossetians work in mining and steel industries.

There are approximately 583,000 Ossetians, of whom an estimated 40 percent, or 233,000, are Muslim. The rest are Christian. In the north, where three-fourths of the Ossetians live, there is little reported animosity between the two groups. One reason for this may be the relative isolation of the Muslim Digiron in the mountainous northwestern Ossetia, limiting to a degree the amount of contact between this minority and the overwhelming number of Ossetian Christians. In Georgia, which is almost totally Christian, Muslims are traditionally looked down upon.

Thought to be descendants of the ancient Scythians, Sarmatians and Alans, the Ossetians consider the *Narts*, epic legends said to have parallels with Icelandic and Scandanavian sagas, to be the earliest items in their folklore.

Unlike most Muslims of the Caucasus, Ossetians do not have large families— the average number appears to be about four or five members despite the fact that polygyny, while illegal, is widespread among both Muslims and Christians. Traditionally, Ossetian men have had concubines (*nomylus*, "wife in name"), whose children were once considered illegitimate; Soviet law now legitimizes such offspring.

One explanation for smaller families is the increasing independence of women under Soviet laws of equality. Widows and divorcees tend today to preserve their own homes rather than return to the homes of their parents or brother, as was customary in the past.

Larger families often consist of the husband's kin, rarely his wife's. Financial control is held by the husband or his mother. Property is shared by all members of the family. Family ties are strong, esteem for older members is high and affection for children is profound. Control of family life is exerted by the extended family, neighbors and co-workers whose opinions are respected.

Ossetians follow certain formal relationships among family members. Wives are expected to serve their husbands at the table and help him dress and wash; she is not allowed to precede him to bed. Children are not supposed to initiate conversation with their father and never stand or dance in his presence. Spouses are not often seen together in public, nor do they show affection towards each other or their children in the presence of non-family. The wife refrains from communicating with her older in-laws for several years after marriage and even then does not pronounce their names or eat at the same table. The husband avoids his in-laws, especially his mother-in-law, until he is granted special permission. The extent to which these restrictions are observed vary from family to family, but polls as recent as the 1970s show more than 50 percent favoring and actually practicing them, particularly in rural areas.

Marriage rites also contain numerous restrictions. The groom conceals himself from his bride's parents, and, to a lesser degree, the bride from the groom's. A more archaic practice requires the almost total absence of the newlyweds from the marriage ceremony. The marriage itself is preceded by an exchange of visits by the two families involved. Brideprice is paid in two steps: first payment is made to the parents of the bride, second payment to the bride herself. This custom persists at all levels of Ossetian society even if in a simplified manner, such as the transfer of several months' salary to the bride's family. Sometimes cash payments are replaced by costly but practical gifts such as furniture, television sets and cars.

In recent years changes have occurred in the customs of the Ossetians. For instance, there has been a noticeable drop in the marrying age of young men (at least for their first marriage) and a rise in the marrying age of girls. Endogamous class divisions are giving way to intermarriage between different social and occupational groups. Studies show that less than half of both the white collar and unskilled workers are married to members of their occupational group.

Marriages arranged by parents are decreasing also. Most young people select their mates, but with the approval of their parents. Pre-marital courtship, totally unthinkable and alien to both Muslim and Christian traditions, is now acceptable, and pre-marital sex is not unknown; abortions are rare. Interethnic marriages are also accepted, even in rural areas, although the percentage of such marriages is low.

Funeral and burial rites include pre-Islamic elements and are attended by entire villages. Muslims have at least seven wakes in the year following burial, a custom which draws heavily on the wealth of the family survivors.

BIBLIOGRAPHY

Books

Abaev, V. I. *A Grammatical Sketch of Ossetian.* Translated by Steven P. Hill. Bloomington: Indiana University Press, 1964.
Birney, Charles, and Lang, D. M. *The People of the Hills.* London: Weidenfeld and Nicolson, 1971.
Pereira, Michael. *Across the Caucasus.* London: Geoffrey Bles, 1973.
Wixman, Ronald. *Language Aspects of Ethnic Patterns and Processes in the North Caucasus.* Department of Geography Research Paper, No. 191. Chicago: University of Chicago, 1980.

Articles

Bennigsen, Alexandre. "The Problem of Bilingualism and Assimilation in the North Caucasus." *Caucasian Review* 15:3 (1967): 205–211.
Trilati, T. "Literature on Ossetia and the Ossetians." *Caucasian Review* 6 (1958): 107–126.

Sergei A. Shuiskii

P

PALAWANON   The island of Palawan hosts five groups of Muslim Filipinos, including scattered communities of Tausug, Jamá Mapun and Pangutaran Sama. The two other groups are the Molbog and the Palawanon. Nearly all are found in the five southern municipalities of Palawanon Province: Aborlon, Balabac, Batarasa, Brooke' Point and Quezon.

The Palawanon, who number around 70,000, of whom approximately 10 percent are Muslim, live in the mountainous, forested interior regions of southern Palawan. A few live along the west and east coasts of southern Palawan and also in the midst of Muslim groups on Balabac-Bugsuk islands. Islamization has occurred among these coastal Palawanon only in recent generations and is continuing, a function of increasing interaction with other Muslims. Palawanon in the interior are primarily traditional in religion.

The Palawanon, unlike many other groups, but like the Muslim Yakan, live in houses out of sight of each other, distributed among their plots of farm land. Probably for this reason they are called Ira-an, or "people in scattered places." They are primarily subsistence farmers cultivating upland rice.

BIBLIOGRAPHY

Book

LeBar, Frank M. *Ethnic Groups of Insular Southeast Asia. Vol. 2, Philippines and Formosa.* New Haven: Human Relations Area Files, 1975.

Articles

Abbahil, Abdulsiddick. "The Molbog and Palawanon." *Dansalan Junior College Staff Gazette* 29 (1980): 3.
———. "The Yakan and Kolibugan." *Dansalan Junior College Gazette* 18 (1979): 1.

Gowing, Peter G. "The Growing List of Filipino Muslims Groups." *Dansalan Research Center Reports* 2 (1975): 5–6.

                                                                    Peter G. Gowing

PASHAI   Although Afghanistan is no longer quite the "ethnic mystery" some have called it, there are still segments of its population for which there is little reliable information. Of these, the people who speak what linguists call Pashai particularly stand out. No mention is made of the Pashai speakers in many general works on Afghanistan, and one will look in vain for some indication they exist on most maps which purport to show the distribution of ethnic groups—this despite the fact that the Pashai number close to 100,000.

Pashai is generally classed by linguists as a Dardic language, a term used to categorize a number of archaic Indic hill languages not all of which are closely related. Although the viability of Dardic as a linguistic category is somewhat questionable, it is widely used by scholars working in the area (see Shina-speaking Peoples).

While Dardic languages are spoken in a wide area ranging from Afghanistan to Ladakh, Pashai is spoken only in Afghanistan, north of the Kabul River, in a territory extending some 95 miles from Gulbahar on the Panjshir River in the northwest to the vicinity of Chaga Serai in the east. With few exceptions, the Pashai inhabit the side valleys of major river valley systems and in many instances are found only in the highest parts of these.

"Pashai" is used in native terminology for the language spoken in the western section of the Pashai area. In other places it is called by different names. For example, in the villages of Oygal and Mangu, located respectively in the Darra-i-Nur and the Alingar valleys, it is called Sare, while in Korungul, the easternmost village of Pashai speakers, it is called Korashi.

Pashai has linguistic borders with several languages. There are Farsi speakers to the northwest; Pashto to the southwest, south and northeast; and the Nuristani languages of Ashkun and Kati in the north (see Nuristanis; Pushtun). In addition there are intrusions of other Dardic and Indic languages; in the northwest near Bulbahar, Parachi, an Indo-Iranian language, is spoken, while in the southwest in the upper Mazar Valley a Dardic language called Shumashti is found.

Not surprisingly, there is evidence that these bordering languages have influenced Pashai. This undoubtedly reflects intense social interaction between speakers of these languages that has probably been going on for some time.

There are conflicting positions among specialists regarding the history of the Pashai. Karl Jettmar and Georg Morgenstierne, scholars whose work on the languages and cultures of the area is well known, argue that the progenitors of the present-day Pashai were expelled from their original homes in the lowlands of classic Gandhara culture by the invasion of Pashto-speaking Afghans from the Suleiman Mountains; they found refuge in the high mountain valleys of the Hindu Kush, where their descendants live today. These descendants, the contemporary Pashai mountain people, are thus seen as relics of a once higher civilization.

Although historical records indicate that the population of the Pashai area converted to Islam fairly recently, Morgenstierne feels that this is no way means that the Pashai religion of the immediate pre-Islamic period was similar to that found among the pagans of what is now Nuristan. This latter religious system was comprised of symbols, rituals and beliefs strikingly similar to those found in ancient Indo-Iranian religions. According to Morgenstierne, the paganism of the Pashai was rather a debased form of Hindu-Buddhism.

In contrast, there are those who argue that the Pashai are probably not the descendants of lowland refugees but are more likely a population that has inhabited their high mountain valleys from a time before the rise of Gandharan civilization. This argument is based mainly on evidence gathered in the course of field research among the Pashai speakers of the Darra-i-Nur Valley. The author, who worked in Oygal, and Jan Ovesen, who worked in the main Darra-i-Nur Valley, both found that in terms of social structure and culture the valley's inhabitants closely resemble the neighboring Nuristani and Dardic-speaking tribes of the Hindu Kush and Karakorum. Because of the strongly similar themes that thread through the social structure and culture of all the mountain people of the area, it seems probable that they share in general common historical roots. The ethnographic evidence does not support an argument that the Pashai, as opposed to their Dardic and Nuristani neighbors, have fallen from a previously more "civilized" state.

Ethnic terms for the Pashai-speaking people are confusing. The term "Pashai" is used here to refer to those who speak the Pashai language. In a few villages in the Alingar Valley there are Pashai speakers who are actually called Pashai. However, in the majority of cases the speakers of Pashai neither call themselves Pashai nor are called this by their neighbors. In many instances the Pashai are known as Tajik (generally meaning "Persian-speaking agriculturalists") or Safi (the name of a Pashto-speaking tribe in the Kunar Valley). However, they are also called Kohistanis (meaning non-Pushtun mountain dweller) and in some instances even classified as Nuristanis.

The Pashai are Sunni Muslims who in terms of formal religion are no different from their Nuristani and Pushtun neighbors. There are shrines of famous saints in the area, and it is not unknown for Pashai men to leave their home communities and become followers of well-known Pakistani or Afghan holy men. However, in the remote villages, saints do not play a particularly important role in local politics. In other ways as well, the Pashai living in the more remote areas differ from their neighbors. In many of these villages, women are not secluded, are able to interact freely with men and have a degree of sexual freedom unheard of in most rural areas of Afghanistan.

Although the Pashai are in general mixed herders and cultivators, in the relatively low elevations agriculture is of greater economic importance than herding. Staple crops are rice in the lower elevations and wheat and maize in the higher parts of the valleys. They also grow various vegetables as well as walnuts, mulberries and poppies. Herds consist primarily of goats, with some sheep and cattle.

The divisions of labor in the more remote villages is similar to that found in neighboring Nuristan; men are responsible for herding activities, while women do all but the heaviest agricultural work. In villages at lower elevations, where herding is not so important, this pattern is not found. There men are involved in all aspects of crop cultivation.

Although social relationships based on patrilineal descent are recognized in many Pashai-speaking communities, the political importance of patrilineal descent groups varies. In Oygal, membership in such groups is not a factor in political allegiances but does relate to the structure of village councils. Allegiances in fights and feuds are more directly related to kinship reckoned through both males and females. In the main Darra-i-Nur Valley patrilineal descent groups appear to have more importance in determining political allegiances than they do in the Ishpi Valley.

Political leadership among the Pashai is based on age, ability to mediate disputes, reputation for honor and generosity. In general, Pashai leaders have influence rather than authority. Although under the previous Mohammadzai government there were village *maliks*, or "headmen," those who held these positions lacked political authority; *maliks* functioned instead as intermediaries between village members and government officials.

Authority is held by village councils consisting of representatives from patrilineal kin groups. Council authority is typically limited to the regulation of the agricultural cycle and distribution of irrigation water. In some instances, particular village councils have formulated regulations limiting the cost of bridewealth, betrothal, weddings and funerals, as well as setting rates for carpenters, blacksmiths and barbers. However, councils are not involved in matters concerning wrongs against individuals. Each person is responsible for enforcing his own rights and avenging wrongs committed against him. The obligations of kinship, marriage and friendship relations define political allegiances in instances where individuals have been wronged.

Sometimes disputes between individuals and their allies are peacefully settled with the aid of mediators. Until recently in the Darra-i-Nur Valley, particularly serious disputes were sometimes mediated by influential leaders, who periodically travelled from village to village for this purpose. Other times, however, disputes cannot be settled without fighting and bloodshed, making feuds an important part of Pashai life.

Pashai cultural values are related to the importance of the feud; masculinity and honor are values pivotal to the cultural system. These values provide important themes in many stories and songs, and men are careful to cultivate the image of the proud warrior loyal to kin, dangerous to enemies and always ready to engage in a feud when necessary. Every man carries at least a knife and learns at an early age to be proficient with it. Many men own rifles and handguns, and at present modern small arms of Soviet manufacture are widely distributed among the male population. If men fail to act in terms of the values of honor and masculinity, they risk strong sanctions. Their enemies may call them men without honor and belittle what they say, people may joke at their expense and, in extreme cases, women may even pour ashes on their heads.

The Pashai in Darra-i-Nur are divided into hierarchically ranked cultural categories based on occupation. The highest ranked of these is the *siyal*, or "equals." This category consists of men (and related women) who own property, that is, those individuals who own fields and share rights to pastures. The lowest-ranked group is the *peishawar*, or "artisans." The *rayat* ("landless tenants") are thought to be descended from the pagan population of Darra-i-Nur conquered by the ancestors of the *siyal*. In the main Darra-i-Nur Valley these categories form caste-like groups in that marriage is permitted only between members of the same "caste" category. In Oygal some informants denied that these categories were in fact a barrier to marriage. It remains to be seen, however, if in Oygal marriages actually take place across category lines, since detailed census data is lacking. There is some evidence contained in songs and stories that similar categorical distinctions are important in the western Pashai-speaking area.

In many instances Pashai villages are linked together into larger units of various sizes. It is questionable whether it is always meaningful to refer to these as tribes since they are not always territorially bounded and are not always based on the same inclusion principles. Specifically, in some instances these units are based on a belief in common descent, while in other instances they are based on a belief in a common place of origin, usually a particular valley. For example, the Shenganek, or "people of the horn," are believed to be the descendants of an infant boy abandoned in the mountains. This infant was discovered when a goat scraped away the leaves covering it with its horns. In contrast, the Chugani are those people whose ancestors came from the Kordar Valley. Their "tribal" appellation is derived from the Pashai name for that valley.

There is still little information on the majority of Pashai. Given the current (1982) situation in Afghanistan, it is doubtful this will change in the near future. However, the Pashai are an important segment of the Afghan population; they warrant study if and when it again becomes possible to do research in Afghanistan.

BIBLIOGRAPHY

Books

Grierson, G. A. "Specimens of the Dardic or Pisacha Languages." In *Linguistic Survey of India*. Vol. 8, 2. Calcutta: Superintendent of Government Printing, 1919.
Humlum, Johannes. *La Géographie de l'Afghanistan, Etude d'un pays aride avec des chapitres de M. Kie and K. Ferdinand*. Copenhagen: Gyldenal, 1959.
Masson, C. *Narrative of Various Journeys in Balochistan, Afghanistan and the Punjab*. London: Richard Bentley, 1842.

Morgenstierne, Georg. *Indo-Iranian Frontier Languages, Vol. 3, The Pashai Language, Part 2, Grammar*. Instituttet for Sammenlignende Kulturforskning. Olso: Universitetsforlaget, 1967.
———. *Report on a Linguistic Mission to Afghanistan*. Instituttet for Sammenlignende Kulturforskning, Serie C1-1. Oslo: Aschehoug, 1926.
———. *Report on a Linguistic Mission to North-Western India*. Instituttet for Sammenlignende Kulturforskning, Serie C111-1. Oslo: Aschehoug, 1932.
———. *Indo-Iranian Frontier Languages, Vol. 3, The Pashai Language, Part 2, Texts and Translations*. Instituttet for Sammenlignende Kulturforskning. Oslo: Aschehoug, 1944.
Wutt, Karl. *Pashai: Lanschaft-Menschen-Architektur*. Graz, Austria: Akademische Druck-u. Verlagsanstalt, 1981.

Articles

Jettmar, Karl. "Urgent Tasks of Research Among the Dardic Peoples of Eastern Afghanistan and Northern Pakistan." *International Union of Anthropological and Ethnological Sciences, Bulletin of the International Committee on Urgent Anthropological and Ethnological Research*, no. 2 (1959): 85–96.
Keiser, R. Lincoln. "The Relevancy of Structural Principles in the Study of Political Organization." *Anthropos* 76 (1981): 430–440.
———. "Social Structure in the Southeastern Hindu-Kush: Some Implications for Pashai Ethno-History." *Anthropos* 69 (1974): 445–456.
Morgenstierne, Georg. "A Kafir on Kafir Laws and Customs." *Goteborgs Hogskalas Arsskrift* 39 (1933): 195–203.
Ovesen, Jan. "The Continuity of Pashai Society." *Folk* 23 (1981): 221–234.
———. "Marriage and Social Groups Among the Pashai." *Folk* 24 (1983): 195–203.
Wutt, Karl. "Zur Bausubstanz des Darrah-e-Nur." *Afghanistan Journal* 4:4 (1977): 54–65.
———. "Uber Kerkunft und Kulturelle Merkmale einiger Pashai-Gruppen. *Afghanistan Journal* 5:2 (1978): 43–58.

Unpublished Manuscripts

Keiser, R. Lincoln. "Social Structure and Social Control in Two Afghan Mountain Societies." Ph.D. dissertation, University of Rochester, 1971.
Ovesen, Jan. "The Construction of Ethnic Identities: The Nuristani and the Pashai, Eastern Afghanistan." Paper presented at the Symposium on Identity—Personal and Sociocultural, Uppsala University, January 1982.
———. 'The Position of Goats in Pashai Society." Paper presented at the Ninth Nordiske Etnografmode, Uppsala University, January 1979.

R. Lincoln Keiser

PERSIANS   Because of its unique position as a land bridge of rugged mountains and barren plains between Europe and Asia, the Iranian Plateau exhibits among its inhabitants a degree of ethnic and linguistic diversity unsurpassed by any other area in Southwest Asia. In this heterogeneous culture area encompassing

Iran and Afghanistan, the Persian-speaking inhabitants, 23 million in Iran, and 600,000 in Afghanistan (where they are generally known as Farsiwan or Parsiwan, i.e., Persian speakers) comprise nearly 50 percent of the population. (Tajik, who speak various dialects of Persian, are treated separately here.)

Persian belongs to the Indo-Iranian branch of the Indo-European family of languages and is related to such diverse languages as English and Bengali. It is the official language of Iran, the language of Iran's government bureaucracies, educational institutions, the mass media and literature. Dari, a dialect of modern Persian, is the language of the elite in Afghanistan. Standard Persian, called Farsi by its speakers, stems from Pahlavi, also known as Middle Persian, which was the language of the Sassanian period (A.D. 224–642) prior to the Arab conquest of Iran in the seventh century. During the succeeding centuries, Pahlavi underwent structural transformation by absorbing large amounts of Arabic elements. The rapid diffusion of Arabic, however, owed its success not so much to political domination by the Arabs as to Iranian men of letters who adopted Arabic as their literary medium.

Language was not the only profound change caused by the Arabs. The Islamization of the Persians was even more consequential. Their religion before the advent of Islam was Zoroastrianism, a belief system based on an eternal conflict between the forces of good and evil. As a universal doctrine, it recognized Ahura Mazda as the God of Good and the Divine Light. (An estimated 50,000 Zoroastrians known in Iran as Gabres and concentrated in the area of Yazd and Kerman; a much larger number known as Parsees form small, tightly knit economic and political elites in South Asia and East Africa.) Today nearly all Persians are Shia Muslims of the Ithna Ashari denomination.

The Persians were not the earliest inhabitants of Iran. Archeological investigations near Behshar on the Caspian coast indicate that as early as 10,000 B.C. the Iranian Plateau was already settled by a hunting and gathering people who in many ways resembled those of the Upper Paleolithic Europe.

At the beginning of the third millennium B.C., a new ethnic element of Indo-European origin appeared. The newcomers probably left their Eurasian plains in southern Russia as a result of population pressure. Archeological evidence supports the theory that they were pastoralists affected by drought and in search of pasturage. They came in successive waves but split into two sections. The western branch rounded the Black Sea and spearheaded into Asia Minor; the eastern branch consisted mainly of warrior horsemen who went around the Caspian Sea into the plateau, supplanting the indigenous populations.

The beginning of the first milennium B.C. marked the arrival of the Iranians (Aryans). Like others of Indo-European origin who came before them, they penetrated the Iranian Plateau in waves lasting several centuries, apparently using the same Caucasus and Transoxiana routes as the earlier invaders. They were pastoralists and, to a lesser extent, agriculturalists.

The Iranians consisted of several tribal groups: Medes, Persians (Parsa), Parthians, Bactrians, Soghdians, Sacians and Scythians. Over the next four centuries, Iranians formed nuclei of power within certain areas and absorbed the cultural influences of existing civilizations. By the first half of the first millennium B.C., they were strong enough to overcome all political obstacles and pave the way for the formation of the first world empire.

Between 625 and 585 B.C., the Medes developed an impressive civilization centered at Echbatana, the modern Hamadan. They completely destroyed the power of Assyria and extended their hegemony far into Asia Minor. Persians, who had initially settled to the northwest of Lake Urmia about the eighth century B.C., moved farther south and occupied Parsa, the modern province of Fars, from which they receive their ethnic title. This loosely federated tribal group became a more cohesive political unit under the Achaemenian clan. In 553 B.C. Cyrus, the ruler of Parsa, overthrew the Median dynasty and consolidated the Medes and Persians into the great Achaemenid Empire.

From the fifth century B.C. to the seventh century A.D., the social structure of Persia contained rulers, priests, warriors, artisans, scribes and producers, a structure which became progressively more complex and rigid. Towards the end of this period, a small privileged class dominated a growing mass of disfranchised people with few avenues for mobility. This condition, exacerbated by long and costly campaigns against the Eastern Roman Empire, led to an internal decay which prepared the way for the Arab invasion.

The 13 centuries from the Arab invasion of Persia until today have seen a fluctuation in monarchical powers and also a steady Persianization of the heterogeneous society. Politically, Persians were able to maintain their independence from invaders and their dominance over non-Persian minorities within the country. Since 1925 and the beginning of an intense nationalistic period, including the official adoption of the name "Iran," governments have sought to spread the use of Farsi and to encourage the best in Persian culture.

Persians are a sedentary people found in every part of Iran and western Afghanistan. Their concentration is in and around a number of cities in the interior of the plateau—Kerman, Shiraz, Yazd, Isfahan, Kashan, Tehran and Herat in Afghanistan. Each city is the economic and political hub of a dozen or more towns. Each town in turn integrates hundreds of villages into a regional economic network.

Urban Persians may be grouped into a number of distinct occupational categories, with social classes based largely on the degree of control over the economic and political resources. At the top of the hierarchy are the former landlords. Frustrated by the agrarian reform of the 1960s, they have become the principal investors and speculators in the real estate market, as well as major industrial and commercial entrepreneurs. Until a few decades ago, this was the only class which could afford an education abroad. As expected, most of the deputies, senators, ministers, ambassadors and provincial governors have traditionally belonged to this urban elite. Next in line are the high-echelon administrators, who are either part of the elite or derive power from them.

Merchants and shopkeepers, the Bazaaris, form the third component of the urban social system. Despite sharp differentiation into social and economic levels, the Bazaaris are the most cohesive segment of Iranian society. Culturally traditional and deeply religious, they have developed a close alliance with the clerical class in opposition to the excesses of secular authorities.

Ever since the introduction of Shiism as the national religion of Iran in the Safavid period (1501–1722), the *ulama* as the interpreters and practitioners of Islam have played an increasingly important role in the social and political life of the nation. They have been, at least for the past 100 years, the vanguard of significant protest movements against despotic rulers or policies which compromised the cultural and political integrity of Iran. The success of the Constitutional Revolution (1905–1911), for example, owed much to the *ulama* supported by the Bazaaris and secular liberals. The subsequent process of secularization of education and judicial system by the Pahlavis gradually undermined the social and moral leadership of the *ulama*. Nevertheless, they still enjoy the respect and devotion of a sizable segment of the Iranian population.

In the early 1960s the relationship between the bureaucratic state and the *ulama* entered a new phase when Ayatollah Khomeini began challenging the legitimacy of the Pahlavi regime on grounds that monarchy is incompatible with Islam. The Quran and Tradition, he stressed, contain all the laws needed for human guidance. It is incumbent upon the *ulama* to purify Islam and apply its laws. Furthermore, in the absence of the last infallible Imam, who is in occultation, the Islamic jurists must accept the responsibility to govern. Ayatollah Khomeini was imprisoned and then exiled to Iraq. He returned in 1979 to topple the monarchy.

A fifth urban category is what might loosely be called the middle class. A relatively recent phenomenon, the middle class is different from all other social groups in Iran in a number of respects. Although predominantly Shia Muslim and Persian, it incorporates other ethnic and religious elements. It includes a large proportion of the educated white collar workers, civil service employees, doctors, teachers, engineers and a wide variety of specialists in both public and private sectors, including the military. The middle class is growing in size and political importance. With a far better standard of living than ever before, the middle class is attempting to rectify the enormous economic disparity that has always existed between the elite and the rest of the population. Those more affluent can now attend universities abroad.

The urban proletariat form the sixth social category. They comprise between one-third and one-half of the city inhabitants and include factory and construction workers, city service employees and menial laborers. They inhabit the older sections of the city, often in run-down, crowded quarters. The urban proletariat is also ethnically heterogeneous, although not to the same degree as the middle class.

Finally, there is the sub-proletariat, unskilled and often under-employed or unemployed. Largely Persian, the bulk of this group consists of landless villagers and some impoverished pastoral nomads who come to the city in search of seasonal wage labor. A growing number of these rural migrants form permanent shantytowns around the outer edges of the cities, the men combing the streets for any menial task and the women and children begging for money or food.

In contrast to the city, the town is far more homogeneous. Religious observances, though less sophisticated than in the city, are practiced regularly and with deep conviction, particularly the fast of Ramadan and the Ashura ceremony during Muharram. Many towns still organize passion plays commemorating the martyrdom of Hussain. While deprecating the religious laxity of the city and what is perceived to be decadent Western behavior and values, in many ways townspeople, especially the more affluent members, try to emulate the city lifestyle.

A large but diminishing segment of the Persian population (about 50 percent) lives in thousands of villages and hamlets, mostly along the interior rim of the plateau. A village population may vary from a few households to more than a thousand people living in one-story houses. The size of a village depends on two important factors: arable land and water, both of which can be privately owned. Usually, however, rights to water for irrigation are determined by membership in the community. The allocation of water follows a complex procedure which in larger communities is relegated to a *mirab*, or the distributor of water. A common technique of channeling water in Iran is through *qanats*, miles-long underground tunnels.

A major proportion of agriculture in Iran is based on dry farming. Farming methods and implements are primitive by Western standards, but well adapted to the steep and rocky terrain and shallow humus. The chief crops are wheat, barley, some legumes and a few cash crops, such as tobacco, sugar beets and sesame. Few villages can boast an appreciable surplus.

The basic social and economic unit in Persian society is the elementary family. Some families combine into larger units comprised of a man, his wife or wives (Persians practice polygyny) and married sons and their families. Extended family units occupy independent quarters facing a central courtyard.

The Persian family is patriarchal. The wife defers to her husband in public and when children are present, but in private she may wield considerable decision-making power. Usually the father is an aloof disciplinarian, the mother permissive and affectionate. She is also an intermediary between her children and husband. In the father's absence, the eldest son is accorded respect and is shown deference by his siblings as the master of the household. Men are the guardians and defenders of the family honor, the locus of which are the female members. Essentially this attitude has been responsible for the sequestering of women in the more traditional segment of the society.

Selecting a future spouse is seldom a matter concerning only two individuals. Even in modern urban communities marriage often involves two blocs of kinsmen whose approval must be given some consideration. Compatibility is normally judged on the basis of education and socioeconomic status. In spite of the recent trend among the urban educated people to avoid endogamy, there is widespread preference for marrying one's paternal or maternal cousin.

Persians possess a strong patrilineal orientation, which is reflected in their descent and inheritance systems. Descent is traced strictly through the male line. Although the inheritance of property follows the same rule, certain items of property, usually movables, can be passed through the female line.

Much like the structure of the family, the social system of the Persians is hierarchical, paternalistic and authoritarian. The dominance of a superior over a subordinate is such that the individual must constantly look upward for sources of initiative and decision making. Thus, subordinates seldom assume responsibility or bear the burden of failure. The unrewarding aspects of this vertical system of social relations is mitigated by informal and intimate relationships between friends of equal status. Close and lasting friendship is greatly valued, particularly between males, but the strict ethics of mutual sacrifice and absolute loyalty place such a burden on the participants that these friendships are hard to maintain.

Another important value is hospitality. Persian folklore is replete with accounts of lavish hospitality shown to total strangers, particularly a display of hospitality made possible through self-denial. On the other hand, generosity is expected from those who have the means. To incur a reputation for miserliness is in many ways socially damaging.

Interpersonal relations are often accompanied by *ta'aruf*, or ceremonial politeness, involving elaborate formalities in speech and gesture during social intercourse. Essentially, *ta'aruf* is a symbolic demonstration of one's hospitality, generosity, humility and modesty. While some foreign visitors may interpret it as duplicity or hypocrisy, Persians themselves seldom confuse what is in the realm of *ta'aruf* and what should be taken seriously.

Persians have always prided themselves on the rich esthetic aspects of their culture. Artistic expressions are found in a variety of forms ranging from the intricately designed tilework and highly stylized Quranic inscriptions decorating the walls of major mosques to handicrafts, miniature painting and calligraphy. They all reflect an underlying sense of symmetry, unity and orderliness.

The universally admired Persian art form is poetry. With its uncompromising insistence on meter and rhyme, Persian poetry is much more than an expression of emotion. It contains subjective truth and the wisdom of the past. Sometimes it functions as an effective medium of satire and social commentary on inequality, injustice and repression in masterly use of metaphor and allegory. The epic poetry of Fardousi recounts the heroic heritage; other poets guide the reader through the labyrinth of Sufi mysticism. An appreciation for poetry is cultivated early in Persian life. Primary school children are required to memorize long passages from Fardousi, Saadi, Hafez and other poets.

A frequent theme in both literature and ordinary conversation is Qesmat (Kismet), or fate. Knowing the caprice of all natural and supernatural forces, Persians commonly use the phrase *Inshallah* (if God wills) when declaring a future event or action. It is also this unpredictability in life which justifies to a Persian the pursuit of pleasure, as reflected in the hedonistic philosophy of Omar Khayyám.

The concept of face, or *aberu*, in Persian society is extremely important. In order to earn respect and approval of others, close attention must be paid to the impression one gives. Face-saving involves maintaining an appropriate bearing and appearance commensurate with one's social status. Anxiety over *aberu-rizee*, loss of face, can be overcompensated by defensive behavior, conspicuous consumption or adopting a life-style beyond one's means. An important male value is *gheyrat*, assertive masculinity, the challenge of which evokes an immediate defensive reaction.

While many aspects of Iranian society have remained traditional, some areas have undergone profound change especially in the last few decades leading to the structural contradictions which were finally manifested in the revolution of February 11, 1979. The seemingly invincible Pahlavi regime and centuries of dynastic absolutism were suddenly swept aside. Chief among the causal factors were the worsening economic conditions of the mid-1970s. Windfall oil revenues were rapidly dissipated through ill-conceived development programs, uncontrollable administrative waste and corruption and huge arms purchases by the Shah.

These processes widened the gap between the affluent elite, often reveling in ostentatious extravagance, and a poverty-stricken majority. The source of the growing malaise, however, was the increasing capitalistic penetration of Iran and the attendant economic dependency. The mounting discontent was met with widespread repression. Although secular liberals and various leftist groups took up active opposition to the regime, it was the religious faction under the leadership of Ayatollah Khomeini that mobilized the masses.

The succession of events since the adoption of the Islamic Republic by a plebiscite has altered fundamentally the social and political character of Iran. The ascendancy of the clerical class is leading, step by step, to the Islamization of the entire social order.

Golamreza Fazel

BIBLIOGRAPHY

Books

Arasteh, A. Reza. *Education and Social Awakening in Iran, 1850–1968*. Rev. ed. Leiden: E. J. Brill, 1969.
———. *Faces of Persian Youth: A Sociological Study*. Leiden: E. J. Brill, 1970.
———, and Arasteh, J. *Man and Society in Iran*. Rev. ed. Leiden: E. J. Brill, 1970.
Bagley, F.R.C. "The Iranian Family Protection Law of 1967: A Milestone in the Advance of Woman's Rights." In *Iran and Islam*, edited by C. E. Bosworth. Edinburgh: Edinburgh University Press, 1971.
Bill, James Alban. *The Politics of Iran: Groups, Classes, and Modernization*. Columbus, O.: Charles E. Merrill, 1972.

Coon, Carleton S. *Caravan: The Story of the Middle East*. Rev. ed. 1958. Reprint ed
    New York: Holt, Rinehart and Winston, 1962.
Critchfield, Richard. *The Golden Bowl Be Broken: Peasant Life in Four Cultures*. Bloom-
    ington: Indiana University Press, 1973.
English, Paul Ward. *City and Village in Iran: Settlement and Economy in the Kirman
    Basin*. Madison: University of Wisconsin Press, 1966.
————. "Culture Change and the Structure of a Persian City." In *The Conflict of
    Traditionalism and Modernism in the Muslim Middle East*, edited by Carl Leiden.
    Austin: University of Texas Press, 1966.
Jacobs, Norman. *The Sociology of Development: Iran as an Asian Case Study*. New
    York: Praeger, 1966.
Keddie, Nikki R. ed. *Religion and Politics in Iran: Shi'ism from Quietism to Revolution*.
    New Haven: Yale University Press, 1982.
————. "Stratification, Social Control, and Capitalism in Iranian Villages: Before and
    After Land Reform." In *Rural Politics and Social Change in the Middle East*,
    edited by R. Antoun and I. Harik. Bloomington: Indiana University Press, 1972.
Lambton, A.K.S. *Landlord and Peasant in Persia*. 1953. Reprint ed London: Oxford
    University Press, 1969.
————. *The Persian Land Reform, 1962–1966*. London: Oxford University Press, 1969.
Lerner, Daniel. *The Passing of Traditional Society*. Glencoe, Ill.: Free Press, 1958.
Minorsky, Vladimir. "Iran: Opposition, Matyrdom, Revolt." In *Unity and Variety in
    Muslim Civilization*, edited by G. E. von Grunebaum. Chicago: University of
    Chicago Press, 1955.
Pierce, Joe E. *Understanding the Middle East*. Rutland, Vt.: Charles E. Tuttle, 1971.
Smith, Harvey H., et al. *Area Handbook for Iran*. The American University FAS, DA
    Pam 550–68. Washington, D.C.: Government Printing Office, 1971.
Szyliowicz, Joseph S. *Education and Modernization in the Middle East*. Ithaca: Cornell
    University Press, 1973.
Youssef, Nadia Haggag. *Woman and Work in Developing Societies*. Population Mono-
    graph Series, No. 15. Berkeley: University of California Press, 1974.
Zonis Marvin. "Higher Education and Social Change in Iran." In *Iran Faces the 1970's*,
    edited by E. Yar-Shater. New York: Praeger, 1971.
————. *The Political Elite of Iran*. Princeton: Princeton University Press, 1971.

Articles

Ajami, Ismail. "Social Classes, Family Demographic Characteristics, and Mobility in
    Three Iranian Villages." *Sociologia Ruralis* 9:1 (1969): 62–72.
Gulick, J. and M. "Varieties of Domestic Social Organizations in the Iranian City of
    Isfahan." *Annals of the New York Academy of Science* 220:6 (1974): 441–469.
Keddie, Nikki R. "The Iranian Power Structure and Social Change, 1800–1969: An
    Overview." *International Journal of Middle East Studies* 2:1 (1971): 3–20.
————. "The Iranian Village Before and After Land Reform." *Journal of Contemporary
    History* 3:3 (1968): 69–91.
Miller, William G. "Hosseinabad: A Persian Village." *Middle East Journal* 18 (1964):
    483–498.
Paydarfar, A., and Sarram, M. "Differential Fertility and Socioeconomic Status of Shirazi
    Women: A Pilot Study." *Journal of Marriage and Family* 32:4 (1970): 692–699.

Unpublished Manuscripts

Alberts, R.C. "Social Structure and Culture Change in an Iranian Village." Ph.D. dissertation, University of Wisconsin, 1963.
Rotblat, Howard J. "Stability and Change in an Iranian Bazaar." Ph.D. dissertation, University of Chicago, 1972.

POMAKS   In Bulgaria the designation "Pomak" is now taken to be derogatory and is no longer found in print or in public use. Yet the Pomaks exist, Bulgarians who converted to Islam during the early centuries of the Ottoman occupation. They live chiefly in the Rhodope Mountains and on the southeast slopes of the Pirin Mountains. Many thousands also live in Greece and Turkey, where they settled during migrations over the past century.

Because Bulgaria has not released census data on ethnic minorities since the Communist regime came to power in 1944, the current number of Pomaks there can only be estimated at 75,000. Earlier census reports indicate that in 1878 there were half a million Pomaks, and by 1934 there were 134,000. This decline is the result of repeated exchanges of population between Bulgaria and Turkey. In 1950 Pomaks were given the option to change their nationality designation from "Bulgarian-Muslim" to "Turk" and thereby be allowed to emigrate to Turkey. Many thousands of the 200,000 "Turks" who went to Turkey were actually Pomaks. Turkey now has a population of Pomaks numbering around 200,000 living in the northwest and south central parts of the country. Greece also has a Pomak population of possibly 80,000, mostly living in the prefecture of Xanthi. A rough guess is that today there are at least 300,000 to 400,000 who consider themselves Pomaks.

The Bulgarian Pomak population seems to be increasing. Most of the Muslim villages in the Rhodopes have grown steadily since the 1920s (with a slight drop in the 1950s), in contrast to Christian villages, which are being depopulated due to urbanization. The Pomak birthrate is higher than that of the Christians; families of four to six children are common, whereas the Bulgarian average is approximately two children. Most Pomaks still live in villages, although there is a sizable population in the towns and cities of southwest Bulgaria.

The word "Pomak" does not appear prior to nineteenth-century Ottoman documents. It is a word the Pomaks did not use for themselves. It was originally used by Bulgarians (Eastern Orthodox Christians) for those who had converted to Islam. The origin of the word is not agreed upon by scholars. Since 1878 Bulgarian scholars have used the term "Bulgaro-Mohamedanin" to avoid any connotation whatsoever.

There is also no consensus as to the nature of Pomak conversion to Islam. It is certain that the Ottomans reached the Rhodope area in 1371 and that by the 1700s a majority there were Muslims. Bulgarian scholars claim the Pomaks were forced to convert en masse through unprecedented terror and torture. Although historical evidence is scant, the "forced" conversion of Pomaks has become part of the national consciousness of the Bulgarian people and is detailed in many songs and legends.

Non-Bulgarians concur that conversion was almost everywhere voluntary in response to various economic, legal and religious pressures. No doubt many Christians converted to avoid the *jizya* (*cizye*) tax demanded of non-Muslims by the Ottomans, or to gain preferred legal status. The Bektashi order of Islam may have been particularly attractive to villagers since it embraced many pre-Christian and Christian customs. The Turkic nomadic Yoruk and the Bogomils (a persecuted heretical Christian sect) probably accepted Islam to the degree to which it coincided with their own folk practices. Actually folk Christianity and folk Islam were quite similar, both based on agricultural rites and shrines. Conversion may well have been a mere pragmatic decision requiring at first only minor concessions to Islamic practice, such as the use of a Muslim first name. Only later did Pomaks adopt other Muslim customs such as the wearing of veils by women in front of strangers.

Interaction between Pomaks and Christians has varied depending on location and era. In general, Pomaks have lived in separate villages. In the central Rhodopes, where the Christians predominated, Pomaks had frequent and friendly contact with Christians, including holding common orchards and grazing lands and celebrating holidays together. Where Pomaks have predominated there was little contact with Christians. This may account for the anti-Christian attitude of these Pomaks and for the fact that many of them fought on the Turkish side of the Bulgarian War of Liberation in 1878.

The major crops of the Pomaks reflect the ecology of the mountainous terrain— rye, barley, corn, flax, hemp, potatoes and tobacco. Bread is a staple food, supplemented by potatoes and beans, dairy products from sheep and cow such as yogurt and cheeses and lamb and goat meat. While in the past only the wealthy ate wheat bread and the majority ate corn or rye bread, today wheat bread and grain mixtures are common.

Pomaks live in nucleated villages surrounded by agricultural and grazing land and dense forest. Like Christians, their houses are usually two-storied with the first floor for animals and farm equipment and the second floor for human habitation. Houses are made of stone, wood and clay, with sloping slate roofs. Recently brick and cinderblock and ceramic tile roofs have been introduced. The interiors of wealthy homes often have elaborate carved ceilings.

Bulgarian ethnographers have thoroughly documented nineteenth- and twentieth-century Pomak life with an eye to proving that Pomak culture is purely Slavic. The Pomak language, which is the Rhodope dialect of Bulgarian, preserves many archaic Slavic grammatical and lexical features. Pomak speech also includes some specifically Pomak words, which are best preserved in song texts. The Turkish words in the Rhodope dialect were introduced in connection with Ottoman administration, the Muslim religion or the shepherding activities of the

Yoruk (see Yoruk). There are also many Turkish place names and Turkish personal and family names, although they have been Slavicized.

Pomak culture is a combination of pre-Christian, Christian and Muslim elements. The Pomak ritual calendar, like the Christian, is based on an agricultural cycle and includes magical and propitiatory acts to ensure a good harvest, good health and fertility for men and animals. Pomaks, especially women, have continued to enact Christian and pre-Christian rites such as keeping holy water and crosses, venerating Christian shrines and priests and making offerings to saints and pagan deities. Pomaks share with Bulgarian Christians many institutions such as fictive kinship (god-parenthood) and such customs as exchange of red eggs on Easter, the tapping of cornel branches on New Year's Day, the divining of young girls' fortunes on St. John's Day and the decoration of the house on St. George's Day. Shepherding rituals are noticeably absent since the Pomaks are not commonly shepherds. Pomak life-cycle celebrations, such as weddings, conform to Christian practice with the addition of such ''Muslim'' elements as the dyeing of the bride's hair and hands with henna. Their lack of familiarity with official Islam, caused by their mountain isolation, has made the Pomaks better preservers of the folkways of the area than the Christians.

The Pomaks practice many traditions of Islam. They do not eat pork or drink alcoholic beverages; they celebrate the circumcisions of young boys (*sunet*). Men and women are segregated in public while men congregate in village coffeehouses, women visit and pray at home and remain secluded from the public. Other Muslim customs observed in the past are no longer practiced today. Until recently Pomaks observed the Ramadan fast and the two major feast days, Id al Fitr and Id al Adha (''Maluk'' and ''Golem Bajram,'' respectively). In areas where there was little contact with Christians, Pomak women wore veils (*jashmak*) in public and wore a black outer coat (*feredzhe*). Everywhere, women could be distinguished immediately as Christian or Muslim by their costume. Today traditional dress is only seen in the more isolated villages.

Polygyny, now forbidden by law, was always rare among the Pomaks. Marriage was (and continues to be) endogamous and arranged by the parents of the couple. The bride does not participate in the dancing and merrymaking, but remains indoors on display for the guests to admire. She may be quite young, in her mid-teens, with the groom only slightly older. She is expected to prepare an extensive dowry of handmade items for her new home, including carpets, blankets, clothing and gifts for wedding guests. Virtually all Pomak women weave, and some of the finest Rhodope weavers are Pomaks.

Pomak society is patrilineal and patrilocal, based on the extended family (*zadruga*), which shares resources and money and divides agricultural, herding and household work among members by sex and age. Indoor and outdoor communal work parties are regularly called to aid villagers with handiwork such as spinning and tobacco stringing and with construction projects. Men and women usually work separately, but socializing and courting do occur.

Many changes have come into Pomak life in the twentieth century. With the closing the the Greek border in 1919 and the cutting off of Aegean grazing lands and markets, the economy declined. Cash crops such as tobacco and potatoes have become the mainstays; farmwork has become mechanized except on steep slopes; logging, mining and construction have greatly expanded. Most important, since 1944, land and flocks have been collectivized; only small garden plots remain in private hands.

Since the Communist regime, a policy of assimilation has been in effect, conforming to the general anti-religious attitude of the government and its promotion of ethnic unity. (Due to international pressure, ethnic Turks living in Bulgaria have relative freedom of religion.) In the late 1960s Pomaks had to assume Slavic names; the official designation ''Bulgarian-Muslim'' which appeared on identification papers was replaced by the unspecified ''Bulgarian''; and the word ''Pomak'' was proscribed in official and public statements.

While in the privacy of their homes Pomaks observe the basic requirements of Islam such as the fast and celebrations, they have modernized like the rest of Bulgaria, but perhaps not as rapidly. Paved roads and railroad and bus lines now link their villages; running water and electricity have been introduced; cars, radios and television are common in villages. So far, however, the Pomaks have retained their distinctiveness simply because they feel themselves to be different from the Bulgarian Christians.

BIBLIOGRAPHY

Books

Andreadis, K. G. *The Moslem Minority of Western Thrace*. Salonika, Greece: Institute for Balkan Studies, 1956.
Bajraktarevic, Fehim. ''Pomak.'' In *Encyclopedia of Islam*. Vol. 3. Leiden: E. J. Brill, 1936.
Dellin, L.A.D. *Bulgaria*. New York: Praeger, 1957.
Georgeoff, John. ''Ethnic Minorities in the Peoples Republic of Bulgaria.'' In *The Politics of Ethnicity in Eastern Europe*, edited by George Klein and Milan J. Reban. New York: Columbia University Press, 1981.
Hasluck, F. W. *Christianity and Islam Under the Sultans*. Oxford: Clarendon Press, 1929.
Inalcik, Halil. ''Bulgaria.'' In *Encyclopedia of Islam*. New ed. Leiden: E. J. Brill, 1960.
———. *The Ottoman Empire: The Classical Age 1300–1600*. New York: Praeger, 1973.
Keefe, Eugene, et al. *Area Handbook for Bulgaria*. Washington, D.C.: Government Printing Office, 1974.
Pundeff, Marin V. *Bulgaria: A Bibliographic Guide*. Washington, D.C.: Library of Congress, 1965.
Shoup, Paul. *The East European and Soviet Data Handbook: Political Social and Developmental Indicators 1945–1975*. New York: Columbia University Press, 1981.

Sugar, Peter. *Southeastern Europe Under Ottoman Rule 1354–1804*. Seattle: University of Washington Press, 1977.

Carol Silverman

PUNJABIS   Panj-aab, the land of the five rivers (Jhelum, Chenab, Ravi, Beas and Sutlej), lends its name to its people, the Punjabis. Numerically and politically, they are the dominant people of Pakistan and the Indian Punjab, numbering approximately 73 million.

The Punjab has been the most productive land in South Asia ever since the British in the nineteenth century constructed on the Punjabi plains the largest irrigation system the world had yet seen. Even 3,000-4,000 years earlier, the banks of the five rivers and the Indus River into which they flow supported civilizations which created cities—Harrapa, Mohenjodaro and Kot Diji—whose ruins exhibit marked similarities to those of the Mesopotamians. The Aryan migrations of these eras established the base of modern Punjabi culture.

The mountain passes leading down from Afghanistan, the Khyber, the Kurram, the Tochi and the Gemal, served as doorways for successive waves of invaders; the forces of Darius and of Alexander the Great, the Persians, the Mauryas, Greco-Bactrians, Sakas, Parthians and Hepthalite Huns, each adding to the heritage of the Punjab. In 712 the Arabs extended their power to the lower Punjab, but Islam failed to take root until after the eleventh century, when the Turks under Mahmud of Ghazni invaded the land. The religion spread rapidly during the 300-year suzerainty of the Turkish sultanate of Delhi. Another period of growth came with the founding of the Moghul Empire under Babur in the sixteenth century, particularly upon Emperor Aurangzeb's enforcement of the *jizya*, a tax on non-Muslims. Lahore became a center of Muslim dynamism.

Following the disintegration of Moghul power, the Punjab was conquered first by the Sikhs and then by the British, who, after the Muslim ''mutiny'' of 1857, suppressed Islamic leadership. Under the British, Hindus assumed ascendant social and political power.

As independence approached in India in the 1940s, relations among Sikhs, Muslims and Hindus in the Punjab turned from coolness to hostility. The promise of a country of their own prompted each group to seek positions of strength at the expense of the others. Fear of violence and the hope for prosperity led Hindus and Sikhs in western Punjab to migrate eastward to India, while Muslims in India moved westward to Pakistan. At the cost of thousands of lives lost in communal violence, nearly 12 million people moved to new homes after the partition of the Punjab and the independence of Pakistan and India in 1947. The tenuous border between Pakistani Punjab and Indian Punjab has several times witnessed warfare between the two countries. Today the Punjab of Pakistan is 98 percent Muslim; the Punjab of India is 99 percent Hindu, Sikh and Christian and perhaps 1 percent Muslim.

Punjabi, an Indo-Iranian language, is the mother tongue in a triangular area defined by the cities of Rawalpindi, Multan and Ambala. About 58 million people in Pakistan, 61 percent of the country's population, and 14.6 million people in India are native speakers of its four major dialects: Eastern Punjabi, which shades into Urdu of Delhi; Dogri, the distinct dialect of Jammu; Majhi, or Standard Punjabi, of central Punjab; Lahnda or Western Punjabi; and Bahawalpuri, Hindko and Pahari, the pure forms of which are so variant from Standard Punjabi that they are sometimes classified as distinct languages.

Historically, Punjabi not only served to convey the primarily oral traditional poetry and lore of the Muslims but became the Sikh scriptural language. Partly because of this identification of Punjabi with the Sikh religion and because of the inherent importance and prestige of the Arabic script for Muslims, the latter cultivated Urdu as the official medium of their culture. Thus, Urdu has become the primary language of literature and education (English is second), particularly since the arrival of tens of thousands of Urdu-speaking *muhajirs* (refugees) from India after the partition. Even so, Urdu speakers today represent only 9 percent of Pakistan's population. An activist movement in the cause of the Punjabi language, although suppressed in the 1960s by the Pakistan military, remains vigorous in the Punjab's cities.

Since it was the Turks who brought Sunni Islam to the Punjab, the Hanafi school of the Sha·iah dominates Punjabi Muslim doctrine. However, about 1 out of every 12 Punjabis is Shia, in most cases of the Ithna Ashari branch. The Ahmadiya and its more liberal Qadiani branch have large followings. However, anti-Ahmadiya riots occurred in West Punjab in 1953 and 1974, ostensibly on religious grounds, but also motivated by resentment of the disproportionately great political and military prominence achieved by the more educated Ahmadi. The National Assembly of Pakistan in 1974 amended the constitution to provide that, for purposes of law, Ahmadi are not Muslims. Thus the entire sect was deprived of the benefits afforded Muslims in the country (see Akan).

Punjabi folk religion weaves a rich variety of local mysticism—such as beliefs in the evil eye, the predictions of astrologers and the potency of amulets and potions—into the scriptural, universalizing traditions of Islam propounded by the *ulama*. Sufi influences are pervasive. The principal Sufi orders found in Pakistan Punjab are the Qadiriyya, Naqshbandiyya and Suhrawardy. The Chistiyya order, in which ecstatic singing and music are combined with the *dhikr* (recitation), was concentrated in East Punjab prior to Partition but since then has experienced a revival in the west, especially in the major urban centers. Many Punjabis are lifelong devotees (*murid*) of hereditary Sufi spiritual guides (*pir*), men, usually of Sayyid pedigree, who are believed to possess divine inspiration and the ability to heal, protect and purify. Enshrined tombs (*mazaar*) of *pirs* and other legendary saintly figures are ubiquitous throughout the Punjab, both in the countryside and in the cities, the more famous serving as places of homage and meditation and as sites of ritual festivals and commemorations which yearly attract hundred of thousands of pilgrims.

An individual's place in the traditional Punjabi social scheme is fixed by membership in a series of inclusive units. The unit with the widest scale is the *qaum* or *zat*, of which there are two basic types: those, like the Sayyid, Jat, Rajput and Awan, which are defined in terms of putative patrilineal descent from a historical or mythical figure; and those, like the Jullaha (weaver), Mussali (sweeper) and Mirasi (bard and genealogist), which are defined occupationally. In general, the former are considered hereditarily superior to the latter, the greatest esteem and prestige being accorded to the Sayyids and Sharifs, who claim direct descent from the Prophet Muhammad or his family, and the least to the Mussalis, who are associated with defiling tasks and materials. Punjabi society as a whole consists of many *qaums* or *zats* theoretically arranged in a hierarchy of status but with no clear order of precedence in the middle ranks. In this respect there are broad similarities with the Hindu scheme of *varnas*, or castes, and indeed the literature abounds with references to "Muslim castes," despite the fact that a religiously sanctioned caste ideology is lacking. Punjabi Muslims themselves, particularly those claiming high status, are apt to draw analogies to the Hindu caste system. The Rajputs will say they are a martial race descended from warrior princes and therefore are "like Kshatriyas."

Although rural-to-urban migration has taken place on a massive scale in recent years, the bulk of the Punjabi population still resides in discrete agricultural communities or associated outlying hamlets. A village settlement usually is nucleated and may range in size from a few hundred to even 20,000 people residing in densely packed clusters of mud-brick houses. It serves as a basic unit for purposes of government, revenue collection, the provision of social services and the implementation of economic programs. A person's ties to his or her ancestral village, in addition to being practically important, are of great sentimental value. They are used as a primary means of identification and are never fully severed even after many years of absence.

In the village context political and collective economic affairs largely are organized in terms of *biraderi* relationships. The *biraderi* is the constituent unit of the *qaum* or *zat* and is composed of the descendants of a known ancestor two to six generations removed from the eldest living cohort. *Biraderis* constitute relatively tightly bound and well-defined groups. Their members share a common patronymic, are able to trace specific ties of kinship to each other and are expected to engage in close cooperation for the sake of common prosperity and the protection of persons and property. *Biraderi* relationships are sustained through constant visiting, consultations, gift exchanges at birth, circumcision and marriage and by respect shown to group elders. Conversely, lack of material resources and the wherewithal for hospitality and the dispersion of members are seriously detrimental to effective *biraderi* organization. Hence, large and solidary *biraderis* typically are found among those who are prosperous or politically and economically interdependent, while small and fractionalized *biraderis* are characteristic of the economically disenfranchised and dependent.

Within the context of the village, another division of key importance is that which separates the landholders (*zamindar*) from the artisans, domestic servants and field laborers whom they employ (collectively designated *kammi*). A given village may be dominated by a single *zamindar biraderi* or, more often, will include segments of several *zamindar biraderis*, of different *qaums/zats*, contending for political and economic hegemony over the local population of *kammis*, sharecroppers and tenants. Individual *zamindars* and *kammis* solidify their relationships by entering into long-term contracts for the performance of work—such as harvesting, sweeping, clothes washing or smithery—in exchange for fixed quantities of grain and other subsistence commodities.

The pivot of social life for Punjabis, rich and poor, is the household (*ghar*), conceived as the group which contributes to and eats from a single hearth (*chula*). The household encompasses the personal bonds of marriage and parentage and provides the framework of care, support and instruction through which an individual is morally and legally incorporated in the society at large. The household also serves as the basis for economic organization. Not only are daily activities organized in terms of it, but so are the principal forms of private wealth and productive assets, including labor. Members of a household must pool their earnings and engage in joint decision making regarding savings, investment and major transactions. The schooling and supervision of children, attending the aged or sick and holding life-cycle rites are tasks coped with similarly. Residential separation does not necessarily preclude these practices. Some of the largest, most extensive business empires in the country are managed in this way—essentially as household enterprises—as are most of the independently held farms, shops and trades.

Families form and develop within the fold of the patriarchally or fraternally governed *ghar*. While a man's daughters are destined to be given away in marriage by the time they are 15 or so, his sons remain a part of his *ghar* throughout his active lifetime, even after having children of their own. Upon his death partition of property does not occur right away; instead his sons continue their association for some time afterwards, often for many years. In such cases the elder brother assumes the role of household head, and typically his wife takes charge as the senior woman of the establishment. However, stress and strains between brothers' competing family interests eventually lead to separation and the beginning of new *ghars*. Ideals of household unity are then upheld anew. Thus, Punjabi households may grow exceedingly large and complex before splitting into smaller, nuclear family-based units.

Differences in male and female rights of inheritance underly the structure and continuity of the Punjabi household. All substantial property, such as land, houses, livestock and businesses, passes in the patriline and is divided equally among a man's sons after he dies, or retires, and his sons partition their joint *ghar*. Daughters and sisters receive their share of the estate at the time of their wedding in the form of dowries consisting of jewelry, clothing, domestic equipment and the like. Only some of the Punjabi elite conform to the Shariah in allowing daughters to inherit substantial productive assets.

The preservation and enhancement of familial *izzat* (honor) are prime concerns in Punjabi society. *Izzat* is preserved by offering generous hospitality to guests, holding life-cycle rites for household members in a timely and proper manner, safeguarding the chastity and modesty of female relatives and defending close kin against threats and public accusations. *Izzat* is enhanced by gaining freedom from the need to perform manual labor, making arrangements for the seclusion and veiling of women, acquiring formal education, giving alms to the poor, employing a *maulvi* (cleric) to tutor children in the Quran and performing the Haj.

Marriage is a momentous event for it involves a crucial test of *izzat* and an indication of relative social standing. Punjabi Muslims prefer to marry within the *biraderi* and, in particular, idealize marriage with children of paternal uncles, as this makes for a match between known social equals, conserves wealth in the patriline, gives women effective recourse to their agnates in case of ill treatment and keeps marriage-related disputes out of the public eye. The preference for in-marriage produces the reticulated kinship system characteristic of Punjabi Muslim society, as opposed to Hindu lineage exogamy and preference for marriage outside one's natal village.

Next to the Urdu-speaking *muhajirs*, the Punjabis are the ethnic group most closely identified with the ideology and interests of the Pakistani state. They dominate its civilian bureaucracies and armed forces and constitute its essential political constituency. National power in Pakistan rides on the balance of calm and disorder in the cities of the Punjab. In turn, the Punjabi world view and Punjabi aspirations increasingly are shaped by socializing institutions developed within an urban-oriented, nationally organized cultural framework. These include schools, colleges and universities following standardized curricula, mass political parties, the literary and artistic genres purveyed through the cinema, radio, TV and popular press and spectator sports, particularly cricket and hockey.

Rising numbers of the rural poor stream into the cities of the Punjab in search of jobs and better living conditions. The newly arrived indigent form an underclass in relation to four principal groups in the Punjab's burgeoning urban population: skilled and industrial workers, students, bazaar merchants and traders and the elite. The last are mainly civil and military officials, doctors, lawyers, engineers and landlords-turned-investors. They are markedly Western oriented and widely travelled, have been taught from English-language texts and read English-language newspapers, journals, books and magazines.

While illiteracy remains an acute problem in village society, the cities are filled with secondary school and university graduates who lack technical training and thus face uncertain prospects. A large number are from rural backgrounds but have no wish to return there. Concern for *izzat* leads them to spurn blue collar jobs and instead accept clerical posts in the city, if any are available. This results in estrangement between them and the rural families, who looked to their returning sons for leadership, support and the continuity of the *biraderi* and *qhar*.

BIBLIOGRAPHY

Books

Ahmad, Makhdum Tassaduq. *Systems of Social Stratification in India and Pakistan.* Lahore, Pakistan: Punjab University Press, 1972.

Ahmad, Saghir. *Class and Power in a Punjabi Village.* New York: Monthly Review Press, 1977.

————. "Social Classes in a Punjabi Village." In *Caste and Social Stratification Among Muslims of India,* edited by Imtiaz Ahmad. Delhi: Manohar Book Service, 1973.

————. "A Village in Pakistani Punjab: Jalpana." In *South Asia: Seven Community Profiles,* edited by Clarence Mahoney. New York: Holt, Rinehart and Winston, 1974.

Critchfield, Richard. *The Golden Bowl Be Broken: Peasant Life in Four Cultures.* Bloomington: Indiana University Press, 1973.

Darling, Malcolm L. *The Punjab Peasant in Prosperity and Debt.* London: Oxford University Press, 1946.

Eglar, Zekiya. *A Punjabi Village in Pakistan.* New York: Columbia University Press, 1960.

Pastner, S., and Flomm, L., eds. *Current Anthropology in Pakistan.* Ithaca: Cornell University Press, 1982.

Raza, Muhammad Rafique. *Two Pakistani Villages: A Study in Social Stratification.* Lahore, Pakistan: Punjab University Press, 1969.

Waheed, Zuhra. *Contacts Between Villages and Public Officials in Three Villages of Lyallpur Tehsil.* Lahore, Pakistan: Pakistan Administrative Staff College, 1964.

Weekes, Richard V. *Birth and Growth of a Muslim Nation.* Princeton: Van Nostrand, 1964.

Westphal-Hellbusch, Sigrid. *The Jats of Pakistan.* Berlin: Drucker and Humbolt, 1964.

Articles

Ahmad, Imtiaz. "Social Stratification Among Muslims of Pakistan." *Economic Weekly* 10 (1965): 1093–1096.

Alavi, Hamza. "The Politics of Dependence: A Village in West Punjab." *South Asian Review* 4:2 (1971): 11–28.

Eaton, Richard M. "The Profile of Popular Islam in the Pakistani Punjab." *Journal of South Asian and Middle Eastern Studies* 2:1 (1978): 74–91.

Leaf, Murray J. "The Punjabi Kinship Terminology as a Semantic System." *American Anthropologist* 73:3 (1971): 545–554.

Shackle, C. "Punjabi in Lahore." *Modern Asian Studies* 4:3 (1970): 239–268.

Unpublished Manuscripts

Chaudhri, J.J.M. "A Typical Support Structure of Leadership in Punjab: The Faction." Ph.D. dissertation, University of Manchester, 1968.

Izmirlian, Harry. "Caste, Kin and Politics in a Punjab Village." Ph.D. dissertation, University of California, Berkeley, 1964.

Tahir Ali
Richard V. Weekes

PUSHTUN   Before the Soviet invasion of 1979, about 15 million Pushtun lived almost equally divided between Afghanistan and Pakistan. To most Pushtun tribesmen and their neighbors, Pushtun and Afghan are virtually synonymous and refer to the entire body of Pashto speakers on both sides of the Durand Line of 1893, one of those legacies of European imperialism which clutter the political landscape in Africa and Asia. These boundaries often threaten regional peace. Pushtun are also called Pukhtun and, especially in Pakistan, India and Great Britain, Pathans, a Hindustani bastardization.

Pashto, an Indo-Iranian language of the great Indo-European family, has several mutually intelligible dialects. Depending on the linguistic authority consulted, Pashto has from two to four dialects, but all agree on the basic "soft" Pashtu of the Kandahar (Afghanistan) area and the harsher Pakhtu variant of Peshawar and the North-West Frontier Province of Pakistan. Pashto differs from neighboring Farsi (or Persian) in that nouns have gender and a complicated two-case, two-number declension system. To be a "true" or "pure" Pushtun, a man's father and mother must both be native Pashto speakers.

Physically, the Pushtun are basically a Mediterranean type. Compared to most of their neighbors, the Pushtun are tall.

Pushtun men wear distinctive turban caps and often tie the turban cloth in a special way to indicate tribal identity. Usually they wear long cotton or light woolen shirts (*pyran*) buttoned at one shoulder which hang outside baggy trousers (*yizar* or *tombon*). Over the shirt is a sleeveless, embroidered vest. In zones of relative inaccessibility, rifles, pistols, knives or other assorted weaponry are considered essential items of dress.

Village and nomad women wear head shawls (*chadar*), seldom the *chadry* or *burqa* (head-to-toe sack-like garment), which is basically an urban manifestation. Such a veil would hinder rural women from working in the fields or tending flocks. Women wear basically the same clothing as men, but of more colorful material. Nomadic women ride camels and horses dressed in their best clothing and often sew coins into their garments. So laden, they become travelling banks. Woman stealing, a not uncommon practice, has both monetary and sexual objectives.

All Pushtun (except the Turi of Kurram, Pakistan, who are Imami Shia) are Hanafi Sunni Muslims. Many pre-Islamic localized beliefs and customs permeate the religious scene. Shrines of saints abound. The chief religious leaders, the *mullahs*, are found throughout the society, performing traditional rites at life-cycle ceremonies and festivals. Occasionally, they assert considerable political influence.

The Pushtun are basically farmers of both irrigated and unirrigated farmland or herdsmen. They raise wheat or barley and herd sheep, goats, cattle, camels or horses. In some regions, they have specialty occupations. For instance, in the North-West Frontier Province they grow sugar cane; in northern Afghanistan, cotton. Several groups in Paktyia (Afghanistan) monopolize the lumber trade between Afghanistan and Pakistan; the Andar Ghilzai in east central Afghanistan specialize in construction and repairing underground irrigation canals.

Most Pushtun are evolving towards either semi-nomadism, in which more than 50 percent of the group moves from winter (*kishlak*) to summer quarters (*yaylla*) with the herds while the rest remain behind to farm, or semi-sedentariness, when fewer than 50 percent make the annual trek. Before the 1979 invasion, more than 300,000 nomads crossed annually into Pakistan.

More enterprising herders use the annual move as a time to engage in commercial activities along the route by trading or lending money to needy farmers. Improved road networks have made it easier for some to haul heavy equipment such as tents and poles in trucks, but the camel and donkey are still important beasts of burden. Horses are prestige animals everywhere.

Pushtun on the move live in black goat-hair tents supported only by a guy rope. An entire camp of these portable dwellings can be set up or struck in less than an hour.

Houses in the winter quarters and sedentary villages vary with the terrain and available building materials but almost always occupy non-productive land. The most common house is square or rectangular, made of sun-dried brick covered with mud and straw plaster. Bricks are made in wooden molds and placed on the ground to dry. Flat roofs of rammed earth interlaced with twigs are supported on mat-covered beams. In mountainous regions, most have stone foundations. Extended families live in several huts surrounded by a high *pise*, a pressed mud wall, with tall, cylindrical watchtowers overseeing the village complex. Enemy surprise attack is a much-used tactic in Pushtun warfare, and survival depends on constant vigilance.

In general, Pushtun society can be categorized as patriarchal (authority of the *spin geray*, white beards or old men), patrilineal and patrilocal, with strong matri-influences. The preferred marriage mate is father's brother's offspring or another near relative. Since endogamy is preferred, women seldom move far from their female kin, so the matricore remains intact. Pushtun women have little formal power and seldom appear in public when strangers are in the area. However, behind the mud walls and inside the tent, their influence is great, not only in decision making concerning domestic affairs but often also in influencing their husbands and sons on political and extralegal issues discussed at local *jirgah* (village camp or councils). Divorce is rare, the levirate still occurs and polygyny is permitted but seldom practiced except by the wealthier *khans* or chiefs.

A vertical kin system stretches from the nuclear family to the ethno-linguistic group. Each unit embodies a system of reciprocal rights and obligations concerning society, economics and politics. The system involves a genealogy of real or assumed ancestors, and the blood aspect permeates the entire fabric of the society, for even the blood feud (*badal*) is inherited.

The ideal kinship-tribal structure from bottom to top is as follows with an example in parentheses: nuclear family, *hastani, aulad* (Ghazi); extended family, *plarghaney* (Musahiban); sublineage, clan if group has residential unity, *khel* (Yahya Khel); lineage, *p'sha* (Mohammadzai); tribe, *qaum* (Durrani); ethnic group (Pushtun). Not all tribes have so elaborate a structure, and some have eliminated several of the above steps.

The *qaum* of Afghanistan include Durrani, Ghilzai, Safi, Mangal, Jadran, Khostwal, Jaji, Khugiani and Shinwari. Major tribes in Pakistan include Afridi, Mohmand, Yusufzi, Wazir, Mahsud, Khattak, Bangash, Bannuchi, Darwesh Khel and Orakzai. Many of these as well as others reside across the Durand Line in both countries.

Although most Pushtun live in either Afghanistan or Pakistan, they have always felt a closer loyalty to their locally oriented tribal system than to the nation-state, unless the larger unit was threatened by an outside power. Several late nineteenth- and twentieth-century events have had considerable impact on the functions of the units within the tribal system, however.

The migrations, some forced, some voluntary, of certain Pushtun groups to northern Afghanistan during the time of Amir Abdur Rahman (1880–1901) caused a breakdown in the residential clan community. It ended the importance of the section and subtribe as political entities and forced the decline of the integrated section. Small-scale migrations occur even today, as land hungry peasants move to land newly reclaimed by irrigation projects in both Pakistan and Afghanistan.

A shift of the economic functions from the clan village to the extended family occurred in spite of the loss of residential unity among many groups. Whenever a man is away from his extended family, working on a development project or in the city, he maintains close economic ties with his extended family, sending them money and seeking out jobs for his close kin. Some of the surplus village labor force moves to the town and cities, thus helping maintain the balance in rural areas.

Shifts in population have also resulted in intergroup marriages between neighbors. Generally, Pushtun males might marry non-Pushtun females; rarely do non-Pushtun males marry Pushtun females. Such miscegenation has produced many males calling themselves Pushtun who have blond or red hair and blue eyes.

The independence of Pakistan in 1947 gave rise to the Pushtunistan issue, in which the Afghan government, headed by a Pushtun king, sought political unity for all Pushtun over the objections of the Pakistan government. The issue has strained relations between the two countries ever since.

In Pushtun culture warfare plays an important role, as it does in most nonliterate, peasant-tribal societies, either in its pursuit or avoidance. Students of warfare, however, often ignore the relationship between leisure time and fighting in the ecological cycle of agricultural and herding peoples. The Pushtun engage in feuding in the off-agricultural season or when the herders are not moving.

Idle young men in villages or nomadic winter quarters, who have suppressed their anxieties during the periods of maximum work, come dangerously close to in-group violence. The underlying sexual competition of male cousins for female cousins tends to exacerbate the problem.

Feuding with outsiders, therefore, channels the potential violence away from the village or camp. Relatively few people are killed in tribal fighting, but the safety valve aspect cannot be underestimated. Group unity threatened by individual outbursts of violence is maintained.

The idealized Pushtun male is the warrior-poet, brave in battle and eloquent in *jirgah*. Few men fulfill both requirements, but those who do become heroes of their age, as did a special hero, Khushal Khan Kattak (1613–1690).

The general traits of a Pushtun are suspicion of outsiders modified by a traditional code of hospitality; indifference to religion unless an outsider challenges his beliefs; brutality tempered by a love of beauty; industriousness when work is to be done, but easily swayed to indolence; avarice combined with compulsive generosity; conservatism in their mountain homeland, but quickly adaptable to new ideas when removed to cities; rugged individualism limited by the accepted role of their aristocratic *khans*; belief in masculine superiority, yet yielding to woman's persuasiveness; contentment in isolation overlaid by curiosity about the outside world.

The essence of Pushtun culture is expressed in the Pushtun code called the Pushtunwali (Pukhtunwali) or *nang*, Pushtun honor. The code incorporates these major practices: *melmastia* (being a genial host; throwing lavish parties); *mehr-man-palineh* (elaborate hospitality for guests, invited or not); *nanawati* (the right of asylum and the obligatory acceptance of a truce offer); *badal* (the blood feud or revenge); *tureh* (literally, sword, therefore, bravery); *meraneh* (manhood, chivalry); *isteqamat* (persistence, constancy); *sabat* (steadfastness); *imamdari* (righteousness); *ghayrat* (defense of property and honor); *mamus* (defense of the honor of one's own women). This is a stringent code, a tough code for tough men, who of necessity lead tough lives.

The Pakistani Pushtun live mainly in the North-West Frontier Province, Baluchistan Province and the Federally Administered Tribal Agencies (FATAs): Bajaur, Mohmand, Khyber, Kurram, Orakzai, North Waziristan and South Waziristan; but different patterns have been emerging in the 1970s and 1980s.

In 1973, Prime Minister Zulfikar Ali Bhutto launched an unprecedented socioeconomic development program in the FATAs, which led to a 30-fold increase in expenditures in four years. He also reopened several deserted British cantonments, including Razmak and Wana. Violence erupted but roads continued to creep into the FATAs.

Many local Pushtun integrated themselves into the economic mainstream (transport, trade, smuggling) of Pakistan. In addition, thousands of Pushtun left Pakistan (and Afghanistan) to seize new work opportunities in the oil fields of the Arab world and Persian Gulf. Along with other Pakistanis, they returned home with new wealth.

Conflicts between generations arose as groups began to adapt to the new economic and political situations. Junior lineages and junior members within lineages began to challenge the political power of the *spin geray*, who generally had not taken advantage of the accelerated economic opportunities. ''Business is not Pukhto,'' they said.

In the past, ownership of honor (*nang*), coupled with ownership of land (*zamin*), had been the most important prestige factors among the Pakistani Pushtun. This is changing, and money increases status, even in the political arena.

In spite of this, the Pushtun in both the Settled Districts of the provinces and the FATAs still cling to the paramount ideal of honor as articulated in the various versions of the Pukhtunwali. Some ''frontier-wallas'' may mourn the passing of the old frontier as they knew it, but for better or worse, the roads have come in to stay, and they are highways of cultural change as well as conquest and commerce.

Demands for meaningful regional autonomy within Pakistan continue to be a dominating force in politics. No Pakistani government has taken a postive view of the problem since Partition. The battle for the Pakistani Pushtun tribal soul is far from over.

On the Afghan side of the Durand Line, the Soviet-Afghan War has totally altered the political picture. The Pushtun (and other Afghan ethnic groups) will never be the same.

The process began with the *coup d'état* of July 17, 1973, when former (1953–1963) Prime Minister Mohammad Daoud (first cousin and brother-in-law of King Mohammad Zahir) seized power in association with leftist officers and established the Republic of Afghanistan.

A second coup occurred in April 1978 which broke the power of the Mohammadzai Durrani Pushtun tribe, the dominant political force (at least at the center) for about 150 years. The Democratic Republic of Afghanistan (DRA) was born. Subsequent sociopolitical and economic reforms introduced by the Khalqi (Masses) Party alienated virtually every segment of Afghan society. Widespread revolts swept the country after the summer of 1978, a manifestation of the seasonal aspects of Pushtun warfare.

The initial series of uprisings followed a traditional Central Asian-Iranian Plateau pattern. The revolts merely expressed an opinion. They informed the central government that it had stepped beyond the allowable bounds of cultural deviance. Such insurrections are not necessarily launched to overthrow a regime in power.

The new DRA did not respond in the traditional manner by sending just enough military force into the field to halt the movements, then calling for a Loya Jirgah (Great National Assembly), consisting of the regional power elites, both religious and secular. Instead, the Soviet-trained and equipped Afghan armed forces (with Soviet advisors) bombed and napalmed dissident villages. Much blood was shed, which triggered off a *badal* between the government and the people. The spring of 1979 approached, and the tribes sent out another culturally oriented signal to Kabul.

Normally, local annual feuds pause in time for the spring planting or herd migrations. But the tribes continued to fight and escalated the fighting in the spring and summer of 1979. Now, they were saying, we are fighting to overthrow. At this time, Afghan military units (all draftees) began to desert. Many joined the Mujahidin (freedom fighters).

In order to salvage the DRA (among other reasons), the Soviet Union invaded Afghanistan on December 24, 1979, and established a puppet regime under the Parchami (Banner Leader), Babrak Karmal. But the Soviet leadership had forgotten—or ignored—the history and culture of Afghanistan. Twice in the nineteenth century (1838–1842, 1878–1880) Afghan tribes and ethnic groups united regionally to drive the invading British from their country. Relatively speaking, few Afghans were involved in the fighting before the Soviet invasion; afterwards, they all became involved.

Pushtun kin units were based on regionally oriented, vertically structured, segmentary lineages. Neighboring lineages compete on the off-agricultural season. Part of this competition includes the blood feud. But when an outside, horizontal force threatens the vertical lineages, these neighboring kin units unite to resist. Traditional enemies such as the Nangal and Jadran in Paktya united to fight against the Soviets in 1980, just as they did when the British invaded their area in 1880.

Soviet tactics thus helped accelerate the localization and expansion of regional power. Conventional tactics have failed to destroy the Mujahidin or gain control of Afghanistan. The most effective Soviet tactics involved the use of the Mi-24 helicopter gunships. These armored weapons systems systematically roamed up and down selected valleys, destroying villages with their massive firepower, a process of "rubbleization" which resulted in migratory genocide. As of August 1982, Afghan refugees in Pakistan totalled about 3 million, becoming the world's largest refugee population. The majority were Pushtun.

"Rubbleization" has not worked. Guerrilla leaders, their villages destroyed and their families safe in Pakistan, returned to their own areas to fight. Because they no longer had to worry about the safety of their families or the sanctity of their villages, groups coalesced into larger units and expanded their zones of activity. Although disparate ethnic groups may seldom cooperate, they do maintain closer communication and on occasion have fought alongside one another.

A new leadership is emerging inside Afghanistan. Although the war is being fought under an overall Islamic banner, most of the leadership, both outside and inside, is more modernist than fundamentalist in orientation. Young men, often trained in the Soviet Union or by Soviet military advisers, have risen to dominance in many regions. Most still consult the traditional *spin geray*, but the mantle of power is gradually slipping in the direction of the younger military commanders.

Whether the Soviets leave Afghanistan or not, Pushtun culture (and that of

other Afghan ethnic groups) will never be the same. This is also true for the
Pakistani Pushtun, who must tolerate (not always peaceably) the increasing
number of refugees in their midst.

BIBLIOGRAPHY

Books

Ahmed, Akbar S. *Millennium and Charisma Among the Pathans*. London: Routledge
    and Kegan Paul, 1976.
———. *Pukhtun Economy and Society*. London: Routledge and Kegan Paul, 1980.
———. *Religion and Politics in Muslim Society: Order and Conflict in Paki.tan*. Cam-
    bridge: Cambridge University Press, 1982.
Anderson, Jon, and Strand, Richard, eds. *Ethnic Processes and Intergroup Relations in
    Contemporary Afghanistan*. Occasional Paper No. 15. New York: Afghanistan
    Council, Asia Society, 1978.
The Baluchis and Pathans. Report No. 48. London: Minority Rights Group, 1981.
Barth, F. *Selected Essays of Fredrik Barth: Features of Person and Society in Swat:
    Collected Essays on the Pathans*. Vol. 2. London: Routledge and Kegan Paul,
    1981.
Dupree, Louis. *Afghanistan*. Princeton: Princeton University Press, 1980.
———. "Afghanistan, 1880–1973." In *Commoners, Climbers and Notables*, edited by
    C.A.O. van Nieuwenhuijze. Leiden: E. J. Brill, 1977.
———. "The Durand Line, 1893." In *Current Problems in Afghanistan,* edited by T.
    Cuyler Young. Princeton: Princeton University Press, 1961.
———. "Language and Politics in Afghanistan." In *Contributions to Asian Studies XI:
    Language and Civilization Change in South Asia*, edited by Clarence Maloney.
    Leiden: E. J. Brill, 1978.
———. "The Political Uses of Religion: Afghanistan." In *Churches and States: The
    Religious Institution and Modernization*, edited by Kalman H. Silvert. New York:
    American Universities Field Staff, 1967.
———. "Religion, Technology and Islam." In *Aspects of Religion in Indian Society*,
    edited by L. P. Vidyarthi. Meerut, India: Kedar Ram Nath, 1961.
———. "Tribalism, Regionalism and National Oligarchy: Afghanistan." In *Expectant
    Peoples: Nationalism and Development,* edited by K. H. Silvert. New York:
    Random House, 1963.
———, and Albert, Linette, eds. *Afghanistan in the 1970s*. New York: Praeger, 1974.
Dupree, Nancy Hatch. *Kabul City*. Special Paper. New York: Afghanistan Council, Asia
    Society, 1975.
———. *Revolutionary Rhetoric and Afghan Women*. New York: Afghanistan Council,
    Asia Society, 1981.
———, ed. *History and Geography of Central Asia: Afghanistan*. Vol. 1. Essex, England:
    Susil Gupta, 1972.
Grassmuck, George; Adamec, Ludwig; and Irwin, Frances H., eds. *Afghanistan: Some
    New Approaches*. Ann Arbor: University of Michigan Press, 1969.
Gregorian, V. *The Emergence of Modern Afghanistan*. Stanford: Stanford University
    Press, 1969.

Howell, Evelyn. *Mizh: A Monograph on Government's Relations with the Mahsud Tribe*. Karachi: Oxford University in Asia Historical Reprints, 1979.

Kakar, H. K. *Government and Society in Afghanistan*. Austin: University of Texas Press, 1979.

Knabe, Erika. "Women in the Social Stratification of Afghanistan." In *Commoners, Climbers and Notables*, edited by C.A.O. van Nieuwenhuijze. Leiden: E. J. Brill, 1977.

Miller, Charles. *Kyber: The Story of an Imperial Migraine*. London: Macdonald and Jane's, 1977.

Newell, N., and Newell, R. *The Struggle for Afghanistan*. Ithaca: Cornell University Press, 1981.

Poullada, Leon B. *The Pushtun Role in the Afghan System*. Occasional Paper No. 1. New York: Afghanistan Council, Asia Society, 1972.

Scott, Richard. "Tribal and Ethnic Groups in the Helmand Valley." Occasional Paper No. 21. New York: Afghanistan Council, Asia Society, 1980.

Shahrani, Nazif, and Canfield, Robert, eds. *Revolutions and Rebellions in Afghanistan, 1978–1982*. In press.

Singer, Andre. *Guardians of the North-West Frontier: The Pathans*. Amsterdam: Time-Life Books, 1982.

Spain, James W. *Pathan Borderland*. The Hague: Mouton, 1963.

Steul, Willi. *Paschtunwali* (in German with English summary). Wiesbaden, Germany: Franz Steiner, 1981.

Tapper, Richard. "Nomadism in Modern Afghanistan." In *Afghanistan in the 1970s*, edited by Louis Dupree and L. Albert. New York: Praeger, 1974.

Van Oudenhoven, Nico J. A. *Common Afghan Street Names*. Lisse and Zeitlinger, 1979.

Articles

Ahmed, Akbar S. "An Aspect of the Colonial Encounter in the N-WFP." *Asian Affairs* 9:3 (1978): 319–327.

———. "Order and Conflict in Muslim Society: A Case Study from Pakistan." *Middle East Journal* 36:2 (1982): 184–204.

Anderson, Jon. "Tribe and Community Among the Ghilzai Pashtun." *Anthropos* 70 (1975): 575–601.

Boesen, Inger W. "Women, Honour and Love: Some Aspects of the Pashtun Women's Life in Eastern Afghanistan." *Afghanistan Journal* 7:2 (1980): 51–59.

Christensen, A. "The Pashtuns of Kunar." *Afghanistan Journal* 7:3 (1980): 79–92.

Dupree, Louis. "The Changing Character of South-Central Afghanistan Village. *Human Organization* 14:4 (1956): 26–29.

———. "Functions of Folklore in Afghan Society." *Asian Affairs* 66:1 (1979): 51–61.

———. "Involvement: A Key to Development." *Economic Development and Cultural Change* 13:4 (1965): 490–504.

———. "Islam in Politics: Afghanistan." *The Muslim World* 56:4 (1966): 269–276.

———. "Militant Islam and Traditional Warfare in Islamic South Asia." *Universities Field Staff International (formerly AUFS), Asia Series* 21 (1980): 1–12.

———. "Peshawar University: The Role of a University in Pakistan's Regional and

National Development." *American Universities Field Staff Reports: South Asia Series* 7:6 (1963): 1–26.

———. "Political Processes in Afghanistan: 1963–1970." *Asia: A Journal Published by the Asia Society, N.Y.* 22 (1971): 1–19.

———. " 'Pushtunistan': Parts I, II, III." *American Universities Field Staff Reports: South Asia Series* 5:2–4 (1961): 1–11; 1–16; 1–7.

———. "Red Flag Over the Hindu Kush" (6 pts.). *American Universities Field Staff Reports: Asia Series* 44 (1979): 1–17: 45 (1979): 1–16; 23, 27 (1980): 28, 1–15; 29, 1–10.

———. "The Saints Come Marching In." *American Universities Field Staff Reports: South Asia Series* 21:1 (1977): 1–4.

———. "Settlement and Migration Patterns in Afghanistan: A Tentative Statement." *Modern Asian Studies* 9:3 (1975): 385–400.

———, with Nancy Hatch Dupree. "Women and Men: Afghanistan." *Common Ground* 2:1 (1976): 29–35.

Dupree, Nancy Hatch. "An Interpretation of the Role of the Hoopoe in Afghan Folklore and Magic." *Folklore* 85 (1974): 173–193.

Lindholm, Charles. "The Structure of Violence Among the Swat Pukhtun." *Ethnology* 20:2 (1981): 147–156.

———, and Lindholm, Cherry. "Marriage as Warfare." *Natural History* 88 (1979): 11–20.

Pedersen, Gorm. "Socio-Economic Change Among a Group of East Afghan Nomads." *Afghanistan Journal* 8:4 (1981): 115–122.

Tapper, Nancy. "Pashtun Nomad Women in Afghanistan." *Asian Affairs* 8 (o.s. 64): 2 (1977): 163–170.

Weinbaum, Marvin. "Legal Elites in Afghan Society." 12:1 (1980): 39–57.

Unpublished Manuscripts

Anderson, Jon. "Doing Pakhtu: Social Organization of the Ghilzai Pakhtun." Ph.D. dissertation, University of North Carolina, 1979.

Evans-Von Krbek, J.H.P. "The Social Structure and Organisation of Pakhto Speaking Community in Afghanistan." Ph.D. dissertation, University of Durham (U.K.), 1977.

Tapper, Nancy Starr Self. "Marriage and Social Organization Among Durrani Pashtuns in Northern Afghanistan." Ph.D. dissertation, School of Oriental and African Studies, University of London, 1979.

Zadran, Alef-Shah. "Socio-Economic and Legal-Political Processes in a Pashtun Village, Southeastern Afghanistan." Ph.D. dissertation, State University of New York, Buffalo, 1977.

Louis Dupree

Q

QASHQA'I The Qashqa'i, one of Iran's many ethnic, tribal and national-minority groups, are Turkic speakers who live in the country's southwest. They number between 500,000 and 700,000. The term "Qashqa'i" applies to groups and individuals of different origins who were united politically in the past and who continue to share cultural features and notions of distinctiveness.

A major criterion of Qashqa'i identity is Turkic speech (western Oğuz Turkic language called Turki). Because of the predominance of the Qashqa'i among Turkic populations in southwest Iran, the words "Qashqa'i" and "Turk" are virtually synonymous there. Cultural criteria such as customs (especially weddings and hospitality), traditions and values also identify the Qashqa'i. The hat worn by men, made of tan or a gray felt with two distinctive "ears," is unique to the Qashqa'i and is a political symbol.

Most Qashqa'i are nomadic pastoralists, herders of sheep and goats who migrate long distances between winter and summer pastures in the lowlands and highlands of the Zagros Mountains. In the 1960s and 1970s, many were forced to become settled agriculturists or urban wage laborers, but under the conditions of the Iranian Revolution in 1978–1979 and the establishment of the Islamic Republic of Iran in 1979, many of these same Qashqa'i have returned to nomadic pastoralism.

There are five large Qashqa'i tribes (Amaleh, Darrehshuri, Kashkuli Bozorg, Farsi Madan and Shish Boluki) and many small ones. Each tribe consists of a number of named subtribes, which are represented by headmen and which have their own traditional areas of winter and summer pastures.

The Qashqa'i tribal confederacy, whose exact date of origin is unknown, probably came into existence in the eighteenth century. It consisted primarily of the descendants of Central Asian Turkic groups that entered Iran between the eleventh and fifteenth centuries. The name "Qashqa'i"—meaning "those of a horse with a white-starred forehead" or "those who fled"—is not well known outside of Fars Province, which was the gathering place of the diverse peoples who were the ancestors of the contemporary Qashqa'i. Turkic groups were joined by Lurs, Kurds, Arabs, Persians and Gypsies, who took on, to varying degrees,

Turkic identity, speech and custom. These populations were united by strong political leadership centered on a dynasty of powerful tribal khans. Beginning in the late eighteenth century, the paramount Qashqa'i khan was recognized by the Iranian central government with the title of Il Khani and given official administrative responsibilities, including tax collection, army conscription and maintenance of law and order in Qashqa'i and surrounding territories. By the early nineteenth century, the Qashqa'i confederacy had grown to be a strong political and military force, and through the nineteenth and twentieth centuries it has been a leading center of power in Fars Province, actively involved in pro-government and anti-government actions, intertribal alliances and disputes and some intrigue with foreign powers. During World War I, the Qashqa'i were perceived as a major impediment to British interests in Iran, and British military forces were used against them.

Reza Shah (1925–1941), founder off the Pahlavi dynasty, dealt severely with Iran's nomadic tribes. He stopped migrations by military force and enforced the settlement of nearly all pastoral nomads. He removed, imprisoned and in some cases executed tribal leaders. He confiscated tribal firearms. Many tribal populations, including the Qashqa'i, were forcibly settled on land that could not support flocks or produce crops, and many people and animals died. With the abdication of Reza Shah in 1941, the Qashqa'i, like many tribal populations, reacquired weapons and resumed their migrations. Leaders who had been imprisoned returned, and the Qashqa'i once again assumed political and military control of the area.

Qashqa'i leaders supported Prime Minister Mohammed Mossadeq (1951–1953), who nationalized Iran's British-owned oil company. After Mossadeq's overthrow, Mohammed Reza Shah moved against Qashqa'i power by exiling paramount tribal leaders and installing military governors. The confederacy was formally disbanded by government decree. Between 1956 and 1979, state action against the Qashqa'i was less dramatic, but the impact of the government policies of the 1960s and 1970s was severe nonetheless (see Lur).

Changed economic conditions, removal of tribal leaders, government control of land use and movement and loss of pastureland all had detrimental effects on the Qashqa'i. Pastoralism became increasingly commercialized, with more work and products oriented to the market instead of the home. Qashqa'i needs for cash (for agricultural products, grazing rents, bribes to government officials and newly felt needs) exceeded their income. They were unable to increase pastoral production because of pasture shortage, and they were forced to buy dry fodder for their animals. Many nomads fell heavily into debt to urban moneylenders, whose practices included interest rates up to 100 percent a year and below-market-value prices for pastoral products. Many Qashqa'i had to transfer ownership of their flocks to pay their creditors, only to become the hired shepherds of these same animals.

In the period from 1962 to 1978, the Qashqa'i were moving in three general directions: settlement in villages, continuation of impoverished nomadic pastoralism and urban wage labor. Most Qashqa'i settled or planned to settle, aware that only land ownership and agriculture offered them security. They had difficulty finding affordable productive land, and increasingly the settler depended on the wages of family members who were migrant laborers in the city. Most settlers tried to combine agriculture with pastoralism and divided household labor accordingly; some members cultivated crops, while others migrated with the herds. Those who settled did so in groups, often in winter or summer pastures where local ties already existed. Climatic conditions were, however, extreme: terrible heat and aridity in winter pastures in the summer and heavy snow and severe cold in summer pastures in the winter. Areas at middle altitudes were already heavily populated, and land was either unavailable or too expensive for most Qashqa'i. The land reform of the 1960s did not provide land for nomadic pastoralists, and purchase of nationalized land that had formerly belonged to tribes was forbidden by law.

The ecological richness and strategic importance of Qashqa'i territory combined with their political system helped to make the Qashqa'i one of the wealthiest of Iran's tribally organized, nomadic pastoral populations, despite political and military repressions against them by the Pahlavi shahs.

At the apex of the Qashqa'i socioeconomic system in the 1970s were the khan families, who, by virtue of noble lineages and hereditary tribal leadership, comprised a small, exclusive and wealthy group. They were members of Iran's national and regional political elite, were well educated and travelled and had urban residences and Western life-styles. Their income was derived from land, agriculture, orchards, flocks and, until the 1960s, tribal taxes.

The second level, also small, consisted of wealthy, landed, but non-elite Qashqa'i. This group, which had not existed to any degree until the 1960s, was created by the forces of land reform, pasture nationalization, agricultural mechanization and Qashqa'i depoliticization. Many were tribal headmen or held other positions of political power. In the 1970s most had life-styles similar to the urban, land-owning, upper middle and middle classes in Iranian society, while they simultaneously retained Qashqa'i culture and roots in Qashqa'i territory.

The vast majority of Qashqa'i constituted the third socioeconomic level, those who subsisted on animal husbandry and some agriculture. Wealth differences within this group depended on land availability, political contacts and market relations.

The fourth level consisted of hired shepherds and agricultural workers. Their life-styles were similar to those of the third level, but they were poorer and subsisted on contract herding, wage labor and their own small flocks.

The fifth level was a diverse collection of servants, craft specialists, camel drivers and wage laborers, all of whom depended on tribal or nontribal employers for a livelihood. In the 1970s many had left the paid employ of wealthy Qashqa'i for wage labor in Iranian cities, on construction sites and even in the Persian Gulf states.

For the majority of Qashqa'i for whom animal husbandry and agriculture are the primary sources of livelihood, the basic social unit—and the unit of production and consumption—is the nuclear or extended family, which resides in a small, rectangular, black goat-hair tent. A man, a woman and their children are responsible for the many tasks that sustain the household. Older boys and men do the daily herding, while younger boys and girls care for young animals and pack animals. Adolescent girls and women do most of the milking, milk processing, weaving, cooking and child care. Men perform most economic and political tasks that establish contacts with the market and with wider kinship and tribal groups. All household members help to migrate and make and break camp.

Qashqa'i males and females, as members of households and wider kinship and tribal units, view their roles and tasks as interdependent and mutually beneficial. The economic, political and social inequalities between men and women in many Muslim and Middle Eastern rural, lower and middle-class settings are much greater than among the Qashqa'i. Qashqa'i women are not devalued in ideological and symbolic systems to the degree that many other Muslim and Middle Eastern women are. Qashqa'i women do not wear veils except when visiting bazaars and shrines, where they feel obliged to conform with prevailing practices.

Qashqa'i dress is a matter of pride for the tribespeople, and the men's two-eared tan or gray felt hats and the woman's tunics, scarves and multilayered skirts set the Qashqa'i apart from their Persian and Luri neighbors. Before Reza Shah outlawed ethnic dress in the 1930s, Qashqa'i men wore cloaks, cummerbunds and wide pants. Since then, all but a few of the most elderly wear plain dark colored trousers, suit coats and white or light-colored shirts. At weddings, however, young men sometimes wear the cloaks and cummerbunds.

The Qashqa'i are Shia Muslims, unlike some other national minorities in Iran such as the Kurds, who are Sunnis. The Qashqa'i are not active in the performance of Islamic rites, and their knowledge of Islamic beliefs and practices tends to be slight, due partly to their lack of interest in and infrequent contact with religious institutions and personnel. No religious figures are part of Qashqa'i society. The Qashqa'i follow some Islamic requirements during the rites of marriage and death, but few observe the daily prayers, the Ramadan fast or the pilgrimage to Mecca. Some provide supposedly Quranic justification for some customs and behaviors. A few adult Qashqa'i males in each tribal section who are literate in Persian (Qashqa'i Turki is not written) and who have some expertise write marriage contracts and recite Quranic passages at funerals. Many families sacrifice a lamb and charitably distribute its meat on the Day of Sacrifice.

Islamic law codes are not particularly relevant to the position of Qashqa'i women within their society. Qashqa'i women are less knowledgeable in the formal aspects of Islam than are the men. However, they have less chance to gain this knowledge than many Muslim women because of their distance from urban and religious centers. Itinerant dervishes supply cures, prayers and amulets for women and children. Qashqa'i women attend local shrines if migration routes afford them access, and some every year make pilgrimages to a major shrine in

Shiraz to make or discharge vows. Qashqa'i women, therefore, use the more accessible and supposedly efficacious aspects of Islam, while Qashqa'i men, who also clearly and unambiguously identify themselves as Muslims, tend to be skeptical concerning the Islam they see practiced in bazaar economics and (after 1978) state politics and associate themselves with more specifically tribal customs and codes of ethics.

The revolution against the rule of the Shah in 1978–1979 and the ensuing establishment of the Islamic Republic of Iran in 1979 brought about many political, economic and social changes for the Qashqa'i. Qashqa'i tribespeople quickly rearmed and seized control of former pastoral and agricultural land. Nontribal encroachers were forced to leave. Prices of pastoral products tripled, interest taking (a practice that had been a major cause of poverty in the past) was forbidden and debts were reduced to the actual value of the goods or money borrowed; many Qashqa'i did very well economically after the revolution and found pastoralism to be more profitable than many of the livelihoods adopted in the 1960s and 1970s.

Attitudes of the Qashqa'i concerning Islam changed after the forced imposition of theocratic rule in Iran. Before 1979 they had been critical of what they regarded as the irreligious behavior of the moneylender-merchant *hajjis*, on whom they had been economically dependent, and offered this behavior as evidence that daily prayer and fasting had little to do with being a good Muslim. After 1979 they were suspicious of the ruling clergy's political repressions, which were said to be justified by religious doctrine. Persecutions against Iran's national minorities, with whom many Qashqa'i identified and sympathized, were viewed with alarm. Qashqa'i women who went to town not properly dressed were harassed, and coeducational classes at the tribal schools in Shiraz were forbidden. Also forbidden by the new Islamic regime were the music and dancing performed at Qashqa'i weddings.

But it was in the area of Qashqa'i politics that the Islamic Republic had the most impact. With the revolution of 1978–1979, Qashqa'i leaders who had been exiled and deposed by the Shah returned to tribal territory and attempted to resume leadership of the Qashqa'i population. This was a difficult task given their many years of absence and the socioeconomically diversified and geographically dispersed population.

During the uneasy first year of the Islamic Republic, Revolutionary Guards were sent out to enforce state rule among Iran's national minorities. They interfered little in Qashqa'i activities. That the Qashqa'i were Shia and not Sunni, as were the Kurds, Turkmen and Baluch, was one reason. Ayatollah Khomeini attributed peaceful conditions in Fars Province to the presence of the Qashqa'i khans who had returned from exile. However, in 1980 relationships turned hostile when conservative clerics denied Khosrow Khan Qashqa'i, a popular Qashqa'i leader, his seat in the newly elected parliament. When he was arrested and imprisoned, military confrontations between the Revolutionary Guards and Qashqa'i forces broke out in southern Iran. Paramount Qashqa'i leaders and their families, many of whom had spent much of the past 25 years under Pahlavi-imposed exile, sought refuge in the mountains to avoid capture and arrest. For two years, Revolutionary Guards attacked the insurgent camp and its small supporting military force. In the summer of 1982, after the death or departure of some key Qashqa'i leaders, the insurgents were defeated. Khosrow Khan, by this time the paramount Qashqa'i leader, was captured, arrested and condemned to death by an Islamic revolutionary court and publicly hanged in Shiraz. Other Qashqa'i leaders were imprisoned or subjected to house arrest, while some went underground or managed secretly to flee the country.

The vast majority of the Qashqa'i people, who did not participate in any way in the insurgent movement, were unobstructed by the government in their pastoral and agricultural livelihoods after 1979 and were allowed to continue their migrations. However, all Qashqa'i in rural areas were heavily armed and prepared to resist the reestablishment of state control in their territories and to defend their local interests.

BIBLIOGRAPHY

Books

Allgrove, Joan. "The Qashqa'i." In *Yoruk: The Nomadic Weaving Tradition of the Middle East*, edited by Anthony Landreau. Pittsburgh: Museum of Art, Carnegie Institute, 1978.

Bahmanbegui, Mohammad. "Qashqa'i: Hardy Shepherds of Iran's Zagros Mountains Build a Future Through Tent-School Education." In *Nomads of the World*, edited by Melville Grosvenor. Washington, D.C.: National Geographic Society, 1971.

Barker, Paul. "Tent Schools of the Qashqa'i: A Paradox of Local Initiative and State Control." In *Modern Iran: The Dialectics of Continuity and Change*, edited by Michael Bonine and Nikki Keddie. Albany: State University of New York Press, 1981.

Beck, Lois. "Economic Transformations Among Qashqa'i Nomads, 1962–1978." In *Modern Iran: The Dialectics of Continuity and Change*, edited by Michael Bonine and Nikki Keddie. Albany: State University of New York Press, 1981.

———. "Iran and the Qashqa'i Tribal Confederacy." In *Tribe and State in Afghanistan and Iran from 1800 to 1980*, edited by Richard Tapper. London: Croom Helm, 1983.

———. *The Qashqa'i Confederacy of Iran*. New Haven: Yale University Press. In press.

———. "*The Qashqa'i People of Southern Iran*. UCLA Museum of Cultural History Pamphlet Series, No. 14. Los Angeles: UCLA Museum of Cultural History, 1981.

———. "Women Among Qashqa'i Nomadic Pastoralists in Iran." In *Women in the Muslim World*, edited by Lois Beck and Nikki Keddie. Cambridge: Harvard University Press, 1978.

Douglas, William O. *Strange Lands and Friendly People*. New York: Harper, 1951.

Duncan, David Douglas. *The World of Allah*. Boston: Houghton Mifflin, 1982.
Oberling, Pierre. *The Qashqa'i Nomads of Fars*. The Hague: Mouton, 1974.
Tapper, Richard. "The Tribes in Eighteenth and Nineteenth Century Iran." In *The Cambridge History of Iran*. Vol. 7. Edited by Peter Avery and G. Hambly. Cambridge: Cambridge University Press, 1983.
Ullens de Schooten, Marie Therese. *Lords of the Mountains: Southern Persia and the Kashkai Tribe*. London: Chatto and Windus, 1956.

Articles

Beck, Lois. "Government Policy and Pastoral Land Use in Southwest Iran." *Journal of Arid Environment* 4:3 (1981): 253–267.
———. "Herd Owners and Hired Shepherds: The Qashqa'i of Iran." *Ethnology* 19:3 (1980): 327–351.
———. "Nomads and Urbanites, Involuntary Hosts and Uninvited Guests." *Journal of Middle Eastern Studies* 18:4 (1982): 426–444.
———. "The Qashqa'i Nomads of Fars (Pierre Oberling)." *Iranian Studies* 10:1–2 (1977): 116–119.
———. "Revolutionary Iran and Its Tribal Peoples." *MERIP Reports* 10:4 (1980): 14–20.
———. "Tribe and State in Revolutionary Iran: The Return of the Qashqa'i Khans." *Iranian Studies* 13:1–4 (1980): 215–255.
Soraya, Mehdy. "Ghashghai Social Structure." *Islamic Culture* 43:2 (1969): 125–142.

Unpublished Manuscripts

Beck, Lois. "Local Organization Among Qashqa'i Nomadic Pastoralists in Southwest Iran." Ph.D. dissertation, University of Chicago, 1977.
Ghashghai, Houshang. "The Question of Settlement of Nomads of Iran." Ph.D. dissertation, United States International University, 1981.
Marsden, David. "The Qashqa'i 'Tribe' and Tribal Identity." Occasional Paper No. 6, Centre for Development Studies, University College of Swansea, Wales, 1978.
Salzer, Richard E. "Social Organization of a Nomadic Pastoral Nobility in Southern Iran: The Kashkulu Kuchek Tribe of the Qashqa'i." Ph.D. dissertation, University of California, Berkeley, 1974.
Swee, Gary. "Sedentarization: Change and Adaptation Among the Kordshuli Pastoral Nomads of Southwestern Iran." Ph.D. dissertation, Michigan State University, 1981.

Lois Beck

QIZILBASH Throughout their existence, the Qizilbash have had an importance which far overshadows their numbers. No current accurate population figures can be quoted, for many Qizilbash in Afghanistan and Pakistan, who are Shia, practice *taqiyya* (dissimilation) and pass for Sunni, Tajik, Farsiwan or Pushtun. In Pakistan, some even claim to be Punjabis or, if their families came to Pakistan in 1947 (or after), refer to themselves in relation to the place in India from which their ancestors sprung, for example, Hyderabad (Deccan), Bombay or Delhi.

Estimates for Qizilbash in Afghanistan vary from 30,000 to 200,000. Some enthusiastic Qizilbash in Afghanistan insist the true figure is close to 1 million, an indication of the widespread practice of *taqiyya*. In Pakistan estimates also vary with the source, but no one denies the importance of the Qizilbash in the upper strata of power and among the intelligentsia. Few Qizilbash in the upper strata of power live in Iran, their original home.

The Qizilbash grew out of the hodgepodge of Turkish Shia groups living in northwest Persia (Azerbaijan), militant refugees from oppression by the Osmanli Turks during the emerging Ottoman Empire. Shaikh Haider (1460–1468), a charismatic Sunni religious leader, gained a large following among the Shia of Azerbaijan. He designated his most loyal Turkic followers as "Qizilbash" and created a special headgear for them to wear, a common practice when new orders are formed. The Haider hat was red, with 12 red tassels, 1 for each Imam. "Qizilbash" is alternately translated "red hats," "red heads" or even "red beards."

In 1488, Shaikh Haider was killed in a battle between his Qizilbash and other Turks, and civil war rent Azerbaijan. But in 1501, one of Haider's sons, Ismail (1501–1524), founded the Safavid dynasty (1501–1732) and conquered most of what is called Iran today. Shah Ismail spread Ithna Ashari Shiism throughout Persia, and the religion is still dominant in Iran.

The Qizilbash could put over 70,000 armed horsemen in the field and constituted a formidable force. Some hired themselves out as mercenaries, but most loyally supported the Safavid Shahs, particularly in their struggles with the Sunni Ottoman Turks in the west and the Sunni Uzbek Turks in the east. But subsequent Shahs began to distrust the Qizilbash, who returned the distrust. As the end of the sixteenth century approached, the mutual distrust reached a climax.

Shah Abbas the Great (1588–1629) ruled Persia for 43 years, the climax period for the Safavids. The Shah formed a new corps of janissaries, consisting of Georgians and Armenians who had been converted from Christianity to Islam. He also gave a prestigious title to the Turks living in the Moghan steppes of northwest Azerbiajan: the Shahsevan, "Friends (or Protectors) of the Shah," or "Those Who Love the Shah" (see Shahsevan).

Civil wars and revolts spread throughout the Safavid Empire after the death of Shah Abbas, culminating in the invasion of Persia by the Ghilzai Pushtun from the Afghan area. The Ghilzai chief, Mahmud, ruled parts of Persia from Isfahan, the old Safavid capital, from 1722 to 1725, when he was overthrown by his cousin, Ashraf. Mahmud gained the enmity of the Qizilbash by slaughtering 3,000 of them in an Isfahan bloodbath. But a new Turk was waiting in the wings to drive out the Afghan usurpers.

An Afshar Turk, Nadir Quli Khan, led the resistance to Ashraf and, with the aid of the Qizilbash (among others), defeated the Afghans and drove them into

Afghan Khorasan and Baluchistan. Nadir proclaimed himself Shah in 1736 and launched a series of religious reforms and military campaigns against the Moghul Empire. He forced the Persians to give up the Ithna Ashari Shiism of Abbas the Great but did not force them to accept Sunnism. Instead he accepted a new orthodox school named after the Imam Jafar Sadiq (the Jafarites, who in modern times consider themselves Shia).

At the classic battle of Panipat in 1739, Nadir Shah defeated the "pleasure-loving carpet knights" of the Moghul court with his toughened Georgian and Qizilbash mercenaries. Along his route of invasion, Nadir Shah had left behind garrisons of Qizilbash (and others) to protect his route of communication and supply, to maintain law and order and to collect revenue and tribute from the conquered populations. Nadir Shah had besieged Kandahar in 1737–1738 and left behind a sizable garrison, mainly Qizilbash. He also left behind a 12,000-man Qizilbash garrison in Kabul. They established a separate fortified quarter in Kabul named Chandiwal ("rear guard"), which exists today.

After looting Delhi, Nadir Shah led his troops past Kandahar and Herat into Central Asia, taking Samarkand, Bokhara and Khiva. He returned to Mashad, which he made his capital in 1741. Increasing brutality marked the final years of Nadir Shah. Convinced that his son, Raza Quli, wanted to assassinate him and seize the throne, Nadir had him blinded. Nadir became morose and suspicious and had many of his loyal followers (among them Qizilbash) executed at the slightest hint of opposition.

While in camp outside Kuchan, Nadir Shah confided in a young Afghan (Pushtun) commander, Ahmad Khan, that officers from his own tribe, the Afshar Turks, were plotting to kill him. Nadir asked for the loyalty of Ahmad Khan. Indeed, the Afshar and Qizilbash officers were plotting, and they slipped into Nadir's tent and beheaded the Shah as he slept. As the regicides looted the camp, Ahmad Khan and his 4,000 Sunni horsemen sped away, fearing that the Shia Afshar and Qizilbash would probably use them as scapegoats. Ahmad Khan had been a treasury official in Nadir's camp, so he lifted much of the Shah's portable wealth, including the fabled Koh-i-Noor diamond, which Nadir had taken from the Moghul treasury in Delhi. (The diamond now resides in the crown of the Queen of England.)

At a *jirgah* (tribal council) outside Kandahar, Ahmad Khan became Ahmad Shah Durrani, ruler in the Kandahar area, but first he had to defeat the Qizilbash in Kandahar who had declared independence of Nadir Shah while he campaigned in Central Asia. The local Pushtun tribal leadership ruled jointly with the Qizilbash.

From his capital in Kandahar, Ahmad Shah Durrani spread the final Afghan Empire from eastern Persia to northern India, from the Arabian Sea to Turkistan. The Afghans were able warriors but had little experience in the administration of empire, so the Qizilbash colonies proved invaluable to the founder of the Durrani Empire (1747–1793). Next to the Ottoman Empire, the Durrani Empire was the greatest Muslim state of the second half of the eighteenth century.

Having conquered almost all the area administered by the Qizilbash in Af-

ghanistan and India, Ahmad Shah retained them to help him govern but did not
let the Qizilbash maintain their formidable military organization—with one important exception. Qizilbash made up his personal bodyguard, the household
troops called *ghulam khana*, which included both cavalry and artillery units. (In
the eighteenth and nineteenth centuries, many Qizilbash served in the irregular
cavalry in India, sometimes for the British, sometimes for opposing princely
states.)

Originally Turkic speakers, the Qizilbash gradually accepted Dari (Afghan
Farsi or Persian) as their primary language, although many still learned Turkish
as their mother tongue. But the use of Dari was logical, since dialects of Persian
were the languages of empires from Persia to Central Asia to Moghul India,
before English replaced Persian as the language of empire in South Asia.

Timur Shah (1772–1793) succeeded his father to the throne in Kandahar and
inherited a political can of worms. The Kandahari Afghan (Pushtun) tribal khans
and Sunni religious leaders resented the fact that Shia Qizilbash held many
important administrative positions in the royal court and the provinces. In addition, a 12,000-man Qizilbash personal guard protected (and had influence on)
the Shah.

The court of Timur had become Persianized in language, attitudes and customs.
He went so far as to dismiss virtually all of his non-Qizilbash advisors. The
Qizilbash came to be known as *ghulam-i-Shah* ("slaves of the Shah"). Timur
further alienated the Sunni Kandahari Pushtun by utilizing his Shia Qizilbash
bodyguard as trouble-shooters in his trouble-ridden empire. Several threats from
the local Kandahari were systematically suppressed by the Qizilbash mercenaries.

Relations between Timur Shah and the Afghan population around Kandahar
continued to worsen, so the Shah moved his capital to Kabul in 1775–1776. The
rapidly disintegrating scene exploded into civil war after the death of the Timur
Shah. The wars had begun before his death but now escalated. In rapid succession, Shahs rose and fell, with the Qizilbash usually supporting the line of Ahmad
Shah Durrani.

Intermarriage also helped the position of the Qizilbash in the Afghan court.
Leading members in the Afghan power elites married Qizilbash ladies to cement
inter-family alliances, but few (if any) Sunni Pushtun ladies married Shia Qizilbash men. Probably the most important product of the Sunni male-Shia female
liaison was Dost Mohammad Khan, another great figure in Central Asian history.
He ruled twice (1819–1839, 1842–1863) from Kabul and came closest to unifying
Afghanistan before the reign of Abdur Rahman Khan (1880–1901). Dost Mohammad rejected the term "Shah," and called himself Amir, which Afghan
rulers preferred until Amanullah proclaimed himself Padhshah (king) in 1923.

Qizilbash today say that Dost Mohammad's Qizilbash mother had a great
influence on his life, and that is why he is still lionized by most Afghans. The
following saying is commonly heard: "Where is justice in the land, now that
Dost Mohammad Khan is dead?"

In spite of their considerable influence in the Afghan court, the Qizilbash constantly felt waves of discrimination emanate from the dominant Sunni population. Also, not all Qizilbash were administrators, clerks, traders and craftsmen. Many pockets of them existed in the countryside and still do. For example Qizilbash make up one of the four villages known as Chahardeh-i-Ghorband (the four villages of the Ghorband Valley). The other three are occupied by Sunni Pushtun and Sunni Tajik.

But the real impact of the Qizilbash in Afghan history relates to the urban scene. Many groups lived not only in Kabul but also in Kandahar Herat and Mazar-i-Sharif, among other places. Nineteenth-century European travellers reported the following Qizilbash subdivisions: Jawansher, Kurd, Rika, Afshar, Bakhtiari, Shahsevan, Talish, Bayat and others. (Several names relate to the Persian origin of the Qizilbash and even include names of other ethnic groups, such as Kurd, Bakhtiari, Shahsevan.)

The British invaded Afghanistan twice in the nineteenth century, during the First Anglo-Afghan War (1838–1842) and the Second Anglo-Afghan War (1878–1880). The wars were a result of real or imagined threats to British India by czarist Russia. In both instances, groups of Qizilbash (and others) who opposed any Afghan government in power supported the British. According to British sources, at least 6,500 Qizilbash served as tax collectors, clerks, commissary suppliers and mercenaries. For example, 600 Qizilbash cavalry accompanied Captain Richard Shakespear on a mission to rescue the British hostages being held at Bamiyan in September 1842.

Some Qizilbash left with the British army after both wars. They settled in British India and became influential in the army, bureaucracy and commerce both before and after the 1947 Partition, which divided the subcontinent into India and Pakistan. The British also hired a number of Qizilbash as ''news writers,'' actually spies, who represented the British Indian government in Afghan cities from 1880 to 1919, at which time the Afghan government permitted the British to send Englishmen as diplomatic representatives.

Qizilbash influence in the Afghan court continued to diminish after Abdur Rahman Khan (1880–1901) became Amir in Kabul and spread his influence, if not actual control, over most of what is now Afghanistan. He engaged in ''internal imperialism,'' conquering and attempting to pacify the countryside, while the British and czarist Russia drew his boundaries.

One of the bloodier fights of Abdur Rahman was the 1891–1893 conquest of the Hazarajat (see Hazaras). The Shia Qizilbash were accused of supporting the Shia Hazaras, some openly, some secretly. Because of this, many Afghans today consider all Hazaras also to be Qizilbash. In April 1893, the Qizilbash refugees in Mashad (Persia) declared a holy war on Abdur Rahman. The Sunni population of western Afghanistan supported Abdur Rahman, and the revolt failed.

Abdur Rahman Khan attempted to convert forcibly the Qizilbash to Sunnism. Those who refused were forced to wear red turbans. Partly because of the blatant discrimination, many Qizilbash outwardly accepted Hanafi Sunnism but practiced *taqiyya* (secretly remained Shia).

Twentieth-century Qizilbash have moved from being mercenaries to being merchants as well as mainstays in the urban professions—doctors, teachers, engineers and lawyers—and they continue to be important cogs in the administrative structure.

The leftish coups of 1973, 1978 and 1979 and the Soviet invasion of Afghanistan in late 1979 once again divided the Qizilbash into two camps: those supporting the leftist regime in the hope that a genuine Afghan socialism would emerge from the chaos, and those opposed to the leftist regime on both religious and secular (ideological) grounds. Most of the latter have either fled Afghanistan or joined the Mujahidin (freedom fighters).

The Qizilbash are a classic example of a cohesive group tossed about by history and split among several nations, losing their cohesion and influence but never their ethnic pride—in spite of the fact that many must practice *taqiyya* in order to survive.

BIBLIOGRAPHY

Books

Brockelmann, Carl. *History of the Islamic Peoples*. New York: Putnams, 1947.
Caroe, Sir Olaf. *The Pathans, 550 B.C.–A.D. 1957*. London: Macmillan, 1958.
Dupree, Louis. *Afghanistan*. Princeton: Princeton University Press, 1980.
Hanifi, M. Jamil. *Annotated Bibliography of Afghanistan*. New Haven: Human Relations Area Files Press, 1982.
Kakar, M. Hasan. *Afghanistan: A Study of Internal Political Developments: 1880–1896*. Lahore, Pakistan: Punjab Educational Press, 1971.
———. *Government and Society in Afghanistan: The Reign of Abdal-Rahman Khan*. Austin: University of Texas Press, 1979.
Lal, Mohan. *Life of the Amir Dost Mohammad Khan*. 1846. Reprint ed. Karachi: Oxford University in Asia Historical Reprints, 1978.
Lockhart, Laurence. *The Fall of the Safavi Dynasty and the Afghan Occupation of Persia*. Cambridge: The University Press, 1958.
Tapper, Richard. *Pasture and Politics*. London: Academic Press, 1979.
Watkins, Mary Bradley. *Afghanistan: Land in Transition*. Princeton: Van Nostrand, 1963.

Articles

Dupree, Louis. "Afghan Studies." *American Universities Field Staff Reports: South Asia Series* 20:4 (1976): 1–32.
———. "Anthropology in Afghanistan." *American University Field Staff Reports: South Asian Series* 20:5 (1976): 1–21.
———. "Further Notes on *Taqiyya*: Afghanistan." *Journal of the American Oriental Society* 99:4 (1979): 680–682.

Louis Dupree

R

RESHAWA   They call themselves Reshawa, but throughout the Yauri Division of Sokoto State in Nigeria many call them Gungawa, a Hausa term for "island dwellers." Their homeland is on the banks and islands of the Niger River, where they excel in fishing, farming and becoming Hausa-ized. Numbering some 50,000, of whom perhaps 70 percent are Muslim, they share their remote area with the Shangawa, Dukawa, Lopawa, Kamberi and the dominant Hausa (see Hausa; Kamberi; Shangawa).

The origins of the Reshawa are a matter of conjecture. Their language, Reshe, is of the Benue-Congo division of the Niger-Congo language family, similar to that of most of the ethnic groups in northern Nigeria. A Muslim opinion of origin is that they came to Yauri from northeastern Nigeria, the land of the Kanuri, whose language is Nilo-Saharan. Other opinions include a southeastern origin, where other Niger-Congo languages are spoken.

The Reshawa probably settled on the islands in Yauri before the fourteenth century. They came as migrants who adapted to a riverine environment, becoming hoe farmers who grew (and still grow) millet and guinea corn on the highlands and onions along the river. They supplemented their food supply and income through fishing. Although they were not themselves traditional fishermen, they incorporated members of other ethnic groups who were.

By the sixteenth century, the Reshawa had been ruled by five emirs, according to their kings' lists. In the sixteenth century they expanded their political control from the islands to the mainland. They seized Bin Yauri, then the capital, from the Hausa and the first Emir of Yauri was a Reshawa. The Hausa reestablished themselves after the death of the second emir and have remained in power ever since.

Islam came to Yauri with traders, itinerant *mallamai* (clerics) and Hausa administrators. They were reinforced by Fulani slave raiders; those who were openly Muslim were relatively safe from capture. Being a practical people, the Reshawa found that their future was enhanced not only by becoming Muslim but by becoming Hausa, or "Yaurawa," the name for Reshawa who enter the governing group.

There are many interethnic ties between the Reshawa and Yauri's other ethnic groups. They hunt with the Kamberi, fish with the Serkawa, market with the Hausa, joke with the the Shangawa and in general maintain connections with all groups. Members of all ethnic groups in Yauri except the Dukawa, intermarry. But Reshawa are the most active in incorporating people of other ethnic groups into their own, making themselves stronger. The prevalence of polygyny increases the frequency of interethnic marriage. The traditionally high incidence of Hausa divorce works to the benefit of the Reshawa, who then acquire Hausa wives. The bridewealth for a Hausa divorcee is much less than for a Hausa virgin. Reshawa intermarriage with Hausa eases their political life as Hausa people have a high regard for Reshawa. Hausa women are considered more reliable than Reshawa women, who cannot take secondary husbands since polyandry is prohibited among Muslims.

Male–female hostility and distrust is common among Reshawa, who traditionally have both high divorce and secondary marriage rates. Men are free to marry as many women as they can afford unless they are Muslim. Sexual hostility permeates most relationships, except between mother and son. Men state that mothers and grandmothers are the only women they really trust. Close male friends find themselves competing for the same women and becoming suspicious of their designs on their wives.

The traditional economic pattern fosters such problems as there is little need for genuine economic cooperation between men and women. Resettlement has exacerbated this problem since men must leave the villages for extended periods and often must go miles to work on farmland instead of on nearby fields.

The strong male–female antipathy among Reshawa is emphasized in the organization of the primary work team, a male kin-based group. Marriage does not provide a mechanism for crosscutting kin ties. The young non-Muslim Reshawa males form intervillage wrestling teams, however, that do crosscut lineal ties. Wrestling emphasizes all the essential Reshawa values while tying non-kinsmen together. Islamic teachers have forbidden Reshawa converts to engage in wrestling because of the drinking and the performance of religious rituals taking place.

One major deviation from the Hausa model of Islam among converted Reshawa concerns the child-avoidance (*dan fari*) practice in which Hausa avoid their firstborn son or daughter. Among the Hausa, child avoidance pushes the children into ties outside the nuclear family, emphasizing the separation of generations and stressing the importance of marriage and childrearing as status markers. The Reshawa do not ignore their children in such manner and maintain close parent–child relationships.

There are two Sufi brotherhoods in Yauri, the Tijani and the Qadiri. Unlike other cases in Nigeria, the two have not established different mosques; they pray together even at Friday service. At other times they pray separately. The *imam* refrains from praying as a member of an order on Fridays since each has a special method of praying.

Muslims in Yauri accept the beliefs of traditional religion and superimpose an Islamic layer on them. For their part, those who believe in traditional religion believe in Allah, at least as a Creator God or Supreme One. But Allah appears too far away to concern Himself with man's affairs. Muslims and traditionalists both pray to the spirits for help. Muslims call them *jinn* and name them. Islam appears to be more a matter of outward conformity rather than inward conviction in Yauri. As long as a person prays five times a day, keeps the Ramadan fast, gives alms, refrains at least from guinea corn beer, gives children Muslim names and, if possible, goes to Mecca no one blames the person for going to a traditional priest in a crisis.

The Reshawa possess a number of significant religious leaders. One such leader was Jugun Halla, who enjoyed widespread acclaim. He died under mysterious circumstances in 1976. His statement to the author helps to explain both his power and death: "Even those who became Muslims at the time of the Sardauna (Ahmadu Bello), before the British left, come to see me. Yes, there is Allah, but He is too far away to help men. He cannot be bothered with men. But my spirits will travel to me from even America in a twinkling of an eye and will help anyone I ask them to help."

The Reshawa have a pragmatic outlook on Islam and Western cultures. They emphasize the maximization of opportunity. Thus, at any given time, the Reshawa attitude towards any other group is shaped largely by what that group has to offer them. Since cooperation with the politically dominant Hausa is best assured by Islamic conversion, the Reshawa view such conversion positively.

Especially since their forced move to the mainland in 1968 as part of the Kainji Dam project, the Reshawa perceive benefits in becoming Muslim. First, court cases go more smoothly. Second, government jobs and taxes are more equitable for Muslims. Third, the cost of renting equipment is lower for Muslims. Moreover, *mallamai* more easily contact resettled Reshawa now that they are near the town of Yelwa rather than on the islands.

The dam has had other effects. The traditional way of life has been disrupted. Reshawa have no room to expand from their resettlement villages. The tin roofs on the houses make them unbearably hot, up to 144° F. Work teams are disrupted, as some of the men must remain behind to watch after the women.

Finally, modernization in the form of new roads, wells, schools, welfare agencies, farm experts and all the paraphernalia of modern government facilitates the control of central government over traditional peoples. The weight of the state favors Islam. The Reshawa who have a pattern of Islamic conversion will continue to follow it. Most of them, however, will no longer be as easily able to pass as Hausa, for the path is now crowded and the Hausa can be more selective in conferring ethnic membership.

BIBLIOGRAPHY

Books

Arnett, E. J. *Gazetteer of Sokoto Province*. London: Waterlow, 1920.

Duff, E. C. *Gazetteer of the Kontagora Province*. London: Waterlow, 1920.

Greenberg, Joseph. *The Influence of Islam on a Sudanese Religion*. Seattle: University of Washington Press, 1946.

Gunn, Harold, and Conant, Francis. *Peoples of the Middle Niger*. London: International African Institute, 1960.

Harris, P. G. *Provincial Gazetteer of Sokoto Province*. London: Waterlow, 1938.

Jeness, Jonathan. *Fishermen of the Kainji Basin*. Rome: F.A.O., 1970.

Roder, Wolf. *The Irrigation Farmers of the Kainji Lake Region, Nigeria*. Rome: F.A.O., 1970.

Salamone, Frank. A. *Gods and Goods in Africa*. New Haven: HRAFlex, 1974.

―――. "Religious Change in a Small Emirate." In *The Realm of the Extrahuman: Actors and Audiences*, edited by A. Bharati. The Hague: Mouton, 1976.

Articles

Harris, P.G. "Notes on Yauri, Sokoto Province, Nigeria." *Journal of the Royal Anthropological Institute of Great Britain and Ireland* 68 (1930): 283–334.

Salamone, Frank A. "All Resettled at Kainji?" *Intellect* (1977): 231–233.

―――. "Becoming Hausa: Contributions to the Theory of Cultural Pluralism." *Africa* 45(4):(1975): 401–424.

―――. "Competitive Conversion and Its Implications for Modernization." *Anthropos* 75 (1980): 383–404.

―――. "Gungawa Wrestling as an Ethnic Marker." *Africa und Ubersee* (1974): 193–201.

―――. "Religion as Play: Bori, a Friendly Witch Doctor." *Journal of Religion in Africa* 8:3 (1976): 201–211.

―――, and Swanson, Charles. "Identity and Ethnicity." *Ethnic Groups* 2 (1979): 1167–183.

Unpublished Manuscripts

Balogun, Sake Adegbite. "Gwandu Emirates in the Nineteenth Century with Special Reference to Political Relations, 1817–1903." M. A. thesis, University of Ibadan, 1970.

Mahdi, Adamu. "A Hausa Government in Decline: Yawuri in the Nineteenth Century." M.A. thesis, Ahmadu Bello University, Zaria, Nigeria, 1968.

Frank A. Salamone

S

SADAMA   The Ethiopian people who refer to themselves as Sadama (adjective: Sidamo) may number more than 600,000 and include several differing, but related, ethnic groups in the southwest part of Ethiopia. Perhaps 10 pecent are Muslim. They live in a trapezoidal-shape area marked by Lake Awasa, Lake Abaya, the upper branches of the Loghita River and the Billate River. To the north are the Arussi people; the Walamo are situated on the western boundary, the Guği and Darasa on the south and Jamjam (Northern Guği) on the east. They form part of the Highland East Cushitic language group.

Without adequate census data one can only speculate as to the present number of Muslims in the Sidamo population. Though it is likely that the interethnic trade of the last century would have provided the Sadama with some knowledge of Islam, informants are of the belief that only recently (within the last 20 years) have there been any significant numbers of converts. J. Spencer Trimingham in his book *Islam in Ethiopia* reports Islam is professed among such Sidamo groups as the Tamboro, Garo, Alaba and Hadiya. Since, however, Islam places more stress on behavior than doctrine, it is possible to make an estimate of whether the numbers of converts are increasing by observing the adoption of Islamic clothing styles, performance of prayers and presence of mosques and cemeteries. Based on these criteria there was a noticeable increase in the decade from 1964 to 1974. For example, by 1973 more men could be seen wearing turbans or Islamic skullcaps. And the cemetery of one small town, originally designed for both Muslims and Christians, had been completely filled with graves of the former.

There is also an indirect indication of Islamic influence in the expanding cultivation of kat (*Catha edulis*). The major cash crop of the Sadama since World War II has been coffee, but by the mid-1970s a number of farmers were beginning to realize a substantial portion of their income from the production of kat in market towns like Yirgalem. (Kat is a plant whose leaves, when chewed, produce a mild narcotic effect. It was introduced by Muslims for ritual purposes but is now also used by others, particularly adolescent high school students).

Fundamental to understanding the Sidamo life is the symbiotic relationships between ensete production and cattle. The banana-like ensete is a durable drought-resistant plant which provides a starchy grain eaten as a porridge mixed with vegetables or made into a pancake to be eaten with vegetables. Cattle dung is necessary for continuous cultivation on the small garden plots, which are seldom larger than two or three acres. Productivity centers around this relationship in the sense that the household is nearly always to be found on the edge of the garden, convenient for the transport of dung from the cattle byre on one side of the house to the garden. The households of a Sidamo community are generally adjacent to a large communal pasture where the cattle graze. Women and girls are responsible for all household tasks such as removal of animal dung from household to garden and the preparation of the raw ensete into food, while men and boys take care of the heavy tasks of gardening by preparing and weeding the land, as well as maintaining the usually small herd of cattle.

Men have virtually complete authority over this production process as they control the land and animals, which are transmitted to their sons through patrilineal descent. Their daughters, who usually marry out of the community, since exogamy is the rule, help provide the bridewealth, which in turn supports the marriage of their brothers and the continuous reproduction of the system. In recent years male authority and production have been enhanced through cash cropping in coffee, though traditional subsistence practices and control of land remain largely unchanged. The cash economy has provided new opportunities for trade, has increased considerably the value and scarcity of land and has provided new opportunities for improving individual wealth and prestige for men.

In the past there were no urban marketing centers in Sidamo land, but trade and markets were, and continue to be, of importance. For example, the four days of the week are named for the principal marketing centers, providing people with knowledge of where trading will be occurring at any given time. In addition to trading markets, there are several Sidamo towns which serve as administrative centers. As cash cropping has expanded, so have the towns and the variety of merchants from other parts of Ethiopia and beyond. It is in such centers that one observes the most obvious symbols of Islamic penetration such as small mosques, men with the characteristic turbans and skull caps, special burial places and trade in cash rather than barter.

The elders (*čimessa*) are the sanctioning body for authority at the community (*kača*) and neighborhood (*olaun*) levels and within the descent system, which consists of patriclans (*gurri*) linked by an elaborate generational class system (*lua*) crosscutting descent group boundaries. A man is promoted to elderhood not on the basis of chronological age but when he is initiated into his *lua* class, which in turn is related to the promotion of his father's class to elderhood. So important is this latter event that, unlike most of the world's societies, which utilize bodily mutilation and elaborate ritual for puberty rites, the Sadama reserve these practices for the transition from maturity to an estate of wisdom and circumspection associated with elderhood. It is these men, who may or may not be chronologically old, who are expected to make public policy and settle disputes. Their authority is organized in various levels or elders' councils (*songo*) at the community, neighborhood, lineage and clan levels of organization. The distinctiveness of their position and the awe in which they are generally held by the population rests upon the belief that they are the guardians of the "true" way of life (*halili*) and emblematic of good fortune (*iyani*). Indeed, there are even exemplary elders known as *woma*. These are men who are usually chronologically old, having survived two cycles of the *lua*, and are supposed to be especially adept at interpreting tradition and settling disputes. It is the emphasis upon their role as guardians and interpreters of a traditional way of life developed by founding ancestors which provided a convenient basis for a syncretic link with Islam.

The traditional belief system of the Sadama involves the concept of a Creator God who continues to be the ultimate influence on all events and phenomena in the universe, a concern with spirit beings that may bring good or evil fortune and the honoring of dead elders. There are numerous variations on the theme of how Magano (Creator Sky God) created man out of earth and then having become dissatisfied with his work returned permanently to his home in the sky. Despite the remoteness of the Creator, his blessing is always sought on ritual occasions, and there is a certain fatalism in the view that all events are ultimately dependent upon Magano's will.

Spirit beings (*shatana*), on the other hand, do not affect all persons and at best are viewed ambiguously. With a few exceptions, such as Dorissa, the spirit of insanity, who clearly dwells in bodies of water, the abodes of others are only vaguely identified with trees, caves and other natural habitats. Their presence is known only by the way in which they affect people and cattle through the occurrence of unexplained illness, as well as the dialogue they carry on through the mouth of the possessed. There is also a behavioral aspect involving a jerking motion of the head and shoulders when the spirit enters the body. Although the ritual of calling and honoring these spirits brings to the host's household a great deal of attention from the community, the propitiation process is often expensive, and in time *shatana* usually become feared and resented. Nevertheless, there are unusual occurrences of spirit possession in which the host obtains great power, enabling him or her to settle disputes and predict the future. In such instances a following is attracted, and great wealth devolves upon the host from those who come to honor the spirit and bring gifts for assistance in settling disputes. The spirit is then referred to as an *iyani* rather than a *shatani*.

Honoring spirits of dead elders is universally accepted and fundamental to the underpinning of the Sidamo world view. When a man's dead father appears to him in a dream requesting to be fed a bull or honey, the son is obligated, upon pain of death or illness for himself and his descendants, to perform the ritual feeding. The spirits of even the recently dead are closer to the founding heroes who established *halali* (the true way of life), which when followed provides the individual with *iyani* (good fortune). Consequently, the dead provide continuity for the charter which sanctions the authority of the living elders in settling disputes and making public policy by revealing their wishes, primarily through dreams.

There are several aspects of Sidamo culture which provide for ease of syncretic accommodation with Islam. These include dreams as a means of communication with the supernatural, importance of a traditional life code, revered elders as code interpreters, the use of conditional vows and reverence for spirits in the healing process.

The principal means of conversion to Islam is through dreams, an important element in Sidamo culture. One informant, after losing four of his children through serious illness in the space of a few months, dreamed that the loss was a message from Magano that he should become a Muslim. Three of his relatives had the same dream at approximately the same time. One convert suggested that the dream is conditional, like the one in which a dead father appears demanding to be honored. In the Islamic dream, however, the spirit of Shaikh Husain is manifest, and if one does not obey his summons death will occur. (Shaikh Husain was one of the first Muslim missionaries in the region. His revered tomb is in Balke on the plain near Goba.) The Shaikh is said to have been beloved by Magano, hence given the power to transform himself or other mortals into anything he desires. This is in keeping with the orthodox Muslim belief that saints are especially favored by God and after death constitute a link between the latter and the material world. For this reason saints signify their presence to mortals by appearing in dreams.

Even though the Quran is a written code, its meaning for contemporaries must be interpreted by lawyers, scholars and saints. And in making their interpretation the latter must be sure of a consensus for acceptance within the community. In like manner Sidamo elders meeting in the *songo* (council) seek to settle disputes and make community policy in keeping with *halili*. Sidamo converts see a definite parallel between the revered ancestors and Islamic saints. Abo, one of the most prominent of the ancestors and founder of the Holo and Garbico clans, is said to have been revealed in a dream as a relative of Shaikh Husain. Consequently, Muslims, regardless of clan affiliation, now make pilgrimages to Abo's grave, and in the mid-1970s a small mosque was constructed just outside the gates leading to the grave site.

The widespread use of conditional vows by Muslims provides a means for syncretism with the Sidamo concept of *tano*. In honoring saints a vow is made, along with the presentation of votive offerings, that in return for the gift of a child or the curing of an illness the supplicant will pledge an expensive gift. If the saint then blesses the supplicant by providing the request, and the latter fails to reciprocate, the blessing becomes a curse. Similarly, the Sidamo practice involves pledging a valued animal and other offerings in return for increased wealth or fertility. The request is always directed to one of the ancestral heroes such as Abo.

There is apparently no problem for Islam in accommodating to the realm of minor spirit beings in other cultures. Muslim healers, for example, have been effective among the Sadama in counteracting the negative effects of spirit possession. Typical is the situation of small children being possessed by Dorissa, the spirit of insanity. In one known case, a small girl showed symptoms of possession by tearing off her clothing, grinding her teeth and running amok. A Muslim healer came and slaughtered a black goat, passed the lung of the animal in a circular motion over the head of the child and beat her with a whip while ordering Dorissa to leave. Another case involved a small boy who had been guarding millet from marauding flocks of birds along the Gidabo River, the reputed home of Dorissa. The boy was taken with violent seizures of sobbing and inability to recognize people. The healer was called and by using the same techniques succeeded in driving Dorissa back to the river. These techniques show a syncretic relationship with those of the Sidamo curers, who require the possessed to drink an infusion from the bark and roots of a special tree before whipping the person and ordering Dorissa to leave.

Trimingham has suggested three stages in the Islamic change process: adoption of superficial elements, acquisition of new techniques for supernatural control and genuine belief. The Sadama appear to be in the first and second stages of assimilating Islamic beliefs and practices, as indicated by the adoption of clothing styles, dietary practices, certain ceremonial and dreaming techniques, as well as resort to Islamic healers. There is also evidence for the beginnings of the third stage in the building of the first crude mosques, sporadic performance of ritual prayers, the keeping of the Ramadan fast and, in at least one instance, participation in the pilgrimage to Mecca. Nevertheless, from observation and accounts of behavior and belief by Muslim converts, there is no indication of significant change in traditional kinship practices, belief in spirit beings like *shatan* or honoring the spirits of dead elders.

Converts, while participating in all aspects of the generational class promotion rituals (*lua*) and animal sacrifices, avoid the custom of putting blood on their foreheads. Despite the development of a syncretic relationship between these elements of certain aspects of Islam, there is no evidence of an awareness of the Shariah and other aspects of Islamic law.

There will continue to be Sidamo converts to Islam, but it is unlikely that the faith will come to dominate Sidamo culture. A pervasive commitment to Islam seems unlikely given the contradictions and competition with Christianity and traditional beliefs. Adherents of the latter are still predominant in numbers despite several decades of proselytization by the universalistic religions. Instead, there is a greater possibility for increased syncretization of all three belief systems, especially in times of crisis. Recently, for example, the Wando Magano movement has combined Christian and Islamic concepts and symbols with traditional ones, at a time when many Sadama have felt threatened from the pressures of an increasingly cash-oriented economy and dramatic political changes affecting all of Ethiopian society.

BIBLIOGRAPHY

Books

Central Statistical Office. *Estimates of Rural Households and Population in Thirteen Provinces*. Mimeographed. Addis Ababa: Government Printer, 1972.
Trimingham, J. Spencer. *Islam in Ethiopia*. New York: Barnes and Noble, 1965.
Von Grunebaum, G. *Islam: Essays in the Nature and Growth of a Cultural Tradition*. American Anthropological Association Memoir, No. 81. New York: A.A.A., 1955.

Articles

Hamer, J. "Crisis, Moral Consensus, and the Wando Magono Movement Among the Sadama of Southwest Ethiopia." *Ethnology* 41 (1977): 399–413.
———. "Dispute Settlement and Sanctity: An Ethiopian Example." *Anthropological Quarterly* 45 (1972): 232–247.
———. "Myth, Ritual and the Authority of Elders in an Ethiopian Society." *Africa* 46 (1976): 327–339.
———. "Sidamo Generational Class Cycles: A Political Gerontocracy." *Africa* 40 (1970): 50–70.
———, and Hamer, I. "Spirit Possession and Its Socio-Psychological Implications Among the Sadama of Southwest Ethiopia." *Ethnology* 5 (1966): 392–408.

John Hamer

SALARS   The Salars have a reputation of being the most zealous Muslims in China, having participated in every Muslim uprising since the seventeenth century. Today numbering about 70,000, nearly all are concentrated in the Zunhua Salar Autonomous County in the eastern part of Qinghai Province in north central China. Most of the rest live in small groups in Gandu of neighboring Hualong County and in Linxia, a city southwest of Lanzhou, capital of Gansu Province. A few Salars are scattered in other parts of Qinghai and Gansu provinces as well as in the Xinjiang Uygur Autonomous Region. Xinhua Salar County, with its seat at Jishi, was established in 1954.

The Salar area belonged to Gansu until 1928, when it was incorporated into the newly created Qinghai Province. At that time the most important local administrative division was the *gong*, which, on the average was slightly smaller than the subsequent township and commune. Of 13 *gong*, 8 were called Zunhua, lay south of the Huang (Yellow) River and were composed mostly of Salars. Five *gong*, called Hualong *gong*, were north of the river, where mostly Tibetans, Han and Hui lived. The old Zunghua *gong* became the present-day seven southern communes, while the Hualong *gong* corresponded to today's four northern communes.

The self-appellation "Salar" is believed to have derived from the word "Salor," the name of a Turkmen tribe. This tribe was mentioned in the eleventh century by Mahmud al Kashgari and later by Rashidu-'d-din (fourteenth century) and Abu-'l-Gazi (seventeenth century). The Salars' oral history supports the idea of the Salars having originated as a Turkmen tribe when speaking of the progenitors Haraman and Ahman setting out from Samarkand and arriving in the Xunhua area around 1370. While still in Central Asia, the Salars were governed by a hereditary *darugachi*, a post established by the Mongols to supervise both military and civilian affairs in the conquered territories. After arriving in the Xunhua area during the Ming dynasty, the Salars were governed by their own hereditary *tusi*, a kind of headman, of whom there were three grades; one in charge of 100 households, and two (a chief and an assistant) for each 1,000 households. They had authority over the militia, taxation, legal matters, and the provisioning of officials passing through the area.

By the time of the Yongzheng reign (1723–1735), the Salar population had increased to the point that the area was divided into 13 *gong*. At the same time and continuing almost until the end of the eighteenth century, the Qing dynasty extended its control of the Salars by establishing military and civilian posts in Xunhua.

The Salar language belongs to the Öguz branch of the Turkic group of the Altaic family of languages. It is related to the East Turkic spoken in parts of the Xinjiang Uygur Autonomous Region, and its lexicon contains mostly Turkic words (see Turkic-speaking Peoples.). In addition, about 7 percent of the words are Arab-Persian, and 17 percent are Chinese, with a few words of Tibetan and Mongolian origin. Before 1949, some Salars could read the Arabic script of the Quran and other religious material. Today literacy has greatly increased, but it is almost exclusively in Chinese. There is no independent script for Salar.

Xunhua Salar County grows a number of food crops, but it is best known for its many orchards, which grow winter melon, grapes, apricots, jujube (Chinese dates) and apples. Xunhua is also famous for its hot spice, called *xunhua huajiao*, or simply, *xunjiao*. Its walnuts are sold far beyond Xunhua Salar County. In the mountainous parts of Xunhua are found Chinese ephedra and other medicinal herbs. The 1978 food crop was 150 percent higher than in 1953, and the number of cattle increased 71 percent over the same period. As in many other counties in this part of China, afforestation has been promoted for many years.

Industry is relatively underdeveloped; only electric generators and building materials are presently manufactured. There are also a few shops for repairing farm implements. Dirt roads connect all communes and most production brigades, and a bridge has been built across the Huang River to link the two parts of the county.

Before 1949 the literacy rate is said to have been as low as 3 percent, whereas official statements report almost universal literacy today. Whatever one's definition of literacy may be, education has unquestionably progressed among the Salar. When Xunhua Salar County was established in 1954, only 24 schools existed. By 1978 they had increased to 164, including a new teachers' college.

The Salars are devout Muslims. They are Hanafi whose religion was introduced to the area around 1750 by a certain Muhammad Amin. Every village has one mosque. Before the attack against the clergy in 1958, there was a chief *mullah* for the entire county, and each *gong* had its own *mullah*, assistant (*fu*) *mullah* and junior (*xiao*) *mullah*, known collectively as the "three heads" (*san tou*). During the so-called Cultural Revolution (1966–1976) all religious practices were banned. They are now once again permitted.

BIBLIOGRAPHY

Books

Qinghaisheng Xunhua Salar zu zizhi xian gaikuang. Xuanhua, China: 1963.
"Salar zu." In *Zhongguo shaoshu minzu*. Beijing: Renmin chubanshe, 1981.
Tenishev, Edgem Rakhimovich. *Salarskii yazyk*. Moscow: Nauka, 1963.

Articles

Kakuk, Suzanne. "Sur la phonetique de la langue salare." *Acte Orientalia Hungaricai*
    15 (1962): 161–172.
Poppe, Nicholas. "Remarks on the Salar Language." *Harvard Journal of Asiatic Studies*
    16 (1953): 438–477.

Henry G. Schwarz

SAMA Sometimes called Samal, the Sama are the most widely dispersed ethnic group indigenous to Southeast Asia. Their villages are scattered over a maritime territory extending from northern Philippines to southern Indonesia, from Borneo to the Moluccas. Land-based Sama in the Philippines, except for the Yakan and Abak, are generally referred to as Samal, a Tausug term also used by the Christian population. In Malaysia and Indonesia, they are referred to by some variant of the Malay term, Bajau (also spelled Badjau or Bajaw). Nomadic, boat-dwelling Sama are known as Bajau in the Philippines, and as Orang Laut ("sea people") or Bajau Laut in Malaysia and Indonesia (see Bajau). The most common self-designation is Sama, almost always with a modifier to indicate geographical and/or dialect affiliation. (For example, Sama Baangingiq refers to a group of Sama who trace their origin and dialect to Balangingi Island in northern Sulu.) "Sama" used by itself is often considered pejorative. Their numbers in Southeast Asia are close to 760,000.

Sama-Bajau has recently been suggested as a general term for languages spoken by the various Sama populations. It includes approximately ten distinct languages, several with numerous local dialects. The group as a whole is probably coordinate with Malay and the Philippines languages as a member of the Hesperonesian branch of Austronesian (see Malayo-Polynesian-speaking Peoples).

Following are the major subdivisions of the Sama.

The Abak appear to be the only Christianized group among the Sama. They derive from a migration into the central Philippines that took place about 1,100 years ago, and in the intervening centuries they have been heavily influenced by their Bisayan neighbors.

The Yakan are descended from another early offshoot of the parent stock, although one that has remained within the ancestral homeland. They number in the vicinity of 116,000, with the majority concentrated on Basilan Island south of Zamboanga City. Unlike the majority of Sama, they are an agricultural population with no close ties to the sea (see Yakan).

The Sibuguey Bay Sama are small Sama groups indigenous to the Zamboanga peninsula and the coasts of Sibuguey Bay in western Mindanao. Relatively isolated and few in number, they probably represent the only surviving remnant of the Sama penetration into the northern part of the bay about 1,000 years ago.

The Jama Mapun are a predominantly agricultural people concentrated on the island of Cagayan Sulu, about 60 miles off the coast of northeastern Sabah. In the past, they engaged in fairly extensive maritime trade under the loose jurisdiction of the Brunei and Sulu sultanates. In recent times, their economy has become increasingly centered on subsistence agriculture and copra production. Recent estimates place the Jama Mapun population at about 21,000.

One offshoot of the southwestward expansion of the Sama is currently represented by the Land Bajau of western Sabah. They are an agricultural people, though cattle raising also enjoys some prominence. Settlements take the form of compact communities located in the low foothills bordering the coastal plain. The Land Bajau, comprising only a small portion of Sabah's population, have nevertheless played an important role in the recent political history of that state. No reliable estimate of their population is currently available.

Scattered across a wide area of central and eastern Indonesia is a series of closely related Sama groups, termed Indonesian Bajau, that together comprise another major offshoot of the original southwestward expansion. Their subsequent movement outward from southern Sulawesi leading to the remarkably wide dispersion that exists today, appears to have taken place only within the last 300 years or so and was probably connected with the expanding economic and political influence of the Macassarese and Buginese with whom many Indonesian Sama still maintain close ties. Today the majority follow a more or less settled existence in compact shore-line communities, with an economy based on fishing and other maritime pursuits. Their settlements are often found closely associated with those of indigenous ethnic groups with whom they maintain a close economic relationship.

Although fleets of nomadic Sama have been reported throughout this region for the last century or two, their precise ethnic affiliation is not understood at this time. Some appear to be far-flung outliers of Sulu nomads, while others may belong to the Indonesian branch.

The Suluan Sama (386,000) are the largest concentration of Sama found in the Sulu Archipelago and along the adjacent coasts of southwestern Mindanao and eastern Sabah. They are the most widely studied and best documented of the Sama peoples and have achieved the greatest relative strength in numbers and economic influence. Allowing for differences in local context, a description of the Suluan Sama should apply equally well, at least in broad outline, to other Sama groups in Malaysia, Indonesia and the Philippines.

Suluan Sama communities, and especially those with a strong maritime component to their economy, typically take the form of densely clustered houses situated along a stretch of well-protected shore line: at a river mouth, for example, facing a narrow channel, or where a fringe reef affords some protection against heavy seas. In central Sulu villages, and particularly in those of recently settled Sama Dilaut (Sea Sama, the nomadic and semi-nomadic Bajau of the southern Philippines), the village is usually built directly over the tidal shallows. Elsewhere, settlements are normally found on the beach front or immediately behind it. Most houses are built on piles with three to six feet of clearance between the floor and dry ground or high water, as the case may be. Construction materials and size generally vary with the wealth of the owner and, to a certain extent, family size. A relatively poor dwelling might have framing materials of mangrove or other locally available woods, split bamboo flooring, walls and roof of thatch and possess a total floor area of 435 square feet or less for its single room. A wealthier family might use commercially produced sheet lumber and corrugated roofing to build a house with several sleeping rooms, a porch and a separate cooking area. Occasionally, there is a spacious, Western-style "bungalow," built at ground level from concrete blocks, painted inside and out and expensively furnished.

The basic unit of Sama social organization is the independent nuclear family, normally consisting of a married couple (or a divorced or widowed individual) and one or more dependent offspring. Although the most common type of household consists of a single nuclear family, membership is frequently augmented by the addition of other dependents, such as an elderly parent, unmarried siblings, newly married offspring or others who are unable to establish an independent residence. The constituency of large extended households tends to be fluid. It is not uncommon for dependent adults and juveniles to maintain a sort of circulating membership in the households of several closely related although geographically separated kin, spending a few weeks or a few months with each in turn. Children past the age of six or seven are permitted a great degree of latitude in choosing their household, and one occasionally finds a youngster moving out of his or her natal home to establish temporary or permanent residence elsewhere with a favorite sibling or other close kinsman.

The households within a community are generally divided into larger units known as *tumpuk*, or residence clusters, composed of households both physically adjacent to one another and closely related genealogically. One head of household from within the cluster will be commonly acknowledged as its leader or spokesman within the community, often as a parish, a larger unit whose members attend a single mosque and recognize one of their number (usually the mosque's owner or sponsor) as their common leader in political and legal matters. Large communities may contain two or more parishes, with one of the parish leaders serving as a headman for the village as a whole.

The Suluan Sama, as well as other Sama groups of maritime orientation, depend primarily upon the sea for their subsistence and livelihood. Fishing has been and continues to be the dominant form of economic activity for most Sama households, though other activities consistent with a maritime environment are also present where local conditions permit. The production of firewood from various species of mangrove, collecting of intertidal invertebrates and food plants, seaweed (*agar-agar*) mariculture, and maritime trade, for example, are also practiced to a greater or lesser extent among the Suluan Sama, although usually as secondary alternatives to cash and subsistence fishing. Copra production has a relatively high ratio of income to labor investment and is thus a desirable alternative to fishing for many Sama, but unless a substantial amount of capital is available for purchase of land and/or bearing palms, it remains at best a source only of supplementary income.

One of the more important features of the Sama economy is the almost symbiotic exchange relationship usually established with agricultural groups in their immediate area. The Sama produce considerable quantities of protein in the form of fish and other marine life, but little starch, while the agricultural groups produce the starch (generally in the form of rice and root crops), but very little in the way of animal protein. The establishment of social arrangements to facilitate the exchange of these essential commodities is to the obvious benefit of both parties, but perhaps with some additional payoff for the Sama. In the Sulu area the Sama have for centuries had something close to a monopoly on the production of fish for local consumption, and this has afforded them a certain amount of security from the often more powerful and politically dominant agricultural groups in the vicinity. The maritime Sama have not always been treated well by the latter, but they have generally been spared from the intergroup conflict that has often embroiled their largely immobile and increasingly land-hungry agricultural neighbors.

Except for the Abak, all of the Sama groups of the Philippines, Malaysia and Indonesia are at least nominally Muslim in their formal religious orientation. Beyond this point, however, there is a great unevenness in the degree to which Islam has actually penetrated the various Sama groups. Some, like the nomadic Sama Dilaut, are still effectively pagan (but not in their own estimation), while others, such as the Sama Baangingiq, have gone much farther towards a full-scale adoption of orthodox belief and practice.

The close association between Islam and trade in insular Southeast Asia probably had much to do with the development of such variation. Those groups with extensive economic, political or military interests outside their own immediate area generally found an advantage in the adoption of Islam. Among the Sama groups of Sulu, therefore, it is not too surprising that the most Islamicized were those with the strongest political and economic links to the powerful sultanates of the region.

Since 1970 there has been considerable organized violence in Mindanao and Sulu. What began as a series of isolated conflicts between local Muslim communities and immigrant Christians over land titles in the Cotabato hinterlands rapidly escalated into civil war. The situation was exacerbated by animosities between Muslim and Christian that go back to the Spanish period and the days of widespread Muslim piracy, by a sense among Muslims that martial law and military intervention of the Philippine government was a loosely disguised attempt to eradicate Islam and perhaps its followers and by the intervention of foreign governments willing to supply the Muslim warriors with arms and moral support.

With the burning of Jolo and the steady erosion of the Tausug military and economic base, Tausug dominance in Sulu was finally brought to a close, capping a decline that began over a century ago. The heavy fighting in the Yakan home of Basilan turned thousands of this group into landless refugees on the Zamboanga mainland, destroying the economic and political basis of their independence. Other Sama groups of Mindanao and Sulu did not stay aloof from the conflict, nor did they remain untouched by the destruction. Sama refugees numbered in the tens of thousands, many of them moving into the already crowded Zamboanga City area.

The mobility and adaptability of the maritime Sama have smoothed the way for their geographical expansion and their survival through periods of war and alien domination. The recent troubles in the southern Philippines constitute just another chapter in that story as far as the Sama are concerned and probably not the last, if history contains any predictive value for the future.

BIBLIOGRAPHY

Books

Benton, Nena Eslao. "Child-rearing Among the Samal of Manbul, Siasi, Sulu." In *The Muslim Filipinos: Their History, Society, and Contemporary Problems*, edited by Peter G. Gowing and Robert D. McAmis. Manila: Solidaridad Publishing House, 1974.

Casino, Eric S. "Jama Mapun." In *Ethnic Groups of Insular Southeast Asia*, edited by Frank M. LeBar. Vol. 2. New Haven: Human Relations Area Files Press, 1975.

Chaffeee, Frederick H., et al. *Area Handbook for the Philippines*. The American University FAS, DA Pam 550–72. Washington, D.C.: Government Printing Office, 1969.

Geoghegan, William H. "Balangingi." In *Ethnic Groups of Insular Southeast Asia*, edited by Frank M. LeBar. Vol. 2. New Haven: Human Relations Area Files Press, 1975.

LeBar, Frank M., ed. *Ethnic Groups of Insular Southeast Asia*. Vol. 2. New Haven: Human Relations Area Files Press, 1975.

Majul, Cesar Adib. *Muslims in the Philippines*. Quezon City: University of the Philippines Press, 1973.

Pallesen, Kemp. "Reciprocity in Samal Marriage." In *Sulu Studies*, edited by Gerard Rixhon. Vol. 1. Jolo, Philippines: Notre Dame of Jolo College, 1972.

Sather, Clifford. "Bajau Laut." In *Ethnic Groups of Insular Southeast Asia*, edited by Frank M. LeBar. Vol. 2. New Haven: Human Relations Area Files Press, 1975.

Spoehr, Alexander. *Zamboanga and Sulu: An Archaeological Approach to Ethnic Diversity*. Ethnology Monographs, No. 1. Pittsburgh: University of Pittsburgh, Department of Anthropology, 1973.

Stone, Richard L. "Intergroup Relations Among the Tausug, Samals, and Badjaw of Sulu." In *The Muslim Filipinos: Their History, Society, and Contemporary Problems*, edited by Peter G. Gowing and Robert D. McAmis. Manila: Solidaridad Publishing House, 1974.

Warren, James F. *The North Borneo Chartered Company's Administration of the Bajau, 1878–1909: The Pacification of a Maritime Nomadic People*. Southeast Asia Series, No. 22. Athens: Ohio University Center for International Studies, 1971.

Articles

Casino, Eric S. "Jama Mapun Ethnoecology: Economic and Symbolic." *Asian Studies* 5 (1967): 1–32.

Rixhon, Gerard. "The Religious Attitude of the Manubul Samal: An Appraisal." *Notre Dame Journal* 1 (1969): 1–18.

Sather, Clifford. "Social Rank and Marriage Payments in an Immigrant Moro Community in Malaysia." *Ethnology* 6 (1967): 97–102.

Unpublished Manuscript

Pallesen, Kemp. "Linguistic Convergence and Culture Contact." Ph.D. dissertation, University of California, Berkeley, 1976.

William H. Geoghegan
Population figures updated by Richard V. Weekes

SANGIL   The Sangil Muslims number about 4,000 and live for the most part in the Sarangani and Balut islands off the southeastern coast of Mindanao in the Republic of the Philippines. Their language is usually classed with the Central Philippine subgroup of Malayo-Polynesian languages.

The Sangil are not to be confused with the several thousands of Sangir, who are Indonesian nationals, mostly Christians, inhabiting the southern coast of mainland Mindanao in the Sarangani Bay area. The Sangir are recent migrants of one or two generations standing from the Sangihe or Sangir and Talaud island chains of Indonesia between northern Sulawezi and southern Mindanao.

The Sangil represent a much earlier migration from the same island dating back at least to the seventeenth century. Today they are regarded by both Indonesia and the Philippines as Philippine nationals. The substitution of the *l* for the *r* in their name probably came about through contact with the Maguindanao and other coastal Mindanao Muslim groups with whom the Sangil have been undergoing a process of acculturation and absorption.

As early as 1602, the Spaniards in their campaigns against the Muslims (Moros) noted that the Sangils were among the forces marshalled by the Sultan of Ternate to aid the Mindanao Muslims. Subsequently there were reports of Sangils attacking settlements in the Visayas in the company of Sulu Muslims and then of Spanish operations against them in the 1620s.

Culturally, the Sangil retain some features of the culture of their Sangihe origins, though their former home islands are now predominantly Christian. The Sangil raise food crops and engage in fishing and boatbuilding.

BIBLIOGRAPHY

Books

Conklin, Harold C. "Preliminary Linguistic Survey of Mindanao." In *Papers Read at the Mindanao Conference.* Vol. 1. Chicago: University of Chicago, Department of Anthropology, 1955.
LeBar, Frank M., ed. *Ethnic Groups of Insular Southeast Asia.* Vol. 2. New Haven: Human Relations Area Files Press, 1975.

Articles

Gowing, Peter G. "The Growing List of Filipino Muslims Groups." *Dansalan Research Center Reports* 2 (1975): 5–6.
———. "The Sangil Moros." *Dansalan Junior College Staff Gazette* 19 (1979).

Peter G. Gowing

SASAK   Between the Indonesian islands of Bali and Sumbawa lies the island of Lombok, about 2,000 square miles in size and dominated along the north by high mountain ranges culminating in the second highest volcano in the country, Gunung Rinjani, 10,000 feet high. Lombok and Sumbawa comprise the province of Nusa Tenggara Barat; its capital is Mataram on Lombok's west coast. The Lombok Straits is one of the most important waterways in the world of petroleum transportation. The Sasak, who number 2 million, form the major ethnic group of the island.

Apart from the Sasak, Lombok is inhabited by Balinese, Sumbawanese, Makassarese and some smaller groups of Chinese, Javanese and Arabs. Balinese and Sumbawanese comprise about 71 percent of this non-Sasak population.

Lombok is drier than Bali and the islands to the west and has more precipitation than Sumbawa and the islands to the east. The arid zones of the island are located in both the north and the south. The western part gets rain even during the dry season between May and July.

The fertile central plain running from east to west has the greatest population concentration, while areas of the south and east are more sparsely populated. The Sasak are primarily agarian, with the cultivation of irrigated rice the major occupation. In the mountainous and more arid regions, some dry field and shifting cultivation occurs. The southern part is so dry that no irrigated rice can be grown, and it is here that recurrent food shortages occur.

The Sasak language belongs to the Malayo-Polynesian family and is closely related to Javanese and Balinese. The language has high, middle and low levels, the usage of which relates to the ranking system (sometimes called the caste system) and the relative ages of the persons conversing. A person in the lower ranking system, or younger in years, will use the higher level when addressing and speaking about a person higher in caste or older than himself; the older person, or one of higher rank, will use the lower level of vocabulary when speaking to or about a younger, or lower-ranking person.

The Sasak are divided into two groups: the more numerous Waktu Lima, who tend to be located in the plains and near roads and towns; and the Waktu Telu, located in the more marginal areas. Waktu Lima Sasak are more involved with production for market and with the cash economy in general than are the Waktu Telu, who are geographically, economically and culturally more isolated. Both are Muslim, but the Waktu Lima are more orthodox, while the Waktu Telu are more syncretistic and traditional.

Waktu Telu villages are physically different from those of the Waktu Lima. In the former there is greater uniformity of house style as well as the presence of rice storehouses, which are not present in Waktu Lima villages, because the latter sell their rice and do not store it. Waktu Lima villages have marketplaces, orthodox-style mosques and *madrasas*.

The Sasak have a ranking system of aristocrats and commoners which crosscuts ethnic and village boundaries. Not all of these ranked levels occur in every village, some of which may have only commoners; both Waktu Lima and Waktu Telu villages may have aristocrats. Caste regulates marriage, ritual position and, in some villages, occupation and acquisition of political office, especially in villages in which there is an aristocracy.

Kinship systems are bilateral with a tendency to stress certain groups of kinsmen in the male line in terms of rights and obligations, such as provision of the brideprice. Marriage regulations differ between Waktu Lima and Waktu Telu. The Waktu Telu consider cross-generational marriage between kinsmen (between parent's child and parent's sibling) to be incestuous. Waktu Lima do not prohibit such marriages. Marriages between first, second or third cousins is preferred. In some villages, land is inherited by sons only, while in others daughters may inherit one out of every three shares.

Waktu Telu and Waktu Lima differ in their religious beliefs, practices and values. For the Waktu Telu, these beliefs and rituals are acquired through the process of socialization, as a Sasak is a Waktu Telu through community and family membership and is considered to be related to the ancestors and other local supernaturals through birth or marriage. Although one cannot become a Waktu Telu through conversion and study, one may become a Waktu Lima in this manner. Waktu Telu tend to be traditional and do not rigorously observe the five tenets of Islam except for the belief in Allah with Muhammad as his prophet.

Waktu Lima place more emphasis on Islamic tenets, including prayers five times daily, the fast, the pilgrimage and religious tithe. While the Waktu Lima emphasize *agama* (the Islamic religion), Waktu Telu values and behavior are focused on *adat* (customary law), which differs somewhat in each village. This is expressed in the Sasak saying, *"lain desa, lain adat"* ("different villages have different customs"). The Waktu Lima consider *adat* pagan and regard Waktu Telu as backward. The differences have repercussions on village culture in general.

Waktu Telu give much of their attention—and allocate much of their production not consumed in daily living—to ritual feasts, called *gawe*. These are held for life-crisis events such as naming rituals, first hair cutting, circumcision, tooth filling and death, including specified mourning ceremonies.

Waktu Telu villages are more homogeneous occupationally. So, too, are their values. This relates in part to land ownership, as almost all Waktu Telu households own and work small farms. Barter has been commonly used to obtain the few goods not produced in the village. Labor for projects such as house building or farming which require labor groups larger than the household is cooperative or voluntary. While wage work is increasing, Waktu Telu villages still tend to resist economic, religious and cultural influences from the outside.

Religious expenditures by household are more widespread among the Waktu Telu. In their villages all households have ceremonial expenses, often amounting to 30 percent or more of their income. Among Waktu Lima less than one-quarter of the households may spend money for such purposes.

A decline in *adat* ceremonies seems to be occurring in some Waktu Telu villages, not because of Islamic pressures but because of an increase in commercialization. So, for example, even in the Waktu Telu villages where rituals are still held for irrigated rice, a sacred crop, the abandonment of dry field rituals can be traced to the period when dry season crops became cash crops.

Waktu Telu religion tends to be village specific. It is acquired through membership in the village, which is acquired by birth or marriage. The land by which one earns one's livelihood is considered a sacred trust from one's ancestors and may not be alienated. Even rice, the major crop, is believed to be endowed with sacred properties and may not be sold outright.

Waktu Lima are money oriented. Landless villagers sell their labor to wealthy landlords or produce handicrafts for sale in the market. They value making a profit, often justifying the accumulation of wealth by one of the highest Waktu Lima ideals, making the pilgrimage to Mecca. A surprising number of Waktu Lima have made the holy journey (20 percent of the households in one Waktu Lima village have been able to send a member on the Haj). Most villagers admit that they have no hope of ever saving enough to achieve the ideals of either making the Haj or acquiring land to farm. Approximately 75 percent of the Waktu Lima villagers are landless.

The religious organization of Sasak villages varies for the two groups. Waktu Telu villages have religious officials called *pemangku*, who function as mediums between the spirits of local holy places and the villagers. They are especially important in curing ceremonies at which sacrifices to local supernaturals are made. These officials do not appear in Waktu Lima villages.

The villages of both groups have religious officials called *kijaji* as well as *penghulu*, the Islamic leader in each village. But their functions are different depending upon the group. In Waktu Lima villages the religious leaders conduct Islamic ceremonies; the other religious obligations are performed by the individual villager. In Waktu Lima villages, Islamic obligations such as the abbreviated fast of Ramadan and any formal prayers in the village mosque are carried out by the religious leaders on behalf of the villagers, who need do nothing themselves.

The *tuan guru*, influential Muslim teachers and leaders on Lombok, are highly revered by the orthodox Muslims. Some also have a significant following among the Waktu Telu. The *tuan guru* may have political as well as religious importance in Sasak society. Some function in a mode similar to the traditional messianic leaders of the early part of this century. They are intent upon making Indonesia strictly a Muslim nation governed by the Quran. One such *tuan guru* created Islamic schools, published religious literature and has a sizable following amounting to about half the Muslim population of Lombok. Under *tuan guru* auspices, the number of mosques and religious schools on Lombok is increasing. The *tuan guru* see themselves as opponents of *adat* and position themselves against the traditional Sasak aristocracy.

It appears that the *tuan guru* are successful to the point that there is an erosion of *adat* in traditional aristocracy. While Waktu Telu villages remain traditionalist, there is increasing evidence of Waktu Lima exploitation through incursions into the market of the village economies. But despite the pressures of the *tuan guru* and their followers, *adat* regulations pertaining to Sasak aristocracy, the ranking system, marriage and land inheritance persist.

BIBLIOGRAPHY

Books

Cederroth, Sven. *The Spell of the Ancestors and the Power of Mekkah: A Sasak Community on Lombok*. Gothenburg Studies in Social Anthropology, No. 3. Göteborg, Sweden: Acta Universitatis Gothoburgensis, 1981.
Krulfeld, Ruth. "The Influence of Land Availability on Market Involvement in Two Sasak Villages in Indonesia: A Problem in Cultural Ecology." In *Cultural-Ecological Perspectives on Southeast Asia*, edited by William Wood. Papers in International Studies, Southeast Asia Series, No. 41. Athens: Ohio University, 1977.
———. "The Sasak." In *Ethnic Groups of Insular Southeast Asia*, edited by Frank M. LeBar. New Haven: Human Relations Area Files Press, 1972.

Articles

Bousquet, G. H. "Researchers sur les deux sectes musulmanes (Waktou Telous et Waktou Lima) de Lombok." *Revue des etudes islamiques* 13 (1939): 149–177.
Krulfeld, Ruth. "Fatalism in Indonesia: A Comparison of Socio-Religious Types on Lombok." *Anthropological Quarterly* 39 (1966): 180–190.
Polak, A. "Some Aspects of a Process of Change in an Indonesian Community." *Tropical Man* 4 (1971): 108–116.

Unpublished Manuscripts

Ecklund, Judith. "Marriage, Seaworms and Song: Ritualized Responses to Cultural Change in Sasak Life." Ph.D. dissertation, Cornell University, 1977.
Krulfeld, Ruth. "The Village Economies of the Sasak of Lombok." Ph.D. dissertation, Yale University, 1974.

Ruth Krulfeld

SENUFO The Senufo of West Africa number more than 2.7 million and live in Ivory Coast, Mali and Upper Volta. The geographical area in which they live is called the Middle Volta, a region to the east of the Bagoe River, to the south of the Bani River, to the west of the Black Volta, and occupying the northern-center portion of Ivory Coast around Korhogo and Odienne. Located in the less fertile regions of the Sudanic zone and between the major traditional routes of trade, the Senufo are agrarian with little history as traders or warriors.

Despite the fact that they have not been geographically isolated as have other small ethnic groups in the same general region, the Senufo resisted Islamization until contemporary times. Only about one-quarter are Muslim.

Dyula traders were the first to introduce them to Islam and its cultural adjuncts. With the decline of the Songhay empire in the early seventeenth century small groups of Islamic traders from that polity migrated and settled among the stateless peoples in the northern part of Ivory Coast. These Dyula (see Dyula) were Islamized during the first period of Islamic expansion below the Sahara. Arab historians indicate that the religion had penetrated peoples on the banks of the upper Senegal and in the Sahel region by the beginning of the eleventh century. During this first period, Islam was a class religion limited to chiefs and traders with a group of professional clerics. Islam was one of the dynamic forces in the empires of Mali and Songhay (see Songhay).

The migrating traders and warriors settled among the eclectic groups in the Sudanic region and attached to these people the term "Bambara" and/or "Senufo." Bambara was the name the Dyula applied to all non-Muslims in the Niger Bend and Senufo to the cluster of people living around present-day Odienne and Korhogo. Because of the Dyula's political and economic importance in the Middle Volta Basin during the period of French expansion, French explorers and military leaders accepted the Mande terms "Senufo" and "Bambara" and applied them to the people living in the region. The term "Senufo" was specifically applied to the majority of the people living in the city of Kong and to those in the kingdom of Kenedougou during the latter half of the nineteenth century.

Historically, the people called Senufo do not refer to themselves or their language by this name. The exact etymology of the Mande term Senufo is unknown. Sienamana is the vernacular name for the Senufo in the region around Korhogo, and Senadi is the language spoken by the people. Supide is the language and the name which the people use to refer to themselves in the region of Kenedougou. The early Muslim migrants who settled among the Senufo kept their cultural identity in that they remained in contact with other Mande peoples. Thus, the Dyula who settled among the Senufo were able to build a communal autonomy and cultural identity in which the Mande dialect was spoken as the first language. Islamization of the Senufo can be closely attributed to the degree of Mande Dyula influence in early times.

The Senufo may be divided into three broad subdivisions or branches: northern, central and southern Senufo. The northern Senufo are the speakers of Supide, the purest dialect of the language of Mali whose population numbers approximately 600,000. This group, often referred to as the people of Kenedougou, is the least Islamized of the three branches. The northern Senufo, normally viewed as being indigenous to the region, are a cultural syncretization of the people who migrated northward from the area around Odienne along the route east of the Bagoe River and west of the mountainous region of Fourou and who mixed with other indigenous groups bordering the Kenedougou region, for example, the Samogos, Gana and Minianka.

Islam first penetrated the northern Senufo with the settlement of the Dyula Traores in Finkolo and the establishment of the kingdom of Kenedougou in the nineteenth century. However, the Traores, who were of Mande origin, had been ''Senufo-ized'' linguistically and culturally by the time Sikasso was established as their administrative capital. Sikasso, originally a Senufo village, became the capital of the kingdom of Kenedougou, the second largest empire in the western Sudan by 1890. Tieba Traore, as king of Sikasso for approximately three decades, limited the spread of Islam to his court, and during his reign the religion was not accessible to his warriors or the masses of Senufo. However, Islam did spread among the ruling elite and chiefs during the reign of Tieba's successor, Babemba.

The southern Senufo were among the first groups in the Middle Volta to be influenced by Islam. These Senufo, founders of Kong, permitted Dyula traders to settle in the city and by the eighteenth century were consequently overthrown by them. With the advent of the Dyula rulers, Kong became a thriving commercial city and center of Islamic learning. Thus, this branch of the Senufo was greatly influenced by the Manding and Dyula and the Qadiriyya Muslim order of northern Ghana. During the nineteenth century, because of the political and economic importance of the Dyula, many of the Senufo chiefs became affiliated with Islam. In many instances Senufo families changed their patronymic and took on Dyula surnames, for example, Fofana, Kulibali, Traores. Despite the conversion of chiefs and leading families to Islam, the masses of Senufo remained traditionalists in their religious practices. Today, fewer than 20 percent of the southern Senufo could be classified as Muslims.

The central Senufo includes the groups in the area of Banfora and Bobo-Dioulasso, Upper Volta. Culturally, this group is a mixture of Samogo, Lobi, Turkas, Toussian and the Bobo-Dyula. Numbering probably less than 30,000, this branch is numerically the smallest of the three Senufo branches. Also, because of the limited amount of field research carried out among this group, the central Senufo are the least culturally delineated among the three major divisions of the Senufo. Although often classified as being indigenous to the region, the central Senufo have been heavily influenced by the political and economic forces originating in Kong, northern Ghana and Sikasso, as well as the local influences of the Bobo-Dyula.

Senufo society successfully resisted large-scale conversion to Islam until after World War II. Several major factors account for the small percentage of Senufo Muslims. Senufo society has developed cultural institutions and practices which resist change. Senufo are primarily cultivators, with much of their mythology associated with the earth. Rituals honor nature spirits. Strong ancestor involvement in life discourages acceptance of a religion which removes the dead from participating with the living.

The communal nature of Senufo society discourages individual initiative in changing the value system. Among the Senufo the economy and social structure of the society negate the existence of the individual except as a member of a particular group. Thus, no man may stand alone within Senufo society. He is the member of an extended family, hamlet or village. A brother is either the first, second or older of younger, for the general term "brother" has meaning only in relationship to a group. One eats in a group, and according to age one will dip into the common dish. The oldest receives the best and the youngest the least piece of meat. At all times, one knows his place in relationship to others in the group. The fields are worked collectively, and food is stored collectively by family; each family contributes towards the communal store for the hamlet or village to help those in need in times of crises. The individual Senufo is conditioned from birth to death to subordinate his individuality for groupness for the common good. Unless the entire group converts to Islam, no one does.

With the advent of national independence and the drive on the part of the national leaders to mold a national citizenry, in contrast to tribal identity, Senufo society has entered a period of political, economic and cultural transformation. Islamic affiliations and conversions are increasing among all branches of the Senufo. The acceleration of affiliations with Islam is most noticeable among those who migrate to the cities in search of work. In Mali, for instance, in seven districts formerly regarded as traditionalist, the number of Muslims has doubled in the last 20 years.

In recent field work undertaken among the Malian and Ivory Coast Senufo, some of the reasons stated for conversion to Islam were that Islamic affiliation offered a sense of belonging to a larger community; conversion complemented ancestral beliefs in the earth spirits once the individual settled in urban areas; by accepting Islam, the individual was not embarrassed at having to explain his traditional beliefs; local administrators were usually Muslim or Christian, and by identifying with one of these religions the Senufo believed that he had greater social and economic security. The nature of Islam allowed the Senufo to keep more of his traditional beliefs than did the Christian sects.

Under current influences the Senufo conversion to Islam can be expected to accelerate in years to come. In the past the communal nature of Senufo society, combined with the religious role of the patriarchal head of family, served as a cultural brake on Senufo conversion to Islam. Now, however, with the decline of patriarchal influences, since the son can now earn money in the cities, and the concurrent decline in the communal nature of traditional Senufo society, more and more Senufo are becoming Muslims.

BIBLIOGRAPHY

Books

Fraser, Douglas, and Cole, Herbert M. *African Art and Leadership*. Madison: University of Wisconsin Press, 1972.
Goldwater, Robert. *Senufo Sculpture from West Africa*. New York Museum of Primitive Art. Greenwich, Conn.: New York Graphic Society, 1964.
Laude Jean. *The Arts of Black Africa*. Translated by Jean Decock. Berkeley: University of California Press, 1971.
Obichere, Boniface I. "The African Factor in the Establishment of French Authority in West Africa, 1880–1900." In *France and Britain in Africa*, edited by P. Gifford and William R. Louis, New Haven: Yale University Press, 1971.
Roberts, T. D., et al. *Area Handbook for Ivory Coast*. 2nd ed. The American University FAS, DA Pam 550–69. Washington, D.C.: Government Printing Office, 1974.
Trimingham, J. Spencer. *The Influence of Islam Upon Africa*. London: Longmans, 1968.

Articles

Grindal, Bruce T. "Islamic Affiliations and Urban Adaptation: The Sosala Migrant in Accra, Ghana." *Africa* 43:4 (1973): 333–352.
Holas, Bohumil. "The Sacred in Social Life: The Senufo Example." *Diogenes* 61 (1968): 114–131.
O'Brien, Donal Cruise. "Towards an 'Islamic Policy' in French West Africa." *Journal of African History* 7:2 (1967): 303–316.
Welmers, Williams E. "Notes on Two Languages in the Senufo Group: I. Senadi." *Language* 26 (1950): 126–146.

————. ''Notes on Two Languages in the Senufo Group: II. Sup'ide.'' *Language* 26 (1950): 494–531.

LeVell Holmes
Population figures updated by Richard V. Weekes

SERER   The Serer are an agricultural people who inhabit an area south and west of Dakar, the capital of Senegal. There are also a few Serer villages in Gambia.

The term ''Serer'' is actually used for two very distinct groups of people. The first is a series of fairly small groups speaking Cangin, so named by W. J. Pichl, author of *The Cangin Group: A Language in Northern Senegal*. The Cangin languages are Safen, Ndut and Non. Although no accurate census has ever been made, it is doubtful whether Cangin speakers exceed 10,000 people. Located in the immediate hinterland of the Dakar-Thies-Rufisque urban triangle, the Cangin speakers are being assimilated by Senegal's dominant Wolof culture (see Wolof). They are probably the descendants of an aboriginal population which was over-run by southward migrations of Serer, Wolof and Fulani (see Fulani) during the first two or three centuries of the current millennium.

The larger group, numbering more than 940,000, of whom about 80 percent are Muslim, traces its descent to migrants from the Senegal River area. There are traditions that this migration involved a rejection of Islam, which was then taking root along the Senegal. This group, in turn, divides in two. The first, the Ndyegem from the Mbuur area and the Nyominka fishermen from the islands of the Saalum estuary, is stateless. The second group inhabits the ''kingdoms'' of Siin and Saalum. The ruling family of these kingdoms is the Gelowar, a matrilineage of Manding extraction, which traces its arrival to the thirteenth or fourteenth century, when the Manding were colonizing Gambia (see Manding-speaking Peoples). Siin is virtually a homogeneous Serer state, but Saalum has a large Wolof majority and Kaolack, the capital of the region, is a Wolof city surrounded by Serer peasants.

The Serer language is the westernmost of the Niger-Congo family. As a member of the West Atlantic subgroup, it is akin to Wolof, Fulani and Temne. Culturally, the Serer are closest to the Fulani-speaking Tukulor, with whom they have a joking (relaxed, informal) relationship.

The Serer live in compact isolated villages and are noted for their intensive agricultural system. Traditionally, they alternated between millet and fallow with their cattle staked out so that manure would be distributed on the fallow field. With the development of peanuts as a cash crop in the nineteenth century, they moved peanuts into a three-field cycle. They also protect a species of tree which drops its leaves at the beginning of the rains and gives the Serer landscape a parklike atmosphere. In the 1960s this tradition began to break down, largely as a result of high population densities in some parts of Siin. Serer peasants began planting the fallow field and sending their cattle into the semi-desert Ferlo during the rainy season. The result was a decline in productivity.

Of all the people living north of the Gambia River, the Serer resisted Islam the most vigorously. Both Serer kings kept *marabouts* at court to handle correspondence, make amulets and pray for their royal masters. In Saalum, two *marabout* families received enough land as a reward for these services that they formed major provincial commands. In each case the provincial chiefs were clerics and the population was solidly Muslim. By the nineteenth century, much of the Wolof population of Saalum was Muslim. From 1861 to the French conquest in 1887, Siin and Saalum found their existence threatened by a *jihad* led by Ma Ba Jaxoo, a Muslim from the neighboring Manding state of Badibu. Ma Ba was killed when he tried to invade Siin in 1867, but Saalum was almost destroyed by the *jihad*.

One result of the *jihad* and the way in which colonization and the extension of cash crop cultivation took place was that the traditional order broke down more quickly in Saalum. By the beginning of World War I the Wolof areas were heavily Muslim and the Serer about 40 percent. In Siin the traditional order proved more resilient. The French felt it wise to operate through the chiefs. Catholic missions were kept out, in part because the Serer blamed an early mission (founded in 1848) for the French invasions of 1859 and 1861.

Traditional religion remained dominant in Siin until after World War II. At this point, there were important Christian and Muslim communities among the Serer. Young Serer men were working in the cities in increasing numbers; many were also going to school. Modern transportation and communications were breaking down the isolation of the village. The result was a rapid process of conversion, which in the 1950s and 1960s moved heavily in favor of Islam.

Today, most Serer have converted, although many still continue their earlier religious practices. Over four-fifths of the converts have chosen Islam. A major factor in Muslim success has been the assimilation of Serer in the city to the dominant culture. The Serer have a reputation for being more lax in their practice of Islam than the Wolof or Tukulor.

The Serer live in exogamous matrilineages. A son lives with his father until circumcision (which used to occur in his twenties), but land is inherited in the matrilineal line, and his mother's brother is responsible for arranging his marriage. A woman joins her husband's community.

The social structure is very hierarchical and consists of four status groups. The first is the Gelowar matrilineage. The second, and probably the largest, is the *jaambuur*, or free men. The third is a series of endogamous artisan castes—smiths, leatherworkers, bards and woodworkers. The fourth and lowest status group, from pre-colonial times, is composed of former slaves.

Martin A. Klein
Population figures updated by Richard V. Weekes

BIBLIOGRAPHY

Books

Gamble, David P. *The Wolof of Senegambia, Together with Notes on the Lebu and the Serer*. London: International African Institute, 1957.

Klein, Martin A. *Islam and Imperialism in Senegal*. Stanford: Stanford University Press, 1968.

Diarra, Fatoumata-Agnes, and Fougeyrollas, Pierre. "Ethnic Group Relations in Senegal." In *Two Studies on Ethnic Group Relations in Africa: Senegal, The United Republic of Tanzania*. Paris: UNESCO, 1974.

Murdock, George P. *Africa: Its People and Their Culture History*. New York: McGraw-Hill, 1959.

Nelson, Harold D., et al. *Area Handbook for Senegal*. The American University FAS, DA Pam 550–70. Washington, D.C.: Government Printing Office, 1974.

Pichl, W. J. *The Cangin Group: A Language Group in Northern Senegal*. Pittsburgh: Duquesne University Press, 1966.

Unpublished Manuscript

Klein, Martin. "Serer and Wolof of Senegal." Paper presented at the Fifteenth Annual Meeting of the African Studies Association, Philadelphia, November 8–11, 1972.

SHAHSEVAN   There are several tribal groups called Shahsevan in Iran, numbering some 310,000 people. They are Shia Muslims and speak Azerbaijani Turkish (see Azeri). Their ancestors are said to have been formed into a special tribe in about A.D. 1600 by Shah Abbas of the Safavid dynasty.

The Safavids, who ruled Iran from 1500 to 1722, descended from a line of Sufis. Their rise to power was based on the fanatical spiritual devotion of a number of pastoral nomad tribes, warriors known as Qizilbash (redheads) after the red cap they wore as the symbol of their sect. The Safavid shahs had difficulty controlling the chiefs of these unruly tribes until Shah Abbas managed to tame them. Among the methods he used was a personal appeal to the shah lovers (Shahsevan), in response to which many Qizilbash tribesmen abandoned their rebellious chiefs and became Shahsevan (see Qizilbash).

Most Shahsevan are now settled villagers or townsmen and preserve little of their tribal organization or culture, but more than 5,000 families still live a nomadic or semi-nomadic life in the province of Azerbaijan, close to the Soviet frontier.

In the last 250 years, Azerbaijan has often been a battleground between Iran and her neighbors, and the Shahsevan nomads figured prominently in the history of the period. Early in the last century the Russians established the present frontier, depriving the Shahsevan of the greater part of their traditional winter quarters in the Mughan steppe. From then until they were disarmed in 1923, they became increasingly lawless. Their raids sometimes disrupted trade and settlement far into both Russia and Iran and caused friction between the two countries. Old men today preserve vivid memories of those times and of their defeat of the Cossacks sent against them by Russia.

Apart from their distinctive frontier location, the most obvious way the Shahsevan differ from other nomads is in their tents. Most tribes in Iran have rectangular goat hair tents, similar to those of the Arab bedouin. Shahsevan tents resemble upturned saucers and are related to the yurts of the Central Asian nomads. The wooden framework of curved struts, held together by long girths radiates from a central roof ring, which is anchored to the ground by a massive peg. The covering of thick felt mats keeps out both heat and cold. Such a tent, both heavier and sturdier than other types, costs up to the equivalent of $500. The wooden parts should last 20 years and are bought in the bazaar, while the felts, which need replacing every three years, are made in camp from the wool of the flocks. Only about two out of three households can afford such a tent.

In each tent lives a household of seven or eight people on the average. The Shahsevan prefer large households, and often brothers and their wives and children or an old couple and their married sons stay together. There are no partitions in the tent except in the first year of a son's marriage, when he and his bride sleep behind a curtain. The hearth, focus of all domestic life, lies between the door and the central peg.

The staple food is bread. To obtain wheat flour and other supplies, the Shahsevan sell wool and surplus animals. Herding, milking, shearing and the marketing of produce are the work of men, who also see to the erection and maintenance of the tents. The household head is rarely at home during the day unless he has guests. Younger men and boys help with the herding and fetch fuel.

Women and girls may fetch water, but normally stay in camp to run the household. Their regular chore, at least once a day, is baking bread over the hearth. For home consumption they also turn milk into cheese, yogurt and butter, spin the wool and weave various colorful storage bags and rugs, given in a girl's trousseau on marriage. Other containers are made of dung and straw.

Shahsevan women do not wear veils, but cover the lower part of the face in the presence of unrelated men. This rule is strictly observed by newly married women; young girls and old women are more casual.

For herding purposes, four or five households cooperate. The men are usually brothers or paternal cousins, but may include relatives through marriage and perhaps a hired shepherd, who is paid 5 percent of the animals he tends for every six-month contract period.

People in these herding units know each other intimately, of course, but they also have intense social relations within a wider community of 20 to 30 households, the *tireh*. Men of the *tireh* trace common descent from an ancestor some four generations back, whose name they usually bear.

About four marriages in ten involve couples from the same *tireh*, but unlike many Muslims the Shahsevan rarely marry their first paternal cousins. Many boys and girls are able to choose their own partners and say they marry for love. Marriages are most often made between distant kin of the same *tireh* or between neighboring *tirehs*. There is little or no divorce among the nomads. Perhaps three men in a *tireh* have second wives, almost all of whom were widows.

Each *tireh* has rights to defined pastures in summer and winter quarters. The rights have recently been subdivided, so that in summer the small herding units camp separately, while in winter two or three come together in larger groups of 10 to 15 tents. The whole *tireh* migrates as a unit in spring and autumn to and from the mountains. Moreover, the members of the *tireh* form a congregation for important religious ceremonies, such as Ramadan and Muharram.

These communal activities are directed by the "gray beard" of the *tireh*, who has a difficult job as official leader, responsible for all dealings with the authorities. He, or his son, should be literate. Members of the *tireh* look to his life-style as a source and symbol of their honor, and he should be wealthy enough not only to entertain important visitors, but also to provide lavish entertainment at feasts.

There are wide differences of wealth. A gray beard may own several hundred sheep, 5 or 10 camels and some donkeys and horses, while a poor kinsmen may have only 15 sheep and 2 camels and have to work as a shepherd or supplement his income by casual labor or petty trading.

A gray beard rarely displays his authority. Instead, with most of the *tireh*, he uses skillful persuasion. Disputes, especially where women are involved, are not discussed openly but are resolved if possible by private communications between gray beards and participants.

The women, too, have their leaders, who act somewhat differently. Women past childbearing age may reach positions of considerable respect, and a few become influential leaders, "gray hairs," comparable to the male gray beards. These leaders are consulted privately by gray beards, but among the women they exercise their influence in public, at feasts attended by guests from a wide range of *tirehs*.

At feasts, men and women are segregated. While the men are enjoying music and other entertainment, in the women's tent the leaders are likely to discuss matters of importance to both men and women, such as marriage arrangements, disputes, irregular behavior among *tireh* members or broader subjects bearing on economic and political affairs. Opinions are formed and decisions made, which are then spread as the women return home and tell their menfolk and friends. This unusual information network among the women serves a most important function for the society as a whole.

The Shahsevan of Azerbaijan are comprised of 30-odd tribes (*tayfeh*), each led by a chief. The tribes vary in size from two *tirehs* (50 families) to more than 25 (1,000 families). Few contacts, and less than 10 percent of marriages, are made between *tayfehs*, each of which feels itself different in subtle ways from the others. The chiefs no longer have the arbitrary power over their followers they once enjoyed, but several of them and their families remain a privileged class, distinct from ordinary nomad society.

The Shahsevan winter near sea level on the Mughan steppe and spend the summer months in the high pastures of the Savalon range to the south. With a migration of 100 to 150 miles, they gain maximum protection from seasonal variations in climate, which can be extreme in this part of Southwest Asia.

The Iranian New Year (March 21) marks the beginning of spring, the most pleasant season in Mughan. After the shepherds renew their contracts, the winter camps break up to scatter in herding units over the rolling hills, now blanketed by tall grass and flowers, but the season is brief, and by the beginning of May the sun is scorching the steppe into a semi-desert. A few feverish days are spent mowing and stacking hay in preparation for winter before the nomads start the migration southward and upward. Within 10 days of the first departure, Mughan is empty of nomads.

The tents are dismantled the evening before a move is planned. Each move begins well before dawn, so long as the sky is clear, and lasts about four hours. An average household has three or four camels, strung together nose to tail. The first is preferably a hybrid between the two-humped Bactrian and the one-humped dromedary, a huge beast capable of carrying a complete tent weighing nearly half a ton. The others carry bedding, carpets and supplies, with women and small children perched on top. Some men and boys accompany the flocks, which move more slowly and graze on the way. Others lead the camels on foot or astride donkeys. Gray beards and other men wealthy enough to have horses ride ahead to inspect possible stopping places.

On arrival at camp, the camels are unloaded, and the men set about erecting the tents. Women arrange the furniture and prepare a simple breakfast of bread, cheese and tea before setting about their usual chores. Men, unless tending the animals, spend the rest of the day dozing, discussing whether or where to move the next night or perhaps visiting village friends.

Nomads are less than one-quarter of the rural population of this region. They share their language and religion with the settled people, whom they know as Tats. They are involved in close economic and administrative contacts with the market towns and with the villagers, who practice extensive irrigated and rain-fed cultivation.

Tent dwelling and a nomadic way of life are basic to Shahsevan identity. With their annual cycle of movement, their view of time and space differs from that of settled people; winter and summer are places as well as seasons. In the past, all the nomads knew of the mountains in winter was that they were deep under snow, while they thought Mughan in summer to be impossibly hot and infested with snakes. More and more in recent years, cultivation has spread throughout the region at the expense of pasture land, and the Shahsevan have come to settle and adopt a more sedentary view of the world.

BIBLIOGRAPHY

Books

Tapper, Richard. *Pasture and Politics: Economics, Conflict and Ritual Among the Shahsevan Nomads of Northwestern Iran.* London: Academic Press, 1979.

Tapper, Nancy. "The Women's Sub-society Among the Shahsevan Nomads." In *Women in the Muslim World*, edited by Lois Beck and N. Keddie. Cambridge: Harvard University Press, 1978.

Articles

Tapper, Richard. "Black Sheep, White Sheep and Redheads: A Historical Sketch of the Shahsavan of Azarbaijan." *Journal of the British Institute of Persian Studies* 4 (1966): 61–84.
———. "Shahsevan." *Family of Man* 6:84 (1975): 2337–2339.
———. "Shahsevan in Safavis Persia." *Bulletin of the School of Oriental and African Studies* 37:2 (1974): 321–354.

Unpublished Manuscript

Tapper, Richard. "The Shahsavan of Azarbaijan: A Study of Political and Economic Change in a Middle Eastern Tribal Society." Ph.D. dissertation, University of London, 1971.

Richard Tapper
Population figures updated by Richard V. Weekes

SHANGAWA   The banks and islands of the Niger River support the Shangawa in and around the northwestern Nigerian city of Shanga, which they are credited with founding. Shanga District forms a link between the farthest outpost of Hausa culture to the west and the outside world to the south, a link that emphasizes the importance of this ethnic group. Numbering some 30,000, the people are 40 percent Muslim, a percentage that is increasing rapidly.

Shanga, which is 85 percent Shangawa, is one of the six districts in Yauri, a political division in Sokoto State, the heart of Hausaland (see Hausa). Yauri (population 112,000), like most divisions, corresponds roughly to traditional emirates, whose powers have been increasingly taken over by the state governments. In Sokoto and thus Yauri and Shanga, authority is held by Muslims, mostly Hausa, who assert continuing pressures in various ways on the people to become Muslim.

The Shangawa were once a subgroup of the Kengawa (Kiengawa, Kyengawa, Tienga). According to legend the Kengawa and Shangawa are the elder and younger branches of a priestly tribe that served the House of Kisra, reputedly Muhammad's rival "in the East." A number of Nigerian peoples trace their origins to Kisra or one of his sons or daughters. Kisra, who some say was Persian, fought against the spread of Islam. In Persian, the word "Kisra" may have come from "Chosroes," the name of a Persian dynasty. The Prophet Muhammad defeated Kisra in battle, and Kisra then either fled or was allowed to emigrate in recognition of his valor.

By the thirteenth century the Kengawa-Shangawa were part of the Songhay Empire with many of their towns occupied by Songhay troops. In the late sixteenth century a Moroccan army defeated the Songhay; many Songhay soldiers by then had merged with the indigenous populations, and myths take note of the fact. Amidst the invasions the Shangawa found refuge in Yauri, and Shanga District was most likely founded in the early nineteenth century. Invaders and slave raiders forced them to retreat further into the hinterlands, and they found a haven on the islands of the Niger River.

The Shangawa speak Kengawa, a branch of Niger-Benue division of the Niger-Congo language family. They are thus linguistically allied with the Reshawa, Kamberi and Dukawa, although their dialects are not mutually intelligible. Interethnic communication is in Hausa (see Kamberi; Reshawa).

Shangawa are primarily farmers, secondarily fishermen and thirdly traders. Still relying essentially on hoe technology, they grow millet and guinea corn and, along the river, various vegetables. Shanga has three seasons: rainy (June–October), *harmattan* (November–February) and *bazara* (March–May). In general, positive feelings are associated with the rainy season, when temperatures are lower but the climate is still pleasant. Annual rainfall is about 40 inches. Prospects for replenishing storage bins are good and social events are more common. *Harmattan* is colder weather, time to repair farms and compounds, fish and visit friends. The *bazara* means hot weather, when temperatures stay over 100°F. Not much work is accomplished. The recent Sahelian drought severely affected Shanga. Food had to be imported.

Shangawa family life is characterized by an extended patrilateral family structure. Upon the death of the eldest male, fissioning along matrilateral lines tends to occur. Sons of the same mother tend to cluster together. Shangawa marriages, while sometimes arranged at birth, result from considerable freedom of choice for both sexes. Selection often takes place at intervillage wrestling matches, a serious business. A boy begins wrestling at puberty and wrestles with his agemates only until his first marriage. At wrestling matches prospective spouses size each other up. Once selection is made, brideservice (*gormu*) can begin.

Brideservice requires the betrothed young man to work with his work team (composed of his wrestling partners) for seven years on his future father-in-law's farm. The young couple earns increasing conjugal rights as the service progresses. Muslims do not perform brideservice and follow more traditional Islamic marriage patterns.

Because Muslim Shangawa may have four wives and traditional Shangawa males are limited only by their income and inclinations, plural marriage is common. In all cases, however, a woman has a voice in whether she will marry a particular person. That right extends to cases of leviratic marriage as well. A man is required to marry his older brother's widow, who must be wooed, for she is under no obligation to marry her husband's brother. How much real choice she has of course, depends on her value. If she has been a "good" wife, her dead husband's family will try to convince her to remain in the family. A "good" wife is one who has remained faithful, tends her fields (rice, economic trees), minds the children and shows proper modesty.

Birth in a family, while important, does not call for special ceremonies. If a woman has been married two or three years without bearing children, she will go to a priest to obtain magical aid. In return she promises to sacrifice animals—goats, sheep, chickens.

Children belong to the father's family. If a divorce occurs, then only unweaned children accompany their mothers. It is expected that such children will be returned to their fathers upon weaning. Muslim Shangawa are more strict in this observance. No one, however, doubts in theory the rights of a man over his family. That right extends to married sons, who, in theory, should remain with their father and form an extended family compound.

Family decisions are ideally made by males. In reality, women, who are not kept in *purdah* (seclusion), have great influence upon family matters. They may exercise that influence directly or through adult sons. Little overt male–female hostility is noticeable. Indeed, great cooperation appears to be the rule among Shangawa men and women.

Although there is a patrilateral bias among Shangawa, there are no functioning patrilineages. As more and more Shangawa become Muslims, they move towards the Hausa *dengi* system, which includes relatives bilaterally and favors those who happen to be available for help in particular situations.

Traditional Shangawa religion draws heavily upon the Kisra legend. The use of black oxen, goats or chickens reflects Kisra symbolism in that black is sacred to Kisra; all groups "descended" from him make use of it in their rituals. Especially, black animals are necessary for life-crisis observances. When a woman has been unable to conceive, she will sacrifice such an animal, depending upon her wealth. When drought has struck the land, black animals are sacrificed.

Islam, or at least the Hausa version of Islam, has influenced the traditional religion. The major spirits, Gadakassa, Berkassa and Gwaraswa, are considered *jinns* responsible for major events in human life. Each has its own shrines, usually in baobob or tamarind trees. All such trees are sacred in the area.

Although Shangawa chiefs take part in religious sacrifices, there are other traditional practitioners, especially Bori priests. The Bori complex, a spirit possession cult widespread in Yauri, is strong in Hausa areas. Although the Shangawa have their own Sarkin Bori, the Sarkin Bori of the neighboring Reshawa has long been acknowledged as the best of all such priests.

There are two significant sacrifices practiced by Muslim and traditional Shangawa alike. The first is the annual sowing of corn, when a black bull and a red cow are the preferred victims. Other possible combinations include black and white fowl or a red goat and white fowl. The victims are decapitated and their blood smeared on sacred buildings.

At death, a similar sacrifice occurs. Mourners consume the flesh of the animals and inter the bones with the deceased. Burial should occur as soon as possible. The grave should be in the deceased's compound; if this is not possible, then a calabash of earth from the deceased's grave is carried ceremoniously to the compound and buried there.

A corpse is buried with monkey skin around the loins and placed in a round hole 30 inches deep. A tunnel is dug at the bottom, facing north–south. While drummers pound a slow, mournful beat, mourners, usually a man's wrestling and brideservice mates, carry the body around the grave three times. The corpse is lowered into the grave facing the right side of the tunnel with the right hand under the head. For the Shangawa, as for many African peoples, including Muslims, the right side is sacred, the left profane. The corpse's feet must be to the north with the face to the east.

Yauri long ago came under the religious influence of Muslim traders and religious leaders, *mallamai* (singular, *mallam*). In the seventeenth century that influence came predominantly from the Kebbi, whose Muslim leader, Kanta, was a legendary but real slave raider. By the end of the seventeenth century, the Emir of Yauri was a Muslim. Yauri Muslims are Sunni by sect, Maliki in rite. Indeed, the power of Maliki law to organize the government and administration of the emirate was a major factor in its acceptance by the ruling Hausa.

Currently, the government sponsors *mallamai* to effect conversion. The employment of clear-cut role models is a definite art of Islamic conversion strategy. These are males who must know how to read and write Quranic Arabic and have gone through training. The Islamic Education Trust, an association with links throughout the Islamic world and with headquarters in Mecca, sponsors training projects and provides literature and other aid.

The *mallamai* generally live in villages and support themselves through farming. They interact with the Shangawa in every aspect of life, seeking to demonstrate that Islam transcends ethnic identity. Additionally, they attempt to convert groups of people in order to provide a convert with a built-in support group. They are not hesitant either to show that economic and political advantages accrue to Muslims over traditionalists.

The work of the *mallamai* has not been in vain. While today a large minority of the Shangawa are Muslims, soon the majority will be. Shangawa who are not yet Muslim have begun to adopt Muslim names, dress and practices. They consult *mallamai* in religious and other matters. Some *mallamai* are also traditional doctors, and others teach in schools. No strong hostility has marred relationships between the Shangawa and Yauri's rulers. Many Shangawa have served as village heads and counsellors. Therefore, there is no natural impediment in refusing Islam such as the Dukawa, for example, have done. Already the Shangawa celebrate all the Islamic religious holidays that the Hausa do. They do so even though they, like the Hausa in Yauri, tenaciously hold on to the old Bori practices and beliefs and never quite abandon the old religion.

BIBLIOGRAPHY

Books

Meek, Charles K. *The Northern Tribes of Nigeria*. 1925. Reprint ed. London: Frank Cass, 1971.

————. *Tribal Studies in Northern Nigeria*. London: Kegan Paul, 1931.

Salamone, Frank A. *Gods and Goods in Africa*. New Haven: HRAFlex, 1974.

Temple, C. F., ed. *Notes on the Tribes, Provinces, Emirates and States of the Northern Provinces of Nigeria*. Compiled from official reports by O. Temple. 1922. Reprint ed. London: Frank Cass, 1965.

Articles

Jeness, Jonathan. "Fisherman of the Kainji Basin." Rome: F.A.O., 1970.

Nicholson, W. E. "Notes on Some of the Customs of the Busa and Kyenga Tribes at Illo." *Journal of the African Society* 26:102 (1927): 92–100.

Roder, Wolf. "The Irrigation Farmers of the Kainji Lake Region, Nigeria." Rome: F.A.O., 1970.

Salamone, Frank A. "Becoming Hausa: Ethnic Identity Change and Its Implications for the Study of Ethnic Pluralism and Stratification." *Africa* 54:4 (1975): 410–421.

————. "The Work of the Social Welfare Worker in a Small Nigerian Division." *Africanus* 4:2 (1974): 37–51.

Frank A. Salamone

SHINA-SPEAKING PEOPLES   Speakers of the Shina language are distributed throughout the mountainous regions of the upper Indus River and its tributaries, the Gilgit, lower Hunza, Tangir, Kishenganga, Astor and Dras rivers, an area which is now approximately bisected by the cease-fire line between Pakistan and India. Owing to an ambiguity in the distinction between ethnicity and linguistic affiliation among these people, an accurate estimate of their numbers is difficult to obtain, and census data are unreliable. Shina speakers generally refer to themselves by a geographical designation, such as Gilgitis, Kohistanis, or Drasis, and may not call their language Shina but rather use an adaptation of a geographical designation, such as Kohistyō. On the other hand, not all Shina speakers are Shins, which is a social grouping. There may be between 300,000 and 350,000 Shina speakers in all. Nearly all are Muslim.

The Shina language belongs to the Dardic group of the Indo-Aryan subfamily of the Indo-European family of languages, and the region in which it is spoken has been termed Dardistan by some authors; however, this term suggests a political unity which has never existed.

The entire area is arid or semi-arid, and as the topography is extremely rugged, the population centers are found in the narrow valleys formed by the tributaries of the Indus, where irrigation is possible. The Indus itself is useless for irrigation and a poor communication route, as it flows through a steep rocky gorge between banks of sand deposited by recurrent floods. Many valleys are inaccessible, and most habitations exist as small independent communities, ruled by local councils (*jirgahs*) or minor princes.

In pre-Islamic times the region was an important center of Buddhism. The famous Gilgit Manuscripts were found here, and there are inscriptions in Kharosthi, Sogdian, Prakrit, an undeciphered language which is probably Aramaic, and old Chinese. There is also evidence that the Indus was a better route of communication during those times. In recent centuries, the aggressive assertion of their autonomy by the tribes living on both sides of the Indus has discouraged travel along this route—a situation prevailing until the opening of the Karakoram Highway in the late 1970s.

Traces of pre-Islamic local beliefs linger on in some areas, among them belief in fairies and demons, as well as shamanism. But the shamans, who formerly belonged to both sexes, are now exclusively male.

In the nineteenth and twentieth centuries, many Shina-speaking communities were conquered by the Maharajah of Kashmir and thus came indirectly under British influence. Today, the Shina-speaking communities of the Gilgit, lower Hunza, Tangir-Darel, Astor and Chilas valleys, as well as those in the Indus Kohistan, are under Pakistani administration. India administers the Shina communites in the Kishenganga (or Neelam) drainage: the Gures and Tilel valleys, the Dras plain and the Shina-speaking (Brokskat) communities of Ladakh.

Although Shina is fairly homogeneous throughout the region, eight different dialects can be distinguished, corresponding to the distribution of the Shins themselves—except in Gilgit, where Shina serves as a *lingua franca* for a variety of ethnic groups and castes. The original center of the Shina language is Gilgit, and the Gilgiti dialect is the only one with a standardizing influence. It possesses a body of oral literature, and now there are the beginnings of a written literature; it is also used by Radio Pakistan for its Shina-language broadcasts. Some important isoglosses separate the Gilgiti dialect, along with that of the lower Hunza Valley, from the other Shina dialects. This dialect split implies either a somewhat independent evolution of the Shina language and culture in the Gilgit valley or an early division into two groups of the original Shina speakers. However, the reasons for this are obscure.

The other major dialects of Shina are:

1. *Chilasi and the Kohistani Dialects.* Chilas live below Nanga Parbat on the westward swing of the Indus River. Downriver from Chilas lie the Shina-speaking communities of Jalkot, Palas and Koli, whose inhabitants have an oral tradition that their ancestors migrated there from Chilas. Despite the fact that there is about 70 percent intelligibility between the Kohistani dialects and that of Gilgit, the left-bank Kohistanis consider all the Shina spoken north of Sea (slightly upriver from Jalkot) as a separate language, which they call Sunkyo. They call their own dialects by other names: Kohistyō and Kolichyō. Chilasi and the Kohistani dialects are similar; so, with slight differences, is that of Tangir-Darel, which is the southernmost Shina dialect on the right bank of the Indus. The true linguistic boundary between Gilgiti and the southern dialects may be placed north of Chilas, in the inhospitable foothills of Nanga Parbat.

2. *Astori, Guresi and Drasi.* These three dialects form another grouping, separate from Chilasi and the Kohistani dialects, but agreeing with them in certain points, notably, the formation of the infinitive suffix in *-onu*. The Drasi dialect is the most divergent of the three. Relatively little is known about the linguistic and cultural

patterns of Astor and Guresi, areas which abut on a sensitive political boundary.

3. *Brokskat*. Pockets of Shina speakers are scattered throughout Baltistan and western Ladakh as far as Kargil. A few villages in Ladakh are inhabited by Buddhist Shina speakers. Their Shina has converged with Balti (locally called Purki) to such an extent that it is not intelligible to speakers of other Shina dialects.

Linguistic boundaries are roughly paralleled by sectarian religious boundaries. In Hunza and the Gilgit valley west of Gilgit town, the Ismaili sect predominates. In Gilgit town and the eastern Indus Valley (Baltistan and Ladakh), Shias are more numerous, especially among Baltis and those Shina speakers (Brokpas) who have settled among the Baltis (see Baltis). Astor has a mixed population of Sunnis and Shias. Throughout the southern flank of the Shina area, including Chilas, Kohistan, Gures and Dras, the Sunni sect is greatly in the majority. Chilas, Tangir-Darel and the Kohistan were converted by Sunni *mullahs* from Swat and are the home of the most intense religious conservatism. Sectarian differences between the Gilgitis and their Shina-speaking Sunni neighbors have undoubtedly contributed to the differences in dialect, as they have intensified the isolation between Gilgit and its neighbors (see Kohistanis).

Thus, where Gilgit may be considered a center of the Shina language and associated culture traits, the Indus River and Nanga Parbat massif form natural boundaries within the region which correspond to linguistic and cultural variations. The ethnographic generalizations presented below describe the pattern found in Gilgit and adjoining areas, with some variation occurring in other areas noted, where these are known. Much of the region has not been studied at all, or studied relatively superficially. Since all the ethnographic research has been done by men, little is known about life within the family (a unit to which men have no access). It is unlikely that the Gilgiti cultural pattern prevails throughout the region. In the south, Pushtun (Pathan) influence is strong; in the Indian Shina communities there has been some convergence with patterns typical of the Kashmir Valley (see Pushtun; Kashmiris).

The Shina speakers of Gilgit, the lower Hunza Valley and Tangir-Darel are divided into four communities or castes: Shins, Yeshkuns, Kamins and Doms. The Yeshkuns predominate in the Gilgit and Hunza valleys, Tangir-Darel and Astor and appear to be the original inhabitants of the region. The Shins claim a superior status to the other three groups and are numerically strongest in the southern part of the region: Kohistan, Gures and Dras. This inverse distribution, taken into consideration along with the toponymy (place names) of the upper Gilgit Valley, has suggested to some an encroachment by Shins from the south on the indigenous Yeshkun (or Burusho?) homeland (see Burusho). Preliminary observations of the toponymy of the Sind Valley in Kashmir suggest that on the northern fringes of the Kashmir Valley the Shins themselves may have been displaced by Kashmiri speakers. Migration of ethnic and linguistic groups from south to north is thus an unproven (and perhaps unprovable) factor—but a likely one—in the linguistic and cultural patchwork of "Dardistan."

Kamins ("workers") are found outside the Shina area, in the Punjab. Their status as a separate sociological grouping, and the occupational castes classified under this term, vary from one area to another. In Gilgit, blacksmiths and potters are inferior to Kamins, but in Kohistan (Palas) the term "Kamin" is used to describe all non-Shins including Yeshkuns, Gujars, blacksmiths, weavers and even Doms (see Gujars). Thus in Palas only a binary sociological division (Shin–Kamin) exists. In the Tilel Valley of the Guresi-speaking area, the entire population is reported to be Shin, and Shins work as blacksmiths, potters, carpenters, barbers and shepherds (unless these are Gujars).

Doms are the musicians; in Gilgit they also work as blacksmiths. In Gilgit they play musical instruments—kettledrums, drums, clarinets and flutes—but do not sing. In Kohistan, they used to sing and dance as well but have been prohibited from practicing their arts by the *mullahs*. There are no Doms in the Tilel Valley. Where Doms still practice their traditional profession, their performances are an essential feature of weddings, polo matches or official tours by dignitaries of all sorts. A fondness for music and dancing is characteristic of the Shina-speaking people, and all the traditional festivals (winter solstice, spring, harvest and sowing) have special songs to be sung in connection with them.

The Doms of Gilgit and Hunza-Nager have their own language, Dumaki, which is not Dardic but belongs to the Central Indo-Aryan group of the South Asian plains. Both Doms and Kamins appear to have migrated into the area from the south.

The economy is based on farming and herding. In the broader valleys, which can accommodate a year-round sedentary population, most of the valley land is terraced and irrigated, and maize, wheat and barley are grown. Some rice, millet and various kinds of legumes are also cultivated, along with vegetables (potatoes, tomatoes, onions and squashes). Horticulture is a specialty of these valleys which produce apricots, apples, grapes and nuts for home consumption and cash crops. The opening of the Karakoram Highway in Pakistan has recently improved the marketability of nuts and dried fruit in that country. The Indian valleys are located off the major communication routes and have less access to markets.

Goats, sheep, buffalo and cows are raised throughout the region and are taken by shepherds to higher mountain pastures to graze during the summer. In the Gilgit, Hunza and Astor valleys, ponies are raised for the popular sport of polo, but the horse is a prestige animal, and it is the buffalo which is the common beast of burden for plowing. Nineteenth-century explorers observed that the Shins considered the cow and its products polluting; only traces of this ancient taboo remain. Traces of its counterpart are to be found in the attribution of supernatural powers to wild goats (ibor and markhor) and the custom of embellishing the gate and veranda of the residence of a local ruler or important religious leader by the horns of a markhor.

In the steep-sided valleys of the Indus, agriculture and herding are combined in a finely balanced transhumance cycle. At the end of April the community prepares to shift from the lowest elevations, near the rivers, to cultivated fields at median elevations. The cattle and goats are sent ahead with shepherds or tenants to manure the fields. After these fields are sown with maize, the population shifts again to still higher elevations, where barley and vegetables are grown. The months of July and August are spent in the highest mountain pastures, which, because of their location, serve as meeting places for people from dispersed settlements throughout the valley. The high mountain pastures are considered by these people as the most suitable environment for the composition of poetry in the Shina language. In the autumn, the migration process is reversed, with the livestock being brought down by stages after the harvesting at each elevation has been completed.

The extended family and the village are the basic sociological units. Villages usually consist of dispersed hamlets, which tend to be inhabited by people of the same patrilineal descent group. In Gilgit, hamlets are further subdivided into *phari* (neighborhoods or wards). Within the hamlet or ward, women generally do not wear the full veil but only a head shawl, which does not hinder performance of tasks outside the house walls, such as fetching water and firewood, weeding crops and washing pots and clothes in the irrigation channel. As marriages tend to be endogamous, women often stay near their natal home after marriage.

In some remote valleys, villages are constructed as fortresses, with walled perimeters and towers. Fortress-towers are also built in dispersed settlements in the Kohistan when a blood feud occurs. In this case the aggrieved party ceases to till his fields, takes refuge in his tower and, armed with guns and binoculars, waits for his enemy to attack. This strategy is available only to prosperous men; poorer men must either flee or seek asylum with some rival party. The most frequent causes of feuds are adultery and infliction of physical injury or murder. Feuds are more common in Chilas, Tangir-Darel and the Kohistan, where Pushtun influence is strongest, than in Gilgit or the Indian valleys. In Gilgit, fines are more commonly imposed. Associated with factionalism and local warfare is a tendency to establish alliances between localities through marriages of exchange; for example, in Kohistan between Palas and Jalkot valleys and in Tangir-Darel between Tangir and Darel.

Most Shina speakers are in the process of acculturation, at least to some extent, to the dominant patterns of Pakistan or India. Urdu has become the carrier language throughout most of the region, and most men (but not women) are bilingual. Trilingualism (Shina-Urdu-Pakhto or Shina-Urdu-Kashmiri) is not uncommon.

With the construction of the Karakoram Highway, the Indus has again become the best route of communication from the South Asian subcontinent to China, through the core of the Shina-speaking territory. Shina speakers are being integrated into wider economic networks, as well as gaining access to expanded health and educational facilities. In both Pakistan and India, research in the last few years has sought to answer questions about the Shina language as well as about the social structure, religious beliefs and history of its speakers. In India, a government-sponsored project has begun to provide Shina-speaking children primary textbooks in their own language. Thus, after many centuries of isolation, Shina speakers have again begun to participate in the wider economic and cultural spheres of the South Asian subcontinent.

(The author wishes to express her gratitude to Professor Georg Buddress of Johannes-Gutenberg University, Mainz, West Germany, for reading the unpublished manuscript, correcting errors and providing additional information about the Shina speakers of Gilgit and Tangir-Darel. Any inaccuracies which may remain are the sole responsibility of the author.)

BIBLIOGRAPHY

Books

Bailey, T. Grahame. *Grammar of the Shina Language*. London: The Royal Asiatic Society, 1924.

Barth, Fredrik. *Indus and Swat Kohistani: An Ethnographic Survey*. Studies Honoring the Centennial of the Universitets Etnografiske Museum, Oslo. Oslo: Forenede Trykkerier, 1956.

Biddulph, John. *Tribes of the Hindoo Koosh*. 1880. Reprint ed. Karachi: Indus Publications, 1977.

Buddruss, Georg. "Aus Dardischer Volksdichtung (Some Dardic Folk Poetry)." In *Indo Iranica: Mélanges présentés à Georg Morgenstierne à l'occasion de son soixante-dixième anniversaire*. Wiesbaden, Germany: Otto Harassowitz, 1964.

―――. "Neue Schriftsprachen im Norden Pakistans." In *Schrift und Gedächtnis*, edited by Jan Assman. Paderborn, Germany: Ferdinand Schöningh. In press.

―――. *Proben eines Maiyã-Dialektes aus Tanger (Hindukusch)*. Munich: Münchner Studien zur Sprachwissenschaft, 1959.

Fussman, Gérard. *Atlas linguistique des parlers dardes et kafirs*. Paris: Ecole Française d'Extrême-Orient, 1972.

Grierson, George A. *Indo-Aryan Family, Northwestern Group: Specimens of the Dardic or Pisacha Languages (Including Kashmiri)*. Linguistic Survey of India. Vol. 8, pt. 2. 1919. Reprint ed. Delhi: Motilal Banarsidass 1968, and Lahore, Pakistan: Accurate Printers, 1969.

Jettmar, Karl. *Bolor and Dardistan*. Islamabad: National Institute of Folk Heritage, 1980.

―――. *Die Religionen des Hindukusch*. Stuttgart, Germany: W. Kolhammer, 1975.

Keay, John. *The Gilgit Game*. London: John Murray, 1979.

Koul, Omkar N., and Schmidt, Ruth Laila. "Dardistan Revisited: An Examination of the Relationship Between Kashmiri and Shina." In *Aspects of Kashmiri Linguistics*, edited by Omkar N. Koul and Peter Hook. New Delhi: Bahri Publications, 1983.

Leitner, G. W. *Dardistan in 1866, 1886 and 1893. Being an Account of the History, Religions, Customs, Legends, Fables and Songs of Gilgit, Chilas, Kandia (Gabrial), Yasin, Chitral, Hunza, Nagyr and Other Parts of the Hindu Kush. As Also a Supplement to the Second Edition of The Hunza and Nagyr Handbook and an*

Epitome of Part III of the Author's The Languages and Races of Dardistan. 1893. Reprint ed. New Delhi: Manjusri Publishing House, 1978.

Lorimer, D.L.R. *The Dumāki Language: Outlines of the Speech of the Ḍoma, or Bēricho, of Hunza*. Comité International Permanent de Linguistes, Publications de la Commission d'Enquête Linguistique, No. 4. Nijmegen, Netherlands: Dekker & Van de Vegt, N.V., 1939.

Morgenstierne, George. *Report on a Linguistic Mission to North-Western India*. Instituttet for Sammenlignende Kulturforskning, Serie C III-1. 1932. Reprint ed. Karachi: Indus Publications, n.d.

Müller-Stellrecht, Irmtraud. *Feste in Dardistan: Darstellung und Kulturegeschichtliche Analyse*. Wiesbaden, Germany: Franz Steiner, 1973.

————. *Materialen zur Ethnographie von Dardistan: Aus den nachgelassenen Aufzeichnungen von D.R.L. Lorimer*. Vol. 1, *Hunza*. Vol. 2, *Gilgit*. Vol. 3, *Chitral und Yasin*. Graz, Austria: Akademische Druck-u, 1979.

Namus, M. S. *Gilgit Aur Šinā Zabān*. Bahawalpur, Pakistan: Urdu Academy, 1955.

Ramaswami, N. *Brokskat Phonetic Reader*. Mysore, India: Central Institute of Indian Languages, 1975.

Schmidt, Ruth Laila, and Koul, Omkar N., with Vijay Kaul. *Kohistani to Kashmiri: An Annotated Bibliography of Dardic Languages*. Patiala, India: Indian Institute of Language Studies, 1983.

Schomberg, Reginald Charles Francis. *Between the Oxus and the Indus*. 1935. Reprint ed. Lahore: Al-Biruni, n.d.

Zia, Amin, trans. *Sawenō Morye*. Edited by Uxi Mufti and Mazhar-ul-Islam. Islamabad: Institute of Folk Heritage, 1978.

Articles

Fussman, Gérard. ''Quelques ouvrages récents sur les langues et civilisations de l'Hindou-Kouch (1976–1979).'' *Journal asiatique* (Paris) 268 (1980): 451–465.

Jettmar, Karl. ''Ethnological Research in Dardistan 1958.'' *Proceedings of the American Philosophical Society* 105:1 (1961): 79–97. Reprinted Islamabad: National Institute of Folk Heritage, 1980.

Schmidt, Ruth Laila. ''Report on a Survey of Dardic Dialects of Kashmir.'' *Indian Linguistics*. In press.

————, and Zarin, Mohammad. ''The Phonology and Tonal System of Pālas Kohistyō Shina.'' *Münchner Studien zur Sprachwissenschaft* 40 (1981): 155–185.

Strand, Richard F. ''Notes on the Nuristani and Dardic Languages.'' *Journal of the American Oriental Society* 93:3 (1973): 297–305.

Ruth Laila Schmidt

SINDHIS   As the mighty Indus, one of the major rivers of the world, winds its way southward from the ranges of the high Himalayas to the Arabian Sea, it leaves Pakistan's Punjab Province and at its northern end enters the province of Sind, homeland for more than 11 million Sindhis. The Indus, the ancient name of which—Sindhu—is where the name ''Sind'' comes from, flows south, dividing the province into two almost equal expanses of fertile land, upon which most of the inhabitants depend for their livelihood.

Approximately 93 percent (about 10.6 million) of the Sindhis in Pakistan are Muslim. Perhaps 65,000 Sindhi Muslims live in India, although before Partition in 1947 the number was much higher. After Partition, thousands migrated to Pakistan, where they are called *muhajir*. Other Sindhis live and work in the oil-related industries of the Persian Gulf.

Most Sindhi Muslims are descendants of people who have lived in the Sind Province for centuries. These Sindhis are called *pukka*, meaning "real," and are descendants of such central Asian groups as the Sakas, Kushans and Huns as well as the many Rajput and Jat tribes of eastern India, such as the Yadavs and Parwars. In Sind, descendants of the Yadavs are known locally as Sammas, and those of the Parwars are called Sumras and include such tribes as the Bhuttos, the Bhattis, the Lohanos and the Mohanos. Some ethnologists have combined the two names of Sammas and Sumras into Sammat to refer to those Sindhis with indigenous origins. The Mohanos, thought to be among the oldest inhabitants of Sind, concentrate on the rivers and lakes, especially Lake Manchar in Dadu District and in the Indus River delta, where their primary occupations are fishing and ferrying.

There are two other ethnic strains in the Sindhi Muslim population. Some Sindhi Muslims trace their origins to Arab conquerors who came in A.D. 711, the first to bring Islam to the subcontinent, and to subsequent waves of invaders including Persians, Turks, Moghuls and Pushtun (Pathans). By and large these groups have long since mingled and intermarried with the local population and thus are indistinguishable except for some, such as the Sayyid families, who claim direct descent from the Prophet Muhammad, and the Pushtun families of northwestern Sind. The other strain is that of the Baluch, who, attracted by the fertile land of the Indus Valley, have been coming for 500 years from neighboring Baluchistan (see Baluch). Those who settled on the west bank of the Indus, such as the Chandios, the Jamalis and the Khosos, have managed to keep their Baluch identity, but those who settled on the east bank, such as the Jatois and the Talpurs (former rulers of Sind), have largely been "Sindhi-ized" and now speak Sindhi as a mother tongue.

In addition to these main strains that constitute the majority of Sindhi Muslims, there are some minor but influential groups, namely the trading communities of the Memons, the Bohras and the Khojas (including Ismailis). Of these the Memons (Sunni, as opposed to the other two, both Shia) are perhaps the most Sindhi (although at one time the Ismailis were a dominant presence). Their capital was Thatta until the mid-1500s, when it was destroyed by the Portuguese and the Memons were dispersed mainly to Gujarat and Saurshastra in India. Not all left at the time, so that in addition to those who have returned since 1947 (among whom was Mohammed Ali Jinnah, a Khoja and founder of Pakistan), many Sindhi-speaking Memons can be found in the towns and villages of Sind.

The uncertain origins of the Sindhi language have led to conflicting arguments about its true sources and development. Western scholars claim that Sindhi was largely derived from Sanskrit or Prakrit but that it also had close associations with some of the Indo-European Dardic languages such as Kashmiri. They do concede however, that Arabic and Persian did contribute significantly to the development of Sindhi, more in the case of the former than the latter. Present-day Sindhi scholars in Pakistan tend to stress, not surprisingly, Sindhi's close association with and derivation from Arabic, the language of Islam, some of them to the point of denying Sindhi's Sanskrit origins. While the reason they give is that Sindhi antedates Sanskrit, one suspects that Sanskrit's close association with Hinduism has something to do with their thinking.

Classical Sindhi, the form of the language which is dominant throughout the province in spoken and written form, developed in southern Sind in the region known historically as Lar. Other Sindhi dialects that are spoken in the province are Siraiki, in the northern part of Sind (this dialect is written as well and is claimed by Punjabis to be a dialect of their language), Thareli or Jesalmeri, spoken in eastern Sind, and Takkarana, spoken in western Sind.

Prior to the coming of the British to Sind in the mid-nineteenth century, Persian was the language of government and administration in Sind, and Sindhi was largely a spoken language with a few rudimentary written forms. In the early days of British rule, with the need to formalize written Sindhi, a decision was made to devise an alphabet which would have wider acceptance. Using the 29 letters of Arabic, a 52-letter Sindhi alphabet was created. The letters were also designed to be printed, with the result that Sindhi has been a printed language for over a century.

The topography and climate of Sind play a significant role in how the people live. The dominant feature of the land of Sind is the Indus River—a comparison is often drawn with Egypt and the Nile—which provides fertile, alluvial soils and water for irrigation. On the west, Sind is bordered by dry, barren hills which support animal grazing; on the south by the Arabian Sea, where a fledgling fishing industry has developed centered mostly around the port city of Karachi; on the southeast by the sandy wastes of the Rann of Cutch and on the east by the westernmost reaches of the Great Thar or Indian Desert. The climate of Sind is hot and dry in the interior during the summer season; the coastal area's climate is moderated by its proximity to the sea, although humidity is high. During the cold season the weather is moderate to cool throughout the province. Sind does have a monsoon season, though it is characterized by heavy cloud cover with little rainfall.

Despite the tribal origins of most Sindhi Muslims, the family traditionally has been and continues to be the basic unity of society. Most Sindhi Muslims find themselves part of a patriarchal, joint-family structure. The joint family arrangement derives from Hindu or Indian influence, as does the tendency for Sindhi Muslims to organize in caste-like groups along hereditary and occupational lines, such as cultivators, blacksmiths, barbers, weavers and potters. These groups are known as *zats*, and individuals of one *zat* who share a common descent from one ancestor are grouped into a *biraderi* or *paro* (see Punjabis).

In the family the male head is the dominant authority, and he is responsible for the family's affairs. The wife or wives (Sindhis are polygynous) look after the household affairs and in addition, through such economic activities as embroidery, may contribute to the overall family income. The children, once they are old enough, are expected to provide income for the family aside from their school responsibilities.

Marriage takes place within one's *zat* or *biradiri*, ideally between first cousins (man marries daughter of father's brother). If a suitable choice cannot be found for a male within his own clan, then it is possible for him to marry outside, even with a woman from a *zat* inferior in social rank to his own. But this would not be the case for a woman; no self-respecting father would consent to his daughter "marrying down" into a *zat* that is socially below his own.

Marriage is preceded by betrothal (*mangno*), which takes place at varying lengths of time before the marriage, sometimes even in the infancy of the partners, although this is not common in modern times. For the betrothal the bridegroom and his family go to the bride's home, where, seated separately, the men with the men and the women in the women's quarters, they take refreshments brought by the bridegroom's family. They then hear a reading from the Quran, which marks the betrothal's completion.

The day of the marriage is preceded by several days of music and merrymaking. On the marriage day, the bridegroom and bride are dressed in finery. The bridegroom travels by car, donkey cart or camel, with elaborate decorating, to the bride's home for the ceremony. The ceremony is simple, with each partner being asked three times if he will have the other. Then the marriage settlements are agreed to and recorded by witnesses and the marriage ceremony (*nikah*) is authenticated with the reading of the Quran by a local *maulvi*, or religious teacher.

In addition to marriage, the important events in Sindhi Muslim social life are birth and death. Three ceremonies are associated with birth: naming, shaving the head (*akiko*) and circumcision (*khutno*). Naming takes place as soon after birth as possible, with the father or an elderly male relation whispering first "Allah is great" into the child's ear in order that God's name be the first thing the child hears. Immediately afterwards the child is named. The origins of the shaving custom are obscure but appear to be symbolic of a sacrifice of atonement. It takes place at some point in the first few weeks after birth, and a goat in the case of a girl or two in the case of a boy are then sacrificed. The meat is cooked and distributed among relations, and then the bones are buried along with the child's hair at some selected place. Circumcision, with no particular age prescribed, usually takes place after the child has grown to boyhood. On the day of the ceremony the boy is garlanded and taken around the town and then to his home, where the rite is performed by a barber in the presence of relatives and friends. After the child recovers, a celebration is held at his home to which family and friends are invited, each bringing with them a small present which serves to defray expenses.

When a Sindhi is about to die, relatives gather around, and appropriate passages from the Quran are read. The creed (*kalima*) is repeated, and prayers are offered for forgiveness. After death the body is washed, its big toes tied together, and it is prepared for burial by being wrapped in a shroud called a *kaffan*. The body is placed on a bier and covered with a shawl and then carried to the graveyard by four of the deceased's nearest kinsmen. Mourners follow reciting the creed. At the graveside, after prayer for the peace of the departed soul, the body is laid in the grave on its side with the face towards Mecca. On the third day after death, a Soem feast is given at the home of the deceased after prayers and reading of the Quran. This is repeated on the tenth day; a feast for all relatives on the fortieth day marks the end of the period of mourning.

The traditional role of women in Sindhi Muslim society has been one of subservience, and while this persists in the rural areas, it is changing in urban areas as women gain education and become wage earners. Also with the increasing emphasis in Pakistan on Islamic law, which recognizes female inheritance and property ownership, the position of women is improving. Formerly, under customary law, inheritance rights of women were not commonly honored. The custom of veiling is also undergoing some change. Formerly the women of the upper classes were the strictest observers of this custom; now it is more the women of the middle classes. Veiling is still observed in the villages in the families of the land-owning elite, but it is not followed by the women of tenant and tiller (*hari*) families who work in the fields.

In the rural areas the structures of *zat* and *biradiri* still retain their force, and there continues to be interaction within these structures and the extended family. In the urban areas these structures are breaking down, and interaction between these groups is less. For instance, a generation ago a father would typically have a son or two living with him in the home, but today, if this is the case, it is more for economic reasons that out of kinship obligations.

Considerable change is taking place in Sindhi society as a result of such factors as an increase in the number of educational opportunities and an increase in the number of industrial and commercial enterprises in rural as well as urban areas. These factors have worked to speed the rate of urbanization, and they have played a role in the rapid growth of such cities as Karachi and Hyderabad. During the last decade the population of Karachi grew by 31 percent from 3.5 million to over 5 million (placing it in the top 20 of the world's most populous cities) and that of Hyderabad by 21 percent from 630,000 to almost 800,000. A similar trend is true for the other major provincial towns of Sukkur, Nawabshah, Larkana and Mirpurkhas. This movement of people from the rural to the urban areas exacerbates a serious problem present in Sind throughout this century—an inadequate agricultural labor force, which places restraints on Sind's agricultural productivity and contributes to a breakdown of the extended family.

The majority of Sindhis—almost 70 percent—are engaged in cultivation. Most are cultivators (*haris*) who rent the land they till (over 70 percent). Some 15 percent are land owners who till all the land they own, 8 percent are land owners who till part and rent out part of their land, 3 percent are agricultural laborers and 1 percent are those renting and also working for hire.

Crops grown include wheat, rice, millet, cotton, rape and mustard seeds, sugar cane and fruits, of which the most prized are mangoes in many different varieties. Livestock farming—the grazing of sheep and goats and camel breeding—is also a significant occupation in the rural areas, particularly in the eastern and western border areas of the province. Fishing, too, is a noteworthy occupation, inland as well as in the coastal areas.

The huge size of the Karachi metropolis, which helps to make Sind Pakistan's most urbanized province (over 43 percent of the population of Sind reside in urban areas), belies the fact that the major economic activity in the province is agriculture. Next to the Punjab, Sind produces most of the country's food grains, which go to help the deficit provinces of Baluchistan and the North-West Frontier. Also Karachi, as the country's leading commercial and industrial center, places Sind in a dominant position in the country's non-agricultural sector as well.

The majority of Sindhi Muslims are Sunni and subscribe to the Hanafi school of jurisprudence. This is despite the fact that for centuries Sind has been exposed to, and its inhabitants have become followers of, other Islamic sects and Sufi orders. At one time the Shia sect of Ismailis held sway over Sind (A.D. 900–1200), and following their political eclipse, various Sufi orders made inroads through missionary activities. The Suhrawardi, the Qadiri and the Naqshbandi reached their apex in Sind in the fourteenth and fifteenth centuries, but their influence survives today, particularly that of the Suhrawardi in the veneration of Lal Shabaz Qalander of Sehwan, one of the most revered saints of Sind today, and of the Qadiri, to whom the influential Lakiari and Matiari Sayyids pay great respect.

Prior to 1947, when many Hindus lived in Sind, there was considerable syncretization. For instance, it was not uncommon for Hindus and Muslims to venerate the same saint, the most prominent example being the patron saint of the Indus River, known as Khwajah Khidr or Shaikh Tahir to the Muslims and Shah Darya or Uderolal to the Hindus. The veneration of Muslims of Sind for their *pirs* and saints with all the attending rituals may be taken to be a result of Hindu influence. The practice of saint worship or *piri-muridi* persists today with considerable vitality in the rural areas. Probably the best-known living *pir* today is the Pir Pagaro (Pir of the Turban), who is a leading politician with a large following.

Major festivals in Sind center on three men, the occasion being the death anniversary (*urs*) of each. They are Lal Shahbaz Qalander, a religious mystic of the thirteenth century, Shah Abdul Latif and Sachal Sarmast, both literary men of the seventeenth and eighteenth centuries, respectively. Of the three, Latif is probably the most eminent, as his popular book of mystical poetry, *Shah Jo Risalo*, is known and recited by many Sindhis. The *urs* of these are celebrated in the towns where each is buried, and the occasions are marked by much festivity, singing, dancing and reading of poetry.

As most Sindhi Muslims are orthodox Sunnis, they derive their life values from the Quran and the *sunna*. Thus they endeavor to perform faithfully the five main practices incumbent upon all good Muslims. Likewise they follow the Quran and the *sunna* in what those two authorities identify as practice that is optional, allowed and banned. Perhaps the practice that deviates the most from orthodox Islam and is the most widespread is that of *piri-muridi*.

BIBLIOGRAPHY

Books

Abdullah, Ahmned. *The Historical Background of Pakistan and Its Peoples*. Karachi: Tanzeem, 1973.

Ahmed, Manzooruddin, ed. *Contemporary Pakistan*. Durham: Carolina Academic Press, 1980.

Burton, Richard F. *Sindh and the Races that Inhabit the Valley of the Indus*. Reprint ed. Karachi: Oxford University Press, 1973.

Gulraj, Jethmal Parsram. *Sind and Its Sufis*. Madras: Theosophical Publishing House, 1924.

Khan, Ansar Zahid. *History and Culture of Sind*. Karachi: Royal Book, 1980.

Lambrick, H. T. *Sind: A General Introduction*. Hyderabad, Pakistan: Sind Adabi Board, 1964.

————. *The Terrorist*. London: Ernest Benn, 1972.

Nyrop, Richard R., ed. *Area Handbook for Pakistan*. Washington, D.C.: Government Printing Office, 1975.

Pakistan, Government of. *Census Bulletin 1: Housing and Population Census of Pakistan 1980–81*. Islamabad: Population Census Organization, 1982.

Pithawalla, Maneck B. *An Introduction to Sind: Its Wealth and Welfare*. Karachi: Sind Observer Press, 1951.

Sorley H. T. *West Pakistan Gazeteer: Sind Region*. Karachi: Government Printing Press, 1959.

Weekes, Richard V. *Pakistan: Birth and Growth of a Muslim Nation*. Princeton: Van Nostrand, 1964.

Article

Channa, Karim Buksh A. "A Brief Survey of Sindhi Language and Literature." *Sind Quarterly* 5:1 (1977): 34–55.

Unpublished Manuscript

Jones, Allen K. "Muslim Politics and the Growth of the Muslim League in Sind, 1935–41." Ph.D. dissertation, Duke University, 1977.

Allen K. Jones

SINYAR The Sinyar of Chad and Sudan live along the lower reaches and confluence of three seasonal rivers: the Wadi Azum, Wadi Kaja and Wadi Salih. They are bounded to the north by the Masalit, to the west by the Daju-Sila, to the east by the Fur and to the south by a congeries of small ethnic groups with whom contact is minimal—the Fongoro, Kujargé, Fur-Dalinga and Daju-Galfigé (see Daju; Fongoro; Fur; Masalit).

The Sinyar call themselves Shamya after their alleged common ancestor; the Fur call them Zimirra; the Masalit, Simyartá. Today the Chadian and Sudanese Sinyar might number 26,000, scattered through some 40 villages, sometimes together with the Fur or Daju, with whom they intermarry. About half of the villages are in Chad, and only four of these are said to be relatively new settlements. The oldest village is Angaïre, named after a hill that dominates the landscape.

In Sudan, Korenga, marked on the earliest Condominium maps, and Kodoro on the eastern bank of the Wadi Azum are said to be the oldest Sinyar settlements. The Sudanese part of Dar Sinyar hosts settlements of Bornu, camps of Baggara Arabs and a number of multi-ethnic villages inhabited by economic and political refugees from Chad such as Runga, Daggal, Kibeit and Bakha. The main Sinyar center is the multi-ethnic trade town of Foro Boranga, which has an estimated population of 7,500. Another center is a string of seven villages collectively known as Merissa (officially called Gimeiza-Babikr), which is situated along the Wadi Azum near its confluence with the Wadi Kaja. Part of its inhabitants used to live across the river in villages near Jebel Angaïre and in the old administrative center of Mogororo. Destruction of this government post by Chadian rebels and daily exposure to extortion and physical violence prompted many Chadian Sinyar to join their brothers in Sudan.

The Chadian part of Dar Sinyar is hilly and infested with tsetse fly. Although rich in wildlife, the region is sparsely populated because of lack of water, the tsetse fly and the abundance of game, which make cultivation and animal husbandry difficult. The Sinyar who used to inhabit this region have abandoned most of their villages and moved northward over the course of time. The river valleys which constitute the international frontier have clay soils, an average annual rainfall of 18 to 24 inches and a more varied and abundant vegetation and tree stratum than the Masalit territory further north. Dar Sinyar is cut off from the outside world between late June and late September except for travellers on foot or donkey. Descriptions of the region's vegetation and wildlife suggest that the area has suffered from decreased rainfall over the past few decades. In addition, due to the relentless exploitation of the environment by its inhabitants, a large number of game and tree species have disappeared, and the density of the remaining species has decreased sharply. Nevertheless, a large part of Dar Sinyar remains flooded during the rainy season, precluding significant animal husbandry by the settled population. On the other hand, nomadic pastoralists direct their vast herds to the permanent water resources in the valleys during the dry season.

Sinyar oral traditions claim Arab origin for the founding father of the group, and Egypt is mentioned as his place of origin. Kinship and co-residence with the Berti of northern Darfur Province is sometimes claimed (see Berti). Apparently they broke with the Arabs and migrated to their present habitat and now claim they lost their knowledge of the Arabic language because they intermarried with the women of the pagan tribe they found and defeated in battle. Remnants of this original population of Dar Sinyar are alleged to live in the northeastern part of the Central African Republic. They are the Kara, Binga and the Gula-Mamoun, indeed linguistically akin to the Sinyar language, which is Central Sudanic, Sara-Bongo-Bagirmi branch (Chari-Nile language family).

This historical self-portrait is not dissimilar to that of other ethnic groups in the region, which also claim Arab, even Abbasid or Quraysh descent and also use the excuse of intermarriage with pagan slave women to explain their present linguistic and cultural identity. Of immediate relevance to the Sinyar is the fact that non-Sinyar flatly reject this historical self-image and instead designate the Sinyar as former non-Muslim slaves, *fertit*, of the sultanates of Dar Fur and Dar Sila. Linguistically the Sinyar are undoubtedly *fertit*, along with the Kreish, Kara, Yulu and other Sara-Bongo-Bagirmi-speaking populations which in the past constituted the slave reservoirs for the old sultanates. In Sudan, the Sinyar are the northernmost group speaking a *fertit* language; in Chad it is the Barma, who themselves established a powerful sultanate in Bagirmi in the nineteenth century (see Barma). However, there is no historical evidence that the Sinyar have collectively been considered a slave tribe such as the Kreish or Kara. Of course, until as late as the second decade of the twentieth century the Sinyar were individually enslavable once they moved into the territory of another polity or after losing in battle against a superior enemy, but this was the fate also reserved for the neighboring Fur, Daju and Masalit at the time.

From time immemorial the Sinyar have been organized as a quasi-independent, tribute-paying sultanate headed by a dynasty of petty sultans. Until 1863 they paid tribute to the Keira Sultanate of Dar Fur, since then until this century to the Daju Sultanate of Dar Sila, which was initially also subject to Dar Fur. The last two decades of the nineteenth century were turbulent in the region. The area was invaded by the Turko-Egyptian army in 1879, by the infamous slaver Babikr Zibeir in 1881, by Sultan Abu Risha of Dar Sila in 1882, and a few years later by Mahdist units led by Osman Jano. In contrast to the Fongoro, the Sinyar managed to maintain their sultanate intact, although not without bloodshed, by paying tribute to various overlords at the same time.

The British and the French fixed the Chad-Sudan border on the eastern boundary of the sultanate of Wadai in Chad, which meant that Dar Sinyar, Dar Fongoro and Dar Sila, as ancient vassals of Dar Fur, would become part of the British sphere. Subsequent developments in the region, especially two disastrous military campaigns of the French against the sultanate of Dar Masalit in 1910, led to a border settlement in 1924 in which Dar Sila became part of Chad and in which the Masalit, the Sinyar and the Fongoro were to find themselves divided by the new international frontier.

In 1928 a dynastic conflict of succession led to the exile of part of the Chadian Sinyar to Sudan; their leader became chief of the southernmost part of Dar

Masalit Native Administration, and in 1954 he was succeeded by his son. Over the years many Chadian Sinyar have settled on Sudanese soil because of better economic opportunities and the progressive breakdown of services and security in Chad.

In the course of time during which the Sinyar constituted a semi-autonomous buffer state of the Keira sultanate of Dar Fur, they culturally became Fur with admixtures of Daju, Masalit and above all Arab cultures. Today the Sinyar have no kinship terms, songs, dances and stories, or musical instruments such as a special type of drum, other than those adopted from the Fur. Most Sinyar are fluent in Sinyar, Fur and Arabic; quite a few know Daju or Masalit as well. Thus in contrast to the Fongoro, who have also become Fur culturally, the Sinyar have preserved their language.

Today the Sinyar live in two countries and are administered by four different provincial administrations, or rather by two in Sudan and by various rebel groups in Chad. Internally they are segmented into 18 different sections, of which 8 appear to be headed by a land chief, custodian of the land and the drum which symbolizes his offices, which is used sparingly in case of sad and festive occasions and cattle raids. As in surrounding ethnic groups, the land chief is the custodian of the section's land, which he allocates to members and guests. However, among groups such as the Masalit the land chief is also head of the *diya* (blood money-paying community). Owing to their small size, the Sinyar collectively contribute towards the payment of blood money (compensation which relatives of a murderer pay to relatives of the victim).

Matrilineality was once a dominant factor in Sinyar culture, evident today in kinship terms whereby the word for father is the same as that for maternal uncle. Women have significant roles of their own. The compounds often belong to the wives, and husbands move out when they divorce their wives. Wives may be economically independent of their husbands. There is considerable marriage instability, divorce is frequent and fostering of children is common.

More than other groups the Sinyar live and work as extended families encompassing three or four generations and frequently numbering as many as 60 people (apart from those absent as a result of labor migration). In such residence units women frequently outnumber men two to one.

The Sinyar are Muslims, and apart from a few surviving elders who were Ansar (followers of the Mahdi) in the past, they are little inclined to either fanaticism or asceticism. Politically they are indifferent to candidates from the ranks of the traditional rulers and aspirants from the trading and professional strata and will vote for the most generous candidate, entertaining no illusions about electoral promises ever becoming reality.

In 1925, Grossard described the Sinyar and their habitat in terms invoking untempered bliss and contentment: "Living in a fertile country in which the resources of hunting and fishing contribute to those of cultivation, the Sinyar are kind epicureans, fond of music, dance and even more of millet beer." Today, more than half a century later this picture is still largely true, most of all because the Sinyar themselves have changed little in the course of time; they are still kind-hearted hedonists unwilling to forsake today's harvest in favor of tomorrow's promises. However, the circumstances in which they do this have changed dramatically. The land of Dar Sinyar is still fertile but is farmed mainly by immigrant entrepreneurs who employ Sinyar as casual labor in clearing, sowing, weeding and reaping. In the past fishery was so important among the Sinyar that a special priest initiated the fishing season. Today, owing to decreased rainfall, both fishing and the office of fishing priest have disappeared as a means of subsistence. Hunting has lost its traditional importance, too. In the past when game was abundant, its planning and execution cemented several villages together. Days beforehand hunting strategy was discussed and functions assigned. On an individual basis trapping and stalking were feasible means of subsistence. Today, owing to desiccation and the proliferation of firearms among migrant traders, soldiers and policemen, game has retreated southwards to Dar Fongoro and Dar Runga, which are thinly populated. In the 1930s, hundreds of lions and hyenas and tens of thousands of monkeys were poisoned by strychnine. Since then, lions have practically disappeared. There are still monkeys and occasional hyenas.

As for agriculture, it takes no great effort to grow the amount of grain needed for food, beer and seeding, but of all the populations living in Foro Boranga it is the Sinyar who have suffered most from grain shortages during the past few years. One of the reasons is labor migration, not necessarily to the Nile Valley or the oil countries but to agricultural schemes situated to the east of the Wadi Azum. The Sinyar still largely maintain the traditional division of labor and economic responsibility whereby the husband and his wife or wives constitute separate economic households. The husband grows the amount of grain he needs for himself and his guests and cash crops to fulfill his obligation to his spouses and children in terms of clothing and footwear. The wife or wives and children have to grow their own grain and grow a wide variety of vegetables for sale in the women's market and to use as ingredients in meals. Sinyar men often prefer to work as casual laborers during the rainy season in hopes of procuring enough cash to buy their grain afterwards. Sinyar women, on the other hand, still cultivate their own grain and, above all, convert their grain into gin and beer for sale in the market. Sinyar women often earn substantially more than their husbands.

The Sinyar are 100 percent Muslim insofar as they adhere to the Five Pillars of Islam. But they consume alcohol and do not seclude their women (a practice more easily affordable by traders and salaried officials). According to the fundamentalist conception of Islam which is spreading from the Nile Valley to outlying Muslim areas (carried by traders and salaried officials), the peasants, craftsmen and pastoral nomads of Sinyar are lax Muslims.

BIBLIOGRAPHY

Books

Grossard, Lt. Col. *Mission de délimitation de l'Afrique Equatorial Française et du Soudan Anglo-Egyptien.* Paris: Librarie Emile Larose, 1925.
Haaland, G. "Language Use and Ethnic Identity." In *Aspects of Language in the Sudan,* edited by Robin Thelwall. Coleraine: The New University of Ulster, 1978.

Articles

Doornbos, Paul. "A Sinyar Tale of Friendship." In *Sudan Texts Bulletin* (in press).
Tubiana, Joseph. "Les Débuts de la mission de délimitation de la frontière entre le Tchad et le Soudan Anglo-Egyptien (1922)." *Le Mois en Afrique* 16:186–187 (1981): 113–128.

Paul Doornbos

SOGA   The Soga of Uganda are a Bantu-speaking people of the Interlacustrine group. They number nearly 1 million, about 8 percent of the total population of Uganda. Some 150,000 of them are Muslims. They speak their own language, Lusoga, and like other Bantu languages, theirs also has class prefixes. Thus a member of the group is called *Mu*soga, the plural *Ba*soga, the language *Lu*soga and the country *Bu*soga (see Bantu-speaking Peoples).

Busoga today is a district in East Uganda, bounded on the north by Lake Kyoga, on the west by the Nile River, on the south by Lake Victoria and on the east by the Mpologoma River. The southern part of the district along Lake Victoria is fertile and well watered, while the northern part is drier. The majority of the Soga are peasants cultivating small plots. The major cash crops are cotton and coffee, introduced by the British in the beginning of the present century. The staple food includes plantains, sweet potatoes, millet and cassava. In the north, cattle raising is more widespread.

The main town in Busoga is Jinja, the second largest town in Uganda after the capital, Kampala, which has become an important industrial center. Industry was greatly stimulated by the hydroelectric power station of the Owen Falls Dam built near the point where the Nile River departs Lake Victoria.

The Soga are divided into numerous clans, whose members attribute their descent to a common ancestor and recognize a common totem. The children belong to the clan of their father. Their society is characterized also by a hierarchical structure of authority and status. Every man is a member of a clan, and within the clan he could be a peasant, a subchief, a chief or a ruler. The clan's council has authority over succession and inheritance.

The traditional religion, with a belief system involving an ancestors cult, is still strong among the Soga, and some rituals are common even among those who embrace Islam or Christianity. In the traditional religion, there exist many gods and goddesses whose aid is sought in time of trouble and sickness and to whom offerings are made. Among the gods are those of death, plague, earthquakes and also the great Creator God, Mukama. The Soga believe also in tree and rock spirits; in every large tree or large stone reside spirits for good or evil. A person should be careful not to cut down a tree or break a rock unless precautions have been taken. There are also large, sacred trees to which the Soga make offerings. Medicine men or mediums live near the sacred trees and inform the people about the wishes of the spirits. Worship of the dead forms an important part of the religion, and belief in ghosts is the chief feature of regular worship. Indeed, the gods are able to affect the human being, but it is the ghosts that are most feared in day-to-day life. They receive most of the attention during such events as childbirth, sickness and death. Ghosts can damage or help, and people frequently make sacrifices of fowl or other animals to satisfy them.

As with other Interlacustrine Bantu of Uganda, the traditional political system of the Soga was of the centralized type. Nevertheless, unlike their neighbors the Ganda and the Buyoro, the Soga did not form one single kingdom but were divided into numerous states. According to the local traditions, there were as many as 47 Soga states, the oldest established in the mid-seventeenth century. The founders of most of these states were immigrants associated with the Lwo-speaking people of southern Sudan and northern Uganda. Some Soga traditions trace the origin of their royal dynasties to the ruling Babito clan of Bunyoro. In the late nineteenth century, the Soga were divided into 15 petty kingdoms, each forming a distinct political unit. Each state was headed by a paramount ruler, who held his position within a royal patrilineal descent group and had absolute authority over the inhabitants of his state. He was hereditary king, and as in other Bantu kingdoms, the ruler had ritual functions but was not considered a god. Subordinate to him were the chiefs, who administered territorial subdivisions in his name. Foremost among them was the prime minister, who was in charge of the palace and controlled access to the ruler. The royal group in Busoga was part of an endogamous aristocratic caste, and no commoner could marry into this group. Unlike the Ganda or the Nyankole of Uganda, the Soga believed in fundamental inequality between the hereditary royal group and other commoners (see Ganda; Nyankole).

These small states because of their splits and constant rivalries could not stand against their powerful neighbors, Bunyoro and Buganda, which in the nineteenth century dominated them and forced them to pay tribute. With the establishment of the British protectorate in Uganda in 1894, Busoga was unified politically and integrated into Uganda as one of the administrative districts, and the former rulers of the states became chiefs of counties. In 1900, under the terms of the agreement between Buganda and the British government, the King of Buganda relinquished all authority over Busoga. Yet Ganda influence in Busoga continued. The protectorate government engaged Buganda chiefs as administrators of various districts in the protectorate, and they remodeled the political system of these territories along Buganda lines. In Busoga, the administrative system was carried out by the Ganda Semei Kakungulu, who from 1906 to 1914 acted as paramount chief of the district. Gradually the Busoga traditional rulers were salaried by the British and integrated into the civil service. By 1952, all the hereditary rulers, except the constitutional head of Busoga, had been dismissed or retired and their places taken by persons appointed on the basis of personal qualifications. The official title of the constitutional head of Busoga district was *isebantu kyabazinga*, which means "the father who invites all people," and he was elected by the local council. After Uganda's independence in 1967, President A. M. Obote abolished the Kyabazingaship along with the other kingdoms.

The influence of the Ganda on Busoga is reflected not only in politics and administration but also in the religious sphere. The Ganda were the people who did more than anyone else to spread Islam among the Soga, and therefore many of the Islamic characteristics of Buganda can be found in Busoga. Moreover, the Soga Muslims are still largely under the influence of Buganda Muslim religious leaders.

The number of the Muslims in Busoga is the highest after that of Buganda. They comprise about 15 percent of the 1 million inhabitants of the district. The Christians constitute about 45 percent, and the rest retain their traditional religion.

The first Muslims to reach Busoga were the Arab and Swahili traders from the east coast of Africa. They arrived in the second half of the nineteenth century, but the Muslim traders did not leave any significant Islamic mark similar to that in Buganda. Their numbers were smaller due to the fact that Busoga was not as secure as Buganda, where the king was in absolute control of his territory. Besides, the traders were interested mainly in profit and not so much in the diffusion of Islam.

A second group who brought Islam to Busoga were the Sudanese troops who were recruited by the British administration at the end of the nineteenth century, some of whom were stationed in the district. The Sudanese soldiers intermarried with Soga families and also proselytized their servants. Because of the prestige which the Sudanese soldiers enjoyed as part of the British rule, other Soga adopted their religion and a nucleus of a Muslim community developed around them.

A far more important factor encouraging Islam were the Ganda Muslims who arrived in Busoga as refugees in the wake of the religious wars in Buganda at the end of the nineteenth century. In these wars between the Christians and Muslims, the latter were defeated and many of them fled. Later, during the British colonial rule (1894–1962), some Ganda Muslims arrived in Busoga along with other Ganda Christians to serve as assistants and interpreters to the British officials. Muganda Ali Lwanga is a typical example. He came to Busoga as an interpreter of the British district commissioner and then was promoted to county chief. In this prestigious position, he was able to encourage the adoption of Islam. Some of the Soga converts were influential people, such as Munulo, the hereditary chief of Bugweri County, who was converted to Islam in 1896 and then imposed his new religion on many of his dependents and subjects. Christian missionaries who feared lest Islam be the dominant religion in Busoga induced the British to send Munulo into exile. Yet, Bugweri County remained (and remains) one of the most Islamized areas in Uganda. About 80 percent of its people are Muslims, and it has become a center for further diffusion of Islam in Busoga.

Indeed, the progress of Islam in Busoga alarmed the Christian missionaries and the British administrators. The missionaries pressed the government to block the expansion of Islam in Busoga, claiming that the Muslims were less loyal than the Christians and that they might endanger British rule. British officials, at the beginning of the century, usually agreed with them. Thus, Sir Harry

Johnston, the Governor of Uganda (1899–1901), assured the Christian leaders that the government was behind them in restricting the spread of Islam, pointing out:

If there is one thing to which I am doggedly opposed on political grounds putting aside religions, it is the Mohammedising of Busoga. For this country to become a focus of Mohammedanism would be one of the most dangerous threats to the future of the prosperity of the Protectorate. In fact, it would bring Islam down from the Nile to the Victoria Nyanza and what we aim at politically is to thrust Islam as much as possible into the Sudan. (King and Oded 1973, p. 110)

For a long period the British avoided appointing Muslims to key posts in the administration, although as a whole the Muslims were loyal subjects. In 1897 when the Sudanese soldiers mutinied, only a few Soga Muslims joined them.

Another factor hindering the advance of Soga Muslims politically was their lack of education. They did not possess the means to establish schools and hospitals as did the Christians with the support of the British authorities. Muslims were reluctant to send their children to school lest they be influenced by Christianity. Muslim children stayed at home or went to Quranic schools, where they were taught religious subjects only. A wide gap was created between them and the Soga Christians in secular and technical studies.

Despite these handicaps, Islam continues to expand in Busoga. Conversion to Islam progresses quietly through personal contacts with the *shaikhs* and teachers with the local population and by the feelings of brotherhood among Soga. Islam seems to be more flexible, understandable, simple and attractive to the pagan Soga than does Christianity. This is reflected, for example, during the Maulud (the birthday of the Prophet Muhammad) festivals. In these religious gatherings *matali* (tambourines) are used, and the congregation repeats simple, devotional prayers in songs and with rhythmic dances. Then delicious Arab food containing rice and meat is usually served to all the participants. Many Soga join Islam during these popular feasts, as one Muslim *shaikh* observed, saying that Islam in Busoga progressed "through the dishes of meat and rice."

Since the 1940s, the East Africa Muslim Welfare Society, founded in 1945 by the Ismailis, has established advanced Muslim schools, some of which teach secular and technical subjects. When Uganda became independent in 1962, all educational institutions came under the Ministry of Education and Muslim schools received the same government support as the others. Muslims of Busoga have also received financial support from Arab and Muslim countries to build new schools and mosques and have been granted scholarships for studies in Arab countries.

The vast majority of the Muslims in Busoga are Sunni, following the Shafi rite. Shia are found only among the Asian minority. The Ahmadiya is active, with their main center in Jinja. They are opposed by the Sunnis, and their activities produce meager results. While the Ahmadiya missionaries do not insist on circumcision, this is obligatory for the Sunni Muslims.

The recognized head of the Muslim community in Busoga is the Shaikh-Qadi, who is also responsible for the Shariah court, which deals with Muslim personal affairs such as marriage and divorce. The first Muslim *shaikhs* in Busoga were Ganda or Swahili, but gradually local Soga *walimu* (teachers) and *shaikhs* have been trained and have assumed these positions. Among the first well-known Soga Shaikh-Qadi was Juma Waiswa, who did much for the spread of Islam during the colonial period.

The first mosques were built in Busoga in the 1890s, and today in all the main towns and townships there are numerous beautiful mosques. Even in the small villages where Muslims live, one can find small, well-attended mosques. Muslims are easily recognized by their special white head caps and turbans. In the towns and commercial centers, Islam is more strictly observed than in the more remote villages, where traditional beliefs connected with ancestor spirits are still strong.

BIBLIOGRAPHY

Books

Fallers, L. A. *Bantu Bureaucracy: A Century of Political Evolution Among the Basoga of Uganda*. 2nd ed. Chicago: University of Chicago Press, 1965.

King, N. Kasozi, and Oded, A. *Islam and the Confluence of Religions in Uganda 1840–1966*. Tallahassee, Fla.: American Academy of Religion, 1973.

Lubogo, Y. K. *History of Busoga*. Jinja, Uganda: East African Literature Bureau, 1960.

Oded, A. *Islam in Uganda*. Jerusalem: Israel Universities Press, 1974.

Richard, Audrey, ed. *East African Chiefs*. London: Faber and Faber, 1959.

Roscoe, J. *The Northern Bantu*. 2nd ed. New York: Barnes and Noble, 1966.

Trimingham, J. Spencer. *Islam in East Africa*. Oxford: Clarendon Press, 1964.

Uganda, Republic of. *Report on the 1969 Population Census*. Vol. 1. Entebbe: The Government Printer, 1971.

Welbourn, F. B. *Religion and Politics in Uganda*. Nairobi: East African Publishing House, 1965.

Articles

Nabwiso-Bulima, W. F. "The Evolution of the Kyabazingaship of Busoga." *Uganda Journal* 31:1 (1967): 89–99.

Rigby, P. "Political Change in Busoga." *Uganda Journal* 30:2 (1966): 223–225.

Arye Oded

SOMALIS   The Somalis inhabit the Horn of Africa and form one of the most uniformly homogeneous populations of the continent. Somalis speak a common language, adhere to a single faith, Sunni Islam, and share a cultural heritage which is an integral part of their nomadic way of life. The very name, So Maal, when spoken in the imperative, is said to mean, "Go milk a beast for yourself!"—a rough expression of hospitality. The Somali's self-conception is inseparable from his flocks and his traditional grazing lands, although for some, urban life, too, is a new and irresistible trend.

Somalis number at least 7.6 million. Most (4.4 million) live in the Republic of Somalia. About 2.5 million live in Ethiopia, at least 540,000 in Kenya and perhaps as many as 240,000 in the Republic of Djibouti; while a fluctuating and floating expatriate population of at least 100,000 is to be found in a number of Arab countries, mainly in South Yemen and Saudi Arabia. Between 60 and 70 percent of the Somali people, in their traditional setting, are pastoralists with small but increasing communities of cultivators in wetter regions of the extreme northwest and in the riverine southwest. There is a growing urban population in such towns as Mogadishu, the capital of Somali, and in smaller communities along the east coast of Africa. The Somali economy is based principally on the herding of camels, sheep and goats.

There is controversy as to the origin of the Somalis. Traditional ethnologists, such as Enrico Cerulli and I. M. Lewis, believe that the Somalis and the Oromo (Galla) were Hamitic colonizers in the Horn, migrating from the north. The Somalis drove out the Oromo, who were there first (see Oromo). The opposing theory, advanced by historical linguists Harold Fleming and Herbert Lewis, proposes that the Somalis and Oromo, among other people of the Horn, are racially, culturally and linguistically related, having originated in present-day Bale Province in Ethiopia. While the first school draws heavily on ethnographic surveys and oral traditions, the second bases its findings on linguistic evidence arrived at through the application of the comparative method of historical linguistics and lexico-statistical data.

Both Somali and Oromo are languages of the Eastern Cushitic branch of the Afro-Asiatic language family, which encompasses a wide range of peoples, including the Afar, Beja, Rendille and others scattered from Somalia to Sudan and even as far south as Tanzania. Given the linguistic evidence and shared cultural traits, the Somalis cannot be regarded as other than being indigenous to the African continent (see Afar; Beja).

In the early years of the Islamic era, the African coast facing Arabia became important as a place of refuge for the Prophet Muhammad's early followers fleeing Meccan persecution. There followed a period of Islamization and Arab-African cultural exchange via commerce and colonization.

The Somalis are Sunni Muslims of the Shafi rite, with Sufism being an important religious experience for many. This includes ecstasy (induced by chanting or *dhikr* and by narcotics). The main *turuq* (Sufi brotherhoods) are the Qadiri and Salihi. Some are followers of the Ahmadiya sect.

Another important element in the Somalis' way of life is customary law, or *heer* (Arabic, *adat*) which predates Islam and which regulates daily affairs among nomads. In the towns the Shariah takes precedence wherever the two are in open conflict. Two cases in point are the rules and conventions governing the practices of female circumcision and the payment of blood indemnity for murder. In the latter case, there is strict adherence, for the sake of peace, to the prompt payment of 100 she-camels as stipulated in the Shariah, while in the former case, Pharaonic customs prevail and there is more extensive surgery, bordering on mutilation, performed on female genitalia than is allowed for in Islamic convention or is practiced by Muslin Arabs.

The basic building block of Somali tribal society is the family, consisting of a husband, wife and children. The family normally owns a herd of sheep or goats ranging from 100 to several hundred, a few burden camels and, under more favorable circumstance, a herd of breeding and milch camels. The more camels a man possesses, the greater both his prestige and risk. In wetter regions of the country Somalis raise cattle.

The family unit, or *qois*, usually lives in a camp, protected from predators such as lions and hyenas by a fence of thornbushes inside of which is a hut of sticks and grassmats and a corral of thornbushes or a number of such corrals for the herds. The entrances to the fence and corrals are guarded by removable thornbushes. On most occasions, the fence may also contain the huts and corrals of immediately related families, such as old parents and married sons of the husband. Space may also be provided for the huts of extra wives. Aunts, uncles, unmarried and destitute members of the extended family as well as unrelated individuals who may enjoy a client status may also find room within the basic family's camp.

A number of related but autonomous families would, in most cases, congregate on a favorite pasture or near wells for common defense and protection. These family units, which may all be related by blood via paternal descent, constitute the next building block of tribal society, the *rer*. A number of *rers* (*rero*) residing within the same general area (or even scattered and interspersed among other *rers*) constitute a *qolo* or *qabiil*, or clan. When all the *qabiils* claiming descent from a common eponymous ancestor are taken together, the result is a tribe, which may have thousands of members. This, according to one authority, con-stitutes the "agnatic basis of Somali society, where community of social re-lations is expressed genealogically."

The *qois* (family unit) is ruled by the male head of the family; the *rer* (sub-clan) is governed by its male elders, the heads of families meeting together. The *qolo* is governed by an assembly of males presided over by a clan head. He, like a president of a republic, is advised by a council (*gudi*), which can vary in number from a dozen elders to all mature males in the clan. When there is business to transact, the chief may call a council, depending upon the seriousness of the situation. Decisions, reached by open discussion, are carried out through consensus and moral suasion rather than by force. The council also attends to all major business between its own and other mutually autonomous clans.

In time of peace an *ergo*, or peace deputation, is sent to other clans to settle disputes over such tribal properties as wells and pasturelands or to right wrongs in interpersonal disputes, some of which could lead to loss of life, limb, honor or property. Such injuries may include adultery and rape, physical and verbal abuse, theft, robbery and homicide. There is specific compensation for each of the wrongs. For instance, in the case of loss of life, the guilty party (i.e. the corporate clan) must pay from 10 to 100 camels (for the death of a male) to the injured party or clan. Should a man have an affair with another man's wife, he must compensate the husband whose honor he has injured by payment of a certain (negotiable) amount of livestock. In the case of rape or intercourse with an unmarried girl, the offender must either marry her or pay the full prescribed brideprice, as if marriage had taken place. Otherwise he could be killed by the victim's clansmen, as is sometimes the case.

Somalis have traditionally divided themselves into two major lineages, the Samale and Sab. The Samale are predominantly nomadic pastoralists who would not ordinarily accept the Sab as equals in marriage or in other social relations. The Sab are a complex of hunter-gatherers, cultivators and craftsmen—all necessary but despised vocations in the eyes of the warlike Samale.

In addition to the Sab-Samale dichotomy, there are five major tribal confederations in Somali society: the Dir, Darod, Hawiya, Ishak and Digil-Rahanwein, the last group being more a political grouping than a lineage in the traditional Somali sense. The Darod, Hawiya and Ishak, all Samale, are predominantly pastoralists and traders, occupying lands on the coast, in the interior of the Horn, the Ogaden and northeastern Kenya. The Digil-Rahanwein and related Sab tribes live in the wetter southwest between the Shebelle and Juba rivers. Along these rivers are also found agricultural peoples who are believed to be of Bantu origin and who are economically and socially interdependent with the Sab or may even be considered as members of the Sab. The Dir, believed to be the oldest Somali stock, live mainly in southern Somalia and in the northwest, between Harar and the northern Somali coast. The Issa of the Djibouti Republic are counted among the Dir. The Dir may engage in every type of economic activity from herding to farming.

The material culture of the Somalis is limited pretty much to camels and to what a camel can carry. This will include grass mats to cover a collapsible hut, water containers, cutting and cooking implements. It is the non-material culture of the Somalis that is distinctive, from the values of hospitality and manly pride to interpersonal relationships. Even more distinctive and renowned are Somali oral lore and literature, particularly Somali poetry.

Somalis have been called "a nation of poets in search of an alphabet" (the Somali language was without written form until 1972). Somali poetry is primarily didactic in purpose as opposed to lyrical. Memorization is made easy by alliteration and other poetic devices. Its main themes are history, philosophy and propaganda. The enterprising poet may also revel in tribal politics, as both instigator of tribal strife and peacemaker. Praise and ridicule are other favorite themes. Examples of classical Somali poems are Mohammed Abdulle Hassan's "Hiin Finiin," in praise of his favorite horse; Ismail Mire's "The Rewards of

Success,'' a philosophical poem; and Abdillahi Muse's ''An Elder's Reproof to his Wife.'' Each is a rich repository of worldly wisdom, poignant images and practical advice.

The modern history of the Somali people is not unlike that of other peoples of the African continent, a history of Western domination, resistance and anti-colonialism. Following the footsteps of explorers and adventurers, a number of European powers concluded treaties with various Somali tribes along the coast-line. In 1885 Great Britain made a protectorate of the northern Somali coast; the French created the French Somaliland or Somali Djibouti, later known as the French Territory of the Afars and Issas after the two major groups of inhabitants, the Issas being Somali.

With the voluntary withdrawal of Turko-Egyptian control from portions of northern Somalia, Menelik II of Ethiopia occupied the inland Islamic center of Harar in 1887, thus formally entering the colonial scramble for territory (see Harari). Two years later, the Italians acquired a colony in southern Somalia. In 1910, Great Britain formally established the Northern Frontier District in Kenya Crown Colony, the majority of whose inhabitants then, as now, were Somali-speaking pastoralists.

In the north, Ethiopia continued to expand. Under the terms of the 1897 Anglo-Abyssinian treaty, Britain surrendered the Somali-occupied territories of the Ogaden and Haud, the latter being a loosely defined grazing area between Hargeisa and Harar, in 1948 and 1954, respectively.

Somali nationalism was fired by these multiple fractures, leading to resistance, sometimes violent. The most notable was by Mohammed Abdulle Hassan pejoratively known as the Mad Mullah, whose dervish fighters harried the British and other colonial forces from 1900 to his death in 1920. The Somali Youth League, an urban-based political movement, eventually succeeded in leading two Somali-inhabited territories—British and Italian Somalilands—to union and independence in 1960. Two points in the star of the Somali national flag were accounted for; the other three points, representing French Somaliland, the Ogaden and the Northern Frontier District of Kenya, remained under foreign rule.

Believing it had a mandate to unite all Somali peoples, the new government embarked on a diplomatic campaign. Starting with the All-African Peoples' Conference at Cairo in 1961, it presented its case to every African and non-aligned meeting of nations. The Somalis' cry for reunification fell on deaf ears. In 1963, Kenya achieved independence and incorporated nearly 400,000 Somalis within its borders. In 1978 Somalia fought a devastating war over the Ogaden territory with Ethiopia and lost. In the meantime, in 1977, the Territory of Afars and Issas became the independent Republic of Djibouti, a further setback for Somali aspirations.

As a consequence of these setbacks, Somali politics turned inward, with a resurgence of virulent tribalism. Bitter feuding developed among such groups as the Marehan, who in 1982 were in power, and the Majertein, who were once in power. Both groups belong to the Darod tribe, as opposed to the Dir, Hawiya,

Ishak and Sab, each of whom feels excluded from real power. The Majertein and other dissident groups are waging a guerrilla war against Somalia's central government, while the Somali regime in Mogadishu has been aiding and abetting western Somali liberation fighters harrying the Ethiopian army in the Ogaden. Somalia and Ethiopia manage to continue their sputtering border war by proxy, while the majority of Somalis, whose political fate is in the balance, tensely await the uncertain outcome.

BIBLIOGRAPHY

Books

Andrzewski, B. W., and Lewis, I. M. *Somali Poetry: An Introduction*. Oxford: Clarendon Press, 1964.
Contini, Jeanne. "The Somalis: A Nation of Poets in Search of an Alphabet." In *A Handbook of African Affairs*, edited by Helen Kitchen. New York: Praeger, 1964.
Farer, Tom J. *War Clouds on the Horn of Africa*. 2nd ed. New York: Carnegie Endowment for International Peace, 1979.
Fleming, Harold C. *Baiso and Rendille: Somali Outliers*. Rome: Instituto per L'Oriente, 1964.
Greenberg, Joseph. *The Languages of Africa*. Bloomington: Indiana University Press, 1966.
Ibn Batutta. *The Travels of Ibn Battuta, A.D. 1325–1354*. Translated by C. Defremery and B. R. Sanguinetti and edited by H.A.R. Gibb. Cambridge: Cambridge University Press, 1962.
Jardine, Douglas. *The Mad Mullah of Somaliland*. London: Herbert Jenkins, 1923.
Laitin, David. *Politics, Language and Thought: The Somali Experience*. Chicago: University of Chicago Press, 1977.
Legum, Colin, ed. *African Contemporary Records: Annual Survey and Documents, 1978–1979*. New York: Africana, 1980.
Lewis, Ioan Myrddin. "Conformity and Contract in Somali Islam." In *Islam in Tropical Africa*, edited by I. M. Lewis. London: Oxford University Press, 1966.
————. "From Nomadism to Cultivation: The Expansion of Political Solidarity in Southern Somalia." In *Man in Africa*, edited by Mary Douglas and Phyllis M. Kaberry. New York: Tavistock, 1969.
————. *Marriage and the Family in Northern Somaliland*. Kampala: East African Institute of Social Research, 1962.
————. *A Modern History of Somalia: Nation and State in the Horn of Africa*. London: Longman Group, 1980.
————. "The Northern Pastoral Somali of the Horn." In *Peoples of Africa*, edited by James Gibbs. New York: Holt, Rinehart and Winston, 1965.
————. *A Pastoral Democracy: A Study of Pastoralism and Politics Among the Northern Somali of the Horn of Africa*. London: International African Institute, 1961.
————. *Peoples of the Horn of Africa: Somali, Afar and Saho*. London: International African Institute, 1955.

Luling, Virginia. "Somali." In *Muslim Peoples: A World Ethnographic Survey*, edited by Richard V. Weekes. Westport, Conn.: Greenwood Press, 1978.

Thompson, Virginia, and Adloff, P. *Djibouti and the Horn of Africa*. Stanford: Stanford University Press, 1968.

Touval, Saadia. *Somali Nationalism: International Politics and the Drive for Unity in the Horn of Africa*. Cambridge: Harvard University Press, 1963.

Trimingham, J. Spencer. *The Influence of Islam Upon Africa*. New York: Praeger, 1968.

————. *Islam in Ethiopia*. London: Frank Cass, 1952.

Articles

Andrzewski, B. W. "The Development of a National Orthography in Somalia and the Modernization of the Somali Language." *Horn of Africa* (Summit, N.J.) 1:3 (1978): 39–45.

Castagno, A. A. Jr. "The Somali-Kenya Controversy." *Journal of Modern African Studies* 2:1–4 (1964): 165–188.

Laitin, David. "Somali Territorial Claims in International Perspective." *Africa Today* 23:2 (1976): 29–38.

Lewis, H. S. "The Origins of the Galla and Somali." *Journal of African History* 7:1 (1966): 27–46.

Lewis, I. M. "The Politics of the 1969 Somali Coup." *Journal of Modern African Studies* 10:3 (1972): 383–408.

Sheik-Abdi, Abdi. "Ideology and Leadership in Somalia." *Journal of Modern African Studies* 19:1 (1981): 163–172.

————. "Somali Nationalism: Its Origins and Future." *Journal of Modern African Studies* 15:4 (1977): 657–665.

Silberman, Leo. "Somali Nomads." *International Social Science Journal* 9 (1959): 559–571.

Turton, E. R. "Somali Resistance to Colonial Rule and the Development of Somali Political Activity in Kenya, 1893–1960." *Journal of African History* 13:1 (1972): 119–143.

Unpublished Manuscripts

Adam, Hussein. "A Nation in Search of a Script." M.A. thesis, University of East Africa (Makerere), 1968.

Cassanelli, Lee. "The Benaadir Past: Essays in Southern Somali History." Ph.D. dissertation, University of Wisconsin, 1973.

Hersi, Ali Abdirahman. "The Arab Factor in Somali History: The Origins and the Development of Arab Enterprise and Cultural Influences in the Somali Peninsula." Ph.D. dissertation, University of California, Los Angeles, 1977.

Samatar, Said S. "Poetry in Somali Politics: The Case of Sayyid Mahammad Abdille Hasan." Ph.D. dissertation, Northwestern University, 1979.

Abdi A. Sheik-Abdi

SONGHAY   From Timbuktu downstream to Goa, Niamey and Gaya, the Niger River flows through the Sahelian area of Songhay culture. In hundreds of hamlets, villages and towns of this hot and semiarid region of West Africa, the name "Songhay" (also Songhoi, Songhai, Sonhrai) still evokes through popular legend and songs the epic days of migration, conquest and empire of long ago. The cycle of events, though at some points hazy, is clear in its main outlines.

Original congeries of riverine people, among them fishermen (Sorko) and hunters (Gow), moved from the "W" region upstream and settled in the Dendi area between Say and Bourem; eventually in the seventh century, they formed a rudimentary nation under the leadership of the house of Za (Dia). The Za resided at first in Koukya and later moved to Gao, a growing center of Sudanese trade and trans-Saharan traffic. The Za here embraced Islam (ca. 1010), even though his people remained faithful to the spirits which governed their relations with the river, the wild game and the soil. For centuries they lived simply as subjects of states ruled by others: first the Soninké (ca. 900–1077), later the Manding (ca. 1260–1400).

The decline of the Manding left a power vacuum. Rising to the occasion, Sonni Ali (Ali Ber, 1465–1492) audaciously set out to reclaim the Mali empire under Songhay rule and to control the routes of commerce and trade in the name of Islam. Songhay warriors took Timbuktu in 1468, Djenne in 1473, Mopti a few years later and Oualata, a Mossi outpost, in 1483 (see Mossi).

Sonni Ali was a fierce leader and an astute politician, but he was no religious man, although Islam served his cause. He certainly was more feared than lauded by the Muslim notables. When he died in battle, the succession was settled by a coup in favor of a more pious servant of Allah, Mamadu Touré (1493–1529), who reigned as the first *askia*, soon enthroned as Askia el-Hadj Muhammad by the caliph of Egypt in Cairo. He and his successors ruled with luster over a vast, well-administered expanse, the boundaries of which reached Agadez and Kano in the east, Djenne in the south, Oualata in the west and Taghaza in the north.

Ahmad ad-Dehebi, sultan of Morocco, attracted by mirages of gold and treasure, sent a mercenary force armed with muskets across the Sahara in 1590. Six months later the Askia was killed in flight at Tondibi, Bao was devastated and Timbuktu sacked and looted. In Morocco the sultan, upon the sad reports of mud-brick settlements and arid spaces in lieu of fabulous cities and gold mines, soon decided to abandon the project.

Thus, the Songhay state disappeared and the Songhay nation broke up, reverting to the previous condition in which cultural dissimilarities asserted themselves in the different ecological settings to which the various groups wandered or returned. Certain cultural elements would remain to be shared, among these the Songhay language (of the Nilo-Saharan group), which allowed for several dialects and regional variations, a mixed and uneven adherence to Islam and above all, perhaps, the legend of a great past, which allowed for eclectic memories—in Ayorou and Tera, the Mayga's boasted blood ties to the noble Askia. Elsewhere, among the Sohantie, the Sorko or the Gow, the claim of being of the original nucleus, "where it all began," was frequently invoked.

It would hardly be possible to draw the demographic map of the groups and communities of Songhay culture in sharp detail. The diverse groups are dispersed in at least four different countries, let alone the migrant groups scattered in various coastal cities. Also, the available population statistics are only estimates at best.

The Songhay proper form two large clusters. One covers the lake-like region of the river bend in Mali, extending from Lake Debo along the river with strong concentrations in Goundam, Timbuktu, Bandiagara and Gao, and smaller ones in Issa Ber, Mopti, Segou and Bamako. The estimated population here is 420,000. The other spreads out in areas of the westernmost provinces of Niger, with strong concentration in Tillaberi, Ayorou and Tera (estimated population, 600,000). To these must be added the Songhay settlements of Dori in Upper Volta (8,000), of Parakou and Kandi in Benin (46,000), of the Sokoto River in Nigeria (12,000) and of Agadez in Niger (8,000). They are known by various names—the Kado in Tera, Ayorou and the Goroul; the Gabibi (or Gabibi Arbi) north of Gao; the Sorko of the fishing hamlets all along the river; the Fono in the upper lake area; the Gow in the high grass stretches of the W in Anzourou and the Hombori hills; and the Dendi between Gaya and Parakou. A caste of magicians goes proudly by the name of Sohanti, while the descendants of the Askia carry the noble name of Mayga. Less noble, but no less dignified, are the Kourtey on the river banks between Niamey and Say.

By far the strongest subgroup is the Zerma (also called Djerma and Zaberma), whose homelands in Niger are Zermaganda, the land on both sides of the river, and Zaberma, the wadi region around Dosso. In these two areas, which are interspersed with Hausa (see Hausa) and Fulani (see Fulani) settlements, the Zerma form the predominant population of some 500,000. In the Republic of Niger, therefore, the Zerma-Songhay represent roughly 20 percent of the nation's 6.1 million people. One-half of the inhabitants of Niamey, Niger's capital city and largest conglomerate (70,000), are Zerma. In all there are more than 2 million Songhay.

The vast majority of Zerma-Songhay in Niger live in 2,000 villages ranging in size from 100 to 800 people and in 100 small towns averaging 2,000 inhabitants. Life in all these places is organized around four major themes: local subsistence through agriculture, kinship links, nobility ranks and a nature cult modified by Sunni Islam (Maliki school). Every locality is not only spatially distant from others, but also constitutes its own customary-legal authority for most internal affairs. It most often insists upon its peculiar identity to the extent of affirming its own descent lines within the Zerma-Songhay genealogy (even in town, the Zerma are Zerma only for the Fulani and the Hausa; among themselves they are pridefully Kalle, Golle, Kado, Kourtey or perhaps even Loqa), its own idiomatic distinctions and, until recently, its own facial marks.

Outside the capital city, all Zerma except the minute proportion in administrative and commercial activities are agriculturalists. With the use of hand tools, they grow a variety of millet during the brief rainy season and live off what harvest there is the rest of the year. They keep some small livestock and let the

Fulani herd the few heads of horned cattle they possess. Farming is noble labor and for men only. The women grow vegetables and herbs in personal garden plots. They produce enough surplus to cover the cost of necessities, such as salt, sugar, tools and clothing, the expenses for birth, marriage and death ceremonies and to pay taxes. Except in times of drought, which come in cycles, they live well but frugally.

The village community is first of all a lineage group: all the men are linked to one male ancestor. The group is divided into sublineages, each headed by the senior in line and further subdivided into as many household units as there are married sons. Polygyny is practiced: 25 percent of the households count two or more wives, each living in her own separate dwelling within the household's enclosure. Patrilineality is maintained by strict rules of exogamy, the effect of which is that the men stay in their native villages while the women circulate between villages. Since marriage raises a man to senior status, men marry late, in their late twenties, whereas girls marry in their early teens. Whether the marriage bond lasts or not, children belong to the husband's lineage group.

The social organization is complicated in subtle ways by a ranking system which at one end records the gradients of blood relations from ancient rulers and princes and at the other end reflects the developments of indigenous slavery. The resulting intricacies defy summary description, since they involve not only the minutely codified nuances of status granted to the original war captives' descendants, whose assimilation progresses with each generation, but also the more concealed forms which the resulting relations tacitly could take around the decrees of colonial administrators and the manifestos of later regimes. The Zerma-Songhay look up to the most noble among them: the Mayga and the princely Zerma families, and maintain cordial but quietly dominant relations with the lower castes of their community. To these belong the captive domestic servants and dependents (*horso*) and the various castes of craftsmen, blacksmiths, celebrants, *griots* (praise singers), therapists and magicians, whose specialist duties and products are integral parts of Zerma-Songhay custom and community.

The ideological canopy of the Zerma-Songhay world could not possibly be of one cloth. On the surface and for all official figures, the Songhay culture is evidently Muslim. Indeed, the clothes people wear, the calendar and the code of law which regulates civil life from the naming of the newborn to the wake for the dead are manifestly Muslim. Few if any of the freeborn will choose to ignore the five prayers of the day or any of the fasts and feasts of the Muslim year. In fact, the higher one's station on the social ladder, the more publicly exhibited the signs of devotion. On Friday, howling sirens escort the parade of limousines behind the president's to the mosque.

Islam has introduced new elements to the Songhay culture while leaving almost untouched the underlying framework of custom and tradition, for Islam has come to these regions, travelling with the caravans of traders and merchants and settling in marketplaces, fortified towns and administrative centers. On the other hand, more than 95 percent of the Zerma-Songhay reside in the vast spaces between such sites, drawing their sustenance—their "life's strength"—from the soil, the river or other elements of nature in respectful relations with the forces and spirits which govern these realms and in dependence upon the elders and the specialists among them who can transmit the secrets of these relations.

Even in the city, when night falls, after the limousines and the sirens have found their way back to the presidential residence and are quiet, the sound of the talking drums rises from one or another suburb, calling forth the nightly possession dances.

BIBLIOGRAPHY

Books

Humwick, J. O. "Religion and State in the Songhay Empire." In *Islam in Tropical Africa*, edited by I. M. Lewis. London: Oxford University Press, 1966.
———. "Songhay, Bornu, and Hausaland in the Sixteenth Century." In *History of West Africa*, edited by J.F.A. Ajayi and M. Crowder. Vol. 1. New York: Columbia University Press, 1971.
Lewis, I. M. "Introduction." In *Islam in Tropical Africa*, edited by I. M. Lewis. London: Oxford University Press, 1966.
Miner, H. M. *The Primitive City of Timbuctoo*. Garden City, N.Y.: Doubleday, 1965.
Murdock, G. P. *Africa: Its People and Their Culture History*. New York: McGraw-Hill, 1959.
Thompson, V. "Niger." In *National Unity and Regionalism in Eight African States*, edited by Gwendolyn M. Carter. Ithaca: Cornell University Press, 1966.
Trimingham, J. S. *The Influence of Islam Upon Africa*. New York: Praeger, 1968.
———. *Islam in West Africa*. London: Oxford University Press, 1959.
Van Hoey, L. F. "The Coercive Process of Urbanization: The Case of Niger." In *The New Urbanization*, edited by S. Greer, et al. New York: St. Martin's Press, 1969.
———. "Small Scale Society Under Stress." In *The Concept of Community*, edited by D. Minar, et al. Chicago: Aldine, 1969.

Article

Fuglestadt, F ."UNIS and BNA: The Role of Traditionalist Parties in Niger, 1948–1960." *Journal of African History* 16:1 (1975): 113–137.

Unpublished Manuscript

Van Hoey, L. F. "Emergent Urbanization: Increasing Social Scale in Niger, West Africa." Ph.D. dissertation, Northwestern University, 1966.

Leo F. Van Hoey
Population figures updated by Richard V. Weekes

SONINKÉ   The Soninké, often called Sarakolé, form a relatively large western African ethnic group of 2.5 million people, 47 percent of whom are Muslim.

Most live in Mali, Upper Volta and Ivory Coast, while smaller groups are found in Senegal, Gambia and Mauritania. According to their oral history, they are related to ancestors of the Caucasian race from the Saharan-Mediterranean region, probably Berbers, who exercised considerable authority and power in the Sudanese Sahel, in Ghana, near Koumbi, in the Ouagadougou until the end of the eleventh century and, later, at Diara, near Nioro.

Since then the Soninké have formed numerous communities during their migrations and are referred to by their neighbors under a variety of names. They are called Diakhanke, Ouakore or Aswanik by the Moors of Mauritania; Azor (from their original tongue, Azer) and Ahl-Massin in Tagant, Ouadane and in the Niger buckle (5,000 of these live in Marseilles, France). They are also referred to as Dyankanke in upper Gambia and in Futa Jalon, where they may also be called Tubakai. The Fulani, Hausa and Songhay call them Wangarbe, Wangarawa and Wankore, respectively.

Except where they form compact and relatively pure ethnic communities, such as in the regions of Nioro, Nara, Guidimakha between Kayes and Selibaby in Mauritania and Bakel in Senegal, the Soninké have almost everywhere else abandoned Azer and speak the tongues of their larger neighbors in the countries where they happen to live—Songhay at Djenne, Bambara in the region of Bamako, Dyula in Dafina (Upper Volta) and Odienne in southern Ivory Coast.

The Soninké were forcibly converted to Islam by the Almoravids in the eleventh century and subsequently became fervent propagators of the religion. Today, their clerics are among the most learned Muslims and educated people of West Africa. Firmly attached to the soil, the Soninké's occupation is either agriculture or trading, providing intense competition in the field to the Dyula (see Dyula). In Gambia and in Guinea-Bissau (where they are referred to as Ligbe), they are notorious illegal traffickers. More recently, the Soninké have taken to sea and have become excellent sailors.

Generally the Soninké's social life has been deeply influenced by Islam, but the traditional person remains superficially Muslim, leaving the practice of the religion to the clerical clans. Beliefs concerning the nature of man are at present in a fluid stage with much remaining and still believed in from the animistic substratum. The destiny of man after death, however, has been more deeply influenced by Islam. The Soninké, therefore, believe in the "vital force," which is impersonal and which goes to the nether world to be absorbed into the deity. The "shadow soul" which enters the body on the eighth day after birth, upon the naming of the child, leaves the body during sleep, is the element exposed to seizure by witches and, after death, wanders about the earth to be reunited with the body upon resurrection.

Soninké society is highly stratified, and mobility between the levels is still minimal in a traditional milieu. The clergy is drawn from the clerical class. A special distinction is made for those with juridical training. The chief regional cleric is elected for life. The liturgical tongue is Arabic; in some areas, however, *khutba* (the sermon) is recited in local languages.

Unlike other inhabitants of the Sahel and the western Sudan who subscribe to a cult of saints entailing much devotion, the Soninké are more flexible. Most Soninké belong to the Tijaniyya *tariqa*; the others have been won over by a deviationist sect, Hamalism. This is particularly true among those who live in the Mauritanian areas of Kaedi, Assaba and Nema. Among the idiosyncrasies of Hamalism are the recitation of the *jawharat al-kamal* after the eleventh bead of the rosary, the adoption of extravagant *dhikrs* with hysterical convulsive movements and the inclusion of women in many ceremonies. Such ceremonies can lead to ritualistic orgy. Any children born as a result acquire special status in the community and are referred to as "children of light."

Islam acknowledges magic but condemns sorcery and witchcraft; nevertheless, the Soninké clerics, as many of their neighbors do, "pray against" individuals, usually reciting the *fatiha* while holding the palms of their hands downward.

National laws are slowly superseding tribal and Islamic law. While these are bringing about change in tribal behavior, folklore and rituals among the Soninké are still alive, particularly in their attitudes and practices regarding the cycle of life: name-giving, initiation, marriage and death. Mother and child still remain indoors for the first seven days after birth, the eighth day providing the occasion for a significant festival involving the naming of the child and the taking up of one's shadow soul. At sunset on the seventh day the *nyamakhala* (woman *griot*) announces the ceremony. The father arrives on the morning of the eighth day with the *imam* and village notables at his mother-in-law's house, where the birth has taken place. The *imam* and father enter the hut, and, following customary special greetings, the father tells the *imam* the child's Muslim name. In turn, the *imam* announces that day's Muslim saint's name, who becomes the child's spiritual guardian. Women from both parents' sides arrive with presents and profuse congratulations. The official ceremony then begins, with the *imam* preparing two amulets for the child to wear around its neck as a special protection against evil spirits and witches. A sheep is slain, and the *nyamakhala*, having shaved the baby's head, whispers in its ear both the Muslim and ethnic names. The ethnic name is provided by the paternal aunt. The *nyamakhala* then carries the baby outside, where it receives the elders' blessings. The child's hair is placed in a fan along with millet, peanuts and rice and presented to the *imam*, who recites prayers on behalf of the child and his family. The festivities proceed with eating, singing and dancing.

Soninké follow Islamic regulations relating to marriage, although rituals retain some pre-Islamic traditions. The brideprice is usually paid in two installments, the first given to the bride at betrothal and becoming part of her trousseau, while the second installment belongs to her family.

Burial ceremonies are characterized by Islamic simplicity, but inhumation usually takes place in the compound. Cemeteries are being created increasingly in the outskirts of villages, with the women taking part in the cortege but remaining conspicuously absent during prayers.

Alfred G. Gerteiny
Population figures updated by Richard V. Weekes

BIBLIOGRAPHY

Books

Curran, Brian Dean, and Schrock, Joann. *Area Handbook for Mauritania*. The American University FAS, DA Pam 550–161. Washington, D.C.: Government Printing Office, 1972.
Gerteiny, Alfred G. *Mauritania*. New York: Praeger, 1967.
Levtzion, Nehemia. "The Differential Impact of Islam Among Soninké and the Manding." In *Papers from the International Conference on Manding Studies*. London: University of London School of Oriental and African Studies, 1972.
Meillassoux, Claude. *Urbanization of an African Community: Voluntary Associations in Bamako*. Seattle: University of Washington Press, 1968.
Murdock, George P. *Africa: Its People and Their Culture History*. New York: McGraw-Hill, 1959.
Trimingham, J. Spencer. *The Influence of Islam Upon Africa*. New York: Praeger, 1968.
———. *Islam in West Africa*. London: Oxford University Press, 1959.

SOSO   The Soso of West Africa are often referred to as Susu, a word derived from written documents by Europeans who first came to the coast and met the Soso about the middle of the fifteenth century. The Soso people themselves, when speaking in the local language, or in French, the official language, refer to themselves as Soso.

The Soso live mainly in coastal areas of the Republic of Guinea and in the bordering northwestern part of Sierra Leone. There is much ease of movement of the Soso across the border, defying state legislation in both countries. In the Republic of Guinea, one could speak more properly of Soso-speaking peoples as a collectivity, for the Soso dominate this littoral, which is occupied by the original Landuman, Baga, Mikhifore, Mandenyi, Nalou and other peoples. These latter have been at least linguistically absorbed by the Soso and are in many respects regarded as Soso-speaking peoples.

The Soso language, a northern subgroup of Manding, is also mutually intelligible with Yalunka. In the Republic of Guinea, Soso and Yalunka are sometimes regarded as the same people, the latter being called Yalun Soso (see Manding-speaking Peoples; Yalunka).

Though accurate figures are hard to obtain, the Soso in Guinea number about 1 million. The Soso people of Sierra Leone, about 110,000, are peripheral to those of Guinea, from where they originally expanded southwards to northwestern Sierra Leone. Being contiguous to the Temne of Sierra Leone, pockets of Soso settlements came to be found deep in Temne country as the Soso reached this area as traders between the interior and the coast. The Soso settlement of Lungi in the Kaffue Bullum chiefdom, Port Loko District of Sierra Leone, for example, numbers over 15,000.

The country occupied by the Soso consists of low coastal plains, rising in the interior to the Futa Jalon highlands. It is generally marshy coastal plain, a hilly plateau area and mountainous. A few miles from Conakry, the capital of the Republic of Guinea and part of Soso country, Mount Kakulima (3,290 feet) dominates the coastal plain. In the Forecariah region (Republic of Guinea), which is also part of Soso country in the southwest, can be found Mount Benna (3,687 feet) and Mount Gangan (3,657 feet). The part of Soso country in Sierra Leone is an extension of the geographical environment of the Guinea area. The area is extremely well watered, with mangrove swamp on the coast.

Most Soso live in villages, called *ta*, built on the coast with round houses. Villages are usually named after the founder with a -*ya* (or -*ia*) suffix, as in Kindia, Bramaia, Simbaya. Besides the normal *ta*, there are farming villages called *dakha*, which sometimes grow into *ta*. These are usually temporary settlements for the farming season, where farms are situated a distance of a mile or more from the *ta*. In earlier years, *dakha* also signified villages where prisoners were kept as farm slaves. In the bigger towns, there are a number of galvanized metal-roofed houses often built with mud-bricks plastered over with cement, with a veranda where people spend much of the day.

Traditions of the Soso origin would indicate that they were part of the thirteenth-century empire of that same name led by Sumunguru Kante, located in the western Sudan somewhere around the present state of Mali. Upon the breakup of that empire, the Soso moved westwards to Jalonkadu, the mountainous region of which a part is today called Futa Jalon. It was from Jalonkadu that the Soso started migrating towards the coast in stages, reaching the Guinea littoral by the late fifteenth century. Over the years, the Soso spread to occupy what later became northwestern Sierra Leone.

It is maintained in some accounts that the early Soso migrants were animists and their conversion to Islam came with the advent of Muslim Fulani to Futa Jalon by the seventeenth century, especially the Fulani *jihad* there in 1727–1728 and the setting up of a Muslim theocracy. It is in fact suggested in the traditions that the Soso moved out of Jalonkadu in large numbers to avoid the Fulani. Mandinka groups were settling among the Soso on the coast even earlier than the Fulani *jihad*. These Mandinka were Muslims, and they helped to convert some of the Soso. The Portuguese Jesuit priest, Father Balthasar Barreira, visited the Soso country at Bena in 1607 and found Islam already established there (see Mandinka).

With slight variation, partly as a result of a Soso diaspora as in Lungi, the Soso kinship system follows a general pattern. The largest kinship group is termed the clan, called *bankhri*. While *bankhri* has no particular function, it carries a sense of belonging by people who carry the same clan name and have a vague idea of descent from a common ancestor.

Within the *bankhri* (or *bonsoë*, as understood by the Soso of Guinea), there is the *khabilè*, relatives on both their maternal and paternal sides. Members of the *khabilè* do not necessarily live together in the same locality but regard themselves as blood relations. The smallest and most important unit is the *dembaya* or *bankhidé*. This group consists of the immediate household—a man, his wife or wives and children and those living in the household as his dependents, which might include servants or brother's children living with him. It is even claimed that a man's son may still be part of his *dembaya* even if that son has a different compound not contiguous to his father's. It is the *dembaya* which breaks up at the death of its head to create several *dembaya* headed by his sons. A group of *dembaya* may inhabit a compound (*föhkè*), especially those connected by marriage or blood. This is often through the father line, and the *föhkè* is then identified with the suffix *ya* added to the clan name of the inhabitants, as in Banguraya, Sesay-ya.

Soso parentage, inheritance and succession are traced through one's father. Soso society is generally polygynous, and as Muslims they are enjoined to marry no more than four wives; but marriage to more than four is not particularly frowned upon. A child refers to its biological mother with the term *nga* and uses the same appellation for the other wives of its father, but not with reference to its mother's sisters. At the same time it calls its father *n'baba*, the same way it addresses its father's brothers, but never its mother's brothers.

When a child is born, a brief ceremony called *bara akona borun* ("he has been made to eat") is performed in which a member of the paternal family, male or female, chews kola nuts and spits it into a cup and this is fed to the newborn before it receives its mother's milk. This is supposed to introduce the child to this world and to the habit of eating. The same person who chews the kola nut also speaks to the child, advising it to be obedient to God and his elders.

At the naming ceremony eight days later, an *imam* recites passages from the Quran and the father's sister's children, called *gine di*, distribute ricebread and kola nuts to the visitors. Eldest sons usually carry the name *sarè*, while the term *sirè* is attached to the eldest daughters. This nomenclature is important since rank order dictates the way one relates to older or younger people. To distinguish between children in a *dembaya* who sometimes have the same name, the Soso always add the mother's name to precede that given the child. Thus two mothers, Hawa and Atta, having children each called Lamina, would distinguish such children as Hawa Lamina and Atta Lamina.

Marriage above all is an affair between families, with the partners-to-be playing little or no part. Marriage is allowed, even encouraged, between a boy and his mother's family. Thus a boy may marry his maternal cousin. The Soso claim that this helps to cement family ties. A girl's hand can be promised in marriage even before her birth or before she reaches the age of puberty. The prospective husband's family must then look after the girl until she reaches puberty. The future husband gives presents to his future parents-in-law during all of this period of engagement, sometimes in kind like helping them in their rice fields or in building or repairing their house.

The request for marriage is usually made by the boy's father or father's brother. Among the Soso of Lungi, a young man today may sometimes ask a girl to marry him, and if she consents, he goes to her parents or usually sends an intermediary. This follows more current patterns in larger urban or semi-urban centers where Western influence is strong. The engagement is usually sealed with presents of money and kola nuts to the girl's parents.

In polygynous Soso society, one finds that older and more established men tend to have more wives, while young men often have only one since that is all they can afford. The more prosperous a man is, the greater is the tendency for him to have plural wives, which is also seen as a status symbol.

Marriage usually takes place after the girl has reached puberty and been circumcised, the responsibility for the cost of this ceremony being that of the prospective husband or his family, if the girl was already engaged. Whereas formerly all girls were married immediately after reaching womanhood, in present-day Soso society this is not always the case. Some girls who marry after they are no longer virgins are considered a disgrace to their families. In the more traditional setting, this disgrace would sometimes be grounds for them to have their heads shaved or for them to be flogged.

For the marriage ceremony, kola nuts are sent to the parents and the bridegroom does not attend. There is great rejoicing and dancing if the bride is a virgin. Among the Soso of Lungi, marriage is legalized when the groom's parents take a calabash containing small domestic items and the sum of Le 1.75 (1 leone = U.S. $0.80). The groom or his parents later pay a price agreed upon between the two families. The bride goes to her own household during the ceremony, if she had been living at her future husband's household. Eight days after the ceremony, the bride is escorted to her husband's home amidst much merriment and dancing if she is a virgin. Marriage ceremonies are sometimes also sealed in a mosque, with the bride and groom attending as in the Western pattern. This, however, does not preclude the traditional rites.

Husbands are very respectful to their parents-in-law, especially their mothers-in-law. A man speaks with great deference to his mother-in-law and does not speak frivolously in her presence. A father-in-law has the right to request help from his son-in-law. The latter may send money in lieu of his service, but if he flatly refuses, he brings shame on his family.

Women do not attend funerals among the Soso. If a woman dies, her husband prays over her body and is one of those who lowers her into the grave. Burial takes place on the same day of death. The grave of a "big man"—a chief or religious leader—is dug with a cavity on the side where the body is inserted. A child is buried without ceremony if it dies before receiving a name. Otherwise it is given normal burial. Bodies of notorious witches are unceremoniously dragged to their graves with both feet tied.

The Soso are basically a subsistence agricultural people. In the Sierra Leone area, fishing is very common, but this does not appear to be so among the Soso of Guinea, even though they live on the littoral. Hunting for game helps to supplement the diet. Blacksmithery for tools is also an important profession. The Soso are historically and contemporarily known as traders. They travel back and forth between Sierra Leone and the Republic of Guinea, peddling commodities which are cheaper on one side of the border like clothing and footwear, consumer goods and others from one capital city to the other country. They also engage in produce trade, especially in Sierra Leone.

Farming is basically for rice, the staple food. They also plant peanuts, millet and cassava as subsidiary crops and some cash crops, particularly ginger. There are also large-scale banana plantations in Soso territory in the Republic of Guinea. The basic farming unit is the *dembaya*. This group works together on the main family farm, while the women keep peanut or cassava farms with some assistance from their husbands or other members of the *dembaya*. The women have major control over the proceeds of their own special farms on which they concentrate only secondarily to the main family farm.

Apart from this basic labor group, the Soso, like many other ethnic groups in this area, organize cooperative work groups to execute major tasks. The two types of work groups of the Sono are the *kilè* and the *lanyi*. The *kilè* represents a mobilization of voluntary workers by a man who can afford to provide for some "paid" labor for his farm. This is the closest approximation to wage labor. The *lanyi* is often a semi-permanent group of young workers who farm in turn on the fields of the members of the group.

The general political order among the Soso in Sierra Leone follows the pattern of chiefdom administration in that country. Villages have headmen and chiefdoms, which are groups of villages, and paramount chiefs. These latter are often descended from the families described as ruling from the pre-colonial era. The paramount chief is elected by the chiefdom councillors, one councillor representing 19 taxpayers. The position of the paramount chief becomes valid only after it is confirmed by the president of the state. Though he is enjoined not to settle legal matters, for which a court chairman is appointed today, people still take some cases to these inheritors of traditional rule.

The basic unit for the settlement of disputes is the head of the *dembaya* or, above that, the village head. Though these have no legal authority recognized by the central government, their decisions are regarded by the Soso as valid. If satisfaction is not obtained, the case can be taken to the chiefdom headquarters, where a court approved by the central government will consider the matter.

The Soso are almost entirely Sunni Muslim and follow the Maliki school. The form of Islam is laden with pre-Islamic religious practices. Islam is thus understood by the majority of Soso in terms of patterns which they regard as part of their culture. The case of polygyny is an example. Islam permits the practice, but the Soso do not consider it an abomination if even religious elders have more than the prescribed four wives.

In the more orthodox sense, Islam is dominated by certain religious functionaries who direct and interpret the religion. These are the *imam*, head of the mosque and male; the *alhaji* or *alhaja*, males or females who have made the pilgrimage to Mecca and purport to lead pious lives; the *foday* (female, *sewkheno*), one usually learned in the Quran who has pledged himself to follow the laws of God as contained in the Quran or as dictated by his teacher. These title holders generally claim that they are following a "purer" form of Islam than is the general public.

Yet many *imams*, *alhajis* and *fodays* perform the work of the *karamokho*, who often combines the roles of religious teacher, charm maker, diviner and sometimes herbalist. The *karamokho* in Sierra Leone is called a *moriman*. James Thayer, who in 1981 studied the Soso of Sierra Leone, wrote of the *moriman*:

> He can tell a person if a certain day is a good one on which to travel, whether his or her choice of a spouse will result in a good marriage, when a new bride should be de-flowered, and he can also tell the meaning of dreams. If one wishes to take up a trade or profession, the *moriman* will divine to see if the person will have luck; if one is running for political office, to see if he will win; or for a student, if he will pass an examination. A *moriman* is said to be able to tell the sex of an unborn child and whether its life will be long or short. If a person is sick, the *moriman* can tell him if it is the work of witches or not and if he will recover or not. (Thayer 1981, p. 18)

At least among the Muslim Soso of Guinea, besides the observances of Ramadan, Tabaski (Id al Fitr) and Id al Adha, there are ritual ceremonies like the *bari-ki*, in which Muslims participate. The *bari* represents spirits which are either good or evil and are consulted by the Soso. Sacrifices and offerings are still made to these *bari* who are said to inhabit sacred groves or woods. The *bari-ki* is thus a great feast of offering to the spirits in which enormous quantities of rice are consumed. The Soso of Guinea also employ traditional masks for ritual occasions associated with the farming cycle. Thus Islam among the Soso is strongly linked with and understood in terms of traditional cultural practices.

BIBLIOGRAPHY

Books

Fyle, C. Magbaily. *The Solima Yalunka Kingdom: Precolonial Politics, Economics and Society*. Freetown: Nyakon, 1979.
Suret-Canale, J. *La République de Guinée*. Paris: Editions Sociales, 1970.

Articles

Aubert, M. "Laws and Customs of the Susu." *Sierra Leone Studies* 20 (1936): 67–87.
De Hart, J. "Notes on the Susu Settlement at Lungi, Bullom Shore." *Sierra Leone Studies* 2 (1919): 21–44.

Fyle, C. Magbaily. "The Idea of Slavery in 19th Century Sierra Leone: The Career of Bilali." *Journal of the Historical Society of Sierra Leone* 2:1 (1978): 57–61.

Houis, M. "Qui sont les soso?" *Etudes guinéennes* (Conakry) 6 (1947): 77–79.

Sayers, E. F. "Some Susu Proverbs." *Sierra Leone Studies* 15 (1929): 51–56.

———. "The Susu Songs, with Rendering." *Sierra Leone Studies* 15 (1929): 48–50.

Unpublished Manuscripts

Bangua, Mahawa. "Contribution a l'histoire des sosoe du 13e au 19e siècle." Mémoire de fin d'études superieures, Institut Polytechnique Gamal Abdel Nasser, Conakry, 1971–72.

Garfield, Sally. "Kinship and Marriage Among the Susu." Department of Sociology, University of Sierra Leone, 1982.

Thayer, J. S. "Religion and Social Organization Among a West African Peoples: The Susu of Sierra Leone." Ph.D. dissertation, University of Michigan, 1981.

C. Magbaily Fyle

SOUTH AFRICANS   The South African people include 25 million "Blacks" and 4.5 million "Whites." The Blacks are divided, for purposes of apartheid legislation, into three official "race" groups: "Bantu" (African), 22 million; "Coloured" (racially mixed), 2.5 million; and "Asian" (Indian), 750,000. The Whites, among whom there is no official division, are two-thirds Afrikaans-speaking, one-third English-speaking.

There are approximately 360,000 Muslims in South Africa. They are represented in each of the official population groups, but principally in two of them, Coloured and Asian. Within the predominantly Christian Coloured population there is a Muslim subgroup of 182,000 people officially known as "Cape Malays." About three-quarters of these Muslims live in the Cape Town area. Indian Muslims, totalling 160,000, form the second major group. Most live in and around Durban, but there is a significant number living in the Cape Town and Johannesburg areas. In addition, there are nearly 13,000 African and just over 1,000 White Muslims.

Most South African Muslims are a highly urbanized group (more than 90 percent live in towns) with a history of close contact with Western life-styles. While Muslims have always been discriminated against as non-white, they have a privileged position relative to the majority of black Africans. Among Coloured South Africans, Muslims constitute a social and economic elite.

Such advantage has in the past kept Muslims aloof from other non-white groups, has reinforced their intermediary position and has given them a conservative reputation. But the effect of apartheid legislation during the 1960s and 1970s has made Muslims more aware of their separation from Whites and of what they have in common with each other. A growing number of Muslims, especially among the better educated and the young, now call themselves Black and strongly oppose ethnic labels like Cape Malay and Coloured as apartheid terms designed to separate one oppressed group from another in order to control them.

This inclination to stand together as Muslims produced the first national organization in 1975, the Islamic Council of South Africa. Based in Durban, it has 150 affiliated regional bodies. But longstanding historical divisions still persist. For example, Muslim leaders in the two major centers, Cape Town and Durban, are engaged in a power struggle.

It was to the Cape of Good Hope that Islam first came in the seventeenth century. Muslims were introduced as slaves and political exiles by the Dutch, who first settled there in 1652. The latter required cheap labor to build up the new settlement of Cape Town and to work the surrounding farmland and, finding the indigenous Khoikhoia difficult to control, brought slaves in from Batavia (now Jakarta) in the Dutch East Indies (Indonesia).

The political exiles were prisoners of war who had led insurrections against the Dutch in the East Indies. Best known is Shaikh Yusuf (son-in-law of the Sultan of Bantam), who came to the Cape in 1694 with a retinue of 49 kinsmen and servants. He became an ancestral figurehead for succeeding generations of Muslims. His grave became one of several shrines which form an arc around Cape Town and commemorate the lives of seventeenth- and early eighteenth-century Muslim leaders.

The Muslims of the Cape became known as Malays or Cape Malays because Malay (together with Dutch) was their lingua franca. The use of Malay, however, gradually died out except for a few words and expressions retained in present-day Afrikaans conversation. It is now widely, but erroneously, believed that these Muslims came from Malay or that, because they were sent from Batavia (the Dutch administrative center in the East), they were all Indonesian. The first-generation Muslims were a more heterogeneous body of people mainly from India, several Indonesian islands and Madagascar, with a few from Ceylon and other areas on the Indian Ocean. In South Africa they became more heterogeneous through exogamous marriage.

The community was held together by a common faith and set of social practices. The community was Sunni, mostly of the Shafi school. A few became Hanafi during the nineteenth century as a result of the influence of Abu Bakr Effendi, a *mufti* sent to Cape Town from the Ottoman Empire to give guidance on Islamic doctrine. His book, *Bayan al-din*, was one of the first books ever published in the Afrikaans language and is the more remarkable because it is printed in Arabic transliteration.

The ''Malay'' Muslims live in close, if somewhat uneasy, contact with the ''Coloured'' Christians. There was a tendency for Christian Coloured women to marry Muslims and ''turn Malay'' (convert to Islam). This was to their advantage as the Muslims enjoyed a greater degree of economic independence, hiring out their own labor as hawkers of fruit and vegetables, fishermen and fish hawkers and as skilled craftsmen, than the Christians, who were more directly dependent on Whites for employment. There was also a greater degree of mutual support and community life among the Muslims and a sense of dignity in belonging to a religious group that was independent of White hierarchy and organization.

Until recently, a female Muslim convert was *soenated*. This is usually translated as "female circumcision," but it is a small operation, often performed by the *imam*'s wife, to mark the clitoris. It was not uncommon for the convert's daughters to undergo the same treatment just before reaching puberty. This was to ensure that such a woman could be identified as Muslim at her death, in the event of a dispute with her Christian kin over whether the body should receive a Christian or Muslim burial. Nowadays she need only repeat the *shahada* in front of a witness, preferably an *imam*, to be accepted as a Muslim.

Nevertheless the convert's position remains potentially unstable, for such marriages not infrequently break up and the wife reverts to her old religion. This may result from difficulties she experiences in being accepted by her affines, especially if she does not take the trouble to learn to pray in Arabic or teach it to her children, and from her own family's opposition to a marriage which cuts her off from them. Such women, particularly in the poorer Coloured residential areas, fluctuate between adherence to the one religion and the other, fearing above all that they and their children may not belong to either group and that they will be degraded as *deurmakaar*, "mixed up," possessing no religious and, by implication, no social identity.

The loss of their daughters to the Muslim community is one of the main grievances of Christian Coloureds. It has led to accusations against Muslims of using charms procured from a *doekoem* (witch doctor) to further their own ends. The Christians complain that Muslim women are carefully protected from Christians. It is indeed rare for a "Malay" woman to become Christian because of the harsh sanction of social ostracism against one who is branded as *moetat* (apostate).

The number of Hanafis increased rapidly during the late nineteenth and early twentieth centuries with the arrival of Indian Muslims, mostly as merchant traders. Many settled in Durban, where the Hindus were concentrated. Others went to Cape Town and Johannesburg.

In the Cape, Indians set themselves up as shopkeepers in the Coloured community. Some became rich through wholesale businesses and through buying property which they rented to Coloured families. The Indian community has been more endogamous and socially exclusive than the Malays, but there has been some intermarriage with members of the latter group. New immigrants sometimes took a Malay wife while continuing to pay remittances to an Indian spouse and other kin back home. Such hypergamous marriages offered advantages for Malays similar to those for Christian Coloureds marrying into their community; the Indians were generally better off and exhibited a greater sense of dignity with their own distinct cultural heritage. The Indians are now forced by law to live in residential areas separate from those for Coloureds. Though many live in the prestigious township of Rylands Estate, fortunes have been eroded, partly by multiple inheritance, partly by harsh apartheid prohibitions on commercial enterprise outside their own Indian community. It has now become advantageous to Indians to marry Cape Malay women as they can obtain business licenses in Coloured areas in the wife's name. During the 1970s and 1980s Indians also began to marry Christian converts from the Coloured community.

In Durban the Indian community has been much more outward looking, partly because, as the majority Muslim group, it has more strength and confidence. Also, because there are few Coloureds in Natal, there is a stark division between White and Black and less of a tendency to look to the Whites as a reference group.

The Indian Muslim community maintains a strong contact with Pakistan. In recent years it has imported substantial literature and invited Muslim scholars to South Africa for lecture tours. This connection has helped to promote a more fundamentalist and ascetic approach to Islam.

Durban Indians also have maintained close contact with a group of East African Muslims who arrived in South Africa in the 1870s and 1880s. These "Zanzibaris," as they are now called (they were actually from Tanganyika and Mozambique), number 3,000 and live in an Indian residential area in Durban where they are exempted from the Pass Laws and other additional restrictions imposed on Africans.

Until recently, Islam has not had much appeal to most black Africans in South Africa. To them, Muslims have formed an urban elite, distinguished by their lighter skin color, their way of life, which was closer to that of the Whites, and by geographical distance from an essentially rural-based African population. But the migration of Africans to towns (heavily thwarted as it is by influx control) has brought a growing number into contact with Islam, which presents them with an alternative to the Christianity of the Whites. This comes at a time when Muslims are identifying themselves more clearly with the oppressed in South Africa and beginning to proselytize their faith among urban Africans.

The number of African Muslims rose steadily during the 1960s from 5,500 to 7,000, and more dramatically in the next decade to reach 13,000 in 1980. Some estimates put the figure much higher. The number is greatest around Johannesburg, where Muslims from Mozambique and Malawi, working as contract labor on the gold mines, form a nucleus which draws in converts. In Durban the growing number of Zulu converts has made it worthwhile to translate the Quran into Zulu, a task completed in 1982. In Cape Town, where the African population is relatively small and isolated, the major Muslim groups have made a concerted effort to reach them. During the 1970s a mosque was established in the African township of Langa, near Cape Town, to meet the needs of new converts.

The number of White Muslims has always been small, but has increased from 240 enumerated in 1960 to more than 1,000 in 1980. Most live in Cape Town and Johannesburg. A few are South African or foreign Whites who married Indian or Cape Malay Muslims before marriage between White and non-White was made illegal in 1949. But most are recent converts to Islam who live in White residential areas, as the law demands, but identify themselves socially and politically with one of the two major Muslim groups.

More significant than the number of converts is the pervading attitude of Whites towards Muslims. This is largely influenced by coffeetable books on their local traditions in South Africa, and by historical paternalism, in particular towards "Cape Malays." As employers, Whites regard Muslims as more able workers than Christian Coloureds and favor them accordingly. For example, the Malay Choir Board was established in 1939 by a prominent Afrikaaner to promote "Malay" music. During the 1970s substantial public funds were allocated to restore old buildings in the Bokaap area of Cape Town (popularly known as the Malay Quarter), and a Malay Cultural Museum was established nearby.

But the Muslims themselves are becoming increasingly disenchanted with this benign attention. They point out that the Whites are using them as a showpiece to justify separate development based on cultural differences between the two groups. They argue that Whites have only a superficial understanding of their way of life, for it is dictated by apartheid law, not by traditional song and dance, which are dying out anyway.

There are two strong movements among South African Muslims. One is toward religious fundamentalism, the other towards a consciousness of themselves as being oppressed. Both are set explicitly against ethnic divisiveness. The first is reflected in investment in new education and welfare centers to organize joint activities among Muslims and promote Islamic scholarship. Religious influence from Pakistan has brought the *tabligh* (ascetic missionary) movement to South Africa. Muslim women are beginning to wear the *burqa* (a veil covering them from head to waist) instead of a small head scarf. Local traditions are considered anathema to the true religious life. Political consciousness is to be found in nearly every Muslim publication in South Africa. The *Muslim News* (a fortnightly Cape Town newspaper) contains ethnicity as injurious to Black solidarity. Educated Muslims shun the old *kramats* (shrines) venerated by earlier generations and now look to the example of people like *imam* Abdulla Haron, a young and popular Cape Town figure who died while in police detention in 1969 and is now looked upon as a martyr for South African Muslims.

BIBLIOGRAPHY

Books

Boeseken, A. J. *Slaves and Free Blacks at the Cape 1658 to 1700*. Cape Town: Tafelberg, 1977.
Bradlow, F., and Cairns, M. *The Early Cape Muslims*. Cape Town: A. A. Balkema, 1978.
Brandel-Syrier, M. *The Religious Duties of Islam as Taught by and Explained by Abu Bakr Effendi*. Leiden: E. J. Brill, 1971.

Desai, B., and Marney, C. *The Killing of an Imam*. London: Quartet Books, 1978.
Du Plessis, I. D. *Ie Bydrae van die Kaapse Maleier tot die Afrikaanse Volksleid*. Cape
    Town: Nationale Press, 1935.
————. *The Cape Malays. History, Religion, Traditions, Folk Tales, the Malay Quarter*.
    Cape Town: A. A. Balkema, 1972.
Hampson, R. M. *Islam in South Africa: A Bibliography*. Cape Town: School of Librari-
    anship, University of Cape Town, 1963.
Kuper, H. *Indian People in Natal*. Durban, South Africa: The University Press, 1960.
Meet the Muslims in South Africa. Johannesburg: International Relations Committee of
    the Islamic Council of South Africa, 1978.

Articles

Sicard, S. v. "Islam in South Africa." *Islam and the Modern Age* 11:1 (1980): 58–81.
Zwemer, S. W. "Islam at the Cape." *Moslem World* 15:4 (1925): 327–333.

Unpublished Manuscript

Ridd, R. E. "Muslim Images and Identity in Cape Town." Paper presented to the Fifth
    Annual Conference on Southern African Research in Progress at the Centre for
    Southern African Studies, University of York, 1979.

Rosemary E. Ridd

SRI LANKANS   Muslims of Sri Lanka (formerly Ceylon) number some 1.2 million and are found throughout the island, particularly in the towns of the western coast and the agricultural regions of the east coast. They comprise a complex of ethnic groups, of which three are officially recognized in the census: Sri Lanka Moors (1.1 million), Malays (60,000) and Indian Moors (40,000). Their population increase is more rapid than for Sri Lankans as a whole: in 1946 there were 374,000 Sri Lanka Moors, 5.6 percent of the total. This rose to 6.5 percent of the population by 1971. Malays are increasing slower than the population as a whole, and Indian Moors are decreasing because of repatriation and/or absorption into Sri Lanka Moors.

Tamil is the traditional language of the Sri Lanka Moors. Nowadays, in line with political realities, more know the Sinhala language, and some of their children study in that language in school. A few in hill areas even speak Sinhala at home, but most Muslims enter the Tamil stream of education, up through university if they go that far. No mosques use Sinhala, for all religious literature and sermons are in Tamil. Most Indian Moors are also Tamils (see Labbai). Malays speak Malay at home, but do not write it; most know some Tamil through association with the mosque, and they like to educate their children in English. In government publications the term "Tamils" is taken to mean Hindus (and some Christians) who predominate in the northern and eastern parts of the country; Muslims are listed separately as Moors. The reason is political, to show a larger percentage of Sinhalas to Tamil-speakers in the population.

Sri Lanka Muslims have been unable to arrive at a name to call themselves. The term "Moor," derived from Portuguese, while commonly used in English and regarded as pejorative, is used rarely by the Muslims themselves. Sinhalas refer to them as Muslims or as Marakkala men after a prominent Muslim family name. Sri Lanka Muslims may refer to themselves as Sonakar or Sonar, by which they distinguish themselves from the Muslims of south India; the names are derived from the ancient Yona, Yavana or originally Ionian—applied to Greeks, Romans and Arabs, but the words tend to apply more to those of known part-Arab descent; moreover, they are used in a derogatory way by other Tamils, who refer to their dialect as Sona Tamil. Muslims in the upland areas may call themselves Islamiyaranarkal or Islamanarkal, "those who became Islam." The Urdu term "Mussalman" is known mostly around Colombo.

Muslim Arabs came to Sri Lanka in the eighth century, shortly after they had settled in Sind and Kerala. According to tradition, they settled in Bentotta and married Sinhala women. By the tenth century, they controlled considerable trade, and in the thirteenth century, Ibn Battuta, the social historian, reported that Colombo was in the hands of a Muslim, while the Delhi sultanate for a time extended its influence to the tip of India. Muslim traders from Kerala, Mappilla, also came to settle, but most came from Tamilnadu, from such places as Kayal, mentioned by Marco Polo. The source of the hybrid Tamil-Arabic culture of Sri Lanka Muslims is historically not clear. They developed an Arabized dialect written in Arabic script (not used today) and an epic of the life of the Prophet reminiscent of the Tamil version of the *Ramayana*.

The Malays were brought as laborers from Java, Sumatra and the Moluccas by the Dutch. Now they are known as Javar or Java *jati*. They are an urban population retaining their language and food preferences. Other Muslims regard them as rather irreligious, for Malays of the younger generation seldom attend mosque, and they also drink liquor, which other Muslims shun.

The Indian Muslims arrived during the British period, mostly as traders. They have been there since the last century, but like the Hindi Tamils of Indian origin, they are being sent back to India. Only a few are given Sri Lanka citizenship. Most are Tamils and Mappilla, but there are also some Gujaratis, who maintain a few mosques in Colombo. Some of these are Bohras from Bombay, after whom the name "Bohra" or "Borah" is locally given to other merchants from north-western India, even to Parsees (Zoroastrians). The original Bohras were Shia, the only ones on the island, and are now dwindling. There are small immigrant communities of Qadianis and Ahmadis, whose interpretation of Islam is regarded as aberrant.

Many mosque functionaries are not well versed in Arabic. Until recently, those *imams* and *qadis* who wished to pursue higher Arabic studies went to south India, but now in Beruwela and elsewhere there are colleges of Islamic studies. Many mosques have *madrasas* operating Sundays and evenings to teach Arabic letters, and in some of them a little spoken Arabic is taught. Mosque properties are supervised by the Wakfs Board, a government-sponsored agency.

There is considerable variation in observance of Islamic traditions. More than one-half the men, at least in the eastern towns, fail to fully observe the Ramadan fast, although most women do. The government allows only enough foreign exchange for 50 Muslims a year to go on the Haj, but perhaps an equal number go using black market money. Making of vows is popular, as throughout South Asia, and usually the vow is to give to charity. Id al Adha is celebrated with sacrifices of bulls and goats.

There are numerous caste, lineage and family groups. The Maulanas or Sayyids are those who claim patrilineal descent from the Prophet or those close to him. The Marakkayar (also Maraikkar, or Marikkar) comprise a successful business community in and around Colombo. There were merchants of that name in Kerala when the Portuguese arrived. An important Muslim caste or community in port towns of southern Tamilnadu is Marakkalarayara, meaning "wooden-boat lords," which must be the original form of the name. They have histories of how their ancestors traded in wooden ships, one of whom was King Solomon, who came through the Palk Straits in search of gold. Another community in Sri Lanka is the Lebbe or Lebbai, who serve especially as prayer leaders and preachers, the office of which may also be called *lebbe*. These people are related in origin to the Labbai of Tamilnadu. These are not corporate bodies, nor are they geographically localized; they are like lineages but mostly without lineage depth. They have some of the functions of caste, but endogamy is denied as a cultural ideal.

In occupation, most Muslims are in business. The most prominent are the gem-trading families, who virtually monopolize both the extraction and selling of gems. They live principally in Colombo, Galle, Beruwela, Kalatura and Ratnapura. Then there are urban entrepreneurs, in Colombo and elsewhere, who shift their business with the times, profiting from scarce manufactured goods and imported products.

Numerically more important are the petty traders, who have set up shops in villages all over the island; some of them maintain cooperative societies. A few have entered modern professions, but on the whole, modern secular education has been ignored. Beruwela has a community of Muslim fishermen, and Negombo one of Muslim masons. Except for the Muslim peasants on the east side, none does actual farming, coconut tree climbing or hard labor. Barbers, who also circumcise, form the most distinctive Muslim occupational group; they are called Nasuvar in the west and Ostas in the east. They are lowest in status and therefore virtually endogamous, functioning as a separate caste.

In the life cycle the most important event for boys between five and ten is circumcision, accompanied by a celebration that lasts seven days. In some families girls are also "circumcised" by drawing a little blood from a slight cut on the vulva. For girls the puberty ceremony is most important. This occurs upon first menstruation, when adult clothes are donned. Invitations may be printed, and this celebration also may extend for seven days. At the other end of the life cycle marking death, corpses are buried in the mosque yard according to Muslim rites, but today tombstones are rarely erected for lack of space.

Kinship and inheritance practices do not always follow Muslim tradition. Cross-cousin marriage is preferred and parallel-cousin marriage disallowed in accord with Dravidian kinship and Tamil and Sinhala marriage norms. Some urban Muslims, however, now allow parallel-cousin marriage. An eligible girl's parents are responsible for initiating the search for a groom. The two families negotiate the dowry, and the engagement is finalized by the couple exchanging rings. The girl's family bears most of the wedding expense, feeding several hundred people if possible, while the groom gives clothes and jewels to the bride. In urban areas, Western-style wedding attire is favored, and a brass band is hired. While the wedding ritual itself is simple, as in Muslim tradition, the bride must be present because in Sri Lanka the groom ties the *tali* on her, a wedding necklace generally having a crescent on it.

Post-marital residence is at the bride's house among all Sri Lanka Muslims. Symbolic of this is the feeding of the groom during the wedding, when women of the bride's house give him sweets and milk. If the wedding is conducted in a hired hall, the next day when the groom comes to the bride's house, there is another large feast, with the bride seated on an elevated dais. Wedding gifts by relatives are carefully recorded—except among the more urbane Muslims—so that reciprocal gifts may be exchanged. The couple may reside at the bride's house for some months or for many years. Divorce is rare, and polygyny negligible.

A girl receives as much inheritance as a boy, or even more, contrary to Shariah. Her inheritance is dowry, carefully negotiated before marriage, in addition to which she is often given jewels from her mother. Cash is presented to the girl's husband at the time of the wedding, and a year or so later he begins to manage the property part of the dowry. A son may be given shares in a business. Inheritance may also go to a man's sister's son. An ideal arrangement is for daughter's husband also to be sister's son. These practices reflect a submerged matrilineal tradition which has synthesized with Islam to the extent that it is combined with the practice of a certain amount of *purdah*, or seclusion of women, among the more pious or elite Muslims.

The Muslim peasants on the western side have matrilineal clans. They live among Hindus who also have matrilineal clans, but mostly in separate villages. The clan name and membership are inherited from the mother, and there is a tendency for offices, such as in mosque administration, to be matrilineally inherited. For a girl's dowry, the minimum expectation is a house with its land, and, of course, residence is matrilocal.

Two exogamous clans in this region may be in a reciprocal relationship because of cross-cousin marriage. These clans cannot all be ranked, but some are regarded as high and others as low. Hypergamy is neither an ideal nor practiced, and the chief function of the marriage alliance is to promote affinal ties between bilateral cross cousins. Actually, descent is in some respects bilateral, for the Maulanas claiming some Arab ancestry transmit this through males. The Bawas, a Sufi order, also do, but saintliness is enhanced if it is inherited from both parents. In practice, a fair number of men take brides from any Muslim category, except barber. The matrilineal and peasant status of these Muslim communities around Batticaloa and elsewhere on the east coast distinguish them from other Sri Lanka Muslims.

Clarence Maloney

BIBLIOGRAPHY

Books

Arasaratnam, S. *Ceylon*. Englewood Cliffs, N.J.: Prentice Hall, 1964.
Kearney, Robert N. *Communalism and Language in the Politics of Ceylon*. Durham: Duke University Press, 1967.
Leach, Edmund Ronald, ed. *Aspects of Caste in South India, Ceylon and North-West Pakistan*. New York: Cambridge University Press, 1960.
Nilam, A.R.M. *Education—The Birthrite of Every Muslim Girl*. Lahore, Pakistan: Mohd. Ashraf Press, 1940.
Yalman, Nur. *Under the Bo Tree: Studies in Caste, Kinship and Marriage in the Interior of Ceylon*. Berkeley: University of California Press, 1967.

Articles

Mauroof, Mohamed. "Aspects of Religion, Economy and Society Among the Muslims of Sri Lanka." *Contributions to Indian Sociology* n.s. 6 (1971): 66–83.
McGilvray, Dennis. "Caste and Matrician Structure in Eastern Sri Lanka." *Modern Ceylon Studies* 4:1 (1975).
Ramanathan, Hon. P. "On the Ethnology of the 'Moors' of Ceylon." *Journal of the Royal Asiatic Society, Ceylon Branch* 10:36 (1888).

SUNDANESE Nearly 25 million Sundanese live in the western third of the Indonesian island of Java. They call themselves Urang Sunda, and virtually all consider themselves adherents of Islam. The only significant subgroup of whom this is not true is the Badui, whose members follow pre-Islamic customs and beliefs.

West Java, known as Sunda, traditionally is considered to extend westward from the river Cipamali, although Indonesian anthropologist R. M. Koentjaraningrat gives the rivers Citandui and Cidulang as the border. In any case, the area between the Cidulang and the Cipamali can be considered as transitional, both culturally and linguistically, between the Sundanese and the closely related Javanese (see Javanese).

The Sundanese language belongs to the Malayo-Polynesian language family. Like Javanese, it reflects a strong hierarchical social organization through the use of different levels of courtesy in the choice of lexical items. In speaking, a Sundanese must assess whether the addressee is of higher, lower or equal social status with respect to himself, whether they are intimate, as well as the context, including third parties present, in which the speech act takes place. When referring to himself, the Sundanese must be humble. When referring to one's own house one must use *rorompok*; when referring to the house of another, *bumi*. The fact that the former means shack and the latter indicates a nice home has nothing to do with the conditions of either house. Notions of personal development and process are expressed in the language as well.

The Sundanese seem to have used Javanese and Arabic in their oldest manuscripts. Sundanese literati today actively use the Sundanese language, often in preference to Bahasa Indonesia, reflecting a strong ethnic pride and perhaps a fear of being dominated by the Javanese. The Sundanese enjoy using their language; they are generally masters at rhyming games and creative punning.

The Sundanese are culturally similar to the Javanese but see themselves as differing from the Javanese in personality. They say they are more open and informal than the Javanese, whom they characterize as extremely formal. Other Indonesian ethnic groups are not well known in the villages of West Java, except for the Batak of Sumatra, whom they meet in the urban rice trade. These aggressive traders are seen as rather rude by the soft-spoken Sundanese (see Batak).

Traditional values are still strong in the villages. These values are embodied in a behavior code, *adat* (custom). The aim of *adat*, which is said to have been laid down by the ancestors, is the maintenance of harmony in the village and between people and the cosmic whole of which they are a part. One is to share good fortune, offer help when needed and live so as not to attract the envy or approbation of one's neighbors. Respect is owed to one's elders and people of higher social standing. If these and other rules are followed, one lives in harmony both with one's fellows and with the cosmic design, and one's life is sure to be calm and happy. While the emphasis is on the social, the Sundanese tend to be individualistic and will not interfere in another's affairs unless asked. Major obligations are to live according to *adat* and to respect God.

In the cities, these values ideally are adhered to as well, although the anonymity of urban life and the absence of immediate peer pressure combine to create an environment of greater personal freedom and possible deviation from these norms.

Change is coming slowly to the villages. As youths attend schools in the cities or as people go to work there for a while, they bring back with them new ideas, which slowly find a place in the pattern of village life. The power of *adat* acts to slow the influence of these new ideas and to maintain the balance of life. Recent developments such as television and the improvement of roads into the countryside are bringing changes with which even *adat* is hard pressed to cope.

Historically, Sunda has been considered a cultural backwater. The upland peoples, who were at times called *orang gunung* (mountain men) by those inhabiting the lowlands, seem especially to have been little touched by earlier Indian cultural influences as they spread throughout Southeast Asia.

The only major state to arise in West Java was the kingdom of Pajajaran (1333–1579), with its capital at Pakuan near present-day Bogor. It arose after the defeat of the Sumatran kingdom, Srivijaya, by the Javanese kingdom, Singhawari. Srivijaya had controlled the Banten area of West Java and maintained a port there. With Srivijayan power gone, Pajajaran took control of the area and some of its trade.

Islam first was brought to Java in the fifteenth century by Indian traders who had been converted on the trade routes between Egypt and the Spice Islands. Muslim influence was thus first felt in the harbor areas from where it spread. Banten, in northwest West Java, was Islamized by 1525. In 1579, the Sultan of Banten killed the royal family at Pakuan and forced the nobles and officials to adopt Islam.

Before long West Java fell under the hegemony of the central Javanese Muslim kingdom of Mataram, and shortly thereafter European interest in the area altered the course of history. Parts of West Java became important in the Dutch plantation system. An Islamic holy war against the Dutch was waged in 1880, but failed. A similar occurrence came after World War II, when the Dar ul-Islam movement attempted unsuccessfully to establish an Islamic state.

To be a Sundanese villager is, ideally, to be a rice farmer. The non-Islamic rituals and myths pertaining to growing rice are also the rituals and myths of settled life—of being Sundanese. Yet many village households do not own enough rice land to provide all the daily necessities. The average rice landholding is small, and nearly all villagers engage in small trade, crafts, seasonal farm labor or service occupations besides farming. Cash is in chronically short supply in the villages, as these activities usually bring only small rewards. Other crops grown on dry land include corn, root crops, chili peppers and tobacco, which are often sold in the market. Coastal areas tend to have mixed economies of rice, fishing and/or fish farming.

Sundanese kinship has not been well studied. Descent is reckoned bilaterally and seems to contain traces of an ancient veneration of ancestors. While many persons may be recognized as kinsmen, this has not led to the formation of large corporate kingroups. Relationships beyond the second ascending generation and the first degree of collaterality are seldom recognized among the peasants. Some high status villagers, however, are aware of genealogies linking them with illustrious ancestors. The basic kingroup is the nucelar family, which ideally lives in its own home on its own land. Where money and land are in short supply, a married son or daughter may live temporarily in the home of the parents.

While emphasis is on the independent nuclear family, residence tends to be matrilocal with the households of married daughters clustered near or around the parental house, available land permitting. The parental house ideally is inherited by the youngest daughter, who stays home after marriage to care for her parents. Other additions to the nuclear family may include an aged parent or a destitute relative. These, according to the Sundanese value system, must be cared for by the relatives who are in a better financial position.

In the past, marriage was arranged by the parents of a couple. Today, however, young people make their own choices, although parental approval still is necessary. The wedding consists mostly of traditional ceremonies symbolizing the founding of settled life by the rice goddess, Dewi Sri. The contractual aspect of the marriage receives sanction during the strictly Islamic legal ceremony performed by the *naib* (district religious official).

Polygyny is allowed but is rare. Sundanese men claim they cannot afford more than one wife, and besides, their present wife would not like it. Polygyny is more common among lower-level urbanites and orthodox high-ranking families.

While descent is reckoned bilaterally, relations between the male and female sides reflect ancient Indonesian notions of the distinction between inside and outside. The house (inside) is female par excellence, while the outside is male. Thus houses are built for females, and the men's work area reflects their "outsideness."

This is carried further in Sundanese ideas concerning conception and the raising of children. The father is seen as responsible for the physical existence of the child, while the mother is responsible for its socialization. Children claim to be closer to their mothers than to their fathers, and, like the Acehnese, have a *batin* (spiritual) connection with the mother (see Acehnese).

On the death of parents, their property is divided among surviving children. A problem often arises owing to the difference between Islamic rules and *adat*. Islamic inheritance law allots two-thirds of the property to the male child and only one-third to the female, while Sundanese custom gives equal shares to both. The problem is solved by first following Islamic rules, after which the male inheritor gives his sister one-third of his share to bring the division in conformity with custom.

While Islam has been practiced in West Java for a long time, generally it has been taught only comparatively recently. The *lebbe*, who administers village religious affairs, is responsible for entering births and deaths in the village records and the coordination of Islamic religious instruction.

Progress has been made in the teaching of Islam since World War II, with the result that many old beliefs and practices are now beginning to disappear. Religious instruction is offered in the public schools as well as by private teachers. Yet, while most Sundanese claim to be Muslim, only about 60 percent of the men and 50 percent of the women regularly attend services in the mosque. Islam is a factor among other factors to be taken into account in the solution of daily life problems. Spirits and ancestors continue to play an important role and are often seen as intermediaries between a person and Allah. Practices such as visits to ancestral and other venerated graves, which survive from pre-Islamic and probably pre-Indianized times, are integrated in such Islamic festivals as Maulud, as are the ritual cleanings of weapons and amulets. The non-Islamic spirit world is either partially Islamized or otherwise integrated into popular belief. But as Islamic teaching and awareness of modern urban thought progress, these older phenomena will, over time, undoubtedly fade away.

BIBLIOGRAPHY

Books

Boedhisantoso, Soeboer. "Djagakarsa: A Fruit-producing Village near Djakarta." In *Villages in Indonesia*, edited by R. M. Koentjaraningrat. Ithaca: Cornell University Press, 1967.

Boland, B. J. *The Struggle of Islam in Modern Indonesia*. The Hague: Martinus Nijhoff, 1971.

Bruner, Edward M. "The Expression of Ethnicity in Indonesia." In *Urban Ethnicity*, edited by Abner Cohen. ASA Monographs, No. 12. London: Tavistock, 1974.

Jackson, K. D., and Moeliono, Johannes. *Communication and National Integration in Sundanese Villages: Implications for Communication Strategy*. Honolulu: East-West Center, East-West Communication Institute, 1972.

———. "Participation in Rebellion: The Dar'ul Islam in West Java." In *Political Participation in Modern Indonesia*, edited by R. William Liddle. Southeast Asia Studies Monograph Series, No. 19. New Haven: Yale University Press, 1973.

Kartodirdjo, Sartono. "Agrarian Radicalism in Java: Its Setting and Development." In *Culture and Politics in Indonesia*. Ithaca: Cornell University Press, 1972.

Kennedy, R. *Bibliography of Indonesian Peoples and Cultures*. New Haven: Yale University Press, 1962.

Koentjaraningrat, R. M. "Sundanese." In *Ethnic Groups of Insular Southeast Asia*. Vol. 1, *Indonesia, Andaman Islands and Madagascar*. New Haven: Human Relations Area Files Press, 1972.

Suparlan, Parsudi, and Sigit, Hananto. *Culture and Fertility: The Case of Indonesia*. Singapore: Institute of Southeast Asian Studies, 1980.

Thomas, Murray, et al. *Social Strata in Indonesia: A Study of West Javanese Villagers*. Jakarta: Antarkarya, 1975.

Wessing, Robert. *Cosmology and Social Behavior in a West Javanese Settlement*. Southeast Asia Series, No. 47. Athens: Ohio University Center for International Studies, 1978.

———. "Life in the Cosmic Village: Cognitive Models in Sundanese Life." In *Art, Ritual and Society in Indonesia*, edited by E. M. Bruner and J. O. Becker. Southeast Asia Series, No. 53. Athens: Ohio University Center for International Studies, 1979.

Wilcox-Palmer, Andrea. "The Sundanese Village." In *Local, Ethnic and National Loyalties in Village Indonesia: A Symposium*, edited by G. William Skinner. New Haven: Yale University Press, 1959.

———. "Situradja: A Village in Highland Priangan." In *Villages in Indonesia*, edited by R. M. Koentjaraningrat. Ithaca: Cornell University Press, 1967.

Articles

Horikoshi, Hiroko. "Islam and Social Change Among the Moslem Sundanese in West Java." *Kabar Sekarang* 4 (1978): 41–47.

Noorduyn, J. "Categories of Courtesy in Sundanese." *Bible Translator* 14 (1963): 186–191.

———. "Traces of an Old Sundanese Ramayana Tradition." *Indonesia* 12 (1971): 151–157.

Robins, R. H. "Basic Sentence Structure in Sundanese." *Lingua* 21 (1968): 351–358.

———. "Formal Divisions in Sundanese." *Transactions of the Philological Society* (1953): 109–142.

Rosidi, Ajip. "My Experiences in Recording 'Pantun Sunda.' " *Indonesia* 16 (1973): 105–111.

Vredenbregt, J. "Dabus in West Java." *Bijdragen tot de Taal-, Land-, en Volkenkunde* (Netherlands) 128 (1973): 302–320.

Wessing, Robert. "Inchoative Nouns in Sundanese." *Anthropological Linguistics* 18:8 (1976): 341–348.

———. "Language Levels in Sundanese." *Man* 9 (1974): 5–22.

———. "The Position of the Baduj in the Larger West Javanese Society." *Man* 12:2 (1977): 293–303.

Unpublished Manuscripts

Bowers, Ida I. "Factors Influencing Village Receptivity to Agricultural Innovation: A Case Study in Kabupten Krawang, West Java." Ph.D. dissertation, University of Hawaii, 1972.

Foley, Mary Kathleen. "The Sundanese *Wayang Golek*: The Rod Puppet Theatre of West Java." Ph.D. dissertation, University of Hawaii, 1979.

Horikoshi, Hiroko. "A Traditional Leader in a Time of Change: The *Kijaji* and *Ulama* in West Java." Ph.D. dissertation, University of Illinois, 1976.

Wessing, Robert. "The Social Structure of Economic Behavior in West Java Indonesia." Paper presented at the Seventy-first annual meeting of the American Anthropological Association, Toronto, November 29–December 2, 1972.

Robert Wessing

SWAHILI   The East African littoral, including the islands of Lamu, Mombasa, Pemba, Zanzibar and Mafia, stretches from the Somali-Kenya border in the north to the central coastline of Mozambique. This narrow coastal strip, which is separated from the up-country areas of Kenya, Tanzania and Mozambique by a 300–mile expanse of arid land, is the homeland of the 2.4 million Swahili people to whom the Swahili language is the mother tongue.

The Swahili are far from being alone in this geographical area. They share it with nearly 5 million Northeast Bantu peoples, who live mainly in villages along the coastal strip of Kenya and Tanzania. In Mozambique, the coastal Islamic people, while speaking largely Swahili, are nevertheless culturally more heterogeneous than those to the north because of their greater integration with various southern Bantu groups such as the Yao, Makonde and Makena (see Bantu, Central Tanzanian; Yao).

The Swahili live in the cities and towns, principally Lamu Town, Malindi, Mombasa, Vanga, Dar es Salaam and Zanzibar Town, long the centers of trade with the Persian Gulf. Their Swahili language is basically Bantu, but modified through the need for a medium of communication between the largely Arab traders who sailed (and still sail) their dhows to the East African coast on the seasonal monsoons and the Bantu-speaking Africans of the region. The Swahili are distinguished from the Northeast Bantu not only by the fact that they employ Swahili as their first language (rather than as a lingua franca for intergroup communication) but also by their being 100 percent Sunni Muslim and by various aspects of their material culture (see Bantu-speaking Peoples).

Technically, Swahili is an adjective, as in "Swahili people." Within the Bantu noun-class prefix system, the people are *Wa*swahili, the language *Ki*swahili (which is less complex than most Bantu languages, probably because of the simplification characteristic of languages that have been used as trade languages). Linguistically, then, the Swahili people may be thought of as Bantu; culturally, however, they are distinct.

Swahili is not the name of any tribal group; rather, it is the name of the collection of those groups which share a common culture, Uswahili. They are people who consider themselves to be distinct from other Muslim peoples of the coast: Arabs, Asians and converted coastal Northeast Bantu. Much of the existing literature stresses that Swahili are believed to be the descendants of the children of Arab traders and Bantu women, especially those descendants who cannot trace their ancestry back through an exclusively male line. This definition, however, causes the term to appear as a racial one rather than the cultural or organizational term it is, and it downplays the indigenous cultural aspects which are not by-products of the African-Arab admixture. Arab and Persian influences, certainly, cannot be denied; but this aspect of Swahili origins has been overstated. Uswahili is unique; it has been modified and enriched by these influences, but not formed by them.

Given the range of influences and the number of peoples who have visited the coast, and given that the East African littoral covers a great expanse of land, it would be a mistake to assume that the Swahili represent a homogeneous entity. Yet, as a result of their common language and religion, some degree of homogeneity does exist, and it is possible to describe the life-style and social structures as if they represent a single socio-cultural configuration, bearing in mind that regional variations exist and that the boundaries separating the Swahili from various Arab and Northeast Bantu groups are tenuous and often transparent.

Akin to many of the coastal Northeast Bantu groups and some up country peoples as well, the Swahili are believed to have originated in an area known as Shungwaya on the coast of what is now Somalia. Various groups of these people migrated southward and settled along the coast; certain areas, those points at which foreign traders established their ports, developed into the modern urban centers of the region, each forming its own linguistic and cultural variation of the theme. This southerly migration can still be seen in the gradual depopulation of the northern urban centers. Once settled, these groups subdivided into smaller enclaves occupying separate quarters or neighborhoods, each with its own political structure. For example, the people who originally settled in Mombasa were divided into 12 groups (hence their appellation Thenashara Taifa, or Twelve Tribes) in two factions: the Miji Tisa (Nine Tribes—Kilifi, Mvita, Mtapa, Shaka, Pate, Faza, Bajun Gunya, Jomvu, Akatwa) and the Miju Mitatu (Three Tribes—Kilindini, Tangana, Changamwe). Through subsequent migrations and the influx of peoples from countries of the Persian Gulf, these people were joined by other Muslims, predominantly the Shirazi, purporting an ancestry traced back to the Persian city of Shiraz, and two Arab groups: the Omani, descendants of Arabs from Oman; and the Hadrami or Shehiri, more recent arrivals, descendants of Arabs from the Hadramaut. These people are now culturally nearly indistinguishable from the Swahili and are therefore Swahili if the term is employed as a cultural label. Similarly, coastal Northeast Bantu who have become Muslims and who have adopted cultural traits of the Swahili (such as the Digo) may be included within this category.

Central among the goals of the Swahili is to be considered a well-educated individual and a person of exemplary conduct according to Muslim standards, with respectful children. Part of the achievement of the status of the educated is the ability to exploit the full potential of Kiswahili. Kiswahili is a rich source of wit and subtle irony, the sophisticated use of which adds to a person's prestige. This sophistication is not confined to those having formal education; games and contests involving the interpretation of archaic Kiswahili forms, proverbs and riddles are frequent among all groups.

To have well-mannered children is to demonstrate one's own achievement of the Islamic ideal. As a result, for a child to be told "*huna adabu*" ("you have no manners") is a severe admonishment, reflecting on the child's family as well. The ultimate sanction of a parent against a child is disownership. To be thus disowned is to have severed one's ties with the key social institution of the Swahili: the *jamaa*, loosely translated as "family."

It is not possible to describe a typical Swahili family, either in terms of its personnel or its residence patterns, given the lack of consistency. A man may take up to four wives at a time, although this is becoming increasingly rare. When there is more than one wife, each may live apart from the husband in a separate house with her children and possibly other kin. When more than one wife shares the same home, the first wife, regardless of her age, is considered the senior wife and, as such, is shown the deference accorded an elder. The basic kin grouping, the *jamaa*, takes its name from a word which refers to any focal group of people. Thus, men who meet together regularly at a particular mosque may refer to themselves as a *jamaa*, as may neighbors.

Swahili culture (Uswahili) represents a syncretic mixture of coastal Northeast Bantu and Arab elements with some input of Indian and Persian cultures as well. In recent years, Western influences have been strong, especially in the major port cities. Dress is according to Muslim tradition. Although *purdah* is perhaps less strict than before, it remains a source of conflict between the young and the old. Swahili women cover themselves with black robes called *buibui* when in

public, worn over either brightly colored apparel called *kanga*, on which hu-
morous and often risqué sayings are printed, or *kitenge*, the name for the heavier
cloth from which dresses are made. Men, especially when attending the mosque
or when engaged in other religious activities, wear the white *kanzu* robe over
the colorful *kikoi* (loincloth) or *sarani* (sarong); headgear consists of the embroidered *kofia* cap and, for special occasions, the turban (*kilemba*).

Daily life is largely organized around the five daily Islamic prayer hours,
announced by the call of the *wadhini* of the numerous mosques which are
scattered through the towns. Islam is pervasive, especially among the older
Swahili, and most aspects of their daily activities are carried out in at least
nominal accordance with the laws of the Shafi school, as interpreted by the local
qadi and disseminated by means of pamphlets. Dietary laws, rules of dress and
social etiquette, customs of marriage (polygyny, cousin marriage) and divorce
and rituals of birth and death all derive from Muslim tradition.

However, it is those characteristics that are unique to Uswahili which are of
special interest, aspects which diverge from the tenets of Islam but which are
constrained and influenced by them. Central among these cultural phenomena
are various forms of traditional Swahili poetry, symbolic of the long tradition
of oral (and written) literature of the East African coast. Legendary epics, historical accounts, or topical narratives, the form called *utenzi*, have existed in
written form for centuries, a modified Arabic script originally serving as the
medium of transmission. Other forms include *mashairi*, to be recited or sung,
and *wimbo*, songs, the latter distinguished from the others by the absence of a
standardized rhyme scheme.

Dances (*ngoma*) are community affairs marked by audience participation.
Handclapping accompaniments in syncopation embellish the drum beat, and
cadences, signaled by cues inaudible and invisible to the outsider, are clapped
out in unison by the spectators.

Swahili art, fed by the importation of Asian riches, such as rugs, silk, porcelain
and jewels (for which they trade in return ivory, coconut oil, mangrove poles,
resins and spices), flourished over a long period. Recent economic changes have
effected modifications in life-style and material culture, and much of the glory
of traditional Swahili art now lies hidden in the weathered archways of the towns
and in the ruins of settlements long abandoned. Yet certain art forms thrive to
this day. Many homes have elaborately carved wooden doors, usually with a
center post dividing male and female entries and featuring symbolic floral and
geometric patterns. Similar decorations grace plasterwork friezes. Lamu is known
for its large square chairs with cane seats and inlaid patterns of bone and ivory.
Gold jewelry, including ear plugs (*vipuli*), is another developed art form.

Swahili society is distinguished by a number of characteristic practices, such
as weddings, initiation rites for young girls upon reaching puberty, belief in the
mashetani (devils) said to live in the huge baobab trees of the coast, belief in
the "evil eye" (*jicho la hasidi*), the elaborate greeting ritual and local cooking
styles.

Despite the custom of *purdah* (which has been somewhat relaxed in many Swahili homes), Swahili women have in recent years increased the range and variety of their experience while moving closer to social equality with men. The traditional social roles of women were basically limited to the domestic sphere, with the partial exceptions of those of the *wamiji*, the elder women who held positions of authority over weddings; the *masomo*, instructors of girls undergoing initiation; and the *waganga*, women (and men) trained in the practice of folk medicine. Today, partly through the efforts and influence of the organization called Maendeleo ya Wanawake (Women's Progress), as well as changing attitudes regarding the need for educating all East Africans, Swahili women are entering the economic and social worlds, although the political and religious spheres remain largely male-dominated.

Swahili men fill a wide range of occupational roles. Fishing, long a traditional occupation, has lost ground to clerical work, the running of small businesses and teaching. Many urban dwellers own plantations in the hinterland from which they obtain produce as well as income. Some men are trained as chanters of the Quran, others as prayer callers, although these are not full-time occupations.

In much the same manner as they once absorbed and transformed influences from the Persian Gulf, the Swahili are now demonstrating strong interest in certain aspects of Western culture. Current life-style often shifts between traditional and "modern" Western. Medical clinics established by the British provide care for the sick, while not completely supplanting folk medicine. Many homes in the larger towns and cities now have television, by which they are exposed to Western ideas and standards. These ideas are not viewed as alien or threatening, nor as better and therefore to be copied, but as alternatives from which certain elements can be sifted, judged and fitted selectively into the mosaic of their socio-cultural milieu.

BIBLIOGRAPHY

Books

Adamson, Joy. *The People of Kenya*. New York: Harcourt, Brace, World, 1967.

De Blij, Harm J. *Mombasa: An African City*. Evanston: Northwestern University Press, 1968.

El Zein, Abdul Hamid. *The Sacred Meadows: A Structural Analysis of Religious Symbolism in an East African Town*. Evanston: Northwestern University Press, 1974.

Farsi, S. S. *Swahili Sayings from Zanzibar*. Nairobi: East African Publishing House, 1971.

Jewel, J.H.A. *Dhows at Mombasa*. Nairobi: East African Publishing House, 1969.

Kaplan, Irving, et al. *Area Handbook for Kenya*. The American University FAS, DA Pam 550–56. Washington, D.C.: Government Printing Office, 1967.

Kindy, Hyder M. *Life and Politics in Mombasa*. Nairobi: East African Publishing House, 1972.

Lienhardt, Peter. "Controversy Over Islamic Customs in Kilwa Kivinje, Tanzania." In *Islam in Tropical Africa*, edited by I. M. Lewis. London: Oxford University Press, 1966.
Lofchie, Michael. "The Plural Society of Zanzibar." In *Pluralism in Africa*, edited by Leo Kuper. Berkeley: University of California Press, 1971.
Martin, Esmond Bradley. *The History of Malindi: A Geographical Analysis of an East African Coastal Town from the Portuguese Period to the Present*. Nairobi: East African Literature Bureau, 1973.
Middleton, John, and Campbell, I. *Zanzibar: Its Society and Politics*. London: Oxford University Press, 1965.
Mollison, Simon. *Kenya's Coast*. Nairobi: East African Publishing House, 1971.
Nicholls, C. S. *The Swahili Coast*. New York: Africana, 1971.
Prins, A.H.J. *Sailing from Lamu: A Study of a Maritime Culture in Islamic East Africa*. Assen, Netherlands: Van Gorcum, 1965.
———. *The Swahili-Speaking Peoples of Zanzibar and the East African Coast*. London: International African Institute, 1967.
Salim, A. I. *Swahili-Speaking Peoples of Kenya's Coast (1895–1965)*. Nairobi: East African Publishing House, 1973.
Sutton, J.E.G. *The East African Coast*. Nairobi: East African Publishing House, 1966.
Trimingham, J. Spencer. *Islam in East Africa*. Oxford: Clarendon Press, 1964.
Whiteley, Wilfred H. *Swahili: The Rise of a National Language*. London: Methuen, 1969.
———, ed. *Language in Kenya*. Nairobi: Oxford University Press, 1974.

Articles

Arens, W. "The Waswahili: The Social History of an Ethnic Group." *Africa* 45 (1975): 426–438.
Berg, F. J., and Walter, B. J. "Mosques, Population, and Urban Development in Mombasa." *Hadith* 1 (1968): 47–100.
Chittick, Neville. "Kilwa and the Arab Settlement of the East African Coast." *Journal of African History* 4 (1963): 179–190.
———. "The 'Shirazi' Colonization of East Africa." *Journal of African History* 6 (1965): 275–294.
Eastman, Carol M. "Who Are the Waswahili?" *Africa* 41 (1971): 228–236.
Gower, R. H. "Swahili Borrowings from English." *Africa* 22 (1952): 154–157.
Harries, Lyndon. "The Arabs and Swahili Culture." *Africa* 34 (1964): 224–229.
Hinawiy, Mbarak bin Ali. "Notes on Customs in Mombasa." *Swahili* 34:1 (1964): 17–27.
———. "Social and Moral Concepts in Swahili Islamic Literature." *Africa* 40 (1970): 125–136.
Tanner, R.E.S. "Cousin Marriage in the Afro-Arab Community of Mombasa, Kenya." *Africa* 34 (1964): 127–138.
Whiteley, Wilfred H. "The Changing Position of Swahili in East Africa." *Africa* 26 (1956): 343–353.

Unpublished Manuscript

Sims, Michael. "Kimvita Forms of Address and Greeting in Old Town Mombasa." M.A.
    thesis, Wesleyan University, 1974.

Michael Sims
Population figures updated by Richard V. Weekes

T

TAJIK   The Tajik of Central Asia speak various dialects of the Indo-European language family. About 3.5 million live in northern and northeastern Afghanistan, mainly Badakshan, Parwan, Samangan and Takhar provinces, but also extending into the central Hindu Kush Mountains. Another 3.1 million live in the Soviet Union, about half of these in their own Soviet Socialist republic, but many are scattered throughout the other four Central Asian republics of Uzbekistan, Kazakhstan, Kirghizia and Turkmenistan. About 28,000 reportedly live in Chinese Turkestan. Tajik are also called Sarts or Sarjkolis.

Confusion exists in the literature concerning the Farsi speakers along the Irano–Afghan frontier. Some authorities refer to these flatlander farmers as Tajik, although the people themselves seldom use that designation unless prompted. Usually they call themselves Farsiwan on both sides of the border. It is probably more correct to use the term ''Tajik'' only when referring to the mountain farmers of east-central, eastern, northern and northeast Afghanistan.

The Kohistanis of eastern Afghanistan (along the fringes of Nuristan) and northern Pakistan (along the Afghan border) are sometimes incorrectly labeled Mountain Tajik. This group includes Pashai, Gawarbati, Sawoji, Deghani, Kuwar and Gabr. There is neither ethnic nor linguistic justification for calling these groups Tajik (see Kohistanis; Pashai).

In Afghanistan the Tajik usually refer to themselves by the valley or region where they live, such as Panjsheri, Andarabi, Sanangi and Munjani. Those living farther west in zones dominated by non-Tajik groups often simply call themselves Tajik. The term ''Tajik'' probably comes from *taz* or *taj*, used by early Arab invaders to refer to Central Asian Farsi speakers. In the ethno-historical sense, Tajik tended to differentiate Farsi speakers from Turkic speakers, those two great groups whose struggles for political and cultural dominance preceded Islam—and even continued after its arrival in the seventh century.

Most Tajik are Hanafi Sunni, the major Muslim sect in Central and South Asia. Imami Shia do, however, exist along with sizable numbers of Ismaili Shia, who live scattered from the Bamiyan area to the Wakhan Corridor, the entrance to the Pamir Mountains. Ismaili groups in eastern Badakshan and the Wakhan sometimes speak Pamiri (East Iranian) dialects. Because of the version of Islam practiced by the Ismaili, many Tajik consider them to be a separate, non-Tajik ethnic group, in spite of identical nonreligious cultural patterns.

Ecologically, the Tajik area is mountainous, and the lower hills and valleys are covered with a rich mantle of loess, a natural gift which annually drifts down from the Central Asian steppe. The people usually occupy the parallel valleys which push out of the mountain matrix. No true forests now exist, but scattered stands of holy oak, Asian conifers, plane trees, poplars, willows and pistachio can be found. Seasonally flowering grasses create upland pastures for sheep, goats, cattle, a few camels and some horses. The most popular beast of burden is the donkey.

Most Tajik are mountaineer farmers and herders. They practice a remarkable system of terraced mountainside irrigation and also grow unirrigated wheat and barley at the higher altitudes. The amount and control of water are the key factors. Norse-type water mills line canals and grind the grains into flour. The Tajik bake bread out of anything which can be ground into a flour, including various types of peas and mulberries.

Other crops include maize, potatoes, various vegetables and cotton (called *spinzar*, or white gold), an increasingly important cash crop in northern Afghanistan and a major crop north of the Amu Darya (Afghan–Russian boundary) since before the Russian Revolution. Fresh and dried fruits and nuts, varieties of melons, mulberries, apricots, almonds, walnuts, cherries, plums, figs, apples and grapes (many of which are prepared as red or white raisins) are grown, and many tons are exported.

Fish (trout and *shir mahi*, or milk fish), wild fowl—ducks, geese, partridge, quail, pigeons, doves and sparrows eaten whole—seasonally constitute part of the diet.

Bread literally provides the staff of life among the Afghan Tajik, but a more Russianized diet is followed in Soviet Central Asia, including vodka and champagne, frowned upon by the rural Tajik of Afghanistan.

Settlement patterns occasionally vary from region to region, especially on the collective and state farms of the Soviet Union. Generally, villages in Afghanistan are situated in clustered communities on non-tillable, usually rocky land. Low square or rectangular dwellings, constructed of unbaked mud-bricks and *pise* (pressed mud) with stone foundations dominate the lower valleys. Inside walls are covered with a mud and straw plaster, smoothed by hand. The bricks, also a mixture of mud and straw, are made in wooden molds and dried in the sun. Flat roofs of rammed earth, interlaced with twigs, are supported on mat-covered beams. The roofs must be remudded annually because of the deterioration caused by melting snow and rain. The thick walls and roofs keep the dwellings warm in winter and cool in summer.

Higher up the valleys, the houses become multi-storied and more and more stone is used, until entire huts are constructed of stone. For example, in the Panjsher Valley north of Kabul, the transition is gradual; stone foundations slowly creep up the walls until at Kotal-i-Khawak (Khawak Pass), the four walls and roofs consist of stone, often large rounded river boulders, chinked with mud plaster. Boulders also help hold down the slate roof in the high winds which periodically sweep down the valleys.

Many Tajik dwellings in Afghanistan have two or more stories, and in the winter livestock sleep on the ground floor, which along with the third story may also be used for storage. The family sleeps on the second floor, which becomes warm as the heat from the bodies of the animals rises. The farther west one moves in Afghanistan, the more frequent become the domed beehive huts of the Iranian Plateau.

Basically, agricultural production in Afghanistan involves the control of five elements: land, water, seeds, animal or mechanical power (tractors and accessories increase annually) and human labor. Theoretically, whoever contributes one of the five elements receives one-fifth of the resulting crop. Land and water rights often, although not always, go together. In the Tajik area of Afghanistan, farms are individually owned or owned jointly by extended families. In Soviet Central Asia, although collective and state farms dominate, individually owned plots are important to the economy as a whole.

Most Tajik groups in Afghanistan lead fully sedentary or semi-sedentary lives. Completely sedentary groups are apparently in the minority, but rarely does a group travel more than one day from the *kishlak*, the village winter quarters to which all segments retire. Two semi-sedentary patterns exist. For several weeks in the late summer, whole families move to the highland, unirrigated fields to reap wheat and pick melons. Second, young males (at times accompanied by wives) take the group's livestock to summer alpine grazing meadows. Those moving to the *yayla* (summer quarters) live in either yurts or less sturdy portable dwellings called *chaparis*, which unlike yurts have no latticework foundations. Donkeys, horses and even cattle are used to transport families and their possessions to the *yayla*.

In addition to the localized, short-range, seasonal migration, other seasonal migrations in response to new economic developments have helped diversify the economy of the Tajik. From the mountainous valleys surrounding or adjacent to the various small-scale industrial complexes, men come to work on the agricultural off-season. Many return home from the factories when the agricultural season begins. Many plant operators complain about the resulting instability in the work force. The same pattern has plagued—and continues to plague—the industries of Soviet Central Asia.

Although the migrants, individuals and families, whether seasonal labor or permanently settled, may become urban-based, they remain rural-oriented culturally for at least one generation. Horizontal economic links thrust back to villages, and vertical kin links, including the delicate networks of reciprocal rights and obligations, continue to function. Stresses begin to develop when an urban-based man tries to find a wife in his village or take her away from her extended family to the city or town.

The extra income earned by the part-time migrant is usually used to save for the brideprice, to purchase a truck to enter the transport business, to buy land, or pay off debts, to set up a shop and to buy transistor radios, bicycles, household goods, wristwatches, jewelry and second-hand Western clothes.

Just as the annual cycle is partly dominated by nature, the life cycle of the Tajik is largely shaped by Islam. Birth, puberty (circumcision for the boys; commencement of menstruation for girls), marriage and death are ritually marked, either with a celebration or a mourning. Even in Soviet Central Asia, the intensive anti-religious campaigns have not completely eradicated Islam from the lives of the people.

Although Tajik society is often described as patriarchal (authority vested in elder males), patrilineal (inheritance through the male line) and patrilocal (bride moves to husband's household), many matri-aspects exist. Women are not the "weaker" sex among the Tajik, and their seclusion is more assumed than real. Few decisions are made by the *majlis* (village council) without consulting the women, although they seldom appear at council meetings. Village women rarely wear the *chadry* or *burqa*, commonly a sack-like garment which covers one from head to toe, with an open embroidery face to permit limited vision. Since women work in the fields with their husbands and fathers, wearing such a garment would be impractical. Women do wear a *chadar*, a multi-purpose head shawl which permits the women a modicum of modesty if a stranger approaches, for she can clutch a corner in her teeth, thus partly covering her face. Babies can be wrapped and fed in the privacy of its folds. Small items can be tied in one corner and transported. Women wear distinctive cylindrical caps under the *chadar* and the *chadry*, when the latter is worn.

Sophisticated Tajik urban women in Afghanistan continue to come out of *purdah* (seclusion) and the veil. However, a strange reversal of attitudes occurs when Tajik village women move to towns or cities as their husbands and fathers seek out new economic opportunities. To village women the *chadry* has become a symbol of modernization because to wear it indicates that the wearer no longer has to work in the fields. The new "urban" women flaunt their *chadrys* when they return to their old village homes for a visit.

In the old city sections of the larger urban centers in Tajikistan (and elsewhere in Soviet Central Asia), one occasionally sees a woman wearing the traditional black horsehair veil, although such a costume is illegal in the eyes of Soviet authorities. Tradition and custom die hard.

Among the Tajik (and other ethnic groups) of Afghanistan, most child socialization takes place within the extended family, but more and more schools are being constructed under the new republic (the monarchy was overthrown in July 1973). Literacy, however, is probably no more than 10 percent and remains primarily an urban manifestation. State education dominates in Soviet Central Asia, but family influence is far from finished in rural areas.

A functional, three-generation pattern permeates the lives of the rural Afghan Tajik. The grandparent generation represents the past; grandfathers and grandmothers are walking encyclopedias of the society. The mother-father, aunt-uncle generation represents the present, the actively functioning economic and pro-creating element. The children represent the future and are taught the nonmaterial aspects of life (origin myths, locally oriented beliefs, morality tales, etc.) by grandparents and their economic and social roles by parents, aunts and uncles.

Preferred male marriage is with the father's brother's daughter, which creates competition between male cousins, and sometimes feuds develop and families split. Few Tajik in Afghanistan can afford more than one wife, and Soviet law prohibits polygyny.

The local kinship structure dominates the political processes in the Afghan Tajik areas, although less so in the Soviet Union with its functioning hierarchy based on theoretical Socialist equality.

In rural Afghanistan the *majlis* consist of the heads of all the traditional important families, and the *malik* (headman) is selected from one family, but primogeniture is not necessarily the rule. Charisma and influence with government officials are more important.

The power patterns are gradually shifting, however, as more young men return to their villages after military service or from working on one of the many development projects. The returnees often form informal power groups, based on common experiences outside the village milieu and their pride in newly acquired skills. Out of such grouping have grown incipient worker's unions and political parties which now compete with the *majlis* for loyalty in the village.

The period 1973–1982 brought great changes to Afghanistan's ethno-linguistic patterns. The Republic of Afghanistan (July 1973–April 1978) brought hope that the 3.8 million Tajik (out of a total population of about 15 million) would be able to participate in a broadened political base. Such plans were interrupted by the *coup d'état* of the leftist Khalqi (Masses) Party, which created the Democratic Republic of Afghanistan (DRA) in April 1978. The Khalqi power elite was mainly Pushtun-oriented, however (see Pushtun). Therefore, many Tajik joined the anti-government forces in the civil war which lasted until Christmas Eve 1979, when the Soviets invaded Afghanistan and placed a puppet government in power. The leftist Parcham (Banner) Party became dominant.

The Soviet invasion also sent a signal to the other Muslim countries which border the Soviet Union: Turkey, Iran and Pakistan. The invasion indicated that the Soviet Union would not tolerate the existence of Islamic regimes which might infect its own Muslims in Soviet Central Asia, such as the Tajik, Uzbek, Turkmen, Kirghiz and Kazakhs.

In addition, the Soviet Union has never been able to completely Russify its Central Asian republics, and many Soviet Central Asian Muslims have always felt culturally at home with their ethno-linguistic cousins to the south. Some have actually crossed over into Afghanistan to fight with the Mujahidin (freedom fighters). The numbers are not large, but any number would be a significant dissident indicator to the Soviet leaders.

A sizable number of Central Asian Muslim reservists were called to active duty to participate in the occupation of Afghanistan. The Soviets reasoned that "their" Muslims would be able to fraternize and propagandize freely among Afghans (including the Tajik) because the two groups had languages in common and similar cultural heritages.

The Soviet estimate proved to be correct, but it backfired. Tajik (and other Muslim troops) had been told they were going to Afghanistan not only to "help a fellow Socialist regime in trouble" but to "drive out the interventionists"— the Americans, Chinese, Pakistanis, Iranians, British, Israelis and Egyptians. Finding only Afghans on the scene, many Soviet Muslim troops became disgruntled, and they were withdrawn by the end of February 1980. Before leaving, however, they purchased all the Qurans they could find in the bazaars and took them home to their families.

Inside Afghanistan, the successful resistance of the Tajik of the Panjsher Valley north of Kabul continues to inspire the Afghan Mujahidin in all areas. Four major Soviet offenses have been unsuccessful in gaining control of the valley.

It is little wonder that the Tajik pride themselves on being Tajik, distinct from the other ethnic groups around and among them.

BIBLIOGRAPHY

Books

Baghban, Hafizullah. "Afghanistan." In *Folktales Told Around the World*, edited by Richard M. Dorson. Chicago: University of Chicago Press, 1975.
Caroe, Sir Olaf K. *Soviet Empire: The Turks of Central Asia and Stalinism*. New York: St. Martin's Press, 1953.
Carrere d'Encausse, Helene. *Decline of an Empire*. New York: Newsweek Books, 1980.
Coates, W. P., and Coates, Zelda K. *Soviets in Central Asia*. Westport, Conn.: Greenwood Press, 1969.
Dupree, Louis. *Afghanistan*. Princeton: Princeton University Press, 1980.
————. "Aq Kupruk: A Town in North Afghanistan." In *Peoples and Cultures in the Middle East*, edited by Louise Sweet. Vol. 2. New York: Natural History Press, 1970.
————. "Tajik-Soviet Central Asia and Afghanistan." In *Peoples of the Earth*, edited by Sir Edward Evans-Pritchard and Andre Singer. Danbury, Conn.: Danbury Press, 1972.
————, and Albert, Linette, eds. *Afghanistan in the 1970s*. New York: Praeger, 1974.
Dupree, Nancy Hatch. *An Historical Guide to Afghanistan*. 2nd ed. Kabul: Afghan Tourist Organization, 1977.
Krader, Lawrence. *Peoples of Central Asia*. Bloomington: Indiana University Press, 1963.
Poulton, Michelle, and Poulton, Robin. *Ri Jang: Un Village tajik dans le nord de l'Afghanistan*. 3 vols. Paris: Collège Cooperatif, 1979.

Slobin, Mark. *Music in the Culture of Northern Afghanistan.* Tucson: University of
    Arizona Press, 1976.
Uberoi, J. P. Singh. "Men, Women and Property in Northern Afghanistan." In *India
    and Contemporary Islam*, edited by S. T. Lokhandwalla. Simla, India: n.p., 1971.

Articles

Canfield, Robert. "The Ecology of Rural Ethnic Groups and Spatial Dimensions of
    Power." *American Anthropologist* 75:5 (1973): 1529–1541.
———. *Faction and Conversion in a Plural Society: Religious Alignments in the Hindu
    Kush.* Anthropological Paper, No. 50. Ann Arbor: University of Michigan, 1973.
Carless, Hugh. "The Tajiks of the Panjshir Valley of the Hindu Kush." *Revue iranienne
    d'anthropologie* 1 (1956): 40–54.
Davydox, A. D. "The Rural Commune in the Tadzhik Areas of Afghanistan." *Central
    Asian Review* 13:2 (1965): 121–130 (summary).
Dupree, Louis. "The Green and the Black: Social and Economic Aspects of a Coal Mine
    in Afghanistan." *American Universities Field Staff Reports: South Asia Series*
    7:5 (1963): 1–30.
———. "Saint Cults in Afghanistan." *American Universities Fields Staff Reports: South
    Asia Series* 20:1 (1976): 1–26.
———. "Tajik: Afghanistan and the Soviet Union." *Family of Man* 7:88 (1976): 2442–
    2445.
———. "Two Weeks in Soviet Tajikistan and Uzbekistan: Observations and Trends."
    American Universities Field Staff Reports: South Asia Series 3:4 (1959): 1–27.
Naby, Eden. "The Ethnic Factor in Soviet–Afghanistan Relations." *Asian Survey* 20:3
    (1980): 237–256.

Unpublished Manuscripts

Baghban, Hafizullah. "The Context and Concept of Humor in Magadi Theatre." Ph.D.
    dissertation, Indiana University, 1976.
Hunte, Pamela Anne. "The Sociocultural Context of Perinatality in Afghanistan." Ph.D.
    dissertation, University of Wisconsin, Madison, 1980.
Mills, Margaret Ann. "Oral Narrative in Afghanistan: The Individual in Tradition."
    Ph.D. dissertation, Harvard University, 1978.

Louis Dupree

TAMA-SPEAKING PEOPLES   Seven populations with different names and
separate but neighboring territories speak or have spoken the same language or
dialect belonging to the Tama group of Nilo-Saharan (Eastern Sudanic). Geographically they constitute one body of people straddling the Chad–Sudan border
between longitudes of 21° and 23° 05′ east and latitudes 13° 30′ and 15° north.
Their population is approximately 280,000.

   The Tama proper (63,000) and the Gimr (47,000) are distinguished from the
other five groups by having once formed independent polities. The remaining

five—in Chad, the Abu Sharib (45,000), Asungor (56,000) and Mararit (17,000); in Sudan, the Erenga (33,000) and the 8,000 Mileri (called Jebel by outsiders)— have always been dependent upon more powerful neighboring sultanates.

In literature, the seven groups have been classified according to ethnic names and corresponding territories, suggesting a degree of material and cultural separateness which does not really exist, except for the Tama and Gimr. The Mararit and Abu Sharib are in every respect similar; the same applies to the Asungor, Erenga and Mileri. Linguistically, the two western groups cannot be understood by the three southern and eastern groups, and only to some extent by the Tama proper; the Gimr have spoken Arabic for a long time.

The seven groups may not have common ancestry and origins, and they appear never to have acted in common in case of warfare. The Mararit and Abu Sharib have always been part of the sultanate of Wadai (ca. 1680–1912), while the Mileri, Erenga and probably also the Asungor became part of the Keiri sultanate of Darfur at an early stage of its existence (ca. 1650–1874). Despite occupation by the respective hostile sultanates, this situation remained more or less intact until 1874, when the Darfur sultanate was conquered and became a province of Turko-Egyptian Sudan (see Fur).

The Islamization of the region is associated with the collapse of Tunjur rule towards the middle of the seventeenth century in Darfur and a few decades later in Wadai (see Tunjur). However, the process by which Islam became the religion of the subjects rather than the court and ruling classes was slow and gradual, especially on the fringes of the two empires. A more thorough Islamization of western Darfur began in the 1880s, when its peoples, including the Erenga, Asungor and Mileri, joined the Mahdiyya (1881–1898). The Mahdi, who led the holy war against the Turko-Egyptian conquerors of Sudan, did not distinguish between the religious and political dimension of his struggle. Propaganda for the Islamic faith and for the state which he founded went hand in hand. The peoples of western Darfur accepted and continued to believe in the religious message of the Mahdiyya, but they turned against the oppressive government of the Mahdi's successor, the Khalifa Abdullahi, in what has been called "the revolt of Abu Jummayza."

Abu Jummayza was a simple *faqi* (cleric), born in Dar Erenga of Tama parents. Yet, in 1888 he became the leader of a general revolt in western Darfur which failed. Of the seven Tama populations, only the Mararit and Abu Sharib appear not to have taken part in it. Despite a punitive expedition, the Mahdist state never succeeded in reasserting its authority in the area on a permanent basis, and as soon as the Mahdist threat subsided, the political leaders of the area became locked in a power struggle among themselves. The Masalit made themselves independent from their previous rulers and subjugated the Erenga, Mileri and perhaps also the Asungor (see Masalit).

These peoples have always resented their subjugation. When the Masalit became involved in a series of three wars with the ruler of the restored Darfur sultanate in the first decade of the twentieth century, they tried to shake off the

Masalit by offering to make a separate peace. The same occurred in the period 1910–1912, when the Masalit fought the French conquerors of Wadai, and in 1918, when the British prepared to occupy Dar Masalit. All these attempts ended in failure. The Anglo-Egyptian colonial government ruled Dar Erenga and Dar Jebel as sections of the Masalit sultanate until its demise in 1956. The Asungor became part of French Equatorial Africa in 1923.

The social organization of the different groups is very similar. Extended families form lineages which, in turn, constitute strongly localized clans. Today, members of different clans co-reside, and the main function of the clans is payment of *diyya* (blood money). The Mileri consist of seven clans, while the Asungor and Erenga have several dozen. In fact, the two populations are one and the same, calling themselves Birrung; Erenga is probably the name given to them by the Fur. Their largest clans are the Girga, Awra, Asungor, Shali, Daromi and Dula. There is no data on Mararit and Abu Sharib clans. Internally, all groups are ruled by village chiefs who answer to larger territorial chiefs who, in turn, answer to a high official or even the ruler of the polity to which they belong.

There is little difference in natural resources and climate. All groups inhabit sandy, hilly regions at altitudes varying between 3,000 and 4,000 feet. The eastern Sudanese part is drier during the rainy seasons and has poorer underground water resources, and, as a result of natural and human causes, its vegetation is rather poor. Crops sown are identical: sorghum, maize, peanuts, sesame, watermelons, cucumbers and okra. Where irrigation is practiced, farmers grow tomatoes, onions and chili peppers. The Abu Sharib and Mararit yields appear to be highest. These groups own the most livestock and therefore have the most manure.

Nearly all people in this area live in compounds composed of cylindrical houses 15 to 20 feet in diameter. They use coarsely made, rope-tied reed mats for walls and a conical thatched roof, also from reed.

Tama

The Tama live in the mountainous region of eastern Chad, close to the Sudan border. Their territory, called Dar ("home of") Tama, is bounded by the Mimi and Zaghawa peoples in the north, the Abu Sharib and the Mararit in the west, the Asungor and Masalit in the south and the Gimr in the east. Except for the pastoral Ereigat Arabs, who transhume on Tama territory for part of the year, Dar Tama does not host other ethnic groups. The Tama intermarry with the Gimr, Zaghawa, Asungor, Maba and Ereigat Arabs, but not with the Masalit. Those Tama who inhabit the northwestern part of Dar Tama intermarry only with the Abu Sharib. Tama immigrants in western Sudan intermarry with their hosts, including the Masalit (see Arabs; Beri; Maba; Mima-Mimi).

Although their languages are not mutually intelligible and despite their wide geographical separation, members of both the Tama and Daju-Sila acknowledge kinship ties (see Daju). Today this sense of kinship is expressed, for example, in Sudanese cattle markets, where Daju guarantors sometimes also act on behalf of Tama livestock sellers. The friendly relations between the two populations are probably based on an oral tradition which claims that the Tama sultanate was established in the seventeenth or eighteenth centuries by a "Wise Stranger," who was a Daju elephant hunter of superior skills from Dar Sila. Later, both the sultanates paid tribute to and fought frequent wars with their more powerful overlords, the sultanates of Wadai and Darfur. This has fostered a keen sense of ethnic identity and common fate.

During French colonial rule (1910/1916–1960) and after independence, traditional systems of government such as those operating in the Daju and Tama sultanates were allowed to remain intact in modified forms. The basic free social strata were the rulers (or nobility) and the commoners. Below the latter free stratum were the slaves, who were owned by both rulers and commoners, and the despised, endogamous and "unclean" Haddad (blacksmith caste), who occupied and still occupy an inferior place at the margin of society, dependent on patronage from rulers and commoners alike (see Haddad). The commoners lived in villages which were administered by the heads of land-owning lineages, who distributed land, settled minor disputes, collected taxes and represented their people to the outside world. The lineage heads were, in their turn, subject to a district chief or estate holder, who was usually a close male relative of the sultan. This system operated, in a more or less sophisticated form, in the sultanates of Wadai and Dar Fur and among lesser states of the Masalit, Gimr, Daju and Tama and other polities in the region.

Today this administrative system is in decline throughout eastern Chad and western Sudan. In Sudan the traditional rulers have lost most of their influence and authority as a result of administrative reform and the steady proliferation of government services, whose officials took over many of the tasks once performed by traditional rulers.

In eastern Chad, the system has broken down as a result of rebel activity. Since the outbreak of civil war in 1965, the rebel movements have considered the traditional sultans and minor rulers as collaborators with the central government, which was dominated by non-Muslim groups from the south of Chad. As a result, many members of the traditional ruling families and sultanic dynasties have been killed or forced into exile over the years. By 1981, the sultans of the Runga, Sinyar, Daju-Sila and Wadai had been exiled to Sudan.

The only remaining sultan in eastern Chad is the Sultan of the Tama, who has refused to abandon his people and has managed to come to terms with a succession of intruders over the past few years. Elsewhere the Tama sultans have been described as feudal autocrats who rule their people with an iron hand. It is highly plausible to assume that the traditional system of government depicted above is still in full force in Dar Tama. Coupled with the present sultan's diplomatic skills vis-à-vis invading armies, this perhaps explains why the number of Tama refugees abroad is small compared to others who did not have a strong ruler to negotiate on their behalf.

Dar Tama is a mountainous area with an average altitude of 3,000 feet. A number of seasonal rivers have their source in the area, and except for the sandy northeastern region, Dar Tama is potentially well watered. The area is also relatively fertile, and in years of good rains Dar Tama produces more than it can consume. However, periodic droughts were and still are a normal rather than abnormal feature of the region's climate. Besides, there are strong indications that the Sahel zone of which Dar Tama forms part is subject to gradual dessication. Together with increasing exploitation of land, flora and fauna via animal husbandry, agriculture, hunting and gathering, environmental degradation is rampant, even on a short term.

There are several historical accounts of grave famines caused by droughts, locusts or warfare. These have forced the Tama to migrate to areas with better and more dependable rains. In the western part of Sudan, a fair number of Tama settlements date from before the twentieth century, whereas over the years countless Tama have been absorbed and co-opted by their host populations. The Tama family usually migrated to the southeast and settled among the Fur and Masalit.

The Tama are sedentary cultivators. Their main crops are millet, sesame, peanuts, onions, chilies, and a number of vegetables. They frequently negotiate manuring contracts with the Ereigat Arabs, who receive grain in return for coralling their livestock on Tama fields for a fixed period. The Tama possess less livestock (camels, cattle, goats, sheep) than most of their neighbors, and their animal husbandry is also sedentary, that is, their livestock is tethered in the village each night. Hunting (guinea fowl, gazelles) and the gathering of edible or otherwise useful products of the bush are still important, especially during the rainy season (June–September). Other economic pursuits are trade, crafts, and labor migration to the Nile Valley, which has been practiced from the early decades of the twentieth century.

Tama material culture is broadly similar to that of their neighbors. However, owing to the profusion of lions and hyenas in Dar Tama, the entrance of their homes is lower and narrower than average. Furthermore, Tama women adorn themselves richly with colorful beads, which more than compensates for the poverty of their traditional clothing. Finally, instead of carrying loads on their head, as is common among the Fur, Maba and Masalit, Tama women employ a yoke from which hang two large baskets.

Apart from Guereda, the sultan's residence and district center, there are no major market centers in Dar Tama, but people visit those of Kulbus and Geneina in Sudan and Am Zoer, the main center of the Mararit, the western neighbors of the Tama. As in other parts of eastern Chad, Dar Tama has no modern schools, and Tama boys attend Quran schools. Only a tiny percentage of the Tama can be considered fully literate; those who are are the religious teachers and a few sons of notables who have been sent to school at the instigation of the French colonial authorities in the 1940s and 1950s. The rate of literacy among Tama in Sudan is substantially higher than in Dar Tama itself. Veterinary services, health care and public works are absent in Dar Tama.

The Tama were Islamized in the seventeenth and eighteenth centuries. Since Islam has spread from the center of the state to the periphery, and from the top of the administrative hierarchy to the lower rungs, the rank and file of the Tama may not have embraced Islam immediately. Until the Mahdiyya (1881–1898) and long after, the Tama had the reputation of being xenophobic, wild and ignorant mountain folk who knew no Arabic and very little about orthodox Islam. Even today the Tama firmly believe in witchcraft and practice many animist rites and beliefs. Until recently, no religious brotherhood had gained adherents from among the Tama, who were largely Ansar. Today the tolerant Tijaniyya brotherhood appears to be gaining ground, while returned labor migrants often espouse the more orthodox tenets of Islam in Dar Tama.

Gimr

The Gimr live predominantly on their ancestral land, Dar Gimr, which is situated on the Sudanese side of the international frontier with Chad. The Gimr are bounded on the north by the Zaghawa, on the west by the Tama, on the south by the Erenga and Mileri and on the east by Arab pastoral nomads such as the Darrok and sections of the Mahamid.

Dar Gimr is hilly and sandy with few natural resources, little underground water resources and an average annual rainfall which permits only the cultivation of low-yielding, early maturing varieties of millet and other crops. The area is thinly populated, and emigration is such an old phenomenon that it can be considered an institution. Long-established settlements of Gimr who left their native country as a result of warfare or a natural disaster (drought, locust plague, epidemics) exist in Sudan's Southern Darfur Province. Many Gimr have settled on an individual or family basis in the urban centers of Darfur and in the Nile Valley. They number perhaps 47,000.

In Dar Gimr, the traditional means of subsistence are agriculture (millet, peanuts, watermelons, okra) and animal husbandry. Modern occupations in which the Gimr engage are salaried government jobs, such as clerk and teacher; skilled labor, such as tailor, tanner, driver and car mechanic; and self-employed professions, such as trader and middleman. Kulbus (population 6,000) is the only commercial and administrative center in Dar Gimr, catering principally to Chadian producers and consumers who live across the seasonal river which divides the town.

Although the Gimr speak only Arabic and claim Arab descent via the Jacaliyyin of the Nile River, they probably constitute an indigenous ethnic group which once formed part of the Tama language group.

Gimr historical traditions are more deeply rooted and better attested and remembered than those of the majority of their neighbors. Before the Gimr were conquered by the Keira sultanate of Dar Fur in the early years of the eighteenth century, the Gimr exercised control over the neighboring Zaghawa, Tama and Mileri. The old capital of this Gimr empire is reputed to be a site of ruins in what is now Dar Tama, in Chad. Many of the administrative titles which were in use at that time have survived in Gimr folklore.

The history of the Gimr during the past century has been extremely checkered. As a minor state situated between the two regional superpowers of the nineteenth century (the sultanates of Wadai and Darfur), Dar Gimr had been a tributary of the latter for most of 150 years, when in 1874 their overlords were conquered by the Turko-Egyptian administration, which had ruled the Nile Valley since 1821. The Gimr paid an annual tribute to their new overlords until 1882, when the Mahdiyya defeated this "foreign" government. For a number of years the Gimr paid tribute to the Mahdists. However, when Mahdist armies made their appearance in the region and threatened the autonomy of the Gimr state, the latter joined other, similarly weak polities, and together they rose into armed struggle.

In contrast to the sultanate of Masalit in the south, which made a clever use of the unstable political situation of the time to consolidate and extend its newly found independence from their Fur overlords, the Gimr suffered heavily at the hands of the armies and raiding parties of the Mahdists, the Masalit, the Fur and the French. Between 1880 and 1910 each of them contributed to laying waste to Dar Gimr and putting its people to flight. The Gimr sultan of that time, who saw all these foreign powers imperil his empire's sanctity, acquired the nickname of "the one whose saddle is outside," meaning that he was always prepared to flee.

Dar Gimr became part of the Anglo-Egyptian Sudan after the conclusion of the border negotiations with the French in 1924. Until his death, the Gimr sultan, Idris (who was convinced that he would outlive the British as he had done all previous aggressors), was given carte blanche to tax and administer Dar Gimr. However, many commoners literally escaped the predations of their countless rulers. Also, poor rains, locust plagues and the introduction of taxes to be paid in cash caused great hardship among the Gimr. This, coupled with their hatred of being administered by "foreigners," caused a large-scale migration of Gimr either to regions with a better rainfall and better trading perspectives or to the Nile Valley in search of wage labor and spiritual guidance on the cotton plantations of the Jazira, which were owned by the one who might free them from the "Christian unbelievers," namely, the son of the Mahdi, Sayyid Abd al-Rahman al-Mahdi.

This kind of spiritually and materially induced labor migration was common among many ethnic groups in the border region of Sudan and Chad. Numerous groups, such as the Fur, Masalit, Tama and Daju, took part. Upon their return, they imbued their societies with a sense of injustice gathered at the hands of modern-type officials and traders and with hopes for redress. This has frequently caused violent outbursts in the region.

To date the offspring of the Gimr royal dynasty have fared well as educated and therefore salaried members of the judiciary and administration. This is altogether in line with the fate of other pre-colonial traditional ruling families, who were the first to be trusted and sent to school by their British and French overlords. The pattern applies to the ruling elites of the Tama, Zaghawa, Maba, Masalit, Gimr and other populations in the border area of Chad and Sudan. In Chad, however, their preeminence was short-lived, and many have been forced into exile by rebel groups against the central government. In Sudan, the authority which the descendants of the traditional rulers have acquired because of their education and diplomas is limited to narrow fields in the professional realm. The decision-making process is no longer the monopoly of traditional rulers but is shared by professional administrators, by various elected councils and informally by influential merchants and traders.

Abu Sharib and Mararit

The Abu Sharib of Chad are bounded to the east by the Tama, to the southeast by the Mararit, to the south and west by the Maba and to the north by the Mimi. Their area has permanent water resources at a depth of 6 to 10 feet. The predominance of acacia trees makes it an ideal environment for keeping goats and camels, but cattle are more numerous. The area is visited by transhuming Arab pastoralists, but the Abu Sharib themselves do not migrate. In case of emergency, when droughts or locusts cause a lack of vegetation, they take their livestock to the area of the Tama and Mararit. The Abu Sharib were Islamized at an early date, and lay priests from their ranks were chosen in the past by the sultans of Wadai to convert non-Muslim peoples in the south. Most men manage to perform the pilgrimage to Mecca. Their main market center is Am Zoer.

The Mararit are bounded to the east by the Masalit, to the south by the Asungor, to the west by the Maba, to the north by the Tama and to the northwest by the Abu Sharib. Whereas the Abu Sharib consider themselves an offshoot of the Tunjur, the Mararit are a mixture of Tunjur and Asungor. Culturally both groups show many Maba traits, but they do not practice female circumcision. The Mararit natural resources and means of subsistence are broadly similar to that of the Abu Sharib and Asungor. They own more cattle but less sheep and goats. Both groups own a fair number of transport camels (mostly male), bought from Arab nomads with savings from labor migration. Mabrone is the Mararit capital.

Asungor, Erenga and Mileri

When considered as a single group, the Asungor and Erenga are bounded to the east by pastoral Arabs, to the south by the Masalit, to the west by the Maba and to the north by the Mararit, the Tama and the Mileri. The Chadian Asungor number approximately 56,000, the Sudanese Erenga 33,000. Both Asungor and Erenga are names given by the French and Fur to a congery of clans which speak an identical language but which have different traditions of origin. The

Shali and Awra clans of the Erenga claim descent from a brother and sister of Qamr, the founding father of the Gimr sultanate. The Girga and other clans claim descent from the Missiriyya Arabs. The Mileri (population 8,000) also claim Missiriyya descent. This small group inhabits the area surrounding Jebel Mun (altitude 4,000 feet) and is bounded by the Gimr to the north, the Tama to the west, the Erenga to the south and pastoral Arabs to the east.

Agriculture and animal husbandry are the main sources of subsistence for these people. Colonial rule has brought little blessing in the region. On neither side of the border were industries established or encouraged. Schools were few and late in coming, and public health provisions were and are almost nonexistent, especially in Chad. All seven Tama groups were forced to pay taxes in cash, which they could not earn easily in their home areas, and many migrated to the Nile Valley to work on the cotton plantations of the new colonial middle class. It was an irony of history that the man they looked upon as their savior from the infidel governments, the son of the Mahdi, was one of the biggest cotton lords of the period. Labor migration continues, often motivated by the chaos and lack of opportunity in the Chadian countryside and by the desire to make the Haj. A fair portion of the Erenga and Mileri are engaged in trade or salaried occupations. The main Asungor trade centers are Molou and Toumtouma. Those of the Erenga are Sirba, Abu Suruj, Tendelti and El Geneina. Sileia is the capital of the Mileri group.

BIBLIOGRAPHY

Books

Carbou, H. *La Région du Tchad et du Ouaddi*. Paris: Ernest Leroue, 1912.
Doornbos, Paul, and Binder, M. Lionel. "The Languages of the Chad-Sudan Border." In *Eastern Sudanic Studies*, edited by M. Lionel Binder. Vol. 2. East Lansing: Michigan State University, 1983.
Grossard, Lt. Col. *Mission de délimitation de l'Afrique Equatoriale Française et du Soudan Anglo-Egyptien*. Paris: Librairie Emile Larose, 1925.
Le Rouvreur, Albert. *Sahariens et sahéliens du Tchad*. Paris: Editions Berger-Levrault, 1962.
MacMichael, H. A. *A History of the Arabs in the Sudan*. 1922. Reprint ed. Cambridge: Cambridge University Press, 1967.
Nachtigal, G. *Sahara and Sudan*. Translated by A.G.B. and H. J. Fisher. Vol. 14. New York: Barnes and Noble, 1971.
O'Fahey, R. S. *State and Society in Dar Fūr*. New York: St. Martin's Press, 1980.
————, and Spaulding, Jay. *Kingdoms of the Sudan*. London: Methuen, 1974.

Article

Hasan, Imam Hasan, and O'Fahey, R. S. "The Mileri of Jebel Mun." *Sudan Notes and Records* 51 (1970): 152:161.

Unpublished Manuscript

Kapteijns, Lidwien. "Mahdist Faith and Sudanic Tradition: The History of the Masalit Sultanate, 1870–1930." Ph.D. dissertation, Free University of Amsterdam, 1982.

Paul Doornbos
Lidwien Kapteijns

TAQALI   The people of Taqali live in the northeastern Nuba hills of Kordofan Province, Republic of the Sudan. Taqali denotes a place rather than a group of people; in the local language, a person from Taqali would be an Aqali or Ugali. But many people have forgotten that language, and they refer to themselves in Arabic as *nas* or *ahl* ("people," "folk," "family") Taqali or Taqalawin. They have a strong sense of common identity while yet recognizing that their ancestors came from many different ethnic groups. They may number perhaps 180,000 (see Nuba).

Taqali people live in two distinct settings, highlands and plains. Highlanders and plains dwellers often speak different languages, live in different styles of houses, eat different foods and seldom attend each others' weddings or funerals. Yet both groups are Muslim. Like a language, Islam is central to both communities and, to some extent, a medium of their culture. Highlanders and plains people communicate through Islam. When they do make mutual visits, they are often under religious auspices. A common language, Islam nonetheless assumes different guises or dialects in the different social settings of highlands and plains.

Reaching altitudes of 4,500 feet above sea level, Taqali's peaks are among the highest in the Nuba hills. Even more important than the hills' height is their distribution. Unlike many other parts of the hills, Taqali's peaks cluster together and their pediplains merge into a single upland plateau above a sharp escarpment. Exposed granite in sheets and domes, as well as high peaks, break the surface of the plateau's gravelly soil. Despite its rockiness, the soil supports a wide variety of trees and other wild plants.

Terraces which rib the steep hill slopes attest to past farming on even the most difficult terrain; now, most highlanders cultivate on the upland plateau. Households—a man, his wives and their unmarried children—grow sorghum, some millet and peanuts. Wives and daughters generally work on separate fields from husbands and sons. Women also devote themselves to the careful planning, irrigation and transporting of onions, as well as gardens of okra, beans and maize. When clearing or harvesting requires more labor than a household can supply, people organize a *nafir*, or cooperative work party. Iron-tipped dibble sticks and short hoes with fan-shaped blades are the farmers' main tools. Growing peanuts as a cash crop ties highlanders to regional and national commercial networks. They plant a large proportion of their land with peanuts but do not influence the system of markets and transport upon which they depend for the collection and distribution of their product. No local men own shares in lorries or trade in large quantities.

Small villages dot the plateau and even fill occasional level spots on the peaks. Round or irregularly shaped thatch fences enclose household buildings, usually a kitchen, sleeping quarters and granaries. People once built houses of stones carefully pieced together, but now they say that this requires too much work and instead simply erect a thatch frame and plaster it inside and outside with mud. Sometimes a woman who shares a husband with another wife supervises her own compound, and widows often live alone. In many villages, a few households include a special room, the *tawrin*, where young unmarried girls from the neighborhood come to sleep together. The *tawrin* survives despite the disapproval of the local religious *shaikh*, whose opinion is usually greatly respected. Unmarried girls and young wives, although they work extremely hard, enjoy relative freedom of movement and independence in the highlands compared to the plains, where the strictures of what people identify as fathers' authority and "our religion" fall most heavily on girls and young women.

Villages often have one large, rectangular building still made of stone—the mosque. Most highlanders now adhere closely to Islam's requirements, especially prayer. Local Islamic institutions are basic to communities. Most villages have a Quranic school, called a *tukaba* locally, where boys come nightly to study and recite by the light of an open fire. Older boys belong to a youth organization, a junior branch of the Qadiriyya brotherhood, which marches on Muslim holidays. On the same occasions, older members of the Qadiri hold a *dhikr*, forming a circle, chanting to a drumbeat and swaying rhythmically until some reach a state of *hal*, or ecstasy.

A single Islamic organization, the Qadiriyya *shaikh's* settlement at Tasi, dominates the social and religious life of many highland villages. The *shaikh* heads a network of clerics and missionaries and receives vows of allegiance from local men entering the Qadiri. He dispenses Islamic and Western medicine, food and advice. Sick or disturbed people recuperate at Tasi. Villagers visit the *shaikh* on holidays and work in his peanut fields. The *shaikh* proselytizes in other parts of the Nuba hills, sometimes as far south as Kau-Nyaro. The easiest way for an outsider to visit the highlands is to find a pilgrim or cleric on his way to Tasi and, once there, to meet people from all over the highlands and travel with them to their villages. The *shaikh's* ties to a large religious center on the Blue Nile provide a major—although not the only—route by which highlanders visit the Sudanese Jazira.

The Tasi settlement and creation of a Muslim society in the highlands probably dates from after the militant, pan-Sudanese Mahdiyya (1881–1898). Before that, highlanders certainly knew of Islam but seem to have incorporated Islamic elements into their own religion, which, like many ideologies in the northern Nuba hills, emphasized spirit possession and sacrifice of animals. Middle-aged people recall their grandparents' descriptions of traditional rituals, which Arabic-speakers indiscriminately refer to as *sanab* or *sibr*. As late as the 1920s, rain sacrifices were practiced publicly in Taqali's outlying hills. Even today, rumor has it that a woman performs such ceremonies in the privacy of her own home. Interestingly, while men reach a state of ecstasy through *dhikr*, some highland women also experience a kind of possession. These hill women, however, could also be drawing on the regional heritage of spirit possession, in which women were frequently mediums.

Although Muslims, people in the hills do not consider themselves Arabs. That ethnic label, in fact, bears the negative connotation of the nineteenth-century Arab raiders who kidnapped highlanders and sold them into slavery. Men, however, and most women speak Arabic as well as the local tongue, one of the Taqali-Taqoi cluster of dialects. The model of people using Arabic in the market and their own language at home holds true only to a limited extent. The actual mix of language and social context is much less clear-cut and sometimes seems coincidental or arbitrary.

The Taqali kingdom's historic center and the ruins of royal compounds all lie in the hills. In 1929, however, the Taqali king, his family and his entourage descended from the hills for better access to roads and markets. They built the town of Abbasiya and the small villages which surround it. Plains villagers and Abbasiya townsmen constantly exchange visits and form a single community.

Members of Taqali's royal family assumed local political offices under Anglo-Egyptian administration (1898–1956) and had considerable independence until the revolution of 1969. Even after they were removed from formal office, however, local people and guests came to them for advice, mediation and hospitality. The king's descendants continue to wield considerable local power and influence, forming Abbasiya's political elite.

Most of Abbasiya's people say that they belong to a *khashm al-bayt* ("mouth of the house"). In other parts of Sudan, the *khashm al-bayt* denotes a lineage of a certain depth. Each *khashm al-bayt*, however, includes the descendants of a particular king, his allies (including maternal kin) and his clients. As a political institution, the *khashm al-bayt* system no longer functions; nevertheless, some people still call on *khashm al-bayt* ties for paying compensation in property damage suits.

At first glance, Taqali would seem to be a patrilineal society. Formal inheritance and affiliation are traced through paternal ties, relations *bi-l-adan*, or "through the bone," as Abbasiya people say. At the same time, however, people speak of the importance of relations *bi-l-lahm*, "through the flesh," or maternally reckoned links. Abbasiya townspeople, as well as highlanders, act on a wide network of relations including those affected by or traced through women and, especially, common residence.

Plains inhabitants work as government employees, farmers or traders. Primary and lower secondary schools and a rural administrative office employ local people. The mosaic of sand, gravel and clay soils which surrounds Abbasiya supports a greater variety of crops than do the hills. Traditionally, the most valued farmland bordered a rainy season watercourse whose yearly floods deposited rich, alluvial soils. These projects are lowland Taqalis' most profitable and most sought after agriculture.

Both men and women farm, but men have access to mechanized and co-operative farming. Old and middle-aged women often insist on working their fields, but such labor is not regarded as proper for young women, especially the daughters or wives of town notables. If these women work, they teach at the local girls' school or type and file at the government office.

Traders whose ancestors came from the Nile Valley after the Mahdiyya live in a separate quarter next to Abbasiya's central market. Their houses are even more prosperous than those of the king's descendants. One of the largest and richest compounds in Abbasiya belongs to a merchant family linked by marriage to both the Taqali political elite and a family of prominent local Muslim clerics. Some local people also trade but often cannot compete on a large scale with the descendants of these Nile Valley immigrants.

A second group of immigrants is much more segregated from Abbasiya's social and economic life. The cotton boom of the 1920s attracted settlers from the stream of northern Nigerians entering the Sudan in the early twentieth century. These people, known locally as Fallata, built a quarter on the northern edge of town. A separate mosque where men meet for daily prayers marks the separation between the Fallata community and the rest of Abbasiya; however, Fallata men join the Friday prayers at the main Abbasiya mosque. Abbasiya's Taqili inhab-itants bear ambivalent attitudes towards the Fallata. On the one hand, they say the Fallata fail to perform the religious duty of circumcising girls, yet their clerics possess great mystical powers. Fallata, they say, are "dirty," yet their experts circumcise Taqali boys and extract babies' incisors for health reasons. Fallata have a low status in the community, yet individuals have become highly respected.

In contrast to the highlands, plains inhabitants, especially Abbasiya towns-people, participate in many institutions which bring them into contact with people from other parts of Sudan and provide services such as schools, busy bi-weekly markets, medical dispensary, local government and agricultural offices, several Islamic brotherhoods including Qadiri, Tijani and Sammani, the large mosque and weekly court hearings. Some of these are primarily religious institutions, and Islam is apparent in all of them. No specifically Islamic institution, however, claims plains people's attention in the same way that Tasi attracts highland villagers.

Aside from its view of the two hill ranges, Abbasiya looks like it could be situated in another part of northern Sudan, probably central Kordofan or the Jazira. In a social sense, the town has turned its back on the hills and faces north and east. Townspeople most often travel to Kordofan and the Nile River valley. As a local elite, descendants of the kings go there for employment or education. Commercial ties pull traders in the same directions.

Taqali people who live in Abbasiya and neighboring villages consider them-selves as sharing a common northern Sudanese culture whose center is in the Nile Valley. Unlike highlanders, they stress the dual Islamic and Arab contri-bution to their history, saying that an immigrant from the northern Nile River valley founded the Taqali kingdom and converted its people to Islam. While even the most devout Muslim highlanders remember traditional religious practices, Taqali's male elite asserts that such rituals disappeared with the establishment of the kingdom. Only a few old women in Abbasiya mention the ceremonies or leaders of the former religion.

BIBLIOGRAPHY

Article

Elles, R. J. "The Kingdom of Tegali." *Sudan Notes and Records* 18:1 (1935): 1–35.

Unpublished Manuscript

Ewald, Janet J. "Leadership and Social Change on an Islamic Frontier: The Kingdom of Taqali, 1783–1900." Ph.D. dissertation, University of Wisconsin, 1982.

Janet Ewald

TATARS   The terms "Tatar" (meaning "archer") and its European pejorative, "Tartar," conjure images of marauding Mongol hordes with all manner of barbaric customs wreaking violent disruption on civilized European communities. Tartar is especially synonymous with terror because it is a term that applies to the legendary people of Tartarus who rose up from the depths of the earth.

One of the most confusing of ethnonyms, Tatar is a name given to a variety of both Turkic- and non-Turkic-speaking peoples long before the coming of Islam. After Islam arrived, Russians tended to call all Muslims Tatar.

Today the name is used to describe several related, but spatially disparate, peoples. Most of the modern Tatars cannot be regarded as direct descendants of the Tatar-Mongols of Manchuria who overran much of Eurasia in the thirteenth century. Instead, the overwhelming majority of Tatars are distant scions of the Turkic-speaking Volga-Kama Bulgars, who first adopted the name as their own in the sixteenth century.

Though racially mixed, Tatar relatives of the early Mongol armies are comparatively few in contemporary Soviet society. These are the Crimean Tatars, who as a whole may number half a million people, or under 8 percent of all Tatars. During World War II, the Soviet government forcibly removed the Crimean Tatars from their homeland in the Crimean peninsula, falsely accusing them of collaborating with German occupying forces. They were resettled in several locations in Siberia and Central Asia, mostly in Uzbekistan. Their precise number is not known; however, they probably compose the majority of the 650,000 Tatars listed in the 1979 census as residents of the Uzbek Soviet Socialist Republic. They, like the Volga Tatars, are Muslim.

The picture is also muddled by the variety of names used by the Tatars themselves. For instance, prior to the Bolshevik Revolution, many Volga Tatars

called themselves Turks, Bulgars or simply Muslims. Today, they declare themselves as Tatar, but scattered rural groups use different names. In Siberia, for
example, Tobol'sk Tatars refer to themselves as Tobolik, while Tara Tatars call
themselves Tarlyk.

Worldwide, the Tatars number more than 7 million people. The majority
(actual percentage unknown) are Sunni Muslims of the Hanafi school. A strong
and apparently growing minority is composed of non-believers or converts to
other religions.

Within the Soviet Union, the Tatars are the sixth largest ethnic group in the
country, consisting of 7.3 million persons. (They are the leading ethnic minority,
after the Russians, in the Russians' own republic, the R.S.F.S.R.) Some 60
percent are found in the Volga-Kama Basin, Uzbekistan, and Kazakhstan. Although barred by Soviet law from possessing their own full republic because
their homeland does not border on a foreign country, almost 2 million Tatars
are located within the Tatar Autonomous Soviet Socialist Republic (A.S.S.R.).
Beyond the confines of their own administrative unit and nearby Bashkiria and
Central Asia, the Tatars are dispersed widely in over 30 different provinces of
the Soviet Union. The majority of them (56 percent) now live in cities, but this
proportion ranges from 35 to 40 percent in parts of Siberia and the Middle Volga
region to 88 percent in the Ukraine. As a general rule, the share of urban Tatars
rises outside of their traditional homeland along the Volga (Tataria and Bashkiria)
and especially in heavily industrialized areas (e.g., the Donetsk Basin).

Non-Soviet enclaves of Tatars are situated in China, Romania, Bulgaria and
Turkey. As many as 11,000 of them reside in the cities of Quququk and Kulja
in Xinjiang Province of the Chinese People's Republic. These Chinese Tatars
derive from traders who settled in the country during czarist times, as well as
from anti-Soviet refugees. European Tatars number close to 76,000, with 40,000
in Turkey, 26,000 in Romania and 10,000 in Bulgaria. Many of these people
descend from emigré Crimean Tatars who fled from czarist rule at the end of
the eighteenth century. Non-Soviet Tatars tend to rank among the best-educated
minorities within their respective countries.

Linguistically, the Tatars belong to the northwest Turkic Kipchak branch of
the Altaic family of languages (see Turkic-speaking Peoples). They and the
Bashkir speak similar tongues (see Bashkir).

As their history would indicate, their anthropology varies from persons with
obvious Mongoloid features to those strongly influenced by neighboring Finno-
Ugric peoples. In general, they have oval faces with scant facial hair.

Despite considerable industrial expansion in Tataria itself, many Tatars seek
work outside of their native region, following a tradition of mobility established
before 1917. In their capital city of Kazan, where they are a minority of less
than 300,000, Tatars head up 30 percent of the small enterprises but only 20
percent of the top management. Among their places of work are shipyards,
railroad yards, auto repair shops, clothing, shoe and felt boot industries, machine
building (agricultural implements, aircraft, typewriters and calculators) and the

Soviet Union's largest polyethylene plant. One-third of the Soviet Union's poly-ethylene and synthetic rubber and half of its movie and photographic film are produced in the republic. Outside of the capital, petroleum processing and pro-duction, along with the new Kamaz truck works on the Kama River, are important realms of employment. Due to their emphasis on education, Tatars make up 30 percent of the faculty of the University of Kazan, one of the most respected institutes of higher learning in the Soviet Union.

Their urban concentrations notwithstanding, many Tatars are employed in agriculture, especially in the Volga region. Here they dwell predominantly on collective farms on which grain (wheat, rye, oats and millet), hemp, legumes and other fodder crops are grown. Dairying and poultry raising are also important pursuits.

Contemporary Tatar city residents live no differently from ordinary Russian families, but in rural areas some pre-revolutionary traditions persist. Soviet studies of the state of Islam in rural Tataria in the early 1970s indicate that the religion is very much alive. More than 30 percent of the Tatars questioned were true believers, whereas another one-fifth were undecided. About 51 percent favored circumcision, and 40 percent said they celebrated Muslim holidays. Kurban Bayram and Uraza Bayram and Maulud, though officially attacked, have not been eradicated, and mosques are full on such occasions.

Prior to the revolution, the Tatars, in comparison to other Muslims in Central Asia, possessed medium-sized extended families and maintained exogamous relations. The modern rural Tatar family on a Soviet collective farm is now reckoned in two, or at most three, generations living under the same roof. With the diminution of even these moderate extended family ties in the Soviet period, the need for a clear knowledge of genealogy has diminished also. The complexity of the pre-revolutionary system of terminology can be illustrated by the fact that almost 200 different names for relatives existed in the Tatar language at one time.

Social structure remains strongly patriarchal, with the father serving as legal head of the household and private plot. His word is final on all issues confronting the family. Work, although not strictly regimented, is divided along traditional lines. The women cook, carry water, wash clothes and tend livestock; the men engage in labor requiring more physical strength. As a further indication of male dominance, the head of the household is also in charge of family earnings, determining when and how the income should be spent. In case of his death, the father is succeeded as family head by his widow or, if his wife is already dead, by his oldest brother or sister.

Despite continuing patriarchy, the rights of women in Tataria continue to improve. Between 1959 and 1970, for instance, the number of women holding higher degrees among Tatars rose 22 percent. (For men, the same increase was 30 percent.) In the Volga-Ural region, women have begun to appear in mosques.

In modern Tatar families, the allocation of property is handled differently than in the past. For example, in the absence of brideprice and, more importantly, substantial private property, there are no allotments of land, draft animals or agricultural implements. Legal inheritance is transmitted according to the traditional system. The demise of the head of the household never requires, as it did before 1917, the division of property among heirs.

Formal religious weddings, while rare, are still observed. Religious weddings are 1 in 10 in Siberia, for instance. Marriage, prior to the revolution, was a complicated process steeped in formality and ritual, lasting for as long as a year or more. Today, the procedure is simplified and varies regionally. The Kazan Tatars conduct a "two-cycle" wedding ceremony after the betrothal of the couple and after the parents on both sides have come to an agreement. The ceremony usually occurs in the bride's house and is followed by daytime celebrations consisting of only the elderly or male guests and by nocturnal festivities including only the young or female guests. Participants in the revelry must be invited. Gifts in money or in kind are accepted after the nuptials. In contrast, Volga-Kama Tatars are married at the groom's house, and guests of both sexes may attend simultaneously. For them, the holiday begins with the taking of the uniquely Tatar "honey and butter," after which the young couple is presented with money by the men and with cloth remnants by the women. The wedding ceremony continues for several days. On two of those days, the groom's parents are guests of the matchmaker, who is still used in traditional Tatar marriage rites.

Although brideprice is forbidden by law, the dowry, consisting of domestic furnishings, is permissible. Before 1917, the bride could not be given away without the dowry, lest her parents lose face. Today, as Socialist civil marriages become more frequent, the importance of the dowry is declining. Polygyny is also forbidden by Soviet law. Although instances of it are alleged to occur in Central Asia, none has been reported among the Tatars.

Compared to other Soviet Muslim groups, Tatars, particularly those living in cities, reflect a relatively high frequency of intermarriage with Russians and Volga Finns. In fact, fewer than a quarter of all Tatars today attach importance to ethnicity in marriage. In the Tatar A.S.S.R., between 3 and 15 percent of the Russian skilled workers and plant managers, respectively, had Tatar spouses in the 1970s. Among Tatar workers in the same categories, the percentages were 10 and 29 percent, respectively. Tatars in Central Asia also often intermarry with local populations.

This relatively high proportion of mixing with non-Muslims, especially with Russians, appears to have taken its toll among Tatars, who continue to speak their native language and do not choose to speak a second language. Because of their geographic position in the Russian republic, Tatars always have had a higher share of bilingual speakers than other Muslims (60 to 70 percent speaking Russian as a second language versus a Central Asian average of about half that), but now Tatars increasingly have begun to adopt Russian as their primary language, a decision that is tantamount to becoming an ethnic Russian. The group experienced the highest rate of Russification among Soviet Muslims between 1970 and 1979.

In keeping with this trend, the maintenance of the faith has become increasingly less visible. The ritual prayer has been made difficult, except among the very old, in modern Soviet society. Today Tatar *mullahs* try to organize prayers in such a way as to avoid interfering with the work day, at the beginning of the day and at lunch breaks. Other practicing Muslims make up for the conflict by attending Friday congregational prayers.

The modern Tatar mosque is much more than a religious center, serving also as a center for socialization and friendship. There were over 2,000 mosques in Tatarstan before 1917; by 1931 these had fallen to 980; today there are far fewer than 400, but "unregistered congregations" are alleged to meet in private homes.

Other traditions have also suffered. Almsgiving (*zakat*) is forbidden by law, although some parishes get around this by making contributions to the mosque. Fasting is similarly condemned because it reputedly weakens the body of the worker, but as many as half the Tatars may fast. Observation of the Haj is limited to a privileged few.

Most Tatars observe *sabantuy*, or "rites of spring," an ancient agricultural festival that is today celebrated simultaneously with the anniversary of the founding of the Tatar Republic (June 25). Contemporary *sabantuy* festivities include instrumental music, singing, dancing, wrestling, horse racing and track and field events. (A few Soviet Olympic champions have been Tatar *sabantuy* winners.) These early summer rites have their origin in shamanism, many of the sects of which are said to exist in rural areas even now, for example, ancestor, tree and animal cults. The chief difference between the ancient and modern festival is that women are active, if not major, participants. In today's Soviet society, Tatar women enjoy near equal status with men in many ways.

As festivals have acquired a "Soviet flavor," so also have customs. Pictures, formerly forbidden in native houses, are seen now on the walls of Tatar homes and apartments. Older collective farm members wear traditional dress, but younger members wear city-style clothes. Customary women's headwear has been reduced in size. More vegetables have been added to the Tatar diet, with wheaten flour a principal staple. Unlike devout Muslims, only slightly more than 25 percent of the Tatars will eat pork, and Soviet ethnographers observe that "few modern Tatars engage in Islamic fasts."

Politically, Tatars may be underrepresented. Already relegated to autonomous rather than full republican status, meaning 11 deputies instead of 32 are sent to the Soviet of Nationalities, the Tatar party representation lags almost six percentage points behind the proportion of its constituency within the republic. Comprising 50 percent of the population, the Tatars make up only 44 percent of the local party membership. The situation is bound to be worse where the group is an obvious minority.

BIBLIOGRAPHY

Books

Allworth, Edward, ed. *The Nationality Question in Soviet Central Asia*. New York: Praeger, 1973.
————. *Soviet Nationality Problems*. New York: Columbia University Press, 1971.
Bacon, Elizabeth, E. *Central Asians Under Russian Rule*. Ithaca: Cornell University Press, 1966.
Conquest, Robert. *The Nation Killers*. London: Macmillan, 1970.
D'Encasse, H. C. *Decline of an Empire*. New York: Newsweek, 1979.
Fisher, A. *A History of the Crimean Tatars*. Stanford: Hoover Institution Press, 1979.
Katz, Zev; Rogers, Rosemarie, and Harned, Frederic. *Handbook of Major Soviet Nationalities*. New York: Free Press, 1975.
Krueger, John R. *The Turkic Peoples*. Bloomington: Indiana University Press, 1968.
Lattimore, Owen. *Pivot of Asia*. Boston: Little, Brown, 1950.
Levin, M. G., and Potapov, L. P. *The Peoples of Siberia*. Chicago: University of Chicago Press, 1964.
Nekrich, A. M. *The Punished Peoples*. New York: Norton, 1978.
Poppe, Nicholas. *Tatar Manual*. Bloomington: Indiana University Press, 1968.
Symmons-Symonolewicz, Konstantin. *The Non-Slavic Peoples of the Soviet Union*. Meadville, Pa.: Maplewood Press, 1972.

Articles

Potichnyj, P. J. "The Struggle of the Crimean Tatars," *Canadian Slavonic Papers* 17:2–3 (1975): 98–102.
"A River of Brotherhood." *Soviet Life* (1982): 47–48.
Rorlich, A. A. "Acculturation in Tatarstan: The Case of the *Sabantui* Festival," *Slavic Review* 41:2 (1982): 316–321.
Shuiskii, S. A. "Muslims in the Soviet State: Islam, a Privileged Religion?" *Oriente Moderno* 7:12 (1980): 383–402.

Unpublished Manuscripts

Bennigsen, Alexandre. "Modernization and Conservatism in Soviet Islam." Paper presented at the Conference on Religion and Modernization in the Soviet Union under the auspices of the American Association for the Advancement of Slavic Studies, San Marcos, Texas, March 21–23, 1976.

Mandel, William M. "Urban Ethnic Minorities in the Soviet Union." Paper presented at the Fifth National Convention of the American Association for the Advancement of Slavic Studies, Dallas, March 16, 1972.

                                                                                    Victor L. Mote

TAUSUG   The Tausug ("people of the sea current"—*taw* or *tao*, "people or men"; *sug*, "sea current") are politically, economically and numerically the dominant Muslim group in the Sulu Archipelago of the Republic of the Philippines. Their other names are Tawu Sug, Taw Suluk, Sulu Moro, Sulus, Joloanos and Jolo Moros. Although the majority reside on Jolo Island, they are also found on the Sulu islands of Pata, Marunggas, Tapul, Lugus and Siasi; in the provinces of Zamboanga del Sur and Cotabato (Mindanao) and parts of coastal Basilan Island; and in Sabah, where they are known as Suluk. They number perhaps 600,000.

The coast-dwelling Joloan Tausug refer to themselves as Parianon or Tau Higad (*higad*—"seacoast"), while Guimbahanon or Tau Gimba (*gimba*—"far from the sea") is used to identify inlanders (who are at most only a few miles from the sea). Tau Pu (*pu*—"island") is the name for Tausug who live on islands other than Jolo. These terms do not signify cultural distinctions but only geographic or occupational differences.

The language of the Tausug appears to be transitional to the Filipino-Bisayan languages (spoken on Negros, Cebu and Leyte) from the other languages of Mindanao-Sulu. All Filipino languages belong to the Malayo-Polynesian linguistic family. The language, concentrated in the Tausug region and exhibiting little dialectal variation, is also the lingua franca of the Sulu Archipelago. A Malay-Arabic script is used primarily for religious materials.

The Tausug probably came to Sulu from northeastern Mindanao; possibly their movement southward was associated with the expansion of Chinese trade in Sulu during the Yuan period (1280–1368). The first penetration of Islam into Jolo is uncertain. The initial contact may have occurred as early as the Sung period (960–1280), when Arab trade was active with south China via the Sulu Archipelago. Another group involved in the diffusion of Islam may have been Chinese Muslims (see Hui). Islam was later invigorated in Sulu by Sufi missionaries, originating in Arabia or Iraq, who came via Malaysia and Indonesia.

The sultanate of Sulu was established in the middle fifteenth century, presumably by the legendary Salip (Sharif) Abu Bakkar or Salip ul-Hassim. By this time, most Tausug were Muslims. Theoretically, all the peoples of Sulu were united under the sultanate, although actual control over some groups was nominal. The Tausug traded extensively with China until the middle of the nineteenth century and adopted some Chinese foods, weights and measures and items of clothing.

After the Spanish colonized the Philippines in the sixteenth century, the Tausug and they were in conflict for nearly three centuries. Catholic Spain wished to contain Islam in the southern Philippines, to stop the slaving and looting raids of the Tausug (and their allies) and to gain control of the Moluccas from the Portuguese. The first Spanish attack on the town of Jolo occurred in 1578. The Spaniards occupied Jolo town between 1635 and 1646, when they were forced to retreat to their garrison on Zamboanga. A permanent garrison was reestablished in Jolo town in 1876.

After Spain was defeated by the United States in 1898, stiff Muslim resistance to Americans delayed their control of Jolo Island until 1913 (Jolo town was occupied in 1899). Under the pax Americana, illegally owned guns were collected, and slavery was swiftly abolished. In 1915, under the Carpenter Agreement, the sultan of Sulu, Salip Jamal ul-Kiram II, relinquished his claim to secular powers but retained his religious authority.

During and after World War II, the Tausug gained possession of American firearms. As a result, the Philippine government has not been able to control completely the interior of Jolo. The Tausug revived piracy and made lightning raids on coastal settlements of Mindanao and Basilan.

The Tausug, and other peoples of Sulu, have never been at ease under a government centralized in Manila, be it run by Spaniards, Americans or Filipinos. They have continually sought a separate state either through revolt or petition. One main cause that initiated the current rebellion in Sulu was the Philippine army's execution in the late 1960s of Muslims trained at Corregidor ostensibly for guerrilla operations in Sabah. The present Moro National Liberation Front had its origins among Muslim students in Manila, many from Sulu. Its leader is from Jolo. Some of the heaviest and most destructive fighting in the recent past occurred in Sulu, especially Jolo. A battle between Muslim and Christian Filipino soldiers in 1974 destroyed nearly two-thirds of Jolo town. Many people fled to Zamboanga, while others went to Sabah.

The livelihood of the Tausug is based primarily on agriculture and fishing, while some meat animals are raised (cattle, chickens, ducks). Although some Tausug are swidden (slash-and-burn) farmers, most raise rice in permanently diked non-irrigated fields. There are three annual harvests: first, corn and other cereals (millet, etc.); second, rice; and third, cassava. Rice is intercropped with maize, millet and cassava. Cassava, often mixed with grated coconut, is toasted, steamed or boiled. Corn often is eaten raw. Alternatively, the kernels are dried, ground, mixed with rice and boiled. Other crops include peanuts, eggplants, string beans, beans, tomatoes, onions and yams.

The major cash crops are coconut (for copra), coffee, abaca (Manila hemp) and fruit. The need for money to buy guns and ammunition has stimulated the production of copra since World War II. Fruit, often growing wild, includes durian, banana, mangosteen, lanzon, jackfruit and oranges. Some fruit is shipped by motorboat to Mindanao, Cebu and Negros. Copra and abaca usually are sold to Chinese middlemen on Jolo Island.

Fishing, which may be either a full-time or part-time occupation, is done in motorized boats in offshore coastal waters. Nets, hook-and-line, and various types of bamboo traps are used. Some fishermen use piscicides and illegal dynamite charges to secure catches. At night, fishermen may use kerosene lanterns to attract squid and sardines to their lines. Other fish caught include tuna, shark and ray fish. The fisherman's surplus often is sold by middlemen to Jolo Island. Another important economic activity is smuggling European and American goods imported to Southeast Asia to Jolo and Zamboanga and selected Philippine products to various Southeast Asian ports.

Except for Jolo town, and for coastal villages and small towns of fishermen, the Tausug typically reside in dispersed communities. They live near their fields (of which a farmer may have several in different localities). Another reason nucleated settlements are rare is that the sense of community among the Tausug is weak.

The typical Tausug dwelling is a lumber and bamboo-walled rectangular room with a thatched gable roof raised six to eight feet above the ground on piles. The house usually is surrounded by a series of elevated porches leading to a separate kitchen. The residence often is enclosed by a stockade for protection of household members and penning of the family's animals.

The smallest territorial unit is the household or a cluster of households, often of kinsmen. The next larger unit is the hamlet (*lungan*), which again may include many related members. Still larger is the community (*kauman*), which has a common name and headman. The solidarity of the *kauman* depends on such factors as the amount of intermarriage among its residents, the effective authority of the headman and attendance at a common mosque.

Jolo town is the political, economic, educational and transportation center of Sulu and the traditional site of the sultanate. Inter-island vessels move daily between its port and other smaller islands to the south and Mindanao to the north. An airport connects the island with the rest of the Philippines. This largest city of Sulu includes several schools, modern stores, hospitals, movies and government offices. The population consists of Tausug, Sama, Bajau, Chinese, Christian Filipinos and some Americans and Europeans. Jolo town was badly damaged in 1974 during the fighting between Christians and Muslims. The population of Jolo town dropped from 45,000 in 1970 to 37,600 in 1975.

The ideal marriage among the Tausug is still one arranged by the parents. However, among younger Tausug, courting may occur and the young people select their own mates. First and second cousins are favored spouses since their parents are kinsmen and the problems of inheritance are simplified. A series of negotiations occur between the two groups until the bridewealth (the bride's outfit and food and drink for the festivities) and other wedding expenses are requested by the girl's family and agreed upon by the boy's family. Popular times for a wedding are after the end of the Ramadan fast and during the month in which Muhammad was born. The bridewealth must be given to the girl's family before the wedding, which is held in the groom's residence with the *imam* officiating. The newly married couple first lives with the wife's family. Later they may reside with the husband's family or, preferably, establish an independent household.

Sometimes a spouse is obtained through elopement or abduction. Although the young man must pay a fine, this costs less than obtaining a wife through formal negotiations. A few well-to-do Tausug have plural wives who live in separate houses. Divorce is permitted, although most Tausug regard it as a drastic and serious decision. Probably fewer than 10 percent of all marriages end in divorce, usually caused by barrenness, gambling, mistreatment of the children or nonsupport.

Most Tausug consider a marriage without children a misfortune. During her pregnancy, a woman observes dietary and behavioral taboos, such as not bathing in the sea to prevent stillbirth. Birth occurs in the woman's residence (or in the hospital in Jolo town), and the new infant's arrival is announced to the community by the striking of gongs. The *imam* comes to pray for the new child, who may be given an Arabic or American name. For the first several years the child is believed to be vulnerable to harmful spirits and may wear a protective amulet. When the child is about two years old the *paggunting* is held. In this ceremony, a lock of the child's hair is cut by the *imam*, who then pours perfume over its head and prays. The elaborateness of the ceremony depends upon the status and resources of the parents.

As the children grow older (5 to 12 years of age), they may study the Quran with a private tutor (*guru*), and a public ceremony (*pagtammat*) is held when they are ready to recite. A son is circumcised (*pag-islam*) in his early teens. A similar ceremony (*pagsunnat*) without surgery is held when a daughter is only six or seven years old. Children attend public schools, although not many finish their elementary education and still fewer graduate from high school.

It is considered improper for the two sexes to mix in public, but they do have a chance to become acquainted at weddings, funerals and religious affairs. Among the younger generation, especially those living in towns, this restriction on the interaction of the sexes has weakened. Tausug women are not veiled and may engage in commercial activities.

The Tausugs' concept of life after death is a melding of Islamic and indigenous beliefs. They believe each person has four souls that leave the body on death. The body of the deceased goes to Hell, where his length of punishment is determined by his misconduct when living. Eventually, however, all Tausug reach Heaven.

The Tausug are Sunni, followers of the Shafi school. They worship God (Tuhan) and accept the Five Pillars of Faith, although only the elderly or pious say their daily prayers and few can afford to make the pilgrimage to Mecca. The *imam* is an important community figure, for he recites the prayers in the mosque and officiates at the life-cycle crises. Since few Tausug understand Arabic, most of their knowledge of Islam is gained through the oral tradition.

The Tausug recognize three categories of law. First is Quranic law, in which God punishes violators after their deaths. Second, interpreted religious law, codified by the sultan and other Tausug officials, deals primarily with such crimes as murder of relatives, slander and adultery. Third, customary law mediates conflicts involving traditional mores including offenses of honor.

All illness, accidents and other misfortunes ultimately are traced to God's will. However, the Tausug have retained many of their pre-Islamic religious beliefs and rituals. Their world is filled with environmental spirits that may cause sickness or good fortune. Folk curers (*mangungubat*), usually older men, may be sought by Tausug when ill, although they also consult the *imam* and physicians residing in Jolo town. The traditional medical specialists, who presumably receive their powers to heal through dreams or instructions by other curers, use herbal remedies and prayers. Good health is also maintained by following various taboos or wearing charms consisting of Arabic words.

The kinship system of the Tausug shares many general characteristics of Filipino society. The Tausug kindred has been defined as a group of relatives traced bilaterally with whom one has intimate ties involving reciprocal duties and obligations. Selected members of the kindred are the primary support of a Tausug during the various life crises and on other occasions when assistance is needed, for example, financial assistance or aid in disputes or feuds. The kindred never act as a unified group, and in crisis a person's support depends on the situation and his persuasive power. One outstanding characteristic of Tausug social structure is the absence of corporate groups.

The typical Tausug family consists of parents, their unmarried children and one married child and spouse and their offspring. In one typical region of Jolo, the average family had seven members. Fully extended as distinguished from stem families are uncommon. Children (*anak*) are taught to respect and obey their father (*ama*) and mother (*ina*). The relationship between the husband (*bana*) and wife (*asawa*) is intimate, frank and usually enduring. Sibling solidarity is intense, especially in supporting challenges to family unity and honor. The eldest son has the right of primogeniture.

The Tausug recognize various types of formal friendships. Among these are ritual friendships created when two men swear everlasting allegiance upon the Quran and in front of witnesses or when the headman, sensing a potential conflict between two Tausug, urges them to become ritual friends. A Tausug who violates ritual friendship bonds is believed to sicken and possibly die. Having many friends is crucial, for their support is essential in either a feud or a dispute.

Tausug social stratification has been described as status-conscious egalitarianism since all men are regarded as equal, although some have greater wealth or power. An individual's power is determined by such factors as the size of his following, wealth, titles, personal courage and the number of guns owned. People of the highest status are those with titles either inherited through relationship with a sultan or bestowed by him. The second level includes most Tausug who lack such titles. The lowest level is slaves (including debt slaves). During the first half of the nineteenth century the raids to obtain slaves reached their zenith. An immense number of these captives were incorporated into Tausug (and Samal) society. Many later improved their lives, while their offspring, by at least the second generation, often were assimilated into Tausug society. At present slavery is rare among the Tausug.

(Author's note: This summary account has drawn heavily on the publications of anthropologist Thomas M. Kiefer, historian Peter Gowing and Dr. Juanito Bruno, a prominent Tausug educator.)

BIBLIOGRAPHY

Books

Bruno, Juanito. *The Social World of the Tausug: A Study in Philippine Culture and Education*. Manila: Central Escolar University Research and Development Center, 1973.

Chaffee, Frederic H., et al. *Area Handbook for the Philippines*. The American University FAS, DA Pam 550–72. Washington, D.C.: Government Printing Office, 1969.

Gowing, Peter G. *Muslim Filipinos: Heritage and Horizon*. Quezon City: New Day, 1979.

———, and Robert D. McAmis, eds. *The Muslim Filipinos: Their History, Society, and Contemporary Problems*. Manila: Solidaridad Publishing House, 1974.

Kiefer, Thomas M. "Tausug." In *Ethnic Groups of Insular Southeast Asia*, edited by Frank M. LeBar. Vol. 2. New Haven: Human Relations Area Files Press, 1975.

———. *The Tausug: Violence and Law in a Philippine Moslem Society*. New York: Holt, Rinehart and Winston, 1972.

———. *Tausug Armed Conflict: The Social Organization of Military Activity in a Philippine Moslem Society*. Philippines Studies Program Research Series, No. 7. Chicago: University of Chicago Department of Anthropology, 1969.

Majul, Cesar Adib. *Muslims in the Philippines*. Quezon City: University of the Philippines Press, 1973.

Tiamson, Alfredo T. *Mindanao-Sulu Bibliography Containing Published, Unpublished Manuscripts, and Works in Progress: A Preliminary Survey. And W. E. Retana's Bibliographia de Mindanao (1894)*. Davao City, Philippines: Ateneo de Davao, 1970.

Warren, James F. *The Sulu Zone: 1768–1898. The Dynamics of External Trade, Slavery and Ethnicity in the Transformation of a Southeast Asian Maritime State*. Singapore: Singapore University Press, 1981.

Articles

Abubakar, Asiri J. "To Win a Tausug Maiden: Love Is a Family Affair." *Philippine Heritage* 3 (1977): 607–611.

Bruno, Juanito. "The Social World of the Tausug." *Archipelago* 2:15 (1975): 38–46.

Escio, Carlos A., Jr. "The Taosug Concept of Marriage in the Light of Catholic Principles." *Unitas* 32 (1959): 230–232.

Ewing, J. Franklin. "Birth Customs of the Tawsug of Siasi Island, Philippines, with Comparative Notes." *Anthropological Quarterly* 33 (1960): 129–133.

———. "Food and Drink Among the Tausug, with Comparative Notes from Other Philippine and Nearby Groups." *Anthropological Quarterly* 36 (1963): 60–70.

———. "Housing Among the Tawsug of Siasi Island, Philippines, with Comparative Notes." *Anthropological Quarterly* 35 (1962): 10–34.

———. "Illness, Death, and Burial in the Southern Philippines with Special Reference to the Tausug." *Anthropological Quarterly* 40:1 (1967): 13–26, and 40:2 (1967): 45–64.

———. "Some Rites of Passage Among the Tawsug of the Philippines." *Anthropological Quarterly* 31 (1958): 33–41.

———. "Subsistence Activities of the Tawsug with Comparative Notes." *Anthropological Quarterly* 36 (1963): 183–202.

Hassan, Irene; Adjawie, Ricardo; and Rixhon, Gerard. "Selected Tausug Poems." *Sulu Studies* 3 (1974): 115–129.

Jainal, Taun Iklali; Ruppert, David; and Spoehr, Alexander. "Kinship in a Tausug Poblacion." *Ethnology* 10 (1971): 73–97.

Jainal, Tuwan Iklali; Rixhon, Gerard; and Ruppert, David. "Housebuilding Among the Tausug." *Sulu Studies* 1 (1972): 81–121.

Kasman, Edward S. "Birth and Death Among the Tausugs of Siasi." *Unitas* 35 (1962): 291–340.

Kiefer, Thomas M. "Institutionalized Friendship and Warfare Among the Tausug of Jolo." *Ethnology* 7 (1968): 225–244.

———. "Modes of Social Action in Armed Combat: Effect, Tradition, and Reason in Tausug Private Warfare." *Man* 5 (1970): 586–596.

———. "Power, Politics, and Guns in Jolo: The Influence of Modern Weapons on Taosug Legal and Economic Institutions." *Philippine Sociological Review* 15 (1967): 21–29.

———. "Reciprocity and Revenge in the Philippines: Some Preliminary Remarks About the Tausug of Jolo." *Philippine Sociological Review* 16 (1968): 124–131.

———. "The Tausug Polity and Sultanate in Sulu: A Segmentary State in the Southern Philippines." *Sulu Studies* 1 (1972): 19–64.

———. "Tausug Thunder." *Filipino Heritage* 4 (1977): 1071–1077.

Rixhon, Gerard. "Ten Years of Research in Sulu. Selected List of Recent Works on Sulu." *Sulu Studies* 1 (1972): 1–18, 143–162.

Stone, Richard L. "Intergroup Relations Among the Taosug, Samal, and Badjaw of Sulu." *Philippine Sociological Review* 10 (1962): 107–133.

Donn V. Hart

TEBU The Tebu, also referred to as Toubbou, Tibbu and Tubu, constitute a large ethnic group (235,000) dispersed throughout the Saharan and Sahelian zones of Niger, Chad, Libya and Sudan. The actual composition of the Tebu is difficult to determine since the term does not refer to a political, social or geographical unit. Depending on the individual and the context, the name "Tebu" can be used to include different groups of people.

The name "Tebu" itself derives from two words: "Te" in the Tebu language is the name of the Tibesti massif on the Libyan–Chad border; *bu* is an archaic suffix still in use in the Kanuri area meaning "people of." The Tebu are, therefore, the people of Tibesti. However, the Tibesti is occupied today by only about 13,000 people, most of whom call themselves Teda. Throughout the ages the formidable volcanic massif of Tibesti has served as a refuge for groups of Tebu. The history of the area is one of constant migration, expansion out of and retreat into the mountains. This constant movement has spread the Tebu peoples, language and culture far from its Tibesti core, and the cyclical pattern has confused any concept of linear development. Intermarriage with other groups and migrants from other areas have also played their part. Today the Tebu lack any concept of a common Tebu ancestor which might link all members by real or fictive kinship ties.

The sense in which the name is used by Tebu themselves is generally as a *yele*, a category or sort of person. In its widest sense, it includes all those people speaking languages of the Saharan branch of the Nilo-Saharan language family, not all of which are mutually intelligible. The larger components of this category would be: the Kanembu in the Lake Chad area, the Daza and Aza in the Niger and Chad Sahel, the Teda in the central Tibesti and Libya, the people of Ennedi, the Bideyat and the Zaghawa of Sudan. They resemble each other greatly in material culture, social organization and culture (see Beri; Kanembu).

In its narrowest sense, Tebu as a category refers only to those groups who speak mutually intelligible dialects of the Tebu language. This is composed of two linguistic groups: those who speak Dazaga and those who speak Tedaga. The groups who speak Dazaga are primarily the Daza and Aza, but there are other smaller groups such as the Dowaza and the Wajunga, in all totalling about 208,000 people. Except for certain rare individuals, the only people who speak Tedaga are the Teda of Tibesti. Dazaga is the lingua franca and the only language in which poetry and songs are composed even by the Teda, whose knowledge of Dazaga is often imperfect. Intermarriage and economic interest have formed multiple kinship ties between groups.

The Teda number perhaps 20,000. There are approximately 13,000 in the Tibesti itself and another 3,000 in the southern-most oases of Libya, and then others scattered in Niger and Chad. Most of the Teda are isolated in the mountains. They have herds of goats and in some areas camels. Their general pastoral pattern is transhumant and cyclical within specific clan-guarded territories. The general economy is tripartite. The women do most of the herding. The men go to market to sell the animals and engage in long-distance commercial ventures. The two together sow and harvest seasonal crops and dates in nearby oases. They are not purely pastoral, but their economy has a definite pastoral base.

Teda are divided into a dozen patrilineal clans. Each member traces descent to a common ancestor, who was generally a rogue escaping from some other area into the Tibesti. Of the clans of the present Teda, few seem older than ten generations. There are clans descendant from Daza, Dowaza, Tuareg, Arab and Bideyat ancestors. At the arrival of the French, the central Tibesti was ruled by a *derdai*, or chief of one of the clans. His authority never reached as far as the northern Tibesti, which was tied to Kufra, the Sanussi and the Italians. There is every reason to believe that he used personal skill to solidify powers under colonial rule that he never could have had in the traditional system. It seems that previously the *derdai* was a guardian rather than a chief.

The dominant rule governing actual social organization is one of bilateral kindred and relationship rather than patrilineality. Marriage is kindred exogamous and ideally virilocal. The last 15 years of drought and revolution have so reduced the economic viability of the Tibesti that men remain absent most of the year and residence has become commonly uxorilocal, as the women stay with the children to care for the herds. The basic unit of social organization is the nuclear family. Friendship plays at least as large a part in determining cooperation as does relationship.

The Teda are 100 percent Muslim. Their Islamization dates very probably to early in the Arab conquest, although most education in the Quran and the intricacies of the legal system was a result of the establishment of Sanussi schools in Libya and Chad within the last 100 years. Although there are some traces of pre-Islamic belief, most of these have been incorporated into the Muslim system. The Islamic calendar is followed. Prayer is regularly practiced by both men and women, as is the Ramadan fast and *zakat*. Inheritance is Islamic. Although the Tibesti does not shelter many *mallamai* (men educated in the Quran) since few return to live permanently in the mountains, there are families boasting five generations of *mallamai*. Two clans' ancestors seem to have been *mallamai* educated in southern Chad and Niger. The Libyan oil boom has enabled more and more Teda, both men and women, to perform the Haj.

The Teda are considered to be solitary, rather tough mountain and desert people. They have been on fairly hostile terms with their Arab and Tuareg neighbors through the colonial period. Independence from rather than cooperation with each other is the modus vivendi. Teda values are basically Spartan in character, softened somewhat by an Islamic sense of the more you give, the more your receive.

The last 10 years have been particularly difficult for the Teda. The Tibesti has served as a refuge for the guerrilla forces fighting the Chad government for the rights of the Muslims, who constitute 50 percent of the population in Chad. One-half of the Tibesti belong nominally to Chad and half to Libya, although since the French left the area has not received the benefits of any government.

The Daza constitute by far the largest and oldest group within the Tebu. There are reported to be 181,000 in Chad and 30,000 in Niger. Generally characterized as cattle and camel pastoralists of the open Sahel, the Daza, like the Teda, engage in commerce and agriculture. Their pastoralism involves frequent moves in the vicinity of clan-owned wells with seasonal movement between wells. They are divided into patrilineal clans which are not linked to those of the Teda. These clans seem to identify more with territory than do the Teda, and patrilineality is slightly more emphasized. Their culture is very similar to that of the Teda. They live in similar loaf-shaped mat tents. Circumcision is performed on boys of 10 to 12. Marriage involves a seven-day ceremony and divorce is frequent, divorcees holding an independent and respectable status in the community. A basic difference in social organization seems to result from the necessity for large family groups of Daza to camp and herd together, creating a sense of community and cooperation. The prolonged presence of the men in the camp and their importance in herding seems to place more emphasis on patrilineality. The openness of the Sahel, the common congregation of large groups of people and the greater wealth derived from cattle have helped make Daza values slightly more hospitable than those of the Teda.

Like the Teda, the Daza are 100 percent Muslim, but most of the Islamic influence comes from Nigeria and West Africa. *Mallamai* are numerous even in the camps, and *hajjis* are becoming more frequent.

Numbered among the Daza population are their vassals, the Aza. These are Tebu of the blacksmith caste. In parts of Niger, they form their own cattle camps and villages with their own cattle brands derived from those of the Daza clan to which they are tied. In most of the Tebu area, however, the blacksmiths travel singly or in nuclear families among their Teda or Daza masters. Called Duude, they are not supposed to have an animal brand, nor to be able to marry a free Teda or Daza. The men are metalworkers and net hunters. The women are leatherworkers, potters and hairdressers. The men also play the big drum, the *kidi*, and sing praise songs to which the free men and women dance. All Aza speak Dazaga, even those in the Teda areas. Slaves also exist among both the Teda and Daza. They are called children of their owners. Rarely do they marry, and their condition is even harder than that of their poverty-stricken masters. Children of freed slaves form a caste called Kamaya (see Haddad).

The Dowaza are Dazaga speakers inhabiting the large oases and pastures just to the south of the Tibesti in Chad. They regard both the Daza and the Teda with some derision as primitive country folk. The Dowaza are town people, with farms and cattle and camels pastured nearby. They appear wealthier than the Teda or Daza, but the Teda scorn them as somehow less "free." They live in stone houses and have had much more significant access to both Islamic and French culture.

The Wajunga live around two small lakes to the east of the Tibesti. Reputed to be of different origin, they now speak Dazaga and intermarry with Teda and Daza. They are, however, considered slightly lower in status and have no animal brands of their own, but their importance was increased by the establishment of a Sanussi school and later by a French post there and by its use as a resting point for caravans on the north–south route. Wajunga also played a part in the Chad revolution when it split into factions by opposing the leaders supported by the Teda. This resulted in several battles between Teda and Wajunga forces in Murdi which were portrayed by both sides in ethnic rather than political terms.

Kim Kramer
Population figures updated by Richard V. Weekes

BIBLIOGRAPHY

Books

Bremaud, O., and Pagot, J. "Grazing Lands, Nomadism and Transhumance in the Sahel."

In *The Problems of the Arid Zone*. UNESCO Proceedings in the Paris Symposium. Arid Zone Research, No. 18. Paris: UNESCO, 1962.

Briggs, Lloyd Cabot. *Tribes of the Sahara*. Cambridge: Harvard University Press, 1960.

Cline, Walter. *The Teda of Tibesti, Borkou and Kawar in the Eastern Sahara*. General Series in Anthropology, No. 12. Menasha, Wisc.: George Banta, 1950.

Greenberg, Joseph H. *The Languages of Africa*. Bloomington: Indiana University Press, 1966.

Johnson, Douglas L. *The Nature of Nomadism: A Comparative Study of Pastoral Migration in Southwestern Asia and North Africa*. Chicago: University of Chicago, Department of Geography, 1969.

Nelson, Harold D., et al. *Area Handbook for Chad*. The American University FAS, DA Pam 550–159. Washington, D.C.: Government Printing Office, 1972.

Nyrop, Richard V., et al. *Area Handbook for Libya*. 2nd ed. The American University FAS, DA Pam 550–85. Washington, D.C.: Government Printing Office, 1973.

Articles

Heseltine, N. "Toubbou and Gorane: Nomads of Chad Territory, Notes on Their Origins." *South African Archaeological Bulletin* 14 (1953): 21–27.

Kramer, Kim St. Clair. "The Effects of the Drought on the Teda of the Libyan Tibesti." *Proceedings of the First Conference on the Geography of Libya*. (University of Benghazi) (1975).

TEMNE   More than one-third of Sierra Leone's 3.8 million people are Temne, of whom some 425,000 are Muslim. The Temne are the country's largest ethnic group and occupy about one-third of the land area of this West African country.

The Temne (Timne, Timmanee) inhabit the northern portion of the coastal bush area and adjacent sections of the central rain forest. They belong to the culture province labeled Kru and Peripheral Mande by George Murdock in *Africa: Its Peoples and Their Culture History*. This entity includes most of the ethnic groups of Sierra Leone and Liberia and some of Ivory Coast and Guinea.

David Dalby, in "The Mel Languages: A Reclassification of Southern 'West Atlantic,' " places Temne in the Mel group of J. H. Greenberg's Congo-Kordofanian language family. Although they have not been well studied, there are dialectical differences manifest among Temne speakers.

Oral traditions suggest that the ancestral Temne inhabited part of the Futa Jalon plateau in Guinea, from whence they moved southwest to their present habitat. Temne were present on the peninsula of Freetown when the Portuguese first arrived. Land for the first settlements in the Freetown area was acquired from Temne rulers. Temne comprise the largest ethnic segment in Freetown and still regard the city as "theirs" since it was built on Temne land.

The majority of Temne, perhaps 80–90 percent, are farmers. The staple crop is rice, both upland (dry) and swamp (wet) varieties. A lengthy list of secondary crops is headed by cassava, peanuts, millet and a wide range of fruits and vegetables. Many of these, together with oil palm products, tobacco, ginger and kola, enter the market as cash crops. Fishing is carried out by a variety of techniques along the coast and in the rivers. The human density is high enough so that hunting is of negligible importance. Limited grazing and other factors prevent the keeping of cattle on a large scale, but some cows and a variety of other domestic animals are found throughout the area. As opportunities have developed, Temne have taken wage work of various kinds. Large numbers participated in the "diamond rush" into Kono District in the years 1952–1961, and before its closure they made up most of the work force of the Marampa iron mine. Many Temne thus have migrated to work sites and to the growing urban areas, both the provincial cities and the national capital, Freetown.

Islam reached the Temne in the seventeenth century, brought by occasional itinerant Muslims. The Sierra Leone area generally escaped the devastating wars of militant Islam in the Sudan, but the victory of Muslim Fulani (Fulbe) in Futa Jalon late in the eighteenth century did affect the Temne, albeit indirectly. Fulani and various Manding-speaking Muslim traders also penetrated the Temne area as a coastal-oriented trade became established (see Manding-speaking Peoples). Muslim traders settled along the developing trade routes, married locally and, on a limited basis, proselytized. The early Muslim centers in the Temne area from Mabun to Forodugu and from Chinti to the Yoni chiefdoms, began in these ways. During the twentieth century, Islam expanded and continues to expand at the expense of both Christianity and traditional belief systems. Non-Temne Muslims who have settled among the Temne practiced the normative Maliki Islam of western Sudan but seem to have made few Temne converts.

In 1949 the Temne were grouped into 44 chiefdoms, each with a paramount chief and several subchiefs. Subsequent amalgamations have reduced the number of chiefdoms. In the Sierra Leone administrative system chiefdoms are grouped into districts; those districts containing Temne chiefdoms make up the Northern Province. Since independence in 1961 individual Temne have been active participants in the national governments of the Sierra Leone Peoples Party (SLPP) and, after, the All Peoples Conference (APC).

Temne chiefdoms may be grouped into those in which a male society (Poro, Ragbenle or Ramena) conducts the installation ceremonies of the chief and those in which Muslim clerics conduct the rites. In non-Muslim chiefdoms most subchiefs bear the title *kapr*. In Muslim chiefdoms they are known as *alimami* or *santigi*. A number of Muslim Temne chiefs, as well as other Temne, have made the pilgrimage to Mecca and add "El Hadji" to their title/name, like El Hadji Alimami Suri, the late paramount chief of Kunike chiefdom. In a paramount chief's court witnesses swear on the Bible, the Quran or traditional medicines, depending on their religion. Muslim chiefs play leadership roles in the ceremonial calendar of the Muslim community. Today each rural Temne village has an elected headman who serves as a liaison with higher authority. Within a village, representatives of households handle most disputes on a moot basis.

Descent among the Temne is traced unilineally through males, that is, patrilineally. Eligibility to chieftancy as well as the inheritance of rights to most forms of property are both patrilineal. Thus the individual, male or female, identifies first with his or her father's patrikin, although a strong secondary relationship is maintained with the mother's father's patrikin. A marriage is sealed by the transfer of wealth from the groom's patrikin group to that of the bride's father; a smaller dowry or counter-payment moves the other way.

Polygyny among the Temne is relatively frequent. Perhaps 30–45 percent of all rural men married at a given time have two or more wives.

An individual's second name indicates his extended kin group or *abuna*; there are 25 to 30 such patriclans among the Temne. Formerly members of each *abuna* observed certain dietary prohibitions, but this custom is largely ignored today. In the late pre-teen or early teen years virtually all Temne girls are initiated into the Bundu or Sane society. Bundu training stresses homemaking skills and ideals of female behavior. Similarly, in southern chiefdoms, where Islam is less strong, most young boys are initiates into the Poro society.

The Poro society is said to have been introduced to the Temne by the Sherbro; the society is also found among the Mende and a number of groups in Liberia and Guinea. Among the Temne it played both political and economic roles. The basic initiation, lasting months or years traditionally, provided ordinary members with "education for life" in terms of Temne values. A small number underwent training initiation later in life to become Poro officers; these provided super-national services for hire.

Conflict between Muslim Temne and Poro Temne is longstanding and on occasion bitter. Historically local Poro lodges closed roads, charged tolls to traders or hid local bad debtors in the Poro bush to avoid repaying Muslim traders. Today Temne Muslims have a lengthy list of charges against Poro men including that Poro men do not believe in God but "worship" stones and spirits, that they smoke, drink and eat foods prohibited to Muslims, that they tamper with the dead and use parts of corpses in medicines and that Poro officers use bad magic/medicine indiscriminately and thus harm the innocent. Poro men are characterized as rude and overbearing towards Muslims, who resent being labeled *anburaka*, uninitiated, since it suggests that they are children—and this is derogatory. Conversely Poro men dislike being labeled *kafiri*, nonbelievers, which they regard as derogatory. The list of charges includes the refusal of Muslims to drink palm wine and eat "bush pig," a traditional delicacy, to sacrifice to ancestral spirits or to the Poro spirit or to let non-Muslim men marry Muslim women. Usually it is stressed that Islam is a non-Temne faith and that Poro is an integral part of the Temne way of life which must be maintained.

With initiation into Poro, a boy receives a Poro name which he henceforth uses as a first name; Muslim youth who are initiates and those who are converted to Islam as adults forsake the use of their Poro name for a "Muslim name" such as Muhammad or Ali.

In both rural and urban areas, Temne form clubs for recreational, mutual aid and other purposes. Temne are active in the Sierra Leone Muslim Brotherhood, which, among other activities, finances and operates both primary and secondary schools. In general the *ikwan* (Arabic, *tariqa*), or Sufi brotherhoods, were and still are unimportant; both Qadiri and Tijani exist, but Muslim communities are not organized about them.

Islam has penetrated Temne social and political life, but the assimilation of Muslim beliefs and practices has been uneven. Immigrant Muslims provided a range of services in the past, both commercial and political, but also included divining and the making of charms. Temne borrowed many elements of Islam which fit traditional cultural practices. A Muslim cleric who wrote a verse from the Quran on paper and put the paper in a small leather pouch worn on one's person was providing a new form of traditional charm and did not pose a threat to the established order. Similarly the traditional Temne diviner used a number of methods; Islamic practitioners provided new methods to answer old questions. Islamic elements are also found in sacrificial practices, including those which are part of the agricultural cycle, funerals and the purification of widows following the husband's funeral. In this process a large number of Arabic loan words were accepted into Temne vocabulary. In the villages, the praying place is usually at the outskirts, not infrequently next to or replacing traditional spirit houses. As the Muslim community grows, a mosque is built in the traditional style.

In the provincial towns there are minority non-Temne Muslim communities and a growing number of Temne Muslims who have more knowledge of Maliki Islam and who are thus more orthodox in their practices and beliefs. Urban mosques are larger and more elaborate, being built by wealthier communities. In the provincial towns and in Freetown, on the twenty-seventh night of Ramadan, young Muslims carry around lanterns or floats with representations of animals or boats.

The Ahmadiya movement reached Sierra Leone in 1937, but early efforts made at Mange Bure and Rokupr, in the Temne area, were unsuccessful. In 1942 the Ahmadi established themselves at Magburak, a provincial Temne town. Some wealthy, influential Temne joined, a mosque was built and then a school. There was some friction between Ahmadi and the Maliki Muslim majority since the Ahmadi seek to purge other Muslims of corrupt practices and in their role as ''modernist reformists'' they seek to make Islam relevant to a new and changing world and thus to challenge Christianity.

BIBLIOGRAPHY

Books

Clarke, John I. *Sierra Leone in Maps*. London: University of London Press, 1966.
Dorjahn, Vernon R. "African Traders in Central Sierra Leone." In *Markets in Africa*, edited by P. Bohannan and G. Dalton. Evanston: Northwestern University Press, 1962.
Ganton, Michael P. "Social Alignment and Identity in a West African City." In *Ur-*

banization and Migration in West Africa, edited by Hilda Kuper. Berkeley: University of California Press, 1965.

———. *West African City: A Study of Tribal Life in Freetown*. London: Oxford University Press, 1957.

Lewis, Roy. *Sierra Leone*. London: HMSO for the Colonial Office, 1954.

McCulloch, M. *People of Sierra Leone*. London: International African Institute, 1950.

Murdock, George Peter. *Africa: Its Peoples and Their Culture History*. New York: McGraw-Hill, 1959.

Thomas, Northcote W. *Anthropological Report on Sierra Leone. Part I. Law and Customs of the Timne and Other Tribes*. London: Harrison, 1916.

Trimingham, J. Spencer. *Islam in West Africa*. London: Oxford University Press, 1959.

Wylie, Kenneth C. *The Political Kingdoms of the Temne: Temne Government in Sierra Leone, 1825–1910*. New York: Africana, 1977.

Articles

Banton, Michael P. "Adaptation and Integration in the Social System of Temne Immigrants in Freetown." *Africa* 12:4 (1956): 354–368.

Dalby, David. "The Mel Languages: A Reclassification of Southern 'West Atlantic.' " *African Language Studies* 6 (1965): 1–17.

Dawson, J. L. "Temne Witchcraft Vocabulary." *Sierra Leone Language Review* 2 (1963): 16–22.

Dorjahn, Vernon R. "The Changing Political System of the Temne." *Africa* 30:2 (1960): 110–140.

———. "The Extent and Nature of Political Knowledge in Temne Society." *Journal of Asian and African Studies* 3:3 (1968): 51–63.

———. "Fertility, Polygyny and Their Inter-Relations in Temne Society." *American Anthropologist* 60:5 (1958): 838–860.

———. "Migration in Central Sierra Leone: The Temne Chiefdom Kolifa Mayoso." *Africa* 45:1 (1975): 28–47.

———. "The Organization and Functions of the *Ragbenle* Society of the Temne." *Africa* 29:2 (1959): 156–170.

———. "Rural–Urban Differences in Infant and Child Mortality Among the Temne of Kolifa." *Journal of Anthropological Research* 32:1 (1976): 74–103.

———. "Some Aspects of Temne Divination." *Sierra Leone Bulletin of Religion* 4:1 (1962): 1–9.

———. "Some Rural–Urban Marriage Differentials: The Temne of Magburaka Town and Its Environs." *Urban Anthropologist* 2:2 (1973): 161–181.

———. "Tailors, Carpenters and Leather Workers in Magburaka." *Sierra Leone Studies* 20 (1967): 158–172.

———. "Temne Household Size and Composition: Rural Changes Over Time and Rural–Urban Differences." *Ethnology* 16:2 (1977): 105–127.

———, and Hogg, Thomas C. "Job Satisfactions, Dissatisfactions and Aspirations in the Wage Labor Force of Magburaka, a Sierra Leone Town." *Journal of Asian and African Studies* 1:4 (1966): 7–24.

Fisher, H. "Ahmadiyya in Sierra Leone." *Sierra Leone Bulletin of Religion* 2:1 (1960): 1–10.

Gamble, David P. "The Temne Family in a Modern Town (Lunsar) in Sierra Leone."
    Africa 33:3 (1963): 209–226.
Harvey, Milton E. "Makeni: A Geographical Study of a Growing Northern Town and
    Its Environs." *Sierra Leone Geographical Journal* 11 (1967): 26–41.
Littlejohn, James. "The Temne Ansasa." *Sierra Leone Studies* 13 (1960): 32–35.
———. "The Temne House." Sierra Leone Studies 14 (1960): 63–79.
———. "Temne Space." *Anthropological Quarterly* 36:1 (1963): 1–17.
Trimingham, J. Spencer, and Fyfe, C. H. "The Early Expansion of Islam in Sierra
    Leone." *Sierra Leone Bulletin of Religion* 2:12 (1960): 30–39.
Turay, A. K. "Temne Supernatural Terminology." *Sierra Leone Bulletin of Religion*
    19:2 (1967): 50–53.

Unpublished Manuscripts

Hopewell, J. F. "Muslim Penetration Into French Guinea, Sierra Leone and Liberia
    Before 1850." Ph.D. dissertation, Columbia University, 1958.
Howard, Allen M. "Big Men, Traders and Chiefs: Power, Commerce, and Spatial Change
    in the Sierra Leone–Guinea Plain, 1865–1895." Ph.D. dissertation, University
    of Wisconsin, 1972.
Ijagbemi, Ade. "A History of the Temne-Speaking Peoples." Ph.D. dissertation, Uni-
    versity of Edinburgh, 1968.
Skinner, David E. "Islam in Sierra Leone During the Nineteenth Century." Ph.D.
    dissertation, University of California, 1971.
Smith, Antony H. "Social and Cultural Factors in Child Mortality Among the Temne of
    Magburaka, Sierra Leone." Ph.D. dissertation, University of Oregon, 1981.

Vernon R. Dorjahn

TERNATAN-TIDORESE   The Indonesian province of Maluku (the Moluccas)
includes dozens of islands between Sulawesi and Timor on the one hand and
Irian Jaya on the other. Two of the most historically important are Ternate and
Tidore off the west coast of Halmahera. The former is an active volcano rimmed
by a road 25 miles long. Tidore, slightly larger, is made up of an extinct volcano.
Both host Muslim populations who speak closely related languages and share a
common heritage.
    There are perhaps 35,000 Ternatan, only half of whom live on Ternate. The
other half mainly live on the major island of Halmahera. One half of the 70,000
or so Tidorese live on Tidore; the rest live dispersed over a wide area of the
sub-province of North Maluku and Irian Jaya. Both islands are suited for agriculture, but because of the population density, a great number have settled
elsewhere. Tidore has a homogeneous population, but the island of Ternate,
once the site of the regional Dutch colonial administration and now capital of
the sub-province of North Maluku as well as an economic and commercial center,
has seen a great influx of non-Ternatan. The non-Ternatan population of Ternate,
amounting to about 47,000 persons, far exceeds the Ternatan.
    The languages of the Ternatan and Tidorese are closely related branches of

the language group of North Halmahera that so far cannot be related to any language phylum, whether Austronesian (Malayo-Polynesian) or non-Austronesian. In former days Ternatan and Tidorese were written in Arabic script. Now the teaching medium in schools is the Indonesian national language, Bahasa Indonesia, written in the Latin script. As a result, the languages of Ternate and Tidore are reduced to a position of minor social importance, used in daily conversation but no longer in writing.

The area of Halmahera and adjacent islands is the homeland of cloves, and until the sixteenth century the cultivation of cloves remained confined to this area. At the time the Portuguese arrived in the Moluccas, in 1512, this area numbered four sultanates: Ternate, Tidore, Bacan and Jailolo. Together these four easternmost sultanates of the world of Islam controlled the total world production of cloves. The sultanate of Jailolo had its capital of the same name on the west coast of Central Halmahera, but this sultanate came to an end as an independent realm in the middle of the sixteenth century, after it was conquered by the Ternatan and the Portuguese. The sultanate of Bacon covered the extensive but sparsely populated islands off the southwest coast of Halmahera, and this sultanate has always been of minor importance. The two most important and always competing realms have been Ternate and Tidore. It is unknown in which century these four realms came into being, but it is an established fact that their power and prestige were based on the control of the sale of cloves to foreign traders and on the allied political and cultural contacts with Javanese, Malays and later on Europeans. In the fifteenth and sixteenth centuries, Ternate and Tidore succeeded in extending their military power and political and cultural influence over the surrounding islands. Ternate directed its expansion mainly on Moti, Makian, North Halmahera, the Sula islands, Buru, Ambon and adjacent islands and the east coast of Sulawesi. Tidore directed its expansion to South Halmahera, the Raja Ampat islands and adjacent coast of Irian Jaya and on East Ceram. Bacan in vain attempted to obtain dependencies at North Ceram.

In the sixteenth century the Portuguese without success attempted to establish a monopoly of purchase on cloves, but later on in the seventeenth century the Dutch succeeded in this objective. The Dutch restricted the cultivation of cloves to Ambon and a few adjacent islands, producing only enough to supply the world market. For any other island in the Moluccas, including Halmahera and adjacent islands, the cultivation of cloves became strictly forbidden. This interdiction was maintained into the nineteenth century. In compensation for the loss of revenues from clove production and allied trade, the sultans of Ternate, Tidore and Bacan and their principal officials were provided with an annual allowance by the Dutch. Nevertheless, the interdiction of clove production and allied trade resulted in a drastic economic decline for the sultanates, and at the same time in an absolute dependency on the Dutch, in cultural isolation and in an internal social and political ossification. The abolition of the interdiction of clove production in the nineteenth century brought no change whatsoever because the price of cloves had fallen to a level that made the cultivation of cloves unattractive, and the system of annual allowances was maintained. Under Dutch protection Ternate, Tidore and Bacan remained semi-autonomous states until Indonesia's independence in 1949.

The Indonesian government has pursued a policy of total integration of the sultanates into the modern state. The autonomous sultanates gradually have been abolished by integrating the internal administration within the provincial administration of the Moluccas; on the death of the last sultans appointed by the Dutch, no successors will be appointed. The sultanates virtually have ceased to exist now, and institutions of the former sultanates survive only in folklore, not as politically significant elements.

The most lasting influence of the Moluccan sultanates is the spread of Islam. The Islamization of Ternate, Tidore, Bacan and Jailolo began in the fifteenth century as a result of contacts with Javanese and Malays, and in the sixteenth century the process became intensified as a result of the political competition between the Portuguese and the Moluccan sultans, both parties using religion as a political device. The Portuguese were finally defeated by the Moluccans and made no lasting significant results in propagating Christianity.

From Ternate and Tidore, Islam spread to the islands off the west coast of Halmahera, to the coastal areas of Halmahera and of the Sula islands Buru and Ceram, to the Raja Ampat islands and to the east coast of Sulawesi. In this way the foundation was laid for a certain amount of cultural homogeneity over a vast area of Ternate and Tidore as the main political and cultural centers. Politically, Ternate and Tidore were rivals, but culturally Ternate and Tidore did not differ very much. Only the populations of the interior of Halmahera, Sula, Buru, Ceram and Irian Jaya never accepted Islam, though recognizing the political authority of Ternate and Tidore. The Dutch accepted the religious situation as they found it at the beginning of the seventeenth century. Only in the nineteenth and twentieth centuries did the pagan island population become the object of private missionary societies.

Ternatan and Tidorese identify themselves by means of descent from one of the traditional units of sociopolitical organization that are called *soas*, each *soa* having its own name. The meaning of *soa* is literally "ward," "quarter" or "hamlet," but the *soas* were by no means pure territorial units. One did not belong to a certain *soa* on account of residence but, rather, on account of descent. Membership in a *soa* was transmitted in the patrilineal line. However, the *soa* was not a clan or lineage because the members of the *soa* did not claim a common descent from one ancestor and because the kinship organization is not unilinear but cognatic. The *soa* was headed by a chief who was appointed by the sultan. With the abolition of the sultanates, the *soas* as units of sociopolitical organization have become obsolete because they are no longer accepted by the government as units of administration and they do not have a function in the field of kinship organization. The *soas* as units of administration have been replaced by democratically chosen village chiefs.

In upper-class families, marriages are frequently arranged by parents in order to protect and enhance the status and honor of the family involved and to avoid misalliance. It often happens that young people are forced into a marriage. However, among most people, pre-arranged marriages are less frequent. As tolerated by Islamic law, marriage may be within the family, for example, between parallel or cross cousins, and these kinds of marriages do occur. Marriages frequently end in divorce. Polygyny also occurs.

Ternatan have a clear division of labor between men and women, husband and wife. The men do the incidental hard labor in the gardens such as felling trees. They do some fishing, and they take care of building and maintaining the house. The women do the daily work in the gardens, do the cooking, take care of the children and try to make some money for the daily budget by selling garden produce and some food. Generally speaking, the men are inclined to take life easy and to depend for the daily subsistence on their wives, who have to work for the daily meals of the family. Labor is not highly valued, and adolescents do not have to work if their parents can afford to feed them and to provide them with decent clothes. For a male adolescent, manual labor would lower his chances to get a white collar job in town. Ternatan are very conscious of status, and manual labor lowers a man's status. Serving other people for wages is a shame that should be avoided as far as possible, both for men and for women. Wage earning is for immigrants.

Tidorese do not shun manual labor as much as do Ternatan, and generally speaking Tidorese are more industrious in gardening, fishing and trade. Tidorese do provide the market of Ternate with a good deal of its vegetables, fruit and other garden produce, fish and products of local handicraft. At the same time the Tidorese are generally less educated and less cultivated than Ternatan. The Tidorese are classified as the more boorish people in relation to the Ternatan. This distinction between Ternatan and Tidorese was noted in the seventeenth century and holds good for modern times.

Ternatan and Tidorese are not aggressive people, and the mutual distrust and rivalry does not lead to clashes, partly because they do not really mix. There have been no reports of clashes between Ternatan and immigrants from other parts of Indonesia. If Ternatan and Tidorese do not like other people, they tend to avoid them rather than to fight them, while individuals are easily integrated into their society.

Traditionally, Islam on Ternate and Tidore has been closely associated with the court and the sociopolitical organization of the sultanate. Formally, the sultan was the head of the Ummat Islam within the sultanate, and in this capacity the sultan was represented by a *qadi*, who headed a fixed number of *imams* and *khatibs*, who were functionaries of state. Both on Ternate and Tidore, a central mosque of state stood nearby the court, and other houses of prayer within the sultanate were subordinated to this central mosque.

Within the sultanates, there were no institutions for religious teaching, but some individual Arabs living on Ternate and Tidore acted as religious teachers. As teachers of members of the royal family, they sometimes were in a position of having a great deal of influence at court. In many respects their teaching had a distinct mystical flavor, and adherents of the modern reformistic Muhammadiya are inclined to call the traditional Arab teaching old-fashioned and in some respects heterodox.

Ternatan and Tidorese are convinced Muslims as is expressed by the rituals at circumcision, marriage and death, in the strict maintenance of the fast during Ramadan, in the celebration of the Islamic holy days and in the high value placed on the pilgrimage to Mecca. At the same time they retain a great number of traditional local customs that are incompatible with orthodox Islam such as the belief in shrines that are visited to pray for recovery from illness and for other practical purposes. There also exists a widely spread belief in guardian spirits that are venerated and beseeched for help by means of shamanistic rituals.

In colonial times Ternatan and Tidorese feared and passively resisted primary schools out of fear that these schools with Latin script might be a tool for Christianization of their children. Under the Indonesian government this fear has disappeared, and elementary education has become acceptable. Indonesia also has created a nationwide educational system for training of religious teachers. The bureaus of the Department of Religion are filled with graduates from the schools for religious teaching. This department has its branches on Ternate and Tidore, where it appoints *imams* and *khatibs* and takes care of religious juris-diction, as it does elsewhere in Indonesia. The traditional position of Arabs as teachers of religion has been strongly undermined by the new educational system for religious teaching. The modern teachers of religion are more orthodox than the traditional Arab teachers and are inclined to purify Islam from traditional customs incompatible with orthodox Islam. The long-run effect of the integration of Ternate and Tidore within the Indonesian polity certainly will be that Islamic observance gradually will be purified and that elements of traditional and local culture both within the sphere of religion and without gradually will be of diminishing importance.

BIBLIOGRAPHY

Books

Clercq, F.S.A. de. *Bijdragen tot de kennis der residentie Ternate*. Leiden: E. J. Brill, 1980.
Polman, K. *The North Moluccas: An Annotated Bibliography*. The Hague: Martinus Nijhoff, 1981.

Ch. F. van Fraassen

THAIS Throughout the major regions of Buddhist Thailand, the silhouettes of the minaret against the skyline attest to the existence there of some 2 million

Muslims. They constitute the largest religious minority, about 4 percent of the population.

Nearly all Muslims of Thailand are either indigenous Malays or descendants of immigrants or refugees of other ethnic groups. Some have been settled so long among the Theravada Buddhists of the northern and central provinces that they have assimilated into the general culture of Thai society. These Muslims are considered, and consider themselves, as "Thai." They number about 200,000. (Malay-speaking Thais in the south number about 1.8 million.)

During the seventeenth century small migrant populations of Iranian, Cham and Indian Muslims came to the ancient capital of Ayudhya in central Thailand. Later in the nineteenth century Indian, Indonesian, Cham and Chinese (Hui) Muslims settled in central and northern Thailand. But the largest segment of Thai Muslims in these Buddhist areas were Malays forcibly relocated from the deep southernmost provinces of Thailand. Today, they speak Thai as their native language and have become socialized into the dominant culture of their Thai Buddhist neighbors. None of these various ethnic groups systematically has passed on their original languages to their offspring. Economic, social, political and Thai culture values have been conducive to this rapid assimilation, or what has been called Thaiification.

Thai Muslims in Buddhist provinces live cordially with their neighbors. Although mutual stereotypes referring to Thai Muslims and Thai Buddhists exist within the cultural frameworks of both groups, they attend each others' household celebrations, life-cycle rites and other social activities. And in general, there seems to be very little evidence of discrimination on the part of the Thai Buddist majority towards the Muslim minority in these Buddhist areas, both in rural and urban areas in central and northern Thailand.

Thai Muslims have adapted to the occupations which developed in connection with the modernization of the Thai economy. Traditionally Muslims in northern and central Thailand were involved in those occupations which corresponded to their original heritages. Thus, originally, the Indians, Iranians, Indonesians and Chinese Muslims were traders or independent businessmen. The Pakistanis were employed in the cattle industry or as butchers. The Cham and ethnically Malay Muslims were engaged in agriculture. But as these various ethnic groups have generally become Thaiified, they have also become employed in all sectors of the Thai economy.

Thai Muslims have essentially the same family structure as other Thais. A married couple may establish an independent household or reside with either of their parents for a period of time. In general the neo-local residence pattern is displacing the bilocal pattern. But among the more wealthy elite in urban areas, the young couple will often move into a separate home in the compound of the groom's or bride's parents. This is also the typical pattern for the non-Muslim urban elite in Bangkok. But in urban areas even among the old elite, both Muslim and non-Muslim, this type of "extended family residence" is beginning to break down. Only among the rich are newlyweds able to remain on their parents' property indefinitely. The nuclear family housed in its own separate dwelling is the ideal.

The Muslim family organization of the lower socioeconomic stratum differs slightly from the upper- and middle-income group. Though the basic social unit is the simple nuclear family consisting of a father, mother and their unmarried children, at times these households are composed of more family members. Some may become small extended families, including married sons or daughters with their offspring. Joint families with several siblings living together with their children in the same household are not uncommon for these lower-income Muslim families.

Thai Muslim children attend the same primary schools as other Thai children. But after regular school hours in the early evening they also attend the religious school maintained by their community mosque. This part-time religious instruction includes the teaching of basic Arabic, Quranic teachings and prayer techniques. There are 80 schools with special curriculum of this type, and they average 90 students to each school. They are under the jurisdiction of the Ministry of Education and are strictly regulated by the Thai government. Another type of Islamic school is the full-time institution devoted to the study of Islamic teaching. Islamic science, history and theology make up the core of the curriculum. Classes are taught in Arabic. There are only 10 such schools in Thailand.

With the exception of the descendants of Iranians and a few Indian Muslims who are Shia, Thai Muslims are Sunni Muslims. Like other Southeast Asian Muslims, Thais' religious traditions have been influenced by the Shafi legal tradition. In actuality, in northern and central Thailand the Shariah plays little part in legal proceedings for Muslims. They are subject to the same secular judicial processes as any other Thai citizen. Shariah does have an effect on ritual complexes and Islamic ideology as it is expressed in the Muslim communities.

In the rural communities where Muslims are in a minority, the Islamic tradition exists as a syncretic blend of pre-Islamic spiritualism and Hindu-Buddhist concepts conjoined with Islamic precepts and obligations. Many observers have noted the "folk" quality of the Islamic tradition in village communities. Beliefs in *phii* (Thai animistic spirits), *mau phii* (Thai spirit doctors), communal feasting practices which parallel Buddhist institutions and other indigenous beliefs are combined with Islamic concepts.

While Thai Muslims have adopted much of the culture of the Buddhist majority, they nevertheless have distinct values. They view Buddhists as "pig eaters" who are inclined towards violence, gambling, sexual immorality, dishonesty, usury and drunkenness. This derogatory stereotype is of course idealized and does not apply universally. Thai Muslims perceive themselves as "people of the Book," a minority group which does not have any of the social problems of the larger Thai society. They are concerned that their fellow Muslims and their children will be contaminated by the larger Thai society. Hence there is a great deal of stress put on these ideals in their Islamic religious activities. Muslims also accentuate a stronger sense of family solidarity than do Buddhists. Many express disapproval of the entire cultural ethos of Thai society and compare it to the ethos of the Jahilliya (the pre-Islamic period in Arabia marked by idolatry and immorality).

An Islamic reformist movement developed in the early twentieth century within the Thai Muslim communities. External events in the Muslim world and internal sociological developments in Thailand stimulated the rise of Islamic reformism. Primarily an urban phenomenon centered in Bangkok, it gained strength among educated Muslims. Reformist Muslims perceived most Muslims as being in a state of *jumud* (inertia) resulting from ignorance of the true spirit of Islam. The most visible sign was the existence of folk or popular forms of the Islamic tradition. They maintained that this dilution of Islam was a consequence of Thailand's isolation from the rest of the Muslim world.

The reformist movement has led to a split within the Thai Muslim communities. Religious and political rivalries developed between *khana mai* (reformist) Muslims and *khana kau* (traditionalist) Muslims. The former are based in urban areas; the latter find support in rural areas and are especially strong in the south among the Malay Thais.

In southern Thailand, Muslims have had a unique historical past which distinguishes them from other Thai Muslims. Especially in the provinces of Pattani, Narathiwat, Yala and Satul, which border Malaysia, they are usually classified as Malay Thai Muslims. This ambivalent classification is in reference to ethnic or cultural factors as well as citizenship. These southernmost provinces were incorporated into the Thai nation during the early twentieth century, the culmination of a long history of Thai expansion. Formerly these southern provinces were independent Malay states which had been Islamized since the fourteenth century.

Almost 90 percent of the Muslim population in these southern provinces speak a Pattani dialect of Malay and have retained their Malay-Islamic cultural heritage. Continual efforts by the Thai government to assimilate or integrate them into Thai society have only led to irredentist and separatist movements. Few speak the Thai language.

Most of the Malay Thai Muslims reside in rural areas, where their subsistence revolves around the cultivation of wet rice and fishing. There is also a small number involved in tin mining and rubber or coconut plantations. Economic development has been slow. Population pressures, fluctuating market conditions for rubber and coconut products and inflation have led to a decline in living standards; many have been forced to mortgage their land to Chinese or other wealthy brokers. All of these economic conditions have led to political unrest and stimulated various separatist movements.

The separatist movements are not consolidated into one political division, and each faction has different goals. One group desires a separate administrative unit in a federation with Thailand. Another wants an independent traditional Malay state under a sultan, while a third favors establishing an autonomous state of

Pattani. All stress the grandeur of the independent Malay states, the teaching of Malay as opposed to Thai and the need for more local autonomy from the Thai government in Bangkok.

Most recently there has been the development of what is known as *dakwah* (Arabic for "call to duty") movements, which are similar to those in Malaysia, Indonesia, Pakistan and the Middle East. They represent the young generation of Muslims in Thailand who are attempting to bring about fundamental changes in the form of Islamic practices and institutions. Though much like earlier reformist movements, the new *dakwah* are more self-consciously based on worldwide trends in the Muslim world. The *dakwah* are likely to be the key elements in generating political and religious change for Muslims in Thailand in the future.

BIBLIOGRAPHY

Books

Ibrahim, Muhammad ibn. *The Ship of Sulaiman.* Translated by John O'Kane. Persian Heritage Series No. 11. London: Routledge and Kegan Paul, 1972.
Teeuw, A., and Wyatt, David. *Hikayat Patani: The Story of Patani.* Vols. 1 and 2. The Hague: Martinus Nijhoff, 1970.

Articles

Burr, Angel. "Group Ideology, Consciousness and Social Problems: A Study of Buddhist and Muslim Conception of Sin in Two Southern Thai Coastal Villages." *Anthropos* 72 (1977): 433–446.
———. "Religious Institutional Diversity: Social Structural and Conceptual Unity: Islam and Buddhism in a Southern Coastal Fishing Village." *Journal of the Siam Society* 60 (1972): 183–215.
Haemindra, Nantawan. "The Problems of the Thai Muslims in the Four Southern Provinces of Thailand." *Journal of Southeast Asian Studies* 7:2 (1976): 197–225, and 8:1 (1977): 85–105.
Scupin, Raymond. "Islam in Thailand Before the Bangkok Period." *Journal of the Siam Society* 68:1 (1980): 55–71.
———. "Islamic Reformism in Thailand." *Journal of the Siam Society* 68:2 (1980): 1–10.
———. "The Politics of Islamic Reformism in Thailand." *Asian Survey* 20:12 (1980): 1223–1235.
Thomas, Ladd. "Bureaucratic Attitudes and Behavior as Obstacles to Political Integration of Thai Muslims." *Southeast Asia: An International Quarterly* 3:1 (1974): 545–566.

Unpublished Manuscript

Soonthornpasuch, Suthep. "Islamic Identity in Chiengmai City: A Historical and Structural Comparison of Two Communities." Ph.D. dissertation, University of California, Berkeley, 1977.

Ray Scupin

TIGRE   The nomadic Tigre practice pastoralism in the hills and lowlands of the northern and western parts of Ethiopia's Eritrea and Tigre provinces. Nearly all Muslim, they number at least 350,000, probably more.

Tigre is a Semitic language of the Afro-Asiatic family, closely related to Tigrinya. Academic specialists, however, consider the languages mutually unintelligible. It has no script of its own and is written in Gez, the script of the Ethiopian church (Monophysite or Coptic). Many literate Tigre write in Arabic.

Not only a language and a people, Tigre is also the name of a major province in Eritrea, which the Tigre people share with the Tigrinya speakers, who outnumber them considerably. However, the Tigrinya speakers, who are overwhelmingly Christian, are sedentary while the Tigre are pastoralists, herders of cattle, goats, sheep and camels, which they sell in the markets for the produce and manufactured items they need to survive.

Tigre living on Red Sea islands were among the first converts to Islam as it began its expansion from Arabia in the seventh century. Most conversion of the Tigre, however, took place in the nineteenth century, when disciples of Sayyed Ahmad ibn Idriss left Arabia to found Sufi orders. One of his pupils, Sayyed Muhammad 'Uthman al-Mirghani, was sent to Sudan and Eritrea to engage in missionary work. The Mirghani remains the dominant Muslim *tariqa* in eastern Sudan and Eritrea.

A large number of Tigre, perhaps as many as 175,000, are part of the Beni Amer, a confederation of various groups that have formed a single unit. Numbering at least 260,000 in both Ethiopia and Sudan, the Beni Amer are a pastoral polity connected with the larger Beja peoples (see Beja). Their most striking feature is the division of the Beni Amer into two classes, the rulers, who are Beja, and the serfs, who are largely Tigre. A system of mutual obligations and rights maintains the structure (see Beni Amer).

Eritrea has been rent with violence for many years as the government of Ethiopia attempts to incorporate the province forcibly into the Ethiopian political and economic system. Many Tigre have left the country to settle in Sudan. The future of those who have remained will continue to be one of hardship, not only because of the fighting but because a new Marxist government in Addis Ababa is not sympathetic to those who lead a non-sedentary life-style, especially if they are Muslims.

BIBLIOGRAPHY

Books

Bauer, Dan F. *Household and Society in Ethiopia: An Economic and Social Analysis of Tigray*. Committee on Ethiopian Studies, African Studies Center, Occasional Papers Series Monograph, No. 6. East Lansing: Michigan State University, 1977.

Lipsky, George. *Ethiopia: Its Peoples, Its Society, Its Culture*. New Haven: Human Relations Area Files Press, 1962.

Thomas R. DeGregori

TOMINI   The Tomini of Indonesia occupy the northern Sulawesi peninsula from Donggala to Gorontalo. The name "Tomini" is both a geographic and linguistic designation. Geographically, Tomini is a thin strip of land which borders the western edge of Tomini Bay; linguistically, Tomini is a subgroup of western Central Sulawesi languages which include Toli-toli, Dondo, Bolano, Tinombo, Kasimbar, Dampelas and Ndau. Although linguists formerly thought all Tomini languages were mutually intelligible and the different names merely referred to dialects, recent research has asserted that each group forms a separate language. Supposedly these multiple languages originated from the area's many political-trading empires, which remained historically and culturally insulated from each other until Islam unified them in the sixteenth century.

Despite local differences, these empires conformed to a general cultural pattern similar to that of the Toraja and Minahasa. Even though Minahasa and Toraja were influenced by Islamic traders at the same time as Tomini was, today Tomini forms a pocket of Islam, bounded on the north by the Christianized Minahasa and on the south by the equally Christianized Poso Toraja. Both Minahasa and Poso were sites of Dutch schools and Protestant missionary training centers during the nineteenth and twentieth centuries. Because Tomini was bypassed by Dutch missionaries, it has retained its strong Islamic character and thus is quite distinct from its neighbors.

Of the 74,000 Tomini, nearly 90 percent are Sunni Muslims, the rest being animist and Christian. All of the Muslims live along the coast rather than in the mountains, which span the center of the area and are home for animists and Christians. Highlanders cultivate dry rice, grow maize and sago and gather rattan and *damar* (resin) for trade along the coast. The Muslim coastal people work on clove, copra and palm plantations, cultivate wet rice fields or work as traders, lumberers or sailors.

The cultural history of the area can be divided into four periods: 1) the coming of Islam, 2) the Dutch colonial period, 3) the Japanese occupation and 4) post-independence. Islam came to Tomini in three waves. The first arrived from the eastern Indonesian trading empire of Ternate in the sixteenth century (see Ternatan-Tidorese), the second from the southern Sulawesi traders, the Bugis and the Mandar, beginning in the sixteenth century and increasing in the seventeenth century, and the third in the eighteenth century from Minangkabau (Sumatran) travellers (see Bugis; Minangkabau).

Islam first penetrated and unified Tomini's disparate kingdoms by converting the nobility, especially the rajas' or kings' families, who after conversion married each other rather than non-Muslims within the realm. The initial ties between kingdoms were thus between elite Muslims.

Even though all the pre-Islamic kingdoms were distinct, they shared common rules for political and economic organization, including maintenance of regional sovereignty through a system of tribute. Subjects either gave labor service or prestige objects to the ruler indicating they were willing to be of service to the stronger raja. The raja's right to rule or his sign of power was signified by a collection of sacred regalia such as gold objects, trays and umbrellas which were inherited from the former ruler (usually matrilineally). Each of the kingdoms ruled with their own particular regalia until Muslim rulers from outside the Tomini area introduced new royal symbols. In 1556 the Muslim raja, Harian of Ternate, wished to develop new trade networks on the eastern and northwestern coasts of Tomini, especially in Moutong and Buoll, which were rich in gold deposits. As a sign of friendship, Raja Harian gave a scepter and a letter written in Arabic script to each of the rajas of Buol, Mouton and Toli-Toli. The Tomini rajas regarded these gifts as sacred. In acknowledgement, the Buol raja sailed to Ternate in 1595, presenting a golden goat to Harian on behalf of these northern Tomini rajas.

This exchange of gifts signalled the beginning of an epoch in which the Tomini rajas fell under the influence of the Ternate kingdom and also accepted the ruler's religion. Tomini kings changed their official titles to Arabic ones, their families began to recite Islamic prayers in the home and they sought sons in other distant Islamic kingdoms to the north to marry their daughters and consolidate power.

The second wave of Islam actually began at the same time as the first, but rather than Ternate traders introducing Islam, the south Sulawesi Bugis and Mandar traders brought Islam and unified the southwestern coast of Tomini. This pattern was almost identical to that of the Ternate kingdom's but did not reach a peak until later in the seventeenth century. The result was an area divided into two parts, the northern influenced by Ternate, the southern by the south Sulawesi polities of Goa, Bone and Luwu.

Gradually the Bugis and Mandar realms became more powerful than the waning Ternate so that by the early seventeenth century the Tomini nobles oriented themselves towards the southern rulers, especially the Mandar rajas. During this time a strict class system emerged such that nobles were divided into two groups, both Islamic. The first were those with direct genealogical and patrilineal connections to the Mandar nobility and inheriting the right to rule. The second group of nobles were those who were not so related to the Mandar rajas and whose children could not inherit governmental office.

This second wave was significant in the bifurcation of the noble class, the shift from matrilateral inheritance of property and right to office to an emphasis on patrilater inheritance. In addition, funeral rites became more Islamic, especially in regard to stipulations for washing and praying over the corpse and using the white shroud over it. General house architecture (on stilts), clothing styles (sarongs) and types of gifts used in elite brideprice exchanges (coins, trays, krisses and plates) were all adopted from the south Sulawesi Mandar and Bugis society and persist to the present. Generally, however, the Muslim nobility still recited their prayers in private. There were no mosques, organized clergy or *madrasas*. Islam was for the nobility.

It was not until the third wave of conversion that Islam became more popular. In the eighteenth century, Minangkabau visitors acting as Muslim missionaries travelled throughout the Tomini area introducing Islam to the commoners. Public mosques were built, and each area acquired its own *imam*. The vassals paid religious taxes to the rajas as they had always done, but now Muslim subjects paid tribute following the Shariah and not pre-Islamic law, *adat*. Although the rajas began reciting their prayers with the masses in the mosques, they still retained esoteric religious knowledge which distinguished noble from commoner. It was always the raja who started Ramadan by quoting Arabic *pantuns* passed down from Ternate and Bugis contacts. It was during this period that nobler and wealthier Tomini reportedly first made the pilgrimage to Mecca.

Although Islam was firmly established in the Tomini area by the eighteenth century, its character was drastically affected by European contact, especially after the Dutch, who had been attracted by the region's gold mines, became the effective ruling power. In response to European contact, Islam became a political rallying point of anti-colonial sentiment. For instance, the Dutch East Indies Company made frequent stops in Buol and Toli-toli, trading rice for gold. Early in the 1800s, one agricultural season was particularly unfruitful so the raja raised the amount of rice imported in exchange for gold. The Dutch head officer was enraged that the raja had violated the specified trade agreement and declared that if the Buol raja were indeed so hungry he could eat pork. Naturally, the raja refused so the Dutch officer ordered his public execution. The raja was tied to two horses, which ran in opposite directions until his body was split apart. The people rebelled, gold trade in the area was suspended and Islam became the vehicle through which anti-Dutch sentiments were expressed.

In 1862 the Dutch built a fortress in Tinombo and attempted to control the island. Each raja was asked to sign a trade contract relinquishing all regional authority to the Dutch. The southern Mandar had already been defeated by the Dutch military forces and could not longer help their Tomini vassals. The Dutch did not defeat the Tominis until 1904; by then, all the Tomini rajas had been forced to sign the contracts, surrendering their authority. The Dutch let them keep their Arabic titles (and gave them Dutch titles as well) in order to take advantage of the raja's access to the people's labor service. Because the local system of religious taxes required commoners to give a certain amount of labor service (or goods, if they could afford it) to their raja, the Dutch forced the rajas to order their own people to work on plantation and public works projects. Coffee, coconut and palm plantations were begun by the colonial government throughout the coastal Tomini area. Wet rice agriculture was introduced to supplement the traditional maize, sago and dry rice production, and an elaborate network of roads and bridges was built to connect the region and facilitate commercial transport—all using the forced labor of the commoners.

In several regions the people directed their anger at the severity of the forced labor against the rajas. In some regions, however, the rajas helped the people as best they could by covertly supporting local chapters of nationalist religious parties. For instance, in Buol and Toli-toli, a chapter of Syarekat Islam was founded in 1916; a chapter was started in Donggala and Parigi the next year. The Syarekat Islam movement spread quickly into all of the Tomini area until the Dutch arrested and exiled its leaders and threatened to execute the rajas who were suspected of allowing it to persist. In 1917 the Raja of Moutong was arrested; in 1919 the people rebelled but were quickly squelched. Some local commoners escaped into the mountains.

Persecution by the Dutch served to strengthen the Islamic Party in Tomini, its major focus being anti-Dutch and nationalistic. In 1941 in Toli-toli a large rebellion broke out in response to being forced to work a full day during Ramadan. The precipitating event occurred when several laborers, weak from hunger and exhaustion, ostensibly unable to work, escaped from the plantation to the mosque. Dutch overseers marched into the mosque and shot the laborers while they were praying. Total rebellion broke out. The Dutch eventually regained control, but the families of the rebels fled to the mountains.

In the same year, 1942, the Japanese ousted the Dutch, but the situation for the Tomini people changed little. The rajas were given Japanese names rather than Dutch names and were required to work as slaves on the plantations along-side the commoners. In 1943 another rebellion broke out in Toli-toli, again because the Japanese colonialists had violated religious mores. Underground Islamic groups grew more fanatic, culminating in the declaration of *fisabillah*, or holy war. They sabotaged the bridges and roads so that plantation products could not be marketed. In 1945, the Dutch returned but were unable to reopen the plantations as viable economic units before independence was declared.

Tomini remained quiet during the early 1950s as the people adjusted to Indonesian national concerns. Some of the former rajas and their families found positions in the new bureaucracy; others became private entrepreneurs. In the late 1950s, separatist movements against the Indonesian government of Sukarno were led by youth groups throughout the entire island of Sulawesi. In the Tomini region this reached a peak with the Permesta Rebellion of the 1960s. Reportedly coconut farmers joined the movement initiated by the "Parmesta rebels" because they received so little return for their work. Without a renewed transportation system, laborers were exploited by private businessmen; farmers quit working, and for several years the area produced no marketable products.

Since these times, however, the government has made an effort to integrate the area into the national and international economic system. For instance, government cooperatives for poor farmers have been established to encourage continual production; new forms of transportation are subsidized by the government. The trans-Sulawesi highway, which runs along the east coast of Tomini, was opened in 1980, and on the west coast, Buol and Toli-toli have airfields in addition to their harbors. In the 1970s the cash crop sector of the region's economy blossomed. Cloves were introduced in large plantations and were successful (in the Toli-toli area, clove trees produce three times more often than in any other region). National and international lumber firms have established themselves throughout the area, and rice production has increased to the point that the area has the highest ratio of rice per person in both north and central Sulawesi combined.

Despite this economic boom, social and political problems persist, especially among the mountain animist peoples, now called *suku terasing* (foreign tribes). These are the descendants of the Tomini people who fled from the forced labor service in the colonial period and the same people who never adopted Islam. Only minimal trading ties currently exist between the Islamic and animist neighbors, even though they once recognized a common heritage and once married each other. Coastal Muslim Tomini consider themselves to be modern Indonesians looking towards a relatively bright economic future. The Indonesian government has made attempts to acculturate the *suku terasing* by moving them down the mountains into settlement camps, but so far these efforts have not been successful. As clove production in the Tomini area develops and encroaches on the mountain territory of these animists, more concerted efforts will probably be made to relocate them along the coast among the Muslim Tomini.

BIBLIOGRAPHY

Books

Barr, Donald F.; Barr, Sharon G.; and Salombe, C. *Languages of Central Sulawesi, Checklist, Preliminary Classification, Language Maps, Wordlists.* Ujung Pandang, Indonesia: Hasanuddin University Press, 1980.
LeBar, Frank W., ed. *Ethnic Groups of Insular Southeast Asia.* New Haven: Human Relations Area Files Press, 1972.

Unpublished Manuscript

Kennedy, Raymond. "Ethnology of Great Sunda Islands." Ph.D. dissertation, Yale University, 1935.

Jennifer W. Nourse

TUKULOR Tukulor refers to an ethnic group of some 700,000 Muslims in West Africa. Arab geographers called them Takarir, inhabitants of the kingdom of Tekrur. As for themselves, the Tukulor use the term "Haopholaren" (Pholarphone) or "Futankobe," if they come from Senegal. They speak Fulani (Ful-

fulde), a West Atlantic language of the Niger-Congo family. They are distinguished from the Fulani by the important role they played in the history of West African Islam and their sedentary occupations, which contrast with Fulani pastoral nomadism (see Fulani). They are a mixed group through intermarriage with Fulani and, to a lesser extent, Moors and Soninké. The Tukulor's main concentration is in Senegal, where they inhabit both banks of the Dagana (a tributary of the Senegal River) to halfway between Matam and Bakel. They are numerous also in and around Kayes, Nioro-du-Sahel, in the region of Segu on the Niger River, in eastern Massina and Dinginray. About 140,000 live in Mauritania.

Traditional beliefs in the nature of man and his destiny after death play a significant role in the Tukulor's outlook on life; the animistic stratum in which they are imbedded is tenacious. The impersonal vital force, *fittandu*, is upon death absorbed into deity, while the shadow soul, *belu*, is the personal spirit subject to reward in Heaven or punishment in Hell. The distinction between these two spirits, however, is not as clear as might be expected, and they are often confused.

Tukulor differentiate among their clergy according to whether they lead the prayer, teach, specialize in the study and interpretation of canon law or head a parish. The common word for a cleric is *midibbo*, the teacher is the *tyerno*, while the jurist and highest priest is the *fodio*. The parish head, often also the chief administrative officer in a village, is called *almami*.

Islam came to the Tukulor in the eleventh century with the conversion of the ruling class. The common people followed during the next few centuries, and today nearly all Tukulor are Muslims.

Islam has brought no significant change in psychological attitudes towards magic. Supernatural power, or *baraka*, may be possessed by a renowned cleric, or it may simply emanate from him, reflecting a strong Berber Islamic influence. In the Senegal River valley the fabrication and sale of charms and amulets are the preserve of Tukulor clerics. Witchcraft persists in spite of Islam; in the Futas, each village has its own recognized witch family. Tukulor believe that the witch substance is inherited through women but that it does not necessarily affect all the children. The people also make uninhibited use of exorcists, who may also act as herbalists and rainmakers. Divination flourishes, with people more concerned about the diviner's power than with Islamic prescription; in fact, in most cases, the diviner is a Muslim cleric.

In the past the Tukulor have been associated with various Sufi orders. Early in the nineteenth century the Shadhili was introduced among them by a Fulani cleric, Ali As-Sufi, but they ultimately adopted the Tijani upon the rise of Al-Hajj Umar. Practices, tendencies and devotion vary greatly within this *tariqa*, depending on the training of the clerics.

Tukulor society is divided into four main social strata, each permitted to own slaves. First are the *torobe*, who are traditionally concerned with the learning and propagation of Islam. This aristocratic class emerged when the first Tukulor *almami*, Suleyman Ball, established the *almamyat* of Tekrur in Futa Toro in 1778.

The middle class, *rimbé*, comprise the following: the *subalbé*, who hold and manage the fishing industry along the river; the *sebbé*, farmers who, because of the seasonal nature of agriculture, comprise a martial establishment during slack periods and are often referred to as the warriors; the *dyawambé*, who are administrators or courtiers and often middlemen or tradesmen.

The lower middle class includes the *nyenbé*, skilled craftsmen, who may be smiths, jewelers, carpenters, boat builders, weavers, leatherworkers, shoemakers, singers, storytellers and oral historians or musicians.

The lower class, made up of servants and the manual unskilled laborers, includes the *gallunkobé*, or freed slaves, and the *matyubé*, or slaves.

Social mobility in the traditional Tukulor milieu is practically nonexistent except that slaves become free at the third generation.

Tukulor social life displays a mosaic of indigenous and Islamic elements associated in complex and often poorly integrated combinations. Thus wives, upon the death of their husbands, are returned to their respective families, while those with grown children who refuse to leave the conjugal compound come under the authority of the eldest son. He may give women in the compound, including his own mother, in marriage. Yet the relationship between maternal uncle and nephew are as strong as in pre-Islamic times. Indeed, the Tukulor teach their children that on the day of resurrection they will be recognized not by their own mother or father, but by their maternal uncle. The clans, or *woda*, continue to be a social-political institution, honoring a particular totem—primarily a taboo.

The Tukulor strictly observe the Islamic categories of prohibited persons in marriage and marriage equality regulations. A brideprice, including obligatory gifts of animals, or *nafore*, goes to the couple to guarantee the stability of the union. Part of the *nafore* is turned over to the bride as a dowry, but if she seeks a divorce, the *nafore* is restored to the husband. Tukulor do not regard the levirate as obligatory. Customarily, Tukulor prefer to marry in Shawwal, the month that the Prophet Muhammad married Aisha. Fridays are reserved for virgins, while Mondays are for divorcees and widows.

When death seems imminent, the dying person's face is turned towards Mecca, and he is encouraged to recite the *shahada*. If this is not possible, it is said for him. The room is then fumigated with incense to keep the spirits at bay. Immediately after death the cleric (in the region of Kayes a woman, usually the wife) performs the ritual washing of the corpse with water perfumed with herbs and roots.

Alfred G. Gerteiny
Population figures updated by Richard V. Weekes

BIBLIOGRAPHY

Books

Behrman, Lucy C. *Muslim Brotherhood and Politics in Senegal*. Cambridge: Harvard University Press, 1970.

Curran, Brian Dean, and Schrock, Joann. *Area Handbook for Mauritania*. The American University FAS, DA Pam 550–161. Washington, D.C.: Government Printing Office, 1972.

Diarra, Fatoumata-Agnes, and Fougeyrollas, Pierre. "Ethnic Group Relations in Senegal." In *Ethnic Group Relations in Africa: Senegal; The United Republic of Tanzania*. Paris: UNESCO, 1974.

Gerteiny, Alfred G. *Mauritania*. New York: Praeger, 1967.

Nelson, Harold D., et al. *Area Handbook for Senegal*. The American University FAS, DA Pam 550–70. 2nd ed. Washington, D.C.: Government Printing Office, 1974.

Oloruntimehin, B. O. *The Segu Tukulor Empire*. New York: Humanities Press, 1972.

Trimingham, J. Spencer. *Islam in West Africa*. London: Oxford University Press, 1959.

TUNJUR   Tradition, supported by archaeological remains, records the existence of a Tunjur kingdom seated in northern Darfur (Sudan), powerful in the sixteenth century and destroyed by the rising power of the Fur at the beginning of the seventeenth century. A perhaps less important Tunjur kingdom flourished in Wadai (Chad) at about the same time until it was ended by the Maba supporters of Abd al-Karim early in the seventeenth century. The Tunjur, or at least some of them, migrated to the west and settled among the Kanembu of Mao (Kanem), where they failed in trying to found an autonomous kingdom.

It is their pride in past glories and bitterness against those who later oppressed them which today prevent the few remaining Tunjur from disappearing altogether.

At the most there are no more than 10,000 Tunjur. In Sudan they live chiefly in Darfur Province, where they were once the rulers. Ruined citadels or palaces on nearly every hilltop witness the past power of the Tunjur sultans. Descendants of the former royal clan live in Jebel Hires south of El Fasher not far from the former seat of the Fur sultanate, which succeeded them in power in the seventeenth century. Some Tunjur are traders in the Kutum area as well as traders and farmers in the Fatta Borno area, but it is in the hills of Dar ("home of") Furnung that one meets the clans of the poor peasantry. Other Tunjur are scattered in Dar Forok, Dar Hamra, Jebel Gubba and Jebel Si. In Chad, where they number perhaps 5,000, they live in a few villages in the Am Dam district of Wadai Province near the Batha River, in the Abu Telfan hills and in Dar Ziyud. In the Dagana, there is a large group west of the big village of Massakori. In Kanem, apart from a tiny group in the Motoa district, the largest group of all is found in and around the big village of Mondo, perhaps the former seat of the short-lived Tunjur sultanate in Kanem. First-hand (and sound) information about the Tunjur is scarce except in Dar Furnung and Kanem.

The Tunjur language has apparently disappeared. In Dar Furnung, the first language of the Tunjur is Fur; the second is local Arabic used by educated people and traders. In the Kutum-Fatta Borno area, they speak mainly Arabic, although some speak Beri (see Beri). In Kanem, Arabic is considered their own language— some say that anyone speaking only Arabic in Kanem may be Tunjur, but that leaves open the question of the Arab migrants in Kanem. Tunjur may speak Kanembu or Dazaga as a second language (see Kanembu; Tebu). Such dispersal of the Tunjur supports the local tradition that the people migrated westward from Sudan after the fall of their sultanate.

It is not easy to distinguish the Tunjur from the various peoples living in the same area such as the Fur, Maba, Arabs and Kanembu. This may be accounted for by the constraints of the natural environment, to which all of them must submit, and to the unifying factor of Islam. However, close observance reveals distinctions. One of them is the Tunjur's bitter pride, the pride of a beaten people, destroyed as a nation, hunted from place to place, surviving only in a kind of diaspora, having found refuge in secluded areas, a pride which creates a strong will to survive. Every Tunjur keeps the cherished memory of the glories of the lost Tunjur kingdom as if every one of them belonged to the royal clan. They often despise the people around them, especially the Fur, who deprived them of their dignity. While they claim Arab ancestry, like nearly every people in the area, and are proud of it, they put even greater pride in being Tunjur and in the fact that their ancestors were Muslim as far as one can remember. Lacking such pride, they would not have survived as a people.

Another distinctive feature of the Tunjur is their success in growing date palms. They are the only ones to do this; their neighbors do not even try to imitate them.

Dar Furnung is a cold, hilly country with fertile foothills and sandy hollows where water is never far underneath. Villages and fields of bulrush millet flourish on the plateaus. In the hollows are groves of palm trees. From the outskirts of the hills and as far eastwards as Fatta Borno, the wide bed of the Wadi Kutum opens like a large avenue of date palms.

Kanem is a large sandy area of ancient dunes and hollows, a monotonous landscape covered with wild grass and few trees. Annual rainfall is not above 14 inches. Water is collected by the sandy hollows, never far from the surface. There the Tunjur bore permanent wells, and their cattle graze in the hollows.

The Tunjur are grouped in settled villages of houses, usually built on higher positions such as ridges or hilltops. Their round reed-walled houses with conical thatched roofs are identical with those of the neighboring peoples but sometimes look more miserable. Poverty may account for it, but colonial officers usually considered the material inferiority of the Tunjur to be evidence of lower technological ability. This opinion does not consider the skill shown in the stone buildings attributed by tradition to the Tunjur.

In Dar Furnung, the Tunjur grow bulrush millet in fields of various sizes. This is men's work. Women participate in weeding and harvesting. They take care, too, of small irrigated gardens, where they grow vegetables and sometimes fruit (onions, tomatoes, bamya, lemons, watermelons); this practice is not common among neighboring peoples. Date palms are planted and cared for by the men. Local blacksmiths (*haddad*) make the tools needed for cultivation of the date palms. The surplus of dates is sold in the local markets. Wild grass seeds are still harvested in order to brew the local beer (*märisä*). Camels and cattle are few, sheep and goats numerous, at least they were before the great drought of the 1970s.

The Tunjur of Kanem cultivate millet, sorghum, maize, haricot beans. One typical crop rotation is millet, beans, sorghum; afterwards the land lies fallow a few years. Cattle are pastured on the fields in the dry season in order to have them naturally manured. Wild fruit (jujube, *Balanites aegyptiaca*) is collected in some areas; gum is collected when available. Cattle raising in Kanem is sedentary; there is no transhumance. The Tunjur of Kanem raise sheep and goats for their meat, skins and hair; camels and oxen are used for transport.

In Kanem and in Dar Furnung, wealthy Tunjur ride horses and own donkeys for transport and for their women; the poor have only donkeys. Traders live in the big villages or towns and cannot easily be distinguished from traders of different origins. They still own fields in the countryside, cared for by members of the family. Usually they have one wife and household in the trading center and another in the country.

Tunjur social organization rests on segmentation into clans. Six clans are known in Kanem, and a much greater number are in Darfur. The royal clan seems to be present in both regions, far apart as they are. Very little else is known of these clans except for the cattle brands used in Darfur. Clan founders, taboos, exogamy need further investigation.

The Tunjur may marry a non-Tunjur, but never the son or daughter of a blacksmith (see Haddad). Marriage customs such as brideprice are similar to those of the surrounding peoples; in Darfur the brideprice is not excessive, as it is among the Zaghawa. Family life is governed by the Shariah (Islamic law), interpreted by the local *faqi* (cleric). Polygyny, while legal, is not common among the peasantry. Male circumcision is practiced between 8 and 16 years of age. They say that they do not practice female circumcision.

Political leadership was destroyed by the defeat of the Tunjur at the hands of the Fur, Maba and Kanembu. In Darfur, the Fur rulers placated Tunjur by appointing one of the highest dignitaries of the Fur sultanate, the *takanyon*, from among the Tunjur clan of the Kunyanga. Otherwise, clan authority was vested in foreigners. This practice was continued by the colonial powers.

Tunjur leaders consider that their people as a whole have been kept out of any kind of governmental positions in the nation where they live. However, one may discover among the national elite prominent personalities who soberly claim a Tunjur ancestry.

The Tunjur are zealous Muslims and may be described as orthodox Sunni following the Maliki school of jurisprudence and following mainly the teachings of the Risala. Traces of pre-Islamic rituals do exist and deserve further research, but this is a difficult and sensitive matter.

For this humiliated people Islam is a link with the outside world. Only religion permits them to regain access to the large community on an equal footing with the people who destroyed their states. Through it, they assert a kind of superiority both in the past (precedence in adopting Islam) and in the present as learned and pious members of the Islamic intelligentsia. Restoring their former dignity, if not their former leadership, seems to be their common purpose.

BIBLIOGRAPHY

Books

Balfour-Paul, H. G. *History and Antiquities of Darfur*. Khartoum: Sudan Antiquities Service, 1953.
Gros, R. "Histoire des toundjour de Mondo (Kanem)." In *Quelques Populations de la république du Tchad*. Paris: C.H.E.A.M., 1971.
Le Rouvreur, A. *Sahariens et sahéliens du Tchad*. Paris: Editions Berger-Levrault, 1962.
Nachtigal, G. *Sahara and Sudan. IV. Wadai and Darfur*. New York: Barnes and Noble, 1971. (English translation.)
O'Fahey, R. S., and Spaulding, J. *Kingdoms of the Sudan*. London: Methuen, 1974.
Tubiana, M.-J. *Un Patriote tundjur: Le Faki Adam ab-Tishêka*. Valbonne, France: Centre National de la Recherche Scientifique, 1981.
————; Khayar, I. H.; and Deville, P. *Abd el-Karim, propagateur de l'Islam et fondateur du royaume des Ouaddaï*. Contributions à la connaissance des élites africaines, No. 2. Valbonne, France: Centre National de la Recherche Scientifique, 1978.

Articles

Arkell, A. J. "Darfur Antiquities." *Sudan Notes and Records* 19:1 (1936): 301–311; 20:1 (1937): 91–105; 27 (1946): 185–202.
MacMichael, H. A. "The Tungur-Fur of Dar Furnung." *Sudan Notes and Records* 3:1 (1920): 24–32.

Record

Adam Ab Tishêka (*faqi*). *Autobiography* (in Arabic). Valbonne, France: Centre National de la Recherche Scientifique, 1981.

Joseph Tubiana

TURKIC-SPEAKING PEOPLES   More than 100 million Turkic-speaking peoples of Europe and Asia, here called Turks, occupy an almost continuous band of territory extending from the Balkans to northeastern Siberia. While the peripheries of their lands are but sparsely populated by Turks, they comprise the predominant ethnic communities in the Anatolian peninsula and in the Central Asian borderlands of the Soviet Union, Iran, Afghanistan and China.

The heterogeneity of the Turks in religion (they are 98 percent Muslim of various sects), racial type, social structure and modes of livelihood renders untenable any attempt to classify them as a separate and distinct ethnic entity on any basis save that of linguistic affinity. Turkic subgroups are distinct and self-identified. The shamanistic Yakut, engaged in reindeer breeding along the upper reaches of the Aldan River in eastern Siberia, and the Christian, sedentary Surguch of Bulgaria possess no distinguishing feature in common other than the fact that their mutually unintelligible languages are descended from a common parent language. That language, Proto-Turkic, is related through common descent to the precursors of the Mongolic and Tungus-Manchu languages. The Turkic, Mongolic and Tungus-Manchu languages together comprise the Altaic family of languages, to which Yukagir, Korean, Japanese and the Uralic languages (Finno-Ugric and Samoyedic) are commonly throught to bear a more distant relation.

The primordial homeland of the Turks is generally thought to have been in the eastern portion of the Eurasian plain, approximately in the area now occupied by the Mongolian People's Republic. Thus, the ancestral Turks would have faced Tungus and Paleo-Siberian tribes on the north and east, Mongols to the south and Tocharian and Iranic-speaking peoples on the west.

The present disposition of the Turks is largely the result of a series of migrations out of the original homeland. One of these movements, that of the Yakut, whose northward exodus to their present habitat in Siberia probably began in the twelfth century, is of little consequence to the historiography of the Muslim world. The other migrations consisted of four overlapping waves of Turks and other Altaic people, whose penetrations into Central Asia, the Middle East and Europe exerted an enormous influence on world history. The four migrations were those of the Huns, the Ogüz Turks, the Kipchaks and the Mongols.

The Hunnic Empire, which thrust itself westward until checked in France at the Battle of Catalaunian Fields in A.D. 451, was comprised of numerous ethnic groups, including Turks, who formed the nucleus of the Bulgar and Khazar states in the Russian steppe lands between the fifth and tenth centuries. Meanwhile, a confederation of Turks consolidated power in the area formerly occupied by the Huns, between the Amur and Irtysh rivers. The westward advance of these Turks brought them increasingly into contact with Indo-Europeans under the domination of the Persian Sassanid dynasty. The subsequent history of Central Asia is largely concerned with the defeat and assimilation of the Bactrians, Sogdians and others by the Turks, whose westward progress continued without serious interruption, even though the internal political status of the Turks underwent frequent and radical alterations. The Tajiks, the former Sogdians, have retained their Persian speech, but most of the outlying Iranic peoples were assimilated to the language of the Turks, while at the same time assimilating many of the Turks to their more sedentary cultures. Even today the extensive intermingling of the western Turks with Persians is reflected in the predominantly Caucasian features of the Turks living west of the Amu Darya, as opposed to the mainly Mongoloid features of the Turks living east of the region. The Persian influence is also manifested in the strong Zoroastrian substratum underlying the Muslim practices of many Turks.

In the area between the basins of the Volga and Don rivers, the Turkic Khazars had established a khanate which, with the assistance of Byzantium, dominated the area until the eleventh century, when the Kipchak Turks defeated and assimilated the Khazars. Meanwhile, west of the Khazars the Turkic Bulgars had advanced to the western shore of the Black Sea, where most were Slavicized by their sedentary subjects within two centuries. Some, however, were able to maintain their Turkic speech, which was subsequently altered and augmented by later influxes of Turks.

A new and important element was injected into the Turkic migrations by the Arabs, whose armies marched into Central Asia in the eighth century, captured Samarkand and Bukhara and imposed Islam on the subject peoples. Their proselytizing was continued under the Islamic Seljuk confederation, composed of Ogüz Turks, which dominated most of Turkestan from the eleventh century to the Mongol conquest of the area in the early years of the thirteenth century. The Ogüz Turks, constituting the second important wave of Turks, held sway over Persia, Transcaucasus, Mesopotamia and much of Asia Minor by the end of the eleventh century.

The northern element of the Ogüz, the Pechenegs, was soon displaced by the third wave of Turks, that of the Kipchaks, whose position in Central Asia and in the Volga basin was strengthened by their alliance with the Mongols, who advanced their conquests to the gates of Vienna. The establishment of the mainly Turkic Golden Horde at the border of Europe and Asia, the conquests of Tamerlane (Timur Lenk, or Timur the Lame) and his successors and the establishment of the Moghul dynasty in India were fundamentally extensions of the expansionism initiated by Gengis Khan and those who succeeded him.

The period between the thirteenth century, when the Altaian alliance burst into the heart of Europe, and the fifteenth century, when the empire of Tamerlane was at its height and the Ottomans conquered Byzantium and the Balkans, constitutes the high-water mark in the geopolitical fortunes of the Turks. Their subsequent history is largely one of retrenchment from national independence movements and subjugation at the hands of the revivified empires of Russia, China and Persia.

In terms of their inner structure and borrowings from other languages, the various languages of the Turks can be divided into an eastern and a western branch. The languages of the western branch, being products of overlapping migrations, exhibit copious evidence of the intermixture of Turkic dialects and of extensive borrowings from Arabic, Persian and Russian. The western branch may be divided into four groups, here designated the Bulgar, Ogüz, Kipchak and Karluk groups.

The Bulgar group is represented today by only one living language, Chuvash. The Chuvash live along the middle course of the Volga and in various localities of western Siberia. The Chuvash are not Muslim.

The Ogüz group of Turkic languages originated in the second wave of Turks to enter Central Asia and eastern Europe. The Ogüz probably arrived in Central

Asia in the eighth century. Some two centuries later their northern element crossed the Urals and the Volga. A southwestern group of the Ogüz, the Seljuks, moved westward into Europe and southward into Asia Minor and the Middle East, while a southeastern group remained in the vicinity of the Aral Sea and formed the nucleus of the Turkmen (see Turkmen). The Seljuk subgroup is represented today by Turkish, spoken in the Republic of Turkey and in parts of Cyprus, Bulgaria, Yugoslavia, Greece, Iran, Syria and other countries of the Middle East and by Azeri, the principal language of the Azerbaijan Soviet Republic and of the northwest provinces of Iran (see Azeri; Shahsevan; Qashqa'i).

The third division of the western Turkic languages, the Kipchak group, is derived from the third wave of Turks to advance into eastern Europe. The Kipchaks, also known as Kumans or Polovtsy, were the most numerous element in the Golden Horde, which dominated the areas north of Kwarazm from the thirteenth to the fifteenth century. With the disintegration of the Golden Horde into smaller political units, the Kipchaks continued to dominate the Astrakhan, Kazan and Crimean khanates. There are three subdivisions of the Kipchak group—the Kipchak-Kuman, the Kipchak-Bulgar and the Kipchak-Nogai.

The Kipchak-Kuman subgroup of languages stems from the western Kipchaks, who occupied a vast area in the Balkans, Crimea and the southern Russian plain. The modern representative of this subgroup is Karaim, spoken around the cities of Vilnius and Panevezys in Lithuania, in the southern Ukraine near Lutsk and Galich and in the Crimea around the city of Eupatoria. The Kumyks, who live in the Daghestan Autonomous Soviet Republic, the Balkars and Karachai of the Caucasus and the Crimean Tatars (not to be confused with the nationality referred to simply as the Tatars) all speak languages belonging to the Kipchak-Kuman subgroup (see Daghestanis; Karachai, Balkar).

The Kipchak-Bulgar subgroup is composed of languages derived from the eastern element of the Golden Horde. The modern descendants are the Tatars (see Tatars), who live in the vicinity of Kazan on the middle Volga, and the Bashkir (see Bashkir), located south and east of the Tatars around their capital city of Ufa.

The language of the southern Kipchaks has produced the languages of the Kipchak-Nogai subgroup. Nogai is spoken in the vicinity of Stavropol in southeastern Russia and in the Karachai-Circassian region of the Soviet Caucasus. Karakalpak is the principal language of the Karakalpak Autonomous Soviet Republic on the southwest shore of the Aral Sea. Karakalpak is also spoken in the Kwarazm area of Uzbekistan, in the vicinity of Fergana and Astrakhan and in Afghanistan (see Karakalpak). Kazakh is the principal language of the immense Kazakh Soviet Republic (see Kazakhs).

The fourth division within western Turkic is the Karluk group, whose languages are derived from the language of the Turks occupying the extreme southeastern portion of Turkestan. This area was part of the West Turkic khanate in the sixth and seventh centuries. The modern representatives of this group are Uzbek and Uygur. Uzbek, heavily influenced in its formation by Persian, is the main language of the Uzbek Soviet Socialist Republic. One and one-half million Uzbek reside in the other Turkic republics of the Soviet Union (see Uzbek). More than 6 million Uygur live in the Xinjiang-Uygur Autonomous Region of China (see Uygur).

The eastern branch of Turkic includes far fewer languages and speakers than does the western branch. Most of the eastern Turks are non-Muslim, whereas the overwhelming majority of the western Turks observe one or another form of Islam. The two language groups in the east are the Kirghiz-Kipchak and the Khakas-Yakut.

The Kirghiz-Kipchak group consists of two modern languages, Kirghiz and Altai. There are 2 million Kirghiz in the Soviet Union, mainly in the Kirghiz Soviet Socialist Republic (see Kirghiz). The Altai, known earlier by a plethora of names, live in the Gorno-Altai Autonomous Oblast' in the Soviet Union. Many elements from Kipchak Turkic have been superimposed on the Kirghiz and Altai languages. The Kirghiz, alone among the eastern Turks, practice Islam, albeit with a strong shamanistic substratum.

The Khakas subgroup of eastern Tukic consists of the Khakas, who are located in southern Siberia around the city of Abakan, the Kamasin, who live in the valleys of the Mana and Kan rivers in the Krasnoyarsk region of Siberia, and the Shors, located in the northern Altai Mountains. Related peoples are the Tofalari (also called Karagas) of the Krasnoyarsk region and the Tuvinians, who occupy the Tuvinian Autonomous Soviet Socialist Republic, an area annexed to the Soviet Union at the close of World War II. The Yakut, who form the main population of the Yakut Autonomous Soviet Socialist Republic, are isolated from the mainstream of Turks, being surrounded by Paleo-Siberians and Tungus in northeastern Siberia.

BIBLIOGRAPHY

Books

Dabbs, J. A. *History of the Discovery and Exploration of Chinese Turkestan*. The Hague: Mouton, 1963.
Menges, Karl H. *The Turkic Languages and Peoples, An Introduction to Turkic Studies*. Wiesbaden, Germany: Harassowitz, 1968.
Poppe, Nicholas H. *Introduction to Altaic Linguistics*. Wiesbaden, Germany: Harassowitz, 1965.

Articles

Halasi-Kun, T. "The Caucasus, An Ethno-Historical Survey." *Studia Caucasica* 1 (1963): 1–47.

Menges, Karl H. "Peoples, Languages and Migrations." In *Central Asia: A Century of Russian Rule*, edited by Edward Allworth. New York: Columbia University Press, 1967.

Harry H. Walsh

TURKMEN   The majority of the Turkmen reside in the area surrounding the Kara Kum ("Black Sand") desert east of the Caspian Sea, between the Amu Darya River and the mountains bordering the northern edge of the Iranian plateau. The Kara Kum itself is too arid to support a human population of any significant size, but the semi-arid fringes of this low-altitude desert can support a population through livestock production and, in some areas, agriculture. The region is divided among three countries: Afghanistan, Iran and the Soviet Union. Most of the 4 million Turkmen, about 2.1 million, live in the Turkmen Soviet Socialist Republic. There are about 380,000 Turkmen in Afghanistan and about 1.1 million in Iran.

The Turkmen of these three countries have been effectively separated from one another by international boundaries for only about 50 years. The borders themselves have existed for much longer, but until about half a century ago they were not barriers to travel and communication. There are minor linguistic differences corresponding to tribal identity (which for the most part do not coincide with international boundaries), but none of these differences in language is great enough to interfere with communication. There are also minor cultural differences among the various tribal groups; nevertheless the various tribes consider themselves as a single ethnic group. They define their ethnic identity in terms of three criteria. First, in order to be a Turkmen, one must either be a descendant in the male line of Turkmen, or of slaves of Turkmen or of individuals who have lived for several generations among Turkmen. The other two criteria are linguistic and religious. One must be a native speaker of the Turkmen language, and one must be a Sunni Muslim of the Hanafi school.

In the past, a large number of Turkmen migrated out of the region around Kara Kum into Mesopotamia and Anatolia. As a result, there are scattered groups of people in Iraq, Syria and Turkey who identify themselves as Turkmen. These groups can be referred to as the Middle Eastern Turkmen, or diaspora Turkmen, in order to distinguish them from the main Central Asian group in the vicinity of the Kara Kum. There are about 200,000 Turkmen in Iraq and about 110,000 in Syria. It is difficult to estimate the number in Turkey because no figures have been published. Because of a long isolation from the main group of Turkmen, the Middle Eastern Turkmen have evolved somewhat culturally distinct, the most salient difference being religion. Many are Shia Muslims.

The people's name for themselves is Türkmen, a word which in Anglicized form can be either Turkmen or Turkman. (The fact that the last syllable of this word, "men" or "man," appears to be an English word is purely coincidental.)

An alternative spelling is Turkoman, or Turcoman, derived from the Persian, Turkuman.

The Turkmen language, which the Turkmen refer to variously as Türkmence, Türkmen Dil or Türki, belongs to the southwestern or Oqüz group of Turkic languages and has close affinities to Azeri and modern Turkish (see Turkic-speaking Peoples). Like the latter languages, Turkmen is heavily laden with Arabic and Persian loan words. Before the present century, there was a small body of literature written in the Turkmen language using the Arabic alphabet. This literature until recently was cultivated exclusively by religious teachers who had become literate as part of their religious education. Since the establishment of the Turkmen Soviet Socialist Republic, a fairly extensive literature in Turkmen written with Cyrillic letters has developed.

A little over a century ago, most all of the Central Asian Turkmen were nomads living in felt tents of the Central Asian variety, which are often referred to in English as yurts or trellis tents. The nomadic residence patterns of pastoral peoples in the Middle East are often assumed to have a purely economic function, that of using sparse and seasonably variable pasture for livestock production. But nomadism can also be a means of exploiting mobility for military and political ends, and for the Turkmen this second function was more important.

The mode of economic production of most Turkmen included both production of sheep and goats and agriculture. In regions where production of livestock was more important, some migration was necessary for the care of their flocks. Nevertheless, this economy could be easily combined with a semi-nomadic residence pattern. Such a residence pattern would consist of living part of the year in permanent houses and part of the year in tents while making short migrations.

In regions where agriculture was the mainstay of the economy, a completely sedentary form of residence was possible. Despite these facts, however, until recently all Turkmen lived the year around in tents. In spite of the discomfort of portable dwellings as opposed to more substantial ones, the hard work of migration itself and the expense of maintaining the beasts of burden necessary to move their families with all of their belongings, the military advantage of nomadism made it worthwhile. Being highly mobile and on the edge of the Kara Kum, the Turkmen could easily raid sedentary neighbors and retreat quickly into more arid regions where the armies of sedentary states could not follow. They used this military advantage to maintain de facto political independence despite occasional nominal acceptance of sedentary suzerains. Such independence meant freedom from taxation, conscription and the manipulative government officials common in the traditional Middle East. Government officials were especially threatening to rural people, because they often managed to acquire ownership of the land and thus to add a burden of land rent to that of taxation.

The political organization of the Turkmen was based on genealogies traced in the male line, so every Turkmen was a member of a hierarchy of named patrilineal descent groups. Most of the members of a named descent group lived in a region owned jointly by the group. They were united politically and militarily for the defense of this territory and for the defense of their individual rights of person and property. When a military threat was considered too much for smaller and less inclusive descent groups to handle, they would unite with several other similar groups which together formed a larger descent group based on more distant ancestry. The largest descent groups of this sort are groups like the Teke, Yomut, Göklen, Salor, Saryk, Chaudor and Ersari. These names often appear as tribal designations in various descriptions of the Turkmen.

The Turkmen used their military prowess in fights among themselves over territory or, more frequently, in raids for livestock. They also engaged in slave raiding, usually raiding the sedentary inhabitants of northeastern Persia and northern Afghanistan. Caravans would be surprised on the road, or farmers working in their fields would be attacked swiftly and then carried off as captives. These captives could be kept as second-class members in their captor's household, sold to fellow tribesmen or sent by caravan to slave markets in one of the Central Asian cities, Khiva, Bukhara, Samarkand or Merv.

The nineteenth and twentieth centuries witnessed the demise of Turkmen political independence and military prowess. From the middle of the nineteenth century on, the sort of irregular cavalry the Turkmen could put together was no longer effective against the well-organized armies and artillery of czarist Russia. Later, they also proved ineffective against the modernized Iranian army established by Reza Shah. Most of the Turkmen came under Russian control. The Russian conquest of Merv in 1884 marked the end of any internationally recognized Turkmen polity. However, the transition to effective control by sedentary states was gradual and characterized by occasional reversals. The Turkmen of Iran maintained de facto independence until 1925, and some Iranian Turkmen reasserted de facto independence during World War II and again after the Iranian Revolution of 1978. During the Russian Revolution, many Turkmen asserted independence temporarily as part of the so-called Basmachi movement. Despite this, however, the general trend for all Turkmen has been effective control by government dominated by other ethnic groups—Persians, Pushtun or Russians. These governments are not especially sympathetic with Turkmen traditions and are suspicious of possible desires for an independent Turkmenistan. Sentiment for the preservation of Turkmen identity is not at present translated into an active movement for independence. Within the Soviet Union, however, the Turkmen do enjoy a degree of autonomy.

Loss of political independence has robbed nomadism of its political and military value, and most Turkmen have responded by adopting either a sedentary or a semi-sedentary residence pattern.

The Turkmen are divided into two occupational groups, the agricultural *chomur* and the pastoral *charwa*. The *chomur*, who live in the better-watered regions, traditionally made their living primarily by rainfall cultivation of wheat and barley. Herding of sheep, goats, donkeys, horses, cattle and water buffalo was secondary. Despite their primary reliance on agriculture, the *chomur* traditionally lived only in tents and made short migrations. Since their loss of political independence, however, most *chomur* have become sedentary and have taken up mechanized, commercial cotton production.

The *charwa* live in more arid regions and gain their livelihood primarily by raising sheep, goats, donkeys, camels and horses. High-risk cultivation of wheat and barley is secondary. Both pastoral and agricultural products are traded in urban markets for things the Turkmen cannot produce themselves, or at least cannot produce as well as others.

The Turkmen also derive a part of their income from the production of carpets. These are woven from the wool of local sheep by the women of most Turkmen households. Rug dealers sometimes refer to these carpets as Bukharan carpets, probably because those first brought to Europe were acquired in the markets of Bukhara. Turkmen rugs coming from Afghanistan are sometimes placed under the generic label of Afghan carpets. Most carpet dealers and collectors, however, label such carpets correctly as Turkmen carpets. The large number of fine carpets woven by the Turkmen and the intricate and beautiful designs they have perfected in the process constitute an artistic achievement of the highest caliber.

Though political, and in some areas economic, changes have been extensive, less change has occurred in Turkmen family life. This is well documented for the Turkmen of Iran and Afghanistan, who were accessible until recently to Western observers. The situation is less clear in the Soviet Union, although the available information suggests that the Turkmen there are more conservative in family life and religion than Soviet political leaders would like.

The Turkmen, like many warlike, or formerly warlike, peoples, accord formal authority within the family to men. This, however, does not exclude women from informal influence over family affairs. Turkmen families ordinarily go through a cycle of development which begins when a man separates from his father's household between the ages of 30 and 40. By this time, he usually has been married 10 or 20 years and often has children who are old enough to be economically productive. Once a man has established a household of his own, he marries off his daughters according to the order of their birth. For each one he collects bridewealth of 10 camels, or 100 sheep or the equivalent in cash. In recent years, bridal payments in cash have become more common. Each daughter then leaves his household to become part of her husband's household. Through this process, a man's household eventually becomes an extended family, including his wife, his married sons and their wives and children. Then, again following birth order, the sons separate off, forming independent households of their own. As each son separates, he is given part of his father's capital in land and livestock to form the basis for the livelihood of the new household. Prosperous men sometimes become polygynous in their later years, usually taking a wife about the time their first wife approaches the end of her reproductive years. Roughly 10 percent of men who live past 40 eventually marry polygynously.

Within each family, sons must be obedient and respectful to their fathers. Their subordinate status is symbolized by many rules. They sit in less prestigious locations in the family's tent or house; they must be reserved in manner and avoid light conversation or smoking in the presence of their father. A younger brother must show similar respect to an older brother. The subordination of wives to husbands is even greater. When a husband's guests, or older brothers, are present, a wife must cover her mouth with her head cloth and not speak. She must sit quietly in a section of the tent or house reserved for people of low status and quickly obey any orders from her husband or his older brothers. The relationship of a woman to her father-in-law and mother-in-law makes the same demands but with greater stringency. This may be harsh, but it does maintain a household as a well-disciplined group which is efficient in organizing economic production.

Religion is another area in which there has been little change in Turkmen life. The Turkmen are, on the whole, devoutly religious. Most of them say the prayers which are required of Muslims five times a day, and they observe Ramadan. Men who can afford the expense make the pilgrimage to Mecca and afterward are respected as *hajjis*. Women of wealthy families often accompany a male relative to Mecca and also become *hajjis*. Religious teachers are honored and influential members of each Turkmen community. Also, Sufi orders such as the Naqshbandi are represented in many Turkmen communities. Frequently, religious teachers are also leaders of a Sufi order.

At present, most Turkmen wish to preserve their ethnic identity, their religion and many aspects of their traditional family life. However, few Turkmen believe political independence is a realistic goal. In all probability, they will remain an ethnic minority divided among large states in which they often are second-class citizens.

BIBLIOGRAPHY

Books

Allworth, Edward, ed. *The Nationality Question in Soviet Central Asia*. New York: Praeger, 1973.

Bacon, Elizabeth E. *Central Asians Under Russian Rule*. Ithaca: Cornell University Press, 1966.

Barthold, V. V. "A History of the Turkman People." In *Four Studies of the History of Central Asia*, by V. V. Barthold. Translated by V. and T. Minorsky. Vol. 3. Leiden: E. J. Brill, 1962.

Caroe, Sir Olaf K. *Soviet Empire: The Turks of Central Asia and Stalinism*. New York: St. Martin's Press, 1953.

Coon, Carleton S. *Caravan: Story of the Middle East*. Westport, Conn.: Greenwood Press, 1969.

Freykin, Z. G. *Turkmenskaya S.S.R.* Moscow: n.p., 1954. (Translation on deposit, Human Relations Area Files, New Haven, Conn.)

Irons, William. "Is Yomut Social Behavior Adaptive?" In *Sociobiology; Beyond Nature/*

Nurture? AAAS Selected Symposium 35, edited by George W. Barlow and James Silverberg. Boulder, Colo.: Westview Press, 1980.

————. "Variations in Economic Organization: A Comparison of the Pastoral Yomut and the Basseri." In *Perspectives on Nomadism*, edited by William Irons and Neville Dyson-Hudson. International Studies in Sociology and Social Anthropoloy. Vol. 13. Leiden: E. J. Brill, 1972.

————. *The Yomut Turkmen: A Study of Social Organization Among a Central Asian Turkic Speaking Population*. Museum of Anthropology Anthropological Paper, No. 58. Ann Arbor: University of Michigan, 1975.

————. "Political Stratification Among Pastoral Nomads." In *Pastoral Production and Society*, edited by William Irons. Cambridge: Cambridge University Press, 1979.

Krader, Lawrence. *Social Organization of the Mongol-Turkic Pastoral Nomads*. Indiana University Uralic and Altaic Studies, Vol. 20. The Hague: Mouton, 1963.

Mackie, Louise W., and Thompson, Jon, eds. *Turkmen: Tribal Carpets and Traditions*. Washington, D.C.: The Textile Museum, 1980.

Marvin, Charles. *Merv and the Man-Stealing Turcomans*. London: W. H. Allen, 1881.

Nyrop, Richard F., et al. *Area Handbook for Syria*. The American University FAS, DA Pam 550–47. Washington, D.C.: Government Printing Office, 1971.

Pinner, Robert, and Franses, Michael, eds. *Turkoman Studies I; Aspects of the Weaving and Decorative Arts of Central Asia*. London: Oguz Press, 1980.

Wheeler, Geoffrey. *The Modern History of Soviet Central Asia*. New York: Praeger, 1964.

Articles

Andrews, P. A. "The White House of Khurasan: The Felt Tents of the Iranian Yomut and Goklen." *Iran: Journal of the British Institute of Persian Studies* 118 (1973): 93–110.

Davidow, G. "Women in Soviet Turkmenia." *New World Revolution* 40:2 (1972): 107–109.

Dunn, Stephen P., and Dunn, Ethel. "Soviet Regime and Native Culture in Central Asia and Kazakhstan: The Major Peoples." *Current Anthropology* 8:3 (1967): 147–208.

Irons, William. "Nomadism as a Political Adaptation: The Case of the Yomut Turkmen." *American Ethnologist* 1:4 (1974): 635–658.

————. "The Turkmen Nomads." *Natural History* 77:9 (1968): 44–51.

————. "The Turkmen of Iran: A Brief Research Report." *Iranian Studies* 11:1 (1969): 27–38.

————. "Variation in Political Stratification Among the Yomut Turkmen." *Anthropological Quarterly* 44:3 (1971): 143–156.

Michaud, Sabrina, and Michaud, Roland. "Turkomans: Horsemen of the Steppes." *National Geographic Magazine* 144:5 (1973): 634–669.

Unpublished Manuscripts

Irons, William G. "Hospitality, Turkman Style." Paper presented at the Seventy-First Annual Meeting of the American Anthropological Association, Toronto, November 29–December 2, 1972.

————. "Residence Choice and Fitness Among the Turkmen of North Persia." Paper presented at the Seventy-Fourth Annual Meeting of the American Anthropological Association, San Francisco, December 2–6, 1975.
————. "The Yomut Turkmen." Ph.D. dissertation, University of Michigan, 1969.

William G. Irons

TURKS, ANATOLIAN   To most of the world, Turks are citizens of the Republic of Turkey, occupying that historic bridge of land called Anatolia (and part of Thrace) which links Europe to Asia and where many civilizations have flourished and waned. But the 38 million Anatolian Turks are less than half of the world's 100 million Turkic-speaking peoples, although they are the most conspicuous, independent, organized and internationally active.

While as with most ethnic groups there are variations within the whole, the Anatolian Turks are remarkably homogeneous in language and culture and very much aware and proud of being Turks. More than any other Turkic-speaking groups, they are nationalistic, identifying themselves with their heritage and homeland with an intensity which promotes economic and military strength, as well as aversion to efforts by others to influence their way of life.

The deepest division within Turkish society is that between the urban elite and rural Turks, the former striving for modernity, living in high-rise apartments, driving along broad avenues, employed in government and commerce and attending universities and operas in the cosmopolitan cities of Istanbul, Ankara and Izmir. The rural Turk, who outnumbers the urbanist three to two, lives a life in many ways common to villagers the world over, while yet retaining the values and culture traits which distinguish Turks from non-Turks. Even in the cities, the rural Turk outnumbers the "urban" Turk as more than half the population of the major cities is *geçekondulu*, people one or two generations or less removed from villages, people who do not share in the advantages of cosmopolitan urban life.

Rural Turkey itself can be categorized into different ways of living which usually reflect the people's adaptation to the environment. Central Anatolia is an elevated plateau of rolling, often rocky plains extending eastward into Iran. It is extremely hot in summer, numbingly cold in winter. Villages are far apart, separated by fields of wheat and other cereal grains. Farming these fields and herding sheep and goats requires a toughness that has become a national symbol of the Turks. Traditional and conservative, the Central Anatolian farm family usually owns its own land but has few amenities.

Coastal Turkey along the Black Sea in the north, the Aegean Sea in the west, and the Mediterranean Sea in the south is more diverse. Sheltered from the harsh climate of Central Anatolia by the southern Taurus Mountains and the northern Pontic Mountains, the coastal Turks experience an easier life. They have also had more contact with the outside world. In fact, many are immigrants from Eastern Europe and the Soviet Union. Here, industry and commerce have developed, and farming, which still dominates village life, involves the raising of dates, figs, other fruits, vegetables, tobacco and cattle. Life is less traditional, and change comes more easily.

Southeastern Turkey is dry and mountainous, carved by valleys which can be cultivated seasonally (the melons of Diyarbakir are famous). Here live the descendants of the great nomadic tribes of Kurds, Arabs, Yoruk and Turkmen which once dominated Southwest Asia. Today, while numbers of them still move seasonally to the high mountain pastures with their flocks, most have become settled in valley and lowland villages. They have retained their kinship traditions and tribal allegiances, their pride in horsemanship and a restlessness to travel (many are found in the western cities working as porters).

Turkish villages have long faced problems of isolation, insecurity, poverty, ill health, overpopulation and illiteracy. To deal with these problems, they developed social institutions centering around the extended family and the village community, which provided a degree of security and self-sufficiency. But there was no escape from the worst of these conditions until after the revolution led by Kemal Ataturk following World War I. Since then, villages have come to vary a great deal depending on the degree of social and economic influences introduced into their societies. New roads lessen the isolation in almost all cases, bringing in material goods from the cities and taking out young people and the underemployed in search of new lives, or at least expanded opportunities.

In all villages, however, there remains a strong sense of tradition, despite the in and out flow of goods, people and ideas. The principal tradition is the strength of the extended, patriarchal family. The family functions as a unit, with each individual performing a prescribed task. Family ties are complemented by intimate village community involvement to form a complex of mutual obligations and benefits.

The traditional family consists of a man, his wife, unmarried children and married sons and their families. On the death of the father, each son sets up a separate household to start the pattern anew. This tradition is weakening, but more often than not there are more than just nuclear family members living under one roof.

The greatest social distinctions in the Turkish villages are age, sex, wealth and family prestige. Children are taught to respect their elders; while in public, they do not speak in the presence of older people unless they are called upon to do so. Women are not secluded to the degree of those in most South and Southwest Asian Muslim societies, but they nevertheless hold subordinate positions to men, despite the fact that they work in the fields as well as in the home with the usual duties of raising the children, cooking and serving meals.

Traditionally, parents or intermediaries selected brides for the sons and brought them into the groom's home to live. The bride's status is lower than that of all except the young children and is referred to as *gelinlik etmek*, meaning "on call." She performs under the critical eye of her mother-in-law and may be assigned the most unpleasant tasks of the household. In some families she must avoid contact with her father-in-law. Upon the birth of a son, she gains status.

Family honor depends a great deal on the conduct of its women. A girl must be a virgin at the time of her marriage, and assurance of her virginity is a major concern of the male members of the family. Although she is not veiled, the restriction on her movements makes it unlikely that she comes in contact with men outside her family. She is married off at an early age, or she is kidnapped. Kidnapping is not unusual, but most often it is simply a term to cover a carefully arranged elopement. Once a girl is kidnapped, she is no longer considered a virgin and is therefore no longer in the respectable marriage market, with no alternative but to marry her kidnapper.

Under Ataturk, the 1926 Family Code changed marriage from a family-arranged contract to a civil agreement between two consenting individuals. Villagers for years simply ignored the code and continued old customs, but in recent years a compromise has been reached. Modern marriage still consists of a private ceremony (after the families of the engaged couple have agreed on terms) presided over by the *hoca* (cleric, frequently spelled *hoja* in English transliteration) and a lavish feast, sometimes lasting several days, prepared by the bride's family. In addition, the couple now goes before a civil authority to have the marriage recorded officially so that children from the union will be legitimate in the eyes of the law.

All commemorations are important in village life. Besides weddings, circumcisions, visits by important outsiders and the coming of spring are occasions for festivities, as are various religious observances such as Şeker Bayram (candy festival) at the end of Ramadan and Kurban Bayram (feast of sacrifice). Apart from these times of celebration, everyday village life tends to be monotonous, and Turks cling to the various socializing institutions which relieve the tedium. Men meet daily to exchange gossip, transact business and tell stories. These gatherings took place in the past in the guest room of the most prominent villager's home, but today the coffeehouse (*khavehane*), once an urban institution, is the center of village socializing among males.

One institution for which Anatolian Turks are widely known is the *hamam* (bath). Almost every town and some villages boast a *hamam*, to which men and women go at alternate times, or in some cases there is a separate bathhouse for each sex. Bathers sit on benches, in a steaming room, pouring bowls of increasingly hotter water over their bodies. An attendant then scrubs off the dirt, along with a fair amount of skin, with a coarse cloth. Villagers frequent the *hamam* before important festivals. If they must go to a nearby town, it is the occasion for an all-day outing.

Other areas of public meeting are the water fountain and the mosque courtyard. Popular stories told over and over are those of the ubiquitous Nassradin Hoca, a mythical, comical teacher of Seljuk days, sometimes pictured riding backwards on a donkey. Hoca stories are legend and demonstrate the wry sense of humor of the Turks, which combines the absurd with the practical joke.

Enthusiasm for tough athletic competition is a Turkish trademark. The national sport is wrestling, but other types of contests are popular, among them soccer (*futbol*) and a kind of polo (*cirit*). Spectator sports include camel fighting and cock fighting.

Perhaps the greatest changes in the life-style of Turks have come about through the growth of villages into towns and towns into cities, reflecting not only efforts at industrialization but one of the highest population growth rates in the world, more than 2.5 percent a year. It is in the towns that the impact of Ataturk's social revolution has wrenched the conservative Turk further away from his rural traditions.

Kemal Ataturk, born Mustafa in 1881 and given a second name of Kemal by a schoolteacher, came onto the national scene at the end of World War I. No single leader in modern times has so influenced his people. Nearly 45 years after his death in 1938, the edicts he handed down relating to Turkish culture are still in force and constantly working towards bringing a twentieth-century life-style to the village and town Turk.

Ataturk helped bring an end to the control of rural landlords in Anatolia. These were men who evolved by the end of the nineteenth century from tribal leadership, a process that began in the eleventh century when the Seljuk Turks migrated out of the east and conquered most of the Christian Byzantine Empire. The Seljuks, with their capital in Konya, ruled for nearly two centuries and firmly implanted Islam and Turkish culture into the existing population. More migrating Turks entered Anatolia, among them a tribal leader, Ertoghrul, whose tribesmen grew stronger as the Seljuks grew weaker and eventually disappeared from the scene. Ertoghrul's son, Osman, became tribal emir in 1299, fought the Greeks of western Anatolia, acquired territory and a following and finally in 1326 established the seat of his domain in Bursa, then the largest Christian city in Asia. So began the Ottoman (Osmanli) Empire, which expanded to rule over the entire Middle East and Eastern Europe until the twentieth century.

The 600-year history of the Ottoman Empire left a heritage to modern-day Turks which gives them a militant pride in being Turkish. Under great leaders, such as Muhammad II (The Conqueror), who captured Constantinople in 1453 and Suleiman I (The Magnificent), who captured Belgrade in 1521, Turkish soldiers and sailors, the youth of Anatolia, carried war and diplomacy into the eastern Arabian lands, across North Africa, through Greece and the Balkans to the gates of Vienna. They fought against Napolean, the Italians, the British and the Russians, who persistently tried to acquire land to give them a port on the Mediterranean Sea (Turks feel that the Russians still want that land).

Early Ottoman sultans, ruling from Constantinople, established competent and effective administrative control over the vast territories under their suzerainty, combining the assumed religious role of caliph with their temporal power. Minorities within the empire were left free to govern themselves, provided they paid their taxes and kept the peace. Christians and other non-Turks, including slaves, rose to high administrative positions in the Ottoman military monarchy.

By the end of the sixteenth century and with the rise of industrialization in Europe, the seams in the Ottoman ship began to crack. Corruption in the capital and military losses overseas weakened the authority and prestige of the government. One subjugated country after another rose in successful revolt—Serbia, Hungary, Romania, Bulgaria and, finally, Greece. Successively more despotic sultans imposed such harsh rule on Turkish society that the Turks themselves began to seek reform.

Just before and during World War I, which Turkey joined on the side of Germany, Turkish intellectuals wanted for Turks what Europeans had—a national, political state with a constitution guaranteeing basic political rights. These intellectuals, called Young Turks, succeeded in setting the stage for Turkey's true revolution. This began with Turkey's military defeat abroad and the Turkish army's success in Anatolia in driving out the invading Greeks and Italians. The army's leader was Mustafa Kemal, who had earlier led the Turks in defeating the British at Gallipoli.

Kemal was a dictator or, more precisely, a social revolutionist, determined to rid by force if necessary the power of non-Turks in the Turkish "homeland" of Anatolia, whether British, Greek, Armenian or Kurd. He voiced a revulsion common to Turks by then of overseas adventures. He wanted a modern, democratic Turkey, based on current American and European nationalist, secular and republican principles.

His revolutionary program abolished the caliphate and closed religious schools and Shariah courts, declaring Turkey a secular state. He made the town of Ankara in the Anatolian heartland, rather than the imperial city of Constantinople, the new republic's capital. He outlawed the Sufi orders, the *turuq* so famous in Turkey because of the singular role of Jalaladin Rumi of Konya (during Seljuk times) in developing the mystic philosophy of the brotherhoods. Drawing on Swiss, German and Italian commercial, penal and civil codes, he declared polygyny illegal and introduced civil marriage. Sunday, instead of Friday, became the legal holiday.

Kemal decreed that no longer would names follow the traditional pattern of "son of father," but that each person would adopt a family name, to continue through the generations. Mustafa Kemal himself became Kemal Ataturk, "Father of Turks."

His banishments touched all Turks personally, but some with more effect than others. Forbidden was the conical red fez, worn by Turkish Muslims as a symbol of their loyalty to the caliph. European clothing in general was recommended, and brimmed felt hats for men were mandatory (in 1972 a Turk in Bursa was arrested for wearing a brimless hat). The fezzes rapidly disappeared, but Ataturk's attempt to emancipate women met stiffer resistance. City women discarded their veils soon enough, took to European dress and in many other ways enjoyed newfound freedom. Village women were not veiled, but they continued to clutch their head coverings over their faces in the presence of strangers, and their traditional place in society remained subservient. The degree of change in towns depended on the character of the town—whether it was a small city or a large village—and the amount of urban contact.

Another drastic and dramatic change ordered by Ataturk involved the Turkish language. Osmanli, or Anatolian Turkish (see Turkic-speaking Peoples), had been written in Arabic script. Ataturk introduced Roman script with a modified Latin alphabet, more suited to Turkish language sounds. Ataturk personally went on tour to demonstrate the intricacies of the new alphabet, sometimes standing in the village square before a blackboard and a cluster of curious onlookers. Along with this change, Ataturk attempted to ''Turkify'' the language by purging words derived from Arabic or Persian and supplanting them with ''pure'' Turkish ones (today English and French words with Turkish spelling have crept in, especially into city usage).

Three sentiments guided Ataturk's course of government until he died in 1938, and these continue today in varying degrees: nationalism, industrialization and secularization.

The first of these is the strongest. Turks are loyal and devoted to their country. Following World War I, attempts were made to wrap all Turkic-speaking peoples in the same blanket and create a political unity among the Uzbek, Kirghiz, Turkmen, Kazakhs, Azeri and all those groups speaking Turkic languages, particularly in the new Communist-dominated areas of the Caucasus and Central Asia. Pan-Turanism was a dream that never came to reality, not only because the Soviet Union would have no part of it but also because the Anatolian Turks came to identify themselves exclusively with their new Republic of Turkey.

Industrialization has not overtaken the whole of the country in the same manner as nationalism, but impressive gains have been made. Education has reached the rural areas in varying degrees, modern technical schools have produced thousands of engineers and businessmen and cities have grown with new industry. The urban Turks of Istanbul, Izmir, Adana, Zonguldak, Samsun, Trabson, Eskişehir and Ankara differ not too much from French, German, British and American urbanites. While maintaining strong families ties, they nevertheless generally marry partners of their own choosing (usually in their own social stratum), observe office hours, commute from their homes to their jobs along clogged avenues and go out to restaurants, movies, beaches and parks for recreation. They maintain their health and seek their security through public institutions; they join labor unions and the Kiwanis and participate with intensity in party politics.

Secularization is the least successful part of Ataturk's revolution. About 85 percent of Turks are Sunni of the Hanafi rite; 15 percent are Alawi or Shia. Traditionally, the *hoca* was an inspirational figure in Turkish communities, leading services in the mosques, reading the Quran, teaching the young and presiding over life-cycle ceremonies. When their sultan was also the caliph, *hocas* spoke with great authority.

Bit by bit, Ataturk's revolutionaries clipped away at the religious fabric, abolishing the caliphate and the Shariah courts. Many, if not most, of the *hocas* were made government servants. Religious instruction, government controlled, was offered in the primary schools, not private *madrasas*. As recently as 1982, the military government banned head scarves on female teachers and students, despite strong protests.

Yet religion is deep in the Turkish heart. Among the 27 million villagers of Anatolia, it is pervasive. Most villagers attend mosque services and pray more than once a day, provided the exercise does not interfere with work needed to be done. Saints are revered, spirits abound. Calamity or reward is the result of God's will, although recent studies have shown that the rural Turk increasingly believes in the efficacy of his own efforts to change the future.

Whether their home is in a village, town or city, Turks observe the formalities of being Muslim. They condemn those who do not demonstrate publicly some degree of religious observance, especially the fast of Ramadan. And while the villager may not be completely orthodox in religious life, the modern urbanist may also practice customs unacceptable to Islamic purists. City fathers may wait for the blood of a sacrificial animal to be poured onto the ground before laying the cornerstone of a new building. A city mother may hang a handkerchief hammock on a sacred tree in a mosque courtyard in the hope that her married daughter will become pregnant. A university student may go to the mosque to sacrifice a chicken in order to get better marks on the examination.

Turkish society remains bifurcated. The urban–rural distinction has been socially, culturally, politically and economically dynamic. The attraction of many Turkish youth to radical leftist organizations in the 1960s and 1970s is in part the result of perceived and real political-economic distinctions in Turkish society, with strong antagonisms between right and left. The Islamic fundamentalist revival in the Middle East is apparent in Turkey, with mosque attendance rising and the number of young people appearing in public in traditional Islamic clothing increasing. Membership in the fundamentalist National Salvation Party is swelling. While the military government and its urban backers push ahead with Ataturk's continuing revolution, resistance to it, especially on the religious level, grows.

BIBLIOGRAPHY

Books

Allen, Henry Elisha. *The Turkish Transformation*. Westport, Conn.: Greenwood Press, 1968.
Bates, Daniel G., and Rassan, Amal. *Peoples and Cultures of the Middle East*. Englewood Cliffs, N.J.: Prentice-Hall, 1983.
Beck, Lois, and Keddie, Nikki, eds. *Women in the Muslim World*. Cambridge: Harvard University Press, 1978.
Benedict, Peter. *Ula: An Anatolian Town*. Leiden: E. J. Brill, 1974.

————, and Tumertekin, Erol, eds. *Turkish Society*. Istanbul: Istanbul University Press, 1971.

————, Tumertekin, Erol; and Mansur, Fatma, eds. *Turkey: Geographic and Social Perspectives*. Social, Economic and Political Studies of the Middle East, No. 9. Leiden: E. J. Brill, 1974.

Berkes, Niyazi. *The Development of Secularism in Turkey*. Montreal: McGill University Press, 1964.

Cohn, Edwin J. *Turkish Economic, Social, and Political Change*. New York: Praeger, 1970.

Fallers, L. A. *Turkish Islam*. Chicago: University of Chicago, Department of Anthropology, 1971.

Henderson, Celia. *Cyprus: The Country and Its People*. London: Queen Anne Press, 1968.

Hinderink, Jan. *Social Stratification as an Obstacle to Development: A Study of Four Turkish Villages*. New York: Praeger, 1970.

Hotham, David. *The Turks*. London: John Murray, 1972.

Karpat, Kemal H. *The Gecekondu: Rural Migration and Urbanization in Turkey*. New York: Cambridge University Press, 1976.

————, ed. *Social Change and Politics in Turkey*. Leiden: E. J. Brill, 1973.

Keefe, Eugene K., et al. *Area Handbook for Cyprus*. The American University FAS, DA Pam 550–22. Washington, D.C.: Government Printing Office, 1971.

Leder, Arnold. *Catalysts of Change: Marxist Versus Muslim in a Turkish Commuity*. Austin: University of Texas Press, 1981.

Lewis, Bernard. *The Emergence of Modern Turkey*. London: Oxford University Press, 1961.

————. "Turkey: Westernization." In *Unity and Variety in Muslim Civilization*, edited by G. E. von Grunebaum. Chicago: University of Chicago Press, 1955.

Lewis, Geoffrey. *Modern Turkey*. New York: Praeger, 1974.

Magnarella, Paul J. *Tradition and Change in a Turkish Town*. Cambridge, Mass.: Schenkman, 1975.

Mansur, Fatma. *Bodrum: A Town in the Aegean*. Leiden: E. J. Brill, 1972.

Meeker, Michael E. "The Great Family Aghas of Turkey: A Study of a Changing Political Culture." In *Rural Politics and Social Change in the Middle East*, edited by R. Antoun and I. Harik. Bloomington: Indiana University Press, 1972.

Nyrop, Richard F., et al. *Area Handbook for the Republic of Turkey*. The American University FAS, DA Pam 550–80. 2nd ed. Washington, D.C.: Government Printing Office, 1973.

Rathbun, Carole. *The Village in the Turkish Novel and Short Story: 1920–1955*. The Hague: Mouton, 1972.

Roos, Leslie R., Jr., and Roos, Noralou Preston. *Managers of Modernization: Organizations and Elites in Turkey*. Cambridge: Harvard University Press, 1971.

Spencer, William. *The Land and People of Turkey*. Philadelphia: Lippincott, 1958.

Stirling, A. Paul. "The Domestic Cycle and the Distribution of Power in Turkish Villages." In *Mediterranean Countrymen: Essays in the Social Anthropology of the Mediterranean*. Paris: Mouton, 1963.

————. *Turkish Village*. New York: Wiley, 1965.

Szyliowicz, Joseph S. *Education and Moderation in the Middle East*. Ithaca: Cornell University Press, 1973.

Tugac, Ahmet. "Indices of Modernization: Erkenoy, a Case of Local Initiative." In
    Turkey: Geographic and Social Perspectives, edited by Peter Benedict, Erol Tum-
    ertekin, and Fatma Mansur. Leiden: E. J. Brill, 1974.
Tumertekin, Erol. "The Development of Human Geography in Turkey." In *Turkey:
    Geographic and Social Perspectives*, edited by Peter Benedict, Erol Tumertekin,
    and Fatma Mansur. Leiden: E. J. Brill, 1974.
Tunckilek, Necdet. "Types of Rural Settlement and Their Characteristics." In *Turkey:
    Geographic and Social Perspectives*, edited by Peter Benedict, Erol Tumertekin,
    and Fatma Mansur. Leiden: E. J. Brill, 1974.
Tütengill, Cavit Orhan. "A Summary of Change: A Contemporary Study of a Turkish
    Village." In *The Emergence of the Modern Middle East*, edited by Robert G.
    Landen. New York: Van Nostrand Reinhold, 1970.
Weiker, Walter F. *The Modernization of Turkey: From Ataturk to the Present Day*. New
    York: Holmes & Meir, 1981.

Articles

Albaum, Melvin, and Davies, Christopher S. "The Spatial Structure of Socio-Economic
    Attributes of Turkish Provinces." *International Journal of Middle East Studies* 4
    (1973): 288–310.
Aswad, Barbara C. "Key and Peripheral Roles of Noble Women in a Middle Eastern
    Plains Village." *Anthropological Quarterly* 40:3 (1967): 139–152.
———. "Visiting Patterns Among Women of the Elite in a Small Turkish City." *An-
    thropological Quarterly* 47:1 (1974): 9–27.
Beeley, Brian. "The Turkish Village Coffeehouse as a Social Institution." *Geographical
    Review* 60:4 (1970): 475:493.
Benedict, Peter. "The Kabul Günü: Structured Visiting in an Anatolian Provincial Town."
    Anthropological Quarterly 47:1 (1974): 28–47.
Casson, Ronald W. "Paired Polarity in the Formal Analysis of a Turkish Kinship Ter-
    minology." *Ethnology* 12:3 (1973): 275–297.
Dobkin, Marlene. "Social Ranking in the Woman's World of Purdah: A Turkish Ex-
    ample." *Anthropological Quarterly* 40:2 (1967): 65–72.
Eisenstadt, S. N. "Social Transformation in Modernization." *American Sociological
    Review* 30 (1965): 663.
Erdentug, Nermin. "Age Groups." *Antropoloji* 1:2 (1964): 1–7.
———. "Family Structure and Marriage Customs of a Turkish Village." *Antropoloji*
    1:1 (1963): 5–16.
Ergil, Dogu. "Secularization as Class Conflict: The Turkish Example." *Asian Affairs*
    62:1 (1975): 69–80.
Guseinov, A. "Turkey: The Class Struggle Goes On." *Africa and Asia Today* 4 (1974):
    35–37.
Kagitcibasi, C. "Social Norms and Authoritarianism: A Turkish–American Comparison."
    Journal of Personality and Social Psychology 16:3 (1970): 444–451.
Kandiyoti, D. "Some Social-Psychological Dimensions of Social Change in a Turkish
    Village." *British Journal of Sociology* 25:1 (1974): 47–62.
Le Compte, William, and Le Compte, Gurney. "Effects of Education in Intercultural

Contact on Traditional Attitudes in Turkey." *Journal of Social Psychology* 80 (1970): 11–22.

Levine, N. "Old Culture—New Culture: A Study of Migrants in Ankara, Turkey." *Social Forces* 51:3 (1973): 355–368.

Magnarella, Paul J. "Aspects of Kinship Change in a Modernizing Turkish Town." *Human Organization* 31 (1972): 361–371.

———. "Conjugal Role Relationships in a Modernizing Turkish Town." *International Journal of Sociology of the Family* 2:2 (1972): 179–192.

Mardin, Serif. "Center–Periphery Relations: A Key to Turkish Politics?" *Daedalus* 102:1 (1973): 169–190.

Meeker, Michael E. "The Black Sea Turks: Some Aspects of Their Ethnic and Cultural Background." *International Journal of Middle East Studies* 2:4 (1971): 318–345.

Ritter, G. "Rural–Urban Migration and the Growth of Cities in Turkey." *Erdkunde* (Germany) 26 (1972): 177–196.

Schnaiber, A. "Rural–Urban Residence and Modernism: A Study of Ankara Province, Turkey." *Demography* 7:1 (1970): 71–86.

Scott, Richard B. "Qur'an Courses in Turkey." *Muslim World* 61:4 (1971): 239–255.

Srikantan, K. S. "Regional and Urban–Rural Sociodemographic Differences in Turkey." *Middle East Journal* 27:3 (1973): 297–298.

Suzuki, Peter. "Encounters with Istanbul: Urban Peasants and Village Peasants." *International Journal of Comparative Sociology* 5:2 (1964): 208–216.

Tumertekin, Erol. "Changing Picture of Female Participation in Turkish Agriculture." *Professional Geographer* 16:2 (1964): 17–20.

Yalman, Nur. "Islamic Reform and the Mystic Tradition in Eastern Turkey." *European Journal of Sociology* 10:1 (1969): 41–60.

———. "Some Observations on Secularism in Islam: The Cultural Revolution in Turkey." *Daedalus* 102:1 (1973): 139–168.

Unpublished Manuscripts

Carson, R. W. "Kinship Terminology and Kinship Organization in a Turkish Village." Ph.D. dissertation, Stanford University, 1971.

Magnarella, Paul J. "Education and Value Conflicts in a Turkish Community." Paper presented at the Seventy-First Annual Meeting of the American Anthroplogical Association, Toronto, November 29–December 2, 1972.

Ozertug, B. "Household Composition in a Turkish Village." Ph.D. dissertation, Stanford University, 1973.

Sertel, Ayse K. "Forms and Determinants of Elopement in Rural Turkey." Paper presented at the Seventy-First Annual Meeting of the American Anthropological Association, Toronto, November 29–December 2, 1972.

Tarhan, Maurie. "Migration and Social Change in a Turkish Village." Paper presented at the Seventy-Third Annual Meeting of the American Anthropological Association, Mexico City, November 19–24, 1974.

Ava S. Weekes
Richard V. Weekes

TURKS, RUMELIAN Rumelian Turks are literally the Turks of Roman lands. The term "Rumeli" in Turkish refers to the Balkans, which were, before their occupation by the Ottomans, in the hands of the Eastern Roman or Byzantine Empire. The Balkan peninsula includes the modern states of Romania, Bulgaria, Greece, Albania and Yugoslavia. Historically, the lands of Rumeli also encompassed Hungary, Cyprus, Rhodes and Crete, as well as the smaller Greek islands. The term "Rumelian Turk," then, refers to those Turks who came to Eastern Europe from Anatolia, along with Turkmen and others from Central Asia and the Crimea. It also has come to apply to Circassians from the Caucasus who settled in the Balkans.

Occasionally in local usage it may also encompass other non-Turkic Muslim populations, such as the Bosnians in Yugoslavia (see Bosnians). Strictly speaking, however, it should be used to designate intrusive Turkic communities as opposed to Muslim converts from indigenous populations. In fact, not all Rumelian Turks in this sense are Muslims. A small number are converts to Christianity or Judaism.

The largest concentrations of the 7 million Rumelian Turks, whether in villages or towns, are in Bessarabia (formerly northern Romania, now part of the Ukraine S.S.R.), Dobruja (eastern Romania), eastern and central Bulgaria, northern Greece and Thrace in modern Turkey. The numbers and political status of Turks in the Balkans have closely reflected historical events. With the exception of the Turkish inhabitants of the five provinces of Turkey located in Thrace, Rumelian Turks in the Balkans are everywhere minorities whose political and social status varies greatly from country to country.

The earliest recorded settlement of Muslim Turks in Rumelian lands occurred in 1249. Sultan Izzeddin Kayka'us, ruler of the Seljuks of Anatolia, having lost his crown to his brothers, took refuge in Byzantium and was given land by the Byzantines in Dobruja. He was followed by about 30 to 40 *obas*, or small groups of closely related families, of nomadic Turkmen from Anatolia, who settled there. When Dobruja and Bessarabia fell to the Mongols of the Golden Horde in the late thirteenth century, there were further settlements of Turkic peoples who mingled with the Turkmen and became Muslim. Under the pressure of the Christian Bulgars, the majority of these early Turkish-Mongol settlers returned to Anatolia in the fourteenth century. Those who stayed became converts to the Greek Orthodox religion. Today some 3,000 to 4,000 of these Christian Turks remain in Romania and are known as Gagaus, a derivation from the name of Sultan Kayka'us.

The more permanent and large-scale settlement of Turks in the Balkans took place during the long period of Ottoman domination of the peninsula, beginning in 1350. The lands gained in Europe by Ottomans were united until the mid-sixteenth century under one administrative system, and the Rumeli territory was headed by a *beylerbeyi* or "lord of the lords." He retained a status equivalent to that of a vizier and attended cabinet meetings at the Ottoman court in Constantinople. After 1550 the Balkans were divided into smaller administrative territories, following more or less ethnic divisions of the area, such as Bosnia, Macedonia or Morea.

Although Ottomans were the rulers in Rumeli until about the mid-nineteenth century, or until various Balkan nations gained their independence, Turks have always been in the minority except in Turkish Thrace. Because of religious, linguistic and social differences, Turkish settlers in the Balkans did not intermarry in large numbers or mix with the indigenous Christian and Albanian or Bosnian populations. Probably such intermarriage as occurred involved men marrying non-Turkish women. The Turks were mostly settled in towns in the Balkans and served as military personnel and administrators, and as artisans. Land was granted to individuals, usually of the military class, as fiefs in the Balkans from the Ottoman crown holdings. Since ownership of such land was not inherited, it eventually reverted back to the state. Therefore, no Turkish landed noble class developed, and Turkish peasants in the Balkans were rare, with the exception of Dobruja. After annexation of the Crimean khanate to czarist Russia in the late eighteenth century, many Tatars from the Crimea and Circassians from the Caucasus migrated to Dobruja and were given land by the Ottoman government, where they formed villages and became farmers. The Dobruja Turks remain a distinctive cultural entity to this day.

After Yugoslavia, Greece, Albania, Bulgaria and Romania became independent countries in the nineteenth century, many urban Turks living in the Balkans left, and the population of Rumelian Turks was reduced by several million. Following World War I, 400,000 Turks from Greece and the Greek islands were exchanged with Greeks in Anatolia who moved to Greece. After World War II, about 200,000 more Turks were repatriated to Turkey from Bulgaria and Romania. Today there are only about 1.5 million Rumelian Turks living in Romania, Bulgaria, Yugoslavia and Greece. In Turkey many of the returning Rumelian Turks, estimated at 5.5 million, have been given land, and today one finds their villages throughout Anatolia referred to as *goçmen*, or "immigrant villages," by the local people. The Dobruja Turks returning to Turkey have been assimilated in large numbers into the Turkish professional classes and serve in most governmental organizations.

Even today the signs of long Turkish-Ottoman domination are apparent everywhere. The most obvious is in architecture, especially in the still Muslim areas of southern Yugoslavia. Ottoman-style domed mosques with their pencil-thin minarets modeled after those in Islanbul, wooden houses with latticework windows and separate quarters for men and women and marketplaces where specialty stores are grouped together are living legacy of Turkish rule. Less obvious to the casual observer are the cuisine, the social customs and a large number of loan words from Turkish that are still very much in use in all Balkan states. Turkish words are especially widespread in conjunction with clothing, household items, parts of a building, cooking, farm products, hunting and things equestrian. Turkish dishes containing lamb and vegetables, milk products—such as yogurt and cheeses—and, of course, Turkish coffee, are served in homes as well as restaurants. Turkish-style dress has been adapted by Muslim populations in Yugoslavia, but has also affected Christian peasants living in the same or neighboring provinces.

BIBLIOGRAPHY

Books

Birge, John Kingsley. *A Guide to Turkish Area Study*. Washington, D.C.: Committee on Near Eastern Studies, American Council of Learned Societies, 1949.
Davison, Roderick H. *Turkey* Englewood Cliffs, N.J.: Prentice-Hall, 1968.
Holt, P. M.; Lambton, Ann K. S.; and Lewis, Bernard. *Cambridge History of Islam*. Vol. 1. Cambridge: Cambridge University Press, 1970.
Inalcik, Halil. *The Ottoman Empire: The Classical Age, 1300–1600*. Translated by Norman Itzkowitz and Colin Imber. New York: Praeger, 1973.
Stavrianos, Leften Stavros. *The Balkans Since 1453*. New York: Rinehart, 1958.
Vaughn, Dorothy Margaret. *Europe and the Turk: A Pattern of Alliance, 1350–1700*. Liverpool: University of Liverpool Press, 1954.

Article

Fisher, S. N. "Ottoman Feudalism and Its Effects Upon the Balkans." *Historian* 15 (1952): 3–22.

Ulku U. Bates
Population figures updated by Richard V. Weekes

U

URDU-SPEAKING PEOPLES   The Urdu-speaking Muslims of north India and Pakistan are not an ethnic group in the strict sense of the term, but a collection of ethnic groups. Nor are they, strictly speaking, a regional group, but rather are widely dispersed geographically. Nevertheless they possess a sense of group identity based on cultural and historical factors. These include the Islamic religion, a Persian cultural tradition and its Indian offspring, the Urdu language and the tradition of Muslim political supremacy in north India, especially during Moghul rule. Added to this is a sense of political and cultural dispossession, the legacy of British rule which resulted in the creation of a separate Muslim political consciousness and ultimately the establishment of Pakistan.

The more than 48 million Muslims who speak Urdu as their first language are found not only in Pakistan, where they number no more than about 6 million, but also in the northern Indian states of the Punjab, Uttar Pradesh (U.P.) and Bihar. There are also pockets of Urdu speakers in other areas, including West Bengal, Orissa, Bombay and Hyderabad (see Deccani), and in Bangladesh. This geographic spread reflects the historic extent of Muslim rule in India, from the Khyber Pass to the Bengal delta, from Kashmir to Mysore. In recent years Urdu-speaking Muslims have emigrated to the Persian Gulf and Saudi Arabia in search of economic opportunities. The emigrés tend to retain their citizenship of origin, remit the bulk of their wages to their families in Pakistan and India and ultimately return home. Skilled laborers and highly educated professionals have also emigrated to Western Europe, North America and Commonwealth countries as individuals or in family groups. One thus hears Urdu spoken in Toronto, Manchester, Singapore, Sydney and Houston. These latter emigrants tend to stay in their adopted countries as new citizens, and the second generation may lose contact with its native language and culture unless settled in neighborhoods where there are numbers of other Urdu speakers.

Migration was important in the early history of north Indian Muslims as well as in their more recent quests for political autonomy and economic opportunity. This factor helps to account for their ethnic diversity. Muslims in north India are ethnically differentiated by their descent from immigrant groups of Arab merchants and soldiers who entered the subcontinent in small numbers as early as the eighth century A.D. Others descended from Turks, Persians and Pushtun who came as conquering armies beginning in the eleventh century and who established political dominance in the area lasting from the thirteenth to the eighteenth centuries. Among these immigrant groups were both Sunni and Shia Muslims, adding a sectarian dimension to their diversity. The Turkish sultans of Delhi, the Moghul emperors who succeeded them and smaller regional princes patronized the emigré Muslim culture in all its heterogeneity: Islamic jurists of the Hanafi school, Persian literati who were Ithna Ashari Shias and Sufis of several orders, including Chishti, Qadiri and Naqshbandi. The Sufi orders were particularly instrumental in converting Indian Hindus to the new faith.

Indian converts to Islam ultimately outnumbered immigrant Muslims and were similarly diverse in origin. Conversions came from among both high and low Hindu castes, were made for reasons varying from conviction to convenience and continued from the earliest period of contact with Islam down to the present. Sunnis generally outnumbered Shias, although there were concentrations of Shia populations in areas where the princely ruler was Shia (such as Lucknow). Ismailism was embraced by entire castes of coastal merchants such as the Khojas and Bohras, who came into contact with Islam through the Indian Ocean trade. Such merchant groups, while Gujarati speakers, often used Urdu as their language of commerce (see Gujaratis). Another element of diversity among north Indian Muslims was the phenomenon of incomplete conversion, such as the persistence of Hindu rituals and caste identities even after formal acceptance of Islam.

Ethnic diversity has been offset somewhat over time by intermarriages among the different groups and by periodic reform movements aimed at Islamizing ritual practice and spreading knowledge and observance of Islamic personal law. Nevertheless, endogamous groups remain today among the Urdu-speaking Muslims who identify themselves according to their claimed immigrant origins: Sayyids (descendants of Muhammad or his family), Shaikhs (Arabs or Persians), Moghuls (Central Asian Turks) and Pathans (Pushtun).

Members of these four groups are known as *ashraf* (nobles), and their claimed foreign origin places them at the top of the Indo-Muslim social ladder. Nobility (*sharafat*) implies not only noble lineage but also cultivation in the cultural sense. Hence a man may acquire *ashraf* status if he maintains a certain style of life and is a magnanimous host, charitable towards those less fortunate, pious— but not to a fault—and able to sprinkle his conversation with extemporaneous Urdu couplets.

Beneath the *ashraf* are ranged the *ajlaf*, Indian convert groups which retain their Hindu caste or occupational names. Headed by the Rajputs (warriors and landholders who, because of their high status in Hindu society, often successfully claim *ashraf* status), they include other occupational groups such as the Momin Julahas (weavers), Qassabs (butchers), Darzis (tailors) and many more, with Muslim ''untouchables'' at the bottom (see Maharashtrians). These Muslim groups function in society very much as Hindu caste groups. They are endogamous (although there are some hypergamous marriages among *ashraf*) with interdining prohibitions and restricted mobility. Despite the often-quoted adage concerning the greater degree of social mobility among Muslims than among Hindus (''We used to be butchers and now we are Shaikhs; next year if the harvest prices are good for us, we shall be Sayyids''), the fact remains that there is considerable social stratification based upon birth and a corresponding continuity of occupation based upon caste identity.

While among the *ashraf*, religious identity is marked by a cultivated style incorporating certain Islamic virtues, among the *ajlaf* Islamic identity is expressed through popular piety. Examples of this include discipleship of Sufi saints and pilgrimages to their *dargahs* or tombs. The ritual at Sufi shrines, with offerings of food, flowers and incense, resembles similar rituals at Hindu temples. These syncretic observances, in which an essentially Hindu ritual has been endowed with Islamic meaning, give vital evidence of the process of conversion to Islam in India. These practices are not found uniquely among convert groups, for the *ashraf* also participate in them as both patrons and as worshippers.

The *ashraf* enjoyed a sense of political entitlement derived from a long tradition of military and administrative service, first to the various Indo-Muslim rulers and then, after the collapse of the Moghul Empire, to the British. It has often been claimed that Muslim officials were ruined by the British takeover, but this was far from the case in north India. The Urdu-speaking ex-Moghul officialdom retained its prominence in the legal profession and in education in the U.P. and the Punjab until the beginning of the twentieth century. Under the guidance of Sir Sayyid Ahmad Khan and Aligarh College, the Urdu-speaking Muslim elites of north India sought to retain their position of political and administrative importance by reconciling their Islamic and Moghul culture with English education.

The Aligarh movement was a political as well as an educational movement. Through the medium of English education, the Muslim elite sought access to the new corridors of power in order to maintain not only their material interests but also their cultural heritage, including the Islamic religion and Urdu language and literature.

A somewhat different educational movement was led by the *ulama* of Deoband, who founded a religious school designed to revitalize Islamic learning among north Indian Muslims. They also sought to Islamize the religious practices of all strata of Muslim society via an active program of proselytization and Urdu publication.

Aligarh and Deoband both gave currency to Urdu as a medium of modern communication. Urdu is an Indo-Iranian language developed during the 500-year period of Muslim rule from the Hindi vernacular spoken in the Delhi region, heavily laden with Persian and Arabic words and written in the Persian script. Persian was the language of the court, but Urdu was the lingua franca, providing a means of communication among the court, the army (Urdu means ''language of the camp'') and the population. As the Moghul court declined, so, too, did the use of Persian, and Urdu gradually gained standing in the eighteenth and

nineteenth centuries, becoming the language of polite society and of local administration throughout northern India. It gained a body of distinguished literature,
especially poetry, written in the forms and with the imagery of Persian poetry.

Urdu was of great symbolic importance to the education of the Muslim elite,
who perceived any opposition to the use of the Urdu script as a threat, not only
to their professional positions but also to Muslim culture in general. This threat
became a reality in the late nineteenth century when the advocates of Hindi
pushed the claim of that language to equal recognition with Urdu as a judicial
language, first in Bihar and then in U.P. (Hindi is a language very close to Urdu
in its spoken form but written in Devanagari-Sanskrit script and laden with
vocabulary of Sanskrit origin; hence it is of symbolic religious importance to
Hindus.) The Hindi–Urdu controversy at that time was crystallized into a Hindu–
Muslim rivalry which foreshadowed more serious misunderstandings to come.

The role of the Urdu in the creation of Muslim political self-consciousness in
the early twentieth century was significant. Urdu-speaking Muslims formed numerous *anjumans*, or associations, for the improvement of Muslim education
and the regeneration of the Muslim community in India, a community whose
identity was only beginning to emerge from the welter of ethnic, sectarian and
regional groupings of which it was composed. These early Muslim associations
formed the nucleus for the All-India Muslim League, founded in Dacca in 1906
at the annual meeting of the Muhammadan Educational Conference.

As Muslim politics developed in the period before 1947, the Urdu speakers
of north India became the leaders of the Muslim League, which aimed at establishing itself as the major spokesman for a united Indo-Muslim constituency.
This emerging nationalism centered around the symbols of Islam, past Muslim
supremacy, the Urdu language and, after 1940, a territorial demand. Pakistan
was to be the new homeland for Indian Muslims in the areas where Muslims
were already in a majority: Sind, Baluchistan, the Punjab and the North-West
Frontier Province in the west; and Bengal in the east. The irony was that the
heartland of the Moghul heritage and of Urdu lay in the U.P., an area of fervent
political support for the Muslim League which would not be a part of Pakistan.
The holocaust which accompanied the partition of the Punjab and Bengal has
been held up as proof both of the need for a territory for the political and cultural
survival of Indian Muslims and of the needless sundering of a cultural heritage
which belonged to all north India.

The Partition has not only divided the Urdu speakers and their cultural heritage
but has made it even more difficult to generalize about them than before. Urdu
today is the national language of Pakistan, although only about 7 percent list it
as their mother tongue. Many of these are *muhajirs*, migrants or refugees from
areas now in India. It is, however, impossible to estimate the numbers of Pakistanis who speak or understand Urdu but who count Punjabi, Sindhi, Baluchi
or Pashto as their native language. In the area of north India stretching from
Punjab to West Bengal, there are some 53 million Urdu speakers, not all of
whom are Muslim. In Bangladesh the Urdu-speaking minority, most of whom

are known as Biharis after the Indian province from which they fled, found themselves in the uncomfortable position of being labeled Pakistani collaborators during the Bangladesh war of independence in 1971. Subsequently some Biharis migrated or were repatriated to Pakistan, becoming latter-day *muhajirs*.

The diversity of the Urdu-speaking Muslims persists into the present, further complicated by the Partition, which has divided ethnic groups and even families. The situation has particularly affected the *ashraf* groups, many of whom are cut off from their former landholdings in India by the migrations of partition. Some middle-class and professional *muhajirs* remain true to their Moghul (or Aligarh) traditions and have joined the administrative and commercial elites of their new country, and they include many of the most powerful families in Pakistan.

This is not the case of all Urdu speakers, many of whom were totally dispossessed at Partition and who have become part of the urban labor force in Pakistan and often a source of economic and political discontent. This urban discontent is expressed in several ways. Among the lower middle class, which includes those who are able to articulate their resentment, religious fundamentalism is a growing force, not as a refuge but rather as a political ideology. Among the less articulate, discontent may be expressed through social violence among linguistic groups, Sindhis or Punjabis versus *muhajirs* in Pakistan, Bengalis versus Biharis in Bangladesh. Lack of significant land reform in Pakistan has left the peasantry voiceless, though also a potential source of unrest. The majority of the population of Pakistan, the peasantry, is not generally Urdu-speaking, except for purposes of communicating with the government bureaucracy.

Those Muslims who stayed in India following Partition, whether by choice or from lack of opportunity to emigrate, have maintained a diversity of economic and social statuses. In the wake of land reforms, landholders and their retainers underwent a drastic change in fortune. The urban middle class has felt discriminated against in jobs and educational opportunities, often joining the migrants to the Persian Gulf and elsewhere. But laborers, artisans and petty merchants in the urban areas have held their own, and many enjoy prosperity in India. The Muslim peasantry shares the economic situation of its Hindu counterpart, doing well in areas of "green revolution" prosperity (western U.P. and the Punjab), doing poorly in eastern U.P. and Bihar, where the soil is poor or exhausted, landholdings small and landlessness on the increase.

The role of women among the Urdu-speaking Muslims is also subject to wide variation. In the Islamic state of Pakistan, Muslim family laws have been reformed, after considerable debate, placing constraints on men's abilities to contract polygynous marriages and obtain easy divorce. The secular state of India, on the other hand, has not been able to legislate in the matter of Islamic personal law. This means that social change, in the legal sense, may be greater in Pakistan, although here, too, it is hard to generalize. For one thing, legal reforms rarely extend beyond urban areas, and for another, the social pressure to maintain *purdah* (the seclusion of women) is greater in Pakistan, making it hard for women to assert or be aware of their legal rights. The increasing political power of the

Islamic fundamentalists in the early 1980s today threatens to reverse many of the legal protections women were able to win in the 1970s.

Purdah is a custom with many gradations, from the total veiling provided by the *burqa* to the "modern" *purdah* of a head scarf and dark glasses. A phenomenon observed in recent years in Pakistan is the fashion of the *chador*, a brightly colored, printed version of its somber Iranian prototype which permits greater flexibility in veiling and movement than a *burqa*. The custom of *purdah* restricts a woman's interaction with non-kin males even when she is not formally *purdah*-observing. To go out of the house unveiled, she should have a male relative as an escort, or she risks public opprobrium. Women entering the professions tend to choose such occupations as teaching and medicine, in which their clientele will be female. A woman's social life is generally spent in the company of other women. Even at mixed parties, women will gravitate to a separate corner or room, exchanging little conversation with men. Women also have a separate religious life from men, praying and conducting *milads*, or ceremonies celebrating the birth of the Prophet, at home. These ceremonies often mark an engagement or birth or other family life-rite and thus are of particular importance to women's domestic concerns. Sufi devotionalism is common to men and women, although women may worship at a shrine at separate times or in separate areas.

The upheavals in the lives of Urdu-speaking Muslims began centuries ago and continue today. To an extent the resurgence of Islamic religious consciousness among them represents a new upheaval, the results of which cannot be predicted. But it is safe to say that these results, too, will be diverse.

BIBLIOGRAPHY

Books

Ahmad, Imtiaz. "Caste and Kinship in a Muslim Village in Eastern Uttar Pradesh." In *Family, Kinship and Marriage Among Muslims in India*, edited by Imtiaz Ahmad. Delhi: Manohar Book Service, 1976.
———, ed. *Caste and Social Stratification Among the Muslims*. 2nd ed. Delhi: Manohar Book Service, 1979.
———. *Family, Kinship and Marriage Among Muslims in India*. Delhi: Manohar Book Service, 1976.
———. *Modernisation and Social Change Among Muslims in India*. Delhi: Manohar Book Service. In Press.
———. *Ritual and Religion Among Muslims in India*. Delhi: Manohar Book Service, 1980.
Ansari, Ghaus. *Muslim Caste in Uttar Pradesh*. Lucknow, India: Ethnological and Folk Culture Society, 1960.
Bhatty, Zarina. "Muslim Women in Uttar Pradesh: Social Mobility and Directions of Change." In *Women in Contemporary India*, edited by Alfred de Souza. Delhi: Manohar Book Service, 1975.
———. "Status and Power in a Muslim Dominated Village of Uttar Pradesh." In *Caste*

and Social Stratification Among Muslims, edited by Imtiaz Ahmad. Delhi: Manohar Book Service, 1973.

———. "Status of Muslim Women and Social Change." In *Indian Women: From Purdah to Modernity*, edited by B. R. Nanda. New Delhi: Vikas, 1975.

Brass, Paul R. *Language, Religion, and Politics in North India*. Cambridge: Cambridge University Press, 1974.

Das Gupta, Jyotirindra. *Language Conflict and National Development*. Berkeley: University of California Press, 1970.

Hardy, Peter. *The Muslims of British India*. Cambridge: Cambridge University Press, 1972.

Husain, Shaikh Abrar. *Marriage Customs Among Muslims in India*. Delhi: Sterling, 1976.

Imam, Zafar, ed. *Muslims in India*. New Delhi: Orient Longman, 1975.

Jacobson, Doranne. "The Veil of Virtue: Purdah and the Muslim Family in the Bhopal Region of Central India." In *Family, Kinship and Marriage Among Muslims in India*, edited by Imtiaz Ahmad. Delhi: Manohar Book Service, 1976.

Jeffery, Patricia. *Frogs in a Well: Indian Muslim Women in Purdah*. London: Zed, 1979.

Mandelbaum, David G. *Society in India*. Vol. 2. Berkeley: University of California Press, 1970.

Metcalf, Barbara. *Islamic Revival in British India: Deoband, 1860–1900*. Princeton: Princeton University Press, 1982.

Minault, Gail. *The Khilafat Movement: Religious Symbolism and Political Mobilization in India*. New York: Columbia University Press, 1982.

Mujeeb, M. *The Indian Muslims*. London: Allen and Unwin, 1967.

Naipaul, V. S. *Among the Believers: An Islamic Journey*. New York: Knopf, 1981.

Papanek, Hanna, and Minault, Gail, eds. *Separate Worlds: Studies of Purdah in South Asia*. Columbia, Mo.: South Asia Books, 1982.

Robinson, Francis. *Separatism Among Indian Muslims: The Politics of the United Provinces' Muslims, 1860–1923*. Cambridge: Cambridge University Press, 1974.

Roy, Shibani. *Status of Muslim Women in North India*. Delhi: BR Publications, 1979.

Saiyed, A. R. "Indian Muslims and Some Problems of Modernisation: A Theoretical Exploration." In *Dimensions of Social Change in India*, edited by M. N. Srinivas, S. Seshaiah, and V. S. Parthasarathy. New Delhi: Indian Council of Social Science Research, 1978.

Vreede de Steurs, Cora. *Parda: A Study of Muslim Women's Life in Northern India*. Assen, Netherlands: Van Gorcum, 1968.

Weekes, Richard V. *Pakistan: Birth and Growth of a Muslim Nation*. New York: Van Nostrand, 1962.

Articles

Ahmed, Imtiaz. "The Ashraf–Ajlaf Dichotomy in Muslim Social Structure in India." *Indian Economic and Social History Review* 3:13 (1966): 268–278.

Gupta, Raghuraj. "Caste Ranking and Inter-Caste Relations Among the Muslims of a Village in Northwest Uttar Pradesh." *Eastern Anthropologist* 10 (1956): 30–42.

Khan, Zillur. "Caste and Muslim Peasantry in India and Pakistan." *Man in India* 48 (1968): 133–148.

Papanek, Hanna. "Purdah: Separate Worlds and Symbolic Shelter." *Comparative Studies in Society and History* 15:3 (1973): 289–325.

———. "Purdah in Pakistan: Seclusion and Modern Occupations for Women." *Journal of Marriage and the Family* 33:3 (1971): 517–530.

Gail Minault

UYGUR   The name "Uygur" is a general term given to a Turkic people who live for the most part in the Xinjiang-Uygur Autonomous Region of China, where they number approximately 6 million. Only a few (227,000) live in the Soviet Union. Presumably, a few families moved to Taiwan from mainland China when the Communist government took power in 1949.

As an appellation, Uygur (pronounced U-ee-gur and also spelled Uighur, Uigur, Uyghur, Uighar) derives from one of the oldest known Turkic peoples, the Uygur of the Mongol steppe of the eighth century. The name may be even older than that. With a single exception, there is no direct link between those historic Uygur and the Uygur of the twentieth century. The exception is the Yellow Uygur of Gansu Province in China, a group of about 3,800 people who are probably directly descended from the eighth-century Uygur. They are today shamanist or Buddhist by religion.

The bulk of today's Uygur acquired the name only in the twentieth century. By that time the name had long since fallen out of usage. Perhaps as early as the sixteenth century, it became customary for the Uygur of China to identify themselves with their places of habitation, using such names as Kashgarliq, Turfanliq and Taranchi (people of Kashgar, Turfan and Taran). Not until 1922 did the name "Uygur" again come into wide usage and begin to be applied across the Soviet Union and China. The disappearance of the name resulted from the political fragmentation of the Uygur after the Mongol conquest. Its reappearance came from the reintegration of a variety of eastern Turkic peoples after the establishment of the Republic of China, with its emphasis on nationality identity. They assumed the name "Uygur" without regard to their actual or imagined link with the historical Uygur.

All the Uygur of the Soviet Union live in either the Uzbek or Kirghiz Soviet Socialist Republics, with some 25,000 of that total living in the city of Tashkent alone. For the most part, these Uygur are only recently arrived in the Soviet Union, coming as refugees of various upheavals in China after 1880, and again after 1950.

The Uygur of China are spread across all of Xinjiang in the province now known as the Xinjiang-Uygur Autonomous Region, which has also carried the designation East Turkestan or Chinese Turkestan, although the latter term properly applies only to the Tarim basin. They live in or near the many oases scattered along the old northern and southern "silk roads" branching out from Tunhuang to Kaxgar (Kashgar). North of the Tarim basin, Uygur are found at oases on both the northern and southern slopes of the Tien Shan (mountain) range and on either side of the Bogdo-Ula range separating Turfan from Pei-ting. South of the Taklimakan wastes, other Uygur occupy settlements on the northern slopes of the Kunlun ranges. A rather large group is concentrated in villages just to the west of the Lop Nur desert and marshes.

Around 1960 the Uygur were the largest single nationality unit in the Xinjiang-Uygur Autonomous Region. Their total population, then 3.9 million, represented more than 60 percent of the entire population. Although no exact figures are now available, it is probable that the massive influx of Han Chinese into Xinjiang from 1950 to 1960 has altered this percentage.

The Uygur began to make the transition from pastoral nomadism to settled agriculture almost as soon as they settled in Chinese Turkestan after their flight from the Mongol steppe in the ninth century. Although some continued as nomads for a time, the oasis life-style, with its emphasis on irrigated agriculture and caravan trade, eventually became dominant.

By the twentieth century the Uygur were almost all settled agriculturalists or urban dwellers working small independent farms producing melons, cotton, maize, peaches, plums and wheat, all crops unknown to lowland China. Urban Uygur lived in a relatively more sophisticated life as landlords, merchants, shopowners, caravansary keepers, Muslim *shaikhs*, poets and a variety of other occupations. All this changed with the advent of the People's Republic of China and the social change introduced after 1951. As Chinese influence and authority have grown in Chinese Turkistan, there have been great alterations in the traditional life-style of its population. Most of the previously independent farmers have been drawn together into communes. In addition, new programs to reforest mountain slopes are opening up millions of acres of land to irrigation, while expansion of the industrial base of the new territory has led to a massive re-shuffling of the populace. It seems probable that the Uygur are being intermixed with other nationalities to the point that much of their previous national identity will be lost.

The Uygur are relatively tall people with brown hair, brown or lighter eye color, aquiline noses and light skin. The men wear thick moustaches and beards of the Turkic peoples of Central Asia.

There are many schematic linguistic arrangements used to describe and categorize the Turkic language family, of which Uygur is a part (see Turkic-speaking Peoples). In most such schemes, modern Uygur is linked with certain Uzbek and Kirghiz dialects and with other quite small language groups, such as the Yellow Uygur and yet another Turkic group of China's Gansu Province, the Salars. A more general designation for all these languages as a group is Turki (see Salars).

The origin of the first Uygur may be found in the struggles of various nomadic peoples for control of the Mongolian plateau in the sixth century. Among the major protagonists were two hostile Turkic confederations. One, the Toghuz-oghuz, included nine major Turkic tribes of which one was the Uygur. The other, the Kao-ch'e, was composed largely of forest dwellers from the Altai and the west Siberian plain. Although the Toghuz-oghuz eventually triumphed in 552, the steppe empire they built was never successful in making a lasting transition from steppe-nomadic military strength to urban-centered political dominance.

Through the first (552–630) and second (680–744) Turkic imperial periods, the Uygur were erratic allies at best, often siding with enemies of the ruling Turkic line as it suited their interests. Finally, the Uygur seized the opportunity coincident with the failure of the ruling dynasty in 743 to establish themselves as rulers of the Mongol steppe in 744.

Islam began to make inroads in the tenth century, eventually becoming the religion of almost all the Turkic peoples of Russian and Chinese Turkestan. For all of their history as Muslims, the Uygur have been Sunni and extremely devout. As with almost all the Turks of Central Asia, the Uygur have also been heavily influenced by the Sufi orders. That influence reached a peak during the Timurid era in the fourteenth, fifteenth and sixteenth centuries, when the considerable weight of Timur's imperial house was thrown to support a myriad of dervish orders, especially the Naqshbandi.

The Uygur were hardly distinguishable from all other Turkic peoples of eastern inner Asia. They were shamanist in the beginning, later Buddhist and finally, after 760, Manichaean, clearly indicating their eclectic search for a religion. Not until 840, when they were expelled from Mongolia, did the Uygur take up residence in present-day Chinese Turkestan. By the time of the Mongol conquest of the thirteenth century, the Uygur were almost entirely urban and agricultural with a well-developed Muslim civilization. In the twentieth century the Uygur remained devout Muslims until the advent of communism. It has become difficult to know how firm that commitment has held or how seriously it has been challenged.

Larry W. Moses

BIBLIOGRAPHY

Books

Bacon, Elizabeth E. *Central Asia Under Russian Rule*. Ithaca: Cornell University Press, 1966.
Krader, Lawrence. *Peoples of Central Asia*. Bloomington: Indiana University Press, 1963.
Lattimore, Owen. *Pivot of Asia*. Boston: Little, Brown, 1950.
———. *Studies in Frontier History: Collected Papers, 1928–1958*. New York: Oxford University Press, 1962.
Lu, David (Ta-Wei). *Moslems in China Today*. Hong Kong: International Studies Group, 1964.
Mackerras, Colin, ed. and trans. *The Uighur Empire According to the T'ang Dynastic Histories: A Study in Sino-Uighur Relations*. Newton, Conn.: The East and West Shop, 1973.
Moslem Unrest in China. Hong Kong: Union Press, 1958.

Pickens, Claude L., Jr. *Annotated Bibliography of Literature on Moslems in China.* Hankow, China: Society of the Friends of the Moslems in China, 1950.

Whitaker, Donald P., et al. *Area Handbook for the Peoples' Republic of China.* The American University FAS, DA Pam 550–60. Washington, D.C.: Government Printing Office, 1972.

Wixman, Ronald. "Recent Assimilation Trends in Soviet Central Asia." In *The Nationality Question in Soviet Central Asia*, edited by Edward Allworth. New York: Praeger, 1973.

Yang, I-fan. *Islam in China.* Hong Kong: Union Press, 1957.

Articles

Bodde, Derk. "China's Muslim Minority." *Far Eastern Survey* 16 (1946): 281–284.

Mei, Y. P. "Stronghold of Muslim China." *Moslem World* 31 (1941): 178–184.

Shung, Ibrahim C. C. (Hsiung Ch'en-chung). "Moslems in China." *Free China Review* (April, 1960): 13–20.

Wiens, H. H. "Change in the Ethnography and Land Use of the Ili Valley and Region, Chinese Turkestan." *Annals of the Association of American Geographers* 59:4 (1969): 753–775.

UZBEK The most numerous non-European peoples in Central Asia are the nearly 15 million Uzbek. By far the greatest number (13.4 million) live in the Soviet Union, particularly in the Uzbek Soviet Socialist Republic. A large number (1.3 million) live in Afghanistan, while a few live in China and Mongolia. The Uzbek comprise the third largest ethnic group in the Soviet Union, after the Great Russians and Ukrainians. They are the world's second largest Turkic-speaking group after the Anatolian Turks.

The Uzbek language is classified in the Chagatai (sometimes called Eastern or Karluk) group of Turkic languages. Uzbek is comprised of a large number of dialects and subdialects, which can be classified roughly into two groups, one which has the characteristic Turkic vowel harmony and another which has the Iranized dialects without vowel harmony. The present Soviet Uzbek literary language is based largely on the Iranized dialects of the Tashkent area; mass media, both printed and electronic, are causing a homogenization of the Uzbek language. In 1940 a Cyrillic-based alphabet was adopted, yet many older Soviet Uzbek still use the Arabic script for their personal writings. Uzbek in China and Afghanistan still use the Arabic script.

With few exceptions, those terming themselves Uzbek are speakers of the Uzbek language. Many Uzbek of the Samarkand and Bukhara areas also speak Tajik, an Iranian language. Due to an intensive Soviet education program, 52.9 percent of the Uzbek also speak Russian. In Tashkent there are some upper-class Uzbek who are more comfortable speaking Russian than Uzbek. Many rural Uzbek young men do not gain an adequate knowledge of Russian until they serve in the military. Some of the non-Uzbek Turkic-speaking peoples in Uzbekistan are adopting the Uzbek language.

The Soviet Uzbek, both men and women, have adopted European-style clothing, while at the same time maintaining some of their traditional attire. Business suits, neckties, white shirts, dresses and even blue jeans and footwear patterned after European design are encountered everywhere in Uzbekistan. The items of traditional clothing most commonly worn by Uzbek men is the *duppi*, a dark-colored skullcap which is usually black with white embroidery; the *duppi* is worn outdoors and indoors with both traditional and modern clothing. Wearing the *duppi* is becoming less prevalent in the urban areas. Women, especially in rural areas, frequently wear colorfully embroidered *duppis* or head scarves. In their wardrobe of traditional clothing most men have a *chapan*, a long robe open in the front and tied together with a knotted scarf. Everyday *chapans* are lightly padded and worn as an outer garment. The best-quality *chapans* are of silk and frequently have multi-colored stripes. Younger Uzbek more often wear the *chapan* at home or on festive public occasions. The distinguishing traditional apparel of Uzbek women is a short-sleeved, knee-length dress of silk or synthetic material in a pattern of radiant colored stripes or contrasting black and white.

The early Uzbek were probably one of the components of the Turko-Mongolian Golden Horde, which dominated Russia and western Siberia from the thirteenth through fifteenth centuries. The ethnonym ''Uzbek'' may have its origin in the name of Uzbek, Khan of the Golden Horde from 1313 to 1340. The term itself means ''self-lord'' or ''one's own prince.'' With the breakup of the Horde during the fifteenth century, the nomadic Uzbek moved southward and established themselves by mid-century in the lower reaches of the Syr and Amu rivers. There they challenged the power of the Timurid rulers of Transoxiana, the last of whom, Babur, they displaced in the early sixteenth century. (Babur went on to found the Moghul dynasty in India.) Further Uzbek expansion southward was blocked by the Safavid dynasty of Iran.

Over the years the Uzbek became increasingly sedentary, engaging mainly in agriculture, but with some involvement in commerce and crafts. They became participants in the area's Turko-Iranian variant of the Islamic civilization. Three Uzbek-dominated khanates had emerged by the eighteenth century: Kokand, Bukhara and Khiva. The majority of the Uzbek were incorporated into the Russian Empire during the latter half of the nineteenth century. In the course of the Russian Revolution and Civil War (1917–1923) more than 500,000 Uzbek migrated to northern Afghanistan, where they are a major component of the Uzbek community found there presently (see Uzbek [Afghanistan]). In 1924, Soviet authority having been established in Central Asia, the Uzbek Soviet Socialist Republic was organized, incorporating within its boundaries most of the Uzbek in the Soviet Union. The first capital of the Uzbek republic was Samarkand, a traditional cultural center; Tashkent, the former czarist administrative center of Turkestan Province, became the capital in 1931. Under Soviet Russian direction a modernization program was pursued, consisting of secularization, collectivization, industrialization and education.

Contemporary Uzbekistan contains 16.5 million people. The 11.4 million Uzbek constitute 69 percent of the population. Russians number 1.8 million and are 10.8 percent of the population. Other peoples of Muslim heritage number 15.7 percent, and various other nationalities make up 4.8 percent. Uzbek occupy most of the prominent public administrative positions.

The Uzbek are Hanafi Sunni Muslims, with some pre-Islamic shamanist and Zoroastrian influences remaining in folkways. Islam was brought forcibly to Transoxiana by the Arab conquerors during the eighth century. Conversion to Islam did not become extensive in the steppes until the fourteenth century. At the end of the fifteenth century, when the early Uzbek began their move into Transoxiana, they were already Muslim. The Uzbek khanates supported Islamic cultural institutions. With the establishment of Soviet power the religious life of the Uzbek changed; they became subject to officially sponsored secularization, which included invalidating Muslim law, abolishing *adat* and Shariah courts, confiscating *waqfs* and closing *maktab* and *madrasa* schools. Many mosques were closed, and the Islamic clergy persecuted. The overt practice of Islam was discouraged.

In recent decades there has been an official relaxation of limitations on the practice of Islam for several reasons. A reliable secularized Soviet Uzbek leadership has emerged; the supremacy of the state over religion has been established, and Uzbekistan has become a Soviet developmental "showcase" for visitors and students from Muslim states. Since 1956 schools for training a small number of Islamic clergy have operated in Bukhara (the Barak Khan *madrasa*, for one) and in Tashkent (the Mir-i Arab *madrasa*). The clergy graduated are too few to meet the needs of the functioning congregations. A limited amount of religious publication is allowed, mainly calendars and prayer books in the Arabic script. Recently in Uzbekistan a few old mosques have been restored and reopened, and a few new mosques have been built (for example, the new cathedral mosque in Jizzak built in 1981).

Islam has its strongest overt manifestation in rural areas, mainly in the persistence of social customs long associated with religion. Almost all Uzbek male infants are circumcised, and the event is usually an occasion for family ritual and feasting. Traditional Islamic feast days are observed in gatherings of family and friends, although the religious significance is often minimized or ignored. It is common for Uzbek to observe the Ramadan feast. Most Uzbek do not eat pork, but drinking alcohol is widespread. Children are given names from the Turkic or Islamic tradition; an Uzbek with a Russian name is rare.

Among adults, especially among the laboring classes, informal occupational fraternities with a religious-type ritual and patron Islamic saint persist from the pre-Soviet period. Many Uzbek still venerate Islamic shrines, and among some, belief in supernatural beings continues. In some rural areas there are pilgrimages to nominally Islamic holy sites which have been venerated since before Islam.

Many Uzbek, though not religiously involved or concerned during their youth or mature years, in their old age turn to religion as a social and philosophical support. Funerals, even for the educated urban upper classes, are often conducted with Islamic ritual. Traditional funeral processions can be observed even in modernized Tashkent. Gravestones with inscriptions in the Arabic script and Quranic verses are not uncommon. Although adherence to the beliefs and practices of Islam varies widely among the Soviet Uzbeks and some profess to be atheists, self-identification as a Muslim is nearly total and can be considered an important aspect of Uzbek ethnic identification.

In the Uzbek republic most Uzbek are located in the central and eastern areas, which are watered by the melting snows of the eastern mountains, the Bukhara–Samarkand zone, the Tashkent area and the Fergana Valley. Most of western-central Uzbekistan is an arid, sparsely inhabited desert or steppe, with the exception of the lower reaches of the Amu River (the Urgench–Nukus zone), where mainly the Turkic-speaking Karakalpak live (see Karakalpak).

Uzbek are for the most part a rural people. In Uzbekistan, approximately 60 percent live in villages and towns with populations of less than 2,500. There is a recent trend towards urban living; in part this is due to migration to the existing traditional urban centers such as Tashkent, Samarkand, Andijan and Fergana, but it is also due to the development of new, though smaller, urban centers in the countryside with varied economic, cultural and social activities. Urban high-rise apartment living does not appeal to many Uzbek. There is a continuing strong preference for rural, small town/city or suburban living, which provides the opportunities for having a separate house with a garden and courtyard where fruits, vegetables and animals can be raised and several generations can live together. The new towns being developed in Uzbekistan to an extent take traditional housing preferences into consideration. As a result, it is not uncommon for highly qualified Uzbek in the main urban centers to seek employment in the smaller towns.

Although almost two-thirds of the Uzbek live in a rural or small town setting, mainly on a collectivized agricultural enterprise, only half of that number are directly engaged in agricultural work. Seventy percent of the Soviet Union's cotton is grown in Uzbekistan; its cultivation is highly mechanized. Fruit, vegetables, grain and livestock are also produced. Approximately half of the rural labor force is engaged in other rural or small town activities, much of it in direct or indirect support of agricultural labor: mechanics, communications, construction, light manufacturing, crop processing, education, health care, commerce and administration. Some of the countryside Uzbek work in a variety of activities such as commerce, administration, education, communications, transportation and industry (textiles, electronics, refrigeration, aircraft construction, mineral refining). The Soviet educational system is producing increasing numbers of technicians and professional persons, enabling the Uzbek to move from traditional occupations to the more sophisticated technical and administrative positions which previously were held by Russians and other European nationalities.

In pre-revolutionary Transoxiana, educational facilities were few. The literacy rate among the native population was 3.6 percent in 1897. Very early the Soviet government established an effective secular mass educational system, which soon displaced traditional forms of instruction. Soviet sources claim that in Uzbekistan in 1979 the literacy rate was 99.7 percent, and literacy rates for men and women for the first time were nearly equal.

During their nomadic stage the Uzbek had an extensive tribal and clan structure, but centuries of sedentary agricultural and town life have caused this system to almost disappear, except among those rural Soviet Uzbeks with a more recent pastoral or nomadic background and among the current Afghan Uzbek. Nevertheless, kinship ties among immediate blood relatives are strong, and most Uzbek go to great efforts and expense to maintain contact with relatives, despite population movements due to education, work opportunities and the development of new towns. There is a strong sense of mutual obligation among those who are related by blood or marriage. The three-generation household is common; married sons and their families generally live with their parents. However, modern housing, especially in urban areas, is less spacious, thus preventing the co-residence of different generations and discouraging large families. Also, because of educational opportunities, more Uzbek are finding work away from their home areas. Furthermore, as more women enter the work force, they desire fewer children; and as older women remain in the work force, there are fewer grandmothers at home to assist in childraising.

Soviet law requires that marriages be registered and a civil ceremony performed, but some couples are married in a second traditional ceremony. Marriage feasting often follows traditional patterns, with a series of banquets, gift-giving sessions, going to the bride's home to take her to the groom's home and friends and relatives waiting outside the wedding chamber until the marriage is consummated. Young people now have greater personal freedom in spouse selection, but parental approval is almost always sought. Some marriages are still arranged by parents, and among some Uzbeks, the custom of marrying only within certain lineages persists, for example, among the ''white bone'' (descendants of former nomadic aristocracy) or among the *hoja* lines (descendants of former religious aristocracy). Marriage to non-Muslims is rare and is generally between an Uzbek man and a European woman. In such instances, especially in rural areas, the woman is expected to conform to Uzbek social practices. Divorce is not uncommon in such marriages. Uzbek girls are expected to be virgins at the time of marriage. The brideprice (*kalim*) is forbidden by law; however, it is sometimes manifest in the form of wedding gifts. Rural girls frequently marry young but most now wait until completing the middle school (tenth grade—age 17). Polygyny, of course, is outlawed, but it is sometimes encountered in both rural and urban areas under the subterfuge of not registering subsequent wives. Uzbek marriages are relatively stable; the divorce rate is approximately one-third that of the average for the Soviet Union as a whole; divorce more commonly occurs among urban and more highly educated people.

Soviet laws have declared the equality of women with men, but full implementation of the laws has not yet dispelled the influence of traditional male dominant patriarchal values. Generally, those Soviet Uzbek women who are well educated and live and work in urban areas are able to enjoy more fully the benefits of social legislation. The seclusion of women is no longer practiced, being discouraged by the educational and work opportunities provided by the Soviet system. However, in rural areas agricultural work teams are often of separate sexes.

Large families continue to be an Uzbek ideal and contribute to a high rate of natural increase, despite more women in the work force. Families with 4 children are common, and 8 or 10 not unusual. Considering the much lower birthrate of the European ethnic groups in the Soviet Union, the Uzbek and other high birthrate peoples of Muslim heritage have the potential for an increased role in all aspects of Soviet life.

Under the dictum "national in form, but Socialist in content," the Soviet Uzbek have developed their artistic culture. The abandonment of the Arabic script for the Cyrillic alphabet has cut off many Uzbek from their pre-Soviet literary heritage. There is a tendency to link the Uzbek culture more with the past of geographical Uzbekistan than with the broader Turkic tradition. Thus, pre-Uzbek figures of the past of Transoxiana are linked to the Uzbek cultural heritage, including the scholar-physician Avicenna (tenth century), the poet-administrator Ali Sher Navai (mid-fifteenth century) and the poet-biographer and general, Babur, the last of the Timurids (early sixteenth century). In athletics the traditional pastimes of horsemanship and wrestling are popular. *Ulaq*, a rough and tumble confrontation between teams of riders vying for the carcass of a goat, is still popular in rural areas.

The Soviet Uzbek in some ways style themselves as the leading people of Soviet Central Asia and consider Tashkent to be the real capital of Central Asia. The less numerous Soviet peoples of Muslim heritage (Kazakhs, Turkmen, Kirghiz, Karakalpak and Tajik) are considered by some Uzbek to be on a lower level of development. Though the Uzbek are proud of their attainments during the twentieth century, there is no enmity to the other Central Asian peoples. Among some Uzbek, a small minority, there remains some resentment towards the Russians for their conquest and domination of Central Asia. The majority of the Uzbek have accepted Russian domination with a realization of the material benefits that they have received. They recognize that they and other Soviet Muslims probably have the highest standard of living of any Muslim people. As they view the past of Central Asia, when it was a backwater of the Muslim world, many Uzbek intellectuals state that the Russian conquest and Soviet-directed modernization have brought them from obscurity into the mainstream of world historical development. The Uzbek accept most aspects of modernization and have proven capable of utilizing a wide range of technology. They are generally optimistic about the future as they consider their growing numbers and increasing standard of living. The Soviet Uzbek have an interest in other

Uzbek communities both within and without the Soviet Union. Since the 1979 Soviet intervention in Afghanistan, there has been a great interest in the Uzbek population there. Some Soviet Uzbek have gone to Afghanistan as political, technical and educational advisors to the Afghan Uzbek.

BIBLIOGRAPHY

Books

Carlisle, Donald S. "Uzbekistan and the Uzbeks." In *Handbook on Major Soviet Nationalities*, edited by Zev Katz, Rosemarie Rogers, and Frederick Harned. New York: Free Press, 1975.
D'Encausse, Helene Carrere. *Decline of an Empire*. New York: Newsweek Books, 1979.
Montgomery, David C. "The Uzbeks in Two States: Soviet and Afghan Policies Toward an Ethnic Minority." In *Soviet Asian Ethnic Frontiers*, edited by William O. McCagg and Brian Silver. New York: Pergamon Press, 1979.

Articles

Lubin, Nancy. "Assimilation and Retention of Ethnic Identity in Uzbekistan." *Asian Affairs* 12 O.S. 68:3 (1981): 277–285.
Montgomery, David C. "Return to Tashkent." *Asian Affairs* 10 O.S. 66:2 (1979): 166–179, and 3 (1979): 292–303.

David C. Montgomery

UZBEK (AFGHANISTAN) The Uzbek habitat, which they share with the Tajik and other ethnic groups in northern Afghanistan, is an arid zone that has inland drainage systems and a continental climate. It includes sedentary agriculturalists, but the pattern of semi-sedentary groups dominates, particularly in Afghanistan. Local ecology greatly influences livestock distribution. Fundamentally, sheep and goats are mountain animals, although sheep are less adaptable than goats and tend to flounder in the snow. Both fat-tailed (fat used as cooking oil) and karakul (Persian) lamb skins are major exports from both sides of the Amu Darya River. Cattle and camels (dromedaries) thrive in transitional forest steppes and semideserts. The most important modern beast of burden, however, is the donkey. Horses, prestige animals, are ridden, and sometimes the Uzbek drink *kumyss*, fermented mare's milk.

Clothing and diet closely resemble those of the Tajik (see Tajik). Until recently, it was possible to distinguish Uzbek from Tajik and regional subgroups from each other by their distinctively embroidered turban caps. Now, however, the two groups wear each other's caps indiscriminately.

The diet also exhibits an Uzbek–Tajik flavor. Green tea is the hospitality drink and is preferred over black tea. Seldom do the people consume it with sugar and milk. The pasta complex that stretches from the Far East to Italy and beyond had its origin somewhere along the Silk Route. Possibly the complex developed because it was easier for caravaneers to transport food grains in pasta form rather than as flour. Among the pasta dishes enjoyed by the Uzbek, Tajik and others in northern Afghanistan are: *ash* (minestrone-type noodles and vegetable soup) and *ashak* (ravioli with meat, cheese or leek filling). A steamed meat dumpling called *mantu* is a winter favorite, and similar dishes with identical names are found across the Himalayas to Tibet. As among the Tajik, dairy products are popular.

The classic, free enterprise-through-bargaining Central Asian bazaar exists in towns throughout northern Afghanistan and even in Soviet Central Asia. Traditionally, towns have two bazaar days a week, Monday and Thursday. Many Uzbek have become skillful bazaar artisans (silver- and goldsmiths, leatherworkers, woodcarvers and rug makers), but no matter how competent, the artisan always leaves one flaw in his work to conform to the idea that only Allah can produce a perfect thing.

The social structure of the Uzbek is more stratified and hierarchical than that of the Tajik, and their leaders (*begs*, *boyers*) have more authoritarian power, a reflection of the disciplined nomadic past of the Uzbek. In addition, they still refer to themselves by old tribal names of the days of the Golden Horde: Laka, Haraki, Kamaki, Mangit, Ming, Taimus, Durman, Chinaki, Toghul. Others, such as the Dasht-i Kipchak, have lived in the area since the time of the Shaibani Khan (sixteenth century).

The general mixing of the Uzbek and Tajik in both Afghanistan and Soviet Central Asia has affected kinship terms in both groups. The basic terms dealing with marriage relationships will normally be those of the dominant group, usually Tajiki Farsi in the east and south and Uzbeki Turkic in the west and north. Interethnic marriages tend to identify the dominant group in any given area; if Uzbek dominate, Uzbek males will marry Tajik females, and vice versa if Tajik dominate. Since World War II, this pattern has been breaking down, but more slowly in rural areas.

The brideprice, which really refers to an economic exchange, still exists in most areas. The bride's dowry should equal the so-called brideprice given to her family, and in any event, most marriages take place within close kin lineages.

In addition to the usual square and rectangular, or domed-roof, sun-dried and mud-brick houses, a special type of Uzbek house is found in Afghanistan. It is an oblong, rectangular hut with individual rooms leading off from a long, covered porch and situated inside a walled compound. The Central Asian yurt is also common in northern Afghanistan, used by most semi-sedentary groups when they seasonally migrate to *yayla* (summer quarters) with their herds or move to highland fields to reap wheat or pick melons. The classic portable yurt has a latticework wooden frame covered with reed matting, with a number of colorful woven woolen bands wound around the latticework outside the matting. A series of long poles tied with special knots support the structure at the top of the wooden frame. Felt *namad*, often elaborately decorated, are tied over the poles, the designs usually facing the interior. A two-part, wooden frame door, often carved with ethnic designs, serves as the entrance. Many Uzbek (and others) use yurts as summer dwellings *inside* their compounds, even if they do not make short migrations.

Some migrants prefer to live in a *chapari*, another portable dwelling but simpler to construct and smaller than a yurt. The *chapari* has no latticework foundation. Curved or straight poles are either placed in the ground or securely braced and then sided with matting and roofed with matting or felt *namad*. *Chapari* are often used as summer cooking huts inside compounds.

Sports and games often reflect the ethos of a people's culture. Only a few centuries ago the Turko-Mongol peoples, direct ancestors of the Uzbek and Turkmen, thundered across Mongolia, south Siberia, Central Asia and deep into Russia, creating empires from yurts. The epic poetry of these Turkic speakers resounds with memories of past greatness—and past recreation, some of which continues to the present.

Launching falcons after game birds remains an important pastime, and hunting with *tazi* (Afghan hounds) for desert gazelle, rabbits and other rodents occupies some of the leisure time of the Uzbek. The *tazi* hamstring gazelle and wait for their masters to cut the throat of the animal, thus making it *halal*, or clean. Animals that die without their throats cut are considered *haram*, unclean, and cannot be eaten.

One contact sport is *buzkashi*, seldom played in Soviet Central Asia but remaining popular on the Turkestan plains of northern Afghanistan. *Buzkashi* literally means "goat grabbing," but modern play uses a carcass of a small calf instead. Traditionally, the game developed in the steppe lands of Mongolia and Central Asia, where conquering nomads reputedly used live prisoners of war. A released prisoner would try to evade two teams of horsemen, who ultimately dismembered the victim. *Buzkashi* pits one team of whip-wielding horsemen against another, the purpose being to pick up and carry the animal carcass from a starting circle to the goal of one's team. While simple to describe, the actual execution is another matter. The spirit of competition runs high, compounded by limitless numbers of players and a minimum of rules. Besides courage and endurance, *buzkashi* requires skilled horsemanship.

Although mingled with the Tajik (and other groups), the rural Uzbek have not merged with them. The Uzbek's true feelings toward the Tajik can best be expressed in the saying: "When a Tajik tells the truth, he has a fit of colic." To denigrate one's own neighboring ethnic group is, in reality, a way of indicating a positive pride in one's own group.

Since 1973, Afghanistan has been racked by *coup d'etat*, civil war and the 1979 Soviet invasion. The 1 million Uzbek (the largest Turkic-speaking minority in Afghanistan), along with other Afghan minority groups, hoped that the founding of the Republic of Afghanistan in 1973 would guarantee them wider participation in political life above the tribal level. The plans of the republic (never implemented) seemed to move towards more equitable distribution in regional economic development and more regional autonomy for the minority groups.

Even after the April 1978 *coup d'etat* and formation of the Democratic Republic of Afghanistan (DRA), the leftist power elite initially indicated it would respect the uniqueness of the minority groups. Unwise reform programs instituted by the DRA struck at the core of many basic cultural patterns, however, and the Uzbek, among others, felt the government to be anti-Islamic, anti-Uzbek, pro-Communist and pro-Russian.

Most of the ethnic groups of northern Afghanistan are either descendants of refugees from czarist oppression, *basmachi* (freedom fighters) who fought against the Bolsheviks in the 1920s or descendants of the *basmachi*. The overwhelming majority of Uzbek are anti-Russian and anti-Communist. Some Afghan Uzbek did fight in the civil war which raged from late summer 1978 to December 1979, but with the Russian invasion, almost all the Uzbek (and the other peoples of northern Afghanistan) rose against the Soviet invaders. The Soviets have not been able to gain control of the countryside anywhere in Afghanistan (see Pushtun).

Some Uzbek from the Uzbek S.S.R. crossed the Amu Darya to fight with their ethno-linguistic kinsmen. Others on military duty in Afghanistan have deserted and brought their military skills and weapons to the Mujahidin (freedom fighters).

BIBLIOGRAPHY

Books

Azoy, G. Whitney. *Buzkashi: Game and Power in Afghanistan*. Philadelphia: University of Pennsylvania Press, 1982.

Centlivres, Pierre. *Un Bazar d'Asie. Form et organization du bazar de Tashkurghan (Afghanistan)*. Wiesbaden, Germany: Ludwig Reichert, 1972.

Charpentier, C.-J. *Bazaar-e-Tashqurghan*. Upsala: Studia Ethnographica Upsaliensia, 1972.

Dupree, Louis. *Afghanistan*. Princeton: Princeton University Press, 1980.

———. "Uzbek-Soviet Central Asia and Afghanistan." In *Peoples of the Earth*, edited by Sir Edward Evans-Pritchard and Andre Singer. Vol. 15. New York: Grolier, 1973.

———. "Aq Kupruk: A Town in North Afghanistan." In *Peoples and Cultures of the Middle East*, edited by Louise Sweet. Vol. 2. New York: Natural History Press, 1970.

Dupree, Nancy Hatch. *An Historical Guide to Afghanistan*. 2nd ed. Kabul: Afghan Tourist Organization, 1977.

Hanifi, M. Jamil. *Annotated Bibliography of Afghanistan*. 4th ed. rev. New Haven: Human Relations Area Files Press, 1982.

Montgomery, M. A. "The Uzbeks in Two States: Soviet and Afghan Policies Towards an Ethnic Minority." In *Soviet Ethnic Frontiers*, edited by W. O. McCogg, Jr., and B. D. Silner. New York: Pergamon Press, 1979.

Schurmann, Herbert F. *The Mongols of Afghanistan: An Ethnography of the Moghols and Related Peoples of Afghanistan*. The Hague: Mouton, 1962.

Slovin, Mark. *Music in the Culture of Northern Afghanistan*. Tucson: University of Arizona Press, 1976.

Articles

Balikci, A. "Village Buzkashi." *Afghanistan Journal* 5:1 (1978): 11–21.

Centlivres, Pierre. "Les Uzbeks du Qattaghan." *Afghanistan Journal* 2:1 (1975): 28–36.

Dupree, Louis. "Anthropology in Afghanistan." *American Universities Field Staff Reports: South Asia Series* 20:5 (1976): 1–21.

———. "The Green and Black: Social and Economic Aspects of the Coal Mine in Afghanistan." *American Universities Field Staff Reports: South Asia Series* 7:5 (1963): 1–30.

———. "Kessel's 'The Horseman': The Culture, the Book, the Movie." *American Universities Field Staff Reports: South Asia Series* 20:6 (1976): 1–16.

———. "Uzbek: Afghanistan and Soviet Union." *Family of Man* 7:93 (1976): 2577–2580.

Louis Dupree

V

VAI The Vai (also found in literature as Vey and Vei) are an offshoot of northern Manding-speaking peoples of Guinea and Mali (see Manding-speaking Peoples). The Vai seem to have moved into the forest region around A.D. 1500 and finally settled in an area straddling the Mano River on the Atlantic coast in what today is Sierra Leone and Liberia. Although the initial group was probably small in numbers, the Vai have enculturated surrounding peoples into their way of life. In addition, by maintaining contact with the savanna Mandinka they have perpetuated their former savanna culture in the forest region (see Mandinka).

Today the Vai, most of whom are Muslims, number about 63,000 in Liberia, 59,000 in Guinea and 18,000 in Sierra Leone, with all figures awaiting more accurate census and analysis. Some Vai living in Sierra Leone are rapidly acquiring the Mende language and losing Vai. On other cultural levels, they are also acculturating to the more dominant Mende patterns of life. In Liberia, although there has been considerable outmigration to the urban areas, Vai culture survives as a way of life distinct from that of the surrounding peoples (see Mende).

Traditionally, the Vai have based their political structure on patrilineal kinship units with patrilocal residence. Patrilineal clans are territorially defined and form the largest stable political units. Confederations of clans have occurred periodically, but remain unstable, generally based on the personal abilities of particular political leaders. Upon the death of such leaders the confederations usually fragment into single clan units again.

Claims to specific territory are based on a first occupation basis by a particular lineage. Others who arrive later become strangers to the first inhabitants. The late arrivals, with their offspring, remain junior members of the political structure unless they intermarry with members of the original patrilineage or until a sufficient span of generations erases the stranger stigma.

Other forms of stratification exist within Vai society. Various types of servitude occur, including debt bondage, human pawning and chattel slavery. The social distinction and distance between chattel slaves and all other members of Vai society is most notable and particularly affects social, economic and political activities. Chattel slaves as well as their children remain socially distinct from all others in the society, engaging in only the most menial tasks. They are not permitted to participate in any political activity. At certain points in Vai history, this prohibition has led to slave revolts.

The Vai economy depends on a combination of swidden agriculture, with particular emphasis on rice as the staple food, and trade as middlemen between the peoples of the interior and ships stopping along the Vai coast. With these two activities, it has been possible for the Vai to overcome the usual limitations of tropical forest environment. Most forest-dwelling swidden agriculturalists have been unable to sustain any great social stratification, but for the Vai it has been possible because of their access to the additional economic base of trade. Thus, an artisan class has developed. (In about 1830 an indigenous Vai script was invented which permitted the Vai to establish a tradition of literacy. As a consequence, Vai scholars left manuscripts detailing Vai life and history.)

Vai religious activities at the early period of their arrival on the coast encompassed an omnipotent but somewhat distant supreme being, Kongba. The more immediate needs of individuals were supposedly met by a variety of spirits who populated the forests and waters. Ancestors, the "living dead," maintained the most significant place in Vai belief. Old people were venerated, and that veneration continued after death. As parents, the elders-ancestors oversaw and guided the lives of their children, and the strongest manifestation of the ancestors' concern and control was through the men' society, the Poro. It was within this secret society that the ultimate sanction of death, as determined by the will of the ancestors through high-ranking Poro members, was meted out.

Beginning in the middle to late eighteenth century, Islamic influences began to reach the Vai area. The first contacts seem to have been as a direct result of ongoing trade and cultural contacts between the savanna Mandinka and the coastal Vai. By the middle of the nineteenth century, the Vai, particularly in the northern areas, were also coming into contact with Muslim Fulani traders from the Futa Jallon (see Fulani).

Initially, Islam made little impact upon the Vai. Individual political leaders who had consolidated several clans into an unstable confederation might turn to a Muslim divine to sanctify and therefore help sustain their positions. These divines were recognized as powerful, but the precepts of Islam held little interest for Vai people in general.

Beginning in the twentieth century, the central governments of Sierra Leone and Liberia extended increasing political control over the Vai. Political units were stabilized and select individuals and their lineages were designated as the legitimate rulers. Authority to mete out penalties, particularly the death penalty, which had resided with the Poro elders, was taken over by the central governments. Finally, in 1928 in Sierra Leone and 1930 in Liberia, the various forms of internal servitude were abolished. Vai society, resilient through former periods of changing circumstances, for the first time was shaken to its core. The legitimacy of the ancestors' power was undermined. As a consequence, mass conversion to Islam began. Islam provided a belief structure which was respected and which could be accommodated to traditional Vai religious concepts.

Today, Islam is the dominant religion of the Vai countryside. Most Vai are Sunni, with some Ahmadi in the cities, particularly Monrovia. Every town has a mosque, and all men are expected to attend at least the morning and evening prayers and to observe the religious holidays. Both Tijaniyya and Qadiriyya brotherhoods are active, and the process of Islamization continues within the Vai country. The purification of practices is encouraged, and traditional customs, such as masked dancing figures at public festivals, are discouraged. The purification process is not so successful in the urban areas, however. The many Vai men and women who have left the Vai country to find employment in the moneyed economy find that secular distractions have an undermining effect on religious fervor. Physical, social and economic distance is growing between those Vai who have remained in their traditional homes and many of those now living in the urban centers.

BIBLIOGRAPHY

Books

Johnson, S. Jangabaa. *Traditional History, Customary Laws, Mores, Folkways and Legends of the Vai Tribe*. Monrovia: n.p., 1954.
Murdock, George P. *Africa: Its Peoples and Their Culture History*. New York: McGraw-Hill, 1959.

Unpublished Manuscript

Holsoe, Svend E. "The Cassava-Leaf Peoples: An Ethnohistorical Study of the Vai with Particular Emphasis on the Tewo Chiefdom." Ph.D. dissertation, Boston University, 1967.

Svend E. Holsoe
Population figures updated by Richard V. Weekes

W

WANA Most Wana are not Muslim. But as inhabitants of a remote interior region of Indonesia's Central Sulawesi Province, the Wana offer a distinct perspective on Islamic culture. The view from the Wana hinterlands may be unique in details, but it illustrates a pattern widespread in island Southeast Asia, namely, the development of an ethnic self-consciousness on the part of an interior upland population in response to a coastal Muslim presence.

The Wana (known also in the literature as the To Wana) are a population of swidden farmers who inhabit the mountainous region of the Bongka River drainage in Kabupaten Poso regency. Exact census figures are unavailable, but 5,000 was a government estimate for the Wana population in the mid–1970s. If their numbers increased at a net 2.5 percent a year, there would be perhaps 6,000 in 1983.

Wana locate their residences on swidden farm sites. Settlements range in size from two or three households to a dozen or more, each consisting typically of a married couple with dependents, both young and old. New swiddens are prepared and settlements relocate annually. In deference to government demands, many Wana also maintain a house in an officially recognized village. Rice is the principal staple of the diet. It is supplemented with other cultivated foods including maize, sweet potatoes, manioc, bananas, sugar cane, melons and green vegetables. Wana hunt with dogs and traps for wild boar and deer. Wild birds and fish are also an important part of the diet. Community relations are integrated through three key specialists—farming experts, legal authorities and shamans.

While the Wana maintained a high degree of political and economic autonomy into the last quarter of the twentieth century, Wana culture does not make sense apart from its regional and inter-ethnic context. The very name the Wana apply to themselves hints at the source of their cultural identity in relations with outsiders. The word "Wana" derives ultimately from Sanskrit and means "forest" in a number of languages in the Indonesian archipelago. For the Wana themselves, Wana is not a generic term for forest but a specific place name in their territory. It is not unreasonable to suppose that not only the label but their very sense of being a "people" came about through exchanges with coastal populations.

The Wana homeland is located on a peninsula some 80 miles at its widest point. It is bordered on the north and south by narrow strips of coastal lowland that are flanked in turn by foothills that soon change into rugged upland terrain. As inhabitants of the interior, the Wana have been shielded by topography from total hegemony by outsiders. But ties with lowland communities go back into the distant past. Before Dutch authorities entered the region in the first decade of the twentieth century, some Wana were drawn into the spheres of small Islamic sultanates that once dotted the coasts of Sulawesi. In the last century, Wana in the southern reaches of the territory paid tribute in the form of beeswax to the Raja of Bungku, a principality located to the southwest of Wanaland. Likewise Wana in the north presented tiny bamboo tubes filled with uncooked rice to the Raja of Tojo, a sultanate to the northwest of the Wana area. Some Wana were appointed local representatives of these rajas and carried special titles. While Wana homage no doubt enhanced the stature of local sultans and may have conferred certain privileges on Wana middlemen, by no means did these demonstrations of vassalage imply that coastal rulers exercised thoroughgoing suzerainty over the Wana. Then, as now, Wana had the option of fading back into the interior forests when threatened or oppressed in their relations with coastal authorities. For their part, the rajas occupied themselves with issues of status and prestige at political centers, not with territorial concerns in the hinterlands. But through contact with these principalities, Wana adopted and reworked for their own purposes some key political and cosmological concepts basic to the Islamic sultanates, including the idea of *baraka* (magical powers associated with royalty), a tripartite social class system made up of nobles, commoner and slaves (unrealized in Wana social life, but nonetheless present in their thought) and an association of cosmic well-being and political order (a model that Indonesia's Muslim kingdoms had in turn reworked from earlier Hindu-Buddhist constructions). And Wana, who attribute all power to sources external to their own society, claim that their legal code was obtained from the Raja of Bungku.

Wana accounts of the pre-colonial past stress political relations. The nature of economic ties between the Wana and their coastal neighbors before the Dutch period is unclear. But since the Dutch entered the region in the first decade of the twentieth century, trade relations between coast and interior have been an important feature of Wana life. While the Dutch Protestant heritage of the colonialists did not make itself felt until after the Dutch departure, trade brought pagan Wana and Islamic traders together. A flourishing resin trade developed in the Dutch period and continued after World War II in the first decades of the Indonesian Republic. Wana exchange resin for salt, cloth and metal goods. This trade encouraged the growth of small coastal communities made up principally of immigrants from other areas of Sulawesi. Refugees were added to their numbers during the political and religious turmoil of the 1950s and 1960s. More recently, with the development of petrochemical substitutes for natural resins and a decline in quality of resins from central Sulawesi, the resin trade has fallen off. In the mid–1970s, Wana were selling rice for coastal goods, a hardship in a subsistence-based economy. The rice helped to support the coastal settlements, whose largely Muslim populations engage in copra production and sea-oriented activities like fishing and trading.

Wana vaccilate in their coastal-mountain orientation. While drawn to the coast as a source of much desired trade goods, many Wasa resist the loss of autonomy lowland life entails. Many move to foothill settlements to improve their economic lot. Often such moves entail conversion to Islam or Christianity. Financially disadvantaged, many return to interior settlements, where they shed their religious affiliations and resume their former existence.

Wana culture bears the imprint of generations of contact with such coastal Muslim peoples as the immigrant Bugis (see Bugis). Like hill peoples elsewhere in island Southeast Asia, Wana use the image of siblingship to express the relation between themselves and the lowlanders. Once there were two brothers, they say. The elder one remained in the Wana homeland to maintain the traditional ways. The younger one moved to the lowlands and became a Muslim. Indeed, this myth may very well reflect historical experience. The To Ampana, Muslim farmers living along the northern coast of the Wana area, speak a dialect of Taa, the Wana language, and are recognized as cultural neighbors. In recent years, a third sibling has been added to the story, reflecting the increasing importance of Christianity in the Wana region, due in part to a small but significant influx of Christian Mori into the area.

With their shamanistic tradition unfettered by orthodoxy and open to entrepreneurial innovation, Wana borrow freely from the Muslims. Be they pagan, Christian or Muslim, Wana assert the existence of one God and anticipate a heaven modeled along Islamic lines. Their world is inhabited by spirits such as *jimi* (from the Arabic *jinn*), *malaeka* (from the Arabic *malaikat*, the plural form of *malak*, or "angel") and *nabi* (by which Wana mean not prophets in the Islamic sense, but guardian spirits of people and objects). *Do'a*, a variant of the Islamic word for prayer (*doa*), is the Wana word for magical spells, an important resource in Wana society. And spells themselves are laced with potent terms like *bisumila* (Arabic *bi'smi'llahi*, "in the name of God"), *salama* (from the Arabic *salamat, salam*, "peace") and *ala ta ala* (from the Arabic *Allah taala*, "God, may He be exalted").

Religion has become a key element in defining Wana identity. For coastal peoples, the absence of a world religion is a critical feature of the inhabitants of the Wana hills. An argument could be made that paganism is the creation of world religions—there are no pagans except through the eyes of believers in world faiths. That certainly appears to be the case for the Wana. At least as far back as the beginning of this century, Wana have been aware of their heathen status vis-à-vis Muslims. Through longstanding relations with Muslims and, since World War II, with Christians, unconverted Wana have come to articulate for themselves a religion that they call among other things *agama kapir*, or "heathen religion" (from the Arabic *kaffir*).

Spurring their theological inventiveness is an official government policy formulated since Indonesian independence. The Indonesian Republic is founded on a principle of religious freedom within the framework of monotheism. This principle supports the rights of Christians, Hindus, Buddhists and Confucianists in a predominantly Muslim nation. But ethnic minorities who do not belong to recognized world faiths are officially viewed as people without religion and are under considerable pressure to convert. As a consequence, religion has become a major issue in relations between coastal and interior populations in the Wana area. In the 1970s, a gauge of religious affiliation was distance from the coast—the more physically remote the settlement, the more likely its members were to be pagan. But since that time, the New Tribes Mission, an evangelical group that seeks to convert pagans to fundamentalist Christianity, has established a base in the Wana interior. Whether Christianity comes to be the religion of the upland people in contrast to coastal Islam—as is the case in many other parts of Indonesia due to the effects of resident Christian missionaries—remains to be seen.

Jane Monnig Atkinson

WAYTO   The Wayto of Lake Tana in north central Ethiopia are one of the rare remnants of the pre-agricultural African peoples (hunters, gatherers and fishermen) and constitute one of the few instances in the world of Muslim hunters. They live in scattered settlements on the Tana shore and dispersed among Amhara peoples further inland. Wayto in both locations may total as many as 2,000, but they are constantly "passing" and disappearing into the society of the Amhara, the dominant people of Ethiopia. They spoke their own indigenous language and possessed an aboriginal religion in the late eighteenth century, but since at least the mid-nineteenth century the Wayto speak only Amharic (an Ethio-Semitic language) and profess to be Muslims.

Like many other Ethiopian peoples, the Wayto have, without any basis in fact, myths of an origin in ancient Israel. In contrast, many of the surrounding Amhara derisively relate a tale that the Wayto were originally spawned from wood, an explanation they also render for the Qemant Agaw agriculturalists, north of Tana. Actually, the Wayto are undifferentiated somatically from their neighbors, the Amhar and the Agaw (see Bilin). It is quite possible that the ancestral Wayto language was a variety of Agaw, a group of language and dialects spoken today by surviving enclaves of the original pre-Amhara inhabitants of the region. However, there is no record of the Wayto's native tongue.

The Wayto habitat consists of the shores of Tana, offshore islands, the lake itself and, more recently, various plains areas inland from the lacustrine coast. The fresh-water lake is roughly heart-shaped, about 48 by 42 miles. It is quite shallow, few places being deeper than 12 feet, with 55-foot "holes." Tana is a large natural reservoir into which the streams of the region drain and is the source of the Blue Nile. A reliable little rainy season in March and April is followed by the big rains from mid-June through September, in which about 80 percent of the annual precipitation of 40 to 52 inches falls. Vegetation of the shore and islands varies from firm-soil grassland, to papyrus swamp, to deciduous forest remnants.

Over the past 50 years or so, the Wayto have undergone an economic transition from a life-way of hunters-fishers to one of cultivator-craftsmen-fishers. This transition of material base of sustenance has profoundly affected most other aspects of their culture. Wayto culture rested upon the hippopotamus, which thickly populated the Tana shores through the beginning of the twentieth century. At that time, the Wayto were contacted by the price-making market economy of Europe, then spreading over the globe by the impetus of advanced industrial technology. During the course of trade which included rifles for the hippo ivory, the Wayto reduced the teaming herds of hippopotami in the Tana basin to just a few survivors by 1940. Formerly, large-scale hunting was supplemented by fishing, some gathering of plants and exchange of hippo by-products for food and craft items not produced by the Wayto. For several decades now, the very basis of Wayto society literally has been shot out from under it, just as the bison, as the economic foundation of Plains Indians in North America, were destroyed with rifles.

Currently, as in the past, the basic building block of Wayto society is the patrilocal, patrilineal band. Each band contains several families, usually monogamous and rarely polygynous, of a nuclear mode of organization which sometimes develops into an extended mode. The band was and is sedentary with several permanent hamlets of 3 to 5 houses and sometimes a larger settlement, or village, of 10 or more houses. All are in the midst of a demarcated hunting territory along the shore. Houses are a wattle-and-daub or reed-walled cylinder topped with a thatched cone roof. The houses are similar to, but less substantial than those of their non-Wayto neighbors, who are more prosperous. By the 1960s, many band members had dispersed from their home territories to cultivate at places inland from the lake shore.

A band had an informal council of male elders, but this institution is now almost entirely gone. In the past, they adjudicated disputes and also met with councils of other bands to discuss territorial boundaries. Another Wayto wielder of some political authority is the *nagadras*. He is appointed by the government with the consent of the Wayto involved. The *nagadras* leads a band, or today the remnants of more than one band, and generally keeps the peace and attempts to settle local disputes. He also enforces Amhara feudal tax laws on any Wayto who plow land. No taxes exist for foraging activities. Therefore, as long as game and fish were sufficient for Wayto needs, the tax laws had a latent function of reinforcing the traditional foraging way of life. To keep out of the grasp of the state and its taxes, Wayto maintained their hunting ways. Thus, they existed within the territory of the Ethiopian state but were not a part of it.

Consumption of hippopotami engenders a societal boundary-maintaining mechanism around the Wayto which remains almost intact into the present, even though it is impossible to eat hippo meat on a regular basis. The Wayto's neighbors consider hippo to be ritually polluted. Accordingly, the Wayto are considered as unclean pariahs by other people of their region. Until recently, all non-Wayto would not touch or eat with a Wayto. Today, this abhorrence of contact is breaking down, especially on the part of Muslims who are not Wayto.

Nowadays, hunting yields little in the way of food, and fishing does not provide enough of a return by itself to sustain all Wayto. Fishing is supplemented by the making of craft goods and by cultivation. Women make items of basketry from varieties of Tana swamp grasses for sale in local marketplaces. Men arduously mine and hammer to shape flat lava stones used for grinding grain. These are sold to and used by families throughout the region. Wayto men have always gathered select papyrus reeds, bundled them, and formed and tied the bundles into a small boat called *tankwa*. These boats are poled around and across the lake in all kinds of Wayto activities. Some lake trips might take a week or more. Of several millions of inhabitants of the greater Tana region, only the Wayto have a native knowledge of boat building and of navigation. Fishing is done from *tankwas* and along the shore using nets, hook and line, fish spears, basketry fish traps, and specially blended herbal stupificants causing fish to float to the surface.

Cultivation and some tending of domesticated animals are new to the Wayto economy. Except for dogs and cats, the only animals owned by most Wayto are chickens. A few have one or more sheep or goats. Significantly, no Wayto can afford oxen for plowing. Although a few Wayto were given disputed title to some cropland by the government in the 1960s, almost all of the Wayto who now cultivate land must rent or sharecrop land among Amhara who control land. Land rental rates are high, and sharecrop returns are low. A pair of oxen and a plow are rented at the rate of two days of labor furnished to the owner in return for one day of use. Sorghum, barley, maize and the Ethiopian small grain, teff, are cultivated as cereal along with a number of legumes and garden vegetables.

Marriage is by contract between families of a prospective bride and groom. Traditionally, each should be from a different band. The customary practice of the bride's family contributing a modest dowry of household items and the groom's parents paying a moderate amount of bridewealth in goods is now waning. The wedding ceremony is one of the major feasting times of the Wayto and includes song and dance and a *das* (large flat-roofed shelter for seating guests at a ceremony). Ideally, marriage is with those separated by at least seven degrees of kinship. A Muslim practitioner unites the couple in a simple ceremony in which no vows are made by the bridal pair. If the bride is physically immature, marriage is consummated when she comes of age.

Patrilocal residence of the newly married couple is the most common mode. Birth of a boy is greeted far more favorably than that of a girl. Girls assist their mothers and boys their fathers with the daily labors and thus, learn the economic roles allotted to each sex. Boys learn craft, fishing and agricultural skills today, but usually not those of hunting. The values and traditions of the hunting life are now largely pleasant memories. Formerly, a man had to anoint his hair with butter, the mark of a killer of a hippopotamus, and earn the right to sing the songs of hippo killers before he could take a wife. Nowadays, the concerns are no longer on the subjects of hunting prowess and reciprocity in sharing of game but of eking out a living.

Inheritance of property at the death of a parent is said to be by the Islamic principle of inclusion of both daughters and sons. A person who dies is wrapped in a cotton shroud and buried in a large rectangular grave, which is filled with earth and covered with rocks. A funeral and a periodic memorial of the funeral (*tazkar*) are observed for the deceased.

Two kinds of Wayto exist, those who generally attempt to adhere to the tenets of Islam and are somewhat accepted by most other Muslims and those who are nominal followers of Islam and are not accepted. Although ideally subject to Shariah, many Wayto are concerned with little more than the *shahadah*, recitation of the tenet of faith. Some Wayto do attempt daily prayer at prescribed times. Ramadan is observed in a loose fashion, without much fasting, but the feast at the end of this month-long holiday is popularly followed. Most larger villages have a mosque, often without any religious practitioner. A few Wayto have positions of *fuqura* (religious teachers) and one or two of *shah* (*shaikh*, or leader). In pre-Islamic contrast, still others are a *balazar*, master of the pagan *zar* spirit of bodily possession.

Just as the Shariah is known by most Wayto in name only, so, too, is the Quran. No Muslim shrine exists, but the Quran might be read by *fuqura* at an ancient Wayto religious site called *juv*. Some Wayto still drink *baganyia*, their native beer, and others alcohol. Friday is considered the same as any other work day. Wayto are Sunni. Some European scholars allege that they use the Malikite juridical rite, but none of the Wayto is aware of the fact. In all, Islam is not yet even moderately rooted in Wayto society.

The Wayto have become emergent peasants of an agrarian state. By turning to plowing on the land of others, Wayto have become subordinated at the base of a complex, hierarchical social system. By inclusion in an agrarian society, Wayto have been transformed from nonliterates to illiterates. The latter are those who cannot read and write in a society controlled by writing; the former are those entirely within their own independent society, not having writing. Written law requires Wayto cultivators to pay rent and tax upon cultivated land. The feudal agrarian state encompassing the Wayto since the 1940s has recently given way to a socialist one. Its effect upon Wayto life is not yet apparent.

BIBLIOGRAPHY

Books

Gamst, Frederick C. "Wayto Ways: Change from Hunting to Peasant Life." In *Proceedings of the Fifth International Conference on Ethiopian Studies*, edited by Robert L. Hess. Chicago: University of Illinois at Chicago Circle, 1979.

Murdock, George P. *Africa: It Peoples and Their Culture History.* New York, McGraw-Hill, 1959.
Simoons, Frederick J. *Northwest Ethiopia: Peoples and Economy.* Madison: University of Wisconsin Press, 1960.

Frederick C. Gamst

WOLOF   The Wolof inhabit Senegambia in West Africa, from the river Senegal in the north to the river Gambia in the south, and number more than 2.3 million people. They form 36 percent of the population of Senegal and 15 percent of the population of Gambia. The region is ethnically mixed and also includes Mandinka (Soose), Fulani (Fulbe) and Serer (see Mandinka; Fulani; Serer). The Wolof are the dominant element in the former states of Waalo (Oualo), Kahoor (Kayor), Jolof, Baol, Siin (Sine) and Saalum (Saloum) and were already occupying this portion of West Africa when the first Portuguese voyagers reached the coast in the middle of the fifteenth century.

Over time there have been major shifts in population. When they first established contact with the Europeans, many Wolof moved from the interior regions towards the coastal areas. Later, as peanuts became an export crop in the mid-nineteenth century, there was movement into lands in southwestern Senegal where the soil was more suitable for cultivation. In recent years, there has been expansion towards the east and south in search of new areas for peanut cultivation and a drift towards Dakar and its surrounding areas in search of employment. Wolof are also to be found in small numbers in Mauritania and in the Casamance region of Senegal south of Gambia.

Wolof is classified as a West Atlantic language of the Niger-Congo family and is commonly spoken as a second language in Senegal by Serer, Fulani and Mandinka, with perhaps 30 percent of the non-Wolof having a simple understanding of the language. Since independence, increasing efforts are being made to encourage the writing of Wolof—a new script has been officially adopted and a Wolof-French dictionary prepared. Formerly, vernacular material was largely limited to translations made by Catholic missionaries and had a limited distribution. Wolof is also used as the language of trade outside the main Wolof areas. Verbal skill is greatly prized as a sign of a mature adult, and Wolof philosophy is contained in hundreds of proverbs, which are skillfully used in social interaction. Children learn linguistic skills through riddles, storytelling and secret languages. Stories are told by professional storytellers (*griots*) as a form of entertainment.

Wolof have a culture, as well as social and political systems, that are typical of the savanna zone of West Africa. Politically the country was divided into a series of small states, power being concentrated in the hands of certain ruling lineages. Formerly, in certain areas descent was traced through the female line, but with the adoption of Islam, succession to office now follows the male line. Nevertheless, the mother's kin play an important part in a person's life, providing practical help and emotional support in time of trouble, whereas the father's side of the family is held responsible for training and discipline.

Wolof social organization is highly stratified. People are divided into free-born (ranging from high-ranking noble lineages to ordinary peasant farmers who lack real power), those of slave descent (whose status depended on the families to which they were attached; the slaves of a ruler, for example, often being rich and powerful, and the executive arm of the ruler) and a low-caste group of artisans, with three major subdivisions: smiths (blacksmiths and goldsmiths), leatherworkers, and musicians and praise singers, the latter having many subdivisions depending on the instrument played or the role performed. Artisans of other ethnic groups, woodworkers of Laube (Fula-speaking) origin, or weavers of Fula origin, are incorporated into the Wolof ranking system. The major low-caste groups are endogamous units and formerly could also own slaves. Intermarriage across ranks is still rare, even in heterogeneous urban populations, though intermarriage across ethnic boundaries at an equal level has always been common. The families of renowned Muslim scholars are accorded high rank and prestige. Terms derived from Western thought such as class, rank, caste and status group can be applied only to part of the total system, which is maintained largely through the roles that members of each group play in the major rites of passage: naming ceremonies, circumcision of boys, marriages and funerals. The situation is complicated by some regional variations and changes through time. Certain occupations, such as weaving and woodworking, have virtually disappeared among the Wolof, having been taken over by people of different ethnic origins.

The history of the Wolof states is a story of conquests, revolutions, invasions, usurpations and struggles against colonial powers and Islamic warriors. The memories are kept alive in the songs of the *griots*, but many items in the narrations are adjusted to accommodate the audience sponsoring the performance.

The typical rural Wolof village is small, consisting of several hundred people living in fenced-off compounds grouped around a central square shaded by baobab and silk cotton trees. In the center is a platform on which the men can rest, and public meetings are held near that point. Dancing and wrestling matches take place in the square. On the eastern side is to be found a mosque, and behind it the cemetery. Women meet at wells on the outskirts of the village.

The traditional Wolof house is circular with walls of reed or millet stalks, thatched with long grass or palm leaves. In recent years rectangular or square forms are commonly made, with mud walls and corrugated sheeting as roofing material. Just behind the entrance is a short fence, which prevents strangers from seeing directly into the compound. The house of the compound head is opposite the entrance; to the sides are separate houses for the women and their children and, near the entrance, houses for unmarried men and strangers. At the back are storerooms and sheds for goats and sheep. Within the compound lives an extended family—a man, his wives and children, his brothers and their families, and his unmarried sisters. About a quarter of the Wolof men have more than one wife; it is generally the chiefs, village head and heads of large compounds who have more than two. Each wife in a polygynous household has her own house, which she shares with her children, sleeping in turn in her husband's house.

In cities, houses range from shacks occupied by those in low-paying occupations, where the standard differs little from rural housing, to modern dwellings equipped with refrigerators, TV sets and European-type furniture, occupied by those with substantial incomes.

In rural areas Wolof are primarily farmers, growing millet and sorghum, with a little maize, as food crops and peanuts as a cash crop. They keep small numbers of goats, sheep and chickens. Cattle are generally entrusted to the care of Fulani herdsmen. As there is a single rainy season with most rain falling between July and October, farming must be concentrated in this short period. The rainfall varies from about 13 inches in the north to about 40 inches in the south, but it is irregular from year to year.

Vegetation varies from almost desert conditions in the north to the fringes of tropical forest in the south. The coastal zone is bordered with sand dunes, behind which are swamps with saline water, beyond which is a zone of ruhn palm trees. Further inland is the typical savanna zone of long grasses and scattered trees such as acacias, tamarinds and locust-bean trees.

The land is first cleared by a slash-and-burn technique, the seed then planted by hand, after which the farmer faces a long struggle against weeds. When the millets and sorghum begin to ripen, the crops must be protected from flocks of weaver birds. In recent years an increasing number of donkey and horse-drawn agricultural implements for planting and weeding, chemical fertilizers and insecticides have become available to the farmer. The concentration on a single cash crop—though it is clearly the one best suited for the soil and climate conditions—has placed the farmer at the mercy of both the natural elements (drought, soil exhaustion, plant diseases) and of price fluctuations in the world market. Serious droughts in the 1970s, as well as general soil exhaustion, have led to widespread hardship, and many of the younger men have drifted off to the towns to search for employment.

A number of traditional crafts are still practiced. Most villages have a blacksmith to make farming tools. Gold- and silversmiths, renowned for their excellent filigree work, tend to be concentrated in the trade centers and large towns. Pottery bowls in which clothes are washed, water storage jars and steaming pots are still made by women, especially of the smith caste, but metal and plastic utensils are now common. Various types of basketry, both wickerwork and coiled work, are still to be found. With the growth of a tourist industry in Dakar and Banjul, a new market is now available for local crafts.

Practically all Wolof are Muslim, with a small number of Christian Wolof found mainly in the coastal cities (Dakar, Goree, Banjul). Islam came to northern Senegal about the eleventh century, and the early Portuguese travellers of the fifteenth and sixteenth centuries mention that most Wolof rulers, even though they generally followed traditional ways, had religious teachers at their courts. One of the functions of such men was to provide supernatural protection against evil forces—malicious spirits, witchcraft and the evil eye. But Islam was slow in reaching the mass of the people, and Muslim converts often had to form separate communities of their own. It was not until the religious wars of the nineteenth century, particularly as a result of the *jihad* of El Hadj Omar, who was followed by such warriors as Ma Ba in southern Senegal, that widespread conversion took place. Muslim religious leaders were then engaged in a struggle both with traditional rulers, who were opposed to this new threat to their power, as well as with the French. Ironically, though the French were opposed to the expansion of Islam, the period of peace and improved communications that followed the success of the French conquest enabled religious teachers to move more freely, and Islam spread rapidly and widely. A Wolof usually belongs to one of the three main brotherhoods: Tijani (brought by El Hadj Omar), to which about 60 percent of the Wolof owe allegiance; Mouridism, which includes 30 percent of the Wolof, (a group founded by Ahmadou Bamba at Touba, where there is now one of the largest mosques in sub-Saharan Africa and which has become the center of an important annual pilgrimage); and Qadiri, to which about 10 percent belong.

Pre-Islamic beliefs, which survive only marginally, are encountered mainly in isolated rural areas and are generally maintained by women. For example, a woman suffering from a severe mental disorder may be urged to join a cult of spirit possession (*ndep*), the members of which have been through a similar experience and act as a support group. In periods of drought a traditional rain dance may be revived to make the plight of the people known to the forces in the sky that have withheld the rain. In southern Senegal an organization concerned with fertility (*kanyelango*) has spread from the Dyula and Mandinka to some Wolof families.

Wolof social interaction is characterized by a complicated code of etiquette and behavior appropriate to one's social role. An elaborate exchange of greetings shows mutual respect between the parties. The higher one's social status, the greater one's moral obligation to live up to the noblest standards of behavior. These are to maintain self-control and dignity, to show courage in the face of danger, to carry out one's duty, to keep one's word, to show oneself generous even at the cost of hardship to oneself, to be patient in trying circumstances, to avoid actions which would bring dishonor on oneself or one's family and to fulfill one's religious obligations. Within each of the social strata there are differences in the expected type of public behavior. A chief is expected to talk quietly; a *griot* speaks with a loud voice which can be heard over the noise of a crowd. A girl of high rank will dance in restrained fashion in public, while one of lower rank can perform the lascivious motions which characterize many Wolof dances. Outside the house, one must wear dress appropriate to the occasion—one's style validates one's social role. Men going to the mosque, women going to the market or attending social events—marriages, naming ceremonies and so on—place themselves before the public eye and so dress, move and talk in an appropriate way.

In spite of the traditional nature of the culture and its hierarchical social structure, the Wolof, perhaps more than any other Senegalese people, have been influenced by French and British cultures. Wolof have always formed the predominant element in the major cities of Senegal (Dakar, St. Louis, Kaolack) and The Gambia (Banjul). Through the centuries they played a leading role in the import-export business, both as middlemen and as producers of the primary cash crop. They engaged in coastal trade and owned truck and passenger vehicles. They were also dominant in the civil service and played a major role in the development of modern political institutions. In urban centers Wolof women played an important role in the markets, dealing in produce and fish and building up businesses which dealt with fabrics, cloth dyeing and so forth. Wolof women with their flair for display became the fashion setters in matters of hair styles, jewelry and clothing.

Change in Wolof society has been rapid with the increase in educational facilities, the improvement in communications and the influence of cinema, radio, newspapers and magazines. Wolof writers, musicians, actors, filmmakers, poets, politicians, historians and philosophers are known not merely locally but internationally for their achievements. In the cities an increasing number of girls attend school, speak French or English as a second language and expect to have a career which will enable them to live a more independent life. Wolof women work as teachers, nurses and librarians, in department stores, airline offices, post offices and the civil service and in commerce as independent traders in the market and as transport owners. Family planning clinics, infant welfare centers and modern hospital facilities, even though still inadequate to meet the needs of all, provide new amenities for the young Wolof mother. The present generation has greater freedom of choice in marriage. At the same time urban life has brought problems of poor housing and overcrowding, high rents, a high unemployment rate, particularly for teenagers, high food costs, an unsympathetic bureaucracy and exploitation of the illiterate by the literate, with consequent social unrest.

BIBLIOGRAPHY

Books

Behrman, L. *Muslim Brotherhoods and Politics in Senegal.* Cambridge: Harvard University Press, 1970.
Diop, Abdoullaye-Bara. *La société wolof.* Paris: Editions Karthala, 1981.
Gamble, David P. *The Wolof of Senegambia.* London: International African Institute, 1967.
Klein, M. *Islam and Imperialism in Senegal, Sine-Saloum 1847–1914.* Edinburgh: Edinburgh University Press, 1968.

O'Brien, Donal B. Cruise. *The Mourides of Senegal: The Political and Economic Or-ganization of an Islamic Brotherhood*. Oxford: Clarendon Press, 1971.
———. *Saints and Politicians: Essays on the Organization of a Senegalese Peasant Society*. London: Cambridge University Press, 1975.
Venema, L. B. *The Wolof of Saloum: Social Structure and Rural Development in Senegal*. Wageningen, Netherlands: Center for Agricultural Publishing and Documentation, 1978.

David P. Gamble

Y

YAKAN The Yakan are one of the Muslim groups of the southern Philippines who are part of the Sama people. They are practically all Sunni Muslim of the Shafi school and number 116,000. A homogeneous group which has only slight local variations in living and language, they live on the island of Basilan, predominantly in the interior. Information about them traces back only to the latter part of the nineteenth century and is scarce. Probably the Yakan were the original inhabitants of Basilan, but today they comprise less than one-half the population, now sharing the island with later arrivals: Christian Filipinos, mainly living in and around the two municipalities of Isabela and Lamitan, and the Muslim Tausug and Sama, mostly in the coastal villages (see Sama; Tausug).

Basilan is a volcanic island just off the southwestern tip of Mindanao, 495 square miles in area. The interior contains numerous peaks interspersed with undulating hills and tablelands. The climate is tropical with rather equable temperatures and with an adequate rainfall, most of the rains falling from April to November. The rest of the year is relatively dry.

These geographical conditions are suitable for agriculture and therefore of great importance to the Yakan, who are agriculturalists, growing various crops on their individually owned fields. The preferred crop is upland rice, which is grown in nonirrigated fields and harvested once a year. Other important crops are camote and cassava as well as several kinds of vegetables and fruits.

Both men and women, often working together, do the field work. Their combined efforts go toward planting, weeding and harvesting, but men alone tend to the plowing and post-harvest job of cutting and burning off the fields.

The Yakan have no compact villages; houses are scattered among the fields. The dwellings are rectangular pile buildings, with wooden or bamboo walls and a rather steep thatched roof. Apart from the kitchen, the house has only one room and a porch. Although the Yakan are Muslims, they have no special quarters for women. Both men and women—the family as well as guests—gather in the same room or on the porch.

A house is occupied by a family consisting of husband and wife and their unmarried children, perhaps also a newly married son or daughter with spouse.

The center of religious life is the *langgal* (mosque), a simple structure without minaret. A small bamboo drum is used for calling to prayer. An *imam* officiates at prayers and religious celebrations in the *langgal*, as well as at family ceremonies, such as weddings and funerals. Additionally, he is called to pray with any person who has a specific reason to address himself to God. The profession of *imam* has tended to be hereditary, but special study is necessary, too. Since the *imam* has more knowledge of Islam and usually follows the religious rules more strictly than others, he fasts throughout Ramadan while most of his congregation fast only for a few days, just as they usually limit ritual praying to Friday prayers. Very few Yakan make the pilgrimage. On the other hand, *zakat* is paid by all in the form of a contribution at the end of the harvest.

Most Yakan children, both boys and girls, learn to recite the Quran, but as they do not study Arabic as well, they understand very little of the text.

The Yakan follow the Muslim calendar. In seven of the months, they have religious celebrations, three of which are important: the two official Muslim festivals of Id al Fitr and Id al Adha, and the celebration of the birth of the Prophet Muhammad. The latter festival, although a Muslim occasion, contains features of obvious pre-Islamic origin. This is typical of how Yakan incorporate many pagan rituals and traditions into orthodox religious practices. Other examples are the rice ceremonies, performed before both the planting and the harvesting to insure a rich yield. To the individual Yakan, such survivals from an older religion are really Muslim rituals. He sees his religion as true Islam.

On the other hand, if the Yakan consider themselves good Muslims, other Muslims do not consider them so. In recent years Muslim missionaries have tried to instruct the Yakan in more orthodox practices. In parts of Basilan they have gained some influence, but in other places their ideas receive little attention. Christian missionaries, too, have been working for several years among the Yakan with even less success.

Islam affects Yakan family life in the same loose ways as in religious life. According to the Quran, a man is allowed four wives. Theoretically, the Yakan go further, having no limitation, but in fact most men have only one wife and very few have more than three. A man cannot marry a second time without the consent of his first wife.

The initiative for marriage comes from the man. He has to pay not only a brideprice, but also all expenses connected with the wedding ceremonies: a Muslim ritual and a ceremony of pre-Islamic character. Both are performed by the *imam*. After the wedding, the young couple usually lives for some time with the parents of either bride or bridegroom. Later, they build a house of their own, and again, it may be built on the land of either the husband or the wife. In case of divorce, however, the one on whose land the couple lives will keep the house and the spouse must leave. Divorce is not uncommon and is fairly easy to obtain for the woman as well as the man.

The Yakan follow Muslim law in that what property the wife has brought into the marriage, as well as what she may have acquired during marriage, will always belong to her. Inheritance is another matter. According to the Quran, a daughter's inheritance should be only one-half that of a son's, but among the Yakan, sons and daughters inherit equally, from father as well as mother. Kinship and descent is traced through both father's and mother's lineage.

Yakan women are not segregated, nor have they ever been veiled. Both sexes wear tight-fitting blouses and pants. In many kinds of work, especially that connected with agriculture, men and women work together. The women go to market to sell the produce. Many of the women are expert weavers, producing a beautiful material used in making the traditional costume. Recently, they have taken up weaving on a larger scale in order to market their handwoven goods.

The *imam* is the secular as well as the religious head of the community. He serves in cooperation with three elders who sit in judgment of misdemeanors or minor disputes. More serious crimes are supposed to be handled by government authorities since the Yakan are more or less under the Philippine government. This, however, works more in theory than in practice, and greater crimes are usually attended to in the same manner as smaller ones.

Modern times have brought some progress, more roads and schools for example, but progress has also brought difficult problems. Formerly, the Yakan kept mostly to themselves, especially in the interior of the island. They traded some with the Sama, but communication with Christian Filipinos and Tausugs was slight. Now Christian Filipinos have come to settle on the island, a few having acquired large areas for plantations. A Yakan must now have title to his land, lest his ownership be contested and he suddenly find that his land belongs to someone else.

The Muslim rebellion in the Philippines has hit the Yakan severely. Heavy fighting in Basilan made it necessary for most of the Yakan to evacuate their homes. Some joined the rebels while others sided with the Philippine army. But the majority preferred to remain neutral, not because they lacked grievances— they did feel political, economic and religious discrimination—but because they did not believe that supporting either side would resolve their problems. Assuming the rebellion succeeded and resulted in an independent Moro Republic, the Yakan would remain a minority still.

BIBLIOGRAPHY

Books

Frake, Charles O. "Struck by Speech: The Yakan Concept of Litigation." In *Law in Culture and Society*, edited by Laura Nader. Chicago: Aldine Press, 1969.
Gowing, Peter G., and McAmis, Robert D., eds. *The Muslim Filipinos: Their History, Society and Contemporary Problems*. Manila: Solidaridad Publishing House, 1974.
Wulff, Inger. "Features of the Yakan Culture." In *The Muslim Filipinos: Their History, Society, and Contemporary Problems*, edited by Peter G. Gowing and Robert D. McAmis. Manila: Solidaridad Publishing House, 1974.

————. *Habitation Among the Yakan, a Muslim People in the Southern Philippines.* Monographical Series, Vol. 30. Copenhagen: Scandinavian Institute of Asian Studies, 1976.
————. "The Yakan Maulud Celebration." In *Studies in Philippine Anthropology in Honor of H. Otley Beyer*, edited by Mario D. Zamora. Quezon City: Alemar Phoenix, 1967.

Articles

Dapitan, Pilar P. "The Yakans of Basilan City." *Southeast Asia Quarterly* 5:2 (1970): 1–6.
Frake, Charles O. "How to Enter a Yakan House." *Sulu Studies* 3 (1975): 87–104.
Norbeck, Edward. "David Barrows' Notes on Philippine Ethnology: Yakan Rice Planting Ceremony." *Journal of East Asiatic Studies* 5:3 (1956): 252–253.
Wulff, Inger. "Bulan Sapal—A Month of Misfortune: Concepts and Rituals Among the Yakan of Basilan, Southern Philippines." *Folk* (Copenhagen) 16–17 (1974–1975): 381–400.
————. "Burial Customs Among the Yakan, a Muslim People in the Southern Philippines." *Folk* (Copenhagen) 4 (1962): 111–122.
————. "The Yakan Graduation Ceremony." *Folk* (Copenhagen) 5 (1963): 325–332.
————. "The Yakan Imam." *Folk* (Copenhagen) 8–9 (1966–1967): 355–371.
————. "The Yakan of Basilan." *Silliman Journal* 18:4 (1971): 436–440.
————. "The Yakan Rice Planting Ceremony." *Folk* (Copenhagen) 18 (1976): 237–245.

Inger Wulff
Population figures updated by Richard V. Weekes

YALUNKA   The name "Yalunka" is interpreted by the Yalunka themselves to mean "people of the Yalun." This means that they consider themselves to be the original inhabitants of the Futa Jalon plateau in West Africa. The Yalunka (Dialonke, Djalonke, Dyalonke, Jallonke, Jalunka) described here live in the northeastern corner of Sierra Leone and portions of the Republic of Guinea.

The earliest European reference to the Yalunka occurs around 1507 in the form "Jaalunquas." Later references make it clear that the name was long a general one for the original Manding-speaking inhabitants of the Futa Jalon region. Various versions of the name are still applied to the descendants of these peoples, who, as a result of extreme pressure from the Fulani (Fulbe) immigrants into the Futa, migrated to their current locations in the seventeenth century, establishing a group of independent polities, the best known of which is Solima, whose capital was at Falaba in present-day Sierra Leone. Thus there are other groups called Yalunka in the western savanna region of West Africa whose exact relationship with the Sierra Leone–Guinea Yalunka is not known.

The Yalunka number in excess of 85,000, about 90 percent of whom are Sunni Muslims. Their language belongs to the northern subgroup of Manding and is closely related to Soso (see Manding-speaking Peoples; Soso).

Knowledge of the pre-twentieth-century history of the Yalunka is sketchy.

Sporadic relations with the British at Freetown were established in the 1820s and continued throughout the nineteenth century. In the 1820s the Yalunka were strongly pagan and violently anti-Muslim. Although some were drawn to Islam in this period, between the 1820s and early 1880s Islam made only modest headway among them. Itinerant Muslim Quranic teachers, goldsmiths and gunsmiths were in the area from time to time.

In 1884 Solima was conquered by one of the armies of Samory Touré and incorporated into his empire. Touré, a Mandinka, was a great nineteenth-century state builder and proponent of Islam (see Mandinka). There was heroic resistance (the ruler of Falaba blew himself up rather than surrender), but after Touré's conquest all the survivors were forcibly converted to Islam. By 1892 the British and French had driven Touré from the Yalunka area, and with the creation of the Sierra Leone–Guinea border, Solima was divided into two colonial spheres. (The territories of the other former Yalunka polities are entirely in Guinea.)

With the departure of Touré's troops and the imposition of colonial rule, most Yalunka lapsed into pagan ways, although some remained Muslim. In addition, more Muslims came from what was now Guinea into the Yalunka region of Sierra Leone. A Christian mission (Church Missionary Society) was started in the 1890s but had collapsed by the early 1900s. In the 1950s another Christian mission (Missionary Church Society) was begun, but it met with only modest success. Throughout this period Islam gained steadily, and by the 1960s over 90 percent of the Yalunka were Muslim, the remainder being Christian (the last elderly pagan Yalunka died in the 1950s.)

Most Yalunka (over 80 percent) engage in subsistence agriculture. Rice is the staple crop. Many of the larger settlements have been in their current location since the eighteenth century, and the remnants of the moats and stockades that surrounded these towns can still be seen (in the form of large cotton trees which have taken root along the former stockades). The former Yalunka preference for life in large rather than small villages or hamlets continues. A growing number of Sierra Leone Yalunka have migrated to urban centers, especially the diamond areas of Sierra Leone and the city of Freetown. In addition large numbers of non-Yalunka (mostly Mandinka and Fulani) now live in Yalunka country, making up about half the region's population. This process of turning the Yalunka area into a multi-ethnic one began early in this century and encouraged the growth of Islam among the Yalunka, as most of the immigrants were Muslim.

The major social unit of the Yalunka is the family household, ideally headed by a husband and his wife or wives and unmarried children. Additional kin are often present as followers, and extended households of two or more married men (usually father and son or brothers) are not uncommon. The household is the major unit of production and consumption, although the patrilineage is still important. These named, exogamous lineages were once corporate, property-owning residential groups with considerable social and economic power. They are still important as source of social and economic support, but they no longer hold property in common. Each Yalunka also belongs to an exogamous patrilineal clan (clan names are shared with many other Mande-speaking groups), and Yalunka still observe clan food taboos.

Most men still hold polygynous marriage as an ideal, and about 40 percent of married men do have more than one wife. Age at first marriage for men is the early twenties (down from about age 30) and for women is about 15 or 16 (up from about 12 to 14). There is still some preference for matrilateral cross-cousin marriage. A large bridewealth is given to the bride's family and lineage by the husband and his kin. Today women have much more to say about who they will marry than in the past, but desire to control the marriages of daughters is still strong among fathers. The rate of divorce is high.

Boys are circumcised between the ages of 6 and 12. As recently as the early 1950s many boys were not circumcised until nearly 20 years of age. Initiation ceremonies surrounding circumcision are not nearly as elaborate as in the past (when the initiates were dressed as girls until circumcised and emerged as "men" at the end of a period of seclusion). Girls are initiated at puberty by clitoridectomy and are then eligible for marriage.

Traditionally there were a number of hereditary endogamous occupational castes among the Yalunka, a feature shared with many Manding speakers—smiths, leatherworkers, musicians and praise singers. These groups exist, although now only smiths can hope to survive exclusively by the practice of their traditional occupation. In larger towns many newer occupations are also found—clerk, tailor, driver, shopkeeper—although many of these "modern" occupations are filled largely by non-Yalunka.

The Yalunka have always kept some cattle in addition to sheep. Goats and cattle are important both in marriage transactions and in more direct economic activity. Most cattle in the region (the locale of most of Sierra Leone's cattle) are in the hands of the pastoral Fulani.

Islam dominates contemporary Yalunka religious practice. Each large settlement has a mosque with resident *imam*, who is not necessarily Yalunka. Most of the standard Muslim religious festivals are observed, perhaps the most important being the celebration at the end of Ramadan. The Yalunka combine celebrating the end of the fast month with a celebration of traditional chiefdomship, making the holiday doubly important. Traditional Mande hero figures and mythology are well remembered, but religious vocabulary is dominated by words of Arabic origin. This is true even when the supernatural beings involved are clearly of an indigenous character. Origin myths now usually begin with Adam and Eve and recount a truncated version of the Islamic story of creation before introducing Manden Lake, a traditional location of all Manding creation myths, and the classical Mande heroic figures.

Quranic education is important among the Yalunka. While an orthography for the language has been developed by the Missionary Church Association, most Yalunka who use script write in either Arabic or English, depending upon their level of education in the two languages and the purpose of the communication. About 20 percent of the adult men have some Arabic education. Every settlement of any size contains at least one Quranic teacher. In fact, more Yalunka receive some Arabic than English education. A few men leave the area and go to large centers in Guinea for other education in Arabic. These men often return and figure prominently in religious activities.

BIBLIOGRAPHY

Books

Donald, Leland. "Ethnicity and the Occupational Structure of a Yalunka Town." In *Essays on the Economic Anthropology of Liberia and Sierra Leone*, edited by V. R. Dorjahn and B. L. Isaac. Liberian Studies Monograph Series, No. 6. Philadelphia: Institute for Liberian Studies, 1979.
———. "Food Production by the Yalunka Household, Sierra Leone." In *African Food Production Systems*, edited by P. McLoughlin. Baltimore: Johns Hopkins Press, 1970.
Fyle, C. Magbaily. *The Solima Yalunka Kingdom: Precolonial Politics, Economics and Society*. Freetown: Nyakon, 1979.
Laing, Alexander G. *Travels in the Timanee, Kooranko and Soolima Countries*. London: John Murray, 1825.
Welmers, W. E. "Niger-Congo, Mande." In *Current Trends in Linguistics*, edited by T. A. Sebeok. Vol. 7. The Hague: Mouton, 1971.

Articles

Donald, Leland. "Arabic Literacy Among the Yalunka of Sierra Leone." *Africa* 44 (1974): 71–81.
———. "Yalunkayan foloxi di?" *Sierra Leone Studies*, n.s. 22 (1968): 45–51.
Hair, P.E.H. "A Note on Earlier Knowledge of the Yalunka and Kuranko Tongues." *Sierra Leone Bulletin of Religion* 3 (1961): 70–72.
Harnetty E. "A Few Notes on the Yalunka Country and an Outline of Its History." *Sierra Leone Studies* 21 (1939): 75–78.
Harrigan, William. "Christian Literature in the Yalunka Language." *Sierra Leone Bulletin of Religion* 3 (1961): 68–70.
———. "The Form, Function and Distribution of the Definite Nominal Suffix in Yalunka." *Sierra Leone Language Review* 2 (1963): 30–35.
Sayers, Eldred F. "Notes on the Clan or Family Names Common in the Area Inhabited by Temne-speaking People." *Sierra Leone Studies* 10 (1927): 14–108.
Siddle, D. J. "War Towns in Sierra Leone: A Study in Social Change." *Africa* 38 (1968): 47–56.
Thomas, N. W. "The Industrial Pursuits of the Yalunka People." *Sierra Leone Studies* 1 (1918): 39–43.
Warren, Harold G. "Notes on the Yalunka Country." *Sierra Leone Studies* 13:1 (1928): 25–28.

Unpublished Manuscripts

Donald, Leland. "Changes in Yalunka Social Organization: A Study of Adaptation to a
      Changing Cultural Environment." Ph.D. dissertation, University of Oregon, 1968.
Fyle, C. Magbaily. "Solimana and Its Neighbors: A History of the Solima Yalunka from
      the Mid-seventeenth Century to the start of the colonial period." Ph.D. disser-
      tation, Northwestern University, 1976.

Leland Donald

YAO   Known by a variety of names—Wayao, Wahyao, Veiao, Adjao—that
no doubt reflect their mobility over the past centuries, the Yao live in Malawi,
Mozambique and Tanzania. They number close to 1 million. Three other peoples
are sufficiently close culturally and linguistically to be grouped with the Yao.
They are the Mwera, Makua and Makonde, most of whom live in Tanzania; an
unknown number live in Mozambique. Among them they number close to 7
million so that it seems probable that the total Yao group numbers more than 8
million, of whom 3.9 million are Muslims.

The Yao claim that their traditional homeland was between the Lujenda and
Rovuma rivers east of Lake Malawi. For at least two centuries before the colonial
intrusion of the late nineteenth century the Yao were active as traders, bartering
ivory, slaves, beeswax and tobacco for guns, gunpowder, cloth and beads. The
suppliers of these commodities were the Arab and Swahili peoples on the coast,
who did not themselves make any major penetration into the interior until the
early nineteenth century. Not only were the Yao active in the slave trade, but
slaves were also an integral part of their economic and political system before
the coming of Europeans. The rapid spread of Islam among the Yao seems to
have been due partly to their long association with Arabs but much more to their
suspicion of Europeans and Christian missionaries as being antagonistic to their
way of life.

In their home areas the Yao are hoe agriculturalists, growing millet and sorghum.
To replace commercial activities curtailed by the loss of the slave and ivory
trade, many Yao men have had to accept contracts as migrant laborers on estates
and mines. One estimate suggests that as many as 30 percent of adult males
may be away at any one time.

Before the colonial conquest the Yao lived in autonomous villages, each with
a headman. Several villages were grouped under a chief of a district. Because
of the possession of slaves as workers and their value for trade, the chiefs were
very powerful and only submitted to colonial rule by force of arms. Divested
of their slaves, their economic power was undermined, and until recently a
headman or chief lived in a manner little different from anyone else.

The average Yao village consisted of only about a dozen houses, but it was
a highly important unit of social organization. The headman was politically
powerful and belonged to the dominant matrilineage. Matrilineal descent was
the rule and produced conflicts of interest for the headman. Whereas many men

married matrilocally, the headmen often could not move and so his wives came to him. His responsibilities to his matrikin were supposed to be preeminent, but his emotional links to his children sometimes conflicted with these.

In 1967 Tanzania adopted "The Arusha Declaration" with the objective of building a Socialist society. This policy envisaged the voluntary formation of villages based on the principles of *ujamaa* (familyness), which is used to translate the English term "African socialism." By 1974 lack of enthusiasm for the policy prompted the government to pass the Villagization Act, which required that all inhabitants of the rural areas be gathered into villages. In the case of the Yao, much larger agglomerations than had been customary were formed, in some cases involving the compulsory settlement together of Muslims and Christians and of peoples practicing both matrilineal and patrilineal descent. The social effect of these new groupings is hard to estimate, but the combination of radically changed patterns of settlement, land tenure and authority coupled with universal primary education for boys and girls cannot but have profound effects.

The majority—as many as 75 percent—of the Yao claim to be Sunni Muslim of the Shafi school. However, orthodox religious observances are not at all strong, and considerable syncretization has taken place with the traditional cult of the ancestral spirits. Rites for the latter are now regarded as Islamic and are referred to as *sadaka*. Few carry out daily prayers, and the observance of Ramadan is not strict. Few, if any, have made the Haj. Although Islam stresses patrilineal descent and inheritance, matrilineal descent and inheritance continue unchanged for the most part. The Yao regard parallel cousin marriage (*bint amm*—father's brother's daughter) as incestuous, but marriage to cross cousins (father's sister's daughter or mother's brother's daughter) is desirable.

Many Yao have moved to the major cities of East Africa and have adapted to urban living, while still retaining links to their home areas.

BIBLIOGRAPHY

Books

Alpers, Edward A. *Ivory and Slaves*. Berkeley: University of California Press, 1975.
Douglas, Mary. "Techniques of Sorcery Control in Central Africa." In *Witchcraft and Sorcery in East Africa*, edited by J. Middleton and E. H. Winter. London: Routledge and Kegan Paul, 1963.
Iliffe, John. *Tanganyika Under German Rule*. Cambridge: Cambridge University Press, 1969.
Ingham, Kenneth. *A History of East Africa*. London: Longmans, 1962.
Kitambo, I. N., and Temu, A. J. *A History of Tanzania*. Nairobi: East African Publishing House, 1969.
Leinhardt, Peter. "A Controversy Over Islamic Custom in Kilwa Kivinje, Tanzania." In *Islam in Tropical Africa*, edited by I. M. Lewis. London: Oxford University Press, 1966.

Leslie, J.A.K. *A Survey of Dar Es Salaam*. London: Oxford University Press, 1963.

Mitchell, J. Clyde. "The Yao of Southern Nyasaland." In *Seven Tribes of British Central Africa*, edited by E. Colson and M. Gluckman. London: Oxford University Press, 1951.

———. *The Yao Village*. Manchester: Manchester University Press, 1956.

Murdock, George P. *Africa: Its Peoples and Their Culture History*. New York: McGraw-Hill, 1959.

Oliver, R. "Discernible Developments in the Interior." In *History of East Africa*, edited by R. Oliver and G. Matthew. Oxford: Clarendon Press, 1963.

Smith, Alison. "The Southern Section of the Interior." In *History of East Africa*, edited by R. Oliver and G. Matthew. Oxford: Clarendon Press, 1963.

Tew, Mary. *Peoples of the Lake Nyasa Region*. London: Oxford University Press for International African Institute, 1950.

Trimingham, J. Spencer. *Islam in East Africa*. Oxford: Clarendon Press, 1964.

Articles

Kanawire, J.A.K. "Village Segmentalism and Class Formation in S. Malawi." *Africa* 50:2 (1950): 125–145.

Lamburn, R.G.P. "Some Notes on the Yao." *Tanganyika Notes and Records* 29 (1950): 73–84.

Mitchell, J. Clyde. "Marriage, Matriliny and Social Structure Among the Yao of Southern Nyasaland." *International Journal of Comparative Sociology* 3:1 (1962): 29–42.

Rangely, W.H.J. "The Yao." *Nyasaland Journal* 15:1 (1963): 7–27.

James L. Brain

YORUBA   The term "Yoruba" is used to identify a people having, with considerable dialectic variation, a common language (of the Kwa group of the Niger-Congo family) and a common culture, which is remarkably persistent in spite of great political, geographical and religious differences that have arisen over the past three centuries. The language and culture are found as far from their West African origin as Brazil and Cuba, while substantial Yoruba communities are found in most West African states, especially in Sierra Leone and Ghana (230,000). The greatest number, probably over 17 million, are in southwestern Nigeria, adjacent areas of Benin and beyond in Togo. Nearly one-half are Muslim, largely Sunni.

Yoruba constitute virtually the entire populations of the Nigerian states of Ogun, Ondo and Oyo, as well as the great majority of Lagos State, the Ilorin area of Kwara State up almost to Jebba and south and east as well. A few Ondo Yoruba live in Bendel State, and others are in trade or government throughout Nigeria. Until recently, only the Oyo were identified as Yoruba proper, other communities being identified by name with their royal cities. The dialects of Ondo and Ekiti are strikingly different from Oyo, and while gross cultural differences are very few, there exist a great many cultural peculiarities which clearly differentiate, for example, Ife, Ijebu, Ijesa, Ekiti and Ondo from each other and from Oyo.

Recent interpretations of Yoruba traditions of origin agree in identifying Yoruba as a Sudanic people who successfully imposed their rule on an indigenous population in the forest belt of present Nigeria. All traditions confirm Ile-Ife as the first city of the Yoruba and the Ooni of Ife as the spiritual head from whom all other Yoruba kings derive their sanction to rule. Urbanization among Yoruba is both basic and traditional; they have "always" lived in cities. Prior to the wars of the nineteenth century, farming communities extended out from the cities, and hunters served as guardians of boundaries while establishing and maintaining routes for trade. Fulani pressures from the north and colonial changes in the south forced the creation of strategic and defensible towns, such as Ibadan and Abeokuta, as well as the shifting of major cities to the south, notably Oyo. These new cities were built in patterns which can be seen today: substantially walled, largely windowless, large family compounds with internal courtyards, the whole built along intricate access paths.

The compound, containing up to 1,000 people (but rarely that many) may be more than an extended family, since useful strangers may live within it. Beyond the individual compound, the crucial element in social and political organization is the lineage, which has its founding ancestor, its historical myth, its traditional god, its common names (male and female) and perhaps special customs and taboos. Within the compound and the lineage, an intricate social hierarchy controls relations (as an extreme example, a child may be "senior" to a wife who marries into a family a few days after the child's birth). Within the city or town, lineages themselves are hierarchically differentiated (although the ruling lineage may be the poorest and weakest of all), and the lineage chiefs may serve as the town or city council. The economic cohesion of the lineage is based upon agriculture primarily, land being owned communally, as well as upon craft specialization. The introduction in 1955 of free primary education has undercut this economic strength by removing young people from farm work and encouraging career individualism. Nevertheless, the lineages remain remarkably strong.

Substantial numbers of rural Yoruba do not reside in cities even in times of low agricultural activity. They share the common fate of rural dwellers everywhere; they are strangers in the cities, far from the protection of family, ignorant of city ways and certain to be abused unless able to find sophisticated protection.

Apart from these, however, the ordinary Yoruba may feel a high degree of security of place—whether high or low—in his compound and lineage. Further, in spite of dialectical and cultural variations, he can acknowledge a common inheritance from Ile-Ife, as well as the spiritual community that to some extent transcends even orthodox Islam and Christianity. Of the vast pantheon (200 to 400) of *orishas* (loosely, "gods"), Ifa stands apart. Ifa is itself an *orisha*. However, it is cohesive in that when used (as it is almost universally) for divination, it is respectful, indeed promotive, of other deities. It may call for the revival of a forgotten deity, or it may reinforce the inquirer's faith in Christ or Allah.

The cohesion of Yoruba life has prevented any high level of sectarian conflict even where traditional beliefs have been challenged simultaneously by Islam and Christianity. Although some Yoruba felt the influence of Islam in earlier centuries, it was not until the early nineteenth century, following the Fulani *jihad* in the north, that old Oyo came within Muslim influence and Ilorin fell to Muslim rule under a line of emirs that persists to the present. By the time Fulani military pressure forced the resettlement of Oyo to the south, Islam was firmly entrenched in the Yoruba savannas—as far, indeed, as the horse could safely go. Thereafter, the advance of Islam in Yoruba country was peaceful. By the 1830s, Hausa traders, some of whom were also religious teachers, had established themselves in the new city of Ibadan. As British colonial influence grew, freedom of trade movement further facilitated proselytization. During the second quarter of the present century, British "indirect rule," which reinforced powers of emirs and *obas* (kings), led to Islamic domination in the north and a consequent rapid growth in the south. In the 40 years between 1913 and 1953, the proportion of professed Muslims in Ibadan alone increased from 35 to 60 percent. Simultaneously, Christian missionaries—many of them returned slaves from America— were active in the south, and eventually it could be said without great exaggeration that throughout the Yoruba territories fewer than one-seventh of the people remained professed traditionalists, while the remainder divided fairly equally between Islam and Christianity.

One of the most striking characteristics of present Yoruba religious practice is its open tolerance of divergence, even within the family. In hundreds of communities, when the time of the *egungun* ancestor impersonation and festival arrives, drummers go about the streets calling Christians, Muslims and others, often by name, to join in the celebration. Few resist the call. Every city had at one time, and some have still, an active *ogboni* or otherwise named secret society. Largely purged of rites distasteful to the new orthodox, these continue to function and effectively command the allegiance of powerful citizens, regardless of faith. While compounds and even lineages often tend to adopt a common religion, in many families this is not so. Muslim, Christian and traditionalist members of a single family live peacefully together and join happily in each others' festivals, giving the official calendar of holidays a remarkable length and fullness of observance.

This tolerance and even pleasure in diversity arises from the fact that both Islam and Christianity are seen as civilizing in the sense that traditionalists remain outside the ruling cultures, while traditional beliefs are widely shared. Islam demands few overt changes in Yoruba behavior; it is a choice, a preference within a relatively stable lineage-oriented society. The choice can be significant, since in the economy traditionalists are likely to be the least successful, Muslims tend to be more successful and Christians are clearly strongest in professions and large-scale business. Islam's appeal over Christianity is far broader than wealth. While it is true that monogamy is the rule among all Yoruba, it is not the ideal; Islamic toleration of polygyny and also brideprice (condemned by the orthodox churches) have not been inconsequential in influencing free choice favoring Islam. Further, Islam is seen as a black man's religion, Christianity the faith of the white man.

An early dominance of Qadiriyya teaching was later overcome because of the preference (by Hausa clerics) for Tijaniyya. Nevertheless, the stronger Tijaniyya strictures on women have not overcome traditional Yoruba female independence. Seclusion is so rare in most cases as to seem virtually nonexistent.

In the 1920s, the Ahmadiya sect began to gain strength in the south, beginning in Lagos. The movement has remained relatively small in numbers, but its modernist tone and concern for education in the European mode gave it considerable early success in the more affluent community and may have had some influence on the orthodox Muslims. The largest Muslim educational society in Nigeria, the Ansar-ud-Deen, has never been Ahmadiya, but it has been steadfastly nonsectarian (enrolling even qualified Christian students without overt discrimination). It is in large measure a successful attempt to duplicate the Christian mission's school system, which for much of this century attracted thousands of children of ambitious Muslim parents, children who were then lost to the faith. During the 1930s the Young Nawar-ud-Deen Society became active, competing with the Y.M.C.A., and the Islamic Missionary Society challenged the Church Missionary Society.

Islam in southwestern Nigeria may be said to have been more deeply influenced by Yoruba and colonial culture than the reverse. Women's dress was hardly affected at all. Muslim men can often be distinguished by their preference for the loose trousers and jumper top of the *buba* and *sokoto* as opposed to the tight trousers and dress shirts of European fashion. Otherwise, it is hard to identify, superficially, characteristics that differentiate Yoruba from Yoruba. Proud and cohesive, Yoruba dominate three of Nigeria's finest universities, those of Ibadan, Ife and Lagos. At all three some Islamic study is offered, but at the University of Ibadan, the Department of Arabic and Islamic Studies is particularly distinguished.

BIBLIOGRAPHY

Books

Aronson, Dan R. *The City Is Our Farm: Seven Migrant Ijebu Yoruba Families.* Cambridge, Mass.: Schenkman, 1978.

Baldwin, David E., and Baldwin, Charlene M. *The Yoruba of Southwestern Nigeria: An Indexed Bibliography* (to September 1974). Boston: Hall, 1976.

Biobaku, S. O., ed. *Sources of Yoruba History.* Oxford: Oxford University Press, 1973.

Eades, J. S. *The Yoruba Today.* Cambridge: The University Press, 1980.

El-Masri, F. H. "Islam." In *The City of Ibadan,* edited by P. C. Lloyd, et al. Cambridge: The University Press, 1967.

Fadipe, Nathaniel A. *The Sociology of the Yoruba.* New York: Africana, 1970.

Fisher, Humphrey J. *Ahmadiyyah: A Study of Contemporary Islam on the West African Coast.* Lagos: Oxford University Press, 1963.

Gbadamosi, T.G.O. *The Growth of Islam Among the Yoruba 1841–1908.* Atlantic Highlands, N.J.: Humanities Press, 1978.

Lloyd, P. C. "The Yoruba of Nigeria." In *Peoples of Africa*, edited by James L. Gibbs, Jr., New York: Holt, Rinehart and Winston, 1965.

Ojo, G. J. Afolabi. *Yoruba Culture: A Geographical Analysis.* London: University of London Press, 1966.

Article

Peel, J.D.Y. "Religious Change in Yorubaland." *Africa* 37:3 (1967): 292–306.

Robert M. Wren

YORUK   The Yoruk of Turkey are a distinct ethnic-tribal grouping, found widely throughout Turkey but primarily along the Aegean and Mediterranean coastlines. Unlike many groups with a unique cultural heritage in the Middle East, the Yoruk are not linguistically distinct from most of the rural populations among whom they live. They speak the Western Turkish dialect standard in Anatolia (see Turkic-speaking Peoples).

Similarly, religion does not set them apart from the majority of Turkey's population as the Yoruk are Sunni of the Hanafi school of law. What distinguishes the Yoruk is their recognition of a common history in the form of membership in, or descent from, an assortment of Turkic tribes which are presumed to have moved to Anatolia from Iran or Central Asia in the eleventh century.

Historically, the Yoruk are mountain nomadic pastoralists moving, for the most part, from winter pastures (*kishlak*) along the coastal plains to high summer pastures (*yayla*) in the Taurus range. As early as the reign of Bayazid I, there are accounts of Yoruk tribes in Macedonia, Thrace and elsewhere in the Balkans. Following the conquest of Cyprus by Selim II, Yoruk groups moved to that island, where they may be found today as settled villagers. Most historians regard the Yoruk as closely related to Turkmen tribes who came in large numbers after the Battle of Manzikert in 1071, but it is also likely that indigenous nomadic pastoral populations along the coast became Turkified during the early period of Islamic rule in Anatolia. In any event, the Yoruk are distinct culturally, in folklore and traditional distribution, from the Turkmen tribes of Anatolia.

The term "Yoruk" is often thought to be derived from *yurumek*, "to walk." The Yoruk themselves do not make this the case, but regardless of the merits of the etymology, it is a fitting image for a nomadic people moving with their flocks of sheep and goats.

During the Ottoman period, Yoruk tribes were important politically since they were recognized by the government for purposes of taxation, the raising of military levies and local administration. Tribal leaders, for example, supplied 52,000 troops in the eighteenth century. Today Yoruk people continue to speak of tribes, and most of the 88 listed in 1898 as then living in Aydin and Smyrna

(Izmir) provinces still can be located readily. However, the Turkish government now does not recognize tribes or tribal leaders for administrative purposes.

Most Yoruk are settled villagers or townspeople living in the coastal provinces south of Izmir, in Konya, Karaman and Kayseri provinces in central Anatolia and in Gaziantep, Marash, Mardin, and Diyarbakir provinces in the east. The tribe, although not a co-residential grouping, forms the social basis for dispersed villages. The tribe is divided into named patrilineal segments or lineages, called *mahalle* or *kabile*, and these are today often of greater social importance than the tribe itself. It is difficult to estimate accurately the number of Yoruk living in Turkey today. In 1925 their numbers were estimated at 300,000; it is likely that this figure is greater than would result from a survey. (Although often classified as Yoruk by outsiders, the Alevi Tahtaçilar, who are nomadic wood-cutters along the southern coast, should be considered ethnically distinct.)

As might be expected in a rapidly changing society, the way of life of Yoruk people has changed dramatically since World War I and the formation of the Turkish republic. In particular, most have abandoned animal husbandry for agriculture or urban pursuits. This transition resulted from a decrease in available pasturage along the coast rather than from overt attempts by the government to settle them. Nomadic or sedentary, all Yoruk are registered as residents of particular towns or villages, and all are subject to military conscription. Many of the Yoruk villages were established through government programs which offered grants of land to landless farmers and pastoralists willing to settle in places where *hazine*, or treasury-owned, tracts were available. Most who availed themselves did so as groups of families settling together; consequently, Yoruk villages today represent families from the same tribal lineage. Along the coast these farmers, or the ones who have retained their fields after settlement, are sharing in the general prosperity of the region, where commercially grown citrus orchards and cotton production are important. A surprisingly large number of Yoruk have become entrepreneurs as well. Recently many have gone to Europe as laborers.

Travelers to the Turkish southeast may still encounter large-scale Yoruk pastoral migrations. In early spring, April through May, and during the fall months of September and October, the mountain roads around Marash, Pinarbashi, Sariz, Kozan and other areas are filled with flocks of sheep, usually moving at night or in the early dawn to avoid truck traffic, accompanied by shepherds wearing traditional felt cloaks or *kepenek*. The camels and donkeys laden with household belongings which follow are a colorful link with Turkey's past, one part of the national heritage which is rapidly disappearing.

A few Yoruk families continue to move regularly between summer and winter pastures, dwelling in black goat hair tents of their own making and, in most respects, living a way of life that would be familiar to their ancestors. While it is more common today for families to move both belongings and animals by truck or tractor-drawn wagons, some still travel on foot. Each household or tent has several camels, which are loaded with the family's possessions packed in large embroidered bags (made by women and passed from mother to son), with the larger copper pot and tent poles strapped on top. Small infants, too, may be part of the load, but otherwise the camels are not ridden. Each family's camels are led either by a daughter, dressed in her best if she is of marriageable age, or by the most recent bride (*gelin*) to have married into the household. The tent itself, as emerged in one survey of 171 families, houses, on the average, eight individuals. Residence is patrilocal, and extended families consisting of a man and his married sons and their wives and children are common. Polygyny is approved, despite modern Turkish statutes, but is not frequently practiced. Marriage is highly endogamous, with virtually all marriages occurring within the tribal section. Approximately 20 percent of all marriages are between young men and their fathers' brothers' daughters; the Yoruk regard this as a preferred match. Almost 25 percent of all marriages take place through elopement and bride theft (*kiz kachirma*). This is frequently a source of conflict among households as ideal marriages are carefully arranged, with a high brideprice negotiated as part of the settlement.

Like their settled relatives, the Yoruk are part of the national market economy. Virtually all their clothing and most of what they consume is purchased. Furthermore, the pastures they visit have to be rented as today all pasturage is within village borders or is owned privately. Average herd size is large (approximately 270 sheep per family) since the household must face heavy demands for cash. Families whose herds fall much below 100 animals are likely to be forced to settle for lack of sufficient income to rent pastures and buy food. Sources of income are young animals sold each fall, wool sold in the spring and milk sold to Yoruk entrepreneurs, who process it into white cheese for urban markets. Currently the Yoruk herders of southeastern Turkey are heavily involved in exporting livestock to Iraq, a trade which encourages further commercialization of the animal industry. Thus, the nomadic Yoruk, although visibly much like their forefathers, are very much a part of today's world in the Middle East.

BIBLIOGRAPHY

Books

Bates, Daniel G. "Nomadic Settlement in Turkey." In *When Nomads Settle: Processes of Sedentarization as Adaptation and Response*, edited by P. K. Salzman. New York: J. Bergin and Praeger, 1980.
———. *Nomads and Farmers: A Study of the Yoruk of Southeastern Turkey*. Anthropological Papers, No 52. Ann Arbor: University of Michigan Museum of Anthropology, 1973.
———. "Shepherd Becomes Farmer: A Study of Sedentarization and Social Change in Southeastern Turkey." In *Turkey: Geographic and Social Perspectives*, edited by Peter Benedict, Erol Tumertekin, and Fata Mansur. Leiden: E. J. Brill, 1974.

————. *The Yoruk of Southeastern Turkey: A Study of Land Use and Social Organization*. Ann Arbor: University Microfilms, 1971.

————, and Rassam, Amal. *Peoples and Cultures of the Middle East*. Englewood Cliffs, N.J.: Prentice-Hall, 1983.

Dyson-Hudson, Neville. "The Study of Nomads." In *Perspective on Nomadism*, edited by William Irons and Neville Dyson-Hudson. Leiden: E. J. Brill, 1972.

Inalcik, Halil. *The Ottoman Empire*. New York: Praeger, 1973.

Johnson, Douglas L. *The Nature of Nomadism*. Research Paper No. 18. Chicago: University of Chicago, Department of Geography, 1969.

Kolars, John F. *Tradition, Season, and Change in a Turkish Village*. Research Paper No. 82. Chicago: University of Chicago, Department of Geography, 1963.

Planhol, Xavier de. "Aspects of Mountain Life in Anatolia and Iran." In *Geography as Human Ecology: Methodology by Example*, edited by S. R. Eyre and G. R. Jones. London: Edward Arnold, 1966.

Articles

Bates, Daniel G. "Differential Access to Pasture in a Nomadic Society: The Yoruk of Southeastern Turkey." *Journal of Asian and African Studies* 7 (1972): 48–59.

————. "The Role of the State in Peasant-Nomad Mutualism." *Anthropological Quarterly* 44 (1971): 109–131.

Dönmez, Yusuf. "A Yoruk (Nomadic) Settlement West of Karasu." *Review of the Geographical Institute of the University of Istanbul* 9–10 (1963–1964): 161–179.

Eberhard, Wolfram. "Change in Leading Families in Southern Turkey." *Anthropos* 49 (1954): 992–1003.

————. "Nomads and Farmers in Southeastern Turkey: Problems of Settlement." *Oriens* 6 (1953): 32–49.

————. "Types of Settlement in South-East Turkey." *Sociologus* (n.s.) 1 (1953): 49–64.

Kolars, John F. "Community Studies in Rural Turkey." *Annals of the Association of American Geographers* 52 (1962): 476–489.

————. "Locational Aspects of Cultural Ecology: The Case of the Goat in Non-Western Agriculture." *Geographical Review* 56 (1966): 577–584.

Lewis, G. L. "The Secret Language of the Geygelli Yuruks." *Zeki Velidi Togan'a Armagan* (Turkey) (1950): 214–226.

Planhol, Xavier de. "Geography, Politics, and Nomadism in Anatolia." *International Social Science Journal* 9 (1959): 525–531.

Tanoğlu, Ali. "The Geography of Settlement." *Review of the Geographical Institute of the University of Istanbul* 1 (1954): 1–17.

Tunçdilek, Necdet. "Observations on Rural Settlement in Two Different Regions of Turkey." *Review of the Geographical Institute of the University of Istanbul* 8 (1962): 47–56.

————. "Yayla Settlements and Related Activities in Turkey." *Review of the Geographical Institute of the University of Istanbul* 9–10 (1963–1964): 58–71.

Daniel G. Bates

Appendixes

MUSLIM NATIONALITIES OF THE WORLD

Ethnic Groups, Wholly or Partly Muslim, Within Nations

Country	1983 Population (000)[1]	% Muslim	Muslim Population (000)[2]	Ethnic Name	Group's Population (000)	% Muslim	Muslim Population (000)	% of Nation's Population
Afghanistan	14,200	99.0	14,100	Pushtun	6,000	100.0	6,000	42.25
				Tajik	3,527	100.0	3,527	24.84
				Turkic	1,740	100.0	1,740	12.26
				Uzbek	(1,300)[3]	100.0	(1,300)	9.15
				Turkmen	(380)	100.0	(380)	2.68
				Kirghiz	(37)	100.0	(37)	.26
				Kazakhs	(20)	100.0	(20)	.14
				Karakalpak	(3)	100.0	(3)	.02
				Hazaras	1,160	100.0	1,160	8.17
				Persians ("Farsiwan")[4]	600	100.0	600	4.23
				Aimaq	478	100.0	478	3.37
				Baluch	238	100.0	238	1.68
				Pashai	93	100.0	93	.65
				Qizilbash	93	100.0	93	.65
				Nuristanis	65	100.0	65	.46
				Brahui	18	100.0	18	.13
				Moghol (Mongols)[5]	10	100.0	10	.07
				Undetermined			78	.55
				Arabs				
				Jat				
				"Pamir Tajiks"				
				Kohistanis				

Country	Pop. (000s)	%	(000s)	Ethnic group[4][5]	(000s)	%	(000s)	%
Albania	2,900	70.0	2,000	Albanians (Gheg-Tosk)	2,900	70.0	2,000	70.00
Algeria	20,700	99.0	20,500	Arabs	16,210	99.0	16,050	77.54
				Berbers	4,450	100.0	4,450	21.50
				Tuareg	(31)		(31)	.14
Argentina	29,100	.2	58	Arabs	102	56.9	58	.20
Australia	15,300	.2	30	Arabs	200	10.0	20	.13
				Turkic	10	100.0	10	.06
				Anatolian	(10)		(10)	.06
Austria	7,600	.2	15	Undetermined	15		15	.20
Bahrain	150[6]	99.3	149	Arabs	150	99.3	149	99.33
Bangladesh	96,500	82.9	80,050	Bengalis	92,000	86.0	79,130	82.00
				Urdu speakers	920	100.0	920	.95
				Biharis	(820)	100.0	(820)	.85
				Others	(100)	100.0	(100)	.10
Belgium	9,900	.7	68	Undetermined	68		68	.69
Benin	3,800	16.0	608	Yoruba	520	49.6	258	6.79
				Batonun ("Bariba")	508	31.7	161	4.24

1 From "1983 World Population Data Sheet of the Population Reference Bureau, Inc." Washington, D.C. (with exceptions where noted).
2 Includes indigenous Muslims (despite temporary emigration), permanent immigrants; excludes temporary laborers.
3 Figures in parentheses are for subgroup populations.
4 Names in quotes are alternative names.
5 Word in parentheses, not in quotes, is major related group.
6 Does not include 250,000 temporary laborers.
7 South Asians from Bangladesh, India and Pakistan of all ethnic groups who are permanent residents.
8 Unknown, but group is known to include Muslims.
9 Asamiya speakers only.
10 Does not include Gaza, West Bank Jordan River, East Jerusalem.
11 Does not include 600,000 non-Kuwaiti temporary workers.
12 Does not include Druze.
13 Does not include approximately 1 million foreign laborers.

Ethnic Groups, Wholly or Partly Muslim, Within Nations

Country	1983 Population (000)[1]	% Muslim	Muslim Population (000)[2]	Ethnic Name	Group's Population (000)	% Muslim	Muslim Population (000)	% of Nation's Population
				Fulani	92	100.0	92	2.42
				Songhay	76	100.0	76	2.00
				Hausa	13	100.0	13	.34
				Manding speakers	74	11.0	8	.22
				Bambara	(74)	11.0	(8)	.22
Bhutan	1,400	5.0	70	South Asians[7]	U[8]		70	5.00
Brazil	131,300	.1	124	Arabs	131	60.0	79	.06
				South Asians	U	100.0	43	.03
				Turkic	2	100.0	2	—
				Anatolian	(2)	100.0	(2)	—
Brunei	200	64.0	128	Malays	90	100.0	90	45.00
				Kedayan	28	71.4	20	10.00
				Melanau	11	100.0	11	5.50
				South Asians	U		7	3.50
Bulgaria	8,900	11.0	1,014	Turkic	986	76.8	757	8.51
				Rumelian	(976)	76.5	(747)	8.39
				Tatars	(10)	100.0	(10)	.11
				Gypsies	259	68.3	177	1.99
				Pomaks	80	100.0	80	.90
Burma	37,900	3.60	1,364	South Asians	10,813	6.4	694	1.83
				Burmese	26,929	1.9	512	1.35
				Zerbadees				
				Rohinga (Arakanese)				
				Myedu				
				Kaman				
				Malays	152	100.0	152	.40
				Hui	6	100.0	6	.01

Burundi	4,500	1.0	45					
Cameroon	9,100	22.0	2,000	Undetermined			45	1.00
				Fulani	861	80.0	689	7.57
				Hausa	613	80.0	490	5.39
				Mbun	546	60.0	328	3.60
				Gbaya	385	35.0	135	1.48
				Bamun	131	80.0	105	1.15
				Arabs ("Chadian")	73	100.0	73	.80
				Fali	51	80.0	41	.45
				Kotoko	36	100.0	36	.40
				Mandara	35	100.0	35	.38
				Kanuri	22	100.0	22	.24
				Tikar	33	30.0	10	.11
				Vute	30	30.0	9	.10
				Undetermined			27	.30
Canada	24,900	.6	150	South Asians	103	30.0	31	.12
				Arabs	140	10.0	14	.06
				Undetermined			105	.42
Central African Republic	2,500	8.0	200	Gbaya	684	14.0	96	3.83
				Kara				
				Dooka				
				Lai				
				Fulani	83	100.0	83	3.33
				Mbun	173	12.0	21	.83
Chad	4,700	51.0	2,400	Arabs ("Chadian")	855	100.0	855	18.19
				Maba	204	100.0	204	4.34
				Kanembu	190	100.0	190	4.04
				Tebu	184	100.0	184	3.91
				Dazaga	(181)	100.0	(181)	3.85
				Teda	(3)	100.0	(3)	.07
				Tama speakers	180	100.0	180	3.83
				Tama	(62)	100.0	(62)	1.30
				Erenga ("Asungor")	(56)	100.0	(56)	1.20
				Abu Sharib	(45)	100.0	(45)	.96

Ethnic Groups, Wholly or Partly Muslim, Within Nations

Country	1983 Population (000)[1]	% Muslim	Muslim Population (000)[2]	Ethnic Name	Group's Population (000)	% Muslim	Muslim Population (000)	% of Nation's Population
				Mararit	(17)	100.0	(17)	.36
				Haddad	153	100.0	153	3.26
				Lisi	127	100.0	127	2.70
				Bilala	(61)	100.0	(61)	1.30
				Kouka	(56)	100.0	(56)	1.20
				Medogo	(10)	100.0	(10)	.21
				Masalat/Masalit	102	100.0	102	2.17
				Daju	94	100.0	94	2.00
				Beri	61	100.0	61	1.30
				Zaghawa	(41)	100.0	(41)	.87
				Bideyat	(20)	100.0	(20)	.43
				Barma ("Bagirmi")	47	100.0	47	1.00
				Fulani	47	100.0	47	1.00
				Buduma	42	100.0	42	.89
				Mubi	38	100.0	38	.80
				Mimi	30	100.0	30	.54
				Kotoko	18	100.0	18	.39
				Kuri	12	100.0	12	.26
				Sinyar	10	100.0	10	.22
				Tunjur	5	100.0	5	.11
				Fongoro	1	100.0	1	.02
China, Peoples Republic of	1,023,000	1.46	15,000	Hui	7,400	100.0	7,400	.72
				Turkic	7,262	99.9	7,256	.71
				Uygur	(6,146)	99.9	(6,140)	.60
				Kazakhs	(921)	100.0	(921)	.09
				Kirghiz	(109)	100.0	(109)	.01
				Salars	(70)	100.0	(70)	—

Country				Ethnic group				
				Uzbek	(12)	100.0	(12)	—
				Tatars	(4)	100.0	(4)	—
				Dongxiang	307	100.0	307	.03
				Tajik	28	100.0	28	—
				Bonans ("Paoans")	9	100.0	9	—
Comoros	400	99.5	398	Swahili	364	100.0	364	91.00
				Arabs	36	94.4	34	8.50
Congo, Peoples Republic of the	1,700	.4	7	Undetermined			7	.38
Cyprus	700	18.5	130	Turkic	128	100.0	128	18.17
				Rumelian	(1)	100.0	(127)	18.00
				Yoruk	(1)	100.0	(1)	.17
				Arabs	5	40.0	2	.33
Djibouti	300	90.0	270	Somalis	127	100.0	127	42.33
				Afar ("Danakil")	120	100.0	120	40.00
				Arabs	45	51.1	23	7.67
Egypt	45,900	91.1	41,800	Arabs	45,464	91.5	41,600	90.63
				Nubians	136	100.0	136	.29
				Beja	41	100.0	41	.09
				Albanians	16	100.0	16	.03
				Berbers	7	100.0	7	.02
Equatorial Guinea	300	.7	2	Undetermined			2	.67
Ethiopia	31,300	35.1	11,000	Oromo ("Galla")	12,545	55.0	6,900	22.04
				Somalis	1,878	100.0	1,878	6.00
				Gurage	2,312	33.0	783	2.50
				Afar	373	100.0	373	1.19
				Beja	219	100.0	219	.70
				Beni Amer (Tigre)	(178)	100.0	(178)	.57
				Jabarti	207	100.0	207	.66
				Tigre (see also Beja)	178	100.0	178	.57
				Sadama	600	29.2	175	.56
				Saho speakers	158	81.0	128	.41
				Arabs	61	82.0	50	.16

887

Ethnic Groups, Wholly or Partly Muslim, Within Nations

Country	1983 Population (000)[1]	% Muslim	Muslim Population (000)[2]	Ethnic Name	Group's Population (000)	% Muslim	Muslim Population (000)	% of Nation's Population
				Bilin	50	68.0	34	.11
				Harari	30	100.0	30	.10
				Kanuma	U		23	.08
				Baria	U		10	.03
				Argobba	9	100.0	9	.03
				Wayto	2	100.0	2	.01
				South Asians	3	33.3	1	—
Fiji	700	8.0	56	Indo-Fijian	350	16.0	56	8.00
France	54,600	1.0	546	Undetermined			546	1.00
Gabon	700	1.0	7	Undetermined			7	1.00
The Gambia	600	87.0	525	Manding speakers	246	93.8	236	39.33
				Mandinka	(246)	93.8	(236)	39.33
				Fulani	85	100.0	85	14.17
				Wolof	85	98.0	83	13.83
				Soninké	40	100.0	40	6.67
				Diola	42	95.0	40	6.67
				Jahanka	19	100.0	19	3.17
				Moors	13	100.0	13	2.17
				Baga	118	8.0	9	1.50
Gaza	500	98.0	490	Arabs	500	98.0	490	98.0
Ghana	13,900	15.1	2,100	Molé-Dagbane speakers	2,711	30.0	812	5.84
				Dogamba	(352)	60.0	(211)	1.52
				Wala	(74)	90.0	(67)	.48
				Mamprusi	(95)	35.0	(33)	.24
				Chakossi	(16)	19.0	(3)	.02
				Other	(2,174)	22.9	(498)	3.58
				Dagaba				

Group	Country total	Country %	Country no.	Population	%	Number	Index
Lobi							
Talensi							
Kusasi							
Akan				6,600	4.0	264	1.90
Twi				(4,321)	5.0	(220)	1.58
Fante				(1,707)	2.6	(42)	.30
Anyi-Bawle				(224)	1.1	(2)	—
Nzema				(348)	U	U	
Yoruba				232	61.0	142	1.02
Hausa				132	100.0	132	.95
Gurma				584	20.0	117	.84
Kotokoli ("Tem")				124	91.0	113	.81
Songhay				86	90.0	78	.56
Fulani				54	100.0	54	.39
Guang				500	9.0	45	.32
Manding speakers				146	30.0	44	.32
Dyula				(44)	100.0	(44)	.32
Ga-Adangme				1,205	1.5	18	.13
Undetermined						281	2.02
Greece	9,900	2.5	250				
Turkic				185	90.0	166	1.68
Rumelian				(185)	90.0	(166)	1.68
Pomaks				84	100.0	84	.85
Gypsies				U	U	U	
Guinea	5,400	69.3	3,743				
Fulani				1,890	95.0	1,795	33.24
Soso ("Susu")				967	85.0	822	15.22
Manding speakers				1,740	41.0	713	13.20
Mandinka				(1,566)	40.0	(626)	11.59
Bambara				(174)	50.0	(87)	1.61
Soninké				267	87.0	232	4.30
Vai				59	100.0	59	1.09
Yalunka				61	88.5	54	1.00
Koranko				106	30.2	32	.59

Ethnic Groups, Wholly or Partly Muslim, Within Nations

Country	1983 Population (000)[1]	% Muslim	Muslim Population (000)[2]	Ethnic Name	Group's Population (000)	% Muslim	Muslim Population (000)	% of Nation's Population
Guinea-Bissau	800	38.0	304	Kissi	371	8.1	30	.56
				Jahanka	6	100.0	6	.11
				Fulani	160	100.0	160	20.00
				Manding speakers	96	65.0	62	7.75
				Mandinka	(96)	65.0	(62)	7.75
				Balente	240	10.0	24	3.00
				Biafada	52	32.7	17	2.13
				Nalu	17	100.0	17	2.13
				Diola	21	62.0	13	1.63
				Manjaco	104	5.0	5	.63
				Mane	4	100.0	4	.50
				Soso	3	66.7	2	.25
Guyana	800	9.0	72	South Asians	400	18.0	72	9.00
Honduras	4,100	.1	4	Arabs	32	12.5	4	.10
Hong Kong	5,200	.5	26	Hui	15	100.0	15	.29
				South Asians	U		10	.19
India	730,000	10.9	79,570	Urdu speakers	53,175	78.8	41,900	5.75
				Bihari	(24,513)	54.2	(13,286)	1.82
				Deccani	(8,906)	100.0	(8,906)	1.22
				Orissans	(438)	100.0	(438)	.06
				Others	(19,270)	100.0	(19,270)	2.64
				Bengalis	60,000	23.0	14,000	1.92
				Mappilla ("Moplah")	5,840	100.0	5,840	.80
				Maharashtrians	65,448	8.7	5,694	.78
				Kashmiris	2,613	95.0	2,482	.34
				Rajasthanis	35,971	6.9	2,482	.34
				Meos	(584)	100.0	(584)	.08

890

Group						
Gujaratis				35,394	6.6	2,336	.32
Labbai				2,263	100.0	2,263	.31
Assamese[9]				12,463	16.4	2,044	.28
Punjabis				14,600	1.0	146	.02
Tripuris				2,154	6.5	140	.02
Manipuris				1,464	6.5	95	.01
Sindhis				1,806	3.6	65	—
Undetermined						83	—
Shina speakers							
Jat							
Gujars							
Malays							
Indonesia	155,600	80	124,500				
Javanese				58,000	90.0	52,200	33.55
Sundanese				24,912	98.0	24,414	15.69
Madurese				10,890	95.0	10,346	6.65
Malays				7,860	99.0	7,781	5.00
Minangkabau				5,986	98.0	5,866	3.77
Bugis ("Buginese")				4,357	95.0	4,139	2.66
Achenese				2,567	100.0	2,567	1.65
Banjarese-Kutanese				2,334	90.0	2,100	1.35
Makassarese				2,571	95.0	2,443	1.57
Sasak				2,064	95.0	1,961	1.26
Boolaang-Mongondonese				1,556	90.0	1,400	.90
Batak				3,423	30.0	1,027	.66
Ogan-Besemah				1,072	90.0	965	.62
Ogan				(677)	92.0	(622)	.40
Besemah ("Pasemah")				(395)	86.8	(343)	.22
Abung-Paminggir-Pubian				864	90.0	778	.50
Rejang-Lebongers				778	100.0	778	.50
Bimanese (on Sumbawa)				778	90.0	700	.45
Lampungers				662	99.0	655	.42
Butonese				622	100.0	622	.40
Gorontalese				508	98.0	498	.32

Ethnic Groups, Wholly or Partly Muslim, Within Nations

Country	1983 Population (000)[1]	% Muslim	Muslim Population (000)[2]	Ethnic Name	Group's Population (000)	% Muslim	Muslim Population (000)	% of Nation's Population
				Laki	379	100.0	379	.24
				Ambonese ("Moluccan")	622	60.0	373	.24
				Kerinci	311	100.0	311	.20
				Sumbawans	311	82.0	255	.16
				Mangarai	467	50.0	233	.15
				Gayo	202	100.0	202	.13
				Torajanese, West	280	50.0	140	.09
				Ternatan–Tidorese	109	100.0	109	.07
				Batinese	105	100.0	105	.07
				Tomini	74	89.0	66	.04
				Muko-Muko	61	100.0	61	.04
				Pekal	54	100.0	54	.03
				Baweanese	49	100.0	49	.03
				Lembak	45	100.0	45	.03
				Mori	50	90.0	45	.03
				Lamaholot ("Solorese")	254	17.0	43	.03
				Endenese	86	44.0	38	.02
				Simalur-Banyak	30	100.0	30	.02
				Niassim	240	10.0	24	.02
				Kédang	30	53.0	16	.01
				Sama	15	100.0	15	.01
				Bajau	(15)	100.0	(15)	.01
				Balantak	109	10.0	11	.01
				Bonerate	5	100.0	5	—
				Timorese	300	1.0	3	—
				Wana	6	40.0	2	—
				Undetermined			646	.42

Country	Total	%	Number	Group	Number	%	Number	%
				Ampana				
				Arabs				
				Batamese				
				Jambirese				
				Mandarese				
				Palembangese				
Iran	42,500	98.0	41,650	Persians	23,503	96.5	22,680	53.36
				Turkic	10,961	100.0	10,961	25.79
				Azeri	(8,870)	100.0	(8,870)	20.87
				Turkmen	(1,135)	100.0	(1,135)	2.67
				Qashqa'i	(620)	100.0	(620)	1.46
				Shahsevan	(310)	100.0	(310)	.73
				Karakalpak	(26)	100.0	(26)	.06
				Kurds	3,094	100.0	3,094	7.28
				Baluch	1,545	100.0	1,545	3.64
				Arabs	1,030	100.0	1,030	2.43
				Bakhtiari	700	100.0	700	1.65
				Gypsies	620	100.0	620	1.46
				Lur	565	100.0	565	1.33
				Hazara ("Berberi")	204	100.0	204	.48
				Aimaq	120	100.0	120	.24
				Pushtun	63	100.0	63	.15
				Tajik	42	100.0	42	.10
				Khamseh ("Basseri")	26	100.0	26	.06
Iraq	14,500	96.0	13,920	Arabs	11,024	95.0	10,473	72.23
				Kurds	2,950	100.0	2,950	20.34
				Turkic	412	100.0	412	2.84
				Turkmen	(207)	100.0	(207)	1.43
				Azeri	(190)	100.0	(190)	1.32
				Anatolian	(15)	100.0	(15)	.10
				Persians	60	100.0	60	.41
				Lur	15	100.0	15	.10

Ethnic Groups, Wholly or Partly Muslim, Within Nations

Country	1983 Population (000)[1]	% Muslim	Muslim Population (000)[2]	Ethnic Name	Group's Population (000)	% Muslim	Muslim Population (000)	% of Nation's Population
Israel	4,100	12.5	514	Ibero-Caucasians	10	100.0	10	.07
				Circassians	(10)	100.0	(10)	.07
				Arabs	585	87.5	512	12.49
				Ibero-Caucasians	2	100.0	2	.05
				Circassians	(2)	100.0	(2)	.05
Italy	56,300	—	23	Albanians	103	17.5	18	.03
				Bosnians	3	100.0	3	—
				Pomaks	2	100.0	2	—
				Arabs	U			
Ivory Coast	8,900	25.0	2,225	Manding speakers	1,427	73.8	1,053	11.83
				Mandinka	(855)	63.4	(542)	6.09
				Dyula	(374)	100.0	(374)	4.20
				Bambara	(197)	69.6	(137)	1.54
				Molé-Dagbane	1,264	40.0	506	5.68
				Mossi	(1,264)	40.0	(506)	5.68
				Soninké ("Manianka")	1,069	24.8	265	2.98
				Senufo	1,150	22.0	253	2.84
				Fulani	93	100.0	93	1.05
				South Asians	37	9.0	4	.05
				Arabs	2	50.0	1	—
				Undetermined			50	.57
				Hausa				
				Wolof				
				Songhay				
				Moors				
Jamaica	2,300	.2	5	South Asians	150	2.7	4	.18
				Arabs	3	33.3	1	.05

Country				Group				
Japan	119,200	—	2	Japanese	119,200	—	2	—
Jordan	2,700[10]	93.0	2,511	Arabs	2,600	95.0	2,472	91.56
				Ibero-Caucasians	35	100.0	35	1.75
				Circassians	(35)	100.0	(35)	1.75
				Kurds	2	100.0	2	.07
				Turkic	2	100.0	2	.07
				Turkmen	(2)	100.0	(2)	.07
Kampuchea	6,000	2.4	144	Cham	150	95.0	144	2.40
Kenya	18,600	6.0	1,120	Bantu, Northeast	2,073	19.3	400	2.15
				Mijikenda	(902)	34.7	(313)	1.67
				Giriyama	(541)	8.5	(46)	.25
				Taita	(203)	20.2	(41)	.22
				Somalis	433	100.0	433	2.33
				Oromo ("Galla")	84	100.0	84	.45
				South Asians	244	24.4	59	.32
				Manyema	U		57	.31
				Swahili	51	100.0	51	.27
				Bajun	(16)	100.0	(16)	.09
				Shirazi	U		U	
				Arabs	54	50.0	27	.15
				Nubians	9	100.0	9	.05
Korea, Republic of	41,300	—	50	Koreans	41,300	—	50	—
Kuwait	1,000[11]	96.0	960	Arabs	1,000	96.0	960	96.00
Lebanon	2,600	60.0	1,560[12]	Arabs	2,366	65.0	1,540	59.23
				Kurds	20	100.0	20	.77
Liberia	2,100	21.0	440	Manding speakers	63	100.0	63	3.00
				Mandinka	(63)	100.0	(63)	3.00
				Vai	63	75.0	47	2.25
				Kissi	147	10.0	15	.70
				Gbande	60	10.0	6	.28
				Mende	U		5	.25
				Arabs	14	20.0	3	.15
				Undetermined			301	14.35

Ethnic Groups, Wholly or Partly Muslim, Within Nations

Country	1983 Population (000)[1]	% Muslim	Muslim Population (000)[2]	Ethnic Name	Group's Population (000)	% Muslim	Muslim Population (000)	% of Nation's Population
Libya	3,300	98.0	3,234	Arabs	3,009	99.0	2,979	90.27
				Berbers	165	100.0	165	5.00
				Tuareg	(14)	100.0	14)	.44
				Qulaughli	66	100.0	66	2.00
				Tebu	17	100.0	17	.50
				Teda	(14)	100.0	14)	.41
				Dazaga	(3)	100.0	3)	.09
				Beri	5	100.0	5	.16
				Bideyat	(5)	100.0	5)	.16
				Duwwud	2	100.0	2	.06
Madagascar	9,500	2.0	190	Malagasy	9,500	1.0	95	1.00
				Sakalava	568	7.4	42	.44
				Swahili	19	100.0	19	.20
				Malays	14	100.0	14	.15
				South Asians	20	50.0	10	.11
				Arabs	27	37.0	10	.11
Malawi	6,800	16.0	1,088	Yao	951	90.0	856	12.59
				Chewa	1,108	20.0	222	3.26
				South Asians	40	25.0	10	.15
Malaysia	15,000	49.0	7,350	Malays	6,492	100.0	6,492	43.28
				Javanese	465	100.0	465	3.10
				Minangkabau	125	100.0	125	.83
				Sama	123	100.0	123	.82
				Bajau	(105)	100.0	105)	.70
				Sulu	(18)	100.0	18)	.12
				Melanau	78	72.0	56	.37
				South Asians	1,545	3.3	51	.34

Country				Group				
				Bugis	30	100.0	30	.20
				Kalabit	16	18.8	3	.02
				Hui	3	100.0	3	.02
				Molbog	2	100.0	2	.01
Maldive Islands	200	100.0		Divehi	200	100.0	200	100.00
Mali	7,300	80.0	5,840	Manding speakers	3,666	76.0	2,786	38.16
				Bambara	(2,296)	73.0	(1,676)	22.96
				Dyula	(453)	100.0	(453)	6.21
				Mandinka	(360)	90.0	(324)	4.44
				Dafi	(126)	70.0	(88)	1.21
				Sia	(126)	60.0	(76)	1.04
				Dialonke	(144)	50.0	(72)	.99
				Bozo	(55)	100.0	(55)	.76
				Kosanke	(73)	30.0	(22)	.30
				Nono	(20)	100.0	(20)	.27
				Fulani	1,272	95.0	1,208	16.55
				Berbers	438	100.0	438	6.00
				Tuareg	(438)	100.0	(438)	6.00
				Songhay	438	100.0	438	6.00
				Soninké	755	50.0	378	5.18
				Senufo ("Manianka")	1,142	33.0	377	5.16
				Moors	215	100.0	215	2.94
Mauritania	1,800	99.0	1,782	Moors	1,105	100.0	1,105	61.41
				Berbers	354	100.0	354	19.65
				Tukulor	145	100.0	145	8.05
				Fulani	90	100.0	90	5.00
				Soninké	68	90.0	61	3.41
				Wolof	17	100.0	17	.94
				Manding speakers	15	66.0	10	.59
				Bambara	(15)	66.0	(10)	.59
Mauritius	1,000	17.0	171	Indo-Mauritians	680	25.0	171	17.00
Mayotte (French)	48	98.0	47	Swahili	46	100.0	46	95.83

Ethnic Groups, Wholly or Partly Muslim, Within Nations

Country	1983 Population (000)[1]	% Muslim	Muslim Population (000)[2]	Ethnic Name	Group's Population (000)	% Muslim	Muslim Population (000)	% of Nation's Population
				Yao	1	100.0	1	2.08
				Makua	(1)	100.0	(1)	2.08
Mexico	75,700	—	20	Arabs	71	28.0	20	—
Mongolia	1,800	9.5	171	Turkic	150	96.0	144	8.00
				Kazakhs	(94)	100.0	(94)	5.22
				Khoton	(20)	100.0	(20)	1.11
				Uzbek	(16)	100.0	(16)	.89
				Uygur	(14)	100.0	(14)	.78
				Mongols	1,450	1.9	27	1.50
				Alashan "Left Banner"	(27)	100.0	(27)	1.50
Morocco	22,900	99.0	22,670	Arabs	12,824	98.2	12,594	55.00
				Berbers	7,786	100.0	7,786	34.00
				Tuareg	(12)	100.0	(12)	—
				Moors	2,290	100.0	2,290	10.00
Mozambique	13,100	13.0	1,700	Bantu, Central	4,725	23.4	1,106	8.44
				Yao	(4,725)	23.4	(1,106)	8.44
				Makua	(4,141)	18.0	(745)	5.69
				Yao	(288)	80.0	(231)	1.76
				Makonde	(296)	43.9	(130)	.99
				Swahili	589	100.0	589	4.50
				South Asians	15	33.3	5	.04
Nepal	15,800	5.0	790	South Asians	3,800	19.1	790	5.00
				Terai	(768)	100.0	(768)	4.86
				Churaute ("Hill")	(19)	100.0	(19)	.12
				Kathmandu Valley	(3)	100.0	(3)	.02
Niger	6,100	87.4	5,330	Hausa	3,259	85.0	2,770	45.41
				Songhay	1,104	100.0	1,104	18.10

898

Zerma	(526)	100.0	(526)	8.62
Fulani	546	95.0	518	8.50
Berbers	488	100.0	488	8.00
Tuareg	(488)	100.0	(488)	8.00
Kanuri	262	100.0	262	4.29
Arabs ("Chadian")	146	100.0	146	2.40
Tebu	32	100.0	32	.52
Dazaga	(30)	100.0	30)	.48
Teda	(2)	100.0	2)	—
Kanembu	6	100.0	6	—
Buduma	4	100.0	4	—
Nigeria 84,200 45.0 37,890				
Hausa	17,635	90.0	15,872	18.85
Yoruba	16,840	50.0	8,420	10.00
Fulani	8,696	92.0	8,000	9.50
Kanuri	4,092	100.0	4,092	4.86
Arabs ("Chadian" or "Shuwa")	253	100.0	253	.30
Gbari ("Gwari")	495	34.0	168	.20
Songhay	168	100.0	168	.20
Nupe	505	30.0	152	.18
Kanembu	135	100.0	135	.16
Ebira	370	25.0	93	.11
Plateau Chadic	600	15.0	90	.11
Pabir	(204)	25.0	51)	.06
Margi	(129)	10.0	13)	.02
Gwandara	(30)	30.0	9)	.01
Gerawa	(86)	10.0	9)	.01
Others	(151)	5.3	8)	—
Kamberi	758	10.0	76	.09
Gbagyi	300	23.0	70	.08
Yamma	(100)	50.0	50)	.06
Ngenge	(200)	10.0	20)	.02
Batonun ("Bariba")	84	50.0	42	.05

Ethnic Groups, Wholly or Partly Muslim, Within Nations

Country	1983 Population (000)[1]	% Muslim	Muslim Population (000)[2]	Ethnic Name	Group's Population (000)	% Muslim	Muslim Population (000)	% of Nation's Population
				Bantoid	84	50.0	42	.05
				Reshawa	50	70.0	35	.04
				Haddad	25	100.0	25	.03
				Kotoko	18	100.0	18	.02
				Shangawa	30	40.0	12	.01
				Chamba	35	14.0	5	—
				Buduma	3	100.0	3	—
				Undetermined			119	.14
				Busa				
				Berbers (Tuareg)				
				Igala				
Oman	1,000	99.0	990					
Pakistan	95,700	97.0	92,829	Arabs	1,000	99.0	990	99.00
				Punjabis	57,945	98.5	57,075	59.64
				Sindhis	11,422	93.0	10,623	11.10
				Pushtun	8,642	99.9	8,633	9.02
				Urdu speakers	7,300	83.0	6,058	6.33
				Jat	6,316	90.0	5,685	5.94
				Baluch	2,536	100.0	2,536	2.65
				Brahui	861	100.0	861	.90
				Gujaratis	574	90.0	517	.54
				Kho	287	100.0	287	.30
				Rajasthanis	191	100.0	191	.20
				Kohistanis	100	100.0	100	.10
				Arabs	57	100.0	57	.06
				Persians	57	100.0	57	.06
				Undetermined			149	.15
				Gujars				

Country	Total pop.	%	Muslim pop.	Ethnic group	Group pop.	%	Muslim	% of total
Disputed Territories			588	Hazaras				
				Kashmiris				
				Qizilbash				
				Not included in official Pakistan census				
				Shina speakers	346	100.0	346	
				Doms				
				Kamins				
				Shins				
				Yeshkuns				
				Baltis	172	100.0	172	
				Burusho ("Hunzakuts")	70	100.0	70	
				Wakhi	U			
				Dards	U			
Panama	2,100	4.5	95	South Asians	83	66.0	55	2.63
				Arabs	80	50.0	40	1.90
Philippines	52,800	5.6	2,960	Maquindanao	885	100.0	885	1.68
				Maranao	840	100.0	840	1.59
				Tausug	618	100.0	618	1.17
				Sama	624	92.0	575	1.09
				Sulu	(378	100.0	(378	.70
				Yakan	(116	100.0	(116	.22
				Bajau	(42	100.0	(42	.08
				Jama Mapun	(21	100.0	(21	.04
				Sibuquey	(18	100.0	(18	.03
				Kalibugans	16	100.0	16	.03
				Kalagans	8	100.0	8	.02
				Molbog	7	100.0	7	—
				Palawanon	70	10.0	7	—
				Sangil	4	100.0	4	
Qatar	300	95.0	285	Arabs	300	95.0	285	95.00
Reunion	500	2.4	12	Swahili	10	100.0	10	2.00
				South Asians	7	28.0	2	.40

Ethnic Groups, Wholly or Partly Muslim, Within Nations

Country	1983 Population (000)[1]	% Muslim	Muslim Population (000)[2]	Ethnic Name	Group's Population (000)	% Muslim	Muslim Population (000)	% of Nation's Population
Romania	22,700	1.2	272	Turkic	187	97.0	182	.80
				Rumelian	(151)	97.0	(146)	.64
				Tatars	(26)	100.0	(26)	.12
				Nogai	(10)	100.0	(10)	.04
				Gypsies	744	9.0	67	.29
				Pomaks	23	100.0	23	.10
Rwanda	5,600	8.6	480	Undetermined			480	8.60
Saudi Arabia	10,400	99.0	10,300	Arabs	10,320	99.0	10,220	98.27
				South Asians	50	100.0	50	.45
				Hui	30	100.0	30	.27
Senegal	6,100	91.0	5,553	Wolof	2,247	97.0	2,180	35.76
				Fulani	1,080	96.0	1,037	17.00
				Serer	1,008	82.0	827	13.56
				Tukulor	549	100.0	549	9.00
				Manding speakers	540	90.0	486	7.97
				Mandinka	(428)	90.0	(385)	6.31
				Bambara	(122)	83.0	(101)	1.66
				Diola	550	50.0	275	4.51
				Moors	91	100.0	91	1.49
				Soninké	82	63.0	52	.85
				Arabs	31	100.0	31	.51
				Jahanka	25	100.0	25	.41
Sierra Leone	3,800	39.5	1,503	Temne	1,330	32.0	425	11.18
				Mende	1,178	29.4	346	9.11
				Limba	270	70.8	189	4.97
				Fulani	116	95.0	110	2.89
				Soso ("Susu")	109	100.0	109	2.87

Country				Group				
				Manding speakers	211	50.0	106	2.78
				Mandinka	(211)	50.0	(106)	2.78
				Sherbro	128	40.0	51	1.35
				Loko	111	39.0	43	1.14
				Koranko	141	30.0	42	1.11
				Bullom	31	80.0	25	.65
				Yalunka	26	92.0	24	.63
				Vai	18	83.0	15	.41
				South Asians	10	70.0	7	.19
				Krim	15	40.0	6	.16
				Yoruba	10	50.0	5	.14
Singapore	2,500	18.3	458	Malays	375	100.0	375	15.00
				Javanese	55	100.0	55	2.20
				South Asians	175	10.0	18	.72
				Hui	10	100.0	10	.40
Somalia	5,300	99.0	5,250	Somalis	5,038	100.0	5,038	95.06
				Bantu, Northeast	104	100.0	104	1.96
				South Asians	105	57.0	60	1.13
				Arabs	53	93.0	48	.91
South Africa	30,200	1.2	362	Blacks	25,702	1.4	361	1.19
				"Coloured" or "Cape Malays"	(2,527)	7.4	(186)	.61
				"Asians"	(750)	21.6	(162)	.54
				"African"	(22,250)	—	(13)	.04
				Whites	4,500	—	1	—
Soviet Union	272,000	17.3	46,000	Turkic	41,748	96.7	40,385	14.96
				Uzbek	(13,500)	100.0	(13,500)	5.00
				Kazakhs	(7,185)	100.0	(7,185)	2.66
				Tatars	(7,263)	95.0	(6,900)	2.56
				Azeri	(6,000)	100.0	(6,000)	2.22
				Turkmen	(2,180)	100.0	(2,180)	.81
				Kirghiz	(2,100)	100.0	(2,100)	.78
				Bashkir	(1,456)	100.0	(1,456)	.54

Ethnic Groups, Wholly or Partly Muslim, Within Nations

Country	1983 Population (000)[1]	% Muslim	Muslim Population (000)[2]	Ethnic Name	Group's Population (000)	% Muslim	Muslim Population (000)	% of Nation's Population
				Karakalpak	(326)	100.0	(326)	.12
				Kumyk	(245)	100.0	(245)	.09
				Karachai	(140)	100.0	(140)	.05
				Uygur	(220)	52.0	(114)	.04
				Anatolian	(100)	100.0	(100)	.04
				Balkar	(74)	100.0	(74)	.03
				Nogai	(65)	100.0	(65)	.02
				Other	(894)	0		
				Ibero-Caucasian	3,341	90.0	3,000	1.11
				Chechen-Ingush	(1,015)	100.0	(1,015)	.38
				Chechen	(815)	100.0	(815)	.30
				Ingush	(200)	100.0	(200)	.07
				Circassians	(881)	61.0	(540)	.53
				Kabardinian	(581)	59.7	(347)	.13
				Adyghe	(120)	100.0	(120)	.04
				Circassians	(50)	100.0	(50)	.02
				Abkhaz	(130)	17.7	(23)	—
				Abkhaz	(100)	23.0	(23)	—
				Abaza	(30)	0		
				Daghestanis	(1,445)	100.0	(1,445)	.54
				Avars	(544)	100.0	(544)	.20
				Lezgin	(420)	100.0	(420)	.16
				Dargin	(250)	100.0	(250)	.09
				Lak	(110)	100.0	(110)	.04
				Tabasaran	(80)	100.0	(80)	.03
				Rutul	(16)	100.0	(16)	—
				Tsakhurs	(15)	100.0	(15)	—

Country	(total)	(%)	(number)	Group				
				Aguls	(10)	100.0	(10)	—
				Indo-Iranian	3,906	90.9	3,551	1.32
				Tajik	(3,111)	100.0	(3,111)	1.15
				Ossetians	(583)	40.0	(233)	.09
				Kurds	(125)	100.0	(125)	.05
				Persians	(33)	100.0	(33)	.01
				Tat	(24)	100.0	(24)	—
				Baluch	(20)	100.0	(20)	—
				Pushtun	(5)	100.0	(5)	—
				Dungans (Hui)	50	100.0	50	.02
				Arabs	14	100.0	14	—
Sri Lanka	15,600	8.0	1,250	Tamil "Moors"	1,150	100.0	1,150	7.37
				Malays	60	100.0	60	.38
				South Asians	40	100.0	40	.25
Sudan	20,600	72.0	14,832	Arabs	9,857	99.0	9,758	47.37
				Beja	1,223	100.0	1,223	5.94
				Beni Amer	(88)	100.0	(88)	.43
				Hausa	824	100.0	824	4.00
				Fur	721	100.0	721	3.50
				Nubians	659	100.0	659	3.20
				Nuba	1,030	30.0	309	1.50
				Fulani	308	100.0	308	1.50
				Beri	247	100.0	247	1.20
				Zaghawa	(247)	100.0	(247)	1.20
				Masalit	235	100.0	235	1.14
				Taqali	181	100.0	181	.88
				Tama	103	100.0	103	.50
				Gimr	(47)	100.0	(47)	.23
				Erenga	(33)	100.0	(33)	.16
				Mararit	(14)	100.0	(14)	.07
				Mileri ("Jebel")	(8)	100.0	(8)	.04
				Tama	(1)	100.0	(1)	—
				Berti	80	100.0	80	.39

Ethnic Groups, Wholly or Partly Muslim, Within Nations

Country	1983 Population (000)[1]	% Muslim	Muslim Population (000)[2]	Ethnic Name	Group's Population (000)	% Muslim	Muslim Population (000)	% of Nation's Population
				Haddad	52	100.0	52	.25
				Meidob	45	100.0	45	.22
				Daju	43	100.0	43	.21
				Mimi	20	100.0	20	.10
				Sinyar	16	100.0	16	.08
				Tunjur	5	100.0	5	.03
				Tebu	2	100.0	2	.01
				Fongoro	1	100.0	1	—
				Funj				
Surinam	400	14.0	57	Javanese	56	90.0	50	12.50
				South Asians	52	12.0	6	1.50
				Arabs	4	25.0	1	.25
Syria	9,700	87.0	8,440	Arabs	8,368	89.0	7,448	76.78
				Kurds	800	100.0	800	8.25
				Turkic	117	100.0	117	1.21
				Turkmen	(110)	100.0	(110)	1.13
				Anatolian	(7)	100.0	(7)	.07
				Ibero-Caucasian	56	100.0	56	.58
				Circassians	(56)	100.0	(56)	.58
				Gypsies	19	100.0	19	.20
Taiwan (Republic of China)	18,900	.5	95	Turkic	72	100.0	72	.38
				Uygur				
				Kazakhs				
				Hui	23	100.0	23	.12
Tanzania	20,500	30.0	6,150	Bantu, Central	6,959	40.8	2,836	13.83
				Yao	(2,465)	79.0	(1,948)	9.50
				Yao	(913)	85.0	(776)	3.78

Country				Group				
				Makonde	840	90.0	(756)	3.69
				Mwera	302	79.0	(244)	1.19
				Makua	410	41.9	(172)	.84
				Nyamwezi	3,674	13.0	(478)	2.33
				Nyamwezi	717	50.0	(359)	1.75
				Sukuma	2,757	4.0	(111)	.54
				Sumbwa	200	4.0	(8)	.04
				Central Tanzanian	820	50.0	(410)	2.00
				Rangi	267	90.0	(240)	1.17
				Others	553	31.0	(170)	.83
				Bantu, Northeast	2,814	51.0	1,435	7.00
				Luguru	451	89.0	(402)	1.96
				Zaramo	433	90.0	(390)	1.90
				Shambaa	473	65.0	(308)	1.50
				Zigula	330	92.0	(303)	1.48
				Others	1,127	3.0	(32)	.13
				Swahili	1,333	100.0	1,333	6.50
				Shirazi	268	100.0	(268)	1.31
				Arabs	130	90.0	117	.57
				Bantu, Kenya Highland	1,435	8.0	115	.56
				South Asians	300	34.0	102	.50
				Bantu, Rufiji	U		8	.04
				Undetermined			204	1.00
Thailand	50,800	4.0	2,037	Malays	1,824	100.0	1,824	3.59
				Thais	48,945	.4	203	.40
				Hui	6	100.0	6	.01
				South Asians	25	16.0	4	—
Togo	2,800	16.0	448	Kotokoli ("Tem")	196	75.0	147	5.25
				Fulani	122	95.0	116	4.14
				Yoruba	84	71.4	60	2.14
				Hausa	56	89.3	50	1.79
				Molé-Dagbane	28	96.0	27	.96

Ethnic Groups, Wholly or Partly Muslim, Within Nations

Country	1983 Population (000)[1]	% Muslim	Muslim Population (000)[2]	Ethnic Name	Group's Population (000)	% Muslim	Muslim Population (000)	% of Nation's Population
				Chakossi	(28)	96.0	(27)	.96
				Bargu	17	41.2	7	.25
				Chamba	25	16.0	4	—
				Undetermined			37	1.32
				Tamberna				
				Wala				
Trinidad and Tobago	1,200	6.5	78	South Asians	430	18.0	77	6.45
				Arabs	3	33.3	1	.09
Tunisia	6,800	99.4	6,760	Arabs	6,597	99.4	6,557	96.42
				Berbers	203	100.0	203	2.98
Turkey	49,200	99.2	48,800	Turkic	44,098	99.9	44,054	89.54
				Anatolian	(38,020)	99.9	(37,976)	77.19
				Rumelian	(5,466)	100.0	(5,466)	11.11
				Yoruk	(369)	100.0	(369)	.75
				Turkmen	(148)	100.0	(148)	.30
				Karakalpak	(54)	100.0	(54)	.11
				Tatars	(40)	100.0	(40)	.08
				Kirghiz	(1)	100.0	(1)	—
				Nogai	U		U	
				Kurds	3,395	100.0	3,395	6.90
				Arabs	591	89.9	531	1.08
				Bosnians	364	100.0	364	.74
				Ibero-Caucasian	187	100.0	187	.38
				Circassians	(187)	100.0	(187)	.38
				Pomaks	177	100.0	177	.36
				Laze	44	100.0	44	.09
				Undetermined			48	.10

				Group	Pop.	%	No.	%
				Albanians				
				Donmé				
				Gypsies				
Uganda	13,800	6.6	915	Bantu, Interlacustrine	U		690	5.00
				Ganda	(2,515)	20.0	503)	3.65
				Soga	(1,000)	15.0	150)	1.09
				Nyankole	(1,000)	2.0	20)	.15
				Toro	(438)	2.0	9)	.07
				Nyoro	(375)	2.0	8)	.06
				Bantu, Eastern	U		119	.86
				Kedi	(1,000)	8.0	80)	.58
				Gishu	(780)	5.0	39)	.28
				Madi	190	40.0	76	.55
				South Asians	137	10.9	15	.11
				Kakwa	75	13.3	10	.07
				Arabs	10	50.0	5	.04
United Arab Emirates	400[13]	90.0	360	Arabs	400	90.0	360	90.00
United Kingdom	56,000	1.4	785	South Asians	785	50.0	392	.70
				Arabs	200	20.0	40	.07
				Malays	20	100.0	20	—
				Undetermined			333	.59
United States	234,200	.6	1,400	American Blacks	28,000	1.8	500	.21
				Arabs	2,576	10.0	258	.11
				South Asians	928	10.8	100	.04
				Turkic	24	100.0	24	.01
				Anatolian	(24)	100.0	24)	.01
				Persians	48	50.0	24	.01
				Albanians	32	25.0	8	—
				Malays	6	100.0	6	—
				Undetermined			480	.14
Upper Volta	6,800	44.0	3,000	Molé-Dagbane	3,671	35.0	1,285	18.90
				Mossi	(3,671)	35.0	1,285)	18.90
				Yarsé	(172)	90.0	155)	2.28

Ethnic Groups, Wholly or Partly Muslim, Within Nations

Country	1983 Population (000)[1]	% Muslim	Muslim Population (000)[2]	Ethnic Name	Group's Population (000)	% Muslim	Muslim Population (000)	% of Nation's Population
				Manding speakers	1,226	45.0	548	8.06
				Dyula	(237	90.0	(213	3.13
				Bisa	(340	40.0	(136	2.00
				Barka	(223	30.0	(67	.98
				Bobo	(225	20.0	(45	.66
				Dafi	(34	86.0	(29	.42
				Mandinka	(55	40.0	(22	.33
				Samo	(67	30.0	(20	.30
				Sia	(10	90.0	(9	.13
				Tienga	(35	20.0	(7	.10
				Fulani	421	95.0	400	5.88
				Senufo	476	33.0	157	2.31
				Soninké	170	80.0	136	2.00
				Songhay	136	95.0	129	1.90
				Grunshi	404	25.0	101	1.49
				Gourmantche	375	20.0	75	1.10
				Gurma	340	20.0	68	1.00
				Berbers	13	100.0	13	.19
				Tuareg	(13	100.0	(13	.19
				Undetermined			88	1.31
				Masina				
				Wala				
				Hausa				
				Yoruba				
				Wara Wara				
				Quin				
Vietnam	57,000	1.0	570	Cham	172	50.0	86	.15

Country				Ethnic group				
West Bank, Jordan River; East Jerusalem	837	88.7	742	Undetermined			484	.85
				Arabs	837	88.7	742	88.65
Western Sahara	151	100.0	151	Berbers	91	100.0	91	60.26
				Arabs	45	100.0	45	29.80
				Moors	15	100.0	15	10.00
Yemen, Arab Republic of	5,700	99.0	5,645	Arabs	5,633	98.9	5,573	97.73
				Somalis	63	100.0	63	1.11
				South Asians	9	100.0	9	.16
Yemen, Peoples Republic of	2,100	99.0	2,080	Arabs	2,020	99.0	2,000	95.24
				South Asians	52	100.0	52	2.50
				Somalis	25	100.0	25	1.20
				Malays	3	100.0	3	.14
Yugoslavia	22,800	16.0	3,700	Bosnians	4,027	45.0	1,812	7.95
				Albanians	1,416	64.0	906	3.87
				Gypsies	1,604	50.0	802	3.52
				Turkic	180	100.0	180	.80
				Rumelian	(180)	100.0	(180)	.80
Zaire	31,300	1.4	440	Luba ("Kusu")	3,761	11.7	440	1.40
Zambia	6,200	1.0	62	Lozi	182	17.0	31	.50
				South Asians	155	20.0	31	.50
Zimbabwe	8,400	.9	76	Undetermined			76	.90
				Yao				
				Makua				
				Swahili				
				South Asians				

MUSLIMS AND THEIR ETHNIC GROUPS (1983)

Ethnic Group	Group Population (000)	Muslim	Muslim Population (000)	Location
Abkhaz (Circassians[1])	130	17.70	23	Soviet Union
Abung-Paminggir-Pubian	864	90.00	778	Indonesia
Abu Sharib (Tama)	45	100.00	45	Chad
*Acehnese	2,567	100.00	2,567	Indonesia
Adygh (Circassians)	120	100.00	120	Soviet Union
*Afar	493	100.00	493	Djibouti, Ethiopia
Aguls (Daghestanis)	10	100.00	10	Soviet Union
*Aimaq	598	100.00	598	Afghanistan, Iran
*Akan	6,600	4.30	264	Ghana
Alashan Left Banner (Mongols)	27	100.00	27	Mongolia
*Albanians (Gheg-Tosk)	4,467	66.00	2,948	Albania, Yugoslavia
Ambonese	622	60.00	373	Indonesia
*American Blacks	28,000	1.79	500	United States
Ampana	U[2]		U	Indonesia
Anatolians; see Turks, Anatolian				
Anyi-Bawle (Akan)	185	1.08	2	Ghana
*Arabs	148,138	92.89	137,603	Southwest Asia, North Africa
Arakanese; see Rohinga				
*Argobba	9	100.00	9	Ethiopia
*Asians of East Africa (South Asians)	1,026	28.75	295	East Africa
*Assamese[3]	12,463	16.40	2,044	India

Ethnic Group	Group Population (000)	Muslim	Muslim Population (000)	Location
Asungor (Tama)	56	100.00	56	Chad
Avars (Daghestanis)	544	100.00	544	Soviet Union
*Azeri (Turkic)	15,060	100.00	15,060	Iran, Soviet Union
Badakshi	U		U	Afghanistan
Baga	118	7.63	9	Gambia
Baganda; see Ganda				
"Bagirmi";[4] see Barma				
*Bajau (Sama)	162	100.00	162	Southeast Asia
Bajun (Swahili)	16	100.00	16	Kenya
*Bakhtiari	700	100.00	700	Iran
Balantak	109	10.00	11	Indonesia
Balente	240	10.00	24	Guinea-Bissau
*Balkar (Turkic)	74	100.00	74	Soviet Union
*Baltis	172	100.00	172	Pakistan
*Baluch	4,339	100.00	4,339	Iran, Pakistan
*Bambara (Manding)	2,878	70.15	2,019	West Africa
Bamun	131	80.15	105	Cameroon
Banjarese-Kutanese	2,334	90.00	2,100	Indonesia
Bantoid	84	50.00	42	Nigeria
*Bantu, Central Tanzanian	820	50.00	410	Tanzania
*Bantu, Northeast	4,991	38.85	1,939	East Africa
*Bantu-speaking Peoples	134,000	6.09	8,163	Africa
Bargu	17	41.18	7	Togo
Baria	U		10	Ethiopia
"Bariba"; see Batonun				
*Barka (Manding)	233	30.00	67	Upper Volta
*Barma	47	100.00	47	Chad
*Bashkir (Turkic)	1,456	100.00	1,456	Soviet Union
Basseri; see Khamseh				
*Batak	3,423	30.00	1,027	Indonesia
Batinese	105	100.00	105	Indonesia
*Batonun	592	34.29	203	Benin, Nigeria
*Baweanese	49	100.00	49	Indonesia
"Baya"; see Gbaya				
*Beja	1,483	100.00	1,483	Ethiopia, Sudan
*Bengalis	152,000	61.27	93,130	Bangladesh, India
*Beni Amer (Beja)	266	100.00	266	Ethiopia, Sudan
*Berbers	13,995	100.00	13,995	North Africa

Ethnic Group	Group Population (000)	Muslim	Muslim Population (000)	Location
*Beri	313	100.00	313	Chad, Sudan
*Berti	80	100.00	80	Sudan
Besemah (Ogan-Besemah)	395	86.84	343	Indonesia
Biafada	52	32.69	17	Guinea-Bissau
Bideyat (Beri)	25	100.00	25	Chad, Sudan
Biharis (Urdu)	25,333	55.68	14,106	Bangladesh, India
Bilala (Lisi)	61	100.00	61	Chad
*Bilin	50	68.00	34	Ethiopia
Bimanese	778	89.97	700	Indonesia
Bisa (Manding)	340	40.00	136	Upper Volta
Bobo (Manding)	225	20.00	45	Upper Volta
Bolaang-Mongondonese	1,556	90.00	1,400	Indonesia
*Bonans (Mongols)	9	100.00	9	China
Bondei (Bantu, Northeast)	U		U	East Africa
*Bonerate	5	100.00	5	Indonesia
*Bosnians	4,394	49.59	2,179	Turkey, Yugoslavia
Bozo (Manding)	55	100.00	55	Mali
*Brahui	879	100.00	879	Pakistan
*Buduma	49	100.00	49	Chad
*Bugis	4,357	95.00	4,139	Indonesia, Malaysia
Bullom	31	80.64	25	Sierra Leone
*Burmese	26,929	1.90	512	Burma
*Burusho	70	100.00	70	Pakistan
Busa	U		U	Nigeria
*Butonese	622	100.00	622	Indonesia
"Cape Malays"; see South African "Coloured"				
Chakossi (Molé-Dagbane)	44	68.18	30	Ghana, Togo
Chamba	60	15.00	9	Nigeria
*Cham	322	71.43	230	Kampuchea, Vietnam
Chechen (Chechen-Ingush)	815	100.00	815	Soviet Union
*Chechen-Ingush	1,015	100.00	1,015	Soviet Union
Chewa	1,108	20.00	222	Malawi

Ethnic Group	Group Population (000)	Muslim	Muslim Population (000)	Location
"Chitrali"; see Kho Churaute (South Asians)	19	100.00	19	Nepal
*Circassians	1,171	70.88	830	Soviet Union, Southwest Asia
Dafi (Manding)	160	73.13	117	Mali, Upper Volta
Dagaba (Molé-Dagbane)	U		U	Ghana
*Daghestanis	1,445	100.00	1,445	Soviet Union
*Daju	137	100.00	137	Chad, Sudan
"Danakil"; see Afar				
Dagari (Molé-Dagbane)	U		U	Ghana
Dargin (Daghestanis)	250	100.00	250	Soviet Union
Dazaga (Tebu)	214	100.00	214	Chad, Libya
*Deccani (Urdu)	8,906	100.00	8,906	India
Dialonke (Manding)	144	50.00	72	Mali
Digo (Bantu, Northeast)	U		U	East Africa
*Diola	613	53.51	328	Gambia, Senegal
*Divehi	200	100.00	200	Maldives
"Divessi"; see Divehi				
Dogamba (Molé-Dagbane)	352	59.94	211	Ghana
Doms (Shina)	U		U	Pakistan
*Dongxiang (Mongols)	307	100.00	307	China
Donmé	U		U	Turkey
Dooka (Gbaya)	U		U	Central African Republic
*"Dungans" (Hui)	50	100.00	50	Soviet Union
Duwwud	2	100.00	2	Libya
*Dyula (Manding)	1,108	97.83	1,084	West Africa
Ebira	370	25.14	93	Nigeria
*Endenese	86	44.19	38	Indonesia
Erenga (Tama)	33	100.00	33	Chad, Sudan
Fali	51	80.39	41	Cameroon
Fante (Akan)	1,604	2.62	42	Ghana
"Farsiwan"; see Persians				

Ethnic Group	Group Population (000)	Muslim	Muslim Population (000)	Location
*Fongoro	2	100.00	2	Chad, Sudan
Fra-Fra; see Talensi				
Fulbe; see Fulani				
*Fulani	16,016	92.94	14,885	West Africa
*Funj	—		—	Sudan
*Fur	721	100.00	721	Sudan
Ga-Adangme	1,205	1.49	18	Ghana
"Galla"; see Oromo				
*Ganda	2,515	20.00	503	Kenya
*Gayo	202	100.00	202	Indonesia
*Gbagyi	300	23.33	70	Nigeria
Gbande	60	10.00	6	Liberia
Gbari	495	33.94	168	Nigeria
*Gbaya	1,069	21.61	231	Cameroon, Central African Republic
Gerawa (Plateau Chadic)	86	10.47	9	Nigeria
Gheg-Tosk; see Albanians				
Gimr (Tama)	47	100.00	47	Sudan
Giriyama (Mijikenda)	541	8.50	46	Kenya
Gishu	780	5.00	39	Uganda
*Gorontalese	508	98.03	498	Indonesia
Gourmantche	375	20.00	75	Upper Volta
Grunshi	404	25.00	101	Upper Volta
Guang	500	9.00	45	Ghana
*Gujaratis	35,968	7.93	2,853	India, Pakistan
*Gujars	U		U	India
Gungawa; see Reshawa				
*Gurage	2,373	33.00	783	Ethiopia
Gurma	924	20.00	185	Ghana, Upper Volta
Gwandara (Plateau Chadic)	30	30.00	9	Nigeria
"Gwari"; see Gbari				
*Gypsies	U		1,685	Asia, Europe
*Haddad	230	100.00	230	Chad, Nigeria, Sudan
*Harari	30	100.00	30	Ethiopia
*Hausa	22,532	89.43	20,151	West Africa

917

Ethnic Group	Group Population (000)	Muslim	Muslim Population (000)	Location
*Hazaras	1,364	100.00	1,364	Afghanistan, Iran
Hedareb; see Tigre				
*Hui	7,543	100.00	7,543	China, Soviet Union
"Hunzakut"; see Burusho				
Igala	U		U	Nigeria
Indo-Fijian	350	16.00	56	Fiji
*Indo-Mauritians	680	25.15	171	Mauritius
Ingush (Chechen-Ingush)	200	100.00	200	Soviet Union
Iramba (Bantu, Central Tanzanian)	U		U	Tanzania
*Jabarti	207	100.00	207	Ethiopia
*Jahanka	50	100.00	50	West Africa
Jama Mapun (Sama)	21	100.00	21	Philippines
Jambirese	U		U	Indonesia
Japanese	119,200	—	2	Japan
*Jat	U		5,685	India, Pakistan
*Javanese	58,521	90.10	52,715	Southeast Asia
Jebel; see Mileri				
Kabardinian (Circassians)	581	59.72	347	Soviet Union
Kaguru (Bantu, Northeast)	U	40.00	U	East Africa
Kakwa	75	13.33	10	Uganda
Kalabit	16	18.75	3	Malaysia
*Kalagans	8	100.00	8	Philippines
*Kalibugans	16	100.00	16	Philippines
Kaman	U		U	Burma
*Kamberi	758	10.00	76	Nigeria
Kami (Bantu, Northeast)	U	90.00	U	East Africa
Kamins (Shina)	U		U	Pakistan
*Kanembu	331	100.00	331	Chad, Nigeria
Kanuma	U		U	Ethiopia
*Kanuri	4,376	100.00	4,376	Niger, Nigeria
Kara (Gbaya)	U		U	Central African Republic
*Karachai (Turkic)	140	100.00	140	Soviet Union
*Karakalpak (Turkic)	409	100.00	409	Soviet Union
*Kashmiris	2,613	94.99	2,482	India, Pakistan

Ethnic Group	Group Population (000)	Muslim	Muslim Population (000)	Location
Kathmandu Valley (South Asians)	3	100.00	3	Nepal
*Kazakhs (Turkic)	8,220	100.00	8,220	Central Asia
*Kédang	30	53.33	16	Indonesia
Kedayan	28	71.43	20	Brunei
Kedi	1,000	8.00	80	Uganda
Kerinci	311	100.00	311	Indonesia
Khamseh	26	100.00	26	Iran
*Kho	287	100.00	287	Pakistan
*Khoton (Turkic)	20	100.00	20	Mongolia
*Kirgiz (Turkic)	2,247	100.00	2,247	Central Asia
Kissi	518	8.69	45	Liberia, Guinea
*Kohistanis	100	100.00	100	Pakistan
Koranko	247	29.96	74	Guinea, Sierra Leone
*Koreans	41,300	—	50	Korea
Kosanke (Manding)	73	30.14	22	Mali
*Kotoko	72	100.00	72	Cameroon, Chad, Nigeria
Kotokoli	320	81.25	260	Ghana, Togo
Kouka (Lisi)	56	100.00	56	Chad
Krim	15	40.00	6	Sierra Leone
*Kumyk (Turkic)	245	100.00	245	Soviet Union
*Kurds	10,386	100.00	10,386	Southwest Asia
*Kuri	12	100.00	12	Chad
Kusasi (Molé-Dagbane)	U		U	Ghana
Kusu; see Luba				
Kutu (Bantu, Northeast)	U	90.00	U	East Africa
Kwere (Bantu, Northeast)	U	90.00	U	East Africa
*Labbai	2,236	100.00	2,236	India
Lai (Gbaya)	U		U	Central African Republic
Lak (Daghestanis)	110	100.00	110	Soviet Union
Laki	379	100.00	379	Indonesia
*Lamaholot	254	16.93	43	Indonesia
Lampungers	662	99.00	655	Indonesia
Laze	44	100.00	44	Turkey
Lembok	45	100.00	45	Indonesia
Lezgin (Daghestanis)	420	100.00	420	Soviet Union
*Limba	270	70.00	189	Sierra Leone

Ethnic Group	Group Population (000)	Muslim	Muslim Population (000)	Location
Lisi	127	100.00	127	Chad
Lobi (Molé-Dagbane)	U		U	Ghana
Loko	111	38.74	43	Sierra Leone
Lozi	182	17.03	31	Zambia
Luba	3,761	11.70	440	Zaire
Luguru (Bantu, Northeast)	451	89.14	402	Tanzania
*Lur	580	100.00	580	Iran, Iraq
*Maba	204	100.00	204	Chad
Madi	190	40.00	76	Uganda
*Madurese	10,890	95.00	10,346	Indonesia
*Maguindanao	885	100.00	885	Philippines
*Maharashtrians	65,448	8.70	5,694	India
*Makassarese	2,571	95.00	2,443	Indonesia
Makonde (Yao)	1,136	78.00	886	Mozambique, Tanzania
Makua (Yao)	4,552	20.17	918	Mozambique, Tanzania
Malagasy	9,500	1.00	95	Madagascar
*Malays	16,893	99.50	16,814	Southeast Asia
Maldavians; see Divehi				
Malinké; see Mandinka				
Mamprusi (Molé-Dagbane)	95	34.74	33	Ghana
Mandara	35	100.00	35	Cameroon
Mandarese	622	U	U	Indonesia
*Manding-speaking Peoples	11,489	53.23	6,115	West Africa
*Mandinka (Manding)	3,880	60.98	2,366	West Africa
Mane	4	100.00	4	Guinea-Bissau
Manggarai	467	50.00	233	Indonesia
"Manianke"; see Senufo				
Manipuris	1,464	6.49	95	India
Manjaco	104	4.81	5	Guinea-Bissau
Manyema	U		U	Kenya
*Mappilla	5,840	100.00	5,840	India
*Maranao	840	100.00	840	Philippines
Mararit (Tama)	31	100.00	31	Chad, Sudan
Margi (Plateau Chadic)	129	10.08	13	Nigeria

Ethnic Group	Group Population (000)	Muslim	Muslim Population (000)	Location
*Masalat-Masalit	337	100.00	337	Chad, Sudan
Masina	U		U	Upper Volta
Matumbi (Bantu, Northeast)	U		U	East Africa
Mbun	719	48.54	349	Cameroon, Central African Republic
Mbunga (Bantu, Northeast)	U		U	East Africa
Medogo (Lisi)	10	100.00	10	Chad
*Meidob	45	100.00	45	Sudan
*Melanau	89	75.28	67	Brunei, Malaysia
*Mende	1,178	29.40	346	Sierra Leone
*Meos (Rajasthanis)	584	100.00	584	India
Mijikenda (Bantu, Northeast)	902	34.70	313	Kenya
Mileri (Tama)	8	100.00	8	Sudan
*Mima-Mimi	50	100.00	50	Chad, Sudan
*Minangkabau	6,111	98.00	5,991	Indonesia, Malaysia
*Moghols (Mongols)	10	100.00	10	Afghanistan
*Molbog	7	100.00	7	Philippines, Malaysia
*Molé-Dagbane-speaking Peoples	7,674	34.27	2,630	West Africa
"Moluccans"; see Ambonese				
Mongols	U		353	Mongolia, Afghanistan, China
*Moors	3,729	100.00	3,729	Northwest Africa
"Moplah"; see Mappilla				
Mori	50	90.00	45	Indonesia
*Mossi (Molé-Dagbane)	4,935	36.29	1,791	West Africa
Mubi	38	100.00	38	Chad
Muko-Muko	61	100.00	61	Indonesia
Muna-Butung; see Butonese				
Mwera (Yao)	300	80.79	244	Tanzania
Myeda (Burmese)	U		U	Burma
Nabtab; see Beni Amer				
Nalu	17	100.00	17	Guinea-Bissau
Ndamba (Bantu, Northeast)	U		U	East Africa

Ethnic Group	Group Population (000)	Muslim	Muslim Population (000)	Location
Ndengereko (Bantu, Northeast)	U		U	East Africa
Ngenge (Gbagyi)	100	10.00	20	Nigeria
Ngindo (Bantu, Northeast)	U		U	East Africa
Ngulu (Bantu, Northeast)	U	40.00	U	East Africa
Niassim	240	10.00	24	Indonesia
*Nogai (Turkic)	75	100.00	75	Soviet Union, Eastern Europe
Nono (Manding)	20	100.00	20	Mali
*Nuba	1,030	30.00	309	Sudan
*Nubians	804	100.00	804	Egypt, Sudan
*Nupe	505	30.10	152	Nigeria
*Nuristanis	65	100.00	65	Afghanistan
*Nyamwezi	3,674	13.00	478	Tanzania
Nyamwezi (Nyamwezi)	717	50.07	359	Tanzania
*Nyankole	1,000	2.00	20	Uganda
Nyoro	375	2.13	8	Uganda
Ogan (Ogan-Besemah)	677	91.88	622	Indonesia
*Ogan-Besemah	1,072	90.00	965	Indonesia
*Orissans (Urdu)	438	100.00	438	India
*Oromo	12,629	55.30	6,984	Ethiopia, Kenya
*Ossetians	583	39.30	233	Soviet Union
Pabir (Plateau Chadic)	204	25.00	51	Nigeria
*Palawanon	70	10.00	7	Philippines
Palembangese	U		U	Indonesia
"Pamir Tajiks' ; "Mountain Tajiks"	U		U	Afghanistan
"Paoans"; see Bonans				
Pare (Bantu, Northeast)	U		U	East Africa
"Pasemah"; see Besemah				
*Pashai	93	100.00	93	Afghanistan
Pathans; see Pushtun				
Pekal	54	100.00	54	Indonesia
*Persians	24,301	96.51	23,454	Southwest Asia
"Peul"; see Fulani				

Ethnic Group	Group Population (000)	Muslim	Muslim Population (000)	Location
Plateau Chadic	600	15.00	90	Nigeria
Pogoro (Bantu, Northeast)	U		U	East Africa
*Pomaks	366	100.00	366	Southeast Europe
*Punjabis	72,545	78.88	57,221	India, Pakistan
*Pushtun	14,710	99.94	14,701	Afghanistan, Pakistan
*Qashqa'i (Turkic)	620	100.00	620	Iran
*Qizilbash	93	100.00	93	Afghanistan, Pakistan
Quin	U		U	Upper Volta
Qulaughli	66	100.00	66	Libya
Rajasthanis	36,162	7.39	2,673	India, Pakistan
Rangi (Bantu, Central Tanzanian)	267	89.89	240	Tanzania
Rejang-Lebongers	778	100.00	778	Indonesia
*Reshawa	50	70.00	35	Nigeria
Rohinga (Burmese)	U		U	Burma
Rufiji (Bantu, Northeast)	U		U	East Africa
Rumelian; see Turks, Rumelian				
Rutul (Daghestanis)	16	100.00	16	Soviet Union
*Sadama	600	29.17	175	Ethiopia
Sadamo; see Sadama				
Sagara (Bantu, Northeast)	U	90.00	U	East Africa
Saho-speaking Peoples	158	81.00	128	Ethiopia
Sakalava	569	7.39	42	Madagascar
*Salars (Turkic)	70	100.00	70	China
*Sama or Samal	762	93.57	713	Southeast Asia
Samo (Manding)	67	29.85	20	Upper Volta
*Sangil	4	100.00	4	Philippines
Sarakolé; see Soninké				
"Sarts"; see Tajik				
*Sasak	2,064	95.00	1,961	Indonesia
*Senufo	2,768	28.43	787	West Africa
*Serer	1,008	82.04	827	Senegal
*Shahsevan (Turkic)	310	100.00	310	Iran
Shambaa (Bantu, Northeast)	473	65.12	308	Tanzania
*Shangawa	30	40.00	12	Nigeria

Ethnic Group	Group Population (000)	Muslim	Muslim Population (000)	Location
Sherbro	128	39.84	51	Sierra Leone
Shins (Shina)	U		U	India, Pakistan
*Shina-speaking Peoples	346	100.00	346	India, Pakistan
Shirazi (Swahili)	268	100.00	268	Tanzania
"Shuwa"; see Arabs				
Sia (Manding)	137	62.04	85	Mali, Upper Volta
Sibuquey (Sama)	18	100.00	18	Philippines
Sidamo; see Sadama				
Simalur-Banyak	30	100.00	30	Indonesia
*Sindhis	13,228	80.80	10,688	India, Pakistan
*Sinyar	26	100.00	26	Chad, Sudan
Sisala (Molé-Dagbane)	U		U	Ghana
*Soga	1,000	15.00	150	Uganda
Solorese; see Lamaholot				
*Somalis	7,564	100.00	7,564	East Africa
*Songhay	2,008	99.25	1,993	West Africa
*Soninké	2,451	47.49	1,164	West Africa
*Soso	1,069	86.47	933	West Africa
*South Africans	30,200	1.20	362	South Africa
South African "Africans" or "Blacks" (South Africans)	22,250	.06	13	South Africa
South African "Asians" (South Africans)	750	21.60	162	South Africa
South African "Coloured" or "Cape Malays" (South Africans)	2,527	7.36	186	South Africa
South Africans Whites (South Africans)	4,500	—	1	South Africa
South Asians[5]	U		2,881	Worldwide
Sukuma (Nyamwezi)	2,757	4.00	111	Tanzania
Sulu (Sama)	386	100.00	386	Philippines
Sumbawans	311	82.00	255	Indonesia
Sumbwa (Nyamwezi)	200	4.00	8	Tanzania

924

Ethnic Group	Group Population (000)	Muslim	Muslim Population (000)	Location
*Sundanese	24,912	98.00	24,414	Indonesia
"Susu"; see Soso				
*Swahili	2,412	100.00	2,412	East Africa
Tabasaran (Daghestanis)	80	100.00	80	Soviet Union
Taita (Bantu, Northeast)	203	20.20	41	Kenya
*Tajik	6,708	100.00	6,708	Central Asia
Talensi (Molé-Dagbane)	U		U	Ghana
*Tama-speaking Peoples	283	100.00	283	Chad, Sudan
Tama (Tama)	63	100.00	63	Chad, Sudan
Tamberna	U		U	Togo
Tamil "Moors"[6]	1,150	100.00	1,150	Sri Lanka
*Taqali	181	100.00	181	Sudan
Tat	24	100.00	24	Soviet Union
*Tatars (Turkic)	7,347	95.00	6,980	Soviet Union
*Tausug	618	100.00	618	Philippines
*Tebu	235	100.00	235	Chad, Libya, Niger
Teda (Tebu)	19	100.00	19	Chad, Libya, Niger
"Tem"; see Kotokoli				
*Temne	1,330	32.00	425	Sierra Leone
Terai (South Asians)	768	100.00	768	Nepal
*Ternatan-Tidorese	109	100.00	109	Indonesia
*Thais	48,945	.41	203	Thailand
Tiddi; see Meidob				
Tienga (Manding)	35	20.00	7	Upper Volta
*Tigre	356	100.00	356	Ethiopia
Tikar	33	30.30	10	Cameroon
Timorese	300	1.00	3	Indonesia
*Tomini	74	89.19	66	Indonesia
Torajanese, West	280	50.00	140	Indonesia
Toro	438	2.05	9	Uganda
Tripuris	2,154	6.50	140	India
Tsakhurs (Daghestanis)	15	100.00	15	Soviet Union
Tuareg (Berbers)	996	100.00	996	North Africa
Tubu; see Tebu				
*Tukulor	694	100.00	694	Mauritania, Senegal

925

Ethnic Group	Group Population (000)	Muslim	Muslim Population (000)	Location
*Tunjur	10	100.00	10	Chad, Sudan
*Turkic-speaking Peoples	102,239	98.40	100,601	China, Southwest Asia, Soviet Union
*Turkmen (Turkic)	4,162	100.00	4,162	Southwest Asia, Soviet Union
*Turks, Anatolian (Turkic)	38,178	99.88	38,134	Turkey
*Turks, Rumelian (Turkic)	7,085	94.37	6,686	Europe, Turkey
Turu (Bantu, Central Tanzanian)	U		U	Tanzania
Twi (Akan)	U		U	Ghana
*Urdu-speaking Peoples	61,395	79.61	48,878	Bangladesh, India, Pakistan
*Uygur (Turkic)	6,380	99.90	6,374	China, Soviet Union
*Uzbek (Turkic)	14,828	100.00	14,828	Central Asia
*Vai	140	86.43	121	West Africa
Vidunda (Bantu, Northeast)	U	40.00	U	East Africa
Vute	30	30.00	9	Cameroon
"Wadaian"; see Maba				
Wala (Molé-Dagbane)	74	90.54	67	Ghana, Togo
*Wana	6	33.33	2	Indonesia
Wangara; see Dyula				
Wara Wara	U		U	Upper Volta
Waswahili; see Swahili				
*Wayto	2	100.00	2	Ethiopia
*Wolof	2,349	97.06	2,280	Senegal
*Yakan (Sama)	116	100.00	116	Philippines
*Yalunka	87	89.66	78	Guinea, Sierra Leone
Yamma (Gbagyi)	100	50.00	50	Nigeria
*Yao	8,142	48.03	3,911	Tanzania, Malawi, Mozambique
Yao (Yao)	1,201	83.85	1,007	Tanzania, Mozambique
Yarsé (Mossi)	172	90.00	155	Upper Volta
Yeshkuns (Shina)	U		U	Pakistan
*Yoruba	17,686	50.24	8,885	Nigeria
*Yoruk (Turkic)	370	100.00	370	Turkey

Ethnic Group	Group Population (000)	Muslim	Muslim Population (000)	Location
Zaghawa (Beri)	288	100.00	288	Chad, Sudan
Zaramo (Bantu, Northeast)	433	90.00	390	Tanzania
Zerma (Songhay)	526	100.00	526	Niger
Zigula (Bantu, Northeast)	330	91.82	303	Tanzania

* Entry in *Muslim Peoples*.
1 Name of primary ethnic or linguistic group.
2 Population unknown, but group contains Muslims.
3 Only Asamiya speakers.
4 Name in quotes is an alternate, less accurate, name.
5 Emigrants from Bangladesh, India and Pakistan.
6 Under entry "Sri Lankans."

MAJOR MUSLIM ETHNIC GROUPS (1983)

Ethnic Group	No. of Muslims (000)	Ethnic Group	No. of Muslims (000)
Arabs	137,603	Kanuri	4,376
Bengalis	93,130	Baluch	4,339
Punjabis	57,221	Turkmen	4,162
Javanese	52,715	Bugis	4,139
Urdu Speakers	48,878	Yao	3,911
Anatolian Turks	38,134	Moors	3,729
Sundanese	24,414	Albanians (Gheg-Tosk)	2,948
Persians	23,454	South Asian Emigrants	2,881
Hausa	20,151	Gujaratis	2,853
Malays	16,814	Rajasthanis	2,673
Azeri	15,060	Acehnese	2,567
Fulani	14,885	Kashmiris	2,482
Uzbek	14,828	Makassarese	2,443
Pushtun	14,701	Swahili	2,412
Berbers	13,995	Mandinka	2,366
Sindhis	10,688	Wolof	2,280
Kurds	10,386	Kirghiz	2,247
Madurese	10,346	Labbai	2,236
Yoruba	8,885	Bosnians	2,179
Kazakhs	8,220	Banjares-Kutanese	2,100
Somalis	7,564	Assamese	2,044
Hui	7,543	Bambara	2,019
Oromo	6,984	Songhay	1,993
Tatars	6,980	Sasak	1,961
Tajik	6,708	Northeast Bantu	1,939
Rumelian Turks	6,686	Mossi	1,791
Uygur	6,374	Gypsies	1,685
Minangkabau	5,991	Beja	1,483
Mappilla	5,840	Bashkir	1,456
Maharashtrians	5,694	Daghestanis	1,445
Jat	5,685	Bolaang-Mongondonese	1,400

Ethnic Group	Group Population (000)	Muslim	Muslim Population (000)	Location
Hazaras	1,364	Batak	1,027	
Soninké	1,164	Chechen-Ingush	1,015	
Tamil "Moors"	1,150			
Dyula	1,084			

SUMMARY

	Population (000)	% of Total
Major Groups (over 1 million each)	791,800	94.6
Minor Groups (under 1 million each)	40,961	4.9
Undetermined (not yet identified)	4,449	.5
In Indonesia	(646)	
In France	(546)	
In Vietnam	(484)	
In United States	(480)	
In Rwanda	(480)	
In United Kingdom	(333)	
In Other Countries	(1,480)	
Total Muslim Population:	837,210	

INDEX

Due to the encyclopedic nature of this book, a number of subjects are not fully indexed. The text entry for each ethnic group includes available information on the following subjects: dietary practices, economies, family life, heritage, life cycle observations, language, location, population and religious beliefs and practices. These subjects are indexed when an ethnic group displays exceptional or exemplary characteristics. See Appendix 1 for countries and their ethnic groups.

About the Editor

RICHARD V. WEEKES is Adjunct Assistant Professor of Anthropology and Director of the Muslim Peoples Research Project at the University of Houston. He also served abroad as a *Time* correspondent, a USIS officer, and in other capacities in Turkey, Iran, and Pakistan. His earlier publications include *Pakistan, Birth and Growth of a Muslim Nation.*